JAPAN

A COMPARATIVE VIEW

This book is based on a conference
sponsored by the
Joint Committee on Japanese Studies
of the
American Council of Learned Societies
and the
Social Science Research Council

JAPAN

A COMPARATIVE VIEW

EDITED BY ALBERT M. CRAIG

PRINCETON UNIVERSITY PRESS

Published by Princeton University Press, Princeton, New Jersey
In the United Kingdom: Princeton University Press, Guildford, Surrey

Library of Congress Cataloging in Publication Data will be
found on the last printed page of this book

This volume is one of a series on Japanese society based upon five major conferences held in 1973 and 1974. Each conference was attended by Japanese
and foreign scholars; the purpose of the conferences was to increase scholarly
knowledge of Japanese society by enabling Japanese and foreign scholars to
collaborate and to criticize each other's work. The conferences were sponsored
by the Joint Committee on Japanese Studies of the American Council of
Learned Societies and the Social Science Research Council with funds provided by the Ford Foundation.

This book has been composed in linotype Baskerville
Clothbound editions of Princeton University Press books are printed on acid-
free paper, and binding materials are chosen for strength and durability.

Printed in the United States of America by Princeton
University Press, Princeton, New Jersey

Contents

Introduction · ALBERT M. CRAIG   3

I   PATTERNS IN HISTORY

On Foreign Borrowing · MARIUS B. JANSEN   18

Tokyo and London: Comparative Conceptions of the
City · HENRY D. SMITH II   49

II   CHALLENGE AND RESPONSE: MODERN POLITICAL CHANGE IN KOREA, CHINA, AND JAPAN

Response to the West: The Korean and Japanese
Patterns · SEIZABURO SATO   105

Nation-Building in Modern East Asia: Early Meiji
(1868-1890) and Mao's China (1949-1971) · EZRA F. VOGEL   130

III   CULTURE AND PERSONALITY

Love and Death in the Early Modern Novel:
America and Japan · TAKEHIKO NOGUCHI   160

Uchimura Kanzō: Japanese Christianity in Comparative
Perspective · TAKEO DOI   182

Cultural Differences in Family Socialization: A
Psychocultural Comparison of Chinese and Japanese ·
GEORGE DEVOS, LIZABETH HAUSWALD AND ORIN BORDERS   214

IV   ECONOMY AND SOCIETY

Pre-Industrial Landholding Patterns in Japan
and England · KOZO YAMAMURA   276

Industrial Relations in Japan and Elsewhere · R. P. DORE   324

Factory Life in Japan and China Today · JOHN C. PELZEL   371

List of Contributors   433

Index   435

JAPAN

A COMPARATIVE VIEW

Introduction

-»» «-

ALBERT M. CRAIG

Japan offers rich possibilities for comparative research. Its pre-modern history was marked by a succession of distinct stages: the rise of a centralized post-tribal society, a bureaucratized Chinese type of state, feudalism and a warrior society, and then a feudal "monarchy" with a thriving commercial economy and urban culture. Whether in religion or the arts, in economics or politics, the possibilities are many and have been investigated far too little.

During these early stages the pattern of Japan's participation in world civilization was not atypical. In the pre-modern world a few areas were the cradles of the major cultural forms and a few were too remote to participate in them. But most countries, including Japan, became a part of cultures that in important respects had their origins elsewhere. Participation, naturally, involved re-creation, renewal, and further development. Nice comparisons are thus possible between Japan, which, borrowing from China and, through China, India, created its own distinctive forms, and England or countries in northern Europe that borrowed from Mediterranean culture.

Borrowing, of course, can take a variety of forms—as Marius Jansen points out in his chapter. At times a country will reach out for the culture of another. At times conquest or the confrontation with superior military force will thrust another culture upon it. At other times culture will spread almost like a physical process, as is suggested by words such as "osmosis" or "diffusion." In the case of modern Japan all three modes occurred simultaneously, which made the process very complex indeed. Yet the modern era, no less than the pre-modern, abounds in opportunities for comparative inquiries. A representative few are contained in this volume.

In recent years our comprehension of what happened in Japan during the past century has deepened enormously. Yet there are still large questions of conceptualization on which there is little agreement. Consider, for example, the notion of "modernization," which has been a master-category for several decades in Western studies of Japan, and which has been influential, if controversial, in Japan as well.

"Modernization" is a high-level generalization that points to a

3

change in type of society. It is a process word that in turn is defined in terms of a variety of more discrete processes and sub-processes. The consensus in the field of Japanese studies is that it is more useful to study the component processes than to focus for very long on "modernization" per se.

Yet, having said this, we must also say that the master-category "modernization" often furnishes the implicit assumptions contained in research. Discrete studies, like detailed inset maps in a larger map, may be oriented in terms of the more general concept. To the extent this is so, each scholar should be clear as to both his use of the term and its application to Japan. But so diverse are our views on this subject that clarity does not always prevail.

Contrast, for example, the following two sketches of Japan's modern history. They have different comparative implications. The first is the more usual, but the second is at least equally persuasive.

1. *A First View*: Japan is typical or, since it came first, archetypal of most countries in the world in that it wrested its modernity from the West. What was modern, to be sure, came to Japan in an amalgam of Western culture. Spencer and Guizot, Turgenev and Camus, Keynes and Marx, often seem, and perhaps were, as much a part of Japan's transformation as science and technology. The struggle between tradition and modernity in Japan was exacerbated by the fact that initially at least much of what was modern was also foreign. Yet when we consider the ways in which Western elements were transposed, restructured, melded, and made into something new, it is clear that the process is better called modernization than Westernization.

The Japanese family, for example, clearly meets the needs of modern society as well as does the family in the West. It may be slightly less nuclear than, say, the American family; it may be equally well adapted to the requirements of industry; and it may be better geared for educational mobility. But it is constructed on somewhat different lines. Similarly, a Yokohama factory may be less or more modern than one in Detroit, but it will have a different pattern of industrial relations. And the differences are not entirely fading with time. It is as if Japanese and Western developments were on separate tracks, and even at the horizon it does not appear that they will converge.

This view, we note in passing, is held by scholars with very different views of what modernization is. One scholar may define it in terms of rationalization. Another may favor a nuts-and-bolts approach, and view industrialization as the motor of change. An optimist may argue that Japan and Germany became militarist during the 1930's because

4

they were incompletely modern. A pessimist may counter that militarism is one permutation of modernity. Yet all can agree that what happened in Japan is best called modernization.

Of course, that what was modern came to Japan as foreign had implications for the process of change. It meant, for example, that the new elites had to have knowledge of foreign languages and cultures. This brought a certain type of person to the fore. It led to a situation in which Japan's leaders, no matter in what field, were an academic elite. This phenomenon is now appearing in other non-Western countries as well. From a world perspective it was the West, where modernization originated from within, that was atypical; in most countries it came from the outside. Yet most theories regarding change in modern society began in the West and are based on the European or American experience. Japan would clearly provide a better basis.

2. *An Alternative View*: Japan is atypical and what happened after 1868 is better called Westernization.

Japan was atypical because it began its transformation during the nineteenth century, when world conditions were different. Its pattern of development cannot be repeated. And, more important yet, Japan was atypical in that the pre-conditions for a successful adoption of science, industry, and modern culture had been established by the mid-nineteenth century prior to its major contact with the West. Most non-Western countries and not a few Western countries lacked these pre-conditions.

Among the critical pre-conditions in Japan were: an ethic of duty and hard work, the mechanisms of a market economy, a high rate of literacy, an adequate tradition of bureaucracy, a shift from religious to secular thought, and political orientations that in some respects resembled nationalism. All these pre-conditions emerged, and all were interconnected in what might be called the Tokugawa proto-modernization. There is no good term with which to label this process.[1] "Pre-modernization" sounds like a move backward in history. The "transformation of tradition" suggests changes, but changes without any particular direction. Whatever term is used, it is hard to argue that the establishment of these pre-conditions in itself would have been suffi-

---

[1] I resist calling this "early modernization." In European history the "early modern" was the period that gave birth to the modern. Japan lacked such a period. Of course anyone can point out some similarities between the early modern West and late Tokugawa Japan. Bitō Masahide has even suggested that there was in Tokugawa Japan the beginnings of a natural science that was nipped in the bud by the arrival of Dutch studies. ("Edo jidai chūki ni okeru honzōgaku," in *Rekishi to bunka*, Vol. 11, 1957, *Tōkyō daigaku kyōyō gakubu jimbun kagaku kiyō 11*.) But heuristically it is better to distinguish between the conditions that gave rise to science and industry in the modern West and those which led to their adoption in other areas.

cient for an indigenous modernization, though they were, in retrospect, quite adequate as a base upon which to build.

From this perspective, one comparative use of the Japanese experience is vis-à-vis other non-Western countries, to ascertain the kind of changes within the traditional culture that must precede the adoption of modern technology, or, alternatively, to ascertain the kind of tradition that most easily lends itself to the establishment of the necessary pre-conditions. One likely conclusion is that Japan, where the transformation of tradition pre-dated its Westernization, will lie at the extreme end of a continuum, in contrast to many non-Western countries, where the two processes occurred or are occurring more or less at the same time. Another likely conclusion is that the other East Asian nations will be clustered not too far from Japan at the same end of the continuum.

If the notion of necessary pre-conditions is accepted, then perhaps it can be argued that what happened after 1868 is better called Westernization than modernization. After 1868 a great range of Western institutions—universities, post-offices, companies, customs-houses, hospitals, parliaments, banks, etc.—were introduced into Japan. As we look at these institutions even today, the astonishing thing is the degree to which they are recognizable variants of Western institutions. Standing at the intersection of Shijō and Karasuma in Kyoto, even if their names were not given in English, the Western visitor would find it immediately apparent that he is surrounded by banks. They have the same fortress-like construction as in the West, the same stands with deposit and withdrawal slips, the same counters with tellers, the same vaults at the rear, even the same free matches advertising the bank. Studies by economists show a Japanese pattern in the banks' relations with industrial groups. Rohlen's study has illuminated the social relations within the Japanese banks, but the same kind of differences occurs between, say, German and Italian banks. The Japanese variant may be more extreme; it would be surprising if it were not, but it is a variation within the same institution. From this perspective a significant comparative use of the Japanese experience is to test the variability of modern Western-type institutions, to determine the extent to which Western-type values must be internalized for Western institutions to work or to determine the extent to which non-Western values may be functionally equivalent.

One reason for using "Westernization" is that it appears likely that the borrowed institutions are most Western at the point of adoption, but that in time they may evolve in other directions. The parallel with earlier Japanese history may be instructive. The eighth and ninth centuries were the time of Sinification, when Japan was deeply influenced by Chinese culture and institutions. To speak of Sinification does not mean that Japan became a little T'ang China. Then, as the embassies to China came to an end, Japan entered a period of digestion or indigenization, when the borrowed institutions were simplified and reshaped to fit Japanese society and its needs.[2] If we apply this to the modern era, the changes after 1868 would be Westernization and the changes which began in the 1930's or 1940's might be seen as the indigenization of the borrowed Western culture. This third stage of indigenization can be called modernization. But it probably would be better, in order to preserve the sense that the term has in Western history, to use "modernization" as a blanket-term for the three stages of pre-conditionalization, Westernization, and indigenization.[3]

The above interpretations are not given here to present the reader with a choice, much less to convince him of the correctness or utility of one alternative or the other. What I am suggesting is that, in the present state of our conceptualization of modern Japan, both are plausible. Depending on which theory we pick and how we apply it— and the examples given above are merely two modalities in a range of possible positions—a different kind of comparative research will result. The would-be comparativist must examine his assumptions before he begins. But at the same time it is clear that comparative research will also influence modernization theory and its application to

[2] Obviously the earlier parallel is more complex than I have suggested here. There were at least three major waves of Chinese influence. Can such waves, separated by centuries of ongoing indigenization, be compared to the more rapidly occurring waves of Westernization, the first after 1868, the second during and after World War I, and the third after World War II?

[3] Once this schema is laid out, a variety of qualifications are in order: (a) Contact with the West during the past century has been more massive, more constant, and more intrusive than contact with China ever was. Western institutions in Japan, consequently, are continuously reinforced in a way that Chinese institutions never were. It is possible that some Japanese institutions may become more rather than less "Western" over time. (b) Indigenization began earlier in some areas than others. Natsume Sōseki's novels are a case in point. (c) Indigenization may mean the change in institutional forms. But it also means that in the process of assimilation foreign values are internalized, reconciled, or joined with Japanese values at a deeper level than during Westernization. This gives rise to the paradox that the Japanese became more Chinese or Western during the periods of indigenization than they were during the periods of Sinification or Westernization. Thus Sōseki was incomparably more Western than Fukuzawa, even though Fukuzawa was a pamphleteer for Westernization and Sōseki was ambivalent toward the West. (d) in spite of massive contact at many levels, which made Western culture more accessible in Japan than Chinese culture ever had been, in some ways Japan was less receptive to Western culture than it had been to Chinese culture. Once a traditional high culture is in place, a country tends to be impervious to other high traditional cultures. Thus the "filtering out" of Christianity and other aspects of Western tradition during the Meiji period was not simply the result, though this contributed, of the Tokugawa Confucian secularization.

Japan.[4] The relation between them is tandem. More comparative studies are needed to illuminate the universality and the particularity of the Japanese experience. For a balanced, overall perspective we need to test and weigh the Japanese historical experience against a far greater range of national experiences than has been done hitherto. With a few shining exceptions, the comparative study of Japan is only now beginning.

→》《←

The conference of which this book is the product was organized with a number of aims in mind. First, it was intended that this book be a reader or sampler of different comparative approaches. Thus there are papers on personality, on culture, and on a range of economic and political institutions. The authors represent a diverse group of disciplines—sociology, anthropology, economics, history, political science, psychiatry, and literature. Behind these choices lay the pluralist assumption that there are many kinds of legitimate comparisons and many valid ways of making them. A historian will differ from a sociologist, who may again differ from a literary critic. In one study the subject may be hardly visible for the whirring and clanking of the methodological apparatus. In another the methodological assumptions may be invisible or even unconscious. What counts for the scholar interested in Japan, if not always for the social scientist who may be interested primarily in method, is whether the comparison brings forth insights that add to our understanding. Such insights invariably involve some degree of generality that goes beyond the Japanese experience. If these insights result, then even unconscious assumptions are valid. If they do not, then the most magnificent apparatus is a sham.

It was intended that all the papers be dyadic, comparing Japan to one other case, or at the most treating a few cases. The dyadic comparison permits the consideration of many factors in the richness of their cultural or social context. Seeing a phenomenon in the richness of its context is more likely to generate new insights or propositions. Moreover, since all of the comparisons in this volume are cross-cultural, it is especially important to examine as many factors as possible, for one cannot assume as many constants as might obtain in comparisons within a single culture. In contrast, the type of comparison with many cases, though it may be useful for testing propositions, of neces-

---

[4] I am not for a moment suggesting here that "modernization" is the only master category for the field, or even that it is the most useful. There are the Marxist stages of history, the Parsonian systems and sub-systems, and a variety of other more modest schemata. I use the example of modernization here since, however ill-defined, it has been central to Western scholarship on Japan for several decades.

8

sity treats fewer variables in a narrower context. This book would then inevitably be less about Japan.

It was decided that each researcher would integrate the materials from the cases studied and draw conclusions. Too often comparative studies end up as separate studies by two specialists in the respective areas that are no more comparative than a Japanese and a Norwegian sitting side by side on a streetcar. But, since the authors are primarily specialists on Japan, each was given the opportunity to have his paper read by a specialist in the field of the non-Japanese comparative case.

Another goal of this volume was to break out of the intellectual mold that judges Japan by external models.

Comparisons across cultures begin with a proposition held to be true about one society and ask whether it applies to another. If A and B are linked variables in one society, we ask whether A^1 and B^1 can be found in the other, and whether they stand in the same relationship to each other. If the comparison works, it illuminates the situation in the second society and reflects in some measure on the tenuousness or substantiality of the connection between A and B in the first society as well.

Until recently Japanese scholarship has lacked this "reflection." It has stood at the end of a one-way street going the other way. It has compared itself with others, but not others with itself. It has judged Japan in terms of propositions derived from non-Japanese situations, but has not gone on to judge the propositions in terms of their "fit" to Japan. When the proposition does not fit, it has been because Japanese history is "distorted," not because the proposition was deficient.

For most of Japan's history the "universal truths" about men and society were found in China. Japan saw itself reflected in a Chinese mirror. The Japanese used Chinese learning creatively, but the greater their mastery of it, the greater its authority became. History is a case in point. For Japanese scholars, Chinese history constituted an encyclopedia of moral precedents. Over and over again in Tokugawa essays and letters a truth about man or society would be prefaced with the words "in Japan as in China, in the past as in the present." Yet the example used to illustrate the truth would invariably be drawn from Chinese history. The moral significance of China's history was clear and an appeal to it would clinch an argument. Japanese history, in contrast, was murky and lacking in universal significance.

The Tokugawa thinker Kumazawa Banzan straightforwardly acknowledged Japan's debt: "China is the teacher of all lands. To Japan especially, its services have been tremendous. Rites and music, writing and mathematics, palaces and chambers, dress, ships and carts, agricultural implements, military implements, medicine, acupuncture, moxa, offices, ranks, military science, the way of archery, not to mention a hundred arts and crafts—which of them has not come here from China? Is there a single one that we have not learnt from China?"[5]

Banzan allowed that Japan is next best. The Japanese have *jin* and *gi* and so on. But Japan is no China. Its virtue lies in its capacity to partake of Chinese civilization: "Plant shoots of the Cryptomeria Japonica grow randomly here and there. Where the soil is fit and good the shoot will grow. Where the soil is not good it will wither. The Chinese characters too are like that. In the hearts of the Japanese and Koreans there is the stuff culture is made on, naturally. That is why the Chinese characters came and stuck, becoming our own. . . . The people of the southern barbarian lands, of India, and of the northern barbarian lands . . . are half beasts and lack the illumination of heart to make them understand or appreciate culture."[6]

[5] Sajja A. Prasad, "Country of the Soul: Some Japanese Varieties of Patriotic Experience 1600-1770, A Descriptive Essay," Harvard University doctoral dissertation, 1969, p. 13.

[6] *Ibid.*, p. 8. There are two obvious points that need to be made here. One is that the Tokugawa Japanese, reacting in terms of Chinese political culture, had sufficient *amour propre* to judge China by China's own values, and they were not reluctant to point out when it fell short. The Tokugawa *hōken* system was more like the good old days of Yao and Shun, they argued not implausibly, than subsequent dynastic China. The steadfast virtue of Japan's single dynasty, they felt, compared well with the tawdry rise and fall of dynasties in China. Ōhashi Totsuan's comment on the slavish habits of latter-day Chinese who regarded the Manchu conqueror as their lord gives the flavor of the Japanese reaction: "China is the country that gave birth to the sages. During the flowering of the classic culture there was no shame involved in calling it the [central] flowery kingdom (*kaka*). But after that there were ups and downs and its level of civilization gradually declined. By the Ch'ing it was completely in the ranks of the barbarians and unworthy of honor. In such a situation for Chinese wilfully to adhere to old names and see themselves as the flowery kingdom is as if foxes and badgers, dwelling in a human habitation, were to call themselves the glory of creation (*manbutsu no rei*)." (See Watari Shōsaburō, *Nihon dōtoku honron*, Tokyo, 1928, p. 443.) But judging China by Chinese values only underlines the authority of Chinese culture *in the area of scholarship*. (In other areas Japan showed far greater originality and independence.)

The second point is that there was one outstanding exception to these strictures and that was national studies (*kokugaku*). Yet it is interesting to consider the ways in which *kokugaku* was also shaped by Chinese scholarship, both directly and by reaction. It borrowed the Chinese idea of scholarship. It borrowed from the *kogaku* school of Confucianism the techniques of linguistic research on old texts as a means for uncovering old meanings. In the case of Kamo Mabuchi, *kokugaku* quietly borrowed the Taoist critique of Confucianism. This helped the *kokugakusha* to define man's nature in a way quite different from the Confucianists. So there merged in later *kokugaku* elements from the Taoist view of nature as simple, direct, and unadulterate, as something to be directly intuited, and a view of original Japanese man before his contamination by Chinese culture as reflected in certain modal feeling-states found in ancient Japanese writings, especially in the poetry of the *Man'-yōshū*. What was truly Japanese was defined in terms of free, spontaneous, clean emotions *in contrast to* the cramped, rigid, unnatural feelings of the *karagokoro*

After 1868 the authority of Chinese models of scholarship was superseded by those of the West. To industrialize and build military strength, Japan found it necessary to borrow ideas and institutions from the West. The translations of Western scholarly writings were done first by the publicists of the Meiji enlightenment movement and later by scholars at the new universities. English and American scholarship entered first, followed by French and German. The new doctrines produced a revaluation of traditional society and culture. Whatever the field, scholars in the humanities and social sciences took as their models the methods and conceptual categories built into Western scholarship and reflecting the particular Western experience of modernity. Scholarship consisted of translating, of adapting the model for use in Japan, and of interpreting the results in reference to the Western experience. The West, like China earlier, was seen as possessing the lineaments of universality, whereas the Japanese pattern was seen as particular or even as warped.

Much of this scholarship was fruitful. Honjō Eijirō, hoping to find a Tokugawa era Adam Smith lurking in the background of Japan's industrial development, uncovered an enormous economic literature. Marxist historians, searching high and wide for evidence of a "manufacturing stage" in Japan, did important work on the economic structure of Tokugawa Japan. And Maruyama Masao sought in the "school of ancient learning" the Japanese nominalists, who broke through the "realism" of medieval Chu Hsi thought. The most influential analyses were just those that drew the most on Western history.[7]

It has been only in the past decade or so that a new climate has appeared in Japanese scholarship. In part this development was a result of a new maturity and sophistication of method and perspective. In part it was because Western scholarship itself had become less parochial. In part it was because Japan had caught up. The postwar version of the Meiji goal of "enrich the country" was "overtake Europe and America" (ōbei ni oikose). By the early 1970's sufficient parity had

(Chinese heart) typified by Confucianism. The main weaknesses of kokugaku, which consigned it to a minority position in the spectrum of Tokugawa thought, were three. (1) Sensibilities, however refined, are no substitute for philosophy. (2) It was chiefly literary and could not compete with Chinese political doctrines in the domain or bakufu schools. (3) It was an attempt to define the particular characteristics of the Japanese spirit, not an attempt to form a universal view of man based on Japan.

[7] It goes without saying that just as Japanese scholars earlier had reacted against the assumptions of cultural superiority that permeated Chinese scholarship, so they now reacted against similar assumptions in Western scholarship. If anything, the later Japanese reaction was stronger, for it was fueled by direct contact with a militarily more powerful West and by the new Japanese nationalism. Culturally, the reaction was often couched, ironically, in terms of the Japanese version of Confucian values.

been achieved that it was no longer necessary to transform self and society in terms of a Western model. This led to a call for a new comparative scholarship that would "take Japan as one axis, as one constant frame of reference."[8]

The authors of the papers in this volume were inclined, and were encouraged, to compare Japan with non-Western countries, or, when comparing Japan with the West, to see the Japanese experience as an *equally* valid standard for scholarly comparison.

Particular appreciation is due to the Joint Committee on Japanese Studies of the American Council of Learned Societies and to the Social Science Research Council, which sponsored the conference in September 1974, in Cuernavaca, Mexico, and to a number of persons who contributed to the conference but are not represented in this volume. Michael W. Donnelly, representing the Social Science Research Council, supervised the arrangements, participated in the discussions, and later wrote insightful comments on the proceedings. Robert J. Smith, the liaison with the Joint Committee on Japanese Studies, was a lively discussant, as were Nakane Chie, Ōuchi Tsutomu, and Nagao Ryūichi. Several sessions were attended by professors Omar Martinez Legoretta and Tanaka Michiko of El Colegio de México and Lothar Knauth of the University of Mexico. I would also like to express my appreciation to Susan J. Pharr of the Social Science Research Council, who offered valuable help with the arrangements for publication; to Nancy Jarvis, who did a fine job of copyediting the papers while I was in Japan in 1975-1976; and to Patricia Murray and Teruko Craig, for their splendid translations of the Satō and Noguchi papers.

Albert M. Craig
FEBRUARY 1977
CAMBRIDGE, MASSACHUSETTS

[8] From page 2 of "Henshū ni atatte," a brochure introducing the eight-volume work *Kōza hikaku bungaku*, edited by Haga Tōru, etc. (Tokyo Daigaku Shuppankai, 1973—). Another work reflecting the same new intellectual trend is Itō Shuntarō, etc. (ed.), *Kōza hikaku bunka* (Tokyo Kenkyūsha, 1976—).

I
PATTERNS IN HISTORY

There is an immediately recognizable aptness to Henry Smith's comparison of Tokyo and London. Both were the capitals of island empires situated off their respective continents. Both cities saw themselves to some extent in contrast to their continental parallels—to the Chinese capital, and, say, to Paris. Both were relatively old cities; Edo was chronologically less so than London, but as the capital of Japan during its age of late feudal monarchy Edo was old in kind. And in each case divisions and stratifications from an earlier age directed and shaped their evolution into modern cities. Using these historical and structural similarities as his point of departure, Smith examines the cultural and social differences of patterning in a highly original paper.

In contrast, a side-by-side examination of Japan and Russia strikes us at first as unlikely if not impossible. Little island Japan with its homogeneous population and the Russian colossus with its heterogeneous population spread across continental Eurasia! They provide contrasts but not comparisons, or so it would appear. Yet Marius Jansen has discovered certain common denominators. Both were borrowers of their high cultures, Russia from Byzantium and Japan from China. Both were late modernizers, and in both cases their actions as late modernizers were shaped by the dynamics within their earlier cultural patterns. Jansen sets up five categories, five analytically separable aspects of cultural borrowing, and uses them to compare the Russian and Japanese historical experiences. The results of his study bring to our attention aspects of Japan's past that hitherto have been glossed over. For instance, Jansen's observation that it was easier for Russia to be Byzantine with Byzantium dead than for Japan to be Chinese while China was alive produces the sudden flash of understanding that Robert Smith at the conference dubbed the "*naruhodo* effect."

Both Jansen and Smith are historians. Their concern is to illuminate the Japanese experience. They are not just incidentally using Japanese data to test a methodology that is of primary concern. Yet, despite the difference in disciplines, it was noted at the conference that their papers were not unlike those of some of the social scientists. Why should this be so?

One answer is that any comparative study, whatever the discipline of the researcher, at least implicitly has four elements:

1. What the study is trying to explain.

2. Factors which the researcher consciously attempts to hold constant by the design of the study and the choice of cases. These are held to be relevant to what the study is trying to explain. By holding them constant, the researcher can exclude their effect in weighing the connection between the active variables and what is being explained.

3. Active variables.

4. Residual factors which are not held constant by the research design and are not treated. These are assumed either not to be relevant to the subject, or to "randomize," that is, to cancel each other out to the point that they do not interfere with the investigation of the relationship between the active variables and the subject.

So, whether a historian, a sociologist, or an economist, the researcher will define his goal, and then fix the constants as the scaffolding for the comparison within which the variability of other factors can be examined.

A second reason for the similarity between papers is simply that everyone at the conference was doing the same sort of dyadic, cross-cultural or trans-national comparison. In terms of the four elements mentioned above, this kind of comparison has fewer constants than a comparison within a single culture or nation. The factors defined as constants are usually constant at a fairly high level of abstraction. The number of active variables are many, and the likelihood of residual factors that may not simply randomize is moderately high.

This means that, as methodologists are apt to point out, in a dyadic comparison the degree of methodological rigor is low. A scientific proof of a proposition requires the consideration of many cases—if it is possible to talk of science in social studies, where a generally agreed on paradigm, in Thomas Kuhn's sense of the term, has yet to be found.

Yet even while recognizing the virtues of a comparison with, say, fifteen or twenty cases, we feel it is worth pointing out that such a comparison also has certain inherent weaknesses or dangers: if it is trans-national, it is likely to have far fewer constants than the dyadic comparison. Those factors defined as constants will be at a far higher level of abstraction. The active variables will be fewer and the residual factors far more numerous.

Of course, for some kinds of studies the multi-case method is fine: for example, when quantitative data are used to demonstrate cross-nationally the relationship between a nation's balance of payments and the fluctuation of its currency. But in many instances, even for proposition testing, an extended series of dyadic comparisons has distinct advantages over the multi-case approach. Ronald Dore's paper in this volume is close to such a comparison. And, as pointed out in the Introduction, the scope of the dyadic comparison for viewing large numbers of variables makes it ideal for the generation of new propositions.

On Foreign Borrowing*

-》》 《《-

MARIUS B. JANSEN

This essay proposes to compare Japan's borrowing from China with Russia's debt to Byzantium. My interest in this subject grows out of a comparative study of the modernization of Japan and Russia that a number of us at Princeton undertook several years ago, one that has since been brought to completion through the collaborative efforts of four historians, two sociologists, and two economic historians.[1]

Japan and Russia commended themselves to us as the two countries that had responded most strikingly to the challenges posed by the prior development of science and technology in the countries of the North Atlantic world. Their intensive drives for modernization began at almost the same time: the Meiji Restoration and the Great Reforms of the 1860's altered older institutional patterns decisively. Quantitative indexes of changes during the century that followed produce numerous and often striking signs of parallel development, which suggest that, despite the obvious contrasts in institutional and ideological patterns, there may be important things to learn about modernization by looking at Japan and Russia together. Of course neither country developed in isolation; each adapted the institutions and technology of other countries. The development of each was also affected by its participation in the international system of which it became a part. Russia had already been an important element in the European state system since the seventeenth century. Its defeat in the Crimean War spurred the reforms that began its nineteenth-century modernizations, and setbacks at the hands of Japan and the Central Powers speeded and sparked the great revolution. Victory in World War II enabled Russia to emerge as one of the superpowers of the last quarter-century. Japan in turn was successful in three successive wars, enjoyed the support of important allies, and accumulated an impressive empire before its disastrous defeat in World War II, when

---

* In revising the earlier form of this essay I have benefited from thoughtful comments by Cyril E. Black and Donald W. Treadgold in addition to the suggestions that came out of the seminar discussion.

[1] Cyril E. Black, Marius B. Jansen, Herbert S. Levine, Marion J. Levy, Jr., Henry Rosovsky, Gilbert Rozman, Henry D. Smith II, and S. Frederick Starr, *The Modernization of Japan and Russia* (New York: Free Press, 1975).

it had to stand alone. It reemerged in the last quarter-century under American protection, spared the burden of armament experienced by the Soviet Union.

Clearly Japan and Russia can be compared as late modernizers. Both possessed important capabilities for borrowing outside institutions and converting existing patterns. Both accomplished feats of social engineering that resulted in the transformation of their societies. However different the degrees of coercion employed or the patterns of institutions developed, the speed of their development into highly modernized societies sets them apart from other late modernizers.

This raises the question whether the earlier experience of both societies with the importation of foreign culture and institutions which were then adapted and transformed to become part of Russian and Japanese "tradition" may have constituted preparation for the more recent appropriation of foreign thought and institutions. Is it also possible that a consciousness of having borrowed from, or even succeeded to, another tradition became in some sense part of the national consciousness of the two countries? With these quite general, indeed dismayingly inclusive, questions in mind, I propose to examine the earlier approaches of Russia and Japan to the great civilizations on whose periphery they stood.

Although it is usual to make reference to Japan's extensive borrowing from its neighbor, Russia's enormous debt to Byzantium receives less frequent emphasis. All societies have of course borrowed from neighboring and more highly developed civilizations. Western Europe's debt to Greece and Rome, and northern Europe's to Renaissance Italy, have been the fare of history texts for many years. What is unusual about the Japanese and Russian cases, however, is the prolonged domination by a single and overwhelmingly superior cultural model, one that lived on into modern historical consciousness. The European consciousness was of a classical world no longer alive, one that had, in fact, to be rediscovered in early modern times. The Hindu-Buddhist kingdoms of Southeast Asia may provide a closer parallel in their debt to India, but that contact was fated to be overlaid in early modern times by other, non-Indian, layers of influence in both India and Southeast Asia.

Japan and Russia entered world history as societies that took shape on the periphery of far larger and more highly organized civilizations. The Russian relationship to Byzantium and the Japanese relationship to China may suggest something about the possibilities and limitations of foreign borrowing in general. In both cases, departures from the classical model were accompanied by the development of a native and national consciousness, and this common tradition and trend may have helped prepare for the later appropriation of the institutions of the West.

There are also elements of longevity to be noted in comparison of the model states. Byzantium, which endured until mid-Ming China, and Imperial China, which endured until late Romanov Russia, are unusual if only for their endurance, however great the differences in the antiquity and power each could claim.

Cultural borrowing is often considered unusually important in the case of Japan. Although E. O. Reischauer pointed out a quarter-century ago that it was doubtful that Japanese borrowing had resulted in a greater sum total of foreign influences than in any other land of comparable size, the same work referred to China as the "homeland" of Japan's civilization.[2] The Japanese experience was indeed extensive, and it was particularly conspicuous because of Japan's insularity, which restricted borrowing to periods of relatively intense effort. Factors of distance and difficulty produced a spasmodic and episodic contact with the mainland that made it possible to label, modify, and adapt the foreign import. What was even more conspicuous about the process is that it was self-generated. For the most part the Chinese had little interest in Japan, and Japan did not experience the slow but steady expansion of Chinese trade and immigration that characterized the southward movement of Chinese civilization. Perhaps most important was the fact that China functioned as the center of a self-sufficient universal world order. Entry into this ecumene was on sufferance, and it was presumed to represent a desire to conform to the language, values, and even the costumes of the higher civilization. Superiority, magnanimity, and compassion marked the stance of the Son of Heaven in his reception of envoys from lands on China's borders.[3] Japan's existence at the periphery of this order, which it never fully joined, produced a consciousness of distance and of difference that gradually helped define a "Japan" in distinction to a "China."

The Japan-China relationship was one of great complexity. It could produce self-abasement, but also a combative tone in Japanese addresses to the Chinese throne. In modern times it has produced political and commercial exploitation combined with talk of shared culture and values. There was attraction and repulsion, admiration and ambivalence. These points are well-known to Japan specialists. What

[2] *The United States and Japan* (Cambridge, Mass.: Harvard University Press, 1950), pp. 105 and 101.

[3] Described and discussed in John K. Fairbank, ed., *The Chinese World Order* (Cambridge, Mass.: Harvard University Press, 1968).

is worthy of note is that all or most of these characteristics can also be found in the Russian relationship with Byzantium.

Organizational convenience makes it useful to center this examination around five categories for thinking about the range of influence one culture can exert on another.

1. *The "Lender."* The inappropriateness of this term shows what is wrong with the terminology of "borrowing," but no better word is yet at hand. What is involved is the character of the model state and civilization. Is it alone, and the only "model" in sight, or is it one of several, selected from among them, or even utilized together with others? If it stands alone, does it do so as successor to an earlier order, or as the embodiment of an unbroken tradition? The nature of the world order and world view it holds, and the degree to which its other neighbors accept and accommodate themselves to that self-image, help determine the desirability and possibility of participating in that order.

2. *Base-Line*: the receiving culture. The cultural and institutional complexity of the receiving society—its state of development in religion, language, civilization—determine how much from outside can be utilized, and how much will be resisted. A quite inchoate culture— if such there be—may be overwhelmed and submerged completely by outside influence, whereas a more sophisticated and codified system will resist, warp, and adapt what it receives and imports. A structured political society has leaders who can deliberately select what seems to their advantage, whereas a society without central direction cannot discriminate in the same way. It can know only small and local, though perhaps ultimately more pervasive, influence and example.

3. *The Nature of the Contact.* Are there intermediaries or neighbors who have worked out a pattern of borrowing earlier? How direct, how frequent, how large-scale, and how intensive is the contact between the two countries? Does it have a material base in economics and trade, or is it self-consciously political and cultural? Does the contact include political conflict as well as cultural borrowing? What is it that is "borrowed"?

4. *The Turn-Away.* Does the borrowing begin sufficiently early in the national history to become enshrined as part of "tradition," so that the "national" gradually becomes inseparable from the "borrowed" culture? Is there a consciousness of membership in some larger cultural order? How soon, and why, does the borrower turn to other foreign models?

5. *The Residue.* The preceding considerations will in large measure determine what there is of enduring importance for the civilization and institutional patterns of the borrower in the relationship.

Questions remain as to how long, and in what way, the import is seen or labeled as foreign. In turn, this affects the psychological complexity of modern attitudes, thrusts of modern scholarship and interpretation about the cultural debt, and, not infrequently, assumptions of cultural and even of political and international responsibility.

Because the Japan-China story will be familiar to most of those who read this essay, the paragraphs that follow discuss the Russian relationship with Byzantium in considerably greater detail than they do the Japanese relationship with China.

THE "LENDER"

The nature of the model state or "lending" culture provides the first point for examination. The Chinese world order and ecumene have been the subject of extensive analysis, much of it brought together in a volume of essays edited by John K. Fairbank.[4] Byzantium may strike one as an unlikely subject for comparison, but in some ways it provides the only comparable case in world history. Its status as successor to Rome and its millennium of continuity provide impressive evidence of greatness, and its magnificence, its institutions, and its culture combined to project an influence throughout Eastern Europe that helped to civilize and stabilize the societies there.

It can nevertheless be granted that as a model state China had even more to offer its neighbors. It was far larger and remained puissant into modern times, despite occasional conquest from without. The area under its control grew fairly steadily, and sharply at the last, in contrast to the steady shrinking of Byzantine territory. Although the full systematization of tribute relations with nations on its borders was a development of relatively recent date,[5] there was seldom question of the vast superiority of civilization and of power that China developed over its neighbors. This was never more true than when the Japanese first contacted China directly. After several centuries of Chinese disunity, during which Japan met Chinese civilization through its Korean neighbors and immigrants, official contact with the Korean state of Paikche in the sixth century led to the importation of Buddhism, and then to direct missions to the Sui and T'ang courts. It was a period when Chinese attractive power and influence were probably at their zenith. The entrance of the Chinese writing system,

[4] *Ibid.*

[5] And not unchallenged even then. See the doubts expressed by Inoguchi Takeshi, "Dentōteki Higashi Ajiya sekai chitsujoron—Jūhasseiki no Chūgoku no Betonam kanshō o chūshin to shite," *Kokusai hō gaikō zasshi*, vol. 73, no. 5 (1975). It is also worth pointing out that Japan, China's nearest completely independent neighbor, does not fit, or figure, in the *World Order* volume.

of Chinese governmental institutions, and of Confucian culture and Buddhist worship in the decades that followed is too well-known to require description here.

The Byzantine empire, which began as part of a larger Roman whole, outlasted Rome by far. It saw itself as full successor, and its citizens long called themselves "Romans."[6] The eastern Mediterranean world was a culture zone of its own, however, and by the eleventh century it is probable that few officials knew Latin. The Byzantine church, an essential part and expression of the claims of universality, was also conscious of the pull of Rome until the formal schism of 1054. Byzantium's Slavic satellites also experimented with ties with the Roman church, possibly to increase their areas for maneuver. Byzantium was probably strongest in the eleventh century, and its later claims to majesty were much diminished by its obvious political weakness. In 1204 the Fourth Crusade sacked the city and brought Latin rulers for a period, and in 1438-1439, in the empire's final extremity, the Orthodox Church accepted church unity at the Council of Florence. Thus this "universal state" was always conscious of limitations. It also had important trade and cultural links with the West through Venice and Norman Sicily. At the extreme edge of Byzantine influence, however, early Russia never experimented with the Roman church. Instead there was a consistent and bitter anti-Latin tone, suggested by the *Primary Chronicle*'s warning (under 988), "Do not accept the teachings of the Latins, whose instruction is vicious."[7]

Yet the concept of Byzantium as center of a world order was real and strong. The concept of a Byzantine commonwealth is argued by Dimitry Obolensky in "Russia's Byzantine Heritage" and applied by him in *The Byzantine Commonwealth*.[8] Eastern Europe, he demonstrates, is an "intelligible area of study" and is made up of the "heirs of Byzantium": Serbs, Albanians, Greeks, Bulgarians, Rumanians, and Russians. Within this sphere, Byzantium was the cultural colossus, the center of a world order whose members were arranged in a carefully ordered hierarchy.

The Imperial City—Tsar'grad, as the Russians termed it—was the

[6] F. Dolger, "Die Kaiserkunde der Byzantiner als Ausdruck Ihrer Politischen Anschauungen," *Historische Zeitschrift*, vol. 159, no. 2 (1939), pp. 229-250. Also G. Ostrogorsky, "The Byzantine Emperor and the Hierarchical World Order," *Slavonic and Eastern European Review*, vol. 35, no. 84 (Dec. 1956).

[7] Translated and edited by S. H. Cross and O. P. Sherbowitz-Wetzor, *The Russian Primary Chronicle: Laurentian Text* (Cambridge, Mass.: Mediaeval Academy of America, 1957), p. 115. The setting is one of doctrinal instruction given the Russian ruler Vladimir at his baptism.

[8] The 1950 essay is reprinted as selection 3 in *Byzantium and the Slavs: Selected Studies* (London: Variorum Reprints, 1971). *The Byzantine Commonwealth: Eastern Europe, 500-1453* (London: Weidenfeld and Nicolson, 1971).

center of culture, wealth, and trade. "The city of the world's desire," Vladimir's envoys reported to him upon their return. It was not only the seat of the empire and of the church, but also a holy city by virtue of the supernatural forces present within its walls; relics and memorials, repositories of prayer and devotion, abounded, and the whole was crowned by the temple of divine wisdom, St. Sophia, and the Mother of God, whose robe was "venerated as the city's palladium."[9] Eastern European pilgrims felt themselves in the New Jerusalem when there, and, as Vladimir's envoys reported to him, "We knew not whether we were in heaven or on earth." Small wonder that it was the beauty of the service that drew the most striking comments from those same envoys. As the *Primary Chronicle* reports this discussion of alternate forms of religion: "The Bulgars bow down and sit, and look hither and thither, like men possessed; and there is no joy among them, but only sorrow and a dreadful stench. Their religion is not good. Then we went to the Germans, and we saw them celebrating many services in their churches, but we saw no beauty there . . . [but of Constantinople] on earth there is no such vision nor beauty, and we do not know how to describe it, for we know only that there God dwells among men." At an early stage of theological sophistication, the beauty of the liturgy thus counted for as much as the complexity of the theology. Sansom made the same point about the Japanese reception of Buddhism many years ago: "If the Japanese mastered somewhat painfully and slowly the learned and literary elements of Chinese culture, their hearts leaped to welcome all its beauty."[10]

Meetings with foreign emissaries were designed to dramatize the majesty of the world emperor. The costliness of his raiments and the worshipful nature of his court combined to stress his nearness to God. Constantine had converted the pagan god-emperor to a Christian emperor who was called to rule by God. Medallions showed God, or Christ, placing the crown on his head. However unruly and unseemly the times, his succession, once accomplished, was evidence of his selection by divine providence. The palace itself was under divine protection; it was a holy place, characterized by a solemn stillness. The Hellenistic influence of late Roman times, and the theocratic aspirations of the rulers, combined to form the ritual of the court, which

9 *Byzantine Commonwealth*, p. 290.

10 Extract, *Primary Chronicle*, p. 111. The Russian selection of religion is given as a decision based on the report of commissioners sent to examine the claims of "the Bulgars of Mohammedan faith," Jewish Khazars, and German "Emissaries of the Pope." In Constantinople the emperor accompanied the Russians to St. Sophia, "calling their attention to the beauty of the edifice, the chanting, and the pontifical services and the ministry of the deacons." Sansom quotation from G. B. Sansom, *Japan: A Short Cultural History* (London: Cresset Press, 1932), p. 139.

was supported by the ceremonies of the church. Ceremonial prostration had entered from the East; in theory the subjects were the ruler's slaves. By the tenth century these theocratic tendencies had increased, with special religious liturgies for each holiday. One finds the emperor taking the place of Christ, and his magistrates and patricians that of the apostles in some rituals.

Those outside the pale were barbarians, the critical element in this distinction being one of religion. The church patriarchate was supportive of the divinely ordained emperor, though there were also rare instances of strong-minded patriarchs who resisted ungodly emperors by direct insubordination. The Roman emperor in Constantinople was head of the Christian empire, father of all Christians, and head of the family of nations. To be impressed was to be converted, and vice versa.

Moral eminence came to be supplemented by technological wizardry that would have provided Okakura Kakuzō with additional evidence of a "spiritual East" in contrast to a material West. Liudprand, the bishop of Cremona, headed a mission to Constantinople in 949 and made this report of court ceremonial: "Before the emperor's seat stood a tree, made of bronze gilded over, whose branches were filled with birds, also made of gilded bronze, which uttered different cries, each according to its varying species. The throne itself was so marvelously fashioned that at one moment it seemed a low structure, and at another it rose high into the air. It was of immense size and was guarded by lions, made either of bronze or of wood covered over with gold, who beat the ground with their tails and gave a dreadful roar with open mouth and quivering tongue."[11] The scene is set; Liudprand comes in leaning upon the shoulders of two eunuchs, and at his approach these mechanical guardian figures go into action with roars and cries. He then prostrates himself three times, raises his face: "And behold! the man whom just before I had seen sitting on a moderately elevated seat had now changed his raiment and was sitting on the level of the ceiling. On that occasion he did not address me personally, since even if he had wished to do so the wide distance between us would have rendered conversation unseemly." Liudprand had advance knowledge of all this, so that "I was neither terrified nor surprised," but one can imagine that an envoy from the steppes would have been more than a little impressed. Surely, as Baynes puts it, the silent emperor looking down on him would seem as God, regarding mortal men.[12] Add honors, decorations, subsidies, gifts, and perhaps a title in

[11] *The Works of Liudprand of Cremona*, F. A. Wright, trans. (London: G. Routledge and Sons, 1930), pp. 207-208.

[12] Norman H. Baynes, *The Byzantine Empire* (London: Home University Library, 1952), p. 73.

the non-functioning official hierarchy, and the ruffian's heart should be won. The emperor might stand godfather to him for his baptism, and send a bishop subject to the patriarch of Constantinople to preside over the conversion of his land. As in the Chinese order, calendar, costume, and forms of address would then symbolize some degree of fealty.

For its satellite states the empire employed a wide variety of terminology to indicate their place in a very structured hierarchy. The variables were no doubt affected by politico-military considerations, but also by degree of cultural and religious conformity. The Byzantine patriarchate was superior to foreign bishops and appointed them, and the emperor, by virtue of his ecclesiastical stature, enjoyed a nonspecific, but quite real metapolitical eminence over neighboring rulers.

It comes as no surprise that relations so one-sided and uneven produced frictions. The barbarians could be flattered, but also insulted, and at times "internal" documents that revealed the depth of condescension, like diplomatic maneuvers that revealed the sophistication of method, could furnish proof of "Greek" dishonesty. There was often a distinction between the "wise Greek language" and the "difficult Greeks."[13] Nevertheless the claims of Byzantium continued until its fall. In the late fourteenth century a Russian attempt to distinguish between ecclesiastical and political subordination, by omitting the emperor's name from commemorative diptychs of the Russian church, was defended by the Muscovite ruler with the explanation, "We have the church but not the emperor." Not so, the patriarch responded: "It is not possible for Christians to have the church and not to have the empire. . . . The holy emperor is not as other rulers and governors of other regions are. . . . He is anointed with the great myrrh, and is consecrated *basileus* and *autocrator* of the Romans—to wit, of all Christians." He alone was lord of the entire ecumene.[14]

This illustrates the stubborn refusal of state and church to entertain change. "Even the smallest neglect of the traditions," as the Patriarch Photius put it, "leads to the complete contempt for dogma."[15] Even without the fall of Constantinople, the relationship of states within the commonwealth to Byzantium would surely have undergone change. But there is no need to challenge the majesty and comprehensiveness of the world view of the Second Rome. Small wonder that its fall to the Turks was followed by expectations of the end of

[13] Obolensky, *Byzantine Commonwealth*, p. 267.

[14] Obolensky, "Byzantium and Russia in the Late Middle Ages" (1965), reprinted as selection 7 in *Byzantium and the Slavs*; also *Byzantine Commonwealth*, p. 264.

[15] Obolensky, *Byzantine Commonwealth*, p. 294.

the world. It was interpreted as the completion of the works of God, a fulfillment expected at the end of the seventh millennium or chiliad from 5508 B.C., the foundation of the world according to the Byzantine calendar, which was also in use in Russia. The date worked out by these calculations proved to be 1492.[16]

BASE-LINE: THE RECEIVING CULTURE

Russia's appearance on the international scene was later than that of Japan. In contrast to taking form in the prolonged occupation of a clearly differentiated group of islands by the Japanese, Russian culture had to develop in an area that was a highway for population movements and a crossroads for influences. On the north-south axis a river system led from the Baltic to the Black Sea, and on an east-west axis the steppes provided routes for invasion and retreat for Huns, Avars, Khazars, Alans, Pechenegs, and other groups before the "Slavs" and "Russians" finally came into view. The principal routes intersected at Kiev, which became the center for the early state. In the period of the formation of the Russian state about six weeks were required for the journey from Kiev to Constantinople via the rivers and along the Black Sea, and two to four weeks from Belgrade to Constantinople through the mountains to the north.[17] Trade in furs, which could be exchanged for the riches of Byzantium, drew the Russians to the south, while the nomads of the steppe waylaid that trade and later the even more valuable trade in Chinese silk that also wound along the coastal Black Sea route. Byzantine security was intimately involved in the trade routes to the northern frontier, since the barbarians wanted Byzantine wealth. In this respect Byzantium's relations with the Balkans and with Russia were more like those of China with Central Asia than those of China with Japan.

The Byzantines did not have the luxury of being able to concentrate on security problems in one area. The northern border had been critical for them since the establishment of the capital in the fourth century. The empire also had constant problems with its maritime routes and its Near Eastern neighbors; furthermore, in periods of military strength, as under Justinian, it tried to restore the borders of the earlier Roman empire. With limitations of manpower and wealth, it had to develop diplomatic methods to deal with its northern neighbors. A tradition of diplomacy reminiscent of the *Arthasastra* developed; outer

16 A. Vasiliev, "Medieval Ideas of the End of the World—West and East," *Byzantion*, vol. 16, no. 2 (1942/43), pp. 462-502.
17 Obolensky, *Byzantine Commonwealth*, p. 41.

barbarians were persuaded or bribed to attack the neighbors in between.[18] As with Sung China, these methods were often tactically successful but strategically disastrous. Remote barbarians could be persuaded to assail neighboring barbarians, but they often stayed on to
become worse problems than those they had replaced. Byzantium also
paid generously for protection on its borders, with treaty relations
that specified the amounts and times of payments. Once relations were
stable, however, the extension of Byzantine culture through the sending of missionaries was a matter of the highest priority.

The Slavs first entered this system with the establishment of Byzantine relations with a Bulgarian state in 681. Tribute payments were
set, and measures to Hellenize and Christianize the Bulgarians were
immediately launched. Boris was baptized in 865, to the praise of Byzantine patriarchs, who lauded him as the Constantine of his people.
Greek was the language of the new state until 893, by which time Byzantium had worked out writing systems for the vernacular in Gla-
golithic and Cyrillic scripts. Bulgaria (and, slightly later, Serbia) experimented with the advantages of allegiance to the Roman church
instead of to Byzantium, and utilized as well as aggravated the competition between the two. The Byzantine version of the Slavic conver-
sions is reminiscent of the condescension of Chinese annals toward
barbarians: "[The Serbs] sent envoys to the emperor . . . requesting
that they might be placed under the humane yoke of Roman authority
and under that of its supreme pastor. . . . The emperor, like the humane father who received his senselessly rebellious son who repented
and returned to the fold, received and accepted them, and straightway
sent them priests together with a diplomatic agent. . . . When they had
all received divine baptism and returned to the Roman allegiance,
the emperor's authority was fully restored over their country . . . and
he wisely determined that they should be governed by princes, chosen
by them."[19] Conversion and tribute did not rule out "senseless rebellion" when it looked profitable, however; and, in any case, cultural
admiration and commercial aspiration could go hand in hand with
political opposition.

The northernmost outpost of Byzantine intelligence was Cherson,
on the Crimean peninsula; this city served as warning station for
Russian raids and later for cultural relations with the Russians. Toward the end of the first millennium A.D. the area north of Cherson, in-
habited by Finnic tribes and Eastern Slavs, was unified and structured

---

[18] Obolensky, "Principles and Methods of Byzantine Diplomacy" (1964) and "The
Empire and Its Northern Neighbors" (1966), reprinted as selections 1 and 2 in
Byzantium and the Slavs.

[19] Obolensky, *Byzantine Commonwealth,* p. 98.

by Vikings, or Varangians (who also provided a Byzantine palace guard), and became known as Russia. This process of nation-building is described in the *Primary Chronicle*, compiled in the eleventh and twelfth centuries, and the first extant work taken down in the newly acquired writing system.

Greek records indicate earlier contacts from 839 on, and include a surprise Viking invasion of 860. The newcomers seemed unusually rugged barbarians, and the Patriarch Photius described them in a sermon in St. Sophia in terms of horror of the sort agriculturalists have always reserved for invaders from the steppes: "A people has crept down from the north, as if it were attacking another Jerusalem . . . the people is fierce and has no mercy; its voice is as the roaring sea. . . . Woe is me, that I see a fierce and savage tribe fearlessly poured round the city, ravaging the suburbs, destroying everything, ruining everything, fields, houses, herds, beasts of burden, women, children, old men, youths, thrusting their sword through everything, taking pity on nothing, sparing nothing. . . . O city reigning over nearly the whole universe, what an uncaptained army, equipped in servile fashion, is sneering at thee as at a slave!"[20]

The sequence of events that had been seen in earlier Byzantine relations with Bulgaria and Serbia followed. A treaty was worked out in 874, and 907 and 911 agreements extended unusually generous tribute and trade privileges. Russians paid no customs, were granted a special quarter of residence in Constantinople, received free board for six months, and, far from saunas, as many baths as they desired to take. But they were also dangerous; thus they were to come unarmed, never more than fifty at a time, and had to enter through a designated gate.[21] Traditionalists objected to this favoritism much as the Ming ministers opposed the privileges granted piratical bands like the fifteenth-century Japanese. The outsiders soon overplayed their hand; another raid in 941 found the Greeks better prepared, and "Greek fire" sent the invaders reeling back to the north.

Meanwhile the work of conversion had begun. The background of Slavic-Viking popular religion is imperfectly known, but there are accounts of crude paganism and human sacrifices to a thunder-and-lightning God. This seems to have posed little obstacle to Orthodox Christianity for the elite. In 988 Vladimir was baptized in Cherson and was promised an emperor's daughter on the condition that his people convert to Christianity. Soon the church was official, the pagan gods and rituals denounced, and sacred places dishonored. But politi-

[20] *Ibid.*, pp. 182-183.
[21] V. Kliuchevskii, *Geschichte Russlands* 1 Braun and von Walter, trans. (Berlin, 1925), p. 155.

cal conflict was not at an end. The last major war was in 1043, sparked by a brawl between Russian-Scandinavian merchants and their hosts in Constantinople. By then there was a Byzantine metropolitan in Kiev. Artisans, artists, and merchants were coming to Russia from Byzantium and Cherson, and Mount Athos was becoming established as a center for piety and pilgrimage. A considerable trade provided the Russian elite with articles of personal luxury and liturgical necessity, while the Russians brought furs, wax, honey, and slaves to Byzantium.[22]

There are both similarities and contrasts to be observed for pre-Byzantine Russia and pre-Chinese-civilization Japan. The Japanese record, although incomplete and still in controversy, is certainly earlier by half a millennium than the Russian. Geography and a specific habitat provided a clearly defined homeland and limited the racial mix. The assimilative tolerance of Buddhism and an unstructured, formless, native cult produced no contrasts as striking as those of Orthodoxy and Slav paganism, and consequently permitted the survival of much more of the original folk religion. In both cases the imported writing system was first used to compile a national history. But although the *Kojiki* is not without its debt to Chinese annals and tradition in its attribution of virtue and antiquity to the imperial tradition, the mythology it presents stands in clear distinction to any of China. From the first, Japanese poetry also represented a clearly and highly developed native culture. The *Primary Chronicle*, on the other hand, compiled by monks, begins with debts to Greek chronicles in an account of the dispersal of the nations after the Flood and Babel, and it accepts the Byzantine chronology, which begins in 5508 B.C. It then goes on to treat the Slavs and converts them through the work of Cyril and Methodius before introducing the Russians as heirs to all that has gone before. In the course of this, victories over the untrustworthy Greeks receive their full due. In both the *Kojiki* and the *Primary Chronicle* reliance on the written and cultural tradition of an ancient empire is combined with a need for national identification and distinction, and this is resolved through the assertion of a special origin and mission for the fledgling state. In time each work became a major subject for modern philology and nationalism. Motoori's studies of the *Kojiki* in eighteenth-century Japan were contemporaneous with rescensions of the *Chronicle* ordered by Peter the Great, and, by the period of nineteenth-century modernization, both texts had been established by modern scholarly method and could serve as foundation stones for modern nationalism.

[22] *Byzantine Commonwealth*, p. 224.

In other sources Japan is the richer nation. Imperfect as the Chinese accounts of prehistoric Japan may be, they are superior to what is available about early Russia in Greek sources. Constantine VII Porphyrogenitus' tenth-century manual for the guidance of his son, *De Administrando Imperio*, contains one chapter about the empire's northern borders which tells of the Russians' route to Constantinople, but it has a good deal more about route and rapids than it does about society and structure.[23]

A final, but important, difference applies to the timing of the contact between receiving and model state. The Russian state took form during the process of Christianization and civilization via Byzantium. In the case of Japan, the early Chinese influence via Korea was no doubt of considerable importance, although it remains imperfectly known. But by the sixth and seventh centuries there is clear evidence of great and growing central power in Japan. The massive public works that characterize the tomb period immediately prior to the opening of formal relations with China leave no doubt of the development of the ability to marshal population and resources. As a result, the Yamato state that organized missions to the Sui court was far from being shapeless and ineffective. It was ready to investigate specific patterns and solutions to problems of more effective organization, problems of which its leaders were aware.

THE NATURE OF THE CONTACT

Both Japan and Russia emerged at the periphery of a larger cultural sphere, and both profited from the prior exposure of their neighbors to this higher civilization at the center of that sphere. In the case of Japan, Chinese influence had entered Korea during the Han Dynasty, with the founding of the colony at Lolang in 108 B.C., thus establishing a base that survived until A.D. 313. The Korean kingdoms that developed during the latter centuries of this outpost clearly derived much of their knowledge of Chinese civilization from the administrators and artisan-intellectuals it produced. Fourth-century Japan profited also. With the collapse of Lolang and with the political contention that engulfed the Korean peninsula in the years that followed, significant numbers of Koreans and Chinese crossed to Japan, where they were welcomed for the skills they brought. An early ninth-century Japanese listing of the court elite resident in the home provinces provides the names of 1,059 families, of which 304, almost 30 percent, are of conti-

23 Translation and commentary provided as selection 5 in Obolensky, *Byzantium and the Slavs.*

nental origin, and at least one, that of the learned Wani, can be traced via Paikche to Lolang.[24] Knowledge of Chinese script, civilization, and government must have been widespread before the dramatic sixth- and early seventh-century events that signaled the formal turn to China. Korean artisan and scholar immigrants made important contributions to Japanese crafts and culture; no doubt they had their impact on Japanese political decisions to experiment with the invasion of the Korean peninsula as well. When China was reunified by the Sui founder and once again assumed its accustomed leadership in Korea, Japanese rulers were prepared to take the initiative in opening formal relations.

In a somewhat similar way, the extension of Byzantine civilization to Russia's Balkan neighbors helped to speed the conversion of Russia. The transcriptions that had been worked out for Bulgaria speeded up the attainment of literacy for the Russian elite, and the body of translation of religious material into Slavonic served the needs of the early Russian church. There was undoubtedly a fair amount of knowledge of the Christian faith in the early Russian state, and the deliberate process of selection between Christianity, Islam, and Judaism described in the *Primary Chronicle* bespeaks a political decision as much as it does an exclusively spiritual awakening. Byzantium had done its best to enlist Russian power in its campaigns against Bulgaria, and involvement in all aspects of the political and cultural life of the Balkans preceded the conversion of the Russian rulers.[25] Once made, Russian cultural activities undoubtedly attracted the talents of numbers of Byzantines and Slavs, and the missionaries were from many countries.[26] What was different, however, was that the movement of foreigners into Russia was continuous into modern times, whereas the continental immigrants into Japan, absorbed and naturalized into Japanese society, had few or no successors.

The conversion of Russian rulers began in the ninth and tenth centuries. The language of the early Russian church was presumably Slavonic, but there remains little vernacular writing for the same period. No doubt, says Obolensky, there was some diffusion of "Greek" and "Greek learning" alongside the translations in Slavonic, and in the second quarter of the tenth century Iaroslav set up something of a translation bureau in the great cathedral he had built by Byzantine specialists in Kiev.[27] Despite this, there seems nothing quite

[24] Inoue Mitsusada, *Shinwa kara rekishi e* (Tokyo: Chūō Kōron, 1965), pp. 411-415.
[25] George Vernadsky, *Kievan Russia* (New Haven: Yale University Press, 1948), pp. 56-66.
[26] Obolensky, "Byzance et la Russie de Kiev" (1959), selection 4 in *Byzantium and the Slavs*.
[27] Vernadsky, *Kievan Russia*, p. 80.

comparable to the formidable efforts to master Chinese learning in the original language that characterizes early Japan. Perhaps there was no counterpart to the appeal and authority of the Chinese written character.

In church relationships the Russian tie with Constantinople was steady and close. From 1039 to 1448 the Russian church was a metropolitan diocese of the Byzantine patriarchate. The creation of new metropolitan sees was a prerogative of the Byzantine emperor, and consequently brought with it the danger of political subordination. There is good evidence that an arrangement was worked out whereby the Russian primate would alternate between men from Byzantium and Russia, and between 1237 and 1378 this was regularly the case.[28] The details of the relationship, however, are far from clear, not least because contemporary chroniclers did not always see Russia of the tenth to twelfth centuries as an autonomous "country" in the sense that modern national sovereignties desire. Certainly ecclesiastical subordination to Constantinople did not preclude political conflict with Byzantium, as has been noted. Five "raids" or "wars" can be counted in the tenth century. Like their Chinese counterparts, Byzantine chroniclers described these as "rebellions."

The thirteenth century brought sharp changes. Constantinople fell to the Fourth Crusade in 1204, and, even though it freed itself again a half-century later, it never recovered its original power or appeal. Kiev had lost its primacy in Russia before this, and from 1237 to 1240 the Mongol invasions forced a sharp break with the Byzantine commonwealth for a period of 240 years. The church nevertheless kept channels open to Constantinople, even to the extent of arranging transfers of Russian funds for the reconstruction of sacred monuments. The degree of direct Byzantine influence on the Russian church in this period is imperfectly known, however, and it is reasonable to assume that conflicts over the naming of Russian primates, one of which surfaces in accounts of the fifteenth century, provided principal touchstones of conflict.

Concrete political and institutional influence is a good deal more difficult to ascertain. Canon law, clearly, was adopted intact. The Russian church's acceptance of that law in turn brought with it related codes of imperial law, with recognition of the Roman emperor's position. The evidence for secular law is a good deal harder to see, and Obolensky notes that Russian medieval codes have little discernible Byzantine influence. In general terms, as Obolensky sums up the problem: "Christianity, together with the social ideology and material

---

[28] Obolensky, "Byzantium, Kiev, and Moscow: A Study in Ecclesiastical Relations" (1957), selection 6 in *Byzantium and the Slavs*.

trappings that came with it, enabled the East European monarchs of the early Middle Ages to claim divine sanction for their sovereignty, to unite their subjects by the common profession of an exclusive faith, to exalt their own status by royal dress and state ceremonial modeled on the ritual of the imperial court, and through their newly gained association with Byzantium to increase their international prestige. Moreover, it was only by borrowing an ideology and a pattern of culture from abroad that they could hope, like the leaders of 'under-developed countries' of today, to carry out the desired modernization of their societies."[29]

Yet these remain generalities. We have nothing comparable to the massive importation of Chinese institutional structure, official ranks, tax and administrative codes that distinguished seventh- and eighth-century reforms in Japan. The differences, perhaps, lay not so much in intent as in applicability. Japan, an irrigation society with intensive cultivation and control, operating within clearly defined boundaries and free from outside harassment, found in China a model that permitted a kind of emulation that was impossible for Russian rulers.

In terms of trade and economic relations the Russian-Byzantine relationship was probably more important to both partners than was the Japan-China exchange. Byzantium was the natural focus of the commerce that moved along the river system, and the steady growth of church needs guaranteed the continuation of exchange despite political difficulties. The Russian merchant community in Constantinople was important to the acquisition of luxury products for the ecclesiastical and political elite in Russia. The decline of Byzantine commerce after the twelfth century, and the Mongol conquest of Russia, however, cut this back sharply.

Finally, there is the question of the scale and intensity of the contact in human terms. It can be granted at the outset that contact was limited to only the elite. In the Russian-Byzantine instance, there was a measure of dynastic contact through intermarriage and the provision of refuge. In the eleventh century some Russian units also participated in Byzantine campaigns. Ecclesiastical relations inevitably involved a great deal more interchange. Greek bishops would surely have been accompanied by deacons and secretaries, so that each Russian bishopric must have attracted at least a small group of Byzantine intellectuals. In turn, Russian clergy and monks traveled to Byzantium and especially to Mount Athos on pilgrimage. Artists and painters also came to Russia to work on the churches of the Kievan cities, and Russian craftsmen must in some cases have studied in Byzantium 'as well. In

[29] *Byzantine Commonwealth*, p. 282.

addition to all this there was the movement of merchants.[30] Despite this extensive contact, however, there were limitations of cultural influence which derive from the fact that the Russian elite did not learn Greek; the church liturgy itself was in Church Slavonic.

Japanese contact with China had to overcome greater difficulties of distance, and it required state resources to equip the maritime expeditions. Japan also encountered on the Chinese side a more structured officialdom whose ability to regulate and restrain the contact was particularly formidable during periods of dynastic vigor. The first official mission traveled to the Sui court in A.D. 607, to be followed seven years later by a second. During the T'ang period twelve official missions made the journey, and several others were projected but not completed. These were large groups, sometimes numbering as many as six hundred persons, and they represented costly governmental efforts. The movement of Chinese to Japan is much more difficult to determine. No doubt there was additional merchant and clerical travel; on at least one occasion the arrival of the Chinese monk Ganjin, in 753, permitted a true ordination of over four hundred persons to take place. But the difficulties he encountered are also impressive; it was his sixth attempt to cross to Japan, earlier efforts having been thwarted by Chinese authorities, pirates, and storms.[31] The better chronicled travels of the Japanese monk Ennin, who was attached to the last formal mission of 838, illustrate the same degree of difficulty and drive.[32] Artists and artisans had to be numbered among the participants in these voyages, and the Nara temples provide some of the surest guides to T'ang styles of architecture and decoration. The massive body of Buddhist institutional and devotional literature was imported entire and used in the original, and numbers of key figures spent long periods of time mastering it in China. The Japanese elite was expected to read and write in Chinese. There was, however, no talk of intermarriage at the top, nor of military cooperation, and only the most limited possibility for private merchant activity.

The Mongol invasions of Russia interrupted Russian institutional development and hampered mercantile and ecclesiastical relations with Byzantium. The Mongol invasions of China were followed by unsuccessful attempts to invade Japan in 1274 and 1281, the only instances of direct conflict before Hideyoshi's armies encountered Ming armies in northern Korea at the end of the sixteenth century. Yet,

[30] The preceding draws on Vernadsky, *Kievan Russia*, pp. 348-353.

[31] G. B. Sansom, *Japan: A Short Cultural History* (London: Cresset Press, 1932), pp. 121-122.

[32] Edwin O. Reischauer, *Ennin's Diary: The Record of a Pilgrimage to China in Search of the Law* (New York: Ronald Press, 1955).

curiously, even that political hostility between Japan and China did not rule out continued cultural contact; significant numbers of Zen monks traveled to China to seek the new learning, and Chinese abbots managed to make their way to Japan to head Zen establishments.

In sum, no one can dispute the importance of the contact to both Japan and Russia. The Russian-Byzantine contact was probably on a larger scale, and less easily controlled by political authority. Yet on neither side was native culture submerged by that of the higher culture. Both Japan and Russia took care to avoid the appearance or fact of formal incorporation into the international system of the higher culture on anything resembling a vassal or tributary status. In both cases the contact was largely deliberate, controlled, and managed. Religion was at its core, but institutional experimentation and appropriation, particularly marked in the Japanese case, was also of great importance.

The Turn-away

The end of apprenticeship to the model state provides a new set of problems. In some ways these are the most interesting of all, for they illustrate the manner and extent to which the "import" has become "tradition." The complexity of psychological relationships, the mixture of attraction and repulsion, resonate with the development of early sentiments of nationalism in the borrower.

The Russian relation with Constantinople changed with the Mongol victories in Russia. One of the few ideological conditions of Tatar overlordship, James Billington points out, was "the requirement to pray for only one tsar: the Tatar Khan"; this encouraged a sense of having superseded Byzantium and "tended to remove from view in Muscovy the names of the later Byzantine Emperors. Muscovy found it only too easy to view the collapse of this increasingly remote empire in the mid-fifteenth century as God's chastisement of an unfaithful people."[33]

The unfaithfulness had been the ill-fated attempt of Constantinople to obtain Latin support against the Turks by agreeing to an act of union with Rome at the Council of Ferrara-Florence in 1437-1438. The news of this was brought to Moscow by the Primate of Moscow Isidore, a Greek who had been hand-picked by the emperor in 1436. When this worthy, now named Cardinal, brought the startling news of union to Moscow in 1441, he was quickly deposed as heretical. In 1448 a Russian synod consecrated Iona as Metropolitan, and from that

[33] *The Icon and the Axe: An Interpretive History of Russian Culture* (New York: Knopf, 1966), p. 57.

date the Russian church was autocephalous. The Russian ruler Basil II wrote the last emperor: "In all things we hold to the ancient Orthodox faith transmitted to us, and so we shall continue to do. . . . We beseech your Sacred Majesty not to think that what we have done we did out of arrogance, nor to blame us for not writing to your Sovereignty beforehand; we did this from dire necessity." He assured Constantinople of Russia's obedience to the "holy, divine, oecumenical, catholic, and apostolic Church of St. Sophia, the Wisdom of God," and requested of her "all manner of blessing and union, except for the present recently appeared disagreements."[34]

Nevertheless this profession of "obedience" was prompted by just such a "disagreement," and the early fall of Constantinople—Basil's letter was never even sent—seemed God's judgment on the Byzantine acceptance of union with Rome. Within a few decades there appeared the doctrine of Moscow as the Third Rome in the letter of the monk Filofey of Pskov. He painted a vision of the apocalypse in which the "woman clothed with the sun" (the church), having fled from Rome to Constantinople, now, after Florence, came to a Third Rome, "the new, great Russia." There would be no fourth.[35]

This new confidence coincided with Russia's liberation from the Mongol yoke and the expansion of Muscovy. Evidence of wealth and power was to be found in the building of stone churches and fortifications under Ivan III, and the extension of political power over the church through the seizure of its properties. Byzantine refugees from Turkish rule swelled the reservoir of scholars and artisans. "Moscow," Andreyev writes, "began more and more clearly to emulate the 'grand style' of Byzantium in jurisdiction, administrative organization, and court life; and the position of its key-stone, the church, was also subject to the general tendency towards far-reaching changes."[36]

The disappearance of Constantinople (by that name, at least) and the empire facilitated Russian ideas of independence and emergence as successor state with institutional appropriation. The "Third Rome" had little practical intent or capability of re-creating the second, but it did come to see itself as self-sufficient. The Japanese had no comparable opportunity, as the Chinese empire continued its sway. Yet there are a number of parallels worth noting.

---

[34] Obolensky, "Byzantium and Russia," selection 7 in *Byzantium and the Slavs*, pp. 271-272. Gustave Alef, "Muscovy and the Council of Florence," *Slavic Review*, vol. 20, no. 3 (1961), pp. 389-401, points out that the Russian stand was influenced by the need of the Grand Duke to have church support against a usurper, and that he did not act from simple nationalism.

[35] N. Andreyev, "Filofey and His Epistle to Ivan Vasil'yevich," *Slavonic and East European Review* 38 (1959-1960).

[36] *Ibid.*, p. 15.

The Heian court's abandonment of direct relations with T'ang China was signaled by the successful efforts of Sugawara no Michizane to get his nomination as emissary canceled in 894. The T'ang Dynasty, he argued, was in decline, the voyage dangerous and expensive, and the project unnecessary and unwise. Ennin had already brought word of the persecution of Buddhism in China. The time for the great embassies, which may be compared to the learning missions to the West in the nineteenth century, was at an end. Private contact continued and, indeed, increased, as Korean and Chinese ships continued to cross to Japan. But except for artists and Buddhist monks, who sought to master and import the new teachings of Zen and, later, Neo-Confucianism, the time for "learning" had come to an end. Within a few centuries, as the Japanese warriors were preparing to stand against the Mongol invasions from China, the Buddhist monk Nichiren proclaimed Japan the center of a world Buddhist order.

The fifteenth century saw a brief return of official Chinese-Japanese relations, with the Ashikaga shogun Yoshimitsu even willing to accept the status of tributary in order to attract Chinese approval. Although the cultural tastes of the period put almost unprecedented weight on Chinese goods and objects of art, and although the import of Chinese copper currency was important for Yoshimitsu's budget, institutional borrowing or adaptation was no longer any part of the Japanese purpose. By the middle years of the century, official exchange had given way to unofficial booty as pirate bands harassed the Ming, and at the end of the sixteenth century the Japanese invasions of Korea brought political conflict as well. The abortive peace negotiations, in which both Hideyoshi and the Ming court thought the other was submitting, revealed how total the gap had become. Yet, throughout the period, private trade, much of it in luxury goods and precious metals, became steadily more important to both countries.

With the Manchu invasions of the seventeenth century there was some possibility for Japanese assertions of a role as homeland of the true learning in contrast to a China ruled by "barbarians." The eighteenth-century Confucian scholars who rejected Sung Neo-Confucianism and suggested, with Ogyū Sorai, that true teaching could better be found in Japan than in the country of its birth, showed some awareness of such a position; popular dramatists who derided Chinese submission to barbarian rule, as did Chikamatsu in his popular *Battles of Coxinga*, attacked even more frontally the idea of China's functioning as a model state.

But these openings for usurping the role of China were only possibilities, and they were never realized. After all, China continued to exist, whether Ming or Manchu. Japanese Buddhism continued to grow and change, often in response to newer trends on the mainland, and as it lost its place among Japanese intellectuals, the new attraction of Confucianism (which became fully domesticated only in the seventeenth century) fastened the attention of the elite even more securely on China. The struggle of modern nationalism to separate Japanese tradition from that of China was consequently more difficult and time-consuming, and it did not take place until the eighteenth century.

For both Japan and Russia, a gradual turn to the West for new cultural models provided the real evidence of liberation from earlier cultural authority. In Russia, this coincided from the first with the growth of interest in the West, and was shown in ties with Renaissance Italy and between Novgorod and the West.[37] But in both cases the picture was confused by identity struggles in which part of the original import, now appropriated as national tradition, was assimilated to a presumed national essence or character.

In Russia the split began with the ecclesiastical reforms sponsored by Nikon against the Old Believers in the seventeenth century. Minor changes in translation and ritual became symbolic of cultural and theological treason for the Old Believers. Though harassed and cowed by vigorous persecution, their roots among their illiterate countrymen guaranteed their survival. Greek learning, they argued, was altogether corrupt, and the petty changes and corrections were indicative of a far more profound desertion of the principles which could spare Russia the fate of Byzantium. This was combined with reiteration of the doctrine of Moscow as the Third Rome.

A half-century later, Peter brought the tide of Westernization to its crest. His efforts were directed to the sources of national strength. For almost a century before his time Russian kings had made increasing use of Western arms, Western mercenaries, and Western military officers and technicians. Peter intensified these trends, made them national policy, and took a personal interest and role in the importation and transfusion of Western technology and the employment of Western experts. In the course of this came changes in religious administration. Peter saw in the Greek failure evidence of military weakness, civil disobedience, and treachery, and his scorn of Byzantine orthodoxy and monasticism was total. To mock the bigotry of Orthodoxy, he took part in derisive processions, and, to guarantee his control of the religious establishment, he ordered that the governance of the

---

[37] Obolensky, "Russia's Byzantine Heritage" (1950), selection 3 in *Byzantium and the Slavs*.

church should lie in a Holy Synod, which replaced the Patriarch in 1721. Church authority was now secularized and no longer a possible danger. One could compare the late sixteenth-century willingness to import and manufacture Western-style armament in Japan, the crushing of Buddhist and Christian sectarian opposition by the great unifiers, and institutional measures designed by Ieyasu to divide, control, and utilize popular faith Buddhism. Ieyasu was personally a Buddhist, as Peter was a hymn-singing Christian.

The eighteenth century saw continued Russian appropriation of Western knowledge. Eighteenth-century Leyden numbered 120 Russian students among its matriculated students, and unknown numbers of unregistered Russians. Some of these, the aristocrats, had private tutors, and others, including serfs and servants, were permitted to audit informally. From this number came 6 members of the Academy of Sciences, over 30 doctors, and 30 aristocrats educated in the humanities and social sciences of the Western tradition.[38] If one adds the considerable numbers of Russians of Western European origin who came to technical and professional posts in Imperial Russia in this period, the total "influence" was very great. During the same years a tradition of "Dutch studies" developed in Japan, though more slowly and at second-hand. In addition to the interpreters' college at Nagasaki, which totaled as many as 150, "Dutch" medicine became widely practiced throughout the country. Sugita Gempaku's translations in anatomy in the 1770's marked a strong step forward and inaugurated a new age of translation. By the end of the century Shizuki Tadao had translated a Dutch translation of an Oxford physicist's popularization of Newton.[39] The Japanese and Russians were now drinking in the same learning, but because Japan had been closed to outside contact since 1640 only the Russians were getting theirs at first-hand.

In Russia the late eighteenth- and nineteenth-century dispute between Slavophiles and Westernizers brought issues of cultural identity to the surface. The former built their conception of a Russian essence on nostalgia and romanticism. The Westernizers denounced "tradition" as bigotry and superstition. Chaadaev, in his *Lettres philosophiques* (published in 1836, written 1829) blamed what he saw as the sterility of Russian culture on "*la miserable Byzance, objet du profond mépris*," because it had cut Russia off from the civilized

[38] Nicholas Hans, "Russian Students at Leyden in the Eighteenth Century," *Slavonic and East European Review*, vol. 35, no. 85 (June 1957), gives names and details for the 120 students.

[39] Tadashi Yoshida, "The *Rangaku* of Shizuki Tadao: The Introduction of Western Science in Tokugawa Japan," Princeton University Ph.D. dissertation, 1974.

Christian countries of the West.[40] One can go to early Meiji "enlightenment" writers to find equally sweeping denunciations of the Chinese tradition in Japan.

Still other comparisons can be drawn with the *kokugaku* developments in eighteenth-century Japan. The search for a true Japanese past brought a conscious effort to separate national essence and integrity from the corrupting influence of China. The effort to relate China's political turbulence to its moral failings also repeated themes or at least psychological motivations common to the slavophiles. But one suspects that the Japanese had the easier time of it; they were not arguing the case for a successor state or "purified" import, and they had somewhat more of a genuine antiquity to work with in the imperial institution, Shintō, and poetry. In origin both movements were nevertheless non-political, somewhat anarchistic, contemplative, and scholarly.

The nineteenth century saw both nativist traditions put to political use. The uses of *kokugaku* and Shintō thought for Japanese nationalism are well known. The *kokugaku* tradition could focus on the throne and could, with Hirata, justify Western borrowing as fully consonant with a national tradition that had in the past included reliance on China. Asia-firsters talked with fervor and conviction of Japan's duty to repay its cultural debts by taking the lead in a new amalgam of Eastern culture and Western technology, and philosophers and aestheticians argued the superiority of "Eastern" spirit over "Western" matter with the same enthusiasm that their slavophile contemporaries did. In Russia the political potential of slavophile enthusiasm was clearest in discussions of rescuing the territory of Byzantium from the control of the now weakening Ottoman Empire. Pan-Slavism, which grew out of slavophilism in the third quarter of the nineteenth century, found its classical expression in Danilevsky's argument that Russia had a historic mission to restore the East Roman Empire, and that there should be a new federation centered in Constantinople to include all the nations of the old Byzantine commonwealth.[41]

Duty and opportunity extended to areas of cultural and scholarly challenge. Byzantine history as a modern discipline was inaugurated in late-nineteenth-century Russia by Russian scholars of German origin. Obolensky quotes one of them, Kunik, as asking, "Where shall we

---

[40] Obolensky, "Modern Russian Attitudes toward Byzantium," selection 8 in *Byzantium and the Slavs*. For a fuller discussion of Chaadaev, see Donald W. Treadgold, *The West in Russia and China*, vol. 1: *Russia, 1472-1917* (Cambridge: At the University Press, 1973).

[41] Obolensky, "Modern Russian Attitudes." Ihor Sevcenko, "Byzantine Cultural Influences," in C. E. Black, ed., *Rewriting Russian History: Soviet Interpretations of Russia's Past* (New York: Praeger, 1956), p. 151.

find enough Byzantinists to enable us to take our stand in this field alongside other nations?"[42] This note of national duty and opportunity—the point that such scholarship was an area in which Russian scholars would have a decided comparative advantage—also appeared in late-nineteenth-century discussions of Chinese history in Japan. Some of the pioneer Sinologists saw China studies as the one area in which they could have an immediate opportunity to contribute to world knowledge and Japanese reputation.[43] Like their Russian counterparts, they saw such study as a dimension of their examination of Japan's cultural identity. Tsuda Sōkichi found that his efforts to deal with Japanese intellectual history required turning to the study of Chinese thought. Naitō Konan came to the study of Chinese history through his apprenticeship to the *kokusui* publicists of the magazine *Nihon*. His historical vision was of an East Asian civilization which had its origins in the plains of north China, moved down to central and south China, and then flowed to Japan.[44] The political disintegration and social compartmentalism that developed in China had doomed it to impotence in the modern world, but the tide of that civilization was now little more "Chinese" than it was "Japanese," and it had come to center in the political and social dynamism of twentieth-century Japan.

THE RESIDUE

After initial high-level generalizations are offered, it becomes difficult to define with any precision the long-range result of the cultural borrowing I have discussed. In both cases sweeping observations are common. For Russia, Norman H. Baynes says, "The assertion that the early Russian state owed its very existence to Constantinople would hardly be an exaggeration"; and he goes on to say that in addition to the ecclesiastical forms of church and monasticism, "The Russian sovereign may . . . be regarded as the heir of the Byzantine emperors. A Russian scholar has recently shown that the coronation ceremony of the princes of Moscow reproduced the forms of the coronation of the Byzantine 'Caesar,' i.e., the chosen successor of the reigning emperor."[45] Dimitri Obolensky, slightly more cautious, agrees that "the

[42] *Ibid.*, p. 67.

[43] Marius B. Jansen, "Japanese Views of China during the Meiji Period," in Albert Feuerwerker, Rhoads Murphey, and Mary C. Wright, eds., *Approaches to Modern Chinese History* (Berkeley and Los Angeles: University of California Press, 1967), p. 175.

[44] Yue-him Tam, "In Search of the Oriental Past: The Life and Thought of Naitō Konan (1866-1934)," Princeton University Ph.D. dissertation, 1975, pp. 302-314.

[45] Baynes, *The Byzantine Empire*, pp. 232, 236.

influence of Byzantium on Russian history and culture was far more profound and permanent than that of the Turko-Mongol hordes and more homogeneous than that of the modern West. Russia owes her religion and the greater part of her medieval culture to the Byzantine Empire, both directly, through her connexions with Constantinople in the ninth and tenth centuries, and indirectly, through the Slavo-Byzantine schools of the tenth-century Bulgaria. . . . An essay might well be devoted to an illustration of Mr. Sumner's comprehensive formula 'Byzantium brought to Russia five gifts: her religion, her law, her view of the world, her art and writing.' "[46]

Japanese specialists are more circumspect, and Japanese writers themselves are sensitive to the frequently advanced views about Japan as borrower. The theorists of Japanese nationality in the nineteenth century, themselves steeped in Chinese learning but also in *kokugaku* values, stressed Japan's independence during the learning process, its selectivity, and its ability to avoid any kind of bondage to Chinese culture. The tough fiber of the native tradition, they argued, was never extinguished by imports. In comparing political, institutional, and cultural styles, they had little difficulty in making their point. I shall attempt summations under three headings.

In *religion* the Russian importation of orthodoxy apparently extinguished the earlier paganism quite totally, although earlier beliefs and practices lived on for centuries as a "double faith." The church was imported in one piece, as a finished, completely developed institution. It was also, of course, part of an international system; there had been other patriarchates, and Byzantium in one sense was part of a "West," and "not," as Obolensky puts it, "a wall, erected between Russia and the West; she was Russia's gateway to Europe."[47] Western contacts increased from Mongol times on; there was, as Donald Treadgold documents, a considerable and increasing interchange with the centers of Western thought and even institutionalized Catholicism. The currents of Enlightenment and Protestant thought, however, were restricted to a small elite, and never made the impact on peasant life that orthodoxy, especially in its most conservative and Old Believer forms, did. The groundwork was thus laid for that separation of the Russian intellectual elite from the peasant mass that proved so striking and troublesome in modern times.

Buddhism, in contrast, did not enter Japan as a system fully formed, and its continuous transformations in China produced a continuous flow of influence into Japan. It lacked the prescriptive uniformity of monotheist orthodoxy, and possessed an assimilative genius which en-

[46] "Russia's Byzantine Heritage," selection 3 in *Byzantium and the Slavs*, p. 96.
[47] *Ibid.*, p. 119.

abled it to blend with the native cult. Throughout the medieval centuries "dual Shintō" put the two in close relation, with Shintō deities given places in the pantheon of popular Buddhism and Buddhist temple complexes accommodating simple Shintō shrines. Though "foreign," Buddhism did not bring with it the consciousness of built-in alternatives, as orthodoxy did with Rome. There was no central Buddhist structure. By the time Japan met Buddhism it was already in decline in the country of its birth, and no Japanese monks visited India until modern times.[48]

The tide of influence that brought Buddhism also brought with it Confucianism, a code that led even more surely to the center of Chinese culture and values. This too was a continuous process of assimilation that went on into Tokugawa times. The universal nature of Confucianism, however, meant that when fully internalized it needed to carry no national burden at all.[49] Confucianism, in any case, lacked a central religious or philosophical establishment, and it brought no problems of conformity to outside direction. Ultimately, Japan's sanctions and legitimacy for rule, however bolstered by Confucian example or Buddhist ideals, lay with the native cult's ascription of supernatural authority to the sovereign.

In *language* the Chinese writing system gave the Japanese entry to the entire corpus of Chinese civilization. The writing also was used to preserve intact, or nearly so, Japan's oral legends of pre-literate times and adapted to record the poetry which, in form and vocabulary, owed least to Chinese example. Slavic alphabets probably contributed much less to a knowledge of the Hellenistic bases of Byzantine civilization. A minority of church figures might have been formidable scholars on their own, and translations of patristic literature were of course available. But the translations and the revised alphabets had made it unnecessary for Russians to learn Greek, and the religious liturgy was in a version of the vernacular. As a result, there was nothing comparable to the kind of full participation the Japanese elite enjoyed in the literary and historical record of Chinese civilization. Educated Japanese, in effect, added a second language to their own.

In *institutional development* the situation is one of paradox. Clearly the Taika planners reached out to the example of a centralized

[48] When, as Stephen Hay shows, Okakura and others drank in "Asian unity" from Western spirit-firsters like Margaret Noble. *Asian Ideas of East and West* (Cambridge, Mass.: Harvard University Press, 1970), p. 41.

[49] See, for instance, the recent assessment of Hiraishi Naoaki that although the nineteenth-century reformer Yokoi Shōnan "considered himself as a successor to centuries of Confucian tradition handed down from ancient times," he was "fully aware that his Confucian views during his last days had become completely divorced from traditional Confucian teachings as practiced in China, Korea, and Japan." "Universalism in Late Tokugawa Japan: The 'Confucian' Thought of Yokoi Shonan," *Annals of the Institute of Social Science* 16 (1975), University of Tokyo.

state and a powerful court in the hope of building in Japan some of the political majesty they had seen in China. The *ritsu-ryō* codes brought bureaucratic divisions, designations, and ordinances to Japan, and even though one can point to numerous and specific departures from Chinese example, the very conception of such institutions was clearly continental in origin. Yet in practice the idea of a powerful, working emperor proved antithetical to Japanese inclination (as it would again in the nineteenth century, when German constitutional advisers anticipated the monarch would rule). It worked imperfectly, and gradually gave way to the more familistic structure of medieval feudalism. Chinese and Japanese patterns soon diverged. Nevertheless, the alternative forms of organization as Japanese distinguished them, central versus feudal, were both grounded in Chinese history and vocabulary, and the alternative of a central rule and classes open to ability remained into modern times to stir philosophical and political speculation. One of the first acts of even the Meiji government was to order a full translation of the Ming codes, and early Meiji reformers included Chinese examples in their surveys of possible models for reorganization.

In Russia, the development of the central autocracy and "Caesaro-Papism" is often, as by Baynes, related to the Byzantine heritage. "When Peter the Great abolished the Russian Patriarchate and put in its place the Holy Synod (1723)," Baynes asserts, "this was only possible because of the view of the relations of Church and State which Russia had inherited from East Rome: a Western emperor might support a rival Pope, he would never have dreamed of abolishing the Papacy."[50] This Baynes sees as a logical outgrowth of a past in which "His subjects hailed Justinian as priest-king, and it was his bishop that gave classical expression to the theory of Caesaropapism in the words 'Nothing should happen in the Church against the command and will of the Emperor.'"[51] Over against this is Obolensky's distinction between the "theocratic idea of the sacred monarch, ruling his realm in harmony with the church—an idea widely accepted in sixteenth and seventeenth century Muscovy and which owed much to Byzantine influence" and which was, he concludes, "not wholly eradicated by Peter the Great's efforts to subject the ecclesiastical order to the power of the state, in accordance with Lutheran models and Western concepts of the natural law." His assessment is that "the secularisation of the upper-class culture caused by Peter's reforms and its consequent divorce from the beliefs and way of life of the peasantry brought the effective influence of Byzantine cultural patterns on Russian society as a whole to an end in the early eighteenth century."[52]

[50] *The Byzantine Empire*, p. 236.   [51] *Ibid.*, p. 38.
[52] *The Byzantine Commonwealth*, p. 367.

Treadgold, in a somewhat different context, agrees that the earlier tradition ended with Peter: "The Old Belief fought for Old Muscovey, the patriarch fought for Greece, but neither won"; and though "the institutions of Petrine Russia were only the old Muscovite institutions painted over and hung with Western placards, the Western placards themselves eventually had their effect." And yet, ultimately "a revolution which ostensibly rested on the latest Western models and ideas . . . in fact depended on the non-Western model and idea of the all-powerful state."[53] This leaves open the possible origin of that "non-Western model."

It is hardly necessary to point out that generalizations travel poorly over the territory and centuries which have been mentioned. Byzantium's institutions changed with its resource base, and Russia expanded from Moscow to the Pacific, with consequent need for alteration in economic and administrative institutions. China's polity underwent steady change, in which the influence of great families of T'ang days gave way to the solitary domination of the imperial court of early modern times. Japan progressed from imperial centralization modeled on that of China to a shadow court presiding over increasingly feudal baronies, until the unifiers of the sixteenth century constructed an early modern state with late feudal class lines and an increasingly centralized administration. The "model" changed, but no model could long have sufficed to serve the needs to which it was put. Statements about institutional adaptation need to be phrased with greater attention to time and place than has been possible within these limits, which permit only general reference to sources and goals.

Final comparison lies in the fact that both Russia and Japan received their inspiration from universal empires. However they might conceive their role as successor states or phrase their mission, neither was quite able to think of itself in comparably universal terms. Not until Russia became the heartland of a new and messianic view of history would it be possible to approach these goals; by then, of course, the focus had long shifted from "Byzantine" to "Western" orientation. Japan's search for its role was also consistently nationalist and particular; the terminology of Greater East Asia, and Miki Kiyoshi's search for a wider significance in the war against Western imperialism, were desperate but largely unconvincing efforts to meet this need.

→≫-≪-

Is it possible to answer the question posed at the opening of this essay? Did the capacity to borrow that led Russia and Japan to adopt Byzantine and Chinese models in earlier centuries, and led the Rus-

---

[53] *Op. cit.*, pp. 75, 105.

sians to a partial adaptation of the West in the eighteenth century, prepare both countries for the extensive reliance on Western models they have shown in more recent times? It can only be asserted with some confidence that the consciousness of having borrowed in earlier times made it easier to justify doing so again.

First, it made it possible to reject objectionable or obsolete parts of a tradition as "borrowed" and foreign. The eighteenth-century *koku-gakusha* rejection of an "impure" Chinese tradition for a "pure" Japan, and the relief with which a nineteenth-century *rangakusha* like Fukuzawa could greet his liberation from the Chinese tradition,[54] like the venom with which some of the Westernizers dismissed Russia's Byzantine past, gave them a perspective on that past very different from the one held by their contemporaries in China.

Second, those less contemptuous of their predecessors' work could see their role as importers of new wisdom as fulfilling a national tradition, quite in harmony with the decisions, though not the content, of the past. Sugita Gempaku, looking back in 1815 on an eventful life of translating Dutch books, wrote, "I never imagined that Dutch studies would become so important or make such progress. Chinese studies made only slow progress, but Dutch studies were written in plain and direct language."[55] And yet, he adds, perhaps training in Chinese studies "developed our mind beforehand." Forty-five years later, the ambassador sent to Washington to ratify the first treaty with America noted in his diary, "In the old days envoys were sent to China . . . but that is only a neighboring country."[56] And one of the first pronouncements of the restoration government in 1868 justified the decision to continue open access to Japan by citing the relations with China in antiquity.[57]

---

[54] *The Autobiography of Fukuzawa Yukichi* (Tokyo, 1948), p. 98, and Carmen Blacker, *The Japanese Enlightenment: A Study of the Writings of Fukuzawa Yukichi* (Cambridge: At the University Press, 1964), pp. 36, 37.

[55] Eikoh Ma, "The Impact of Western Medicine in Japan: Memoirs of a Pioneer, Sugita Gempaku," part 2, *Archives internationales d'histoire des sciences* 56-57 (1961), pp. 263-264.

[56] *Kōkai Nikki: The Diary of the First Japanese Embassy to the United States of America* (Tokyo: Foreign Affairs Association of Japan, 1958), p. 2.

[57] Thus, the American representative R. B. van Valkenburgh enclosed in his report a translation from the Kyoto government *Gazette* for March 1868: "Intercourse with foreign countries commencing in the reigns of Shujin and Chiuai flourished more and more year after year. Many foreigners of near and distant countries became naturalized and tribute was paid. Subsequently envoys passed constantly between this country and China or went to reside there, and our mutual relations became naturally friendly. At that time no great advance in the art of navigation had been made, and our intercourse was restricted to Corea, China, and other adjacent countries. . . . But of late years, . . . the art of navigation has been brought to perfection, and the most distant countries have been brought into the closest intercourse. . . ." (Department of State, M 133, Roll 10.)

If comparable evidence from the Russian side is at hand, it would seem justified to add this psychological and moral justification of the utility of earlier borrowing for the modern turn to the West on the part of two of the world's great powers.

Tokyo and London:
Comparative Conceptions of the City

❯❯❯ ❮❮❮

HENRY D. SMITH II

INTRODUCTION

The city is never what we think it is: it is always far more complex and changeable than our ideas about it. Yet even ideas of the city are elusive; they are as often implicit as explicit, and it will not suffice to seek out conceptions of the city in self-consciously articulated urban ideologies alone. It is here that cross-cultural comparison provides a valuable tool, for it forces us to deeper and more fundamental levels of differentiation than do culture-bound theoretical speculations on "the city." Comparison is first of all a means, a system of leverage for understanding our own modes of conceptualizing the urban environment. But beyond this, comparison can become an end as well, a technique of appreciating—or at least tolerating—radically different ways of looking at the city.

If we accept the potential benefits of a cross-cultural comparison of ideas of the city, why Tokyo and London? At the broadest level, they provide a comparison of a Western city with a non-Western city, enabling some perspective on the inevitable Western biases of the great bulk of writing on "the" city. Ideally, one would prefer for comparative purposes a non-Western urban tradition which had modernized while remaining free of European cultural influence—unfortunately, none exists. As second best, one would prefer an urban tradition which had been strong and distinctive *before* the impact of the West. Here Japan, probably the most highly urbanized pre-modern society outside Europe, is an excellent choice.[1] In particular, Japan was never subjected to colonial rule, so the continuity of pre-modern urban traditions is much stronger than in many other parts of the non-Western world.

But within the Western urban tradition, why the English variant? The reason is that England offers a revealing parallel with Japan as an

[1] Gilbert Rozman, *Urban Networks in Ch'ing China and Tokugawa Japan* (Princeton, N.J.: Princeton Univeristy Press, 1973), p. 6. Rozman adds the qualification "large-scale" to "society."

island-nation offspring of an older continental culture. A comparison of England and Japan thus implies a comparison of the larger urban traditions of East Asia (defined as the Chinese cultural sphere) with those of Western Europe (or, more simply, "the West"). In fact, the fundamental comparison to be made is precisely that of the Chinese city versus the Western city, and some sketchy but provocative efforts have been made in that direction.[2] The value of Japan and England as a framework for comparison is that they take us one step farther in understanding the range of variability in urban conceptualization, for each evolved urban traditions which were distinctively different from those of their continental relatives. A comparison of England and Japan thus implicitly involves sub-comparisons of Japan with China, and of England with the Continent.

Still further justification for comparing Japan and England is that each has enjoyed a thriving urban culture first as a pre-modern society, then as an industrializing society, and today as a fully industrialized society. I am in general agreement with the arguments of sociological theorists that there is a sharp break in function and structure between the pre-industrial and the industrial city, and again between the industrial and the post-industrial city. But there is far less of a break in the *idea* of the city, which in its many guises remains deeply rooted in pre-modern and early industrial realities. It is for this reason that I have in each section stressed the *modern continuities* of older ideas of the city.

Relevant to the problem of continuity is the most obvious historical similarity of Tokyo and London: both were very large as pre-industrial cities and both have remained continuously very large until the present. They have been so large that for the last three centuries the distinction of the "world's largest city" has gone (or should, from most current evidence, go) to one of these two great capitals; their comparative growth is shown in Figure 1.[3] It bears emphasis, however, that *before* the sixteenth century, neither Edo (renamed Tokyo in

[2] See Etienne Balazs, *Chinese Civilization and Bureaucracy*, ed. Arthur F. Wright and trans. H. M. Wright (New Haven: Yale University Press, 1964), pp. 66-78; Frederick W. Mote, "The City in Traditional Chinese Civilization," in James T. C. Liu and Wei-ming Tu, eds., *Traditional China* (Englewood Cliffs, N.J.: Prentice-Hall, 1970), pp. 42-49; and Arthur F. Wright, "Symbolism and Function: Reflections on Changan and Other Great Cities," *Journal of Asian Studies*, vol. 24, no. 4 (1965), pp. 667-679. The point which bedevils any sustained comparison of the Chinese and the Western city is the essential unity and continuity of the Chinese empire until modern times versus the fragmentation, feudalism, and geographic expansion of Western Europe after the fall of Rome. Japan is much closer to the European pattern.

[3] The only other incontestable holder of the title has been New York City, for a brief period in the second quarter of the twentieth century. Peking may have been larger than Edo at some time in the late eighteenth century.

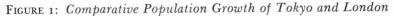

FIGURE 1: *Comparative Population Growth of Tokyo and London*

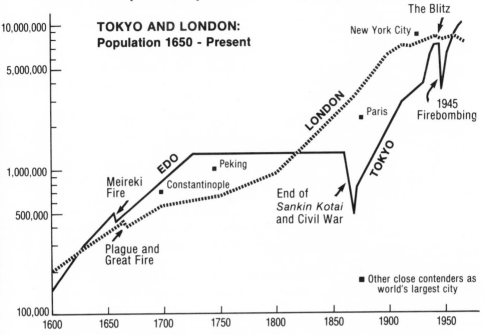

This chart is impressionistic at a number of points, particularly for the early growth pattern of Edo. I have accepted Naitō Akira's estimate of a population of 1.3 million for Edo at its peak, although this is slightly higher than most (*Edo to Edo-jō*, p. 136). The rate and degree of Edo's population decline in the 1860's are likewise pure conjecture. Figures for London from 1870 are for "Greater London," which was defined only in 1898, but are here projected back. Figures for Tokyo from 1876 are for the limits of the post-World War II Tokyo-to, but are here projected back in accord with the calculations of Kishimoto Minoru in Nihon chishi kenkyūjo, ed., *Nihon chishi* [Geography of Japan], 21 vols. (Ninomiya shoten, 1967), Vol. 7, p. 118. Estimates for other cities are taken from Tertius Chandler and Gerald Fox, *3000 Years of Urban Growth* (New York: Academic Press, 1974).

1868) nor London was even in the running as a great world city. Where relevant, I shall mention some of the older urban traditions in Japan and England, both continental and indigenous. But the case of Tokyo and London encourages particular attention to the "early modern" period of the sixteenth through the eighteenth (in the case of Tokyo, through the mid-nineteenth) centuries.[4] It is in part an

[4] The concept of an "early modern" period and its uniform application to Japan and Europe presents many yet unsolved problems. I can only suggest in a tentative way that both Japan and England were from the fifteenth and sixteenth centuries undergoing changes which were in certain ways preparatory to the "modernization" triggered by the Industrial Revolution. The entire problem has yet to be treated in an analytical comparative framework.

assumption, but also an argument of this essay that these centuries were critical in molding ideas and attitudes about the city in both cultures, in ways that persist to the present.

I have also narrowed the scope of this essay to Tokyo and London *as capital cities*. One justification is that these two capitals have played a dominant role in molding ideas of the city in their respective cultures. This is certainly true of London, which has been without a rival as the great English city. It is far less valid for Japan: Edo-Tokyo is a relatively new city which ever since its meteoric rise to dominance in the seventeenth century has continued to share its cultural and economic power with Kyoto and Osaka. At any rate, it is a major but unavoidable qualification of this essay that I have confined my attention to the capital cities, thereby neglecting the wide variety of urban ideas and images deriving from smaller cities and from cities of different functions, of which there are many. The aim here is therefore a comparison of ideas of the city as evolved in the capital, so that any broader comparative implications are limited to capitals or at least to very large multi-functional cities.

In an effort to uncover deep-lying implicit conceptions of the city, I have relied on two types of evidence in particular. First, I have stressed *language* as the critical structure for basic thinking about the city, accepting the hypothesis that language itself structures the processes and categories of human thought.[5] In particular, I have focused on the vocabulary by which urban (and, by implication, non-urban) environments are classified, seeking to capsulize both the defining and the normative powers of such words as "city" and "country" in English, or *"miyako"* and *"inaka"* in Japanese. Particularly revealing for the normative component are adjectival and nominal inflections of these basic urban referents, such as "civic," "countrified," *"miyabita,"* or *"inakamono."*[6]

The second source of evidence is *visual form*, both in the physical city (primarily its plan and architecture) and in visual depictions of

[5] The use of language as a comparative tool for understanding Japan is seen in the suggestive but often misleading cliché, "In the Japanese language there is no word for ————," common candidates being "rights," "guilt," "privacy," "style," and so forth. The point is not that the Japanese "have no word," but rather that they structure comparable realities into isolates of meaning which do not correspond precisely to those of the English language.

[6] Throughout this paper, I have relied primarily on the following sources for the historical uses of words: for English, *The Oxford English Dictionary* (Oxford University Press, 1933), and Raymond Williams, *The Country and the City* (New York: Oxford University Press, 1973), p. 307; for Japanese, Shinmura Izuru, comp., *Kōjien*, 2nd ed. (Iwanami shoten, 1969); Kindaichi Kyōsuke, comp., *Meikai kogo jiten*, new ed. (Sanseidō, 1962); Nihon daijiten kankōkai, ed., *Nihon kokugo daijiten* (Shōgakkan, 1972-   ); and Jōdaigo jiten henshū iinkai, ed., *Jidai-betsu kokugo daijiten: jōdai* (Sanseidō, 1967).

the city in art and literature. It is the visual faculty on which men have always relied as the primary means of identifying and categorizing a city, at least until the twentieth-century proclivity for analyzing the city as a sociological structure. Even today *most* people (including those who have most of the power to change cities) persist in identifying the city by the way it looks. It is my personal conviction that they are not amiss in doing so, and that every city should ideally be, in the words of J. B. Jackson, "a continuously satisfying aesthetic-sensory experience."[7]

In stressing the importance of a visual esthetic in structuring ideas of the city, I do not mean to deny the primacy of social and economic factors in determining the actual patterns of growth in any city. Indeed, it is my conviction that the idea of the city must be approached within a framework of the changing structure of political and economic power within society at large. For this reason, I have delineated four major categories of socioeconomic power within the traditional city as a scaffolding for the comparison: princely, priestly, aristocratic, and commoner. It is my assumption that each represents a coherent "order" within the city as a whole, with its own distinctive visual "aspect" and isolable conception of the city. This typology coincides nicely with the legal segregation of land in the city of Edo into the shogunal domain (primarily Edo Castle), the *jisha-chi* of the Buddhist temples and Shinto shrines; the *buke-chi*, where the daimyo and their samurai retinues resided; and the *machi-chi*, where the commoners lived and conducted their commercial and artisanal activities. While the categories seem more precisely geared to Edo than to London, there are commonsensical reasons for accepting these as the major sociopolitical orders in *any* pre-modern capital. At any rate, I have found them a useful framework for what must in any event be a very rough and simplistic comparison.

URBAN OPPOSITIONS

Every idea of the city harbors an implicit conception of what is *not* a city.[8] Consider the ease with which we grasp such oppositions as "city and country" or "rural and urban" in Anglo-American culture; so with *"tokai to nōson"* or *"machi to inaka"* in Japanese. So rich and com-

[7] Ervin H. Zube, ed., *Landscapes: Selected Writings of J. B. Jackson* (The University of Massachusetts Press, 1970), p. 87. I am indebted at a number of points in this paper to this humane volume of essays on the human landscape.

[8] Since writing this section, I have been greatly stimulated by Yi-fu Tuan, *Topophilia: A Study of Environmental Perceptions, Attitudes, and Values* (Englewood Cliffs, N.J.: Prentice-Hall, 1974), a book which I recommend for those interested in the problem of the conceptualization of urban versus non-urban environments.

plex are these ideas of the non-city that they have had a profound and continuing impact on the way men conceive of cities and aspire to change them. The issue is by no means simple, particularly with respect to the logical relationship between the two members of each pair: they may be, depending on the culture, antithetical, complementary, or coexistent. I would offer a hypothesis that the antithetical relationship is the most prevalent in Western culture, the complementary in China, and the coexistent in Japan. Some evidence for this scheme will emerge from the argument that follows.

The most primitive notion of the non-city in any culture is that of an environment which harbors dangers, a fearful and hostile landscape frequented by natural disasters, terrifying spirits, wild beasts, thieves, and invading armies. In the Western tradition, it is a conception categorized as "wilderness," particularly in its Biblical senses. But in the particular case of England, the conception of the city as a place of safety against a hostile wilderness was far less pervasive than on the Continent. In Japan, where conceptions of a dangerous and hostile environment have been in general far less compelling than in the West, it is difficult even to find a word comparable to "wilderness." In both Japan and England, the non-urban environment had been wholly pacified by the medieval period, and there lingered into the modern era few notions of a hostile anti-urban wilderness. In this respect, both seem similar variants from Continental traditions, where city walls, the prime symbol of the city as safety, often survived into modern times.

Far more persistent in both Japan and England was a conception of the non-city as a settled and working agricultural landscape. Of the many and complex variations within this general category of "rurality," perhaps the earliest and the most unfavorable idea was that of the non-city as a place of ignorance and cruelty. The city, by contrast, was the place of learning, benevolence, and art: in short, a "civilized" environment. Although this conception may be found in both Japan and England, there are subtly revealing differences. In Japan, it was in the early imperial capitals of Nara and Kyoto that such an idea first emerged, centering on the sense of opposition between the *miya*, the palace or court, and the *hina*, the environment distant from the court. The capital itself was known in native Japanese as the *miyako*, or "place of the imperial court," highlighting the crucial importance of the court aristocracy in sustaining this conception of urbanity. In the Nara and Heian periods, this idea took on esthetic overtones of elegance and grace, which are suggested by the word *miyabitaru*, well translated as "courtly." Against this was posed *hinabitaru*, suggesting coarseness of manner. The importance of this conception of city versus country for this essay, however, is that it remained unique to Kyoto and the imperial aristocracy. Indeed, the term *hinabitaru* was used in medieval times as a derogatory label for the provincial samurai class, and it is not surprising that Edo, as a samurai city, was never graced with the idea of *miyabitaru* urbanity.

In London as well, one finds a similar idea of the city as a place of polite and refined manners, as "civil" and "urbane." The contrast with Japan is that the esthetic overtones are less clearly developed, and the application of the terms extends beyond the court. These English words seem to involve a social rather than an esthetic distinction, and are opposed by an imagery far more specifically rural (that is, outside the city) than the classical *hinabitaru*, which seems a matter more of taste than location. Thus one finds in England, particularly in the sixteenth and seventeenth century, the emergence of such terms as "countrified" and "country bumpkin" to suggest the specifically rural content of that which is not "urbane." In Japan, it is not until the modern period that a word such as *inakamono*, closely corresponding to "country bumpkin," comes into common use with comparable nuances of the rural agrarian order.

But in both Japan and England in the early modern period, these older conceptions of the rural environment as a place lacking in taste were overwhelmed by a set of very different notions, which were to prove far more durable. In England, this new rurality is captured by the single word "country," perhaps the most complex and deeply felt environmental word in the culture.[9] In its strong esthetic and literary associations, the English "country" is given much of its structure by the *pastoral* mode. To an extent, this is merely descriptive of the topography of England, where from the sixteenth century pasture accounted for a large percentage of the land area. The comparison in Figure 2 of national land use in England and Japan in 1966 shows a striking contrast in this respect. Despite important fluctuations in these proportions over the past three centuries, the fundamental contrast has remained the same: the "natural" landscape (which in both countries is largely manmade) of greatest familiarity is "pasture" for the English and "mountain forest" for the Japanese.

The "pastoral" qualities of English rurality run far deeper than this physiographical fact, however, for the word harbors a long and complex tradition of esthetic and religious symbolism. Derived in the first instance from the classical tradition, from Hesiod to the most powerful

---

[9] I have drawn heavily on Raymond Williams, *The Country and the City*, for the changing English ideas of the "country." For the pastoral idea, I have drawn in addition on Leo Marx, *The Machine in the Garden: Technology and the Pastoral Ideal in America* (New York: Oxford University Press, 1964).

FIGURE 2: *National Land Use in Japan and England, 1966*

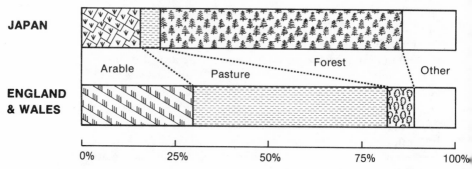

After Prue Dempster, *Japan Advances: A Geographical Study* (London: Methuen, 1967), p. 72.

formulations in Virgil, pastoralism was given deeper religious impact in Western Europe by Judeo-Christian accretions, notably the image of both God and Christ as shepherds: consider the popularity of Psalm 23 in English culture.[10] These ancient traditions enjoyed a great revival in England in the sixteenth through the eighteenth centuries, the crucial period in the formation of the English concept of "country." It was in the literature, painting, and landscape gardening of this period that the esthetic and emotional content of the pastoral "country" was fully exploited.

The socioeconomic key to this pastoral revival was the emergence of a landed elite with national political power: the aristocracy and gentry. This was part of the trend from the fifteenth through the eighteenth centuries toward the increasing concentration of landed wealth in the hands of a small class, through the continuing process of enclosure and the evolution of agrarian capitalism. As a sign of its growing wealth and power, the English landed elite patronized the painters, poets, and garden designers who established the pastoral mode within English culture.

The English conception of the "country" as pastoral, although clearly opposed to that of the city, was not necessarily antithetical to it. The pastoral environment was rather one of *mediation*, offering the innocence of the wilderness but none of its dangers, the arts of the city but none of its corruption. In the course of the eighteenth century, however, as English agriculture was increasingly threatened by urban-based mercantile forces, the idea of the "country" veered in a more

[10] Hallett Smith, "Elizabethan Pastoral," in Eleanor Terry, ed., *Pastoral and Romance: Modern Essays in Criticism* (Englewood Cliffs, N.J.: Prentice-Hall, 1969), p. 13.

defensive and consciously anti-urban direction. There were in fact two quite different directions, that of the agrarianists and that of the Romantics.

Of the two responses, the agrarianist form was the more economically rational, stressing the primacy of agriculture in providing the wealth of a nation. It was far more ethical than esthetic, asserting the essential moral worth of an agrarian way of life in contrast to the moral decadence of the city. It is a form of anti-urbanism which appeared simultaneously in other Western nations, notably in the Physiocratic School in mid-eighteenth century France and in the ideas of Thomas Jefferson in the American colonies. The agrarianist conception of the rural environment has survived to the present day as a dominant form of urban opposition in English culture.

The Romantic response was more emotional and esthetic in its structure and was opposed not only to the city but in a sense to society in general. Central to this response was a reinterpretation of the concept of "nature," which came to signify not an underlying order of which man was an integral part, but rather a substitute order untouched by man, of which an individual could partake only in solitary isolation. It was in a sense a revival of the primitive concept of the wilderness, still seen as the antithesis of the city, but now placed in a favorable light as a place of retreat for those who had had too much of civilization. It is an attitude closely involved with the early stages of industrialization in England and elsewhere, and as such represents perhaps the first distinctly modern conception of the non-urban environment.

Japanese conceptions of rurality offer a number of striking contrasts to the English. The most widely used antonym for the city in Japanese since the sixteenth century has been *inaka*, a word with two distinct implications. On the one hand, it draws on the older imagery of the rural environment as *hinabita*, or "countrified," an idea that has persisted until the present in such a contemptuous term as *inakappei*, or "hick." A more recent use of *inaka*, however, is to indicate "the place one came from," a usage deriving from the continuing waves of rural immigrants into the great cities, particularly Edo-Tokyo. In this meaning, it falls within a tradition of thought extending as far back as the Nara period and captured best by the powerful term *furusato*.

What is revealing in *furusato* is a tradition of rurality not inherently anti-urban, for the word (etymologically "the former place") in classical usage could refer to the city, as for example a capital which had been abandoned. This represents a tradition of rurality in Japanese thought which is basically temporal rather than spatial: such words as *furusato, kokyō, kyōri, kuni,* and *inaka* provide a vocabulary of nostalgia for a place once known. For this reason, it would in most cases be more accurate to translate them as "home" than as "country," although in fact a city-dweller's original "home" has often been—and increasingly so from early modern times—a rural environment. At any rate, these words seem to involve a far lesser sense of antithesis to the city than the English "country," and it is only recently that the terms *inaka* and *furusato* have been affected by elements of anti-urban romanticism, not in small part through Western influence.

Although *furusato* and *inaka* thus present a clear emotional landscape, traditionally they have not formed the basis for either a social ethic or a visual esthetic of the non-urban environment. These are to be sought in different ideas. The social ethic can be detected in such words as *mura* or *nōson*, the agricultural "village," and represent the Japanese version of agrarianism. This ethic first emerged in the writings of a number of Tokugawa thinkers who argued along traditional Confucian lines that agriculture is the "base" of a properly functioning society (whence *nōhonshugi*, the conventional Japanese term for agrarianism—"agriculture-as-the-base-ism"). A new strand in Tokugawa agrarianist thought appeared in the teachings of Ninomiya Sontoku, who as a peasant sage represented the interests not of the national polity but rather of the actual farming population.[11] But in either form, the contrast with England is obvious: Japan had no socially and culturally prestigious class attached to the land which had the wealth and leisure to elaborate the severe moralism of *nōhonshugi* in esthetically persuasive ways.

The dominant sense of the Japanese rural landscape is thus one of a tight *social* order engaged in a highly labor-intensive and land-efficient form of agriculture. It is an order which is suggested visually by the character for a rice paddy, *ta* 田, a sense of geometric patterns of fields and paddies. It is, in short, a landscape of economic production rather than one of esthetic consumption, and as such is not radically different from Jefferson's conception of the countryside. Although it is an order which encourages a defensive sense of moral superiority against the city, the Japanese rural environment as an idea is not aggressively anti-urban. As an order of the ruled rather than the ruling and of work rather than leisure, the Japanese *inaka* has lacked the intellectual articulation which is so distinct for the English "country."

The question which remains is the locus and content of the Japanese *esthetic* landscape and its relationship to the city. A literally pastoral environment simply did not exist in Japan, where animal husbandry

[11] For Japanese agrarianism and its modern fate, see Thomas R. H. Havens, *Farm and Nation in Modern Japan: Agrarian Nationalism, 1870-1940* (Princeton, N.J.: Princeton University Press, 1974).

has always been a peripheral agricultural pursuit, discouraged both by Buddhist proscriptions against meat-eating and, more basically, by constant demographic pressure in favor of more productive arable.[12] In terms of both literal familiarity (see Figure 2) and ancient religious feeling, the esthetic landscape in Japan has always been one of *mountain forests*. (It bears emphasis that in Japan, mountains and forests are rarely separated, either ecologically or conceptually.) It is doubtless this conceptual contrast of landscape—facilitated by an ambiguity of language—that led the Japanese to transpose the American song "Home on the Range" into "Home in a Mountain Pass" (*Tōge no wagaya*).

The structure of meaning in the Japanese mountain landscape is complex. Hori Ichirō, for example, has detected such special meanings of mountains as symbols of procreation in their volcanic aspect, symbols of fertility in their watershed function, and the abodes of the dead in their isolation from the everyday world of man.[13] For the purposes of comparison, however, it may be easiest to envision the Japanese mountain landscape as deriving from two broad traditions, the Shinto belief in the spiritual power of trees and rocks, and the concept—largely Chinese in origin—of mountains and streams as a place of retreat from the cares of the workaday world.[14]

Although there are superficial parallels between the Japanese affection for a mountain landscape and the English romantic love of "wilderness," the contrast is profound. The romantic attachment to mountain wilderness emerged in England very late, following a seventeenth-century metamorphosis in Western attitudes toward mountains, which had until then been viewed as ugly and dangerous.[15] In Japan, by contrast, from the very origins of Japanese history, mountains were looked on with favor as a source of spiritual power and esthetic enjoyment and were never considered a form of flight from civilization. One does find in Japan the rather Sinified and Buddhistic tradition of retreat to a rustic "grass hut" (*sōan*), particularly in old age or in times of political turmoil. Kamo no Chōmei's thirteenth-

---

12 It is revealing that the most common Japanese term for "pastoral" is *den'en* (literally, "paddies and gardens"), a forced equivalent which brings to the modern Japanese mind specifically Western images.

13 Ichirō Hori, *Folk Religion in Japan* (Chicago: Chicago University Press, 1968), Chap. 4.

14 There are major differences between the Chinese and Japanese uses of the mountain landscape, lying principally in the strongly rural bias of Chinese elite ideals. It is interesting to speculate on the strongly "pastoral" qualities of Chinese literati culture in the idealization of a golden mean between civic commitment and natural retreat.

15 Marjorie Hope Nicolson, *Mountain Gloom and Mountain Glory: The Development of the Aesthetics of the Infinite* (Ithaca, N.Y.: Cornell University Press, 1959).

century *Hōjōki* is the classic statement of this tradition. Yet even there, the mountain environment is less a place for self-torturing asceticism than for the spontaneous enjoyment of a simple life in the woods. It was also an exceptional response: rather than communing with mountains in lonely isolation from society, the Japanese on the whole have enjoyed them in highly social contexts, in the form of organized pilgrimages to mountain shrines or temples, or in the sociable group appreciation of gardens and landscape paintings.

Far from representing the antithesis of the city as in the English (and especially American) romantic tradition, mountain forests in Japan bore little or no implication of hostility to or incompatibility with the urban environment. The entire Japanese urban tradition is filled with techniques of *integrating* mountain landscapes into the fabric of the city, both as a way of drawing upon their protective power and as a source of esthetic enjoyment. Thus, for example, one of the few instances of planning for esthetic (as opposed to social) effect in the city of Edo was the orientation of certain streets to provide a vista of Mount Tsukuba to the east or of Mount Fuji to the west: best-known of these was Suruga-chō, which at the hands of woodblock artists came to constitute one of the most famous scenes of the city.[16]

Mountains were also brought into the Japanese city in the form of *gardens*. The distinctively Japanese style of gardening evolved in the medieval period, largely in Buddhist monasteries in urban and suburban locations. Although temples and shrines have continued to provide a strongly gardened aspect to the Japanese city, the practice also spread naturally to the secular elite, both the court aristocracy and the samurai, and in the course of the Tokugawa period to the urban middle classes. Thus the forested grounds of the temples and daimyō mansions in Edo were complemented by a vogue for miniaturized and symbolic forms of landscape gardening, particularly bonsai and other styles of potted plants.

In England, by contrast, the ideal pastoral landscape, as it was expressed in the distinctive English gardening techniques of the seventeenth and eighteenth centuries, was of rural rather than of urban locale, and of secular rather than of religious origin. Reflecting the functional demands of hunting and sport, the "landscape parks" of the English landed elite were of a spacious and "pastoral" aspect, in contrast to the far more compact and symbolic mountain-derived gardens of the Japanese. This created more of a problem in the passage of gar-

[16] Kirishiki Shinjirō, "Tenshō/Keichō/Kan'ei-ki Edo shigaichi kensetsu ni okeru keikan sekkei," in Tōkyō toritsu daigaku, Toshi kenkyū soshiki iinkai, *Edo-Tōkyō no toshi-shi oyobi toshi keikaku-shi-teki kenkyū, I* (author, 1971), pp. 1-22. Kirishiki demonstrates that Edo streets were laid out for views not only of distant mountains but also of hills and bluffs within the city itself.

dening ideals to the middle classes, which in London could scarcely afford expansive parks: at best, they had to be satisfied with small lawns. Thus English popular gardening has remained more in the older monastic tradition of small herb, flower, and fruit gardens, a conception that is more Edenic than Arcadian. Meanwhile, the deeper yearnings of the English remain fixed outside the city, in the direction of the pastoral countryside.

THE PRINCELY ASPECT

The Early Modern Pattern

The concern here is with the manner in which a political sovereign (prince) imposes upon his capital a visual sense of the power he wields. Three characteristic ways for expressing a princely sense of the city are monumental architecture, geometric ordering of the city plan in accord with a cosmic scheme, and permanence of building techniques. These are certainly the most ancient expressions of the idea of the city, and remain today the mark by which most people instinctively identify a city, particularly that of a political capital. Edo and London in this respect bear a revealing similarity: neither has ever *looked* very much like a great capital. To grasp the implications of this similarity, it is necessary to place both cities within the context of the larger continental traditions against which they were inevitably judged.

For Japan, the standards of princely urbanity were set by China, which had provided the model for the first Japanese cities, the capitals of Heijō-kyō (Nara), founded in 710, and its successor from 794, Heian-kyō (now Kyoto). The Chinese model of an imperial capital or *ching* (read *kyō* in Japanese, whence *Kyōto*, "capital city," and Tō-*kyō*, "eastern capital") had gradually emerged from hazy ancient origins during the first centuries of the united empire, culminating in one of its grandest manifestations in the T'ang dynasty capital of Ch'ang-an, planned in the late sixth century, which provided the direct inspiration for the new Japanese capitals.[17]

Although the particular application of the model varied from dynasty to dynasty in China, the basic elements were always the same: careful siting of a new capital in accord with cosmological and geomantic principles, establishment of a basic square or rectangular form with massive walls of copious girth, division of the area within the walls into a basic grid plan, and careful placement of public buildings in relation to the overall scheme. It was a highly *centered* design,

[17] For the evolution of the Chinese model, see Arthur F. Wright, "The Cosmology of the Chinese City," in G. William Skinner, ed., *The City in Late Imperial China* (Stanford: Stanford University Press, 1976).

reaching out through axial roads and gates to the entire empire, and upward through a hierarchical series of enclosures to the imperial palace, the point of contact with Heaven.[18] The entire city was an expression of the power and cosmology of the imperial order, perhaps the purest example of princely urbanity the world has ever known. Its all-encompassing form and intellectual clarity have made the Chinese capital an inspiration for designers of the city until the present day.[19]

Fully as impressive as the coherence of this ancient urban order, as Arthur Wright has stressed, was its persistence, for it served as the model for the design of new Chinese capitals until the Manchu rebuilding of Peking in the seventeenth century. At the same time, he further observes, it was ironically a tradition of urban impermanence, for these cities were built of earth and wood and could last scarcely more than a few decades without rebuilding.[20] These two characteristics were of course related, since both the necessity and the ease of frequent rebuilding helped perpetuate a highly durable tradition of urban construction and design.

These twin characteristics of the Chinese city—persistence of ideal plan and impermanence of physical artifact—were transposed in the history of the city in Western Europe into the persistence of physical remains despite the loss of planning ideas. The ancient Roman imperial model for a city, seen best in colonial towns such as Londinium, was in many respects similar to the Chinese, stressing auspicious siting, square walls with axial roads, and the proper location of public buildings. The crucial difference is that the Roman model of city planning was almost totally forgotten after the fall of the Empire, while the Chinese idea survived intact to modern times. At the same time, the Western ideal has been to build cities which would last as long as possible, with the ironic result that although the Roman *idea* of the city has vanished, its physical relics are cherished in many places to this day.

The very idea of planning a city in princely fashion waned in Europe during the Middle Ages, to be revived in a distinctly new pattern in the renaissance and baroque city. Given the difficulties and expense

[18] Nelson Wu, *Chinese and Indian Architecture: The City of Man, the Mountain of God, and the Realm of the Immortals* (New York: Braziller, 1963), pp. 38-45.

[19] For example, Edmund N. Bacon, *Design of Cities*, rev. ed. (New York: Viking, 1974), p. 244: "Possibly the greatest single work of man on the face of the earth is Peking"; Steen Eiler Rasmussen, *Towns and Buildings* (1949; reprint ed., Cambridge, Mass.: MIT Press, 1969), p. 1: "Peking, the capital of old China! Has there ever been a more majestic and illuminative example of sustained town-planning?"

[20] Wright, "Symbolism and Function"; similar points are made in F. W. Mote, "A Millennium of Chinese Urban History: Form, Time, and Space Concepts in Soochow," *Rice University Studies*, vol. 59, no. 4 (fall 1973), pp. 35-65.

of building entirely new capitals in the increasingly integrated states of Western Europe, most of the baroque urban design techniques involved the imposition of a princely aspect upon existing cities. Walls of course remained an essential feature of the continental capitals, but the strictures of earlier growth patterns rarely permitted the use of ideal geometrical designs. The preoccupation thus shifted from that of regular enclosure to that of *focusing*, in accord with the newly discovered rules of vanishing-point perspective. Primary attention was devoted to monumental structures of great permanence, set off and framed by broad avenues intersecting in ways designed to enhance the monumentality of the buildings.

How did Edo and London relate to these continental models for a capital city? The Japanese had directly borrowed the Chinese model, imposing the continental plan upon the indigenous aristocratic palace, or *miya*, hence *miyako*. The Chinese plan sat poorly with the Japanese from the start, however, for it was economically premature and philosophically alien in its preference for intellectualized regularity. The crucial enclosing walls remained unbuilt in both Nara and Kyoto, and the symmetry of the plan soon crumbled as the city grew eastward into the hills, a more compatible environment for the Japanese urban temperament. Kyoto, the imperial capital for over one thousand years after the late eighth century move from Nara, gradually assumed a relatively unprincely aspect.[21] The private and unassertive quality of the capital, challenged only briefly in the late sixteenth century when Hideyoshi strove to give it a more appropriately sovereign look,[22] was a reflection of the political configuration in the ancient and medieval capital, with power gradually devolving away from the imperial throne and eventually from the city itself.

Hideyoshi's successor as national unifier, Tokugawa Ieyasu, chose to build a new capital in the Kanto plain of east Japan, on the site of a former local castle. The selection of the site of the new city of Edo and its general orientation showed a degree of Chinese attention to auspicious signs, but there the similarity ends. Edo was designed rather on the unique indigenous model of the *jōkamachi*, or "castle towns," which sprang up throughout Japan as power centers of local feudal lords during the sixteenth century.[23] Edo was initially designed, be-

[21] For the planning and evolution of Kyoto, see John W. Hall, "Kyoto as Historical Background," in John W. Hall and Jeffrey P. Mass, eds., *Medieval Japan: Essays in Institutional History* (New Haven: Yale University Press, 1974), pp. 3-38.

[22] For Hideyoshi's rebuilding of Kyoto, see Mary Elizabeth Berry, "Hideyoshi in Kyoto: The Arts of Peace" (Ph.D. dissertation, Harvard University, 1975), chap. 3.

[23] John W. Hall, "The Castle Town and Japan's Modern Urbanization," in John W. Hall and Marius B. Jansen, eds., *Studies in the Institutional History of Early*

ginning in 1590, *not* as a national capital, but merely as the private castle town of a powerful feudal lord.[24] It was not until Ieyasu's emergence as national hegemon after 1600 and the gradual institution of the *sankin kōtai* system, by which provincial lords (daimyō) were required to spend alternate years in residence in Edo, that the city took on a truly national character.[25] And even then, it was never the *miyako*; that ancient courtly concept remained with Kyoto, where the politically impotent emperor and imperial courtiers continued to reside.

The plan of Edo was simply that of a very large *jōkamachi* adapted to the special needs of the *sankin kōtai*, and as such was based largely on considerations of military defense and social control through class segregation. Militarily, the concern was not for the defense of the city as a whole, much less for that of the nation, but purely for the security of the shogun and his immediate retainers. There was no enclosing wall around the city, which blended imperceptibly with the country-side, but merely around the shogunal castle, which sat in the center. Architecturally, Edo Castle was certainly monumental, at least within the context of East Asian building traditions, and particularly the hundred-meter donjon constructed in 1638. But Edo shared with the Chinese city the character of "planned ephemerality" through construction in short-lived materials, and when the donjon was destroyed in the Meireki fire less than two decades later, it was never rebuilt. In time, the many trees in and around Edo Castle came to lend it a hidden and private aspect.[26]

Apart from the castle, Edo was laid out in a highly defensive manner, not from concern with external invaders, as in most cities, but rather with an eye to internal threats either from the resident daimyō or from commoner mobs. The principle was one of strict segregation of classes by residential area. The overall form of Edo was therefore not an ideal geometrical form with cosmic referents, but rather an irregular spiral leading clockwise outward from the castle in a pattern of descent down through the social ladder, passing through the residences of the great lords, into the area occupied by the *hatamoto* retainers of

---

Modern Japan (Princeton, N.J.: Princeton University Press, 1968), pp. 169-188. It is remarkable that no general history of city planning, to my knowledge, recognizes the building of the *jōkamachi* in the period 1550-1650 as one of the world's great efforts in the planned construction of new cities.

[24] For background in English on the design and structure of Edo, see Takeo Yazaki, *Social Change and the City in Japan* (Japan Publications, 1968), chaps. 5, 6.

[25] For details on the *sankin kōtai*, see Toshio G. Tsukahira, *Feudal Control in Tokugawa Japan: The Sankin Kōtai System* (East Asian Research Center, Harvard University, 1970).

[26] Naitō Akira has gone so far as to call Edo "a castle town without a castle." Naitō Akira, *Edo to Edo-jō* (Kajima shuppankai, 1966), p. 64.

the shogun, finally through the central area of the *machi-chi* at Nihon-bashi, and out the Tōkaidō which served as the main approach to the city.[27] This spiral, which seems to have been unique to Edo and was probably not an intellectually conceived design, was defined not by roads but by the wide moats and canals which served for defense and as the primary means of the transport of goods in the city.

Defensive planning was carried out within each of the residential areas as well. The commoner *machi-chi* was laid out, as I shall detail shortly, in a regular grid plan with barriers at every major intersection for close and efficient control. In the samurai *buke-chi* as well, barriers and checkpoints were frequent, with most streets intersecting in **T**'s rather than in crosses so as to deny through access to any rebellious forces.[28] As a further means of control, virtually all wheeled vehicles were prohibited in the streets of Edo, particularly for personal transport. The contrast with contemporary European planning is striking: although baroque monarchs were also preoccupied with military force, the concern was more aggressive than defensive, resulting in long, broad avenues suited for parades and martial display. And while the Japanese were designing streets to discourage carriages, European designers were widening them to allow for still heavier wheeled traffic, particularly the private carriages of the wealthy.

London, in contrast with Edo, was neither planned nor dominated by a sovereign. In fact, "London" was in origin two cities, Westminster and the City of London, which eventually grew into one but continued to maintain separate identities and a clearly defined relationship.[29] National power was entrenched in the Houses of Parliament and the royal palace at Westminster, whereas the commercial City of London lay about a mile down the Thames, encircled by its ancient walls. The English crown made few and never successful attempts to govern or to plan the growth of the entire city, and granted to the corporate City of London a broad assortment of special rights and privileges in return for military and financial assistance, privileges which survive to this day although now of little but ceremonial significance.

[27] See ibid., p. 122, for a diagram. More expressive than "spiral" to describe Edo's form is the shape of the *hiragana* for the syllable *no*. For the general Japanese design principle of "hierarchical access," see Toshi dezain kenkyūtai, *Nihon no toshi kūkan* (Shōkokusha, 1968), p. 32.

[28] This remains true of Tokyo today; one ambitious urban geographer has counted all of Tokyo's street intersections (total 155,676), and found that there are twice as many **T**-intersections as crossroads. Masai Yasuo, *Tōkyō no seikatsu chizu* (Jiji tsūshinsha, 1972), p. 132.

[29] For the structure and character of London, I am indebted throughout this paper to Steen Eiler Rasmussen, *London: The Unique City* (1934; reprint ed., Cambridge, Mass.: The MIT Press, 1967).

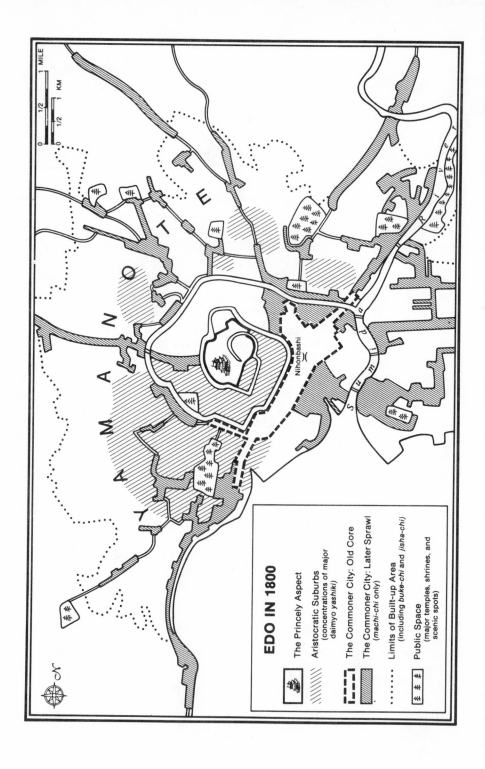

EDO IN 1800

The Princely Aspect

Aristocratic Suburbs
(concentrations of major
daimyo *yashiki*)

The Commoner City: Old Core
(*machi-chi* only)

The Commoner City: Later Sprawl

Limits of Built-up Area
(including *buke-chi* and *jisha-chi*)

Public Space
(major temples, shrines, and
scenic spots)

Nihombashi

Sumida River

0 1/2 1 KM

0 1/2 1 MILE

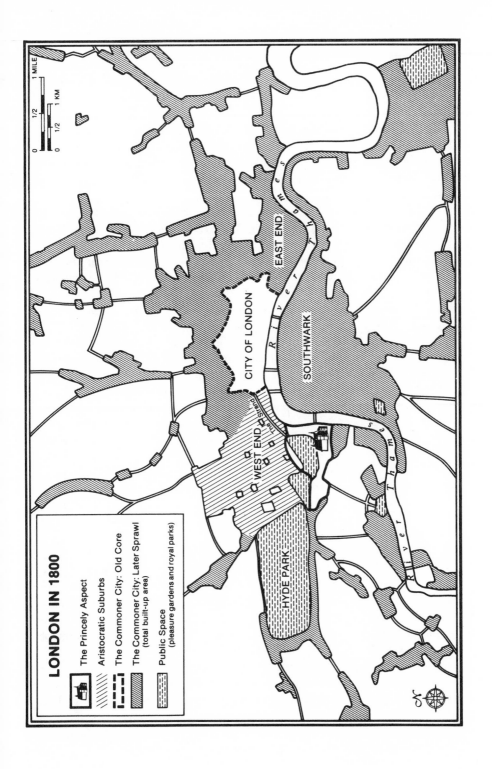

LONDON IN 1800

- The Princely Aspect
- Aristocratic Suburbs
- The Commoner City: Old Core
- The Commoner City: Later Sprawl
  (total built-up area)
- Public Space
  (pleasure gardens and royal parks)

CITY OF LONDON

EAST END

SOUTHWARK

WEST END

HYDE PARK

River Thames

1 MILE

1 KM

1/2

1/2

0

In formal terms, the consequence was a very limited aspect of princely urbanity in London. Baroque planning techniques were, of course, not without influence there. Indeed, if John Evelyn and Christopher Wren had been given their way in the wake of the Great Fire of 1666, the City of London would have been converted into a continental capital with a coherent, geometrical street plan and grand perspectives. Yet here, as with the later plans for rebuilding Tokyo after the 1923 earthquake (when one young Japanese architect fresh from study at the École des Beaux Arts in Paris even produced a textbook baroque plan for reconstruction),[30] or for rebuilding both Tokyo and London after bombing in World War II, plans came to naught. In each case, the result was remarkably the same, with the power of long-entrenched land-holding patterns proving far stronger than the authority, limited by custom and law, of those seeking to impose princely urbanity from above.

London was thus lacking in any visible overall form, existing simply as two contrasting nodes with the space between and around filled in according to the dictates of economic and social advantage rather than political fiat. In this, it was perhaps not so different from Edo, which, despite the vague spiral form, was actually perceived by most residents in a similar fashion—a cluster of commoner commercial activity surrounding Nihonbashi and an unassertive group of buildings composing Edo Castle. In both cases, the princely center was unimposing by continental standards, relatively unframed and unfocused, surrounded by the greenery of the royal (and public) parks in London and the shogunal (but private) gardens in Edo. London's public buildings were far more permanent than Edo's (especially with a general shift from wood to brick after the Great Fire), and its streets grander if not straighter. Yet both within their larger urban traditions were of muted and unpretentious princely aspect.

This similarity is explained most fundamentally by the natural defenses which an island configuration has provided for both countries. For this reason, Lewis Mumford has argued, England and Japan were among the very few cultures in the world (he mentions Egypt as a third) which failed to evolve a tradition of cities with walls, which in both China and continental Europe came to be a sine qua non of princely urbanity.[31] But of equal importance was the fundamentally limited power of the English crown and the Japanese shogunate, in contrast to the absolute sovereigns of the continental mold, who were far more capable of imposing their will on the plan of the city. The

[30] *Asahi gurafu*, May 14, 1924, p. 13. The architect was Nakamura Junpei.
[31] Lewis Mumford, *The City in History: Its Origins, Its Transformations, and Its Prospects* (New York: Harcourt, Brace, & World, 1961), p. 63.

manner of limiting sovereign power in the two countries differed in critical respects. The English crown was limited by long custom, formalized as law, not only vis-à-vis the City of London but also vis-à-vis the peers, who themselves had little concern for a grand capital, their attention being focused rather outward to the "country." The Japanese shogun, by contrast, was limited not by law but by the pragmatic limits of his military power vis-à-vis the daimyō, many of whom were potential enemies. Although the shogun had far greater power over his capital than the English crown over London, the shogunal face of the city remained a surprisingly shy and defensive one.

The lack of an imposing princely aspect at the center of both capitals was exaggerated by their very large size as pre-modern cities, for both grew outward in the seventeenth and eighteenth centuries in a sprawling, unplanned pattern which was greatly accelerated under the impact of industrialization. Lacking any limiting walls or centralized planning authority, both cities came to take on the form of what Steen Rasmussen in the case of London has termed a "scattered city," in contrast to the "concentrated city" typical of the continent.[32] Although it would be difficult to accept the label "concentrated" for the Chinese city, in which the generous area within the walls enabled relatively low densities, it was certainly a highly "coherent city," against which Edo appeared fully as "scattered" as London.

Modern Continuities

Edo and London in their late pre-industrial phases were prematurely modern, in the sense that both already manifested the low levels of formal coherence which were to become characteristic of all great modern cities, at least outside the historical cores. In the absence of defining walls, in the lack of a unitary planning authority, and in their vast and complex structure, both Edo and London in the eighteenth century were far closer to twentieth-century urban realities than their continental relatives. It is thus no surprise that the Industrial Revolution served only to perpetuate their common lack of coherently planned visual form.

Efforts were made to improve the princely aspect of both cities, particularly Edo with its renaming as Tokyo in 1868.[33] In the autumn of the same year, the emperor moved from Kyoto into Edo Castle, which thereby became the Imperial Palace. Yet Tokyo still did not become the *miyako*, for the ancient and dignified urbanity of that term

[32] Rasmussen, *London: The Unique City*, chap. 1.

[33] For a more detailed analysis of the changing conceptualization of modern Tokyo, see my "Tokyo as an Idea: An Exploration of Japanese Urban Thought Until 1945," *Journal of Japanese Studies*, vol. 4, no. 1 (1978), pp. 45-80.

never seemed to befit an upstart city like Edo-Tokyo. Tokyo in the late nineteenth century was less an "imperial" city, home of the emperor, than an "imperialist" city, seat of the empire, a sense best captured by the pretentious sinicism "Teito" ("imperial capital") by which Tokyo was commonly known from the time of the Meiji Constitution of 1889.[34] Visually, Tokyo never lived up to the grand ring of "Teito." The public portions of the central city in the mid-Meiji period were decorated with equestrian statues of military heroes and monumental buildings in a variety of Western revival styles, differing from Victorian London's "obscure and complicated dialogue"[35] of styles only in a generally more austere sense of design and a far greater sense of incongruity. These efforts at a Westernized imperial style climaxed with the completion in 1909 of Katayama Tōkuma's Akasaka Detached Palace, a lavish imitation of Versailles which was as out of place culturally and chronologically as it was costly. From this point, efforts at a grand European continental style of princely urbanity waned, and, despite such grim efforts as the Diet Building of 1936, modern architectural functionalism took easy root in fertile Japanese soil.

Since the collapse of the emperor system and the loss of overseas empire in 1945, Tokyo's appearance has become progressively less ordered and monumental, although the Imperial Palace survives as one of the most curious princely monuments in the world. The massive walls of Edo Castle remain intact, together with a few surviving gates and watchtowers, but most of the buildings in this vast area lying at the heart of the city remain invisible beneath a shroud of trees. For the past three and a half centuries, it has remained a totally private domain, creating a "sacred void" (*le rien sacré*) and making Tokyo, in the analysis of Roland Barthes, the only world capital with an "empty center."[36] One might call it a "concave" princely aspect.

London in the process of industrialization may have outstripped Tokyo in the building of princely monuments, but certainly never enough to offer competition to Paris or Vienna. The city as a whole grew apace, far beyond the bounds of visual comprehension, and like Tokyo it quickly gained the reputation of a metropolis vast in area and numbers but with little sense of a clear and ordered presence befitting a national capital. It is a reputation the two share today, as in the observation in a popular guide to Japan, that "some compare

[34] Tōkyō hyakunenshi henshū iinkai, ed., *Tōkyō hyakunenshi* (Tokyo-to, 1972-1973), vol. 3, p. 7. "Teito" was also commonly used for Japan's first capital Nara in similar circumstances eleven centuries earlier.

[35] The phrase quoted is from John Summerson, "London, the Artifact," in H. J. Dyos and Michael Wolff, eds., *The Victorian City* (Boston: Routledge & Kegan Paul, 1973), p. 311.

[36] Roland Barthes, *L'empire des signes* (Geneva: Albert Skira, 1970), pp. 44-46.

Tokyo's vastness to that of London. The two towns are very different and even their vastness cannot be compared: London is a galaxy of countless villages, Tokyo is an overgrown small town."[37]

This mutual lack of a princely aspect makes Tokyo and London all the more deceptive in terms of their immense integrating influence on a national scale—socially, culturally, and politically. This contradiction between the appearance of power and its reality has been suggested for early modern London in E. A. Wrigley's observation that "the comparative neglect of London as a potent engine working towards change in England in the century 1650-1750 is the more paradoxical in that the dominance of Paris within France has long been a notion in political history." A similar argument has been advanced for Edo by Gilbert Rozman.[38] It would be most revealing to pursue this notion for modern Tokyo and London, not only with respect to social and economic change, but on the cultural and political levels as well. It can here only be hypothesized that the diminished visual aspect of power in both cities has led to a consistent underestimation of their real power.

It must be stressed that the centrality of London within England has throughout the past three hundred years been much greater than that of Edo-Tokyo in Japan. In the eighteenth century, London accounted for about 10 percent of the population of England and Wales, whereas Edo's share in Japan was only between 3 and 4 percent. In the course of industrial growth, similarly, London's proportion rose by the 1890's to over 20 percent, whereas Tokyo by the 1950's accounted for only 10 percent of the national population. Furthermore, the gap between London and other English cities has always been pronounced, with the second largest city (Liverpool until World War I, Birmingham thereafter) having a population of only 10 to 15 percent of that of the Metropolis (a term, incidentally, strongly suggestive of London's centrality) over the past century. Osaka's population, in contrast, has been a consistent 30 to 40 percent of that of Edo-Tokyo ever since the seventeenth century.[39]

London's size has indeed been so great, in the imagery of a head too large for its body, that it appears a striking anomaly among early

[37] George Mikes, *The Land of the Rising Yen—Japan* (London: André Deutsch, 1970), p. 187.

[38] E. A. Wrigley, "A Simple Model of London's Importance in Changing English Society and Economy 1650-1750," *Past and Present* 37 (1967), p. 70, and Gilbert Rozman, "Edo's Importance in the Changing Tokugawa Society," *The Journal of Japanese Studies*, vol. 1, no. 1 (autumn 1974), pp. 91-112.

[39] These estimates are derived from statistics in Wrigley, "A Simple Model of London's Importance"; Irene Taeuber, *The Population of Japan* (Princeton, N.J.: Princeton University Press, 1958); and *The Statesman's Yearbook*.

modernizing nations. It is only in the unbalanced patterns of metro-politan growth in the late-developing nations that one finds such a disproportionately large city, often assigned the term "primate city."[40] Tokyo, on the other hand, has consistently shared its economic and cultural (if not political) power within the nation at large with Kyoto and Osaka, and there is much to be said for a Tokyo-Kyoto-Osaka triangle as the proper approach to Tokyo's centrality. It may also be suggested that this relationship has tended to heighten Tokyo's de-fensive aspect as a political center considerably more than that of Lon-don, which for all of its far longer history has had no such challengers in any sphere.

THE PRIESTLY ASPECT

In ancient capitals, the priestly aspect was typically integrated into the overall princely design of the city, reflecting the degree to which ap-peasement of the gods was considered part and parcel of political rule. In the ideal Chinese and Roman cities, for example, such religious edifices as the Altar to Heaven or the Temple of Jupiter were assigned a proper place in the city and constructed in a style which was har-monious with the more secular buildings. It was only with the rise of universalistic religion—Buddhism in East Asia and Christianity in the West—that religious institutions came to wield political power dis-tinct from and even competitive with that of the secular ruler, evolving a visual aspect which could be clearly distinguished from the princely face of the city.

In both Japan and England, where Buddhism and Christianity were formative cultural influences from an early stage in their urban tra-ditions, the priestly aspect of the city was a distinctive one, reflecting the independent economic and political power of the ecclesiastical establishment. Similarly, however, drastic measures were taken almost simultaneously in the late medieval period to destroy this independent power, through Henry VIII's separation of the Anglican church and dissolution of the monasteries in the 1530's and Oda Nobunaga's sub-jugation of the military power of the Buddhist church in the 1570's. The implications of these moves for the priestly aspect of early modern Edo and London were profoundly different, however, in ways which can be understood only with some initial consideration of the medieval face of the churches in England and of the Buddhist temples in Japan.

In medieval London, religious institutions offered two quite differ-ent aspects to the city, that of the parish churches within the City of

[40] Eric E. Lampard, "The Urbanizing World," in Dyos and Wolff, eds., *The Victorian City*, p. 39.

London and that of the monasteries and convents on the outskirts. The dissolution of the monasteries obliterated the suburban face and with it the landed wealth of the church. The churches at the center of the city remained, serving important charitable and local urban community functions. The spires of the city's churches continued to dominate the urban skyline, and came to provide London with a distinctive visual imagery. It was common, as in Visscher's drawing of the city in the early seventeenth century, to exaggerate the height of the church towers and spires in representing London in panorama.[41] Among the churches, St. Paul's cathedral in particular served as a center of visual attraction by its massive bulk, even though its five-hundred-foot spire was never rebuilt after destruction by lightning in 1561.

City churches in London were thus primarily a vertical presence, for they typically sat on small and crowded plots of land, rarely set off by the plazas and broad avenues which were the preference of continental city designers. As with all important buildings, churches were constructed primarily of stone, conveying a monumental presence characteristic of Western churchly tradition. However diminished the independent power of the church in the city as a whole, London's parish churches have survived as focuses of community activity and persist as a distinctive mark in the cityscape.

East Asia offers a rather different tradition of priestly urbanity. The first appearance of Buddhism, in both the Chinese city and the early Japanese capital of Nara, was marked by a vertical assertiveness not radically different from the medieval Christian church. In the T'ang capital of Ch'angan, for example, the pagodas of the Buddhist temples, "with their gilded finials reaching towards the sky, added color and variety to an otherwise monotonous skyline."[42] In the Japanese capital of Nara, Buddhist temples were a commanding presence both visually and politically. The Great Buddha Hall of Tōdaiji remains today the world's largest wooden structure under a single roof, and every major temple in the city featured a tall pagoda. Less than half a century later, however, the capital was moved to Kyoto, partly in an effort to subdue the growing political power of the clergy, thus putting an end to the brief Japanese effort at a monumental style of priestly urbanity.

From the ninth century, Buddhist temples in Japan were increasingly located in forested mountain settings or in the hills on the outskirts of cities. This shift from "plains Buddhism" to "mountain Buddhism" meant, not that temples deserted the city, but rather that they came to serve as an integrating link between the city and the sur-

---

[41] C. J. Visscher, *London Before the Fire: A Grand Panorama* (c. 1616; reprint ed., London: Sidgwick and Jackson, 1973), p. 1 of commentary by J. S. Wellsman.

[42] Wright, "Symbolism and Function," p. 674.

rounding mountains. Many temples and monasteries maintained a location in or near the center of cities, for they performed the essential functions of the disposal of the dead and the provision of charitable services. But the visual presence of medieval temples was considerably diminished from those of Nara, taking on a certain mountain-forest quality in their hilly locations and generous planting of greenery. Where the spires of London's churches seemed to reach up defiantly to a transcendent Creator, the roofs of Edo's low and hidden temples stretched out to the power of the mountains.

The planning and construction of Edo came only a few years after Nobunaga had broken the independent power of the Buddhist church. Tokugawa Ieyasu, however, was less hostile to Buddhism than Nobunaga, and saw in the ecclesiastical network an effective tool for the control of Christianity. In Edo, the Buddhist establishment was permitted extensive grants of land, amounting to some 15 percent of the total area of the city. Since the total number of temples was over one thousand, the average land occupied by any single temple was less than half a hectare, with only a handful of privileged institutions holding sizable plots. In this way, the political power of the church was effectively fragmented in the interest of close control, but the sense of wealth and power conveyed by such an extensive area of temple land was greater than in the case of London's crowded city churches.

An equally important contrast with London was the presence in Edo of many thriving centers of folk worship. Classified as Shinto shrines (although the object of worship was in some cases a Buddhist deity) and administered as part of the *jisha-chi*, these centers of devotion were considerably more important than the Buddhist temples in structuring the community life of Edo, as today they continue to do in Tokyo. Although perhaps less effective than the parish churches of London in regulating urban community activities, the shrines have nevertheless given Japanese city life an element of cohesion which would not otherwise exist. In Tokyo today, as in Edo before, every established resident will consider himself the *ujiko*—a word aptly translated as "parishioner"—of the neighborhood shrine.

Together with the larger and more public of the Buddhist temples, many of the folk shrines of Edo served a critical urban function as a place of public gathering and recreation.[43] From an early time, temples and shrines throughout Japan had provided the site for periodic markets, and in Edo this commercial function was augmented by that

[43] For a description of Edo's recreational areas (*yūkanjo*), see Tanaka Seidai, *Nihon no kōen* (Kajima shuppankai, 1974), ch. 1. On p. 15 is a map showing the major areas, of which the great majority are shrines and temples.

of general relaxation, sport, and entertainment. In this sense, the shrines and temples should be compared, not with the churches of London, but with the public parks, particularly the royal parks for which Hyde Park provided the precedent in the early seventeenth century.[44] The major difference was in appearance. The parks of London tend to be of the preferred pastoral mode, but religious grounds in Japan were of the mountain landscape style. Located typically on a hill or bluff, the shrines and temples of Edo were approached by a long, winding path, punctuated by teahouses and rows of steps, enshrouded in a natural environment of trees, ponds, and waterfalls characteristic of landscape painting. In panoramic depictions of Edo, these religious centers were conventionally represented as groups of evergreen trees, much as London's churches were shown as spires.

The priestly aspect of Edo was dealt a severe blow in the transformation into Tokyo after 1868. The Buddhist church not only lost the protection of the state but came under strong attack in the early Meiji period, resulting in much destruction of temple lands. Despite some conversion of abandoned daimyo lands into "public parks"—the very idea did not exist until borrowed from the West and rendered as *kōen*—the proportion of open land in Tokyo available for public use rapidly diminished. Ironically this occurred at precisely the time when London was leading the West in a policy of greatly expanding public park area, building on earlier royal precedents. The contrast remains acute to this day, with the proportion of public park land to settled area in Tokyo at only 1.5 percent, compared to over 11 percent in London.[45]

Yet if one conceives of the essential function of the temple and shrine in the Japanese city—apart from the practical matter of caring for the dead—not as the provision of a literal piece of "country" within a hostile city, but rather as a *connection* with the powers and religious feeling of the mountains, the continuity from Edo to Tokyo appears stronger. If sadly diminished in total area, the shrines and temples of Tokyo survive in numbers, providing in hidden and surprising corners of the city a suggestion of the distinctly Japanese conception of the wilderness. They have remained, in short, more tightly integrated with the life of the city through their power as an idea, stemming from the religious meaning which they embody and with which most Japanese spontaneously associate. In London, where

---

[44] For London's recreation areas and parks, I have relied on Rasmussen, *London: The Unique City*, chaps. 5 and 13.

[45] Nihon Chōki Shin'yō Ginkō Chōsabu, ed., *Toshi kaihatsu tōkei* (Nihon keizai shimbunsha, 1970), p. 27.

churches have been proudly aloof from the natural environment and where parks have always been wholly secular, the possibilities for such symbolic uses of the non-urban environment are diminished. Although it would be folly to rationalize the dearth of public recreational space in Tokyo in such terms, it is essential to stress that the meaning of greenery in the city in Japan has been on the whole religious and symbolic, and in the West secular and literal. Such is the price the Japanese have paid for their reluctance to set man apart from "nature."

Commoner Urbanity

The Early Modern Pattern

"Commoner urbanity" refers to the complex range of conceptual and visual orders of the capital which are structured by the non-aristocratic and quintessentially urban classes, from wealthy merchants and skilled artisans to street pedlars and menial laborers. Particularly in Edo and London, where much of the elite class returned regularly to provincial bases and maintained only temporary residence in the city, it was the commoner classes, who identified completely with the city as source of livelihood and place of residence, that were the true bearers of "urbanity."

A comparison of the commoner orders in Edo and London encourages a distinction between two very different conceptions of the city. One is the order of an urban elite which through its wealth is able to assert independent political power against princes, priests, and aristocrats. It is an order which was considerably stronger in London than in Edo, and which is best conveyed by such English terms as "citizen," "civic," and "bourgeois" (the last a term whose French origin suggests the continental roots of this idea). The other is the conception of the commoner city as a plebian mass, deprived of independent political power but conscious of distinctive and autonomous cultural patterns in the face of the social elite: it is, in short, an idea of the city as a *folk* tradition. This latter type was more characteristic of Edo than of London, and is best captured by the complex word *machi*.

The concept of a "civic" order is so much a part of the modern Western idea of the city that many writers have assumed it to be an indispensable element in the urban tradition of *any* culture. However, it is a concept that is either absent or of small consequence in virtually every non-Western culture. Max Weber, who made this conception the basis of a sociological theory of the city, was blunt in his observation that "the concept of the citizen has not existed outside the Occident, and that of the bourgeoisie outside the modern Occident."[46] If one were to take the notion of civic community as *the* idea of the city, a comparison of Edo and London would yield little but a rejection of both as "cities," for even London, as a national capital, had a limited corporate identity. But if one accepts this as *one* conception of the city among many that go into anything as complex as a capital, the notion clearly deserves attention.

The merchant City of London was both visually and politically a fairly good example of the incorporated cities of medieval Europe. It was bounded by tightly encircling walls, and the streets followed irregular patterns characteristic of "organic" growth and the absence of geometrical princely planning.[47] Although by no means wholly autonomous, the City of London was granted by royal charter extensive privileges of self-government and even of participation in the national government, through the traditional if rarely exercised right to select the king. The governance of the City was free from royal interference, and lay in the hands of the powerful urban landowners and eventually of the London guilds. Guildhall in the center of the City served as physical symbol of the civic aspect of London, complemented by the halls of the separate guilds and liveries.

But although the forms and ceremonies of corporate civic identity have survived in the City of London to the present, they ceased from an early date to have any meaning for the city as a whole. With an area of less than 3 square kilometers, the City even with high densities could not support a population of much more than 150,000,[48] so that the residential area from the late sixteenth century began to spill over the walls, growing in a sprawling, uncontrolled pattern over which the City as a corporate power had no authority (the governance of these areas being under the neighboring counties).[49] Nor at the other end of the city did the royal authorities make any special efforts to plan urban growth, so that as London expanded the area within the walls became an increasingly insignificant part of the city as a whole, correspond-

[46] Max Weber, *The Protestant Ethic and the Spirit of Capitalism*, trans. Talcott Parsons (New York: Scribner's, 1958), p. 23. See also Max Weber, *The City*, trans. and eds., Don Martindale and Gertrud Neuwirth (New York: Free Press, 1958), pp. 80-89.

[47] Howard Saalman, *Medieval Cities* (New York: George Braziller, 1968).

[48] The situation was not quite so simple, since some of the City actually lay outside the walls. Dorothy George gives a peak population for the "City within the Walls" of 139,300 in 1700; *London Life in the Eighteenth Century* (1925; reprint ed., New York: Capricorn Books, 1965), p. 329.

[49] For the complex and overlapping patterns of administration in London, see George Rudé, *Hanoverian London, 1714-1808* (London: Secker & Warburg, 1971), pp. 118-119, and Francis Sheppard, *London 1808-1870: The Infernal Wen* (London: Secker & Warburg, 1971), pp. 23, 278-280.

ingly reducing the idea of community. The very survival to the present of the medieval ceremonies of civic power in London is an ironic reflection of the ease with which the power itself was rendered meaningless.

The political landscape of Edo provides considerable contrast with London, for there was no basis for either the form or the content of autonomous "civic" power, or for the evolution of a "bourgeoisie." Edo was founded exclusively as a princely capital, and the commoner class (*chōnin*) was from the beginning wholly subservient to the power of the shogun and his deputies. Commoners were strictly segregated from the samurai class by residence, and the area in which they lived was laid out in a regular grid pattern characteristic of many urban systems which are designed for efficient social and economic control. This pattern was known as the *machi*, a word which etymologically seems to indicate a process of land division and which was written with the Chinese character for a path separating rice paddies (町)[50]. In early Japanese usage, the term referred to regularly divided agricultural land, but was also used in its Sino-Japanese reading of *chō* to refer to the separate blocks in the urban grid pattern borrowed from T'ang China and applied to Japan's first capitals. Conceptually, one finds a clear continuity between the formal structure of the agrarian order and the urban order in ancient Japan: both are systems of efficiency and control.[51]

The next stage in the evolution of the concept of *machi* was a crucial one, involving a sharp deviation from the continental ideal. The Chinese city scheme was basically one of a hierarchy of *enclosures*, at the grandest level that of the city wall and at the lowest level that of the arrangement of rooms around square courtyards in residential architecture. The city was broken down into regular modules, but these were of necessity fitted into larger squares, so that it was a symmetrical and relatively inflexible plan. In Japan, however, the modular concept came to be applied in a different way, as seen in the meanings which in Heian times came to be associated with *machi*, the native Japanese reading of *chō*. One such meaning is "a room attached to a palace or aristocratic residence, especially when a number of identical units are arranged in a row." A second sense is of "an area dense with

[50] Much of my thinking on the concept of the *machi* was stimulated by an unpublished paper by Yoshiyuki Nakai, "Edo," written for a seminar at Harvard University in January 1969.

[51] The relationship between urban grid-planning and such agricultural practices as irrigation and land reclamation has been suggested by Ervin Y. Galantay, *New Towns: Antiquity to the Present* (New York: George Braziller, 1975), p. 22.

houses and divided by a road."[52] While still a subordinated order of control, what is striking here is the evolution from an enclosing block to an extendable row. *Machi* thus refers to an order of modular blocks, unenclosed, asymmetrical, and highly flexible in allowing for change.

This conception of *machi* was reflected in the administrative structure of the Edo commoner district. The entire area was divided by streets into a rough grid pattern of elongated blocks. From these blocks were carved the administrative units known as *chō*, typically the houses on either side of a block-long street, controlled by gates at either end, with an average population of over three hundred persons.[53] The total area covered by these separate *chō* was known as the *machi-chi* ("area of the *machi*") or the *chōnin-chi* ("area of the people of the *chō*"), referring to the administrative realm of the shogunal official known as the *machi-bugyō*. This official did not directly govern the *machi-chi*, for each *chō* was self-governed on principles of collective responsibility similar to those of the rural *mura*. With no overall prescribed boundaries, the number of *chō* could be easily extended by administrative edict, and the total number increased in the course of the Tokugawa period from an initial six hundred to over sixteen hundred by the early eighteenth century, when the population of Edo stabilized.

Although self-government within each small *chō* was the ideal of *machi-chi* administration, some matters required attention at a more coordinated level, such as the allocation of new lands, collection of taxes for the *bakufu*, and so forth. For this, a hierarchy of administrators was chosen from among the residents of the *machi-chi*. As in London, these local urban political leaders were drawn largely from the wealthy classes, the landlords, and guild leaders. The contrast with the City of London lies in their wholly submissive political position vis-à-vis the *bakufu*, which prevented the emergence of an idea of corporate identity against the state. Political identity for the *chōnin* of Edo was fragmented and localized, focused on the local neighborhood *chō* rather than on the commoner city as a whole. Edo's political landscape was thus not essentially different from that of the rural countryside, divided into cohesive and autonomous village units connected to the state by the link of a small number of passive bureaucrats.

How different was this from London? It was very different from the

[52] Kindaichi, *Meikai kogo jiten*, p. 933.

[53] For the number of *chō* and the population of the *machi-chi*, see Naitō, *Edo to Edo-jō*, p. 141. The actual configuration of the separate *chō* showed a variety of complex patterns, which can be grasped from a close study of any map of late Edo, such as that of Hamada Giichirō, ed., *Edo kirie-zu* (1849-1863; reprint ed., Tōkyōdō, 1974).

City of London, to be sure. But what of those Londoners, an increasing majority from the mid-seventeenth century on, who lived outside the City? Most were similarly under village-like regimes, for the most part self-governed and contributing little to an overall spirit of civic community. Although it would be a great mistake to underestimate the acute degree of subservience under which the Edo *chōnin* were placed relative to the shogunal regime, it remains true that *most* Londoners were little different from the residents of Edo in lacking any feeling of corporate civic spirit.[54]

The weakness of *political* identity among the commoner masses in Edo and London should not obscure a real and indeed growing sense of *cultural* identity, a quality which became articulate with the emergence of popular publishing and which tends to be neglected by those who focus on the institutional structure of the city. I would like to suggest the term *machi* as an expressive word for the idea of the city as a folk culture. It is of the utmost importance here to differentiate this use of *machi* from its earliest uses. The ancient uses have in common the meaning of a cell-like order arranged for effective control, a meaning best captured by bureaucratic tone of the Sino-Japanese reading *chō*. The native reading *machi*, however, has no such sense of enclosure or spatial definition: it refers more to the *quality* of an environment than to its physical boundaries, more to the commoner content than the administrative form. In particular, the word began from an early point to develop the sense of the bustling activity of a *market*, in the physical setting of a *street* lined with shops and filled with people. It is a sense of *machi* which has become progressively stronger since the seventeenth century, paralleling the steady growth of popular culture. It is a *machi* best captured when written not with the character *chō*, which suggests regulated order, but with the character *gai*

街 , which in the original Chinese means both "street" and "market."[55]

Whatever the terminology, this sense of urbanity as close, noisy, and

[54] One reflection of the diminished sense of unity in both Tokyo and London is the lack of coordination among administrative jurisdictions for which both cities are frequently cited. For London, see Note 49. For Edo, see Nakai, "Edo," in which the problems of administrative definition are discussed. For modern Tokyo, Charles Beard, *The Administration and Politics of Tokyo* (New York: MacMillan, 1923), chap. 2 is of interest.

[55] Two other words in modern Japanese usage capture this sense of *machi*. One is *chimata*, literally a "fork in the road," hence a place of marketing and street interaction. The other is *kaiwai*, a Sino-Japanese term of Japanese coinage which has the sense of "neighborhood" but without its residential and communal overtones; it is interpreted as an "activity space" in an interesting analysis in Toshi dezain kenkyūtai, *Nihon no toshi kūkan*, p. 44.

cluttered street life is one which crops up with surprising frequency
among observers of both cities in the early modern period, as in the
observation of a Dutchman visiting Edo in the early nineteenth century that "although there are here no carriages to increase the noise
and tumult, I can compare the hurly-burly of Jeddo to nothing but
that of London."[56] The single contrast which he observed is an important one, stemming from the *bakufu* prohibition of wheeled vehicles in Edo. The idea of the street as the site of bustling activity is
thus complemented in Japanese culture by the neglect of the street as
a means of through passage, reflected in the Japanese reluctance to
commemorate or even name their streets.[57] This tradition has left
Tokyo with many narrow, winding back streets poorly adapted to
modern traffic, and a legacy of pedestrian movement that is one of the
most appealing qualities of the city today.

The idea of the city as hurly-burly street life is in certain respects
the antithesis of the idea of the city as a civic corporation. Whereas
the civic concept is highly political, the *machi* notion rejects politics
or at worst suggests resignation to the rule of a narrow elite. Where the
civic concept is narrowly middle class, *machi* is an idea accepted by all
classes. I have used the term "folk" to describe the *machi* idea, perhaps
rashly in view of the common conception that "folk" is the opposite of
"urban." More appropriate is the Japanese *shominteki*, an adjectival
form of *shomin*, in the original Chinese "the multitudes." Like *machi*,
it is a term which originated in the perceptions of the ruling elite, but
came in time to refer to the cultural identity of the ruled. Translatable
only as "popular" but with none of that word's potential political
nuances, *shominteki* captures much of the sense of an urban folk culture which is at the heart of the idea of the city as *machi*.

The sense of spatial homogeneity implied by bustling, commercial
street life does not preclude social distinctions, which were in fact
elaborately observed in pre-modern Edo and London commoner districts. The point seems rather to be, following an interesting theory
advanced by Lyn Lofland, that these distinctions were made not by
spatial segregation but rather by differentiation of *dress*.[58] This perspective explains the relatively minor importance of architecture in
structuring the environment of commoner urbanity, which is rather a

[56] J. F. Fisscher, *Bijdrage tot de Kennis van het Japansche Rijk*, 1833, as quoted
in Andrew Steinmetz, *Japan and Her People* (London: Routledge, Warner & Routledge, 1859), p. 211.

[57] For insight into Tokyo's street and address system, see Barthes, *L'empire des
signes*, pp. 47-51.

[58] Lyn H. Lofland, *A World of Strangers: Order and Action in Urban Public
Space* (New York: Basic Books, 1973), chap. 2.

landscape of the *crowd*. The many colorful prints of street life in both Edo and London in the eighteenth and nineteenth century are prime visual representations of this idea of the city.

Modern Continuities

A middle-class-based civic spirit, which on the eve of industrialization was fading in London and nonexistent in Edo, has survived as little more than a lingering ideal in both cities today. In this respect, they have proved no different from any other great metropolis (small cities are a somewhat different matter) in the world. The lack of a strong civic past may have even enabled both cities to adapt less traumatically to the inevitable process of atomization and loss of community spirit in large modern urban centers.

The civic idea is by no means dead: it simply no longer exists at the city-wide level as an effective political concept. It survives rather in two very different contexts. One is the "city planning" (*toshi keikaku*) profession, which has emerged as a moderately powerful force in both London and Tokyo, particularly since World War II. Despite the tendency of city planners to plead technocratic impartiality, it is inevitable that such a profession harbor ideal conceptions of the city, and one of these seems to be the civic idea of the "public good." The problem is that the middle-class morality which gave rise to the idea is now replaced by technocratic expertise, and the real political issues are obscured. To complicate the matter, the urban planning profession has also absorbed at least two other major ideas: the city as a grand princely monument and the city as a place that deserves to be remade into "country." The former is a continental idea (seen clearly in modern form in Le Corbusier's "radiant city" of 1933), and the latter a distinctive English contribution (formulated first and best in Ebenezer Howard's "garden city" of 1898).[59]

Despite the almost wholly Western bias of the ideology of the planning profession, it has not been without influence in Japan. Hence Tokyo, like London, has over the past few decades come forth with elaborate "master plans" for remaking the city, adopting from the West the notions of green belts, new towns, restrictive zoning, and so forth. It is impossible here to make a detailed comparison of Tokyo and London in terms of the ideology and impact of city planning. It might simply be suggested that city planning in Tokyo has been sub-

[59] Le Corbusier, *The Radiant City: Elements of a Doctrine of Urbanism To Be Used as the Basis of Our Machine-Age Civilization* (1933; reprint ed., New York: Orion Press, 1964), and Ebenezer Howard, *Garden Cities of Tomorrow* (1898, 1902; reprint ed., Cambridge, Mass.: MIT Press, 1965).

stantially less effective than in London, both because its ideas are not wholly compatible with Japanese urban traditions, and because it has a substantially shorter history and less effective institutional framework than in London. At the same time, it should be stressed that English "town planning" (the use of "town" suggests the English ideal of decitification if not countrification) has not created any powerful new idea of London as a city, much less a new reality.

The civic ideal also survives at a much more modest level, that of the neighborhood (*kinjo*), where indeed it was always strong in both Tokyo and London—this is one explanation for the common metaphor of Tokyo and London as conglomerations of "villages." It is dubious whether "civic" is a proper term here, for the "neighborhood" has none of the corporate sense of the city as a self-governing entity: it is rather a narrow, parochial idea of the city as a knowable community, indeed much more like a village than a city. As a result, the political conception of a distinctive *public* realm tends to be lost at the neighborhood level. This tension is particularly evident in Tokyo in recent years, in the emergence of the so-called "citizens' movement" (*shimin undō*) in response primarily to the threat of environmental disruption. Despite the use of the term *shimin*, coined as a translation for the English "citizen," the movement tends in practice to break down into the separate defense of particular local interests. A revealing expression for this tendency is *jūmin egoizumu*, literally "residents' egoism" but more meaningfully, "neighborhood parochialism." Although suggestive of a greater sense of community than in the *chō* of Edo, the idea falls short of that implied by "citizen" in the West.

The dissipation and atomization of the idea of the "citizen" has been paralleled by a complex evolution in the commoner idea of the city as dense and hurly-burly street life. From well before the beginning of modern industrialization, both Edo and Tokyo had each been in a sense two cities, a political-administrative princely city to the west, surrounded by the mansions of the aristocracy, and a commercial-commoner city to the east. This bifurcation was greatly accelerated by industrialization and the resultant rapid growth and heightened spatial differentiation. Two dynamics in particular characterize this process of polarization: (1) the wealthy commercial classes of the old commoner city increasingly aped their aristocratic betters and moved to the upper-class suburbs to the west, while (2) the core of the traditional city was usurped by the commercial institutions of modern capitalism, driving up property values and forcing the poorer classes in the *opposite* direction, to the east. The suburbs to the west—the West End of London and the Yamanote of Tokyo—will be compared in the next section; here the concern is rather with the commoner districts on the other side: the East End of London and the Shitamachi ("under-machi," that is, the *machi* below the castle) of Tokyo.

From the crowded and impoverished lower-class districts of Tokyo and London, there emerged in the process of industrialization a wide range of conceptions of the city, most of which had in common a middle-class point of view. The commoner order has typically been seen in this way, from the outside in, resulting in two rather different responses: that of a lyrical idealization of commoner street life, and that of horrified shock at the deplorable realities of living conditions among the lowest urban classes. The positive conception finds its most appealing articulation in two important urban personifications, the Edokko ("child of Edo") of Tokyo and the Cockney of London, who call for a brief comparison. Of particular interest is the way in which these figures were similarly transformed in the process of industriali-zation.

Both Edokko and Cockney are of clearly pre-industrial origin.[60] The term "Cockney" (in the specific sense of a Londoner) was in use by the seventeenth century, whereas "Edokko" appeared in the late eighteenth century. In origin, both terms appear to have referred in many cases to the upper ranks of the commoner class, living at the heart of the traditional merchant city. The original Edokko seem to have been wealthy rice brokers (*fudasashi*) who catered to the *hatamoto* class of samurai, whereas "merchants and first-rate tradesmen" are said to have qualified as Cockney. As for locale, a Cockney was one born "within the sound of Bow Bells," that is, near the church of St. Mary le Bow in the center of the City of London, whereas a proper Edokko, by a similar tradition, had to be a parishioner of one of the two ancient shrines which lay to either side of the original *machi-chi*, Kanda Daimyōjin or Sannō Daigongen.

In the course of time, however, the locale of these two figures shifted to the east, in Tokyo away from the Shiba-Nihonbashi-Kanda belt north toward Asakusa and across the river to Honjo-Fukagawa, and in London beyond the walls of the City to the area known as the East End.[61] In more recent times, as both Edokko and Cockney have become more and more idealized as folk figures, a considerable tolerance of locale has developed. Thus Julian Franklyn admits that the Cockney can actually be born anywhere in London if he has the proper

[60] For the Edokko, I have relied mostly on Nishiyama Matsunosuke, *Edo chōnin no kenkyū*, 3 vols. (Yoshikawa Kōbunkan, 1972-74), vol. 2, pp. 3-93, and for the Cockney, Julian Franklyn, *The Cockney—A Survey of London Life and Language* (London: André Deutsch, 1953).

[61] Isomura Eiichi, "Tōkyō no Isuto Endo," in Kiuchi Shinzō *et al.*, eds., *Nihon no bunka chiri*, 18 vols. (Kōdansha, 1968-71), vol. 6, pp. 325-327.

qualifications of dialect and spirit, and the recent *Otoko wa tsurai yo* (roughly, "It's Tough To Be a Man," suggestive of the self-conscious masculinity in the Edokko image) film series extends the base of Shitamachi consciousness as far east as Katsushika, some eight miles from Nihonbashi.

At the same time, the class status of both Edokko and Cockney became progressively more plebian in the course of industrialization. As the wealthier commoner classes increasingly aped the aristocracy and moved off to West End houses or country seats, the quintessential mark of the Cockney became his *refusal* to ape his social betters. So too the Edokko came to be conceived as one who stood up defiantly to a samurai, with none of the sycophantic airs of rich merchants and even a positive aversion to the accumulation of wealth. The Cockney similarly is seen as undaunted by airs, self-reliant and self-supporting, tending to side with the underdog rather than ape his betters. In profession, Edokko and Cockney alike came to be typically "street people": pedlars, pitchmen, costers, ricksha-men, cabbies, beggars, on the whole traditional menial urban professions of high mobility and inevitably poor.[62]

The idealization of Edokko and Cockney for their pride and of their locale for its hurly-burly humanity was counterposed in the era of early industrialization in Tokyo and London by a much more unfavorable set of ideas, all identifiably middle-class in origin. One was the idea of the city as a hotbed of sedition and revolutionary radicalism. It is the idea of the commoner crowd now transformed into a "mob."[63] The example of the French Revolution and later the Paris Commune made this a far more pervasive idea in London than in Tokyo, where nevertheless a tradition of pre-modern urban rioting and government fears of subversive Western ideology combined into a similar rhetoric in the late Meiji period. In the end, despite a few small insurrections, neither Tokyo nor London was ever in danger of being lost to the mob. But the specter was there, and created a major new strand in the conceptualization of the city.

Parallel to this was the idea of the city as a place of disease and poverty, an image best captured by the English word "slums." This concept in both cities presents a complex problem in the relationship

[62] There is a revealing overlap between the idea of the Cockney and the idea of poverty, for Cockney professions as described by Franklyn are much the same as those emphasized as poor by Henry Mayhew in *London Labour and the London Poor* (1861-62). For an analysis of the rather special nature of Mayhew's "people," see Gertrude Himmerlfarb, "The Culture of Poverty," in Dyos and Wolff, eds., *The Victorian City.*

[63] The work of George Rudé has emphasized this conception, as in his *Hanoverian London,* especially chap. 11.

between an objective reality of sub-standard living conditions and the subjective discovery of these conditions by horrified and sensitive bourgeois reformers.[64] It can only be hypothesized here that whatever the comparative realities of living conditions among the lower classes in both cities, the English response was far stronger and more sustained, as reflected both in literary sources (Dickens in particular) and in the great investigations into lower-class living conditions by Henry Mayhew and Charles Booth. Tokyo's industrial slums did provoke a similar response, beginning in the 1880's in a series of journalistic exposés, of which the best-known is Yokoyama Gennosuke's *Japan's Lower Classes* (Nihon no kasō shakai, 1899).[65] Yet the Japanese reformers never produced studies as monumental as those of Mayhew and Booth, nor were they stricken with the same ambivalent mix of shock and morbid fascination as the Victorians. One indication of the milder Japanese conception of the city as a place of poverty and disease is the lack of any modern Japanese word as expressive as "slums." For a brief time in the Meiji period, the older Edo word *hinminkutsu* (literally, "caves of the poor people") was used, but was soon replaced by *suramu*, suggesting the degree to which these zones of urban poverty were conceived of as a Western-derived phenomenon.

In the past half-century, these various conceptions of the commoner city which dominated the period of initial industrialization have undergone still further changes. One underlying dynamic of this change has been the evolution of a small and self-conscious middle class intent on aping its betters into a much bigger middle-class mass dedicated largely to the pursuit of leisure and consumerism which seems characteristic of all advanced industrial societies. I would suggest that Japanese society has been more thorough in this process, if only because the tradition of a middle class with a distinct ethic and identity was from the start far weaker than in England. The abolition of the privileges of the samurai class in the early Meiji period had the further effect of converting the entire traditional elite into a new middle class, with the result that the tendency to the aping of social betters has been less persistent in modern Japan than in modern England.[66]

Moralistic bourgeois concern with poverty and disease as metaphors for the commoner city in the nineteenth century has for the most part

[64] For an interesting discussion of the relativity of residential "overcrowding," see Ronald Dore, *City Life in Japan: A Study of a Tokyo Ward* (Berkeley and Los Angeles: University of California Press, 1958), pp. 45-51.

[65] Available in reprint edition (Iwanami shoten, 1949).

[66] For the problem of the Japanese "middle class" in comparative perspective, see Ronald Dore's entry "Modernization: The Bourgeoisie in Modernizing Societies" in David L. Sills, ed., *International Encyclopedia of the Social Sciences*, 17 vols. (New York: MacMillan and The Free Press, 1968), vol. 10, pp. 403-406.

disappeared in the twentieth, less because of the decline of bourgeois attitudes than because of the drastic drop in objective levels of poverty and disease in the contemporary city. On the other hand, the conception of the commoner city as personified in the Edokko and Cockney survives as an appealing ideal in both Tokyo and London. Whether many actual specimens of either breed exist or not, they both live as folk figures who appeal to contemporary commoners for their anti-aristocratic and anti-bourgeois inclinations alike. Coupled with these social implications is the appeal of old-time street life, neighborhood-centered and hurly-burly. Suggestive of the continuing strength of this idea is the great popularity of, for example, London's famous street markets or of the many festivals and markets at the temple of Sensōji in Tokyo's Asakusa, to which vast numbers flock for a taste of *shomin-teki* urbanity.

The idea of the commoner city today is to be found not only in the nostalgia-fueled survival of Edokko, Cockney, and street markets; the twentieth century has given rise to its own distinctive idea of the city, an idea rooted in the urban function of mass popular consumption and entertainment. Both as idea and as fact, it is a type of city which is far more conspicuous in Tokyo than in London, appearing most visibly at the transfer nodes of the rail system connecting central Tokyo with the western suburbs, at Shibuya, Shinjuku, and Ikebukuro. It is an environment, not where one strives to emulate the style and pastimes of one's social betters, but where one can escape into fantasy worlds. It is an environment of signs and lights, a landscape of advertising and consumption, and for a large number of Tokyo dwellers the true contemporary *machi*.[67] This idea of the mass-commoner-consumer city seems less in evidence in London, where such comparable centers of popular entertainment as Picadilly are greeted by most Londoners with disapproval. The contrast seems most clearly rooted in the continuing attachment in London to older conceptions of the city held by the aristocracy and bourgeoisie. To find a counterpart to Tokyo's modern *machi*, one must turn rather to the similarly egalitarian mass society in the United States, where a fundamental contrast in the system of personal transportation has shifted a large part of the world of escape and consumption from the city center to the highway margins on its outskirts.[68]

[67] For an analysis of this environment, see Peter Gluck and Henry Smith, "Shinjuku," *Kenchiku to toshi*, August 1973, pp. 132-156 (in Japanese with English summary).

[68] For interpretations of the American highway strip, see J. B. Jackson's "Other-Directed Houses" (written in 1956), in Zube, ed., *Landscapes*, pp. 55-72, and Robert Venturi, Denise Scott Brown, and Steven Isenour, *Learning from Las Vegas* (Cambridge, Mass.: MIT Press, 1972).

ARISTOCRATIC SUBURBANITY

The Early Modern Pattern

The modern idea of "suburbs" in both Japan and England draws on two different pre-modern traditions. One of these involves primarily a *spatial* distinction, indicating the area lying between the central city and open countryside. The other is a largely *social* distinction, referring to the residential quarters of the aristocratic elite. It was in the course of the transport revolution and rapid population growth which characterized early industrialization in Tokyo and London that these two earlier traditions combined and were transformed into the twentieth century suburban idea.

The spatial conception of the London "suburbs" is seen in the etymology of the word itself, "below the city," that is, lying outside the city walls. The term thus referred from medieval times to a variety of small settlements outside the City of London and of Westminster (a city in its own right), typically at transport junctions where they offered marketing and lodging services. This spatial sense was paralleled by a vague conceptualization of the suburbs as an ambivalent in-between zone, neither really of the city nor of the country. As the walls of the city came to lose their defining power both visually and conceptually from the seventeenth century, this idea of the suburbs became weaker and more diffuse.

In Edo, the idea of such suburbs was still vaguer than in London, although much the same morphology obtained. There was no word for suburbs in Japanese: *kōgai*, the standard modern translation for "suburbs," referred in Tokugawa times simply to the *un*settled land in the outskirts of the city, while *machi-hazure* ("the outer edge of the city") likewise suggested a distinction not between city core and suburban settlement, but between commercial *machi* and agrarian *inaka*. In the Japanese tradition of unwalled cities, there was no conception of a settled zone between city and country which might provide the basis for a "middle landscape" ideal.

More distinctly conceived were the residential quarters of the aristocratic class, which in both Edo and London contributed a quiet and green-enshrouded aspect to the city, catching the eye of many observers for the contrast with the dense, bustling commoner districts in the center. Yet here as well, one discovers a clear ambiguity, less in terms of spatial location than of the *quality* of these districts, which although clearly located *in* the city were in spirit somehow not *of* the city. In neither culture, for example, was there a generic term for these parts of the city, only such specific labels as West End and Yamanote.

One must turn rather to a continental city such as Paris to find a word, *faubourg*, which conveys a more distinct conception of the residential quarters of the aristocracy.

In London, the belt extending over one mile (a long distance in the pre-modern city) between the City of London and Westminster, known as The Strand, provided the obvious site for the initial appearance of an aristocratic faubourg, in the form of elegant residences lining the way.[69] These mansions gave way in time to the more characteristic forms of the West End in the residential squares northwest of The Strand (and later south of Hyde Park) which took shape first in the seventeenth century and continued to grow into the nineteenth. These West End townhouses were in their prototypical form the seasonal residences of the landed elite, and on the whole far smaller and less elaborate than the country houses which were the true elite "seats." They were also relatively modest in comparison with the *palazzos* and *hôtels* of the more city-oriented continental aristocracies. In aspect, the West End suggested the "country" more than the city: most of the houses were nearby the pastoral expanses of the great royal parks, and their monotonous and unassertive facades were often shaded by strategically planted trees.

The *buke-chi* of Edo was comparably green and privatized, but for very different reasons, relating largely to the profound contrast between the elite classes in Japanese and English society in the early modern period. Most obvious was the contrast of size and structure: the samurai class in numbers was far larger than the English landed elite, but at the same time it included a far wider range of status, so that only a small part of the entire class could be considered "aristocratic" in power and prestige as well as in birth. This meant that within the *buke-chi* of Edo resided large numbers of men with samurai status who were in function little more than servants. The West End of London similarly housed large numbers of servants, in all probability more numerous than those they served. But whereas English society involved a straightforward dualism of servants and masters, samurai society had in its pyramidal structure more numerous intermediate levels and was generally more complex.

The residential quarters of the subordinate classes were therefore more conspicuous within the *yashiki*, or daimyo mansions, of Edo than in London's West End. Lower samurai and servants were for the most part housed in linear barracks called *nagaya* ("long houses"), built into the walls which enclosed the *yashiki* complex. In their regular, elongated aspect, the *nagaya* were a version of *machi*, in the

---

[69] These houses stand out clearly on the map "A View of London about the Year 1560" (reprint ed., Ithaca, N.Y.: Historic Urban Plans, 1967).

older sense of a modular order designed for efficiency and control. It is revealing that the barracklike dwellings for the poor constructed in the back alleys of the *machi-chi* were similarly called *nagaya* (or, more precisely, *ura-nagaya*, "back *nagaya*").[70] In London, the distinction was rather a vertical dualism of "upstairs and downstairs," the servants' quarters generally occupying the basement floor of a multistory townhouse and contributing less of a distinctive aspect to the whole than Edo's *nagaya*.[71]

A second major contrast between the Edo samurai and the London aristocracy lies in the terms on which they came to the city. Whereas the English elite came to London voluntarily for the "season" and the pleasures of conspicuous consumption, the daimyo gathered in Edo under the compulsory regulations of the *sankin kōtai*. Like the London elite, the daimyo had their home bases in the provinces, but these bases were the urban *jōkamachi* rather than isolated country estates. Hence for the samurai class, the alternation was not between city and country, but between capital city and provincial city. And although the attendance of the daimyo may have been compulsory, it was doubtless often a welcome escape from the narrow and tedious life in many of the provincial castle towns. So whereas London was typically contrasted with the joys of the pastoral countryside, Edo was set against the loneliness of provincial towns.

The *sankin kōtai* system had some important implications for the visual aspect of the Edo *buke-chi*. First, the population of the *buke-chi*, roughly half of Edo's total population, was far greater than that of the aristocratic quarters of London (including servants). The *buke-chi* was also much greater in area than the West End,[72] and although the actual *yashiki* buildings were densely populated, the large surrounding gardens gave Edo the overall appearance of a great landscape park, particularly in the quarters of the most powerful lords. In the eyes of an English observer in 1860 as he viewed the city from Atago Hill, "the whole surrounding aspect is that of a succession of

[70] For the architecture of the daimyo *yashiki* and the *machi-chi* residences, see Ōkuma Yoshikuni, "Kinsei buke jidai no kenchiku" in Kokushi kenkyūkai, ed., *Iwanami kōza Nihon rekishi*, 18 vols. (Iwanami shoten, 1933-35), 16, 56-69.

[71] The one type of building in London's West End that paralleled the *nagaya* was the mews, or stables, in which grooms were quartered on the second story. These were, however, considerably less conspicuous than the Edo *nagaya*, which had windows fronting on the main streets.

[72] In Edo, the *buke-chi* accounted for over two-thirds of the built-up area of the city (see Naitō, *Edo to Edo-jō*, p. 133), whereas the West End in the mid-eighteenth century could not have been more than a third of the settled area of London, as estimated from the 1747 "Plan of the Cities of London and Westminster and Borough of Southwark" (reprint ed., Ithaca, N.Y.: Historic Urban Plans, 1970).

Hyde Parks or Kensington Gardens—a city of green slopes and over-hanging groves."[73]

Perhaps the most important quality of both the West End of London and the Edo *buke-chi*, particularly in view of modern continuities, was the sense of *privatization* conveyed by both when compared with the commoner order. Neither as a political concept of the common good which typified the civic order nor as a social fact of heterogeneous intermixing in the streets of the folk order was there any sense of "public" in these districts. Architecturally, both the London townhouses and the Edo *yashiki* presented a monotonous and forbidding face to the street, the major contrast being the narrow, multistory, stone-built aspect of one versus the low, long, and wooden form of the other. The description of Laurence Oliphant, an English traveller to Edo in the summer of 1858 is revealing of the general similarity: "This time we soon turned out of the main street, and leaving the dense crowd behind us, dived into the Princes' or aristocratic quarter. We were amazed at the different aspect which the streets here presented from those we had just left; . . . Belgravia in September does not look more deserted than these fashionable thoroughfares, so dull, clean, and respectable."[74]

The collapse of the *sankin kōtai* in the 1860's drastically altered the social structure and visual character of the Edo *buke-chi*, with much of the land either passing into the hands of the new Meiji government as sites for government buildings and military installations, or becoming fragmented among small landholders on the open market. Nevertheless, the cultural concept of a privatized residential area for the respectable classes was perpetuated in the idea of the "Yamanote" (in effect, "towards the mountains"), the term for the hilly areas of Tokyo rising away from the flats and valleys where the commoners resided. This was accomplished as Japan's new ruling class, mainly officials of the Meiji government and officially connected entrepreneurs, took up residence in the spacious hills of the former *buke-chi*. Although these new residents were typically of samurai origin, the dissolution of the samurai class in the 1870's mitigated the exclusivity of the Yamanote, particularly in comparison with the West End of London. The area referred to as the Yamanote in fact includes many lower-class pockets and is far more socially and culturally heterogeneous than the West End. But as a cultural *idea*, the word "Yamanote"

[73] George Smith (Bishop of Victoria, Hong Kong), *Ten Weeks in Japan* (London: Longman Green, 1861), p. 303.

[74] Laurence Oliphant, *Narrative of the Earl of Elgin's Mission to China and Japan in the Years 1857, '58, '59*, 2 vols. (London: William Blackwood, 1859), vol. 2, p. 123.

itself developed the same connotations of a "dull, clean, and respectable" residential district for the social elite as had its premodern version.[75]

Modern Continuities

Modern suburbs are the result of the rail (and later road) transport revolution, which began in London in the 1830's and in Tokyo in the 1880's, enabling increasing numbers of people to hold jobs in the commercial center of the city while residing on the more spacious fringes. This dramatic expansion of the effective residential area of the city most benefited middle-class workers in the tertiary sector, the "white-collar" workers of London and the *"sarariman"* of Tokyo,[76] whose growing affluence and numbers enabled them to leapfrog the crowded lower-class slums and the exclusive aristocratic suburbs into the open land which lay along the new rail lines. This process began on a substantial scale in London from the mid-nineteenth century and in Tokyo from the early twentieth.[77]

Although in the long run the residential orders of these white-collar classes in Tokyo and London have proved to be profoundly different, both are nevertheless dominated by the deep yearning for the central features of the pre-modern aristocratic suburbs in both cities: privacy and greenery. More specifically, the urban middle classes in both Tokyo and London have come to idealize the detached single-family residence with ample space for a garden. Although such an ideal is scarcely unique to Japan and England, it seems to be pursued with particular tenacity in those two cultures. What differs between the two is the motivation for pursuing that ideal and the highly contrasting ways in which it has been approximated in the actual suburbs of Tokyo and London.

In London, the yearning for privacy and greenery is at heart a yearning for the "country," for the pastoral ideals of the landed elite. This is evident in the allurements of early suburban developers, who

[75] For further analysis of the Yamanote-Shitamachi cultural split, see Robert J. Smith, "Pre-Industrial Urbanism in Japan: A Consideration of Multiple Traditions in a Feudal Society," *Economic Development and Cultural Change*, vol. 9, no. 2, part 2 (Oct. 1960), pp. 241-254.

[76] Both the Americanism "white-collar" and the Japanese-coined "salaryman" originated in the years following World War I, the era in which mass suburbanization began in both Japan and England.

[77] For London suburbanization, see H. J. Dyos, *Victorian Suburb: A Study of the Growth of Camberwell* (Leicester: Leicester University Press, 1961), and Alan A. Jackson, *Semi-Detached London: Suburban Development, Life and Transport, 1900-1939* (London: Allen & Unwin, 1973). For Tokyo, I know of no comparable secondary studies on the suburbs—perhaps a reflection of the lack of the idea of "suburbs" —although much source material is available in the local ward histories (*kushi*).

"knew exactly what their potential customers required. Assiduously, often clumsily, they strove to evoke at least a suggestion of that rural-romantic make-believe which was the very spirit of suburbia."[78] Thus there emerged the concept of "suburbia" (the word apparently dates from the 1890's)[79] as a distinct environment, filled not with houses but with "villas" and "cottages," which stand along not streets but "drives," "ways," and "gardens." This conception was even provided with an ideological rationale in Howard's ideal "garden city," which would bring together the best of the city and the country in a new version of the pastoral. Although Howard had in mind the creation of totally new cities, it took little time for the evolution of his concept into the "garden suburb" movement around the turn of the century.[80]

In fact, the London suburbs were as patently urban as their ideology was anti-urban, with the exception of the wealthiest areas, where land was sufficient to allow genuine isolation. The vast majority of London's suburbs were drastically scaled-down versions of the West End, with houses constructed in monotonous rows and token greenery provided front and back. The appearance of the middle-class suburbs owes much to the way in which they were built, largely by speculative developers who took advantage of the large parcels of land offered in the environs of London by estate ownership. Speculation was profitable on both land and buildings, although the two tended to fall into different hands, and the result was the regular and unimaginative planning of many suburban areas. For maximization of profit, houses were built as closely as possible, often in contiguous rows or at best in the "semi-detached" mode popular after World War I. Such methods were enabled by the English tradition of building in brick, which assured substantial privacy even with common walls.

But no matter how cramped the London suburban "cottages," their one indispensable feature was space for a garden in back, occasionally in front.[81] It was the garden, after all, that was responsible for the idea of the "garden suburb," although it is difficult to see how these tiny suburban plots could provide much of the pastoral environment which lay historically and culturally behind their omnipresence in suburbia. In the end, London suburbanites have been forced willy-nilly to ac-

---

[78] Jackson, *Semi-Detached London*, p. 136.

[79] The word "Suburbia" appears to have been sometimes used as a proper noun to refer specifically to the suburbs of London (*The Oxford English Dictionary*).

[80] It is revealing that the Japanese translate "garden city" as *den'en toshi* or "pastoral city," suggesting the Japanese difficulty in finding any native word for "garden" which conveyed the necessary sense of anti-urbanity. Tokyo saw a brief vogue for the "garden suburb" idea in the post-World War I period, the most notable legacy being the upper-class suburb of Den'en Chōfu, planned in 1918.

[81] Jackson, *Semi-Detached London*, p. 149, refers to the suburban garden as a "hallowed plot" and "an essential part of the life style" of the London suburbs.

cept the symbolic uses of nature which the Japanese have exploited spontaneously throughout their urban history.

The monotonously homogeneous aspect of London suburban developments is by no means the fault of profit-hungry developers alone, for it is clear that most English city-dwellers tend to prefer residential areas where social status is clearly announced by the facade of the house, reflecting the deep and persistent attachment of the English to visible distinctions of class and status.[82] Although the neat ordering of suburban facades seems to deny individual identity, it nevertheless enables unmistakable identity in terms of one's place in the social hierarchy.

The ideology and structure of suburban Tokyo differs from London in a variety of ways. Most fundamental is the lack of any conception in Japan of a *rus in urbe*, of an urban environment which looks like the country. Such a conception in fact makes little or no sense in Japanese culture, where there has been no tendency to dichotomize the rural and urban environments. What the Japanese *do* desire, whether in the country or the city, is a residence which is sufficiently protected from neighbors and a garden which will remind them of mountains and forests. Hence Tokyo suburban homes, much like the *yashiki* of Edo, tend to be enclosed by fences and hedges, with heavy planting of trees and shrubs in the spaces between the enclosure and the house itself. Indeed, as is often pointed out, house and garden are considered as an indissoluble whole in Japanese residential building, in contrast to the Western tendency to segregate the two. Whereas English and American suburbanites strive for "better homes and gardens," the Japanese aim at better home-gardens.

But why have Tokyo suburbs not evolved, as in London, in homogeneous developments? The answer lies in strongly contrasting patterns of urban landholding and residential construction in the two cities. In a country like Japan, which unlike most other countries (including England) has been densely populated since early modern times, land has always been precious, and the security which it offers high. One ironic corollary is that the actual occupancy of land is often accorded higher respect, both by custom and by law, than legal ownership. As a result it is very difficult to evict tenants, which makes urban landlordism a far less profitable pursuit than in most other countries, in turn restricting the rental market and intensifying the competition for individual landownership. A final contrast is the ab-

[82] For ideas on the complex problem of "class" in Japan versus England, see Ronald Dore, *British Factory—Japanese Factory: The Origins of National Diversity in Industrial Relations* (Berkeley and Los Angeles: University of California Press, 1973), index references to "class."

sence in Japan until very recently of restrictive use zoning to encourage homogeneous development of land.

Against this intense pressure for urban landholding must be considered the continuing Japanese preference for residential construction in short-lived materials. The result is a far higher premium on land than on houses, so that land speculation is far more profitable in Japan than is building speculation. Unlike London, where most suburban homes are built in a uniform style by developers, Tokyo suburban residences tend to be owner-built and hence less monotonous in appearance than in London. Furthermore, the impossibility of constructing sound-proof common walls between separate residences using conventional Japanese building techniques has obviated the use of row houses for all but the lowest urban classes.

A further obstacle to uniform patterns of suburban development in Tokyo has been a far greater fragmentation of landholding than in London. In the absence of an elite of large landowners, the land available for suburban building in Tokyo, as elsewhere in Japan, was owned by relatively small peasant landlords and owner-cultivators, and even one man's holdings were typically scattered into several different parcels. Hence the development of the Tokyo suburbs was on a piecemeal, ad hoc basis with little regular division of large pieces of land. Even where such large subdivisions have been possible, the tendency has been to sell the land, which is the source of the most profit, and let the buyers erect their own houses.

For all of these reasons, the suburbs of Tokyo have little of the regularity and homogeneity that characterizes London. And just as homogeneity of residential area seems to suit English social preferences, so heterogeneity, although not necessarily sought after, seems no great cause for concern among the Japanese. There are clear notions among Japanese of what constitutes a desirable versus an undesirable neighborhood, but such preferences seem less oriented toward the class status of potential neighbors than among English suburbanites. To a degree, this is a continuation of the tendency of the Edo *buke-chi* to much greater heterogeneity of status than that in the West End of London. London suburban houses clearly announce their owners' status by the outward-facing facades, whereas Japanese suburban houses can be judged only by a furtive look through a neutral and primarily defensive fence. If anything, it is the care and quality of the trees rising above the fence that will mark the wealth of the owner rather than the house, which appears as no more than a low roof.

A final contrast between Tokyo and London suburbs lies not in the external appearance of the two, but rather in the style of life which each has come to represent. In London, there is a clear conception of a suburban way of life, although the normative content varies widely: indeed, no idea of the city has produced such intense feelings pro and con as that of suburbia. Suburbia in England is conceived of as a place for social interaction focused upon the home, whether in competition with one's neighbor for the neatest garden or in the invitation of friends and relatives for dinner in a manner harking back to aristocratic modes of entertainment.

For the Japanese *sarariman*, by contrast, the suburban home is a place of minimal social interaction, limited strictly to the immediate family. For the Japanese suburban male, as for the samurai who was in many ways his predecessor, the focus of attention is rather on the place of work. It might even be suggested that the company is a kind of *mura*, a closely regulated social setting much like the traditional agricultural village. In any case, the suburban residence itself thereby becomes the near-exclusive domain of women and children, who likewise tend to socialize not in their homes but rather in the streets and markets—in short, in the *machi*. In the end, then, the "suburbs" of Tokyo, to the extent that they have any independent identity at all, are simply more *machi*, little different from anywhere else in the city. The fundamental contrast between London's suburbia and Tokyo's amorphous *kōgai* is thus that the one is rooted in rural ideals and the other in urban realities. Whereas London's suburbs represent a way of life, Tokyo's are simply a place to live.

CONCLUSIONS

The various points of comparative interest which have emerged from this tentative analysis may be resolved into a single broad similarity and a single fundamental contrast. The similarity is this: neither Tokyo nor London, either as pre-industrial or as modern cities, has encouraged strong ideas of the city as an isolated entity. Both cities have proved relatively weak in the conception of the city as a clearly defined monumental presence which is found in ancient continental traditions both East Asian and Western. Both have also defied conceptualization as coherent political units in the manner derived from the medieval traditions of Western Europe. In short, Tokyo and London have refused—others would say failed—to conform to either princely or civic standards of urbanity. That Tokyo has been more conspicuous in this refusal (or failure) than London should not obscure their similarity in the broader context of East Asia versus Western Europe.

The significance of this similarity is that Tokyo and London, in their relatively particular, vague, and privatized forms, are far closer to contemporary urban realities than the ancient and medieval notions which continue to structure much thinking about the city today. Over the past several decades, high-speed urban transport and electronic communications have increasingly short-circuited our ability to identify and evaluate the city, both visually and conceptually. In the tendency of the English and particularly of the Japanese to tolerate a vagueness of urban definition, it is possible to detect an easy accommodation to this growing "invisibility" of the twentieth-century city.[83] This perspective is of considerable relevance to many of the debates over the city today, which revolve around such issues as the planned city versus the unplanned city, the inspiring city versus the functional city, the orderly city versus the spontaneous city.

But this passive tolerance of unprincely sprawl and uncivic privatization by no means exhausts the relevance of Tokyo and London, for the traditions of both cities also lend themselves to *alternative* modes for apprehending the city in general. It is here that the fundamental *contrast* of the two is to be sought, in the dominant English conception of the "country" versus the dominant Japanese conception of the *machi*. In the English case, the city is apprehended not directly, but rather is *reflected* through the clear conceptualization and idealization of the rural environment. In the Japanese case, the city is apprehended not through its power of definition (either visually or politically) but through its qualities as a locus of human interaction. In neither case is there any clear sense of the city as an isolate.

To clarify this contrast between the Japanese and English conceptions of the city, it is useful to differentiate two sets of relationships: that of man and his physical environment, and that of man and his fellow men. No conception of the city can be understood by reference to only one of these frameworks, for both interact in complex and wholly symbiotic ways. Thus, for example, the English conception of the "country" can be understood only with reference to the social history of the landed elite, and the Japanese notion of *machi* makes no historical sense without reference to the agricultural environment. But in the relative terms dictated by a comparative analysis, it seems clear that "country" is primarily an environmental concept whereas *machi* is primarily a social one.

The English notion of the "country" is environmental in the sense that it involves a conceptual distinction between the works of man

---

[83] For a photographic essay on the idea of urban "invisibility," see the series "Toshi," 52 installments, *Asahi jānaru*, (March 16, 1973—March 15, 1974, particularly installments 1–38.) This idea is largely the conception of architectural critic Taki Kōji; see his "Aimaisa no kūkan" [The space of ambiguity], *Asahi jānaru*, April 4, 1975, pp. 27-32.

and the works of God, or in the modern secular version, between man and his "natural" environment. The "country" in its dominant pastoral sense is conceived as an idealized middle ground between these two poles of art and nature, of civilization and wilderness. In the more extreme Romantic evolution of this idea, the logic of the resolving mean is sacrificed to a simple dualism of idealized wilderness versus corrupt society; it is this latter idea which has dominated American thinking on the city. In England, the rural compromise is rather the dominant form and has found a modern evolution into the suburban idea. In all of these conceptions, the element of social interaction is secondary to that of man and his physical environment.

The Japanese conception of the *machi* is social in the sense that it involves human relationships, whether that of the ruler and the ruled, as in its ancient meanings, or that of interaction for the sake of exchange and entertainment, as in its early modern transformation into a folk idea. As an environmental concept, the *machi* tends to be neutral, for the Japanese have never conceived of a dichotomy between the works of man and the works of something which transcends man (or, in the secular version, which man transcends). Thus the *machi* is neither anti-rural nor anti-wilderness, and in fact accommodates both, as in the village-like social structure of the Japanese city or in the symbolic use of wilderness in urban gardens.

It must be emphasized again that the environmental and the societal dimensions which structure any coherent idea of the city are symbiotic, and the emphasis on one to the detriment of the other cannot fail to have an unhappy reflection in urban realities. Thus, for example, the English emphasis on man's physical environment has perhaps been related to the conspicuous failures of London as a just and efficient social institution, whereas the Japanese preoccupation with the social efficiency of the city has in the end led to the current failure of Tokyo as a biologically wholesome habitat.[84] At a broader level, this need to *integrate* environmental and societal factors in seeking to comprehend the city has relevance to the evolution of American thinking about the city over the past several decades, among both academic and practicing urbanists. The sociological obsession for seeing the city as a disembodied network of human relations which has characterized much formal American thought about the city since World War II has seen an abrupt shift since the 1960's to the vogue for seeing the city and indeed all human affairs within the context of the "ecological" vogue for biological integrity. Each of these positions tends to neglect the other.

[84] The phrases "just and efficient social institution" and "biologically wholesome habitat" are from J. B. Jackson, in Zube, ed., *Landscapes*, p. 87.

I emphasize that the need is not for a new idea of the city, and even less for a new ideology of the city. Nor is the need for an abandonment of all historical conceptions of the city: most of the ideas mentioned in this essay continue to have their own integrity in the proper part of the city and at the proper time. The need is rather for a tolerance of a diversity of different ways to conceive and appreciate the city, not only among different cultures but within any single culture. The city is nothing if not diversity, and the ultimate comparative use of Tokyo and London is the historical hospitality of these two great capitals to a healthy variety of competing ideas of the city.

II

CHALLENGE AND RESPONSE: MODERN POLITICAL CHANGE IN KOREA, CHINA, AND JAPAN

Most comparisons of the Meiji Restoration and of the building of the new state have been with European revolutions. Or, when a comparison has been made with China, it has been with the 1911 revolution. These two papers break with this tradition, each in a different way.

Seizaburō Satō, in a pioneering paper, examines the parallel between Korea and Japan. He takes as his constants two sets of factors: externally, the encroachment of the Western powers and, internally, the late East Asian Confucian culture of the respective ruling elites. One most interesting finding is that just as there are striking similarities between a Fukuzawa and a Yen Fu, so are there similarities in the response of Korea. Satō calls this the "East Asian response to the West." Then, having defined what the two countries have in common, he goes on to consider the ways in which Japan and Korea were not alike and why their dissimilarities led to such different historical outcomes.

Where Satō compares Japan and Korea in the mid-nineteenth century at a time when their elites had many cultural elements in common, Ezra Vogel compares Japan in the nineteenth century with China after World War II. That is to say, he compares both countries during their periods of nation-building. That Japan's nation-building followed hard on the heels of the previous "dynasty" and China's did not make a difference. Japan used a restatement of traditional doctrines to legitimate its modern state, while China, its tradition crumbling, used Marxist doctrines as its ideological base. That the nation-building took place in different international contexts also made a difference. Vogel argues, however, that any new revolutionary regime, if it is to succeed, must deal with a similar range of problems. Just as Crane Brinton in *The Anatomy of Revolution* inquired into the necessary pre-conditions for the overthrow of the old, so Vogel is asking what are the functional prerequisites for the establishment of a new regime. He looks at officialdom, education, public security, military organization, etc. He compares the Communist oligarchs who emerged from the Long March and the political and military struggles of World War II with the higher level cadres of the Meiji period who survived the purges, politics, and warfare of the Restoration. He then draws conclusions regarding the consequences of the rapid development of the nation-state in the two instances.

One general point regarding the nature of revolution or of forced political change may apply to both papers: any successful revolution has two stages, the overthrow of the *ancien régime* and the establishment of the new. This distinction is initially more useful than talk of revolutions from above and revolutions from below. The overthrow of an *ancien régime*, if it is not a palace *coup d'état*, is always, to a greater or lesser extent, from below. And the subsequent reshaping of society, whether by the Meiji leaders after 1868 or the Chinese leaders after 1949, is always from above. Once this distinction between stages is made, social and other analyses can follow. Satō's paper is primarily concerned with stage one, Vogel's with stage two.

Response to the West:
The Korean and Japanese Patterns*

≫≫ ≪≪

SEIZABURO SATO

I

At some time during the nineteenth century, every East Asian nation found itself in the same urgent situation of having to meet the threat to their national integrity posed by the industrialized Western powers, and having to do so quickly and effectively. That threat was backed by overwhelming strength—strength that no Asian nation could match— and it was impossible to ward off encroachment by the West. To maintain their independence the countries of Asia had no choice but to avoid military confrontation and to comply with the demands of the Western powers to open their doors to "trade and amity" with Europe and America. At the same time, they had to absorb as much Western technology as possible and thereby strengthen their own military and economic capacities in order to develop a defense. They had to act quickly, without destroying their internal order and traditional social system. Prolongation of the process of strengthening themselves meant doom; they would fall victim to the colonial ambitions of the Western powers. But if the rush to dismantle the traditional politico-social order were too precipitous, the result would be chaos. It would risk undermining national integration and political leadership and institutions precisely when they were most desperately needed.

This article is an attempt to compare the Japanese and Korean experience, to show specifically what factors were responsible for the effectiveness or ineffectuality of the response in each case. Korea has been selected for comparison with Japan for the simple reason that, despite their geographical proximity and the shared historical, cultural, and social heritage that binds the two nations together, Korea

* In preparing this paper for publication, I have benefited from useful suggestions made by participants in the Cuernavaca Conference. In addition, I would like to express my special thanks to Professor Choe Yong-ho of the University of Hawaii, Professor Inoguchi Takashi of Sophia University, and Shin Hee-suck of Tokyo University for carefully going over my draft and making many valuable comments. Finally, I wish to acknowledge Patricia Murray of *The Japan Interpreter* for her translation of this article.

responded to the encroachment of the West in a manner strikingly different from Japan.

One of the difficulties in cross-cultural comparative research is how to handle the background factors that are not under direct examination.[1] In a historical analysis of macro-social phenomena, which are molded and modified by innumerable background factors, this problem is further compounded by the difficulty of defining the propositions to be demonstrated in functional terms. The historian is also handicapped by methodological limitations. For example, he cannot reproduce the controlled laboratory experiment of the natural scientist; he cannot use the control-group methodology of the experimental psychologist; nor can he draw random samples from a population, as can a survey researcher. However, the analysis of two different societies that have many traits in common offers a practical means of controlling a considerable number of the background factors. This method seems distinctly primitive, but, given the level of historical research available at present, it nevertheless merits a serious attempt.

II

Both foreign observers and Korean writers have frequently sought to characterize Korean society in terms of its high degree of homogeneity and historical continuity. One American scholar begins his study of Korean politics with the following statement: "Smallness of dimension, stability of boundaries, ethnic and religious homogeneity, and exceptional historical continuity mark Korea."[2] It may be observed, however, that every one of those features also characterizes Japan. Ethnically, Japan is unusually homogeneous. In addition to the indigenous Shinto, numerous sects of Buddhism entered the country, but each was thoroughly Japanized by the Edo period (1603-1868), and any sectarian differences all but lost their significance during the process. Confucianism, though it went through a comparatively rich and variegated development during the Edo period, did not flourish as a comprehensive or systematic world view. On the contrary, it was accepted and came to function within the conceptual framework that focused on moralistic self-discipline and the articulation of a way of life (for example, *bushido*). Finally, *Kokugaku* (National Learning) was fundamentally syncretic, having emerged from and in response to the three older systems of belief.

[1] See Robert T. Holt and John E. Turner, eds., *The Methodology of Comparative Research* (1970, Free Press, New York), pp. 5-20.

[2] Gregory Henderson, *Korea: The Politics of the Vortex* (1968, Harvard University Press, Cambridge, Mass.) p. 13.

Both Japan and Korea are small countries in comparison with China. If one excludes Hokkaido, which was almost uninhabited until the mid-nineteenth century, the total area of the two countries is roughly comparable (Korea: 220,000 square km; Japan: 290,000 square km). In both, about 75 percent of the land is mountainous. The significant difference is that Japan's population during the mid-nineteenth century was about four times that of Korea. (This may be explained partly by the warmer Japanese climate and higher annual rainfall, making it more appropriate for rice cultivation.) The two countries, nonetheless, lie geographically close, are situated at about the same latitude, and share similar climatic conditions. Rice is the basic crop in both.

Historically, the boundaries of insular Japan have been more stable than Korea's. The northern half of the Korean peninsula and Manchuria are contiguous and have been historically subject to dispute. It was only in the Yi dynasty (1392-1910) that the existing boundaries were firmly demarcated. Japan has been involved in disputes over some of the smaller islands, but, with sea on all sides, it has had the advantage of fairly clear boundaries that have remained almost unchanged since the emergence of a unified state under the ancient court.

Japan's historical continuity can also be compared with Korea's "exceptional historical continuity." The imperial court established during the first half of the sixth century has undergone many changes since that time, but it has remained the symbol of national integration until the present. Japan reached a comparatively high level of centralization even in ancient times; since the era of integration of much of the country under the Yamato rulers, the central government has never been completely powerless, except during the Warring States period (1467-1568). Even then one can see a clear trend toward centralization in the struggles among the daimyo to occupy Kyoto and to establish hegemony over the nation.

The similarities between Japan and Korea do not end here. Geographically close, both countries faced the advance of the Western countries into Asia at approximately the same time. Early prodding of Japan to open foreign trade began in 1792 with the coming of the Russian envoy, Adam Laxman. The pressure did not become serious, however, until after the Opium War (1840-1841). Frequently referred to as the "Hermit Kingdom," pre-modern Korea had comparatively little contact with the West. Nevertheless, it was not completely secluded from the Western world. Extant records reveal that between the latter half of the sixteenth and the beginning of the nineteenth centuries Western ships were sighted in Korean coastal waters on more than ten occasions, and in the middle of the nineteenth century this number increased rapidly.[3] It was in 1831 that an English merchant ship first pulled into Korean waters, demanding the commencement of trade. During the 1840's and afterward, the naval fleets of France, Russia, and the United States followed suit, to demand that Korea open its doors to foreign trade. Kanghwa Island, strategically located at the coastal entryway to Seoul, was occupied by French naval forces in 1866 and by American forces in 1871. The 1860 occupation of Peking by British and French troops came as a frightening jolt both to the samurai elite under the Tokugawa bakufu and to the Confucian ruling bureaucracy of the Yi dynasty.

Common cultural features are also abundant. From prehistoric times until the early Edo period the more advanced culture from the continent entered Japan primarily by way of Korea.[4] The writing system using Chinese ideographs and Mahayana Buddhism were introduced to Japan from Korea. The base for Tokugawa neo-Confucianism was laid by Korean scholars; one was Kang Hang (1567-1618). He was captured by Toyotomi Hideyoshi's armies when they invaded Korea in 1592 and 1598 and brought to Japan, together with a great number of scholarly works. Yi Toe-gye (1501-1570), probably the greatest neo-Confucian scholar the Yi dynasty produced, had a profound and lasting influence on scholars in Japan during the Edo period, from Fujiwara Seika (1561-1619) to Yokoi Shōnan (1809-1869).[5] A Korean official who was a member of a mission that came to Japan in 1719 found that "all kinds of books by Korean as well as Chinese scholars" were sold in Osaka. He said, "Of all the books by Korean scholars, the Japanese most respect the works of Yi Toe-gye. . . . When I conversed with Japanese scholars through writing, they always asked about his works first."[6]

As I will discuss later, there were vast differences between the Japanese and Korean attitudes toward the Western incursion, but specific elements in the aggregate social response were strikingly similar. Faced with the advance of the Western nations, for example, both reacted with a xenophobic closing of their gates. In Japan the cry was *Sonnō jōi!* (Revere the emperor, expel the barbarians!), and in Korea

[3] Okudaira Takehiko, *Chōsen kaikoku kōshō shimatsu* (1935, Tōkō Shoin, Tokyo, reprinted in 1969), p. 16.

[4] Regarding Korean influence on Japanese culture, see Chōsen Bunka Sha, ed., *Nihon bunka to Chōsen* (1974, Shin Jinbutsu Ōrai Sha, Tokyo); and Kim Tal-su, *Nihon no naka no Chōsen bunka*, 2 vols. (Tokyo: Kōdan Sha, 1970-1972).

[5] See Abe Yoshio, *Nihon Shushigaku to Chōsen* (Tokyo: Tokyo Daigaku Shuppan Kai, 1965).

[6] Sin Yu-han, *Hae-yu rok*, Japanese title *Kaiyū roku*, Kang Je-ong, trans. (Tokyo: Heibon Sha, 1974), pp. 120, 243.

it was *Wijŏng chŏksa!* (Defend the right, expel evil!) The exclusionism of both countries emphasized the moral superiority of the nation, and both saw the international situation as analogous to that of the Warring States period. Both exhibited hostility and apprehension toward the Western powers, backed by calls for domestic reform that would allow men of ability to take government positions, unify and strengthen public opinion, build a powerful military establishment, and cut back expenditures.[7]

Even the order of events after the onset of the exclusionist movement was similar. Both sought to wed Eastern morality with Western technology; Korea's *Tongdo sŏgi* (Eastern morality, Western technology) was in Japan *Wakon yōsai* (Japanese spirit, Western learning). The appearance of "enlightenment" thinkers followed. Seeking to adopt the social systems and thought of the West, they stimulated a new slogan in both countries: the Korean *Munmyŏng kaehwa* and the Japanese *Bunmei kaika* both meant "civilization and enlightenment."[8] The writings of Yu Kil-chun (1856-1914), a major Korean enlightenment thinker of the time, frequently call to mind the ideas of Fukuzawa Yukichi (1834-1901).[9] Their thinking focused on many of the same themes: natural rights, equality among sovereign states, self-reliance of the individual as prerequisite to national independence, gradual reformism, and belief in the need for improved educational systems. Thus the initial reaction was a heightened xenophobia that advocated total rejection of Western culture. This was followed by an attempt to import only the technology of the West apart from and independent of the cultural background from which it emerged. Finally, "enlightenment thinkers" emerged who had a deep appreciation for the "spirit" of Western culture. As the same sequence can also be found in the Chinese case,[10] this pattern may be called the "East Asian response to the West."

[7] For an analysis of Korean xenophobia, see Kang Je-ong, *Kindai Chōsen no shisō* (Tokyo: Kinokuniya Shoten, 1971), chap. 1. See also Kim Yŏng-jak, "Kanmatsu ni okeru nashonarizumu no shisō to genjitsu" (Ph.D. dissertation, University of Tokyo, 1972), chap. 1.

[8] The phrase "*Munmyŏng kaehwa*" was imported from Japan and widely used after 1882. Prior to this time, the popular slogans for "modernization" in Korea were Chinese words such as "*Koji*" (in Chinese, "*Kengshih*"), "*Pugang*" ("*Fu-ch'iang*"), and "*Jigang*" ("*Tzu-ch'iang*"). The change in usage suggests the growing influence of rapidly modernizing Japan over Korean intellectuals. See Yi Kwang-in, *Hanguk kaehwa si yŏngu* (Seoul: Iljogak, 1969), pp. 21-24; and Kim Yŏng-jak "Kanmatsu," pp. 176, 265-266.

[9] Yu Kil-chun visited Japan in 1881 as part of a Korean cultural mission and studied at Fukuzawa's Keiō College for one year. His complete works were recently published in Korea. Yi Kwang-in, et al., eds., *Yu Kil-chun chŏn so*, 5 vols. (Seoul: Iljogak, 1971-1972).

[10] See, for example, Benjamin Schwartz, *In Search of Wealth and Power: Yen Fu and the West* (Cambridge, Mass.: Harvard University Press, 1964).

The domestic reforms carried out in an effort to resist the incursion of the Western powers also included many elements common to both countries. Taewŏn'gun, the real father of the boy king Kojong, who ascended the throne in 1864, held the court under his control and devoted himself to strengthening the royal prerogative. He was as practical and forceful as the Japanese statesmen who established the Restoration government four years later. One of Taewŏn'gun's ambitions was to destroy the private academies (sŏwŏn) that had become centers of factional groups among the yangban ruling class of the time. He also sought to collect taxes from both the yangban and the common people. Moreover, by expelling the aristocratic families that surrounded the throne, such as the Andong Kim, Taewŏn'gun tried to establish a bureaucratic government. These policies, though not as successful, resemble the actions of Japan's Meiji oligarchs in depriving the samurai and daimyo of their privileges and forcibly centralizing political authority.[11] Subsequently, Korea's reformist leaders—Kim Ok-kyun (1851-1894). Pak Yŏng-kyo (1861-1939), and others—who tried to use the Japanese experience in modernizing their own country, derived many of their ideas from the policies of the Meiji government and the "People's Rights" movement.[12]

III

This brief description reveals some similarities between the experiences of Japan and Korea. Nevertheless, the response of these two nations to the Western impact was on the whole markedly different. For one thing, certain concrete issues made the Japanese far more sensitive than the Koreans to Western encroachment. The outbreak of the Opium War, the first genuine challenge to the "Chinese world order" that had been for centuries the basic framework of international relations in East Asia, had a profoundly shocking effect on the samurai intellectuals. Chinese works concerning the war found their way to Japan, where they were widely read and stimulated an active, serious debate among intellectuals on the significance of the Opium War and Japan's options in dealing with the West. The bakufu proceeded to make detailed inquiries of the Dutch and Chinese in Nagasaki in order to

[11] On the leadership of Taewŏn'gun, see James B. Palais, *Politics and Policy in Traditional Korea: 1864-1876* (Cambridge, Mass.: Harvard University Press, forthcoming).

[12] For discussion of reformist policies, see Kang Je-ong, *Kindai Chōsen no henkaku shisō* (1973, Nihon Hyōron Sha, Tokyo), pp. 112-140; and Kim Yŏng-jak, "Kanmatsu," chaps. 2 and 3. See also Kōin Kinen Kai, ed., *Kin Gyoku-kin den*, vol. 1 (Tokyo: Keiō Shuppan Sha, 1944).

discover the weapons and strategies used by the British navy in China at that time.[13]

By contrast, although—or perhaps because—Korea sent tributary missions to China every year and thus had easier access to information on the situation in China, available evidence indicates that the Korean elite had little interest in the Opium War and its potential implications.

Not only were Japanese more sensitive, they were also more flexible, at least in the sense that they recognized the need for prudence. For example, in 1842, on receiving the report of the Chinese defeat in the Opium War, the bakufu rescinded the 1824 ordinance for the repulsion of foreign ships. This did not mark a change in the seclusion policy, but did indicate the practicality with which the bakufu approached the problem, trying first to avoid risking confrontation with the much stronger Western powers. The bakufu demonstrated the same type of pragmatism in dealing with Commodore Perry's demands. Although the bakufu never intended to take any positive steps to open the country, they were willing to make minimally necessary concessions when they judged that danger of a military confrontation was imminent.

When war broke out between the Ch'ing dynasty and the combined troops of France and England in 1858, Japan was in political turmoil over whether or not to conclude a treaty of commerce with the United States. The bakufu was reluctant to sign the treaty for fear of provoking the court and samurai patriots who stood behind the movement to expel the "barbarians," but when they heard that the second Opium War had begun, they decided to ignore the opposition of the court and loyalist samurai and conclude the pact.

The occupation of Peking by Western forces in 1860 stunned the Korean government as well. It immediately dispatched a special fact-finding mission to China. But the policies that came out of those findings only strengthened exclusionism and isolation. In the same year, Russian forces had advanced as far as the lower reaches of the Tumen River, coming close enough for the first time to share a border with Korea. In 1864 and 1865, the Russians pressed for the opening of trade relations, and in 1866 Russian warships visited Korea, demanding the establishment of diplomatic relations. The Korean government not only rejected all the Russian demands but proceeded to arrest and execute nine French Catholic missionaries who had smuggled themselves into the country, together with several thousand of their Korean

[13] See Nakayama Kyūshirō, "Kinsei Shina yori ishin zengo no Nihon ni oyoboshitaru eikyō," in Shigakkai, ed., *Meiji ishinshi kenkyū* (Tokyo: Iwanami Shoten, 1923).

followers.[14] Moreover, the Taewŏn'gun declared that this religious persecution was justified: "If we do not punish them quickly, the Jehol (Jehe) calamity will befall us."[15] Jehol (Jehe) is the site to which the Manchu emperor fled when the English and French armies occupied Peking. In protest against the wanton murder of the French missionaries, and with the express purpose of protecting two priests still hiding in Korea, a fleet of seven French warships occupied Kanghwa Island in October 1866, blocking the estuary of the Han River which connects Seoul with the Yellow Sea.[16] Even then the Korean government refused to change its position on isolation and the expulsion of foreigners; instead, with all the power at its disposal it fought to resist the French forces. The attitude of the Korean government was articulated in an appeal by the Taewŏn'gun: "If we fail to endure present hardships and accede to the desires of the Western barbarians to establish friendly relations with us, it will amount to a sellout of our country. If we fail to bear up under their onslaught, and thus permit them to trade with us, it will be the ruin of our country. The enemy is pressing on Seoul. Flight from the capital will only endanger the country."[17]

Meeting the unexpected resistance of the Korean army, learning that the two priests had escaped to China, and afraid that they might become icebound as winter set in, the French forces withdrew from Korea in November. The attack of the French fleet had been the result of a personal decision of Admiral Pierre Roze, and it had occurred without adequate preparations. The French government criticized the admiral's precipitous action, and he was recalled. Nevertheless, Korea saw the outcome of the war as a victory for the expulsion policy, a victory that seemed to justify and therefore heighten the feeling of xenophobia. Soon afterward the government placed stone monuments throughout the country on which twelve characters were engraved: *Yangi ch'inbŏm pijŏn chik hwa chuhwa maeguk* (The Western barbarians invaded our country. Had we not taken up arms against them, forced amity with them would have followed, and that would have

[14] At that time, twelve French priests were engaged in missionary work in Korea, and there were more than twenty thousand Korean adherents. Tabohashi Kiyoshi, *Kindai Nitchō kankeishi no kenkyū*, vol. 1 (Seoul: Chōsen Sōtokufu, 1940), pp. 53-55.

[15] Kyu-changgag, ed., *Ilsŏng rok*, the eighth day of the seventh month, 1866, cited in Kang Je-ong, *Kindai Chōsen*, p. 19.

[16] Before he sailed for Korea, Admiral Pierre Roze of the French Far Eastern Fleet notified the Chinese government (suzerain of Korea) that he would conquer Korea and establish a new—virtually puppet—king who would be controlled by the French. Tabohashi, *Kindai Nitchō*, pp. 58-59.

[17] *Yi-jŏng-bu cho-gi* the fourteenth day of the ninth month, 1866, cited in Tabohashi, *Kindai Nitchō*, p. 17.

meant selling out our country). The government went so far as to order all makers of ink blocks to engrave the twelve characters on every stick.[18]

In 1871 Frederick Low, American minister to China, headed a fleet of five warships (the same number Commodore Perry had commanded in 1854), arriving in Korea to demand trade with the U.S. Korea took the same position toward the United States as it had toward France. Low's demands were refused, the situation degenerated into war, and Korea suffered severe damage. However, as the American fleet neither intended to engage in nor was prepared for a drawn-out conflict, it eventually had to withdraw—an act which only served to harden Korea's attitude toward the Western powers.

Neither did Japan escape out-and-out conflict with the Western powers. In 1863 fighting broke out between Britain and the Satsuma *han* (domain) as a result of the Namamugi incident. When England demanded that Satsuma punish those responsible for the incident and pay indemnities as well, Satsuma refused and Britain attacked. In 1864 a combined fleet of British, French, Dutch, and American warships took reprisal on Chōshū for firing at Western ships. There were, however, some striking differences between the Japanese resistance to the Western powers and that of Korea. First, it was not the bakufu—that is, the acting representative of Japan in international matters—which participated in the military clashes, but the powerful *han* opposed to the bakufu. In this sense, these encounters were not strictly confrontations between Japan and the Western powers. Second, although neither Satsuma nor Chōshū was fatally debilitated (in the Satsuma battle, the British fleet was damaged extensively), they called for a ceasefire within a couple of days and made peace with the foreign powers. Third, these two small battles generated a great shock wave throughout the entire *jōi* movement. After the Chōshū extremists abandoned their stand on *jōi*, no organized movement of this nature was seen again.

There was also a great difference between Japanese and Korean enthusiasm for adopting Western technology. Interest in new technology was manifested much sooner in Korea: as early as the beginning of the seventeenth century, several Korean scholars, including Yi Sugwang (Chibong, 1563-1626), were reading about Western technology through books written in Chinese by Matteo Ricci and others. These efforts culminated in an encyclopedic work by Yi Ik (Songho, 1682-1764), covering all known aspects of Western science, and the establishment in the early eighteenth century of the Songho school with its emphasis on practical learning (*Sirhak*). In Japan, works such as

18 Aoyagi Kōtarō, *Richōshi taizen* (Tokyo: Meichō Shuppan, 1972), p. 729.

Matteo Ricci's had been banned ever since Japan shut itself into isolation. Nevertheless, when Yi I-myŏng (Soje, 1658-1722) was studying Western technology and Christianity under the missionaries Joseph Suarez and Ignatius Koegler in Peking, Arai Hakuseki (1657-1725) was interrogating Giovanni Sidotti in Edo about Western culture and society. (Sidotti was a missionary who had been arrested after smuggling himself into Japan.) Both Arai and Yi came to similar conclusions: Christian doctrines were not worth serious consideration, but Western technology had a great deal to offer.

Around the end of the eighteenth century, interest in Western technology began growing rapidly in Japan, both because it seemed exotic and because of an increasing awareness of the foreign threat. In Korea, in contrast, Western learning (Sŏhak) was overwhelmed by the rigid neo-Confucian orthodoxy. Moreover, factional struggles among yangban bureaucrats resulted in the purge and execution of Sirhak scholars in 1788, 1792, 1801, and 1839. Sirhak books and other related works were burned at the same time. During this short interval almost every work on Western technology disappeared from Korea.[19] Nor was there any hope of replenishing these valuable sources. For until it was forced to accede to Japanese demands to open the country in 1876, Yi dynasty Korea lacked even a small window to the West such as Nagasaki provided for Edo Japan.

By the mid-nineteenth century there were few in Japan who could continue to deny the necessity for Western technology, even among jōi fanatics. Although Japanese scholars of Western learning also experienced official suppression, most notably the "Bansha no Goku" of 1839 (suppression of a group engaged in "Dutch learning"), this particular incident involved only a limited number of "unauthorized" persons who had criticized the bakufu's foreign policy and, in so doing, overstepped their rank. Those persecuted at that time included Watanabe Kazan (1793-1841), who was not a bakufu retainer, and Takano Chōei (1804-1850), who was from the merchant class. No bakufu retainers in this group were punished, and ironically one of them was officially rewarded when he formally presented ideas almost identical to those held by Kazan and Chōei. In Korea, on the other hand, it was difficult to openly suggest that Western technology be adopted until after the country finally put an end to its seclusion policy under mounting pressure from Japan. When the seclusion policy was abandoned, a group of intellectual followers of Pak Kyu-su (1807-1876) organized the enlightenment faction (Kaehwa-p'a) and began to promote Tongdo sŏgi. Yet even Kim Yun-sik (1841-1920), a member of

19 Hong I-so, Chōsen kagakushi (Tokyo: Tōto Shoseki, 1944), pp. 427-430; Kang Je-ong, Kindai Chōsen, pp. 41-50.

this enlightenment faction, had remarked in the earlier days: "I understand that in Europe they have slowly improved their vulgar way of living and are now talking of adopting civilization. But Korea is such a civilized country that I wonder if there is anything here that could be improved."[20]

IV

Why did Japan and Korea respond in such totally different ways when they encountered the Western powers and their advanced technology?

First, differences in the nature of nationalism in the two countries undoubtedly played an important role. Both Korea and Japan have had stable territorial boundaries, ethnic and cultural homogeneity, and a long national history. From early times the consciousness of national identity has been strong, providing a sufficient social base for the development of modern nationalism. However, both Korean and Japanese nationalism had to overcome a strong sense of inferiority toward their giant neighbor China.

By maintaining loyalty to the Ming dynasty (to which Korea had been the number-one tributary kingdom) even after it was overthrown, the Koreans were able to deal fairly easily with feelings of inferiority that might otherwise have arisen toward the Ch'ing. The majority of Korean intellectuals saw the Manchurian rulers of China as uncivilized barbarians; and as Korea had been recognized as the "Eastern bulwark of the Great Ming Empire" *(Taemyŏng tongbyŏng)* by the Ming, Korea regarded itself as the legitimate successor of Ming China, the true Middle Kingdom. In the thinking that prevailed among Korean Confucian scholars, their country had no choice, under the existing power relations, but to continue as a tributary to China; but nothing could be learned from the "barbarian Ch'ing." There was even talk of conquering the Ch'ing, expressed in the rallying cry, "*Chon-myŏng yang-i!*" (revere the Ming, expel the barbarians!).[21]

The Pukhak and Sŏngho schools were two of the most influential groups in the study of "practical learning" in late Yi dynasty Korea. The leader of the Pukhak school, Pak Chi-wŏn (1737-1805), was highly critical of the strong tendency among his contemporaries to regard learning from the "barbarians" (Manchu China) as shameful. "If their laws and institutions are good, then we should go to these barbarians and learn from them."[22] The word *pukhak* literally means "northern learning." It referred to the practical willingness to learn

20 Cited in Kang Je-ong, *Kindai Chōsen*, pp. 99-100.
21 *Ibid.*, pp. 16-19.
22 "Pukhakyi sŏ," cited in Kang Je-ong, *Kindai Chōsen*, p. 64.

from the northern barbarians, China of the Ch'ing dynasty. But it was not until the late eighteenth century that a movement to study and learn from the Ch'ing grew up in Korea—strong testimony to the deep Korean identification with Ming civilization in its own nationalism. As a matter of fact, from the beginning of the eighteenth century, members of the Noron school dominated the government and held most of the key posts. Highly critical of the practical learning of the Sŏngho and Pukhak schools, this mainstream faction even went as far as to build a shrine in honor of the Ming dynasty emperors at its headquarters, the Hwanyandong sŏwŏn.[23]

Identification with Ming China placed severe restrictions on the development of Korean nationalism. As the legitimate successor of the Middle Kingdom, Korea felt compelled to cling to its orthodoxy—neo-Confucianism—to the very end. Obsessed by a fanatic "Middle Kingdom" exclusivism, Korean nationalists were *plus royaliste que le roi*. As a result, they were unable to adopt a flexible, practical attitude in the midst of the crisis provoked by the encroachment of the Western powers. If the Ch'ing were to be rejected as barbaric, it is no wonder that Koreans found Western culture totally unacceptable. In his 1876 appeal against opening the country, the famous Confucian scholar Choe Ik-hyŏn (1833-1906) expressed the belief that "Ch'ing may be barbarians, but Western people and Westernized Japanese are beasts. One can associate with barbarians—at least they are humans, but the same cannot be said of animals."[24] "Ming consciousness" also hindered the emergence of the crown as a powerful symbol of modern Korean nationalism. Historically, the king maintained his legitimacy as the ruler of Korea through submission to the Chinese emperor. Consequently, for the king to have rejected the traditional Chinese world order would have been suicidal. In this aspect his position can perhaps be seen as similar to that of the Tokugawa shogun, whose legitimacy was grounded in imperial authorization. Insofar as the emperor advocated *jōi*, the bakufu found it impossible to justify opening the country. In other words, neither the Korean king nor the Tokugawa shogun possessed a legitimacy strong enough to transform the "sacred tradition."

Yet Tokugawa Japan, free of official relations (not to mention tributary relations) with either the Ming or the Ch'ing, was far less bound by the Chinese world order and neo-Confucian orthodoxy. In contrast to the Korean *yangban* intellectuals, who identified with Ming China, Tokugawa Confucian scholars sought to overcome feelings of

---

[23] *Ibid.*, p. 22.

[24] "O pulka so," in Kyu-changgag, ed., *Ilsŏng rok*, the twenty-third day of the first month, 1876, cited in Hatada Takashi, "Kindai ni okeru Chōsenjin no Nippon kan," *Shisō* 152 (Oct. 1967): 62.

inferiority either by separating the *idée* of Chinese culture from the existing Chinese society and abstracting it into universal principles, or by emphasizing the supremacy of Japan's unique virtues, especially in their distinction from Chinese. One of the best examples of the separation and abstraction effort can be found in the works of Ogyū Sorai (1666-1728), who deplored the degeneration of Chinese Confucianism since its inception and flowering in the time of Confucius. He did this by attributing absolute value to the *Sennō no Michi*, the way of governing by the legendary Sage Kings of ancient China. Yamaga Sokō (1622-1685) contended that the three basic virtues of the Sage Kings—wisdom, benevolence, and courage—had been refined to a much higher level in Japan than in China. Most of the samurai intellectuals of the Meiji Restoration years regarded the West in terms of these values, which had by then become so highly abstracted that they no longer had any relation with the cultural milieu or way of life in China. Hence, it is no wonder that a great many samurai were deeply impressed with the Westerner's "wisdom" that could give birth to such powerful technology, the Westerner's "courage" that had brought him all the way to the Orient, and the "benevolence" that had created parliamentary systems capable of checking the emergence of repressive governments.

The scholars of National Learning found it relatively easy to confirm the superiority of Japan by emphasizing their unique, indigenous "virtues," for they were under no compulsion to esteem Confucian concepts. They asserted that Japan was a divine land in which the emperor, a direct descendant of the Sun Goddess, presided over the social hierarchy. Their doctrines provided the emotional basis for growing nationalism. Heirs of a "line unbroken" in historical times, emperors became the symbol of a unique Japanese morality and functioned thereby as a powerful nucleus for the crystallization of Japanese nationalism. Even the extremely ethnocentric thinking of the Kokugaku scholars, however, could not negate the many aspects of Japanese culture that derived from the advanced continental civilizations. For in attempting to make a claim for the universality of Japanese culture in their own terms, the Kokugaku ideologues found themselves reduced either to expounding the far-fetched argument that foreign cultures had all flowed out of Japan into foreign lands in prehistoric times, or to claiming that "openness" to advanced foreign cultures was itself one of the Japanese "virtues." Consequently, even the "divine-land consciousness" did little to encourage a closed attitude toward alien cultures.[25]

[25] Japanese efforts to overcome their inferiority feelings toward China are discussed in my "Bakumatsu ishin ki ni okeru taigai ishiki no shoruikei," in Sato Seizaburo and Roger Dingman, eds., *Kindai Nihon no taigai ishiki* (Tokyo: Tokyo Daigaku Shuppan Kai, 1974).

As I pointed out earlier, nationalism in both countries initially took the form of a vehement xenophobia which expressed itself in acts and exhortations aimed at driving the intruders away. At the same time, however, the political function of this nationalism differed greatly in each case. The function of Korea's *wijŏng* exclusionism was conservative. As the slogan itself indicates, it was a call to protect "righteous traditions." In contrast to this and despite the initial motivations of many of the samurai patriots, Japan's Sonnō jōi movement functioned innovatively in seeking to replace the autocracy of the bakufu with the political authority of a virtually powerless emperor. Most of the early Meiji modernizers were in fact descendants of the Sonnō jōi exclusionists. In Korea, where nationalism remained firmly tied to conservatism, efforts of the enlightenment faction to mobilize nationalism for its cause ultimately proved unsuccessful, thereby placing serious restrictions on the faction's political influence.

As has been suggested, the qualitative and functional differences between the nationalism of the two countries can be partly attributed to the difference in their relationship to China, as well as to the distinctive character of the political systems and the ruling elites that prevailed in each. The Yi dynasty stood on a centralized bureaucracy with the king at the apex of the *yangban* aristocracy. The term *yangban* originally referred to the civil and military bureaucrats of the Koryŏ dynasty (918-1259). The Chinese civil service examination system was imported and imitated as early as the Silla period (654-935), but the adopted Korean version was modified as *yangban* came to be synonymous with aristocratic status, and eligibility for major government positions became in fact hereditary. *Yangban* families were given preferential access whenever a civil service examination (*kwagŏ*) was held. They enjoyed a range of privileges that included special exemption from taxation, and they frequently made use of their official position to accumulate land and wealth.

The *yangban* population continued to grow through the more than five hundred years of the Yi dynasty, both as a result of natural proliferation and the widespread practice of purchasing official rank. Thus they became a varied social group, ranging from top officials and landowning aristocrats to local gentry, on down to poor tenants. Because of that diversity they lost all the cohesiveness that binds those of like social status together. Those who passed the *kwagŏ* examination, however, especially the *munkwa*—the highest level—came from the ranks of a relatively exclusive upper *yangban* group right up through the mid-nineteenth century.[26] That group comprised a closed

[26] Edward E. Wagner, "The Ladder of Success in Yi Dynasty Korea," in *Occasional Papers on Korea*, vol. 1 (Cambridge, Mass.: June 1972), pp. 1-8.

and privileged class, which came closest to what is meant by "landed aristocracy." They were able to maintain their privilege and prestige only through official position, however, for if they lost it, they lost all guarantee of security. Once an official was purged, his wealth, and even his life, were in danger. According to one, perhaps slightly exaggerated, account, "In Korea, a government post meant a source of income. If the prospective official did not receive a position his livelihood was not secure. If he lost the post, it meant starving to death."[27]

Successful candidates for the *kwagŏ* examination were practically, if not legally, limited to the *yangban* elite. The number who passed, however, far exceeded available government jobs. There were also far more applicants who failed, indicating that competition for official positions was stiff. The effort to win profitable positions naturally gave rise to factions in the bureaucracy. In Korea the clans (*munjung*) maintained strong cohesiveness,[28] so bureaucratic factions were almost always based on lineal ties, generating firm factional solidarity and supporting the tendency to institutionalize inheritance of factional affiliation from generation to generation. Since the early sixteenth century, when bureaucratic factions took clear shape, Korean politics began to revolve around the confrontation and competition among tight factional groupings. During the four hundred years from the early sixteenth century until the fall of the Yi dynasty at the outset of the twentieth century, thousands of ranking officials, candidates, and their families were executed, and perhaps an even greater number were sent into exile.[29] In many cases, the charges were trifling, or entirely false.

This kind of factional confrontation served to heighten the influence and authority of the king, who held the ultimate power over bureaucratic appointments. As the fate of the factions became increasingly dependent on the favor of the king, however, the danger that the king and his successors would become enmeshed in factional struggles also increased. During the Yi dynasty three kings were banished between 1495 and 1863, and at least sixteen sons and grandsons of kings were

[27] Hosoi Hajime, *Hōtō shika no kentō* (Seoul: Jiyū Tōkyū Sha, 1926), pp. *i-ii*.

[28] The land where the founding father of a clan first settled is known as *bongwan* in Korea. Until very recently it was taboo for persons of the same *bongwan* to intermarry, regardless of where they lived at the time and even if they did not have the remotest blood relationship. For recent studies on the Korean family structure, see Nakane Chie, ed., *Kankoku nōson no kazoku to saigi* (Tokyo: Tokyo Daigaku Shuppan Kai, 1973); and Vincent S. R. Brandt, *A Korean Village: Between Farm and Sea* (Cambridge, Mass.: Harvard University Press, 1971), chap. 5.

[29] For detailed description of factional struggles under the Yi dynasty, see Hosoi, *Hōtō*, and Aoyagi Kōtarō, "Richō hōtōshi ron," in his *Chōsen bunkashi taizen* (1972, Meichō Shuppan, Tokyo), pp. 901-950.

executed for treason.[30] An extreme example can be seen in the struggle for succession to the twenty-first king, Yŏngjo (r. 1725-1776). His only son and one of his grandsons were executed, and two of the remaining three grandsons were sent into exile. The grandson of one of the banished princes became the twenty-fifth king, Ch'ŏljong (r. 1850-1863). He ascended the throne at the age of nineteen; having been a poor farmer, he could not read nor write.[31]

To undermine the influence of opposing factions and to check actions of the king that were not considered advantageous to one's own faction, a censorate was developed that became a powerful institution in the system. Three separate government agencies, collectively called *samja*, were placed directly under the throne; as a censorate independent of the government administration, this body exerted considerable authority and influence. No act nor writing of any individual official escaped the scrutiny of these censors. Even the king was not free from their surveillance and remonstrations. This system certainly functioned to discipline the behavior of government officials and restrain arbitrary actions of the king, but it also undermined the growth of any criticism of the neo-Confucian orthodoxy. Any intellectual innovation easily became entangled in a power struggle, and heretical views were ruthlessly suppressed. Moreover, constantly involved in factional strife and confronted by the possibility of being punished for the most trifling offense, officials naturally grew passive toward any innovative policy changes. The conservatism of the Korean government in regard to the advance of the Western powers was in large part a result of these severe factional struggles.

It is symbolic that many supporters of practical learning were *yangban* intellectuals who had been alienated from the power structure, and that many of them met tragic deaths. Choe Che-u (1824-1864), founder of Tong-hak, which developed into a popular religion in the latter part of the eighteenth century, was also an unsuccessful *yangban* applicant for the *kwagŏ* examination. The enlightenment faction was another group which attracted many alienated intellectuals. Though the core members of the group were drawn from distinguished families, many Buddhist priests were also among its members.[32] In an environment where Confucianism was the "official religion," Buddhists were regarded, if anything, as the lowest of the intelligentsia; hence their frustration with the establishment and sympathy for the cause of the enlightenment faction.

One way to ease factional rivalry over the allocation of official posts

[30] Henderson, *Korea*, p. 32.
[31] Tabohashi, *Kindai Nitchō*, pp. 2-15.
[32] Kim Yŏng-jak, "Kanmatsu," pp. 143-150.

is to reduce the term of office and assign as many qualified persons as possible to those posts. That is precisely what the Yi dynasty government did. The term of office for some of the important positions was remarkably short. In the ten years between 1864 and 1873, for example, 48 persons were appointed minister of personnel, and 82 held the post of minister of works. The average tenure then was 76 and 52 days, respectively.[33] The term of office for the two most important local posts—governor (kamsa) and magistrate (suryŏng), who directly supervised the local clerks (ajŏn)—was supposed to be two years, but, according to a book written in the 1820's as a guide to morals and conduct for regional officials, actual assignments lasted a year at most, and often no more than several months.[34] It was impossible in such a short time for the official to acquire the knowledge and experience necessary to conduct the duties of his office efficiently. Thus, administrative efficiency of the Yi dynasty government was considerably impaired not only by intense factional strife but also by the frequent rotation system that was designed to ease that strife.

Lacking the necessary knowledge and experience, high-ranking officials had no recourse but to depend on petty officials under them for the conduct of administrative duties. Because governors and magistrates were not permitted to serve in their native provinces, they "governed in virtual isolation from the people."[35] They could not move without the cooperation and assistance of local clerks and influential members of the gentry class of the region. Despite the appearance of a strict hierarchy and merit system based on kwagŏ examination and censorship, the Yi dynasty bureaucracy was actually controlled by the yangban aristocracy on the upper level and supported by the yangban gentry on the lower. It was in the interest of the landed yangban elite to maintain the existing social order, and, being so clearly tied to that group, the Yi ruling bureaucracy was unable to take the initiative in social reform, even under the strong leadership of the king or regent. Efforts for reform by Taewŏn'gun were frustrated whenever they conflicted with the vested interests of the landed yangban.[36]

Most of the yangban elite accepted as orthodoxy the thinking of Yi Hwang, who embraced the ultraconservative interpretation of neo-Confucianism, and that ideological bent increased their hostility to anything that smacked of commerce and industry. One of the major figures in the practical learning school, Chŏng Yag-yong (Tasan, 1763-1836), was no exception; even he favored restricting commercial and

---

[33] Palais, *Politics and Policy*, chap. 3.
[34] Chŏng Yag-yong (Tasan), *Mongmin simsŏ*, Hosoi Hajime, trans. (Seoul: Jiyū Tōkyū Sha, 1926), pp. 1, 121.
[35] *Ibid.*, p. 2.
[36] See Palais, *Politics and Policy*, chap. 3.

industrial activities. He asserted: "The growth of industry and the widening concentrations of workers are symbols of poverty. Where one finds masters of every and any craft but no industry, that is where the noble gentleman should dwell."[37] Before and during the early years of the Yi dynasty there were permanent marketplaces called *changsi* established in many localities, but by the late 1400's they were all banned except in Seoul. The development of commercial cities was inhibited completely until 1876, the year the country "opened." In the interim, commerce and industry were carried out by privileged merchants in Seoul, wholesale dealers in local centers, and peddlers in rural areas. Although there was some development in the late eighteenth and early nineteenth centuries, there were no advances comparable to the commercial and industrial progress in Tokugawa Japan. In the early seventeenth century the minting began of copper coins called *sangp'yong t'ongbo* (ever-normal circulating treasure), but a government agency was never set up to handle coinage and minting exclusively. Instead, a number of agencies minted coins as the need arose. A late nineteenth-century investigation shows that at least 39 agencies coined this particular kind of copper currency at one time or another. The result was a lack of uniformity in shape and quality, and limited circulation.[38] As late as the last century, cotton textile was still used for currency in many local areas, indicating the low level of development in the monetary economy.[39]

The economic development of Korea was inhibited both by the corruption institutionalized within the bureaucracy and by the high degree of extortion that accompanied it. Many of the governors and magistrates who stood isolated from actual duties of governing considered their posts merely a means to augment their personal wealth. By the latter period of the Yi dynasty it had become customary for a newly appointed magistrate to send some gift or money to his friends and the clerks working under him as a token of appreciation for the opportunity to "take fat from the people."[40] The temptation to abuse power in the form of graft and heavy taxes must have been even stronger among the local clerks—they had direct authority in regional government but only low status, and no formal salary. There is evidence that only one-fourth of the actual tax payments reached the government treasury. The rest ended up in the pockets of corrupt

---

[37] Chŏng, *Mongmin simsŏ*, pp. 40, 308.

[38] Takahisa Toshio, *Richō makki no tsūka to sono seiri* (Tokyo: Yūhō Kyōkai, Tokyo, 1967), pp. 12-19.

[39] Rim Byŏng-yun, *Shokuminchi ni okeru shōgyō-teki nōgyō no tenkai* (Tokyo: Tokyo Daigaku Shuppan Kai, 1971), p. 19.

[40] Chŏng, *Mongmin simsŏ*, pp. 2-3.

officials.[41] One reason for the rampant official corruption was probably the strong sense of solidarity among clan members that obligated a person appointed to a government post often to support a large number of relatives.[42]

The political system under the Yi dynasty was a combination of the centralized bureaucracy and landed *yangban* elite whose position in the government hierarchy was not absolutely guaranteed. The political system of Tokugawa Japan, quite differently, was essentially a decentralized structure based on territorial organization of the *han*. The *han* in turn were structured around the political authority of the daimyo and his samurai retainers, who were severed from landownership but guaranteed certain hereditary fiefs or stipends. The bakufu used skillful methods to control all *han*, while placing important cities and mines under its direct jurisdiction. The Edo government also controlled the monetary system and foreign trade and held the largest military force in the country. The threat of attainder or reduction of *han* domain was real, but the daimyo nevertheless governed their territories autonomously and enjoyed the security of hereditary rank and power. By the latter half of the seventeenth century the system had become stable, and the threat of attainder and domain reducion had, in fact, disappeared.

Throughout the Tokugawa period the importance of recruiting the talented was frequently emphasized, but the examination for this purpose was never institutionalized as it was in China and Korea. It was not unheard of for a lower-ranking samurai to attain an important post through a combination of ability and good luck, but most positions in the central and *han* bureaucracies were filled by individuals according to a fixed family ranking. Korean emissaries who came to Japan pointed out that this was an important difference in the political system of Japan and their country. "In Japan there is no examination system for government service. All official posts, important and unimportant, are hereditary. Men of exceptional ability cannot rise to greatness on their own merits. Many people die with a grudge against the system."[43] Family ranking, according to which size of fief and stipend were determined, was hereditary and stable. Whereas the degree to which one could rise in his position was largely predetermined by family rank, competition for positions was accordingly regulated,

[41] *Ibid.*, pp. 75, 160.

[42] Ōuchi Takeji, "Richō makki no nōson," in Keijō Teikoku Daigaku Hōbun Gakkai, ed., *Chōsen shakai keizai shi kenkyū* (Seoul: Keijō Teikoku Daigaku Hōbun Gakkai, 1933), pp. 234-235.

[43] Sin, *Hae-yu rok*, pp. 192, 246-247. See also Pak Chun-il, *Kikō Chōsen shi no michi* (Tokyo: Shin Jinbutsu Ōrai Sha, 1972).

although there were undoubtedly many able and ambitious men of low rank who were ultimately frustrated by the system. As the bakufu and each *han* had maintained a large number of retainers from the battle-scarred Sengoku period, once the "pax Tokugawa" was established, the number of official posts was far smaller than the number of retainers who wanted positions. Many were only semi-employed. Thus, there was some competition among samurai retainers for appointments. When competition became entangled in a rivalry for the place of daimyo or shogun, it often resulted in debilitating in-house strife (*o-ie sōdō*).

In addition to the honor and power that came from official position, there were also bribes and perquisites. Distinguished service often brought about increases in fief and stipend. Even if the official left his position, however, his hereditary grants were not reduced. Consequently, the bureaucratic power struggle was much less intense than in Korea. Samurai retainers were rarely executed or expelled, unless they had committed serious crimes or had become involved in *o-ie sōdō*. We have few reliable statistics, but, compared with Korea, the number of ranking samurai retainers who were punished for criminal acts was minimal.

As opposed to the Korean clan (*munjung*), which is a kinship organization centered on the worship of common ancestors, the Japanese *dōzoku* or clan was a mutual assistance group, significant only to those members who lived in proximity to one another. Blood relations were not of decisive importance. By the early Edo period the ties of *dōzoku* among the samurai class had weakened considerably, whereas for the *yangban* bureaucrats, who had no permanent guarantee of their positions, the clan and clan-based factions served as the only source of identity and support. The Japanese samurai retainers were divorced from the land and could expect no guarantees of support from their kinship organizations, but they were able to depend on the *han* for secure social status and a regular income. Thus their loyalty was directed to the *han*, and it was in that larger organization that they felt group solidarity. In that respect, the samurai-*han* relationship resembles the employee-employer relationship of more recent times. Just as today's employee considers his company almost in the same terms as his family, the samurai was able to relate to the *han* as a pseudo-clan.

The loyalty of the samurai to the *han* and his identification with that domain gave him a sense of responsibility for governing his *han*. Even among the samurai of the Tokugawa period there was a strong sense of competition for better posts. There were certainly those who abused their office to fatten their own pocketbooks, but in general the institutionalization of corruption in the *han* governments was far less advanced than in the Korean bureaucracy. It was rare for a samurai to think of his own personal gain as separate from the gain of his *han*, a fact that gave the samurai good reason to maintain a deep interest in the economic development of their domains. Moreover, as I will discuss later, unlike their Korean counterparts, they were immune to the anti-commercialism of neo-Confucian ethics. Their attitudes and ideas had become an integral part of the thinking patterns of the Tokugawa rulers long before the coming of Perry and the appearance of the slogan *Fukoku kyōhei* (Wealthy nation, strong military).

Throughout the Tokugawa period, irrigation and land reclamation projects were carried out on a large scale by the bakufu, the separate *han*, and the great merchants who were in turn supported by the bakufu and the *han*. New fields were developed all over Japan, but similar projects in Korea lagged far behind; they were not even comparable. In eighteenth-century Japan large volumes of dried sprats and oil cake were widely used as fertilizer in much of the country, but even during the mid-nineteenth century Korean farmers had only their own supplies of nightsoil and barnyard manure for their fields.[44] In commerce and industry Korea's development lagged far behind also. The Korean emissaries who visited the towns of Edo, Osaka, and Nagoya were amazed at the prosperous commercial life there. The failure to develop entrepreneurial institutions is an important factor in the underdevelopment of commercial agriculture at that time in Korea. While nineteenth-century Japanese widely cultivated cotton and rapeseed as commercial products, in Yi dynasty Korea cultivation of commercially viable farm products was restricted.[45] The attitudes of the ruling elites in each country toward economic activity must, in the overall assessment, bear a large part of the responsibility for such differences in the economic development of Japan and Korea, a development that was crucial in shaping the means with which they could face the challenge of the West when it came.

The relationship of the *han*, the bakufu, and the emperor was intricate and complicated. The bakufu was overwhelmingly powerful, but it always recognized a degree of political authority in the emperor. The *han*, especially the big "outside" *han* (*tozama yūhan*), whose founders had equal status with the Tokugawa family under the rule of Toyotomi Hideyoshi, were another locus of political authority. In 1858, Chōshū *han* defined its basic policy as "loyalty to the court, faithfulness to the bakufu, and duty to the ancestors,"[46] demonstrating the plural-

---

[44] Rim, *Shokuminchi*, pp. 15-16.

[45] *Ibid.*, p. 18.

[46] Ishin Shiryō Hensan Jimukyoku, ed., *Ishinshi*, vol. 3 (Tokyo: Meiji Shoin, 1941), p. 6.

istic nature of political authority in Tokugawa Japan. In peaceful times the several sources of authority were integrated around the bakufu. By being "faithful" to the bakufu one was at once loyal to the emperor and dutiful to the ancestors. However, the crisis attendant on the encroachment of the Western powers made it exceedingly difficult to maintain a divided loyalty among bakufu, emperor, and ancestors. Chōshū, for example, could not maintain faithfulness to the bakufu and uphold loyalty to the emperor.

The pluralistic pattern of political authority in Tokugawa Japan made it relatively easy for the *shishi*, or samurai activists, to transfer their loyalty from bakufu or *han* to the emperor in a crisis situation, ultimately facilitating a major shift in the whole traditional order. By contrast, the Korean political authority was unitary. From the Silla dynasty onward, rule by council characterized the Korean political process, and that tradition served to limit the real power of the king, who ruled in symbiotic relation with the *yangban* aristocracy. However, when the Ming dynasty fell, removing the base of authority of the Chinese emperors, the Korean king became the only source of political authority. Even apart from the strongly influential conservative Confucian orthodoxy, it was far more difficult for Korea to transform the traditional order by *using* traditional political authority than it was for Japan.

A strongly pluralistic tendency also marked the political ideology of Tokugawa Japan. Unlike China or Korea, Japan never adopted the civil service examination as an integral part of the system, and no specific Confucian doctrine ever had much chance of becoming official orthodoxy. The warrior class, which had comprised the ruling elite of the Tokugawa period, never developed a strong appreciation for Confucianism, and the rank of Confucian scholars in every *han* and in the bakufu was not very high. One of the Korean emissaries criticized the low level of Confucian training among the samurai: "In Japan public administration is not governed by Confucian doctrine. No one, whether the shogun, daimyo, or retainers, truly understands Confucian learning."[47]

The Hayashi family, which had special prerogatives as bakufu director of higher learning, had almost no influence in policy-making. The neo-Confucianism of the Chu Hsi school, which the Hayashi family upheld, could certainly not be called orthodoxy. The shogun Tsunayoshi (r. 1680-1709) had a Confucian college built in Yushima, Edo, but by the latter half of the eighteenth century the college had fallen into obscurity. The chief of the construction bureau of the bakufu is said to have remarked, "The Yushima College is the most use-

[47] Sin, *Hae-yu rok*, pp. 303-304.

less building. It should be destroyed."[48] The "ban on heterodoxy" (*Igaku no kin*) launched by Matsudaira Sadanobu (1758-1827) toward the end of the eighteenth century shows the extent to which the bakufu tried to make neo-Confucianism an orthodox doctrine. However, it touched only the bakufu and a few *han*, and it was lifted on Sadanobu's downfall.

Reflecting the low status of the Confucian scholar in this period, class origins of the many scholars, far from being elite, were extremely varied. Among the most distinguished, Hayashi Razan (1583-1657), Nakae Tōju (1608-1648), Yamazaki Ansai (1618-1682), and Yamaga Sokō were children of masterless samurai (*rōnin*); Itō Jinsai (1627-1705) and Bitō Nishū (1745-1813) were born into the merchant class; Kaibara Ekken (1630-1714) and Ogyū Sorai were sons of doctors; and Shibano Ritsuzan (1736-1807) and Hosoi Heishū (1728-1801) were farmers' sons. The variety of social origins is in direct contrast to Korea, where Confucian scholars were limited to members of the *yangban* class. Moreover, because the neo-Confucianism under the Tokugawa did not become the orthodoxy of the regime, the period produced many different schools of Confucian thought.[49] This multivaried development led to the rise of schools of thought other than Confucianism, among which National Learning and Shingaku were very important. It became exceedingly difficult to establish any orthodoxy with the rise of such a variety of schools and doctrines. This is probably another reason why Tokugawa Japan was able to handle the impact of the West with flexibility.

V

Japan and Korea collided with the West at about the same time. But when examining the specific details, one finds that even though both countries are geographically close, there were significant differences in the international environment of each, which in turn molded the response to the West. For the traditional Chinese empire, whose capital was in the north, Korea was the closest and most important tributary country. Further, as Toyotomi Hideyoshi also saw, Korea was a corridor in any attempt by Japan to expand into the continent. Neither China nor Japan, both just awakening to nationalism and embarking on the road to modernization, could tolerate the eventuality that the Korean peninsula might fall under the influence of another

[48] Kinugasa Yasuki, "Setchū gakuha to kyōgaku tōsei," in Ienaga Saburō et al., eds., *Iwanami kōza Nihon rekishi*, vol. 12 (Tokyo: Iwanami Shoten, 1963), p. 224.

[49] See Abe Yoshio, "Nihon Shushigaku no hattatsu to Chōsen Min to no hikaku," in Haga Tōru et al., eds., *Kōza hikaku bungaku*, vol. 3 (Tokyo: Tokyo Daigaku Shuppan Kai, 1973), pp. 22-28.

country. Thus, inevitably, the factional struggles within Korea took on the characteristics of a proxy war between Japan and Ch'ing China.

If Korea had set out to modernize at an earlier date, or even at the same time as Japan and China, the resulting situation might have been quite different. However, the Kapsin Reform of 1884, the first genuine attempt at modernizing reforms in Korea, came some twenty-two years after the T'ung-chih Restoration and sixteen years after the Meiji Restoration. The delay proved almost fatal to Korea. This well-known coup d'état of 1884, attempted by Kim Ok-kyun and other radical members of the enlightenment faction, was aimed at the rapid execution of reforms. The radicals were opposed by the Min family faction, with the backing of a Chinese army led by Yuan Shih-k'ai (1859-1916). The government of the enlightenment faction collapsed within three days.

Nine years later, with the victory of Japan in the Sino-Japanese War (1894-1895), the moderate members of the enlightenment faction were able to form a government and institute the so-called Kabo Reform. Faction leaders began implementing reforms, using the presence of the Japanese army to suppress any opposition. It proved impossible, however, to stop the interference of the Japanese army, leaving the enlightenment faction open to attack from the conservatives, who claimed that enlightenment (kaehwa) was nothing but "barbarization through Japanization" (waeihwa). In October 1896 a Japanese conspiracy engineered the murder of Queen Min. The following month proved to be a turning point for the enlightenment government; for when they tried to change old customs through the bobbed hair act and other new laws, anti-government and anti-Japanese riots broke out and the enlightenment government once more toppled. Behind the conservative government that subsequently came into power was Russia, which was beginning to advance into Manchuria.

In the course of the Meiji Restoration there was intervention in Japanese affairs by foreign powers. The French minister Léon Roches supported the bakufu, whereas some of the British diplomats, notably Ernest Satow, favored the anti-bakufu forces. But the home governments of both England and France showed no intention of interfering in the domestic conflicts of Japan, and during the civil war of 1868 foreign emissaries declared themselves neutral. Ch'ing China showed no interest in Japan's political conflicts, and there was no proximate country as vigorous or as ambitious as Japan itself. Thus the Meiji Restoration was carried out mainly in response to the threat from foreign powers, but during the course of that political upheaval there was no serious interference in Japanese affairs by outside powers.

In summary, I have noted the many points in common between

Japan and Korea, geographically, culturally, and socially, and how both were confronted with the forced incursion of the West at the same time and compelled to formulate a response. That response, however, far from being similar, was markedly different in each case. I believe the reasons for the divergent response to the West stemmed primarily from the following three factors:

1. Despite the close geographical proximity of Japan and Korea, the historical context of the international environment of each was significantly different. Korea, adjoining northeast China, became China's number-one tributary state with the establishment of the T'ang dynasty. Japan was separated from the continent by the China Sea and the Straits of Korea and retained a far greater degree of political and cultural independence from the traditional Chinese world order than did Korea. For that reason, Japan was able to develop a more autonomous response to the encroachment of the Western powers, which threatened and ultimately destroyed that order.

2. The landed *yangban* aristocrats had no base of support in any intermediate organization outside the kinship organization of the clan and the factions based on the clan. The aristocracy naturally leaned toward a strong conservatism, and in collusion with the king and his bureaucracy contributed to the institutionalization of corruption and inhibited economic development and social change. The samurai of the Tokugawa period, in contrast, were tied neither to land nor to clan; they received their financial security from the intermediate territorial organization of the *han*, which also guaranteed their social status. They felt a strong sense of responsibility toward, and individual interest in, the economic development of the domain and in the political rationalization of the *han* government.

3. The Tokugawa political system had built into it a far greater degree of pluralism than the political system developed under the Yi dynasty—ideologically, organizationally, and in terms of political authority. It was far easier to reorganize the Japanese system in such a way as to allow a positive response to the Western impact without at the same time uprooting the traditional order.

These factors were all crucial in Japan's comparatively smooth accommodation to radical change in its international environment.

Nation-Building in
Modern East Asia:
Early Meiji (1868-1890) and
Mao's China (1949-1971)

─»≫ «≪─

EZRA F. VOGEL

For many purposes, it is useful to compare countries at a given time period, but for getting at the dynamics of a system it is more fruitful to examine crucial periods when analogous processes were occurring. In Japan the most critical period for modern development was early Meiji, and in China the early years of Communist rule. It was then that the two countries forged the basic outlines of an effective modern political order, developed an educational system which brought virtually universal literacy, standardized national currency and national language, and laid the foundations for modern industry, transport, and communications. This essay compares these modernizing efforts which, considering all the comparisons between China and Japan, have received surprisingly little attention.

Autonomous Late Modernizers:
The Peculiar Opportunities in East Asia

China and Japan not only possessed a historical heritage richer than other late developing countries; they were then able to resist foreign domination. Both Meiji Japan and Communist China had to respond to foreign threats, but native leaders consciously used the threat to mobilize the population to achieve the reorganization they considered necessary. The changes brought about were influenced by Western examples, but the countries themselves selected the foreign models and decided how to adapt them to their own needs and heritage. The basic breakthrough was achieved during periods of relative isolation when the countries could control the small number of citizens who went abroad and the small number of foreign advisers ' invited in. Compared to most late developing countries, neither foreign governments nor foreign businesses nor foreign capital played a major role in determining the basic course of development. It was rather a vigorous centralized native leadership that called the tune.

THE VANGUARD: SAMURAI AND THE COMMUNIST PARTY

In reviewing broad patterns of change in retrospect, one can easily underestimate the tremendous turmoil that existed in Meiji Japan and Mao's China: the starts and stops, the basic arguments, the fights, the confusion, the wild untempered visions, and chaos. In the case of Japan, a vanguard was able to maintain a coherent leadership during this turmoil not only because of its strong determination and sense of national mission, but because it shared a common samurai background. Some have estimated that of the officials in the early 1870's in Meiji about 90 percent came from samurai background. The long stability of the Tokugawa period, combined with certain institutional features like the *sankin kōtai*, which kept representatives of every clan in Edo, gave the clans throughout Japan a base of common culture and parallel structures. As youths, samurai had gone to special schools, where they were trained in the Confucian classics and martial arts. Unlike China, where soldiers had very low status compared to Confucian officials, Japanese united civil and military officialdom under a unified tradition, a romanticized morality centering on the *bushidō* spirit. Despite all the variations in samurai rank and the rivalry between clans, this common samurai culture gave the leaders of early Meiji a coherence lacking among leaders of many countries. Furthermore, because many had served in the clan bureaucracy and had been involved in clan politics before the Restoration, they had a base of appropriate experience for their new leadership roles. Although there was no single disciplined organization which linked the vanguard of Meiji, many leading samurai in the Meiji Restoration were from a small number of clans: Satsuma, Chōshū, Hizen, and Tosa.

The Communist Chinese vanguard had an extraordinarily heterogeneous background. Not only was China troubled by more serious regional linguistic and cultural diversity than Japan, but Communist leaders came from a wide variety of class backgrounds. Some came from declining aristocratic families which had held prominent positions in late imperial China, and a few leaders were old enough to acquire a traditional classic Confucian education. Some had been trained as soldiers at new military academies, but military training was brief and did not provide the coherent base for personal development found in longer samurai training. Communist leaders came from families of shopkeepers, artisans, factory workers, and from farm families all the way from rich landlords to impoverished peasants. Many illiterates served the Communist movement as guerrilla fighters, and many higher intellectuals served as united front propagandists. With such a diversity of social and cultural backgrounds, the unity of the vanguard had to be forged through a disciplined organization, in this case the Communist Party. The party organization was more disciplined and hierarchical than party organization in the West, and a common viewpoint had to be arrived at through argument and maintained through strict discipline. To be sure, the samurai leaders of the Meiji Restoration often held widely diverse views on the proper course of action, but their class and education provided a functional equivalence to ideological uniformity. These variations were minute in comparison with the broader disparities among the Chinese Communist leaders.

The very highest level of Meiji leaders were extraordinarily young at the time of the Restoration. Kido was 34, Ōkubo 38, Inoue 33, Itō 27, Iwakura 43, and Mori Arinori 20. Emperor Meiji at 15 was still too young to rule, but within a few years he and the group around him were together exercising a strong, vigorous leadership. They not only shared a common samurai background with administrative experience, but a number had traveled abroad or at least had been on the forefront of learning about modern and Western affairs.

In contrast, the very top level Chinese leaders were much older by the time they came to power. Mao was 56, Chu Te was 62, Chou En-lai, Liu Shao-ch'i, and P'eng Te-huai were 51, and of the major leaders only Lin Piao at 42 was under 50. Since most of them remained in power for more than two decades, they were soon an aging leadership. Virtually none of them had been in close touch with the most recent developments from abroad in the years immediately before they came to power. Most of them had been young when they joined the Communist movement in the 1920's, but their primary experience before coming to power was not in administrative positions in long-established organizations but in military and political roles in revolutionary organizations. Although in the period of the First United Front, from 1923 to 1927, some of them had briefly held administrative positions in the Kuomintang, these experiences were completely overshadowed by their more rustic experiences in building revolutionary base areas in Kiangsi or Yenan.

The samurai leaders of Meiji had enjoyed positions of prestige and honor in their clans despite their commitment to the revolution. The Communist leaders were men of extraordinary ability, but for the twenty-two years prior to their ascension to power they were the enemies of established authority, their organizations were infiltrated by spies, and their friends and relatives were sometimes hunted, tortured, and summarily executed. These experiences left this dominant Communist leadership core much more alienated, not only toward the Kuomintang, but toward all elites and authority everywhere, be they Western, Russian, or Chinese.

THE TAKEOVER:
SATSUMA-CHŌSHŪ AND THE CHINESE CIVIL WAR

The Meiji government was established with relatively little military activity. Satsuma-Chōshū forces in Kyoto seized the palace and announced the Imperial Restoration on January 3, 1868. With the defeat of the samurai supporting the shogun on January 27, the resistance in the Kyoto area was ended, and in May, when Edo was surrendered peacefully, the emperor could establish his residence in Tokyo. Except for the brief clashes in Tokyo in July and in the following May when Hokkaido surrendered to imperial forces, the Imperial Restoration was achieved with very little fighting.

In China, after the efforts of the Marshall Mission collapsed at the end of 1945, the country was thrown into almost four years of bitter combat, which was not even ended on October 1, 1949, when the establishment of the Chinese People's Republic was declared. Fighting continued into 1950 on Hainan Island, in Tibet, and elsewhere. The fact that the defeated forces were able to find refuge in Taiwan brought a respite but not an end to a determined armed opposition.

The civil war left China in ruins. The KMT (Kuomintang), in staking everything on the short-range fighting, neglected the economy and thus left the country with rampant inflation and a devastated industrial structure when the Communists began restoring order at the end of 1949. The economic disorder was exacerbated by the legacy of internal warfare which, like the American Civil War, left a reservoir of internal bitterness far worse than the Meiji Restoration.

Although civil war brought devastating problems, it provided the Communists with an opportunity to develop a large, dedicated, and disciplined apparatus. By October 1949 the Chinese Communist Party included 4,500,000 members. In addition, the army included millions of non-party members, to say nothing of local guerrillas and civilians who had worked with the Communists in their conquest. This large disciplined core, trained in basic ideology, could be dispatched throughout the country to supervise the implementation of new policies. Compared to the very small number of Satsuma-Chōshū forces who had served to bring about the Restoration, the Chinese Communist forces were incomparably larger, even in proportion to the nation's population. The Chinese Communists could bring their own organization more deeply into the countryside and initiate radical changes more quickly. At the same time, vastness and diversity of organization led to more serious internal dissension, which became more pronounced several years after liberation as the first flush of victory, having first bound the forces together, began to fade.

With the very small number of forces at their disposal, the Restoration leaders from Satsuma-Chōshū had little choice but to work through existing officials, nationally and locally. They did not have the force to do away with local elites and chose instead to buy their cooperation or at least minimize their disaffection. Their success in mobilizing national support by appealing to the disaffection toward the shogunate and the fear of barbarians was such that in March 1869 the four large clans (Satsuma, Chōshū, Tosa, and Hizen) voluntarily offered their fiefs to the central government. The other clans lacked the military power for effective opposition, and in 1871 clans officially ended as daimyō handed over their fiefdoms in exchange for official titles and continuation of half their previous stipends. Although local officials were relieved of their posts, the process of transfer of power from clan to prefectural government was slow and relatively bloodless.

In China, the close links between many local elites and their civil war opponents, on the one hand, and the vast size of their own Red Army, on the other, led the Chinese Communists to a more forceful stand against traditional elites. One might speculate that without the Korean War, former KMT supporters would have judged resistance fruitless and would therefore have yielded to the Communists peacefully. However, with the preoccupation and involvement of Communist troops in Korea, many former KMT supporters chose to resist. Therefore, by late 1950 and 1951 the Communists launched a tough campaign against counter-revolutionaries, rounding up and executing remnants of KMT forces and other local leaders who might have resisted Communist power. Mao told Edgar Snow that some 800,000 counter-revolutionaries were killed during the campaign, but some outsiders estimated these figures to be conservative. The impact of cleaning out a sizable portion of local notables less sympathetic to Communist rule was to pave the way still further for local Communist Party leadership.

Although the Chinese Communists were reluctant to retain former KMT officials, they did retain many former government personnel in economic, educational, technical, and even ordinary bureaucratic work because the Communists did not have enough of their own manpower to staff the more complex tasks of government administration, the economy, and the educational system. Staff retained for such positions were generally given relatively high salary and perquisites, but relatively little power. The Communist leaders, however, quickly trained a new cohort of youth and young adults to staff new positions in an expanded administrative machinery and to replace many older and less cooperative holdover officials at all levels.

In both countries the necessity of maintaining an effective core of coordinated leadership led to a gradual decline in the power of former collaborators. In Japan, for example, the Tosa and Hizen leaders were gradually removed, leaving only a core of Satsuma and Chōshū leaders, while in China larger numbers of former United Front collaborators in literary, educational, and business circles were effectively out of power by 1956 even if they retained honorary titles or positions. To sum up, the Chinese Communists, with more concerted opposition but a larger group of committed followers, were prepared to undertake more penetrating personnel and organizational changes; in short, a more revolutionary program.

FOREIGN RELATIONS:
LATE-BLOOMING IMPERIALISM AND MODERN ANTI-IMPERIALISM

Meiji leaders soon became aware of the superiority of foreign power, but they had great confidence in their military skills and hoped within a short time to stand up to the Western powers. Having confidence in the rapid growth of their own power, Meiji leaders identified not so much with underdogs as with imperialist powers. Even while staving off military dangers and resisting discrimination through unequal treaties, they took the existing world system for granted and opted for raising their position within the system. Within several years after coming to power, many Meiji leaders were prepared to colonize Korea and treat it much as the Western imperialist powers were treating their colonies. Although the internal political forces who opposed invading Korea won the day in 1873 after Iwakura returned from his foreign mission, by 1876, Japan, like Perry twenty-five years earlier, had used a naval display to force open ports for trade. By 1895, at the end of the Sino-Japanese War, Japan had absorbed Taiwan, and by 1910 it had absorbed Korea, creating colonies along the lines of the Western imperialist powers.

China, having been occupied by Japan during World War II, was more worried about invasion from abroad. Clearly it was fear of the American threat which led the Chinese Communists, on assumption of power, to cement their relations with the Soviet Union. In 1950, only a year after coming to power, Chinese Communist leaders were desperately worried that the United States might use the pretext of the

Korean War to launch an invasion. In the late 1950's, fearing domination by the Soviet Union, China attempted to gain more independence. As relations with the Soviet Union began to deteriorate, especially after the 1969 border clash, the Chinese began to look around for allies to counter a possible threat from the Soviet Union. In comparison to Meiji Japan, China, while aspiring eventually to great power status, in the short run identified more with the smaller third-world countries in opposition to the hegemony of the two dominant world powers.

Meiji Japan, finding its representatives readily welcomed in various countries of the world, turned to virtually all countries for advice in building a modern state. Meiji leaders drew freely from the United States and Europe, selecting the most appropriate models and advisers. Perhaps the Chinese Communists had no alternative in their early years, because the United States and many of the Western European powers had sided more with the KMT when they were preparing for takeover. After 1949, American officials, concerned with the Chinese Communist threat, quickly initiated a trade embargo. This, combined with a history of a century of foreign domination of east coast cities, twenty-two years of outpost guerrilla life, including eight years of Japanese occupation and four years of civil war against superior military weaponry provided by foreign powers, caused the Chinese to remain more alienated from the dominant world powers. In the early 1950's they drew heavily on technical advice from the Soviet Union and sent many of their advanced students and scientists to the Soviet Union and other Soviet bloc countries. In the context of the Cold War, their contacts with non-Communist countries were minimal, especially compared to the high level of international contacts then existing among other countries. They procured scientific publications from all over the world, and their best scientists and advisers kept posted on international developments in their respective fields, but the lack of firsthand contact and assistance made the task of approaching world standards immeasurably more difficult.

At times, the Chinese have had a policy of demonstrative friendship with foreign countries, but it has remained within a carefully controlled framework with lingering suspicion and limited trust. Lack of foreign experience on the part of Chinese party and military leaders, combined with their long-standing alienation from foreigners and others in authority, extended their suspicions even to their own foreign-trained politicians and scholars. Foreign returnees have been under great pressure to prove their loyalty. In Japan, although leaders like Mori Arinori, Iwakura, and Fukuzawa Yukichi were not universally popular, they were treated with far more respect and less suspicion than the few Chinese leaders who had the closest contact with the Soviet Union and the West.

Meiji Japanese were not in the least ashamed to take the role of the student learning from the more advanced countries. Mao's China was more anxious to show that it had much to offer the rest of the world, be it acupuncture or ping pong. Since their rise to power, Chinese Communist leaders have criticized their citizens who were too eager to learn from foreigners. Chinese leaders were reluctant to accept openly the role of students of superior foreign technology and remain sensitive about displaying any signs of weakness or inferiority lest they be degraded or taken advantage of by other countries.

In Japan of the 1880's a wave of popular reaction arose against a government that had made too many concessions to foreigners and had engaged in a lavish style of life along foreign lines. But this was an interlude and not the dominant stance, for Japan on the whole remained much more receptive than China to foreign culture and technology.

INSTITUTION-BUILDING: INNOVATIVE ELITISM AND MANAGED SOCIALIST REVOLUTION

Officialdom: The Meritocratic Imperial Bureaucrat and the Commoner "Revolutionary Cadre"

Although the Tokugawa period's formal social classes (samurai, farmer, artisan, and merchant) were abolished in early Meiji, the concern with meritocratic performance remained undiluted by demands for social egalitarianism. Although less than 2,000,000 in a population of over 30,000,000 were from the samurai class, the positions in the bureaucracy and in the new state-supported large enterprises were overwhelmingly dominated by the samurai. To be sure, not all samurai achieved high positions, and some non-samurai were able to rise on the basis of merit. But the samurai had greater opportunities for access to the meritocracy, and most of the population was willing to work under such a meritocratic elite.

About 80 percent of the population was rural in both Meiji Japan and Mao's China. In Meiji Japan, peasants by and large did not expect that their children could rise to leadership positions unless they had unusual educational opportunities. By mid-Meiji it was clear how the officials of the highest bureaucracy were to be chosen. Mainly, they were to be products of the new national university, Tokyo Imperial University. To be a graduate of the new law faculty was tantamount to securing a position as an official. Later, as graduates became more numerous, additional examinations were necessary to select among graduates of Tokyo Imperial University and a small number of other elite universities.

Until 1893, when the Japanese examination system was firmly established, there was considerable experimentation with kinds of examinations, but never with the principle of selection on the basis of ability. Compared to China, loyalty was not an issue because it could be taken for granted. When the system stabilized, higher civil service examinations were conducted by each ministry to fill the prescribed number of vacancies. Tokyo University Law Faculty graduates were exempt from the essay ordinarily required for preliminary screening, for the entrance examination to the university had already proved their talents, but all successful applicants had to pass a difficult written and oral examination.

Communist China never established any such examination system for officials. They preferred officials of proven political loyalty and service from peasant and worker backgrounds, and it was by no means certain that applicants from such backgrounds would fare well on competitive examinations. Instead, recommendations of political advisers and co-workers in a given school or work unit were the crucial criteria for selection. To reduce traditional peasant alienation toward official arrogance, to reduce the gap between mental and manual workers, and to set a proper example for the masses, even high-level officials were expected to spend a certain portion of time each year in physical labor. The program has occasionally languished, only to be revived with new attacks on arrogant bureaucrats, by mass movements sponsored at the highest level of authority in Peking.

As a result, the Chinese have to a considerable extent succeeded in producing a new style of egalitarian non-condescending officialdom which contrasts with the forthright elitism of Japanese officialdom, widely acknowledged in the phrase kanson minpi (respect the officials and look down on the people). The achievement of a plainer style of officialdom in China has been at a cost. In China, where many of the highest officials are in fact not from ordinary worker and peasant families, higher officials are under constant suspicion from peasant and worker officials and therefore subjected to continued surveillance and criticism. This and the occasional purges and rectification campaigns have taken their toll in enthusiasm. In conjunction with the dilution of quality standards in recruitment, administrative effectiveness has been hampered, even if it has enhanced the enthusiasm of certain portions of "the masses." In Japan it was generally assumed that any official who passed the highest civil service examinations would continue a dedicated career until retirement, and the esprit of high civil servants has been impressive.

In Japan it was a well-accepted principle that administrative and policy officials should be distinct at any given time, although by mid-Meiji many former administrators became officials concerned with policy. In China, there was no such sharp distinction between administrative and policy officials. All officials were expected to be involved in and highly committed to the current policies. Because there was no "neutral" bureaucracy, personnel and policy changes at the top led to far more severe administrative shake-ups than in Japan.

The dominant Chinese leaders were more interested in a fundamental social revolution than in administrative structure, even though paradoxically the implementation of revolutionary programs and their management by the state was to require a much larger state administrative apparatus than in Japan.

The early Meiji Japanese bureaucracy was much smaller than the comparable Chinese bureaucracy, even in proportion to the population base. At first the Meiji government had six major executive departments (civil affairs, finance, war, justice, imperial household, and foreign affairs). These divisions were similar to the staff offices (*ban gong shi*) which supervised the ministries in post-1949 Peking, except that in China there was a separate layer of party offices, corresponding to the ministries, for policy-making and supervising the activities of the ministries. In addition to this extra layer of administration, because the Chinese Communists had so many economic activities run by the government, they required a far larger bureaucracy to plan and administer industry, transportation, communications, agriculture, and the like. Because of the scale and scope of Chinese administration they also had more layers of government. Six large regional party bureaus supervised provinces, and below the province level special districts in turn supervised county and city. District government within the city and commune administration below the county were much more comprehensive than their Meiji Japanese counterparts.

In 1871, Japanese clans were officially abolished, and by the end of 1872 the 302 *ken* (prefectures) and the three *fu* (cities) which had been established with the abolition of the domains were combined into 72 *ken*. In 1874, following the establishment of the Home Ministry (from the former Department of Civil Affairs), all the local government officials down to the towns and villages were brought directly under its jurisdiction, providing a tight ring of supervision over all local activities and creating a highly centralized government, especially compared to the federal-type system of the United States and some other countries.

During the Chinese Civil War, as the Communists conquered each part of the country, they established a large administrative region to oversee the provincial governments. By 1949 they had six large administrative regions, each with its own party and government system, which then had considerable degree of autonomy from the central government in Peking. In 1952 there was a vigorous effort to centralize power, and the large administrative regions atrophied. Just as Japan had several large cities (notably Tokyo, Kyoto, and Osaka) directly under central government supervision, so in China several cities (during most of the period it was Shanghai, Peking, and Tientsin) were also directly under the central government. Other cities in both cases were under the next level of government (prefecture and province, respectively).

Because there had been no feudal governments, the Chinese Communists faced no organized resistance from pre-existing governmental structures. The major resistance they faced was from specific leaders and organs which had begun to develop certain vested interests before they were incorporated into the central government beginning in 1952. Like Meiji Japanese, the Chinese had a centralized rather than a federal system, but instead of the Japanese pattern of having a single executive department (the Home Ministry) over all regional governments, the Chinese ministers in Peking played a larger role in supervising their corresponding departments of provincial government, and the provincial government departments in turn supervised the corresponding specialized municipal and county bureaus.

Economic Ownership and Management: Guided Innovation and Nationalization with Collectivization

In Meiji Japan the central government played a key role in economic innovation, especially in key sectors, but at the local level, initiative came largely from local entrepreneurs and village leaders who were anxious to utilize government advice to bring the benefits of modern civilization to their localities. In China, local initiative was much more with party leaders, often dispatched from outside, who persuaded the masses to work for the good of their country.

By 1956, most of the Chinese countryside had been reorganized into higher stage agricultural cooperatives. Families were allowed a small private plot of about 5 percent of available arable land to be used for gardening, small fowl, or pigs, mostly for their own use, although some surplus could be sold on the open market. The rest of the arable land was organized and farmed collectively by teams headed by an official who was ordinarily also a member of the Communist Party. Farm workers were paid according to the measure of their contribution to the team. Except for a brief period from 1958 to 1960, when an effort was made to abolish private plots and individual family cooking and to amalgamate the basic accounting unit of the cooperative into much larger units, the basic system of collective farming with small local units has continued since 1956.

The payment of wages to farmers on the basis of their labor rather than on land ownership has greatly diminished social differentiation among members of a production team. The local team organization under party leadership responds to directives from above for introducing administrative and technical innovations. The collective has been a very effective organization for mass labor projects concerned with irrigation, transport construction, and other public works.

In early Meiji the samurai, who had been administrators and rent collectors during Tokugawa, often moved to urban areas to serve as administrators, teachers, or businessmen. In contrast to China, where many Red Army veterans and other officials were sent to villages both as members of temporary work teams and as long-term officials, Japanese village leadership was largely left to the local village elite. Since Japan had government officials all the way down to the village during Tokugawa, the strengthening of the link between village and higher authority in Meiji was not as striking, as in Communist China. Even in early Meiji, local village leaders were literate and were not only in touch with outside developments but for the benefit of their village they eagerly sought to introduce technological innovation, even without outside directives. In the countryside, as in the society as a whole, Japanese were more willing to tolerate social differentiation. During Meiji there was an increasing concentration of land and slightly increasing tenancy. Except for some areas in northeastern Japan, however, the common pattern was to be found in small-scale farms with the individual owning at least part of the land which he farmed.

In the industrial sector, the Chinese Communists moved with similar dispatch. Only a small portion of industries was publicly owned before the Communists came to power, but by 1956 all large industrial, mining, and commercial enterprises were nationalized, and most smaller enterprises with more than several employees were collectivized. One result was to reduce private wealth, equalizing the distribution of income and making it dependent entirely on salary. Another was to concentrate in state hands the power to decide priorities and allocations. Centralizing so much of economic decisions in the hands of government required a large bureaucratic staff and central planning.

Occasionally it led to bureaucratic bottlenecks and much less flexibility than in Meiji Japan, where administrative initiative was more in the hands of private enterprise.

The Meiji government took the initiative in planning and developing certain key national industries and in such activities as sending technicians abroad, attracting capital, and setting up a national banking system. From the beginning of Meiji until 1881, the government was even directly involved in certain industries. However, in the early 1880's, these industries were sold to private entrepreneurs. Although the government continued to play an active role in providing access to technological information, capital, and in giving administrative guidance, enterprises were privately owned and managed.

Western economists have estimated that the economic growth rate of Japan from the late 1870's until the 1890's was on the order of 4 or 5 percent per year, and economists specializing in Communist China have estimated that the growth rate from 1952 until the 1970's was of roughly the same order. Meiji Japan introduced all the basic modern transport and communications systems: the postal system, railroads, electricity, telegraph, and later the telephone. By 1949, such transport and communication facilities had already been available in China's largest east coast metropolitan areas, but the Communists expanded these facilities into the rural and more remote areas of China.

In the course of this economic development, there were many stops and starts in both countries. In Japan, the government was overextended for its tax base by the end of the 1870's. Matsukata led a vigorous retrenchment in the early 1880's, including selling some government industries, reducing all types of government spending, and increasing their revenues. In China, the retrenchment programs of 1957 and 1960-1962 did not lead so much to the elimination of public enterprise as to greater attention to agricultural production and to decentralization of management and financial responsibility to lower levels of government and from local governments to local cooperatives under the slogan of "self-reliance." The effect of the program was to reduce slightly the amount of revenues which local levels passed on to provincial and national governments and increased significantly the amount of funds local levels would have to raise for their own enterprises and welfare programs. The leadership was still in the hands of party members, but as the responsibility of local leaders increased, some higher level leaders were transferred to lower levels. It was partly to ease grain and other food deliveries to the government for distribution to the cities that China adopted policies of dispersing the urban population to rural areas. In sending down personnel, China concentrated on youth who could bring new skills and energy to the countryside. Sending urban youth to the countryside was not universally popular in a country where the urban-rural gap was still very large, but it did further introduction of new systems of organization, new programs of education, and new technology, perhaps even more rapidly than in early Meiji Japan.

Public Security: Registration and Registration with Remolding

In 1871, Meiji Japan introduced a family registration law and soon began collecting census data. The cities were divided into wards, and local police stations (*hashutsusho*) were introduced into local neighborhoods to maintain public security. Although family registration laws were not codified in China until the mid-1950's, essentially the same program of municipal wards and local police stations (*pai chu suo*, written with the same ideographs as the corresponding Japanese term) were introduced to provide the same kind of registration of the population, control of movement, and to ensure public security in the same manner.

Compared to Japan, which readily acknowledged the foreign origins of institutions, the Chinese have a long history of being borrowed from, and they have been reluctant to publicize to their own citizenry the extent to which modern institutions have been modeled on foreign institutions, especially from Russia and Japan. In many cases, however, the particular form of institutions has been influenced by Japanese patterns brought to China during the Japanese occupation of World War II. The striking similarity of the Meiji household registration and local police stations and those introduced in Communist China suggest conscious borrowing. But in China the "bad" social classes felt more vulnerable to unpredictable attacks, and the government took more initiative in remolding thought at the neighborhood level.

Military: The Creation of a New Army and the Modernization of Infantry and Guerrillas

The military establishment in Communist China was also radically larger than that of Meiji Japan. The Chinese Communists have not published figures on the size of their standing army, but even after the demobilization in 1954 and 1955 following the Korean War, specialists have estimated that their army had several million members. In 1872, the Japanese central government had a force of some 36,000 troops. And even in 1878 there were still only 73,000 troops. In Meiji Japan, there was a most fundamental transition from a military dominated by elite sword-fighting samurai to a modern mass infantry. Commoners began serving as soldiers from the beginning of Meiji, and at the time of Saigō's Rebellion in 1877, they clearly demonstrated that with the new military technology they could defeat the samurai. The conscription system had already begun in 1872, and in 1870 Yamagata, back from Europe, laid plans for the abolition of the clan troops and the establishment of the Imperial Guards. By 1878 he had begun to develop the army along German lines. Since there had been a small central army prior to the beginning of Meiji, it required an entirely new system and new training, although many of the officers of course were former samurai.

In the Chinese Communist case, many of the millions of soldiers who served under Communist direction in the civil war had fought in isolated guerrilla units rather than in a modern army, and in the course of the civil war many former KMT troops surrendered and later fought as part of the Communist army, although they were not always fully trusted. The Communists therefore inherited in 1949 a large military establishment which required rapid modernization during and after the Korean War. The reorganization of former independent guerrilla leaders and incorporation of former KMT troops left a legacy of divisiveness. It was reflected two decades later during the purges of the Cultural Revolution and again in the new round of purges following the demise of Lin Piao in 1971.

With the demobilization following the Korean War in 1954-1955, the Chinese Communists made an effort to discharge large numbers of veterans who were ill-adapted to the more complicated technology of modern warfare and to develop a more literate, highly trained army. Under the direction of P'eng Te-huai, the army underwent a major reorganization along modern technological lines. Like Meiji Japan it relied on the conscription system, and like Japan it had more than enough applicants so it could be selective in choosing personnel for the central army. Although the Chinese retained a regular army, large numbers of young people served one term, lasting usually four to six years.

In both countries, the soldiers were a highly dedicated, nationally oriented group who received training in morality and patriotism as well as in military arts, and could be counted on as a highly loyal national force. Communist China, which took the dangers of direct foreign invasion much more seriously than Japan, especially with the Korean War, Vietnam War, and Soviet border clash, put considerable energy into an extensive civil defense and militia network. This effort inherited the legacy of guerrilla resistance in World War II. The extensive patriotic propaganda network of a country fearing imminent invasion was undoubtedly more similar to the Japan of 1939-1945 than of 1868-1890.

Religion: Building Larger Units of
Solidarity and Eliminating Feudalistic Heterodoxy

With the greater scope of administrative structure and with their own personnel, the Chinese Communists could undertake a more direct and thoroughgoing attack on old institutions. They undertook, for example, strong campaigns against Christian and Buddhist religious groups. Until the Cultural Revolution, they tried to avoid prohibiting religious practices, but the constant pressure of public and private criticism against those who continued "feudalistic" or "capitalistic" practices was sufficient to eliminate virtually all public religious ceremonies. Meiji Japanese never attempted such an onslaught on religion, and even the problem of local religious organization that might resist outside pressures was not dealt with directly but by requiring certain sizes of shrines, which had the effect of forcing the amalgamation of certain local shrines, leading to a new and larger unit of loyalty less embedded in traditional village ties that might have provided a focus of resistance against outside governmental encroachment. In contrast, the Chinese Communists built up their organization in the villages, the production teams, and brigades, approved only leaders who had strong national loyalties, and purged those who did not retain such loyalties.

Education: Meritocratic Training
Undiluted and Under Attack

Ronald Dore has estimated that as many as 40 percent of Japanese males were literate at the beginning of the Meiji period, thanks to the local *terakoya*, the schools for commoners. By 1872, the Meiji government set up a plan for eight national universities to be distributed in each district of Japan, and in each district there were to be 32 secondary schools, with 210 primary schools feeding into each one. At first only sixteen-months' training was to be compulsory. By 1895, 60 percent of the school-age children were in elementary school; by 1900 it was 90 percent, and by 1906, 95 percent. Even the universities were established almost from scratch. The Imperial University was established officially in 1886 when schools of Confucian, Western, and medical studies were combined into a single institution. It became Tokyo Imperial University in 1887 when Kyoto Imperial University was founded. The emphasis in university training was on preparing government bureaucrats. Moral and civic training was an essential part of the curriculum and was especially stressed in the new normal schools for training teachers. In addition to the focus on moral and civic training, the pressure was on developing basic literacy and technical competence for rapid national development.

Communist China shared the same goals, but with the twenty-two years of experience governing base areas and planning for takeover, they were prepared to move more quickly in 1949 when they came to power. At first, they concentrated heavily on short-term special training courses for their own cadres and various special programs for eliminating illiteracy in the countryside, but by 1951 they moved to develop a modern educational system. Because there were many more institutions of higher learning in 1949 China than in early Meiji Japan, the Chinese problem was one of reorganizing and rationalizing the existing institutions. In 1951-1952, they undertook a major university reorganization which required that all medical departments of various institutions in a major east coast metropolitan area be combined into a single medical school, and they did the same for former departments in fields of technology, education, and arts and sciences. In the remoter provinces, which had fewer or lower-quality institutions of higher learning, they established new institutions modeled on the newly reorganized universities on the east coast. The Chinese then began opening lower-level institutes of technology according to national needs in fields like agriculture, public health, mechanics, and education. They expanded elementary schools at a more rapid rate than Meiji Japan, and within a couple of decades virtually all elementary-school-age children were attending school. Lacking proletarian intellectuals, the Chinese Communists had to rely on academics from bourgeois backgrounds whom they did not completely trust. Whereas the Meiji government could assume a minimum loyalty among the intellectual elite, in Communist China there was continued tension between party leaders and academics less committed to the more militant egalitarian objectives of the socialist revolution.

Large-scale research institutions which were hardly a part of the world scene in the late nineteenth century were already part of the Chinese scene when the Communists came to power, and the Communists therefore remodeled the leading central government research institute, the Academia Sinica, into the National Academy of Sciences, focused much more on technical and scientific subjects, following the lines of the Soviet Union. This was heavily staffed by graduates of foreign universities. In certain priority fields, scientists were given substantial government support and encouragement, but in the social sciences and humanities, where their role in economic development was less essential and their opportunities for expressing unorthodox thought greater, they were subject to more continuing supervision and intermittent pressure from less-educated party officials.

Chinese leaders, in their effort to overcome traditional disdain toward physical labor and to reduce inequalities and set an example of hard work, developed systematic programs of physical labor for all youth. Following the Cultural Revolution, they required youths, in order to enter institutions of higher learning, to first spend two years' service in agriculture, industry, or the army. Many poor peasants and workers entered institutions of higher learning and obtained high positions of authority without first being socialized into an elitist subculture. The system of education and research, often elitist in practice, was under constant pressure from radical egalitarians, which led to frequent reorganization and the virtual suspension of all higher education from 1966 to 1971. Although later efforts would strengthen elitism and foreign borrowing, it did not become immune from attacks by radical egalitarians.

Cultural Underpinnings: The Emperor's Divine Right and Mao's Ideological Orthodoxy

Since Japan had had an uninterrupted reign of emperors, the "restoration" of authority once delegated to the shogunate back to the emperor provided Japan with an unassailable natural basis for Meiji legitimation. In the first few years (peaking in 1877), there were military challenges to the leadership but no effective challenge to the government's basic legitimacy. The Japanese people, being essentially unique linguistically, racially, and territorially, had a natural basis for national identity, and by not attacking the upper class categorically, they had little difficulty in pointing with pride to their past history. To be sure, they could be somewhat more critical of certain foreign religions like Buddhism and of the shogunate which they had replaced. But they could rely overwhelmingly on the imperial institution as a fundamental, natural, given basis of legitimacy.

The Chinese Communists had no such natural basis of legitimacy. Since imperial rule ended in 1911, no government had erected a broad new base of legitimacy, although the KMT had come far closer than any of the warlords. With the intensity of the civil war, the Communists felt compelled to introduce a new basis for legitimacy that excluded most KMT leaders. This they constructed on class lines, on the basis of their capacity to represent the will of the workers and peasants against imperialism, the bourgeois landlords, and their "running dogs."

In their rise to power, the Communists announced their willingness to cooperate with representatives of other classes in a united front for the purpose of building China, but they acknowledged that the representatives of the propertyless classes were to exercise a dictatorship over the landlords and bourgeois classes. This stance may have been crucial to their victory in the civil war, but, once they were victorious, the alienation between rich and poor, already given ideological support, made it difficult to erect a basis for legitimation which was broadly inclusive of all classes and of the major trends of Chinese history. Administrators from worker and peasant backgrounds, for example, were often bitterly opposed to serving under children of landlords and the bourgeoisie. Yet many of the highest Communist leaders with early commitment to the revolution had in fact been children of these "bad" classes, and their skills were still required in certain endeavors like science, higher education, cultural affairs, and foreign affairs. Indeed, the question of how severely to attack these class backgrounds became one of the key sore points in internal Chinese Communist debates.

Given the thoroughgoing elitism of traditional rulers, it was difficult for a class-based ideology, sanctified by the thought of Chairman Mao, to reclaim Chinese history as traditionally presented. Chinese Communists accept basically a Marxist interpretation of their own history, but the most promising, more inclusive formulation—that earlier Chinese leaders were progressive for their time—does not satisfy militant cadres who want a harder line against contemporary "bad classes." Archaeological findings are viewed with pride, for they can be seen as products of the labor of the Chinese masses. However, much of the literature and culture of the past is closely interwoven with traditional elitism and provides so many opportunities for intellectual malcontents to present veiled attacks on current leaders that it has been subject to violent, though intermittent, attacks.

Meiji leaders were not unconcerned with the dangers of excessive freedom and potential dissipation of central authority. Indeed, after 1880 they began to exert tighter control over public meetings and public utterances. More care was taken in censorship. Yet a broad range of ideas was considered desirable and not too dangerous for the maintenance of political order. Private universities like Keio and Waseda became symbols and centers of independent ideas and entrepreneurship. Even divergent foreign ideas were recognized as potentially useful for achieving the purposes of the state.

Both Japanese and Chinese traditions emphasized the importance of correct thought and acknowledged the advisability of controlling public utterances to elicit proper behavior. Perhaps because of Japan's natural basis of legitimation, its broader base of unity, and franker acceptance of elitism, orthodoxy was not as brittle as in Communist China. Communist Chinese leaders were acutely sensitive to the danger of weak central authority, which had led to such disastrous results in the first half of the century. Unlike Japan, where the government took a firm but indirect role in propagation of ideas in private institutions and newspapers, all of the cultural educational sector in China was under the direct management of the government. Because media directly reflected party views, censorship was not even an issue except at times of internal party dissension. Soon after the Cultural Revolution, when Aesopian criticisms were confronted directly, the range of permitted cultural activity became extremely narrow, in contrast to the broad range of themes and styles reflected in mid-Meiji culture.

Both Meiji Japan and Communist China made an effort to mobilize public support for government-approved activities. Neither was willing to accept fully the Western "bourgeois democratic" forms of direct mass voting as the basic means for selecting leading officials, but both adopted some procedures for public participation. In 1868, as the Meiji government was inaugurated, the leaders issued a charter oath which promised public discussion as the basis for governmental decision, and in the spring of 1949, as the Chinese Communist government was coming to power, the government released the Common Program in which representatives of a wide variety of classes and special groups expressed their views, offering basic support for the Chinese Communist role. Both countries were wary about uncontrolled private meetings. In Communist China in the early years, there were meetings of People of All Circles and later People's Congresses as ways of representing public opinion, although the role of these institutions diminished in the mid-1950's once power passed to the party committees. In Japan the question of parliamentary discussion was approached with considerable caution. Only in the 1880's, in response to public pressure, did Emperor Meiji reveal that he was planning a constitution to guarantee certain parliamentary forms which finally came to realization in 1890. In Japan, after careful lengthy deliberation over possible options, public participation was increased slowly, within clearly bounded limits. In China, the role of public voting and National People's Congress was quickly introduced amid public fanfare but atrophied after the mid-1950's.

In both countries, however, there was no doubt that the basic power was held by bureaucrats not subject to popular election. In Japan, except for such powers as control over budget increases, the early Meiji Diet did not acquire the most important decision-making authority from the bureaucrats serving under imperial rule. China's National People's Congress had even less power. Its functions were more symbolic. It included members from a variety of localities and strata, but they had limited direct input into the policy process.

DISSIDENCE MANAGEMENT:
PARLIAMENTARY OPPOSITION AND THE SEMI-PURGE

In both countries success in coping with outside opposition is reflected by the fact that the major threats to power, even in the early years, came from among those who had once shared power with the new leaders. In Japan, after Saigō Takamori retired from the government and returned to Satsuma, he opened a private academy, and when government troops went to check his growing power, he resisted. The resulting Satsuma Rebellion of 1877 was suppressed only after months of hard fighting. The other major line of opposition, stemming from former Tosa samurai, became concentrated in pressure in the 1880's to establish the Constitution and the Diet, thus hastening the granting of the Constitution. Once formed, opposition was channeled through parliamentary debate in which elite opponents could publicly criticize government policy.

In China, with less public airing of disagreements, meaningful opposition was largely confined within party circles. From its inception in the early 1920's, the Chinese Communist movement had serious internal factional problems, and the dominant factions at any given time subjected potential opposition to criticism, struggle, enforced study, labor reform, and, in more extreme cases, purge. There are no proved cases of executing top-level Communist leaders following internal purges, but some leaders like Kao Kang and Yao Hung-yen were reported to have committed suicide under pressure, and Lin Piao was reported to have died in an accident while trying to escape from the country. The more common pattern is for dissidents to undergo a semi-purge—a period of reform through study, with the possibility of later reinstatement.

Although Meiji leaders at times were concerned about opposition leaders and limited their access to power, they never undertook a thoroughgoing thought program as in Japan of the 1930's or China after 1949. The most serious opposition for Meiji leaders came from dispossessed samurai. When annual pensions were commuted to final lump-sum payments, samurai who were worried about their livelihood created a storm of opposition. This underlying difficulty fueled Saigō's Rebellion, the last major outbreak. After that, the parliamentary opposition could criticize the government and refuse to raise annual budgets, but the opposition was not so serious as to disrupt the government's capacity to carry out its basic operations.

In Communist China, the major issues of debate were also intertwined with personnel issues. The first serious cleavage in the 1950's (the case of Kao Kang) seems to have been related to the centralization of power from the regions. Subsequent issues involved the speed of collectivization (which continued to be an issue during the anti-rightist campaign in the fall of 1957 after collectivization was completed), the speed and extent of communization (which continued long after the anti-rightist tendency campaign in the fall of 1959), and the Aesopian attacks on Mao and other leaders (which culminated in the Cultural Revolution). In all these cases, policy matters were thoroughly intertwined with personnel issues.

One of the striking characteristics of Japanese internal cleavages is that Saigō Takamori, the leader who created the most serious threat to political order, could still be admired for his devotion to duty and other sterling samurai qualities after rebelling. Dissidents who posed a threat to unity in China were later invariably thoroughly and devastatingly attacked. Despite the turmoil and serious disputes in Meiji, Japanese opposition leaders appear to be recognized more as misguided patriots than as villains. In turn, this undoubtedly reflects the broader base of national loyalty and the greater confidence in the capacity of Meiji leaders to maintain control while permitting a broader range of deviation.

Varieties of Late Modernization: Elite Sponsorship and Semi-Revolutionary Management

Early Meiji Japan and early Communist China both fit the pattern commonly ascribed to rapidly developing late modernizers. Both had the capacity for central coordination and the ability to borrow and absorb new technology and organizational patterns. Both developed programs that enabled them to extend societal controls, expand educational opportunities, and maintain national loyalty—in short, to provide central leadership for rapid modernization.

It would distort the historical record to imply that the preceding descriptions of early Meiji were equally characteristic of Japan in the 1930's and early 1940's, when patterns of control were tightened and extended, or in the 1960's and 1970's, when affluence, advanced technology, and post-industrial organization led to very different patterns of response. It would be equally foolhardy to predict that the preceding descriptions of early Communist China will remain unchanged in the decades ahead. Yet these periods of early modernization clearly did leave a legacy. This legacy created certain patterns which have not yet disappeared in Japan and are not likely to disappear soon in China. The legacy might he summarized briefly as follows.

In Japan, with a higher potential for national unification, a small elite could increase central authority without irreparably alienating traditional power-holders. This required some concessions to their power and wealth. A national elite, of very small size, carefully deliberated over a period of years before initiating particular programs. They chose strategies to stimulate commercial, agricultural, and social changes. Having only a small bureaucratic structure, the local communities and businessmen had great flexibility in adapting and changing their organizational patterns and programs. The technological changes and adaptations, in turn, led to changes even in the local community that were so great as to deserve the term "revolutionary." The able elite in the central bureaucracy did not aspire to control local developments directly, but only to provide the necessary impetus that would bring about these local changes. The impetus for change came from the local communities, businesses, and individual families which competed strenuously with one another to keep pace with change, and to bring material rewards and honor upon themselves.

Chinese leaders not only inherited a more divided and less coherent country, but they sided so strongly with the former underprivileged and mobilized such severe attacks on landlords, bourgeois intellectuals, and KMT officials that it was difficult to retain their enthusiastic cooperation in supporting the new regime. The Chinese leaders were in a sense more ambitious than the Japanese. They endeavored to bring a faster and more thoroughgoing organizational, moral, and social change and to lead it directly. To implement this, they developed a massive party structure (officially numbering 28,000,000 in 1974) and administrative structure (officially over 3,000,000 in 1952 but multiplied by many times since then). Once having acquired an administrative structure of such enormous size, China did not have the flexibility in adapting to local situations of Meiji Japan, which had a looser fit between central authority and local developments. The divisiveness within China also led to tighter control over deviance and variation. The efforts to keep change and progress alive by high-level leaders despite the inflexibility of an enormous bureaucracy required more fundamental shake-ups within their own administrative apparatus. China's more ambitious programs of social egalitarianism did bring about more rapid changes in relationships between persons of different social class backgrounds. Yet it is difficult to say that the social changes China introduced through organizational mobilization by the end of the first several decades were really more profound in their impact than the social changes which occurred through the new technology and the process of local competitive innovation of Meiji. In some ways, the tighter social control in China helped to preserve a more traditional social order despite its revolutionary spirit and aims.

For example, it kept back the pace of urbanization, of individuation, of anomie, and of cultural diversification which proceeded so rapidly in Japan. Furthermore, China, with its huge administrative staff now institutionalized and the revolutionary elan now atrophied, has less organizational flexibility in adapting to changes than in Japan with its looser fit between central authority and the rest of society.

III

CULTURE AND PERSONALITY

The three papers in Part Three were written, respectively, by a literary critic and novelist, a psychiatrist, and a team of anthropologists. So quite naturally they vary in the kinds of materials used, in their approaches, and in their findings. Yet all have a common focus on Japanese personality and its socio-cultural milieu, and some common themes emerge. Noguchi's perception of the fate of love marriages in Meiji Japan bears directly on the outcome of Uchimura's first marriage as described by Doi, and both are related at least tangentially to DeVos' findings on mother-child relationships. This is an area where the concerns of literary analysis and social science overlap. It is a kind of humanistic study of which too little has been done, and it is an area with particularly difficult problems of conceptualization and methodology.

A thorny problem for comparative studies, and for case studies too, is how to handle diffusion. Raoul Naroll cites (in "Galton's Problem: The Logic of Cross-Cultural Analysis," 1965) the anthropological research of Stanislaus Klimek, which "shows that in aboriginal California, patrilineal totemic clans are to be found invariably and exclusively in tribes . . . which also play tunes on flageolets, use carrying frames made of sticks and cords, make oval plate pottery, use a squared muller, and favor twins." Clearly these are not causally related variables: the positive correlation of variables is the result of diffusion. To demonstrate a causal relationship requires an explanation; it requires evidence from areas not reached by the diffusion of cultural traits. Diffusion creates a difficult theoretical problem for the study of nations in the world today, for what country has not been influenced by the West? It is an especially troublesome problem for the study of modern Japan, where a sudden and simultaneous borrowing of a great range of institutions and cultural forms occurred.

One part of the cultural flood from the West was literature. There were reactions against it, but in time Tokugawa patterns were altered, new forms were established, and the novelist as a serious writer emerged. With a few exceptions, the early and mid-Meiji novels were not good literature: they read like parodies of Western novels. For good reasons they have not been translated. But from the turn of the century the great modern Japanese writers began to appear. In Takehiko Noguchi's study of the fate of romantic love in Meiji and Taishō literature, just such a set of diffused cultural elements as are described above are treated. But he avoids the methodological pitfall by asking how these elements, which meant one thing in their American social and religious setting, differed in their reception in Japan; why elements that fit together in America came apart in Japan. Noguchi takes the propositions of Leslie A. Fiedler's *Love and Death in the American Novel* as his starting point. The romantic tradition in American literature as described by Fiedler becomes a precise constant. Noguchi's active variables are the social and cultural forces in Japan that produced the differences. Treating the lives of the authors as well as the fictional lives of the novel's protagonists, his study is rich and complex.

Historians of thought give Christianity, along with Marxism, a special place in Japan's modern history. They are honored as the only systems of belief that enabled Japanese intellectuals to resist the militarism of the 1930's. They are seen as the only doctrines that broke decisively with the orthodox Japanese world-view of the "emperor-system." "Emperor-system" is a vague term that usually includes the mythic origins of Japan, the religious figure of the emperor, the political structure with the emperor at its head, and certain values such as harmony, filial piety, and loyalty that bound together all Japanese within the system. Perhaps the most famous Japanese Christian was Uchimura Kanzō, who, born a samurai, became a convert to Christianity, underwent a series of spiritual struggles, and eventually broke with the missionaries and the established churches to begin the "no-church" movement in Japan. But in his paper on Uchimura, Takeo Doi is not contrasting the universalism of Christianity with the particularism of Japanese ideology. Rather, he is inquiring into the particular character of Uchimura's personality, attempting to define from a psychoanalytic perspective "the distinctly Japanese quality of his Christianity."

Doi's paper is comparative in several ways. First, working over the years with Western as well as Japanese patients, Doi developed a number of modifications of Freudian theory centering on the concept of *amae*. (To *amaeru* is to seek the love of another, to desire to be the recipient of the affection of another, like a child loved by its mother. This is described in his 1973 work, *The Anatomy of Dependence*.) According to Doi the phenomenon of *amae* is universal, though more visible in Japan than in the West since Japan lacks the cultural prescriptions that conceal it in the West. In this paper Doi applied his modified psychoanalytic theory to Uchimura. A second level is the running comparison between Doi's Uchimura and Erikson's Luther. A third occurs in the conclusion, where Uchimura is compared with major figures of Western Christian tradition. And running through the other comparisons is the general question of what specific Christian symbols, such as God the Father, have meant in Japan.

All who study East Asia are of course aware that Chinese are different from Japanese and both are different from Koreans, despite the powerful influences of Confucianism and other common elements of their high cultures. George DeVos, Lizabeth Hauswald, and Orin Borders analyze the Thematic Apperception Test given to sample groups of lower- to middle-class Taiwanese and Japanese families in an attempt to define what the differences are. In this test the respondent is shown a series of deliberately ambiguous pictures; the premise of the test is that in interpreting the picture the respondent will project his own assumptions and feeling regarding human relations. To a student of the two cultures the responses quoted here are fascinating: the brief thumbnail projections embody what might be called the literary imagination of the non-literary classes.

But even the correlations obtained from such data do not in and of themselves say what the tested differences mean. A concern, say, for parental control of children may reflect the importance that such control has for parents in the society, or it may mean that the control is breaking down, which is not quite the same thing. As in the example of the California Indian cultures cited above, correlations of variables must be accompanied by explanations. For these DeVos and his colleagues draw on recent anthropological studies of the two societies and also, to some extent, on the psychoanalytic theory of personality.

Love and Death in
the Early Modern Novel:
America and Japan*

-»» «««-

TAKEHIKO NOGUCHI

AN APPROACH TO THE COMPARATIVE METHOD

Arishima Takeo's novel *A Woman* (*Aru Onna*, 1913) opens as the
heroine, Satsuki Yōko, who has left her husband, is about to depart
alone on a sea voyage to the United States. "Once I am in America,"
the heroine muses to herself, "for the first time in my life I'll be treated as a real woman. I'll be able to live with all my strength, to the
limits of my being, as a woman. And I'll be able to escape from the
kind of narrow-minded society like Japan that shuns a person as a
fallen woman just for having abandoned her marriage of her own
free will." In fact, however, Yōko is still not free from the fetters of
the family system. Her trip to the United States is but a cover for what
is really banishment imposed by her kin. A good and kind-hearted
fiancé awaits her in Seattle. But Yōko will fall in love with the ship's
purser, return to Japan, and cause a fresh new scandal.

At the conclusion of this essay—which one might call a comparative study of romantic literature—I intend to return to Arishima's *A
Woman*, because the setting of this novel sheds a good deal of light
on the course of romantic love in Meiji Japan. Behind Yōko is a half-
feudal Japan which denies the freedom of love, marriage, and divorce,
or at least oppresses it; ahead of her is America, a land where, supposedly, a woman can expect to live as a complete human being—or
so it seems in Yōko's imagination. Her hopes, at least, are real. And
what can be said with equal certainty is that at the very least there
existed in America *a view of romantic love* that was totally different
from the one held by the society in which she grew up.

In their sudden encounter with Western civilization, Yōko and
many other young men and women of the Meiji period were to experience upheavals in their value systems. The notion of "romantic
love" itself was imported from abroad during the early Meiji. To be
sure, the history of love is as old as the history of mankind, but the
sensitivities and ideas attached to "what love is" have differed from

* I would like to express my appreciation to Teruko Craig for her translation of
this essay from the Japanese.

age to age, society to society. The Western notion of romantic love encountered by the young men and women of Meiji differed completely from the nation that had been richly nurtured within the social tradition and literary culture up through the Edo period. And what is crucial in this instance is that the notion of romantic love that the Japanese elite came in contact with was not the one held by the Western world *at large*, but was in the main a peculiarly American product bound up with the atmosphere of Christian education. There is a difference between a teahouse ditty sung to the strumming of a samisen and a serenade accompanied by a guitar, but the emotions of romantic love welling up within the young Meiji intellectuals were those awakened by the singing of hymns to the accompaniment of the organ.

My focal point in comparing the early modern novel of America and Japan—and, more specifically, the romantic love novel—is the conception described in the preceding paragraphs. I have tried to pinpoint a specific dimension within the field of comparative Japanese and Western literature, a discipline in which there has been a tendency simply to juxtapose one against the other. In doing so, I owe no small amount of my knowledge of American literature to Leslie A. Fiedler's *Love and Death in the American Novel*. In contrasting American and European literature, for example, Fiedler developed the following perspective, which I have found suggestive in terms of my own broader, cross-cultural comparison:

"What is called 'love' in literature is a rationalization, a way of coming to terms with the relationship between man and a woman that does justice, on the one hand, to certain biological drives and, on the other, to certain generally accepted conventions of tenderness and courtesy; and literature, expressing and defining those conventions, tends to influence 'real life' more than such life influences it. For better or for worse and for whatever reasons, the American novel is different from its European prototypes, and one of its essential differences arises from its chary treatment of women and sex."[1]

The problem that Fiedler poses, in short, is how even within the same Christian world a new and different kind of literature will develop in a country with a different religious climate and social tradition, and how the same literary prototype will evolve in its own distinctive way. According to Fiedler, "To write then, about the American novel is to write about the fate of certain European genres in a world of alien experience."[2] The question of literature alone convinces us of the immense distance between America and Europe. How much

---

[1] Leslie A. Fiedler, *Love and Death in the American Novel*, rev. ed. (New York: Dell, 1960), p. 31.
[2] *Ibid.*

more so, then, the case of America and Japan. Modern Japan was not a Christian society. In this respect its religious climate was totally different from that of America or Europe. And yet in examining the young literary intellectuals of the late 1880's and early 1890's, one cannot ignore the profound influence of Christian teaching, and in particular of Protestantism, on the formation of their notion of romantic love. Also, in regard to social tradition and custom, in contrast to the relative freedom in the New World, the young Japanese of the time had to bear the almost crushing burden of what had been bequeathed to them from the Edo period.

To follow further the views of Fiedler: the birth of the modern novel in the West was one and the same as the beginnings of what he calls "the Sentimental Love Religion." Behind the emergence of this literary genre was the appearance of a new kind of audience, an audience that can be summed up as middle-class, Protestant, and urban. Speaking from literary history, one can fix the birth of the modern novel with the publication in England of Richardson's *Clarissa* in 1747-1748. Richardson's novel is the story of the seduction and subsequent abandonment of Clarissa, the daughter of a sturdy bourgeois family, by Lovelace, the young aristocrat, a figure clearly drawn from a Don Juan archetype. According to Fiedler, the novel was a protest on the part of a newly emergent urban class which hoped to counter courtly love and aristocratic Don Juanism with solid bourgeois domestic virtues. Eroticism, long-suppressed by the Catholic tradition in European society, had manifested and liberated itself in the heretical passion of courtly love and Don Juan-like seduction. The new urban class formulated a secular ethic alongside Protestant Christianity and established a morality of love precisely where they walled off heretical passion. The tears shed on her death-bed by the virginal Clarissa—seduced, abandoned, but still (!) pure—atone not only for her own sins but for those of her now-repentant seducer, Lovelace. It is for this reason that Fiedler calls "the Sentimental Love Religion" a kind of counter-religion.

How was the prototype of the sentimental novel accepted on the North American continent? To speak of early American literature is to speak of literature in New England. Fortunately for Richardson, the rigorous religious climate of New England which prompted Marcus Cunliffe to say, "Puritan New England laid a curse upon literature and the arts from which America is still suffering,"[3] had softened considerably by the time the American edition of *Pamela* was published in 1744. The teaching of the Sentimental Love Religion that woman

[3] Marcus Cunliffe, *The Literature of the United States* (Baltimore: Penguin. 1954), p. 25.

was pure and that her human purity would be sufficient to save fallen souls from sin ran directly counter to fundamental Calvinist belief. But it was able to take root in New England because Puritan political authority had declined. And as for the novels of Richardson, "With no counter-tradition, cynical or idealizing, to challenge it, the sentimental view came to be accepted as quite *literally* true, was imposed upon actual woman as a required role and responded to by men as if it were a fact of life rather than of fancy."[4]

In the hands of minor American writers who imitated Richardson, the sentimental novel succeeded in projecting the American woman's image of herself as "the long-suffering martyr of love, the inevitable victim of male brutality."[5] It followed, therefore, so Fiedler claims, that serious, gifted writers who had their beginnings in such literary soil had no choice but to seek the central theme of their novels in something other than romantic love. *Moby Dick, Huckleberry Finn,* and *The Last of the Mohicans* were books that fled from society to nature, and the horror stories of Edgar Allan Poe escaped to a nightmare world. All of these, put simply, were emergency exits from the burdensome "facts of wooing, marriage, and child-bearing."[6]

I am aware of the opinion—held by Cunliffe, for example—that Fiedler's analysis of the flight from sentimentalism represents "a sort of inverse chauvinism."[7] It is not within my power nor is it my purpose here to question Fiedler, who is trying to assess the American novel in the light of the Gothic romance. What concerns me foremost is the point at issue in comparative studies: how a literary seed transplanted in an alien spiritual soil develops, as it were, into a sub-species. What, then, was the fate of the modern romantic-love novel in early Meiji Japan, a country dominated by Confucianism for several hundred years, still possessing a heritage of sophisticated popular art at once sensual, hedonistic, and with a philosophy of love peculiarly its own?

THE EDO LEGACY

"Happy love has no history. Romance only comes into existence where love is fatal, frowned upon and doomed by life itself."[8] These words by Denis de Rougemont are famous. Love and Death, Eros and Thanatos, resonate throughout Western literature like the dominant and tonic in music. The author of *Love in the Western World* argues that

[4] Fiedler, *Love and Death*, p. 80. [5] *Ibid.*, p. 97.
[6] *Ibid.*, pp. 25-29.
[7] Cunliffe, *Literature of the United States*, p. 373.
[8] Denis de Rougemont, *Love in the Western World*, Montgomery Belgion, trans. (New York: Fawcett, 1956), p. 15.

what emerges from Europe's long history is the mythic prototype of Tristanism: "There is one great European myth of adultery—the Romance of Tristan and Iseult."[9] What we must not forget here is that also in Don Juanism, which is the counterposition to what is called Tristanism and like it subverts Christian marriage, the themes of love and death run sweetly intermingled. Mozart's *Don Giovanni* and Kierkegaard's interpretations have plumbed the fearful depths that lie beneath Don Juan's search for pleasure. According to the Spanish scholar Gregorio Marañon, in the original story by Tirso de Molina the two elements of the search for sexual pleasure and God's punishment—that is, death and damnation—are already inseparably linked. In either case, the two heretical passions of "the myth of adultery" and "the myth of seduction," which represent the *principle of death*, compete with Christian monogamy (or what Marañon calls *l'organisation de la vie sexuelle*),[10] which represents the *principle of life*. The heretical passions are a reaction to and a transgression against the Christian ideal, and yet at the same time they act as a counterbalance to maintain the equilibrium necessary for a "healthy" sexual social order.

At all times and in all places, man's fantasies about love and sex straddle both his conscious and unconscious mind. Here, before examining the early literature of modern Japan as a chapter in the history of love and Eros, we must touch briefly on the place of love and Eros in the literary tradition of the Edo period, the imprint of which, like a Mongolian spot, was still visible during the following era.

Confucian morality based its teaching of love between human beings (*jin*) on a philosophy which essentially held no view of an afterlife, emphasized the here and now, and stressed the importance of the family. It may be said that in such a Confucian morality there was no room for a code dealing specifically with sex to develop. "A strict distinction must be maintained between husband and wife" (*Fūfu betsu ari*). In Confucianism the ethic governing the relationship between a man and his wife hinged on the concept of their "difference." The question of romantic love was simply not dealt with in the body of its teachings. It is even doubtful whether romantic love and sexual passion were consciously differentiated. The natural and instinctive desires of human beings were defined in Confucianism as "feelings" (*jō*); when the feelings between man and woman become excessive, they may be criticized as heedless passion (*irokoi no sata*), destructive of the social order. Romantic love was simply thrown outside the

[9] *Ibid.*, p. 18.

[10] Gregorio Marañon, *Don Juan et le don juanisme* (Paris: Idée NRF, Gallimard, 1958), p. 15.

main body of Confucian teachings as unworthy of serious theorization. The word for "love" (*ai*) comes from the verb "to spare" (*oshimu*). Unlike *jin*, it was not a basic concept of Confucianism.

The framework of Confucian thought, however, did not prevent the development of the theme of Eros between man and woman in the lives or the arts of the populace—and in particular in the literature of the townsmen or pre-bourgeois society. Rather, shut out from the body of orthodox Confucian thought, Eros formed a current of its own, which was to flow unimpeded from the Edo period into the modern era. The literature of the ruling class in the Edo period, the so-called *shidayū* literature, was fundamentally a moralistic one, whereas the literature of the townsmen celebrated eroticism.

With a rich metaphor, Denis de Rougemont explains the multiplicity of meanings attached to the word "love" in European society: "In that infinitely varied amalgam of phenomenon which only Europe has designated by the single term of love, let us consider the extreme bands of the spectrum: the ultra-violet of the spiritual and the infrared of the sexual."[11] In Confucian society, as well as in Europe, the word *ai* was susceptible of many meanings. In the minds of the people of the Edo period, however, it was clearly divided into two polar concepts: *jin* (human love) and *iro* (sexual love).

The dark forces which escaped the confines of the sexual social order of Edo naturally left traces on the literature and arts of the period. But the phenomenon cannot be explained in terms of a simple analogy with Tristanism or Don Juanism, the European reaction to Christian monogamy. First of all, what corresponded to courtly love and its heresy, Tristanism, was not love between man and woman but the homosexuality that appeared in the *bukemono* tales of Saikaku or in the *Hagakure*. (In this connection one may note that Fiedler disagrees with de Rougemont, who sees the influences of Catharist heresy in Tristanism and points rather to a latent homosexuality.[12]) Second, because Edo society recognized concubinage and the pleasure quarters as a counterpart of *l'organisation de la vie sexuelle*, there did not exist preconditions for the development of Don Juanism in the strict definition of the term. Confucianism in the Edo period, transcending the difference between the Chu Hsi orthodoxy and other contending schools, was extremely lenient toward polygamy in the form of concubinage. The only person who criticized this aspect of the system was the early precursor of anarchist thought, Andō Shōeki.

The consequences of this polygamism via concubinage were bi-

---

[11] Denis de Rougemont, *Love Declared*, Richard Howard, trans. (Boston: Beacon, 1964), pp. 6-7.
[12] Fiedler, *Love and Death*, p. 49.

zarre. The love that finds fruition only in death, the union of Eros and Thanatos, was realized in the double-suicide (*shinjū*), a pact between the ordinary man and woman of the streets, completely without relation either to Don Juanism or Tristanism. It is the world described in Chikamatsu Monzaemon's ballad-tales of everyday life (*sewa jō-ruri*). The famous and not-so-famous *petits* Don Juans who inhabit the pages of the *share-bon* and *ninjōbon* of the late Edo are the extreme vulgarization and popularization of the Hikaru Genji archetype. Or at least, the heroes—for example, Tanjirō in Tamenaga Shunsui's *Shunshoku Umegoyomi*—had pretensions to being Hikaru Genji. In fact, however, these men were not virile and passionate seducers, but only would-be *tsūjin*, those who knew how to dally skillfully with women in the gay quarter, or they were gigolos who lived off one woman after another. The permissiveness toward men's fickleness that was safeguarded by the social system, an emasculated Don Juanist psychology unrestricted by religious or social punishment (even granting an occasional financial ruin), a system of pleasure quarters that reduced relations between man and woman to "play" (*asobi*) in which sexual pleasure was isolated and pursued—all these factors led to this unique philosophy of love. Those who understood Eros as "play" were considered to be *sui*, men of discrimination, whereas those who did not were *yabo*, hopeless boors. I might note here a paradoxical effect: because the pleasure quarters existed as a world outside the orthodox sociosexual order, the relationship between the woman who sold her body and the man who paid for it was like that in a commercial transaction, giving rise to a kind of equal relationship unthinkable in the larger society.

It may safely be said that these sociosexual conditions continued into early Meiji society: a half-feudalistic and half-modern and romantic view of marriage that dominated bourgeois society; a civic code that forbade marriage without parental consent; a system of arranged marriages (*miai kekkon*); subordination of the wife in the family; emphasis on the authority of the family rather than the wishes of husband and wife. But man's yearning for love and sex could not be entirely suppressed by the sociosexual order: now and then, it transgressed its confines; at times it was not possible even to prevent it from blowing the cap off the safety-valve. The 1890's saw the beginnings of a reaction against the dominant moral climate, Eros struggling to assert itself. It took the form of two diametrically opposed forces: one school of criticism was voiced by those attached to the pleasure quarters or prostitution districts of pre-modern times; the other, by writers influenced by the Christian view of romantic love. The former was represented by Izumi Kyōka, Saitō Ryokuu, Nagai Kafū; the latter was dramatized by Kitamura Tōkoku, Kunikida Doppo, Arishima Takeo. Each group was to leave behind a tragic legacy of its own. I will treat first the group of literary intellectuals influenced by Christianity, men who in their youth were either directly influenced by Meiji Protestantism or who stood on the fringe, breathing in a Christian atmosphere.

Protestantism and the Ideal of Monogamous Love

Although one uses the broader word "Christianity," it was the several denominations of Protestantism that exerted the strongest influence on Meiji Japan. This was not unrelated to the fact that the Tokugawa bakufu, which was overthrown by the forces that came to power after the Meiji Restoration, had attempted to ally itself with Catholic France. The new Meiji government was also leery of Catholicism because it was seen to be hand-in-hand with Western colonial policies in Asia—the so-called *Kirishitan* belief of the Edo period. The government was more tolerant of the various Protestant sects.

Many of the Protestant missionaries who came in early Meiji were from North America. One can even say that missionary activity in Japan at the time was a faithful reflection of currents within New England theology. Between New England theology and Meiji Protestantism, however, there existed a time-lag of almost a century. By the time the first Protestant church, the Nippon Kirisuto Kōkai, was founded in Yokohama in 1872, in New England itself the strict Puritan ethic had undergone a radical change, and a liberal theology called Unitarianism had been dominant for some time. Or, to put it another way, the missionaries in early Meiji, whether S. R. Brown in Yokohama, L. L. Janes in Kumamoto, or W. S. Clark in Sapporo, were all idealists who had reacted against the secularization of Christianity in their own country and had come to the new frontier of East Asia to spread the teaching of orthodox Calvinism.

By the 1880's, the Japanese ministers who had been baptized by these missionaries were ready to take charge of the Japanese Protestant church: Uemura Masahisa, Uchimura Kanzō, Ebina Danjō, and Niijima Jō. These men, who from the 1890's were to exert great influence on the young men around them, had without exception received a Confucian education in their childhood. One could say that they had accepted Protestant Christian ethics because they saw in it a close resemblance to Confucian morality. As Yamaji Aizan pointed out in his *History of the Japanese Church* (*Gendai Nippon kyōkai shiron*), most of the Christian intellectuals of the time came from ex-samurai families who had been retainers of the bakufu or were from pro-bakufu *han.* For these men, who were alienated from the bureaucratic society monopolized by cliques from Satsuma and Chōshū, the Protestant ethic which expounded what Max Weber called "worldly asceticism" coexisted subtly with the careerism (*risshin shusse-shugi*) of the Meiji period. On a more vulgar level, the English classes and scholarships to study in America set up by missionaries to entice converts were but aspects of the wave of *bummei kaika* that swept Japan. During the period 1887-1906, the gap between Christian doctrine and Confucian morality and the contradiction between religious morality and secular demands that had hitherto gone relatively unnoticed were to prepare the ground for a series of tragicomedies among the literary intellectuals.

Unitarianism, which entered Japan in the 1890's, caused an upheaval in Japanese Christian society, but the details of its entry are not germane at this point. The problem is to trace the mental turmoil and anguish of the young Meiji intellectuals against the background of controversies within Protestant theological circles and the dissolution of church organization.

Undoubtedly the most important event in the history of love and Eros in early modern Japan was the importation of Western thought based on Christianity and the acceptance *at one and the same time* of the ideal of monogamy and its inherent contradictions. It provided the literary intellectuals who had spent their formative years in the 1890's with moral principles they could use to attack the half-feudalistic, half-modern view of love and marriage held by the ruling generation. But it cannot be denied that it acted at the same time as a double-edged sword which constantly threatened them. For example, the *Magazine for Women Students* (*Jogaku zasshi*), started by Iwamoto Yoshiharu in 1885 for the purpose of giving its female audience a Christian education, also served as a rostrum for the dissemination of enlightened views of romantic love. Together with the proliferation of so-called missionary schools for girls, the founding of the Moral Reform Society of Japan (Nihon Kirisutokyō Kyōfū-kai), the movement to abolish prostitution, and so forth, the magazine served as an impetus for better relations between men and women. The Confucian and feudal view of the male-female relationship expressed in the saying, "At the age of seven boys and girls should be separated," was gradually replaced, thanks to this sort of enlightened agitation (*keimō katsudō*), by Christian and modern ideas of social relations between the sexes and, one step further, by the notion of free love. Or from a somewhat cynical viewpoint, the argument of Meiji youth for free love, legitimated by Protestantism, succeeded in freeing the *id* willynilly from the super-ego of Confucian morality—even if it meant at times a convenient shelving of the Christian super-ego too.

As is shown, perhaps unintentionally, in Shimazaki Tōson's autobiographical novel, *When the Cherries Ripen* (*Sakura no mi no juku suru toki*, 1919), missionary schools were first and foremost a place where young men and women could meet freely. In the book, the young male instructors who come to teach at the Christian girls' school fall in love with the beautiful students, which gives rise to a rash of love affairs and scandals. Kitamura Tōkoku and Shimazaki Tōson are examples. Similar incidents occur in and around the social relations of the church, for example, those involving Kunikida Doppo and Iwano Hōmei. Indeed, the good word of Meiji Protestantism seems to have brought to the young generation religiosity and sensuality in equal proportions, or perhaps even favored the latter.

And yet one step outside the Christian world existed the semifeudal real world in which there was absolutely no room for such notions as romantic love. The split between the idealism of romantic love and the reality of life meant that men could never tally their ego-ideal with their erotic desires. Herein lay the origins of the series of incidents which I earlier called the tragic legacy (*higeki no keifu*) among Christian writers.

In his essay "Misanthropic Poets and Women" (*Ensei shika to josei*), which appeared in *Jogaku zasshi* in 1892, Kitamura Tōkoku attempted to grapple head-on with the problem of the discrepancy between the ideal of romantic love and the reality of marriage: "Love is the key that unlocks the secrets of the human world [*jinsei*]. It is when love exists, and then alone, that the human world exists. If one were to take away love, what savor would be left in life? In spite of this, why is it, then, that these strange beings called poets, who are supposed to see most deeply into the human world and know most widely the secrets of the human heart, are the very ones who make of love an evil practice?"[13] These famous words at the opening of the essay hint at the two opposing themes that the author develops, one light, the other dark. The first, seemingly a paean to the idea of love over everything else, changes abruptly into the second ominous theme, that poets are fated to fail in love and particularly in marriage, its sequel.

Tōkoku draws up a list of those who failed in love: Byron, Shelley, Milton, Carlyle, Marlowe, and Ben Jonson. According to Tōkoku, the poet is the warrior who represents the ideal world (*sō sekai*). He sallies forth to battle with the real world (*jitsu sekai*). But he is doomed to

[13] Kitamura Tōkoku, "Ensei shika to josei," in *Gendai Nippon bungaku taikei*, vol. 6 (Tokyo: Chikuma Shobō, 1969), p. 63.

lose. What shelters and sustains the defeated warrior and gives him strength to fight again is none other than the stronghold of love. To Tōkoku, one of the "misanthropic poets," the real world is false. Only love is real, or *so it would seem*. It alone casts a ray of hope and solace.

It is quite clear that the view of romantic love set forth by Tōkoku is different from Pauline theology, which sees woman as temptress and marriage as a necessary evil. It differs also from Puritanism, which finds "sin" in the physical appeal of woman. It is closest to the modified Protestant version of love which seeks a kind of religious salvation in the "pure" love between man and woman and sanctions it as such in its teachings. Moreover, it shows the heavy influence of Ralph Waldo Emerson's essay on love. Tōkoku had previously written a critical biography of Emerson in which he quoted extensively from this essay. Again, Emerson's influence is clearly discernible in his "Ideals of the Common People during the Tokugawa Period" (*Tokugawa-shi jidai no heimin risō*, 1892), in which he criticized the traditional philosophy of love, saying that true love should take leave of sensuality (*nikujō*), pass through the stage of affection (*jōai*), and reach the realm of sacred love (*shinsei na ren'ai*)—a process during which, he explains, "gentlemanship" and "ladyship" arise by mutuality to new heights.

Tōkoku's philosophy of love, the first theme in his essay "Misanthropic Poets and Women," was exceedingly romantic. Love for him was a kind of romantic escapism. That it was also the Protestant view of love did not seem to him in any way contradictory. Tōkoku and the other literary intellectuals of his time accepted both Protestant Christianity and Emersonian Transcendentalism as a sub-species of romanticism. But as long as love is regarded as a means of romantic escapism, it will always be dealt a harsh blow from reality. Hence, the second theme of his essay: that love is the stronghold of the "ideal world," whereas marriage is the prison of the "real world."

One passage in Emerson's essay on love states: "And nature and intellect and art emulate each other in the gifts and the melody they bring to the epithalamium."[14] In the Christian ethic of love—and it goes without saying that this also was true in the Protestant view of love—it was held to be self-evident that the logical conclusion of a happy love was a happy marriage. Religious salvation was thus worldly salvation as well. The optimistic, all too optimistic, view of love and marriage was never to be realized for Tōkoku. We can read his essay "Misanthropic Poets and Women" in the light of his personal life: he had wooed and won a Christian woman, Ishizaka Mina, who was older

[14] R. W. Emerson, "Love," in *Essays*, vol. 2 of *Collected Works* (New York: AMS Press, 1968), p. 188.

than he, and he had been disillusioned in marriage. It would be unduly harsh to say that this happens in any family, and dismiss it at that. What is problematic in Tōkoku's case is that he embodied certain universal characteristics of his time and place. Men and women who had absorbed Christian culture at school and church fell passionately in love. They dared to marry despite strong opposition, usually from the girl's parents, and in a short time the marriage failed. This was the pattern experienced almost without exception by those who, broadly speaking, may be called Christian writers, such as Kunikida Doppo or Iwano Hōmei. Moreover, in most cases, the troubles were compounded by the fact that the men were idealists with little earning power, and far removed from the world of careerism, and the women were the daughters of affluent families. Tōkoku discovered after his marriage that his angel Mina of the "ideal world" was actually a denizen of the "real world" who scolded her husband day in and day out for being such a poor breadwinner.

The romantic escapism that colored Tōkoku's view of love was permeated by the erotic fantasy of the self, worn out by struggles in the real world governed by the male principle, seeking solace in the embrace of the female principle. He could not, however, steep himself in the *mundus mulieribus*, as did Tanizaki Jun'ichirō or Izumi Kyōka. The figure of the morally responsible Protestant father acted as his ego-ideal throughout his life. His essay put forth the idea that the erotic fantasy would invariably be followed by disenchantment: this made love and marriage incompatible, a problem he could not satisfactorily resolve. What Tōkoku chose, in the end, was not a literary shift of theme from Eros to Thanatos—the prototypical pattern in American literature, according to Fiedler—but the *real* option of suicide.

For most ordinary people the problem is solved in real life by leaving the first wife and finding another. But the problem posed by gifted writers was a metaphysical one, beyond their individual experience, and such a real-life solution was not acceptable. The practical incompatibility of romantic love and marriage, and the ideal unity of the two in the Protestant concept which, embraced by Tōkoku, informed his super-ego, brought Tōkoku to a moral deadlock (*apolia*). If Tōkoku had framed the problem the other way around—as the problem of romantic love which rejects marriage as its logical conclusion—he might have seen a glimmer of salvation, or rather anti-salvation, in Don Juanism. But, curiously enough, there is no indication that Tōkoku even thought of exploring the literary possibilities of such a theme. His dramatic poem *Hōraikyoku*, written in 1891, is clearly modeled on, if not a direct imitation of, Byron's *Manfred*. The hero wanders far and wide searching for the ideal woman, his dead wife. The dead heroine is ill-fated, but never a victim of the hero. In *Manfred*, one can hear the tonality of Don Juanism resonating against a background of "Byronic satanism":

> I loved her, and destroy'd her. (ii, ii, 18)
> But my embrace was fateful. (ii, i, 87)

Tōkoku completely avoids such elements. Not only that: at the conclusion, the spirit of the heroine guides the hero to the other world. Following as he does the obvious theme of *Das Ewig-Weibliche zieht uns hinan*, Tōkoku never realizes that once Faust too was Don Juan when he seduced Gretchen.

For Tōkoku, the immediate task at hand was the negation of the feudalistic notion of love as "play" that had come down from the Edo period. His was a dead-serious attempt to give a dimension of spirituality to love between man and woman. In other words, the idea of love as found in the pleasure quarter was the enemy, and the establishment of a new morality for spiritual love was his strategic aim. Tōkoku had been disappointed, not because he had to choose between love and marriage, but because he had so idealized the unity of the two that he could not but be disappointed by the reality. Given this, he never had the leeway to accept the decadence of Don Juanism. From beginning to end, his view of love suffered from what can only be called an excessive seriousness.

In his famous work *How I Became a Christian*, Uchimura Kanzō, the Christian leader of Meiji Japan whose presence is felt in Arishima's novel *A Woman*, wrote, "God's kingdom was imagined to be one of perfect repose and constant free exchange of good wishes, where tea-parties and love-making could be indulged in with the sanction of the religion of free communions and free love."[15] Although Uchimura's words would seem to deny this, it was true for many frivolous young men and women. The church was a kind of Christian social meeting-ground and nothing more than another manifestation of *bummei kaika*. Tōkoku, who would soon be disillusioned by this and abandon Christianity, must have been a young man who, more than others, moved by this vision, was inclined to fall in love. And this only served to aggravate his despair. Sexual love in the Edo period by the deadly earnestness of its sensuality might have led to double-suicide. But in Tōkoku's case this was not so. For him, unable to share even his intensity with his wife, there was no choice but to die alone in solitude.

If one were to name among the literary figures of the time the per-

---

[15] Uchimura Kanzō, "How I Became a Christian: Out of My Diary," in *Uchimura Kanzō zenshū*, vol. 15 (Tokyo: Iwanami Shoten, 1933), p. 72. See also Doi Takeo's "Uchimura Kanzō: Japanese Christianity in Comparative Perspective" in this volume.

son closest to the Don Juan type, it would probably be Iwano Hōmei. At the age of twenty-two Hōmei married Takenokoshi Kō, an older woman, having practically resorted to force to obtain her. Once his ardor for his wife cooled, he found his home a prison—just as Tōkoku had. Hōmei, however, did not hesitate to declare brazenly to his wife: "This house is really like a graveyard. Any day now, I'll have to leave you and find a fresh young love for myself"[16] (*Hatten*, one of a series of five works by Hōmei). In fact, until he died at the age of forty-seven in 1920, Hōmei went from one affair to another, going through three marriages, two divorces, and numerous scandals. How different from Tōkoku, who committed suicide at twenty-seven! Hōmei's wanderings through the groves of love remind one not so much of the tyranny of the authoritarian head of a household, or of dazzling Don Juanesque adventures shot through with childish egoism, but of the failures of Don Quixote forever tilting at windmills. And yet even Hōmei reflected now and then the influence of Emerson. In his work "Mystic Semi-Animalism" (*Shimpi-teki hanjū-shugi*, 1906),[17] in which he boldly defends the importance of human instincts, he goes to the trouble of quoting from Emerson's essay on love: "From exchanging glances, they advance to acts of courtesy, of gallantry, then to fiery passion, to plighting troth and marriage. Passion beholds its object as a perfect unit. The soul is wholly embodied, and the body is wholly ensouled."[18] But in Hōmei's hands Emerson is transformed rather ingeniously. Following a line of argument incomprehensible to anyone but himself, Hōmei claims that the moment-to-moment satisfaction of sexual instincts leads to the "ensoulment" of the self. He considered the constant search for objects to satisfy sexual desires as a working out of his own philosophy. His Don Quixotic Don Juanism was a serious application of his philosophy, and never "play." Here again, one sees that all-pervasive characteristic of the Meiji writer, extreme optimism and excessive seriousness.

A legend has grown surrounding Hōmei's death. Hōmei lay in bed, dying of acute pleurisy; as he gasped his last breath he called out the name of a woman, but no one could make out whose name it was.

THE CULT OF THE WOMAN

Although the oppressive air of Puritanism had lifted long before, New England in the latter half of the nineteenth century was still

---

[16] Iwano Hōmei, "Hatten," in *Meiji bungaku zenshū*, vol. 71 (Tokyo: Chikuma Shobō, 1965), p. 172.

[17] Iwano Hōmei, "Shimpiteki hanjū shugi," in *Meiji bungaku zenshū*, vol. 71 (Tokyo: Chikuma Shobō, 1965), p. 331.

[18] Emerson, "Love," p. 184.

strongly religious, and, as mentioned earlier, New England theology with its legacy of Calvinism and Unitarianism came to Japan and exerted a strong influence on literary circles. During the decade beginning in 1887, Emersonian Transcendentalism was introduced to young intellectuals through Puritan theology. In dealing with Kunikida Doppo later on, I will show how profoundly affected were the young writers of the 1880's and 1890's—as were Hōmei and Tōkoku—by the pantheistic framework of Transcendentalism.

It is well known that Edgar Allan Poe found the odor of religion he detected in Emersonian Transcendentalism highly offensive. True, Emersonian Transcendentalism spoke of Godliness in Nature, but to Poe this smacked of self-righteousness and didacticism. With characteristic acerbity he wrote, "Mr. Ralph Waldo Emerson belongs to a class of gentlemen with whom we have no patience whatsoever—the mystics for mysticism's sake."[19] To Poe, all of Emerson's writings could be dismissed with one word, *cui bonito?* (so what?). It was the rejection of the didactic heresy of New England literature by one born in Boston but endowed with a Celtic imagination and nurtured by a Southern cultural identity.

Of course, there are many scholars who see a close resemblance between Emersonian Transcendentalism and Symbolism in Europe. Harry Levin has written in *The Power of Blackness*, "For the writer who accepted the Emersonian metaphysic, there was no choice but to be a symbolist."[20] The things of this world are the signs of hidden realities. Religious enlightenment comes, not from the study of Christian dogma but from mystical intuition or poetic insight. In the Emersonian metaphysic, as Levin points out, what lies at the base of the drama unfolded in this world is morality. And it was to this that Poe reacted. The poet and critic Poe says sarcastically that he will "teach us how to go about imitating the 'tone transcendental' ": "Put in something about the Supernal Oneness. Don't say a syllable about the Infernal Twoness. Above, all, study innuendo. Hint everything . . . assert nothing."[21] For a "poet of composition" who had seen into the irrational and terrifying, hellish deep layers of the unconscious, mystical morality of the Emersonian variety must have been intolerable.

I am not one who likes easy comparisons. But I see in a corner of Meiji literature a group of writers who looked with disdain on Westernization, *bummei kaika*, the moralism of Christianity, and asked

[19] Edgar Allan Poe, *The Selected Poetry and Prose of Edgar Allan Poe*, T. O. Mabbott, ed. (New York: Modern Library, 1951), pp. 359-360.

[20] Harry Levin, *The Power of Blackness* (New York: Random House Vintage, 1958), p. 15.

[21] Second-hand quotation from Cunliffe, *Literature of the United States*, p. 84.

themselves, *cui bonito*? And yet they too reacted against the sexual social order that dominated Meiji society. I will focus on one of them, Izumi Kyōka.

Izumi Kyōka and Edgar Allan Poe—East and West, separated by over a century. I am not proposing to present the two writers as a set to facilitate the study of comparative literature, but one cannot ignore a single theme they share: the image of "the fragile, poetic, dying mother," to borrow the words of Marie Bonaparte.[22] Apart from the psychoanalytical question of how much Poe retained the unconscious memory of the mother he lost at three, one cannot deny that there runs throughout his work the theme of intense longing for the dead mother. As Levin says, "motherly or sisterly types predominate in his limited gallery of heroines."[23]

Kyōka was ten when his mother died. In contrast to Poe, the event was etched indelibly in the young boy's memory. It cast a shadow on many of his works. It was no doubt a traumatic experience. Kyōka's yearning for woman which permeates his stylistically and thematically unique novels—the novelistic universe Akutagawa Ryūnosuke so aptly called the Kyōka-world (Kyōka *sekai*)—usually goes by the name *Mahāmāyā* belief. In his novels, a sisterly type of older woman inevitably appears as a substitute for the lost mother; she extends protection and help to a younger boy, who, needless to say, is Kyōka's *alter ego*.

The resemblance between Kyōka and Poe does not stop with a similarity in childhood background. The flirtation between Eros and Thanatos, the mutual embrace of love and death that appears and reappears in the Kyōka-world or, put more succinctly, the almost sadistic sense of beauty, have much in common with the following lines from Poe's "Romance": "I could not love, except where Death was mingling his with Beauty's breath."[24] Again, in the Kyōka-world, there is no dearth of scenes where women of unrivaled beauty expire amid horrendous bloodshed and agony. This essentially sadistic image of woman transformed by the agony of death into something unearthly goes back to the *yomihon* and *kusazōshi* of the Edo period—the literary equivalent of the gothic romance in Europe. But it was also the scar left by the loss of the beautiful young mother who died of tuberculosis. Again, the resemblance to Poe! The juxtaposition of a woman's white skin and fresh red blood was a color-scheme Kyōka used over and over again.

[22] Marie Bonaparte, "Psychoanalytic Interpretations of Stories of E. A. Poe," in *Psychoanalysis and Literature*, H. R. Ruitenbeek, ed. (New York: Dutton, 1964), p. 19.

[23] Levin, *Power of Blackness*, p. 154.

[24] Poe, *Selected Poetry and Prose*, pp. 17-18.

From the viewpoint of thematics, Harry Levin has analyzed Poe's choice of words and phrases from *Berenice* and *Ligeia* to *The Fall of the House of Usher*. He has summed them up as either "the death of a beautiful woman" or "the posthumous heroine." In the Kyōka-world, too, the female heroine either has to die or is already dead. There is, however, one decisive difference from Poe: there is an *otherworldly* aspect to the women in Kyōka's novels. That is, once the woman has died—invariably with great pain—she is purified by it, becomes a supernatural being, and favors the male protagonist, more often than not the author's *alter ego*, with benevolent grace. The woman has become a demoness like Hāritī (*Kishibojin*), who holds the power of death, but, more importantly, she has become a mother who holds the power of life.

We now come across a curious paradox in the history of modern Japanese literature viewed as the intellectual history of Love and Eros. Several of the Christian writers who on strict moral grounds had separated Love from Eros, and could not bring themselves to treat the fatal interplay of Eros and Thanatos in their work, had no choice but to commit suicide. In contrast to these writers, Izumi Kyōka, and later on Tanizaki Jun'ichirō, who inseparably linked the thematics of Thanatos to erotic fantasy, managed to lead a life relatively free from personal disaster.

In 1895 Kyōka published a short essay titled "Love and Marriage" (*Ai to kon'in*). Flanking on one side, as it were, the secure world of petit-bourgeois sexual morality, this essay makes an interesting contrast to Tōkoku's "Misanthropic Poets and Women." Kyōka's criticism of the marriage system of his day is sharper and more insightful. "Love suicide, elopement, disinheritance, all are clearly the offshoots of love. Should we not rejoice, then, for these people, and call such occasions happy and felicitous?"[25] Kyōka proclaimed the absolute nature of love; obversely, he denounced the system of marriage: "In short, marriage as practiced in society is a cruel and vicious law devised to restrict and oppress love, and to destroy freedom."[26]

It followed that the married women who appeared in his novels were almost without exception the unhappy victims of their abusive and highhanded husbands. Kyōka invariably identifies with the youth loved by the older married woman who suffers from the shackles of the marriage system. The youth defies husbands, fathers, rich men, and others in authority. Kyōka's novels are populated by beautiful artistes, prostitutes, geisha, and demonesses, women who are apart from the

25 Izumi Kyōka, "Ai to kon'in," in *Meiji bungaku zenshū*, vol. 21 (Tokyo: Chikuma Shobō, 1965), p. 329.
26 *Ibid.*

restraints of the mundane world (*zokkai*). The locale of his stories is outside bourgeois society with its worldly morality; it is the world of artists and the pleasure quarters. Even if in the long run it was a world where powerful men of wealth trifled with women, Kyōka liked to think of it as a place where pure love between man and woman was still possible.

It did not mean, however, that all the writers who turned their backs on ordinary society and betook themselves to the world of prostitutes and geisha were happy like Kyōka. No matter how one might insist that to persevere pridefully in the way of erotic love was *sui* and to assert one's might with money was *yabo*, there was still the real world to reckon with. In the real world women are not sought as maternal principles but as bodies, material objects for the instant gratification of sexual desire. This basically *misogynistic* attitude can be traced from Saitō Ryokuu to Nagai Kafū. Misogyny was to give rise to a tragic legacy of its own, comparable to that of the Christian writers. Men such as Kyōka, who rejected participation in the ordinary social order through marriage and family and confined themselves to a corner of the pleasure quarters, were, in effect, exiles in the world of prostitutes.

Saitō Ryokuu eventually tired of such an existence. He died in 1904 in great poverty, leaving these lines: "One writes [to earn a living] with one brush but needs two chopsticks [to eat]. One is no match for the many. I should have known this."[27] The anti-feminist Kafū, who lived half a century longer, also shut himself up in the slums. He led a lonely solitary existence, a stingy and miserly man. When he died vomiting blood, in 1958, he was all alone.

THE TRAGEDY OF PASSIONATE LOVE:
The Scarlet Letter AND *Aru Onna*

What most mystifies the Japanese reader of Hawthorne's *The Scarlet Letter* is the opening scene, where before the staring crowd Hester Prynne confesses her crime and remains firmly convinced that what she has committed is a sin. Her sin has been brought to light, she must now wear the scarlet emblem on the breast of her gown, and yet she does not think of leaving the village: "Here, she said to herself, had been the scene of her guilt, and here should be the scene of her earthly punishment; and so, perchance, the torture of her daily shame would at length purge her soul, and work out another purity than which she had lost; more saint-like, because the result of martyrdom."[28]

27 Saitō Ryokuu, "Seigan Hakutō," in *Meiji bungaku zenshū*, vol. 21 (Tokyo: Chikuma Shobō, 1965), p. 385.

28 Nathaniel Hawthorne, *The Scarlet Letter* (New York: Harper and Row, 1968), p. 69.

If what Hester had confessed was regarded as a crime in Puritan society and if she had acknowledged her culpability in that context, one would understand. But she is convinced it is also a sin, or so it would seem to one brought up in an entirely different religious climate. And yet, for all that, the scarlet emblem on her bodice seems to glow a bit too seductively. Harry Levin says, "The color-scheme is all the more arresting because the spot of flaming red is set off against the usual background of sombre blacks and Puritan grays."[29] And when Levin says that "A" stands for "admirable" as well as "adultery," he seems to have grasped the hidden intent of the author.

When the story begins, the adultery has already taken place, off-stage, as it were. The subject of the novel, therefore, is not adultery but atonement. If this is so, then, how account for the mysterious radiance of the scarlet letter? Regarding this, D. H. Lawrence has made a perceptive observation in his "Nathaniel Hawthorne and The Scarlet Letter." In contrast to Fiedler, who sees the minister Dimmesdale as a Faust-like seducer, Lawrence attacks the Puritanism of New England literature without hedging: "The greatest triumph a woman can have, especially an American woman, is the triumph of seducing a man: especially if he is pure."[30]

According to Lawrence, it is Hester, not Dimmesdale, who is the seducer. And just as a demonic nature hides behind the face of contrition, Hawthorne and the entire body of New England literature hide their sensualism behind the mask of moral concern. Lawrence's indictment is severe: "The same old treacherous belief, which was cunning disbelief, in the Spirit, in Purity, in Selfless love, and in Pure Consciousness. They would go on following this belief, for the sake of the sensationalism of it."[31]

And what manner of being was Hester Prynne? It is not an easy question. As Levin points out, in New England literature, which was a literature more of morals than manners, in a novel such as *The Scarlet Letter*, which was allegorical rather than realistic, it is extremely difficult to put one's finger on the reality behind this woman. But when the same question is asked about Satsuki Yōko, the heroine of Arishima Takeo's *A Woman*, we have several important clues to the secrets of her flesh and spirit, the recesses of her psychological and physiological self. For an actual model existed for this long novel, completed in 1920. And that was the love affair between Sasaki Nobuko and Kunikida Doppo, who had died in 1908.

[29] Levin, *Power of Blackness*, p. 74.
[30] D. H. Lawrence, "Nathaniel Hawthorne and The Scarlet Letter," in *Selected Literary Criticism*, Anthony Beal, ed. (New York: Viking, 1970), p. 351.
[31] *Ibid.*, p. 355.

In 1895, Kunikida Doppo, then a rising young newspaperman, fell passionately in love with a nineteen-year-old girl, Sasaki Nobuko. The two were married against the strenuous opposition of her parents. The first blissful days of married love were the fruit of a shared belief in Christianity. Or so Doppo thought. Five months later, Nobuko suddenly disappeared from the house. Doppo's marriage had come to an abrupt end. The two men who had previously blessed the marriage of the religiously united couple now counseled Doppo to divorce Nobuko for her loss of faith. They were none other than those pillars of the Japanese Christian church, Uemura Masahisa and Uchimura Kanzō.

Such was the tragicomedy enacted in Doppo's life. The incident was to have great significance for modern Japanese literary history. First, Doppo emerged from his experience as a serious and creative writer, and, second, in drawing on it and writing his novel *A Woman*, Arishima himself forged a link in a chain of tragedies that was to end in his suicide soon after.

Musashino is known not only as Doppo's most outstanding work but also as the quintessence of writing depicting nature. It is commonly thought that the theme of communion with nature that runs through the work reflects the influence of a Wordsworthian-Emersonian pantheism which sees the oneness and the omnipresence of God in nature. This is undoubtedly true, but if one reads carefully Doppo's diary, "An Account without Deceit" (*Azamukazaru no ki*), one discovers that the depiction of nature in *Musashino* is really the reminiscence of his beloved Nobuko. (Doppo deletes all references to Nobuko in his diary.) What is omnipresent in the woods of Musashino is not the Emersonian oneness, but the image of Nobuko, once the giver of an almost religious salvation, now the object of unremitting regret. It is a pantheism in which God and woman have changed places.

In his diary Doppo speaks of his love affair with Nobuko as "the exchange of a noble and exalted love between two souls and born in Heaven." As for their defiance of parental opposition, he says, "Heaven has summoned me" (*ten ware o mesu*).[32] Truly, this is the apogee of the Protestant view of marriage. The more fervidly involved Doppo became with Nobuko, hopelessly confusing romantic feeling with religious emotion, the more he lost sight of the fact that Nobuko was after all an ordinary mortal. One wonders how fervent a believer Nobuko actually was. Her mother was the executive secretary of the Christian Women's Moral Reform Society (Kirisuto-kyō fujin kyōfū-kai), but one wonders whether Christianity for Nobuko was not just a novel and curious practice.

[32] Kunikida Doppo, "Azamukazaru no ki," in *Gendai Nippon bungaku taikei*, vol. 57 (Tokyo: Chikuma Shobō, 1969), p. 354.

Arishima Takeo knew Nobuko personally, the model for his heroine Satsuki Yōko. Through the eyes of Kotō, Arishima's novelistic alter-ego, who very nearly succumbs to Yōko's charms, Arishima lets the reader see the heroine's willfulness, competitiveness, vanity, coquetry, and the craving lust of her body—all qualities which Nobuko (and Yōko) possessed, but which Doppo either did not notice in his excessive idealization of love or chose not to write about candidly. Confronted by Yōko, Kotō's "rationality" tells him to reject her; but at the same time he cannot suppress "a strange and inexplicable sympathy" for her. This "strange and inexplicable sympathy" was of course the male counterpart of the female's sexual appeal. The author has another alter-ego in the person of the purser, Kurachi. Kurachi's virility, which comes through in the love scenes in the book, makes Yōko a complete woman. Arishima intended it as an unsparing criticism of Doppo's inadequacies as a male. In the novel the character corresponding to Doppo is presented as what Fiedler calls "the pale-faced artist." At the same time Arishima hints at the intensity of the sexual combustion that might have taken place between a man like himself and a woman like Yōko.

A Woman was thus the first novel to portray without prejudice the figure of a woman who struggled against the feudal morality and worldly ethic of her time, who was sexually awakened yet socially still unfree, and who while living a full physical life was gradually destroyed. It must be added, however, that in describing Yōko's downfall in the second half of the novel, Arishima seems a little hasty in judging her from his own Puritanical code of ethics. Taking money from her faithful fiancé under false pretenses so that she may live with her lover, her mad jealousy, her fits of hysteria—all these add up to an impression of a morally depraved woman. The novel ends with Yōko's deathbed scene. She asks Kotō—the author's alter-ego, it may be remembered —to fetch the minister Uchida, her religious mentor of former days who has refused to see her all along. The model for Uchida was Uchimura Kanzō, the strict Calvinist who had refused to compromise with liberal theology and called for a non-church movement (*mukyō-kai-ha*), the last ray of orthodox New England theology in Japan. This formidable man, who did not hesitate to denounce sinners and hypocrites alike, looms over the last scene like a giant-sized super-ego.

The rather minor tragedy that occurred in Doppo's life was expanded and embellished in Arishima's story of a woman who lived before her time. But what I call "the tragic legacy among Christian writers" did not end with this. Three years after the completion of the book (1923) Arishima Takeo committed double-suicide with the wife of another. She was Hatano Akiko, a journalist famous for her wit and beauty and a member of the famous Bluestocking Society. It may be said that their death formed the final link in the chain of tragic events. One wonders nevertheless: in deciding to commit suicide, did the same Puritan super-ego that judged Satsuki Yōko also tower in Arishima's consciousness? No one knows.

Uchimura Kanzō:
Japanese Christianity in
Comparative Perspective

-》》《《-

TAKEO DOI

This chapter is a study of Uchimura Kanzō (1861-1930), particularly his personality development and its bearing on his Christian beliefs. My objective is to define the distinctly Japanese quality of his Christianity as compared with that of non-Japanese Christians. Uchimura himself was a prolific writer, and there are numerous articles and books on his life and work, but for my purposes I shall focus mainly on the book he wrote in English, *How I Became a Christian*.[1]

Uchimura was one of the few pioneers in offering his own experiences as a Japanese for the benefit of non-Japanese. He began writing *How I Became a Christian* in 1893 and wanted to have it published in the United States. However, after the manuscript's initial rejection by an American publisher, it was published in Japan in 1895, followed by the American edition which appeared later the same year under the title *The Diary of a Japanese Convert*. In the preface to the Japanese edition, Uchimura wrote as follows:

"In many a religious gathering, to which I was invited during my stay in America to give a talk for fifteen minutes and no more (as some great doctor, the chief speaker of the meeting, was to fill up most of the time), I often asked the chairman (or the chairwoman) what they would like to hear from me. The commonest answer I received was, 'Oh, just tell us how you were converted.' I was always at a loss how to comply with such a demand, as I could not in any way tell in 'fifteen minutes and no more' the awful change that came over my soul since I was brought in contact with Christianity. The fact is, the conversion of a heathen is always a matter of wonder, if not of curiosity, to the Christian public; and it was just natural that I too was asked to tell them some vivid accounts of how 'I threw my idols into the fire, and clung unto the Gospel'" (p. 9).

---

[1] Uchimura Kanzō, *How I Became a Christian. Complete Works of Uchimura Kanzō*, vol. 1 (Tokyo: Kyōbunkan, 1971). Page references to this volume are noted directly in the text.

One can hardly miss the hidden irony in the preceding passage, indicating a protest against what Uchimura thought to be the patronizing attitude on the part of American Christians. It was evidently to redress such an attitude and make them view his experience of conversion more seriously that he wrote *How I Became a Christian*. Of course, affront was not the sole motivation for writing this book. Uchimura was thirty-three when he began writing it, five years after his return from the United States and still several years before settling on his life-work. It is likely that he wanted to review his experiences for himself, so that he could better face whatever would be in store for him in the coming years. In other words, the book constituted for him an attempt to consolidate his identity. The following words in his introduction to the book suggest such a view:

"I early contracted the habit of keeping my diary, in which I noted down whatever ideas and events that came to pass upon me. I made myself a subject of careful observation, and found it more mysterious than anything I ever have studied. I jotted down its rise and progress, its falls and backslidings, its joys and hopes, its sins and darkness; and notwithstanding all the awfulness that attends such an observation like this, I found it more seriously interesting than any study I ever have undertaken" (p. 15).

It is remarkable that Uchimura found self-observation so interesting, but perhaps even more remarkable that he thought his observations would be interesting to the public as well. What was offered the public could not be exactly what he jotted down in his diary. He certainly edited the material, and it is known that he discreetly withheld any concrete information about his first marriage. Also, he destroyed the diary after completion of the book. Perhaps he reasoned that the book was a distillation of his past experiences, the only thing of value that could be presented to the public.

Valuable in what sense? Uchimura does not specify, leaving that judgment up to the reader by saying, "The reader may draw whatever conclusions he likes from it" (p. 15). Still he was convinced that the book had a message for the wider public and even hoped that it would sell well in the United States. He was disappointed when its sales did not go as well as he had wished. It is reported that the first edition of five hundred copies took several years to be sold, and that the book then went out of print. Against this background one can imagine his pleasant surprise when the German version was published in 1904, and three thousand copies sold at once. He deduced from this that German readers had a better understanding of what he had to say because they were heirs to Martin Luther's Christianity. But, perhaps more significantly, the publication of the German version coincided with the outbreak of the Russo-Japanese War, which certainly aroused worldwide interest in Japan and the Japanese.

In what follows I shall first analyze the contents of the book and compare it with Erik Erikson's analysis of Luther's formative years.[2] I shall then discuss Uchimura's later life from the vantage point provided by this analysis. Finally, I shall attempt to clarify his position by comparison with several Christian thinkers in the West and to summarize the features that characterize his brand of Christianity as uniquely Japanese.

THE FORMATIVE YEARS

In the beginning of the first chapter of the book, entitled "Heathenism," Uchimura gives a brief sketch of his family background. On first reading it, one gets little information about what kind of relationship he had with his parents, except that in describing them he is dutifully filial and treats them with care, affection, and reverence. But if one tries to read between the lines, one glimpses what might actually have transpired between him and his parents. I shall first take up the father-son relationship.

He introduces his father as follows: "My father was cultured, could write good poetry, and was learned in the art of ruling men. He too was a man of no mean military ability, and could lead a most turbulent regiment in a very creditable way" (p. 17). This description clearly indicates the son's pride in his father, but in the following paragraph he reports a curious episode, which apparently taxed his nerves sorely. "My father was decidedly blasphemous toward heathen gods of all sorts. He once dropped a base coin into the money-chest of a Buddhist temple, and scornfully addressed the idols that they would have another such coin if they would in anyway help him to win a law-case in which he was then engaged; a feat wholly beyond my power at any period of my religious experience" (pp. 18-19). This passage comes right after the statement, "But to no one of them do I trace the origin of my 'religious sensibilities,' which I early acquired in my boyhood" (p. 18).

So it appears that Uchimura became religious in spite of his father. As a young boy he surely could not have accused his father of blasphemy. But the first thing he did when he was later converted to Christianity was vigorously to attempt to convert his father. His first attempt, which took place when he returned home from college for vacation, was not successful. He states that "my mother was indifferent, my father was decidedly antagonistic, and my younger brother . . .

[2] Erik H. Erikson, *Young Man Luther* (New York: Norton, 1958).

was so provoking . . ." (p. 47). However, he must have pressed his father hard, because finally, he says, "I succeeded in extracting from my father a promise to examine the faith I implored him to receive" (p. 48). His second attempt at winning over his father, which came two years later, was successful. The idea suddenly occurred to him of giving his father the *Commentary on the Gospel of St. Mark* consisting of five volumes, written by Dr. Faber, a German missionary in China. Why he did it and how it was received by his father is described as follows:

"It [the *Commentary*] was written in unpointed Chinese, and I thought the difficulty of reading it, if not anything else, might whet my father's intellectual appetite to pursue it. I invested two dollars upon this work, and carried it in my trunk to my father. But alas! When I gave it to my father, no words of thanks or appreciation came from his lips, and all the best wishes of my heart met his coldest reception. I went into a closet and wept. The books were thrown into a box with other rubbish; but I took out the first volume and left it on his table. In his leisure when he had nothing else to do, he would read a page or so, and again it went into the rubbish. I took it out again, and placed it upon his table as before. My patience was as great as his reluctance to read these books. Finally, however, I prevailed; he went through the first volume! He stopped scoffing at Christianity! Something in the book must have touched his heart! I did the same thing with the second volume as with the first. Yes, he finished the second volume too, and he began to speak favorably of Christianity. Thank God, he was coming. He finished the third volume, and I observed some change in his life and manners. He would drink less wine, and his behavior toward his wife and children was becoming more affectionate than before. The fourth volume was finished, and his heart came down! 'Son,' he said, 'I have been a poor man. From this day, you may be sure, I will be a disciple of Jesus.' I took him to a church, and observed in him the convulsion of his whole nature. Everything he heard there moved him. The eyes that were all masculine and soldierly were now wet with tears. He would not touch his wine any more. Twelve months more and he was baptized" (p. 72).

The son had used a clever trick, and it worked. Even though the battle was fierce, the son finally prevailed over the father. However, this is not to suggest that Uchimura had no genuine respect and affection for his father. It suggests only that he could not look to him for spiritual guidance. Perhaps his father never meant much as an authority figure for him, and that is why he presented himself as a new authority to his father. Father and son had exchanged their customary roles, and it was as if the son were trying to teach the wayward father without being disgusted by him. It was fortunate for the father that

Kanzō succeeded in this audacious enterprise, for he could from then on count on his father's moral support.

That such was the nature of Uchimura's relationship to his father is supported by information from other sources. Uchimura was made the head of the whole household when he entered Sapporo Agricultural College at sixteen, as his father had retired a few years before in his early forties. This meant that besides his parents, Uchimura had three younger brothers and one younger sister to look after. All this gives credence to the story that he volunteered to go to Sapporo Agricultural College—situated in Hokkaido, still undeveloped and far removed to the north from the capital—only because there he could receive free tuition, plus room and board, with a handsome stipend from which he could contribute to the upkeep of his family. From that time Uchimura and his father switched their respective roles.

Concerning his relationship with his mother Uchimura has this to say: "My mother has inherited from her mother this *mania* for work. She forgets all the pain and sorrow of life in her work. She is one of those who can't afford to be gloomy because life is hard. Her little home is her kingdom, and she rules it, washes it, feeds it, as no queen has ever done" (p. 18). In this thumbnail sketch of Uchimura's mother, what strikes me most is his use of the word *mania* (he italicized it). It is a strong word and can even be slightly pejorative. Prior to describing his mother, he affectionately describes his maternal grandmother as a lovable old lady. She had been a widow for fifty years and had reared all five children by herself—she was a hard worker by necessity. In comparison with this grandmother, however, one gets the impression that Uchimura's mother was a hard worker by compulsion, even though, as he says, she somehow "inherited from her mother this *mania* for work." She is presented as single-minded, indomitable, and perhaps even inaccessible. She appears twice at a later stage in the book, and again she gives the same impression as the earlier one.

I have already mentioned that his mother was indifferent when Uchimura first tried to convert his family to Christianity. He states, "I told my mother that I became a new man in Sapporo, and that she too must become what I became. But she was so much taken up with the joy of seeing her son again that she cared nothing about what I told her about Christianity" (p. 47). Toward the end of the book, where the family reunion after his three-and-a-half-year stay in America is described, he again states that "Mother doesn't care to learn about the world; she is only glad that her son is safely at home," whereas he "talked with father all night" (p. 209).

What kind of mother does not care to listen to what her beloved son wants to tell her? Was she cold? She must have loved him in her own way. But she was only glad to have him back and could not appreciate his experience of growing up in the world. Was she possibly too possessive? Could her attitude have hurt the sensitive Uchimura? He does not say, but instead, right after the briefly quoted description, he relates once more the scene of his homecoming: " 'Mama,' I cried as I opened the gate, 'your son is back again.' Her lean form, with many more marks of toil upon it, how beautiful! The ideal beauty that I failed to recognize in the choices of my Delaware friend, I found again in the sacred form of my mother" (p. 210). This unmistakably suggests a case of idealization of his mother.

From all this I conclude that Uchimura was not close to his mother, much as he might have wished to be. At least he was close to his father. Still, as I suggested before, he could not really depend on his father either. In terms of *amae*, one could say that he did not *amaeru* as a child toward his parents. Perhaps this was partially because as the oldest of five children from an early age he felt keenly the responsibility for the household. Did the frustration in *amae* affect his personality? I think his early religiosity, which I discuss in the next section, is definitely related to this. Also, his reason for attempting to convert his parents to "become what I became" bespeaks his strong sense of being bound to them. He could easily have left them behind and alone. This, however, he did not do. Instead it was as though he had to bind them, precisely because he was bound to them by a hidden need. I think this clearly indicates his frustrated *amae*, a desperate attempt to capture the never freely given affection of his parents.

That Uchimura was particularly sensitive to the feeling of *amae* is shown by his emphatic use of the mother symbol throughout the book.[3] He describes the moment of separation when he left Japan for America in the following words:

"Love of country, like all other loves, is at its best and highest at the time of separation. That strange Something, which, when at home, is no more to us than a mere grouping of rills and valleys, mountains and hills, is now transformed to that living Somebody—Nature etherealized into a spirit—and as a woman speaks to her children, it summons us to noble deeds. . . . The yonder imperial peak that hangs majestically against the western snow—is that not her chaste brow, the inspirer of the nation's heart? The pine-clad hills that encircle the peak, and golden fields that in its bottom lie—is that not the bosom that suckled me, and the knee that took me up? A mother so pure, so noble and lovely—shall not her sons be loyal to her?" (pp. 103-104).

---

[3] *Amae* is the noun form derived from *amaeru*, a unique Japanese verb which signifies a desire for love or behavior indicating such a desire. See Doi Takeo's *The Anatomy of Dependence* (Tokyo: Kodansha International, 1973).

Again, in reminiscing of his college days at Amherst College, he states, "I am exceedingly thankful that I was given another such mother to serve and satisfy" (p. 167). And, there is a passage in which he refers to the Spirit of God as "my Mama" (p. 154). I do not know of any Western Christian who specifically used the mother symbol for the Holy Spirit of the Trinity. From all this one could conclude that Uchimura was always looking for the mother figure who would satisfy his *amae*, as his own parents, particularly his mother, did not.[4]

➤➤➤ ⫷⫷⫷

Let me now turn to Martin Luther's relationship with his parents. He was the first son of Hans Luder, an ambitious ex-peasant who engaged in mining, a new industry in Germany at that time. Hans wanted his son to become a lawyer, and Martin dutifully obeyed the father's wish up to the age of twenty-one, when suddenly, following the famous thunderstorm experience, he quit the study of law he had just begun at the University of Erfurt and entered an Augustinian monastery. Hans was furious and would not give his consent or fatherly blessing. Apparently his wife followed suit. This incident clearly shows that Luther's relationship with his father was quite different from Kanzō's, and it weighed much more for him than his relationship with his mother. Luther's father would not relinquish his hold on the son easily, and perhaps he never did. It is interesting to note in this respect that when Luther, having broken with the Church, was married, he stated as his first and foremost reason that it would please his father.[5]

Luther made two remarks in later life about his parents: "My father once whipped me so that *I fled him and became sadly resentful toward him, until he gradually got me accustomed to him again*"; "*My mother caned me for stealing a nut and afterwards there was blood. Such strict discipline drove me into monkery or the monk-business.*"[6] (The italicized portions are Erikson's literal translation from German.) Erikson concludes:

---

[4] Uchimura Miyoko, who was a devoted disciple of Uchimura Kanzō and later married his son, Yūshi, gives a vivid picture of his personality in her memoir on Kanzō (*Kanzō yakyū seishinigaku*, Tokyo: Nihon Keizai Shimbun Sha, 1973). Her story supports the inference about Kanzō not being favored by his mother. She told me in private conversation that his mother favored his brother Tatsusaburō, a fact which contributed to a future quarrel between the two brothers, as will be discussed later. She also remembers Kanzō's statement when his mother died: "How sad that I must do a funeral for a mother who never loved me." This explains Kanzo's life-long search for the loving mother figure. Again according to Uchimura Miyoko, Kanzō depended very much on his wife, and toward the end of his life particularly enjoyed the company of a few women followers.

[5] Erikson, *Young Man Luther*, p. 91.

[6] *Ibid.*, pp. 64 and 67-68.

"Martin, even when mortally afraid, could not really hate his father, he could only be sad; and Hans, while he could not let the boy come close, and was murderously angry at times, could not let him go for long. They had a mutual and deep investment in each other which neither of them could or would abandon, although neither of them was able to bring it to any kind of fruition. . . . The monk-business . . . refers to his [Luther's] exaggeration of the ascetic and the scrupulous. He implies strongly, then, that such treatment was responsible for the excessive, the neurotic side of the religionism of his early twenties."[7]

About this neurotic side of Luther more will be said in comparison with Uchimura's religious development.

EARLY RELIGIOSITY

I have already mentioned Uchimura's "religious sensibilities," which he says he acquired early in his boyhood. Here I shall quote his description of how excessively religious he was, long before he was converted to Christianity:

"I believed, and that sincerely, that there dwelt in each of innumerable temples its god, jealous over its jurisdiction, ready with punishment to any transgressor that fell under his displeasure. The god whom I reverenced and adored most was the god of learning and writing, for whom I faithfully observed the 25th of every month with due sanctity and sacrifice. I prostrated myself before his image, earnestly implored his aid to improve my hand-writing and help my memory. Then there is a god who presides over rice-culture, and his errands unto mortals are white foxes. He can be approached with prayers to protect our houses from fire and robbery, and as my father was mostly away from the house, and I was alone with my mother, I ceased not to beseech this god of rice to keep my poor house from the said disasters. There was another god whom I feared more than all others. His emblem was a black raven, and he was the searcher of man's inmost heart. The keeper of his temple issued papers upon which ravens were printed in sombre colors, the whole having a miraculous power to cause immediate haemorrhage when taken into stomach by any one who told falsehood. I often vindicated my truthfulness before my comrades by calling upon them to test my veracity by the use of a piece of this sacred paper, if they stood in suspicion of what I asserted. Still another god exercised healing power upon those who suffer from toothache. Him also did I call upon, as I was a constant sufferer from this painful malady. He would exact from his devotee a vow to abstain

---

[7] *Ibid.*, pp. 65 and 67.

from pears as specially obnoxious to him. . . . One god would impose upon me abstinence from the use of eggs, another from beans, till after I made all my vows, many of my boyish delicacies were entered upon the prohibition list. Multiplicity of gods often involved the contradiction of the requirements of one god with those of another, and sad was the plight of a conscientious soul when he had to satisfy more than one god. With so many gods to satisfy and appease, I was naturally a fretful, timid child. I framed a general prayer to be offered to every one of them, adding of course special requests appropriate to each, as I happened to pass before each temple. . . . Where several temples were contiguous to one another, the trouble of repeating the same prayer so many times was very great; and I would often prefer a longer route with less number of sanctuaries in order to avoid the trouble of saying my prayers without scruples of conscience. The number of deities to be worshipped increased day by day, till I found my little soul totally incapable of pleasing them all" (p. 23).

The picture given here is certainly that of a precocious boy who is pitiably scrupulous in offering correct worship to each of the numerous gods. Uchimura prefaces the preceding description with the sentence, "But no retrospect of my bygone days causes in me a greater humiliation than the spiritual darkness I groped under, laboriously sustained with gross superstitions" (pp. 21-22). Very few, if any, however, would dare to laugh at him for his so sincere "superstitions." Surely his scrupulosity would fall into the neurotic range. But what is important is not to label him as obsessive-compulsive, but to understand the underlying anxiety which is so palpable. And speaking of anxiety, he writes later in the book that he used to be afraid of thunder, saying, "I always thought my end did come when it rattled right above my head. In my heathen days, I called in the help of all my protecting gods, burnt incense to them, and took my refuge under a mosquito-net as the safest place to flee from 'the wrath of heaven' " (p. 156). It seems certain that his religiosity was closely tied up with his proneness to anxiety and perhaps could be interpreted as a means of coping with it.

The question to be asked, then, is why Uchimura was given to so much anxiety. By this I do not mean to say that religion is simply a function of anxiety. Again, given his anxiety, why it took the form of "religious sensibilities" is another question which does not concern me at the moment. To get back to the question I originally posed, it is significant that the sentence in which he disavowed any influence from his relatives on his "religious sensibilities" was inserted between the mention of his mother and his father. It is a clinical axiom that if and when a patient tells logically disconnected things together, one can assume the existence of an emotional connection between them. I think this axiom can apply to the case of Uchimura. In other words, I want to propose here that his early religiosity was definitely linked to his parents, notwithstanding his claim that its origin cannot be traced to either of them.

To make the preceding proposition more plausible, I shall relate here something about the background of the Uchimura family. They were *samurai* in one of the pro-Tokugawa domains; the overthrow of the Tokugawa government then led them to personal disaster. This would explain at least partially Kanzō's father's much too early retirement; he must have felt at odds with the revolutionary changes around him. In this connection I also wonder if the recorded blasphemy of Uchimura's father was not more expressive of his anger against the fate that had befallen him rather than against a Buddha. We can be sure at least that he did not inspire the strength and confidence in the members of his family that he should have. Read once more the following passage in the preceding quotation: ". . . as my father was mostly away from home, and I was alone with my mother, I ceased not to beseech this god of rice to keep my poor home from the said disasters" (p. 22). That Uchimura felt helplessness and anxiety in the company of his mother sounds pathetic. It almost reads as if, to the great distress of his mother, his father had deserted the family although presumably he was kept away from home because of work. Or could it be that Uchimura instinctively sensed the hidden anxiety of his mother, which in turn made him so anxious? In this context the word *mania* which he used to describe the way his mother worked acquires a new implication, for was not his way of worshipping gods also mania-like? He went around worshipping gods to ward off his own misgivings, just as his mother has "this mania of work" to forestall any misfortune. There can be no denying a definite resemblance between the two, whether an inherited or infected one.

I would like to make one last comment on Uchimura's early religiosity, particularly with regard to the cult of a god who "was the searcher of man's inmost heart." He says he feared this god more than all others and would often swear his truthfulness by the god's miraculous power. It shows his fine moral sensibility, which in itself should be lauded. But if one asks whether he swore often because he feared the god, the answer must be the converse. The more he swore, the more he must have feared the god. Such is the dilemma of moral scrupulosity. Uchimura's ambivalence had gotten out of hand. In other words, he somehow could not get used to the Japanese custom of solving ambivalence by alternately playing *omote* and *ura* and therefore was more vulnerable to any personal affront. So he swore often, and, swearing, he feared even more the god who was searching his heart. He did not find a way out of this dilemma for quite some time even after Christianity came to his rescue.[8]

Compared with Uchimura's early religiosity, which stands out against the unreligious stance of his parents, Martin Luther's seems to stem directly from his parents, who never questioned the medieval religious Weltanschauung and its many superstitions. Only their harshness in disciplining him must have made him overly docile and scrupulous, as was suggested in his remarks quoted in the previous section. Thus Martin became a sad young man full of conflicts, and it was because of those conflicts that he quit his studies and entered a monastery against his father's ardent wish. It is interesting that in the very act of disobeying his father he called upon St. Anne, the patron saint of his father's trade, for help. Stricken with fear in a thunderstorm, he called out, "Help me, St. Anne . . . I want to become a monk."[9] As Erikson suggests, he probably wanted her to intercede with his father in the confrontation that must follow.

Be that as it may, it is certain that in his decision to enter the monastery Martin was beset with ambivalent feelings toward his father, who had decided on a worldly career for him. Two years later, when he celebrated his first mass, he asked his father, who had been invited as a guest, "Dear father, why did you resist so hard and become so angry because you did not want to let me be a monk, and maybe even now you do not like too much to see me here, although it is a sweet and godly life, full of peace?"[10] He was obviously trying to appease his father at this last moment, but his father retorted in front of the entire congregation, "You scholars, have you not read in the scriptures that one should honor father and mother?"[11] Martin must have cited the thunderstorm experience and argued that his vocation was clearly from God. But his father is reported to have cried out what amounted to a curse: "God give that it wasn't a devil's spook!"[12] Thus Luther's confrontation with his father did not end in an easy victory, as in the case of Uchimura.

[8] About the Japanese custom of solving ambivalence by playing *omote* and *ura* alternately, see Doi Takeo's article, "*Omote* and *Ura*: Concepts Derived from the Japanese Two-Fold Structure of Consciousness," *Journal of Nervous and Mental Disease*, vol. 154, no. 4 (1973), pp. 258-261. To explain it in brief, *omote* stands for the surface that can be shown to others, and *ura* for what has to be kept in back of one's mind or can be confided only to those very close to oneself. Japanese are taught from early years to distinguish between the two, which actually make up the backbone of Japanese morality. Uchimura's failure to acquiesce in the seeming discrepancy between the two modes of conduct again bespeaks his lack of maternal love, because it is the mother who usually habituates children to such dealings.

[9] Erikson, *Young Man Luther*, p. 92.

[10] *Ibid.*, p. 144.   [11] *Ibid.*, p. 145.   [12] *Ibid.*

First Contact With Christianity

Christianity did not come to Uchimura by inner persuasion. It came rather by force. In Tokyo, he had been introduced to church-going by a friend. He enjoyed the exotic sights and sounds of Christian worship but did not take it seriously. When he entered Sapporo Agricultural College, he had no idea he was going into the midst of a totally Christian-spirited group, who were prepared to catch him as if he were a prey. He found himself, along with other classmates, surrounded by upperclassmen who exerted strong pressure on newcomers to sign the "Covenant of Believers in Jesus," a pledge which William S. Clark had penned for his students. Clark had left by then, but his influence was still evident in the zeal he had inspired in his students. Uchimura withstood their pressure for a few months, even after a number of his classmates had signed the covenant, but finally he too signed it although his inner doubts were not completely dispelled. Of this act he relates, "The public opinion of the college was too strong against me, it was beyond my power to withstand. So, you see, my first step toward Christianity was a forced one, against my will, and I must confess, somewhat against my conscience too" (p. 26).

From this one should not surmise that Uchimura was simply coerced into accepting Christianity. He had been susceptible from the very beginning. He states, "The practical advantage of the new faith was evident to me at once. I had felt it even while I was engaging all my powers to repel it from me" (p. 28). The advantage lay in the fact that he now had only one god to worship, whereas before he had agonized over meeting mutually conflicting demands of various gods. After his fateful decision he experienced a new exhilaration of the spirit as well as freedom of his body, as he was no longer hampered by any of his former religious scruples. So he says, "I was not sorry that I was forced to sign the covenant" (p. 29). It is interesting to note here that it was none other than his early religiosity which made him both rejective of and receptive toward Christianity. He confesses later on, "Indeed, the first and greatest fear I had when I was first induced to accept Christianity was that they might make a priest out of me" (p. 171)—an uncanny premonition of what he eventually became! Still, for all the attractions Christianity held for him, it was also true that he had bowed his head to a foreign god in order to take the line of least resistance against group pressure. Thus his first contact with Christianity was both liberating and traumatic. One could say that in a sense he never completely recovered from this trauma.

After signing the covenant he became an active member of the group which met every Sunday for prayer and Bible study. Several months later he was baptized along with six others in his class by M. C. Harris, an American Methodist missionary. He then adopted *Jonathan* as his Christian name because, he says, he "was a strong advocate of the virtue of friendship" (p. 32). In fact he made lifelong friends among this group and enjoyed their company as much in social gatherings or excursions as in religious activities. They always had their own Sunday services, with each of them taking the role of pastor in turn. He records with obvious relish the excitement they shared as well as some squabbles and mischief which they unexpectedly fell into while holding services. Soon they came to realize, however, that Christianity had its own difficulties. What particularly pained them was the fact that they were divided by denomination, whether Methodist or Episcopalian. They came to grips with this problem right after graduation of the upperclassmen, perhaps because they realized that from then on those who belonged to different denominations would seldom have a chance to meet. Uchimura expresses this sentiment thus: " 'Men who ate rice out of the same kettle' is our popular saying about the intimacy well nigh approaching the bond of blood-relationship; and we believed and still believe in the necessity of some other bonds of union for those who are to fight and suffer for one and the same cause than the breaking of bread and drinking of wine by the hand of an officiating minister. Could such a bond be divided into 'two churches' even though ministers of two different denominations wrote the sign of the Cross upon our foreheads?" (p. 58)

They thereupon decided to build a church of their own and a committee of five members including Uchimura was elected. The news of an offer of four hundred dollars by a representative of the Methodist Episcopal Church of America encouraged them, although they did not want to accept it as a gift, but rather decided to borrow it. They clearly wanted to have an independent church with no strings attached. It seems that Kanzō was a leading spirit behind this bold enterprise, as he was, in his own words, "young, idealistic, and impulsive" and "would pour out his heart" whenever he spoke (pp. 64 and 39). After graduation he plunged vigorously into their joint task while conducting fishery surveys as a governmental official to earn a living. Finally a half of one building was procured, and the desire to unite brethren belonging to separate denominations into one independent church was fulfilled. It was a completely lay church, and as in school days some of the members who were recent graduates from the college took turns preaching. Only one problem remained, that of paying their debt, which suddenly became urgent, for the donor requested to be paid back, as he could not approve of their independent church. It was a stupendous feat that they could pay back everything in less than two years, even though they received an unexpected gift of one hundred dollars from Clark, then in America. All of the congregation were still young and barely managing to make ends meet.

What interests me most about their enterprise is not that they succeeded in building an independent church which was completely lay in organization. Neither is it the budding ecumenism, in itself quite striking considering that it has come to see its day only recently the world over. It is rather what inspired them to launch such an enterprise. I have mentioned their initial motivation, and Uchimura further elaborated on this:

"They do err who think that our church-independence was intended as an open rebellion against the denomination to which we once belonged. It was a humble attempt to reach the one great aim we had in view; namely, to come to the full consciousness of our own powers and capabilities, and to remove obstacles in the way of others seeking God's truth for the salvation of their souls" (p. 87).

In short, he attests that what he embarked upon with others was not a protest against the established order. But in actuality it was such. Would it be too farfetched to think Uchimura took revenge for having been forced to bow his head to a foreign god by building an independent church free of foreign influences? Or perhaps this was an attempt to maintain the esprit de corps, which had been such a menace to the lonely Uchimura at the beginning, but later on came to sustain him so much in the name of Christianity. I shall come back to a discussion of this question in connection with his later pronouncement of *Mukyōkai* (Non-church), for I believe it was inspired by a similar spirit. We shall see that in both instances he defends his position in much the same way.

A Vacuum in the Heart

Uchimura left Sapporo for Tokyo in December 1882, apparently in a most dejected state of mind. In the chapter which describes this period of his life in Tokyo, he first introduces a quotation from Hosea (2:14-16), a prophet of the Old Testament, which are the words of God addressing stray Israel to lure her into the wilderness where He may let her recall her first fidelity. He goes on to say:

"So my Lord and Husband must have said to Himself when He drove me from my peaceful home-church. He did this by creating a vacuum in my heart. Nobody goes to a desert who has his all in his home. Nature abhors a vacuum, and the human heart abhors it more than anything else in the Universe. I descried in myself an empty space which neither activity in religious works, nor success in scientific experiments, could fill. What the exact nature of that emptiness was, I was not able to discern. Maybe my health was getting poor, and I yearned after repose and easier tasks. Or, as I was rapidly growing into my manhood, that irresistible call of nature for companionship might have made me feel so haggard and empty. At all events, a vacuum there was, something there was in this vague universe which could make me feel happy and contented; but I had no idea whatever of what that something was. Like a pigeon that was deprived of its cerebrum by the knife of a physiologist, I started, not knowing whither and wherefore, but because stay I could not. From this time on, my whole energy was thrown into this one task of filling up this vacuum" (pp. 90-91).

This passage clearly indicates an acute sense of disillusionment which was instrumental in driving him from Sapporo to Tokyo. But why disillusionment? Was he not happily and proudly working for his church? He wrote in his diary on December 28, 1882, the day he completed the last payment of debt for his church, "Joys inexpressible and indescribable!" (p. 86.) Does this note of joy contradict the preceding passage? It may be that he did not wish to acknowledge the sense of disillusionment which had been plaguing him for some time until he had completed his last duty. Still, why disillusionment? One plausible answer is that he was thoroughly disgusted with what he saw at his job, namely, the corruption among governmental officials in Hokkaido, and thought of resigning his position when he went to Tokyo, which he actually did a few months later. Strangely, he does not mention this, but instead gives a definite impression that his distress was much deeper and that he himself did not understand what could have caused it.

His condition at that time was probably what would have been diagnosed by a clinician as depression. And if I may conjecture further, I should say that his case was rather close to what Freud described as "those wrecked by success,"[13] for so far he had been enormously successful in many ways. He had graduated from college at the top of his class and was launched on a promising career, already having made a scientific discovery in his field. He had converted his antagonistic father and built, against the wishes of foreign missionaries, the only independent church then in Japan. Surely to accomplish all this he must have worked extremely hard, and he was very likely worn out. But if it was a matter of exhaustion, he could easily have recovered, for he was then only twenty-two years old. The cause of his depres-

[13] "Some Character Types Met with in Psychoanalytic Work" (1916), *Complete Psychological Works of Sigmund Freud*, vol. 14 (London: Hogarth, 1957), pp. 316-331.

sion must be sought somewhere deep in his mind. It is quite possible that he somehow felt guilty for his accomplishments, as Freud postulated for "those wrecked by success." And, with or without guilt he might have been feeling, "This is not what I want, though I thought it was." Only he did not know what he really wanted. To go one step further along this line of reasoning, it may be said that he came to realize that those successes which he had to fight for brought no real satisfaction to his hungry soul, and he longed to be given something without fighting for it. The entry for April 22, 1883, in his diary seems to prove the hypothesis: "Repented my past sins deeply, and felt my total inability to save myself by my own efforts" (p. 91).

Uchimura spent the next two years in Tokyo trying to find something that could satisfy him. He participated in the Pentecostal services which were quite popular in Tokyo at the time. He also frequently attended parties given by churches. Outwardly his depression might have disappeared for awhile, and it was then that he fell in love with Take Asada, his first wife. In the book he does not mention this very important episode in his life, but the details surrounding the marriage that lasted only for several months and ended in divorce have become clear, thanks to the research done by his biographers. Take was a "modern" girl, Christian and schooled in the Western style. This was what attracted her to him, but it certainly did not appeal to his old parents, particularly his mother. At one point he gave up the idea of marrying her, but later, encouraged by his friends and with the final though perhaps grudging approval of his parents, he decided to marry her. But once married he found out to his great dismay that he and his bride were not really compatible. Most probably Take irritated him with her too carefree behavior. After some squabble she left him, although he pleaded with her not to. Later when she changed her mind and asked to return, he refused, despite the fact that she was pregnant, and protested that she had been spiritually, if not physically, unfaithful. This sounds self-righteous, but he was serious about it to the end.

The question is why he did not mention this incident in the book. Was it too painful to relate? Undoubtedly. Also, in the light of the depression which he seems to have suffered, his unfortunate marriage and divorce acquires a new meaning. For it seems quite certain that he married out of depression only to sink into it again with the break-up of his marriage. Thus his final rejection of Take, which otherwise might look too cruel, makes sense. Whatever guilt he might have incurred during and after the mariage, it was not, so far as he was concerned, against Take as a person. He must have blamed himself alone for having been too intent on making himself happy by marriage. The unhappy marriage only deepened the sense of disillusionment and guilt which he had been nursing inside for some time. It was in itself a fleeting episode, however painful and tragic. One month after the separation he resigned from a new governmental position he had taken. He then set his mind on going to America. The same impulse which had driven him from Sapporo to Tokyo was with greater force pushing him into an unknown world.

There is one more final note about his failure to mention his first marriage in the book. Its unhappy memory must have naturally weighed heavily on his mind while he was writing the chapter that dealt with this period in his life. Even if he did not specifically mention it, he could not have entirely avoided alluding to it. For instance, when he reflects critically on the prevailing atmosphere in Christian churches during that period—that "God's kingdom was imagined to be one of perfect repose and constant free exchange of good wishes, where tea-parties and love-makings could be indulged in with the sanction of the religion of free communions and free love" (p. 96), he was undoubtedly thinking of what he had undergone. More important than this is the fact that he put the quotation from Hosea at the head of the chapter. Hosea is known to have had an unhappy married life because of his wife's infidelity, and from this bitter experience he understood the love of God beckoning stray Israel to return to Him. It is most likely that Kanzō chose Hosea because of their common unhappy experience. Most interestingly, however, in the passage that follows the quotation he puts himself in the place of stray Israel, saying, "So my Lord and Husband must have said to Himself when He drove me from my peaceful home-church" (p. 90). Does this mean that in addition to identifying with Hosea he put himself in the unfaithful wife's place as well? In other words, somewhere deep in his mind he knew, however vaguely, that he was like his wife after all. Or would it be possible to see here an unconscious admission of his original identification with his mother, that he felt an identity as a woman in some strange way? It must be said then that perhaps he revealed himself much more here than had he simply recorded his unhappy marriage.

What roughly corresponds in the life of Luther to this stage in the life of Uchimura is the period stretching from Luther's entry into the University of Erfurt at seventeen to his ordination as a priest at twenty-three. His entry into the monastery comes in between at twenty-one. Referring to his father's curse at the time of his first mass, he later wrote to his father publicly, "You again hit me so cleverly and fittingly that in my whole life I have hardly heard a word that resounded in me more forcefully and stuck in me more firmly!" (p. 145). What happened then, to quote from Erikson, was as follows: "Incredible as it seems, at this late date Martin was thrown back into the infantile struggle, not only over his obedience toward, but also over his identification with, his father. This regression and this personalization of his conflict cost him that belief in the monastic way and in his superiors which during the first year had been of such 'godly' support" (p. 145).

In other words, he had to combat renewed doubt in his vocation. Thus his scrupulosity, which had found its haven in the monastic life, broke loose, leading to extreme religious preoccupation and erratic behavior which became increasingly noticeable to those around him. His contemporaries reported "the fit in the choir" among others, in which he suddenly fell to the ground in the choir, "raved" like one possessed, and roared with the voice of a bull, *"Ich bin's nit! Ich bin's nit!"* ("It isn't me!").[14]

This incident took place when the passage from the Bible describing "Christ's cure of a man possessed by a dumb spirit" was read. Erikson believes that it refers to a story beginning from Mark 9:17, about a certain father who brings to Christ his son possessed by a dumb spirit and given to convulsions. Erikson also intimates that in the very act of denial—"It isn't me"—Martin revealed his secret identification with the possessed son. Since the fatal reunion with his father, it must have dawned on him that he might be the possessed son after all, an obsession which he desperately fought with all his might.

Experiences in America

Uchimura went to America in November 1884. He states the reason for taking this trip: "To be a man first and then a patriot, was my aim in going abroad" (p. 102). It is as if he were not yet a man and could not be a patriot in his own country! This clearly supports what has been suggested here, that his unhappy marriage brought home to him anew his basic inadequacy. He found himself in the midst of an identity crisis, not only sexually but socially, for he was completely at a loss about what to make of his future. Hence, his use of the word *patriot*, for he was yet to find a lifework which could both satisfy him and earn him recognition by his country. But why did he choose to go to America for these purposes, considering financial and other difficulties in making such a trip? About this he says, "Failing to find the desired satisfaction in my own land, I thought of extending my search to a land differently constituted from my own—even to Christendom, where Christianity having had undisputed power and influ-

[14] Erikson, *Young Man Luther*, p. 23.

ence for hundreds of years, must, I imagined, be found Peace and Joy in a measure inconceivable to us of heathen extraction, and easily procurable by any sincere seeker after the Truth" (p. 101).

He clearly felt that his personal difficulties were intricately and mysteriously tied up with his adoption of the Christian belief. He wanted to see with his own eyes what a Christian country was like and also how he would react to such an environment. No sooner had he arrived in America, however, than his hope of finding a superior society was shattered. Free use of profanity, roaming pickpockets, feigned kindness to exploit the unwary, particularly rampant racial prejudice—all these things struck him deeply. He cried, "O heaven, I am undone! I was deceived! I gave up what was really Peace for that which is no Peace!" (p. 118). He almost regretted having become a Christian. Yet he knew somehow that he had crossed the point of no return. Only, he told himself, he would "never defend Christianity upon its being the religion of Europe and America" (p. 119).

Soon after his arrival he found employment as an attendant in an insane asylum run by Dr. I. N. Kerlin of Pennsylvania, to whom he was introduced through the wife of M. C. Harris, the missionary who had baptized him. About this employment, Uchimura recalls: "I took this step, not because I thought the world needed my service in that line, much less did I seek it as an occupation (poor though I was), but because I thought it to be the only refuge from 'the wrath to come,' there to put my flesh in subjection, and to so discipline myself as to reach the state of inward purity, and thus inherit the kingdom of heaven" (p. 125).

Here looms again the subject of guilt which was tormenting his soul with even stronger force. And I should say it was a well-chosen occupation for a guilt-ridden man. Kerlin on his part, kind and understanding man that he was, sensed the plight of this strange young foreigner and lavished affection on him, at the same time instructing him in the value of medical and philanthropic work. Uchimura felt deep respect and affection for the man and testifies that "he it was who rescued me from degenerating into that morbid religiosity. . . . Indeed it was he who humanized me" (p. 128). For all his good influence, however, Uchimura could not stay with Kerlin for long. Uchimura knew that he was not cut out for the kind of work he was engaging in, for he was, in his own words, too "egoistic." In the meantime "doubts" within him were becoming "impossible to be borne for any length of time" (p. 142). At last, after eight months' service, he left for New England.

The reason for his choosing New England as his next destination was obvious: "I was to see New England by all means, for my Christianity came originally from New England, and she was responsible for all the internal struggles caused thereby" (p. 144). By this he meant that William S. Clark, who originally evangelized Sapporo Agricultural College, came from New England. He reasoned that if there were any place in the world where he could be freed from his internal turmoil, it would be there. It was fortunate for him that J. H. Seeley, president of Amherst College, to whom he was introduced by a friend, gave him an unexpected fatherly welcome and even agreed to accept him as a special student in the junior class. For the first time he felt at ease under the wing of Seeley's protection, however lacking he might have been in material comforts and however lonely without any congenial friends. He states, "I confess Satan's power over me began to slacken ever since I came in contact with that man" (p. 148).

Through Seeley he gradually came to experience the peace of mind he so much longed for. One day, on March 8, 1886, six months after coming to Amherst, he noted in the diary, "Very important day in my life. Never was the atoning power of Christ more clearly revealed to me than it is today. In the crucifixion of the Son of God lies the solution of all the difficulties that have buffeted my mind thus far" (p. 153). Later he reported this experience as "the conciliation of moral schism" (p. 160). The entry for September 13 of the same year is also very moving in that he records a private eucharist he celebrated alone in a dormitory room with juice he pressed out of a cluster of wild grapes and a piece of biscuit. For all his youthful devotion, Christianity had still been something imposed on and not completely assimilated into his soul. But now it was his own. It finally became the substance of himself; he had experienced the wholeness of the faith of Christ.

After completing two years of study at Amherst he entered a theological seminary in Connecticut. From this one might conclude that he had made up his mind to become a Christian minister. But in actuality his decision was a complex one, ridden with doubts and reservations. To become a Christian minister in his day meant to enter the service of a certain denomination whose headquarters existed outside Japan. This his pride could never permit him to undertake. It was completely against the spirit in which he had helped to build Sapporo Independent Church. Also, being exposed in America to many denominations all soliciting his allegiance, he was all the more skeptical about belonging to any. He decided that if he must become a Christian minister, he should become an independent one: "I made up my mind to study Theology, but upon one important condition; and that was that I should never be licensed" (p. 173). With such an unusual decision, how could he have felt at home among seminarians? On the one hand, their worldly ambition to obtain a good position after graduation appalled him. On the other, the academicism in teaching repelled him. And behind all these untoward reactions there lay his mounting nostalgia for Japan. He came to see her good points, which had escaped him before. He even felt that in certain areas Japan might fare more favorably than America. He must have been in agony then as to whether or not he was proceeding on the right path: "Severe mental strains of the past three years unsettled my nerves, and chronic insomnia of a most fearful kind took hold of me. Rest, bromides, prayers proved ineffectual, and the only way now open for me was one leading toward my homeland" (p. 177). He quit the seminary only a few months after admission and departed for Japan. He arrived there in May 1888. And here the book that traces his spiritual journey up to this point comes to its end.[15]

SUMMING UP

Uchimura left Japan in a state of depression like a fugitive and returned there presumably with a troubled mind which was just as bad, if not worse. In the meantime he experienced a new integration in the faith of Christ and acquired a number of lifelong friends. Among them Seeley stands out as the most important, as he became literally Uchimura's spiritual father. This must have meant a great deal to him, because, as noted earlier, he could not look up to his own father for guidance and protection. He had been without a father spiritually and now was given one. However, except for this experience and other similar ones, his days in America were far from pleasant. I have noted his quick disillusionment with America; it had not been like what his missionary friends in Japan had led him to believe. Then in the final stage of his stay he again had to experience a keen sense of disappointment in his hopes for education in a theological seminary. It was this that made him quit the seminary much too soon and return to Japan earlier than he expected. When he returned, did he feel like a man and a patriot, as he had wished to at the time of going abroad? A man, possibly yes, if his deepened faith made him feel like one. But I rather doubt it. And a patriot he was definitely not, as he was still in the dark as to what would become of him. One might almost say

[15] It is known that Kanzō even after he returned to Japan and until his death continued to suffer from insomnia, and that he also had attacks of anxiety from time to time. This indicates that, along with his history of early religious scrupulosity and subsequent depression, he was never completely freed from conflicts over *amae*, not withstanding his firm Christian beliefs. Or rather it may be said that his Christian beliefs even intensified his conflicts, though they certainly helped him overcome his early polytheistic attachments. It seems to lie in the nature of religion to make psychic conflicts more accessible or active so that they must be dealt with (successfully or unsuccessfully).

that Uchimura gained his wholeness of faith at the expense of becoming a man and a patriot. Was faith alone then sufficient to him? I doubt this too. I can only imagine how sad and uncertain he must have felt on his return, though he might not have admitted this to others.

I would like to call attention to the curious fact that Uchimura went through one disillusionment after another within a span of five years or so, beginning with the one that originally drove him from Sapporo to Tokyo. And Uchimura was to undergo many more disillusionments in later life. To exaggerate, it is as though he were born to experience disillusionment. Of course everyone will experience disillusionment of one sort or another, some more, others less frequently in life. But in Kanzō's life this stands out as the most prominent feature; it runs through his life as a common thread. And, most interestingly, whether or not he intended it, his book also begins with the theme of disillusionment: "I was born, according to the Gregorian calendar, on the 28th of March, 1861. My family belonged to the warrior class; so I was born to fight—*vivere est militare*—from the very cradle. My paternal grandfather was every inch a soldier. He was never so happy as when he appeared in his ponderous armour, decked with a bamboo-bow and pheasant-feathered arrows and a 50-pound fire-lock. He lamented that the land was in peace, and died with regret that he never was able to put his trade in practice" (p. 17). (After this comes the description of his father, which I quoted before.)

With this theme of disillusionment as a key concept, I shall make one bold reconstruction of his life. Uchimura as a small child deeply imbibed the feelings of disillusionment and doom that prevailed within his family due to the historical change which drastically altered their fate. His early religiosity, with many superstitious beliefs, can be interpreted as an attempt not to be caught by a fate that threatened to engulf him. Subsequent conversion to Christianity, however, cleared this feeling of impending disaster for him. Thus he could indulge in a feeling of pastoral peace for awhile and become absorbed in various activities. But breaking through these defensive activities, the feeling of being doomed once again set in. From that time on he had to fight one disillusionment after another, as if he had to prove that he could survive them all. We shall see how this theory applies to his later life as well.[16]

Now what is a key concept for the life of Luther? It is the theme of justification, as Erikson amply demonstrates from various sources. First, he had to justify his religious vocation in the face of his father's

[16] It is interesting to note in this regard that the first book he wrote was titled *Kirisuto shinto no nagusame* (The Christian's Consolations).

strong opposition to it. Failing this, he would amount to nothing. Unlike Uchimura, he had to fight despair rather than disillusionment, hence his extreme religious and moral scrupulosity. It looks, then, almost like only one more step from such a scrupulosity to his final doctrine of justification only by faith in Christ. True, he found an understanding father figure in Dr. Staupitz, just as Uchimura had in President Seeley. But the contrast in subsequent course between the two is great. Luther held fast until he became a clerical professor of moral philosophy, whereas Uchimura did not even finish theological seminary. Luther was sent to Rome on a business trip as an official representative of his Order, and his ties with the Roman Church were not affected by it. This contrasts sharply with Uchimura's trip to America, where he went with so much hope only to return with a broken heart.

Later Life

In September 1888, soon after Uchimura returned to Japan, he obtained the position of temporary headmaster at a school in Niigata run by foreign missionaries. He resigned it four months later after quarrelling over school policy with the missionaries. This was his first disillusioning experience after his return, and more followed in rapid succession. In September 1890 he became a lecturer at the First Higher School in Tokyo. Four months later he was unexpectedly the center of a scandal: he reportedly hesitated to bow his head in front of the Imperial Rescript on Education, which had the emperor's signature. The rising sentiment of nationalism at once made a traitor out of him, and he had to hand in his resignation under ignominious circumstances. Following this he became gravely ill with pneumonia, and just as he was recovering, his second wife became ill and died.

In a forlorn state of mind he turned to writing, the only means left to him to express himself and possibly earn a living, as he could count on no gainful employment because of the recent scandal. He produced as many as seven books within a few years, one of which was *How I Became a Christian*. It was his way of coming to grips with the terrible misfortune that befell him and also of seeking to define Japan's mission in the world. He was making his name as a Christian author, and he was quite happy with his third marriage. When war broke out between Japan and China in 1894, he championed Japan's cause in a special essay and was rehabilitated from past ignominy at last. He was now proudly a man and a patriot.

It did not take much time, however, before he became disillusioned with Japan, for she acted entirely differently in her war efforts from what he pictured her as doing in his essay. He then decided to start a movement of social reform, joining with like-minded people. He worked for a while as a columnist for *Yorozuchōhō*, an influential newspaper, and founded with his friends the *Tokyo Independent Journal* in 1898. This came to an end after two years, when a serious quarrel broke out between him and the other staff, including his brother Tatsusaburō. From this time on he and Tatsusaburō never saw each other. It is also known that his mother and other brothers and sister all took the side of Tatsusaburō against him. I might mention in this connection that his mother became psychotic a few years later and died in an asylum, a fact which aggravated even more the feud between him and his brothers.

In 1900 he founded singlehandedly a monthly journal *Seisho no Kenkyū* (Biblical Studies), which became his lifework and lasted for thirty years until his death. Its publication was soon followed by the opening of a Sunday Bible class, which also lasted until he died. He was now ipso facto an independent Christian minister, though he had no ordination nor church. It was then he coined a new word *Mukyō-kai* (Non-church). Interestingly, he declared that it was not meant as a war cry against established churches, but as an invitation to those who did not or could not belong to them for one reason or another. He could have said that Mukyōkai was for those who were disillusioned with or alienated from established churches. At any rate, he never objected to the church institution as such, and besides accepting invitations to speak at many churches he himself occasionally performed baptism and celebrated the eucharist. Thus, the sentiment embodied in his justification for Mukyōkai exactly echoes the defense he once made for the Sapporo Independent Church. While devoting most of his time to missionary work, he still worked as a social critic. But after making the now famous antiwar statement at the time of Russo-Japanese War in 1903, he completely retreated from the public arena and began the life of a full-time Christian minister. By this time he had lost his former passion for social reform. He even began to criticize socialism, the creed of his one-time associates.

The rest of his life was immensely successful and fruitful. His monthly journal of biblical studies promised to be successful from the beginning, with its first issue of three thousand copies being sold at once. His influence was nationwide, and the number of his followers increased yearly. Many of them later became national leaders in their respective fields, and some became independent teachers of Christianity like the master. In spite of this great success, disillusionment did not escape him. He had to endure many more bitter experiences, among which I shall mention two as most noteworthy. One was the death of his nineteen-year-old daughter in 1912. When her condition became very grave, it is reported that he prayed to God earnestly to give her a miraculous cure, being firmly convinced that God would listen to his prayer. One can well imagine how deeply disappointed he must have been when he knew that his prayer was not answered. It looks almost as if he were courting disillusionment so that he could overcome it once and for all. After his daughter's death, his faith became very much heaven-bound or eschatological and this, along with his observations on a world that was soon precipitated into World War I, led to his later movement of the Second Coming of Christ.

The other, also important, source of his disillusionment lay in his relationships with his followers. Some of them whom he loved became apostates later. But it was more painful for him when some of his most trusted assistants disagreed with him on the fundamentals of Christian faith. The most serious conflict occurred toward the end of his life with regard to what Tsukamoto Toraji, his chief assistant who was regarded by all of his followers as his successor, stated as the essence of Christianity. In brief, Tsukamoto attempted to make a logical construct out of Uchimura's life-long teaching that established churches are not only not essential to Christian faith, but harmful. Uchimura vehemently opposed this, saying that his Mukyōkai (Non-church) was not to become an issue in discussing the Christian faith. What he feared most of all was to be looked on as the founder of Tsukamoto's Churchless Christianity, which he instinctively knew would degenerate into another sect, for what he wanted most of all from the beginning was to be independent of any denomination or sect. He could not bear the thought of becoming the founder of a new sect. Soon after virtually excommunicating Tsukamoto, he died a lonely death (on March 28, 1930), leaving word that he wanted to be remembered as having died like a small child clinging to the Cross.[17]

Let us now take a look at Luther's life for comparison. The story of how Luther ignited a revolution throughout Europe when he nailed the ninety-five theses on the door of the Castle Church in Wittenberg in 1517 is so well known that it does not have to be retold. Luther did not dream of a complete break with the Roman Church at the beginning. He only wanted to cleanse the Church of its abuses. But he gradually became involved with the political and social upheaval he helped to stir up, and found himself at a point of no return in his open revolt against the Roman Church, so that he had to establish his own separate church. In all this he vehemently justified his actions, but soon the reaction to it came in the form/shape of a severe depression. Then

[17] Yamamoto Taijirō, *Uchimura Kanzō—Shinkō, Shōgai, Yūjō* (Tokyo: Tōkai Daigaku Shuppankai, 1966), p. 290.

he was unable to believe his own justification of himself, even by faith, as he proclaimed. It is known that he suffered from such depression periodically until he died at sixty-three in 1546. This quick glance at his later life may be sufficient to distinguish it from Uchimura's. After having lived in a cloistered monastery for over ten years, Luther was a most important public figure throughout most of his adult life whereas Uchimura engaged as a journalist in a social movement or national politics only for a short while, and soon after retreated from all this, devoting himself totally to his religious mission. Luther established his own church, whereas Uchimura did not even appoint his successor, refusing to see the birth of a sect in his time.

Conclusion

Among Christian Thinkers[18]

Christianity is a religion which claims universalism. As St. Paul said, "There is one Lord, one faith, one baptism, and one God who is Father of all, over all, through all, and within all" (Ephesians 4:5-6). However, from the beginning of Christianity there was a strong tendency to diversification or even dissension due to personal or regional factors, as can be seen from a reading of the New Testament books. Still, the canonization of the New Testament books in the early period of Christianity indicates an attempt to integrate such diverse views, that is, a manifestation of universalism. This dialectical movement of two opposing tendencies, unification and diversification, runs through the entire history of Christianity to this day.

What attracted Uchimura Kanzō to Christianity was its professed universalism. But it was not long before he was exposed to its diverse denominations. His American experience further taught him a lesson that what goes in the name of Christianity is not necessarily Christian. Then in his subsequent struggle to grasp the essence of Christianity he was gradually led to discover the worth of his Japanese heritage: ". . . looking at a distance from the land of my exile, my country ceased to be a 'good-for-nothing.' It began to appear superbly beautiful—not the grotesque beauty of my heathen days, but the harmonic beauty of true proportions, occupying a definite space in the universe with its own historic individualities" (p. 122). It is not that he placed

---

[18] In preparing this section I was helped by the following books, among others: Augustine's *Confessions*; Erikson's *Young Man Luther*; Pascal's *Pensées*; Walter Lowrie's *A Short Life of Kierkegaard* (New York: Doubleday Anchor, 1961); Mary Bosanquet's *Life and Death of Dietrich Bonhoeffer* (New York: Harper Colophon, 1973).

the Japanese heritage above Christianity. He felt, however, that he had a special advantage as a Japanese in appreciating Christianity, and Japan should have a mission of her own in the scheme of God.

Uchimura wrote the following words on the back of the cover of his Bible while he was studying at Amherst College: "To be inscribed upon my Tomb. I for Japan; Japan for the World; The World for Christ; And All for God." This clearly shows that he felt responsible for the conversion of the nation just as he once felt for the conversion of his family. Thus it became his lifework to present pure Christianity, or one might say orthodox Christianity, to the Japanese people. As he did so, his Christian beliefs and thinking inevitably took a certain shape which distinguishes him from Christian thinkers in the West. I shall try here to compare his position with that of some of the most prominent figures in the history of Christianity.

First, Uchimura shared with St. Paul a strong conviction of being chosen as the minister of the word of God. They were probably similar in temperament, both being passionate fighters. They were also deeply troubled by quarrels among Christians. St. Paul in his first letter to Corinthians admonishes them over fighting among themselves, presumably about who was baptized by whom, and states "Christ did not send me to baptize, but to preach the Good News." These words must have rung true for Uchimura. However, there was an important difference between the two in their dealing with division among Christians. St. Paul firmly believed in the unity of the Church, whereas Uchimura tried to dispense with churches and invented the notion of Mukyōkai (Non-church). One might say that Uchimura's notion of church was sociological rather than theological.

Second, Uchimura shared with Augustine a pagan background, and both left the record of their conversion for the benefit of posterity. But the ways in which they were converted were quite different. In the case of Augustine, his mother had been a Christian and his father a pagan. He tried to escape the influence of his mother, who wanted to make a Christian out of him, and, fleeing her and Christianity, finally reached a point where he could no longer resist becoming a Christian. It was a long spiritual journey with many detours. In the case of Uchimura, Christianity with its accompanying Western culture was forced on him as something far superior to what he had before. So his real struggle began after he was converted. It was the struggle to make Christianity his own. He finally made it, but then he was not quite sure of his standing. Surely he prided himself on his independence, but it cost him life-long suffering, as he was fraught with conflicts over deeply buried dependency wishes. None of his father figures—let alone his own father, or even Seeley who helped him greatly—represented a true authority with which he could identify. For one thing, this was because the type of Puritan Christianity he espoused was no longer a dominant force in American society. Augustine, while not able to identify with his pagan father, could identify himself with the authority of the growing Catholic Church and thereby be saved from being dominated by his mother and at the same time reconciled with her. Thus he became one of the most important spiritual fathers in the history of Christianity. Uchimura was never happy with the fatherly role, refusing to be a father even to his closest disciples.

Third, Uchimura shares with Luther morbidly intense guilt feelings. But the circumstances which led to such an overwrought conscience were different between the two. In the case of Luther the guilt was originally implanted by his much too severe parents. His choice of monastic life was a compromise, on the one hand, of the guilt he imbibed from them and, on the other, a rebellion against his father, who had decided on a secular career for him. But as he could not succeed in appeasing his father, his guilt became intensified until he found for himself justification by faith in Christ. It was by historical accident that he found himself in open revolt against the papacy—a most opportune outlet for his long smouldering fury. In leaving the monastery behind, he became a historical figure who ushered in a new era, finally meeting his father's original expectations of him. Still he would not give credit to his father! One may say that Luther became his own father by eliminating all father figures available on earth. In theological terms, he identified both with Christ and His Father. This Uchimura would never do, as he remained at heart a small lonely child until the end of his life.

Fourth, Uchimura and Pascal were both scientists turned religious thinkers, but they differed considerably in relating their scientific Weltanschauung to Christian beliefs. Perhaps this was because Uchimura was a scientist only by training, whereas Pascal was a great scientist who shaped modern science. Still, the difference in their conceptions of science vis-à-vis religion is remarkable. For Pascal, science was an autonomous domain of human knowledge which was totally independent of religion. One might say that in this respect he was even more Cartesian than Descartes himself. His expressive, "the eternal silence of these infinite spaces terrifies me" foresees the terror of modern man left alone with nothing but science. This sentiment was completely missing in Uchimura. His Christian belief was inseparable from a belief in God as the Creator of all. God was not hidden for him as for Pascal; no dichotomy of science and religion existed. Thus, Uchimura welcomed natural science wholeheartedly, for it helped him to appreciate God all the more as the Creator. Should one say that Uchimura was naive? Perhaps he was, but he certainly was more biblical in this respect. He could perceive the fruits of reason as a blessing (a notion forgotten in the West) precisely because he was naive as a good Japanese should be.

Fifth, Uchimura shared with Kierkegaard a determined refusal to be officially ordained as a minister because of the unique mission each felt destined to fulfill. Uchimura's mission was to bring pure Christianity to Japan, whereas Kierkegaard's was to make the post-Christian age again ready for Christianity. Both suffered periods of depression, which was related to their original experience of Christianity. Uchimura felt that Christianity created new problems for him which it did not solve. For Kierkegaard the crisis which he called the great earthquake came with his growing realization that his religious father, who used to share imaginary trips with him as a child, was in reality a spiritually dead man obsessed with memories of past sins and the idea of impending disaster as a divine punishment. After having been completely immersed in his father's melancholy, he tried to extricate himself from it by vigorously engaging in intellectual life and eventually discovering for himself and others true Christianity. In this process he saw the falsity and emptiness of what ordinarily passed for Christianity, just as he had seen his father's religiosity as impotent. He was perhaps a more unhappy and lonelier man than Uchimura, for he remained single and never formed a group of followers. Uchimura was a self-appointed minister, but Kierkegaard could not permit himself to be one, committing his thoughts only to writing. When he finally plunged into action, he charged like a madman, vehemently attacking official Christianity in public, dying a few months later of exhaustion. It seems then that for all his penetrating insights into Christianity, psychology, and the present age, he was never entirely freed from his father's melancholy.

Sixth, Uchimura can be likened to Bonhoeffer, for his notion of Mukyōkai is very close to what Bonhoeffer spelled out as religionless Christianity. Uchimura is reported to have often said, "Christianity is not a religion,"[19] and in that case his idea and Bonhoeffer's almost become identical. One difference between the two is that for Uchimura the notion of Mukyōkai was a kind of springboard without which he could not have started his mission. It was his point of departure. For Bonhoeffer the notion of religionless Christianity was his terminal point. In his student days he once visited Rome and was deeply impressed by the Catholic Church. Because of this experience, when he became a full-fledged minister he devoted most of his talent

[19] Yamamoto, *Uchimura Kanzō*, pp. 169, 228.

and energy to the task of building up the Confessing Church to which he belonged. This became an urgent matter when the Nazi persecution of churches began. After fighting a losing battle in his attempt to consolidate the Confessing Church against the Nazis, he committed himself to the anti-Nazi movement, but soon was arrested and finally hanged. It was during prison life that he developed a notion of religionless Christianity. He mused on what Christians could do in this godless, religionless world, and came to the conclusion that they could not and should not rely on whatever was left of man's need for religion, and they themselves should be able to get by without such a need, only participating in the sufferings of God at the hands of a godless world. Clearly Bonhoeffer was disillusioned with existing churches, just as Uchimura was. It is interesting to note in this regard that Bonhoeffer's family and its close circle were not particularly religious, though very cultured, loving, and definitely anti-Nazi. His father Karl was a famous professor of psychiatry at the University of Berlin. One could say then that with the idea of religionless Christianity, Bonhoeffer's original identification with his family stood out clearly, as his hope for and identification with the Confessing Church became very faint in his last days.[20]

The Japanese Heritage in Uchimura

As the preceding comparison indicates, one can draw parallels between Uchimura and Christian thinkers in the West. Yet there is something about his life and work that can be attributed only to his Japanese heritage. To stress this point, I shall take up his keen sense of disillusionment, his neglect of things institutional, and the kind of sect he helped to create.

First, there is no doubt that he was particularly sensitive to disillusionment. It was, in my opinion, due to his identification with his disillusioned father and at the same time to what he missed in his early relationship with his mother. It was his mother, not his father, who became a formidable parent with whom he had to deal. Such a family constellation is not rare in Japan; in fact I would say that his was not so uncommon a case. What was remarkable was that he created a historical role for himself out of the sense of disillusionment. Mukyōkai was meant for those disillusioned with established churches, and it appealed strongly to those who were disillusioned for other reasons as well. This explains why Uchimura had a special attraction for Japanese intellectuals, because they were the ones most dissatisfied

---

[20] Another coincidence between Bonhoeffer and Uchimura is that Bonhoeffer's father Karl and Uchimura's son Yūshi were both psychiatrists. Yūshi is now professor emeritus at the University of Tokyo.

with Japanese society. Thus he became a kind of father-figure for them, even though in his personal relations he was not really happy with the father role.[21]

Second, Uchimura was immensely successful as a lay preacher, and his neglect of institutions appealed to many sensitive Japanese, who tended to perceive institutions as something external to themselves, hence lifeless. True, Uchimura occasionally performed the rite of baptism or eucharist when he found it appropriate to do so, in spite of his frequently voiced opinion that the sacraments were not essential for faith. This looks like a contradiction, but he never bothered to explain it. And the fact that he never bothered is superb proof that he regarded institutions or sacraments only from a viewpoint of expediency.

Third, as described here, Uchimura rightly refused to have his idea of Mukyōkai institutionalized. Yet he could not prevent his followers from forming a sect, which consisted of a number of separate groups, each tightly knit around a single teacher. This was a style he himself created. And he created it, I should say, because he was a passionate advocate of friendship and discipleship. Also, as has been hinted here, there is reason to believe that his Mukyōkai mission was a late product of what originally prompted him to establish a church in his Sapporo days. Therefore it would not be too far-fetched to say that the Mukyō-kai sect was an institutionalization of friendship and discipleship, two virtues highly appreciated in Japanese society. It is because of this that only in this sect, among the many Christian churches, does male attendance usually outnumber female. But then why did Uchimura not pride himself on the creation of such a sect? Why did he not acknowledge it?

I have noted here that Uchimura yielded to group pressure in accepting a new faith and as a consequence was subjected to severe internal turmoil. This incidentally represents a typical pattern which has been repeated numerous times in Japan whenever a new ideology

[21] It seems that most of the spiritual leaders in Japan underwent some terribly disillusioning experience to reach a certain enlightenment. This sharply contrasts with the West, where spiritual leaders are usually men of vision. This trend might be attributed to the influence of Buddhism, but I would rather think that it has more to do with the psychology of *amae* which pervades Japanese society. In this regard, see Natsume Sōseki's novel *Kokoro*, in which the chief character called Sensei (meaning master or teacher) is a very impressive person not only to the young man in the story but also to readers. But he is in actuality a terribly disillusioned man bordering on psychosis and eventually commits suicide (compare Doi Takeo's *The Psychological World of Natsume Sōseki*, Harvard University Press, 1976).

It was Uchimura's tragedy that although he became an awe-inspiring and influential teacher he was not happy in the father role, as can be seen from his stressful relationship with his disciples. Furthermore, there is reason to believe that his relationship with his own son was also a strained one. Discretion forbids me to quote his son's remarks on the matter.

is introduced. It usually starts with a small coterie of new adherents which accumulates momentum by virtue of group attraction until it becomes a sizable clique. To step out of one's group after initial identification with it is extremely difficult for Japanese, and many are wrecked in that process, as recent student movements attest. Perhaps Uchimura knew all this instinctively. That is why he came to value his independence more than anything else, and also why he never tried to hold back those who wanted to leave him. He demanded independence of his followers. Is this possibly what was in back of his mind when he refused to see the birth of a new sect in his name? He would not yield to or condone group pressure in his last days as he had earlier. In other words, Uchimura as a person was far above the Mukyōkai sect he helped to create. Therein lies his true greatness.

Cultural Differences
in Family Socialization:
A Psychocultural Comparison of
Chinese and Japanese*

—»» «««—

GEORGE DEVOS

LIZABETH HAUSWALD

ORIN BORDERS

Confucianism, considered either as ideology or as a model for social organization, has had a profound effect on the cultures of China, Korea, and Japan. For example, it has greatly influenced stratified patterns of social belonging, whether to a state or to a community. And it has particularly influenced patterns of precedence and subordination according to age, sex, and family role. This common Confucian heritage, however, has not prevented radical differences in the patterning found today in mainland China or Taiwan, North or South Korea, and Japan. No one with a reasonable knowledge of any of these present-day societies can deny a sense of difference in the way their members conduct themselves in interpersonal relationships. And with detailed observation, one can infer that there are fairly fixed personality modalities that distinguish Chinese, Koreans, and Japanese from one another.

Acknowledging that in all cultures one finds striking dissimilarities and idiosyncracies among individuals, we are seeking nevertheless to suggest some modalities of interpersonal behavior that differ systematically between cultures. In the present discussion, we shall consider differences between samples only of present-day Taiwanese and Japanese, for at present we do not have enough material available to consider Koreans with any degree of cogency and we have no material from mainland China to aid in ascertaining the effects of a revolution-

* This presentation partially incorporates the work reported previously by Lizabeth Hauswald (1974). Many of the conclusions of this paper were anticipated by Ms. Hauswald's work. Orin Borders is responsible for a second scoring and an expansion of the TAT data as well as for this paper's statistical findings; he also was an active participant in the formulation of the final conclusions. George DeVos, the senior author, is responsible for the overall direction of the project and the integration of its findings into a coherent whole.

ary attempt of over twenty-five years to stamp out Confucianism. Our knowledge of Japanese culture far exceeds that which we have been able to learn, mostly indirectly, about Taiwanese family behavior. The latter is derived primarily from continuing discussions with Wolfram Eberhard (a noted scholar on Chinese society) and from various secondary sources (see especially Hsu 1967).

The main arguments here are limited to the results obtained by systematic comparisons of Thematic Apperception Test (TAT) protocols gathered from Taiwanese and Japanese subjects. This project test material on Taiwanese families is but one part of the material obtained in the course of a research project conducted under the supervision of Wolfram Eberhard and George DeVos in San Francisco's Chinatown and in Taipei, Taiwan. In addition to interview schedules on primary family interaction, Kenneth Abbott and teams of Chinese interviewers gathered other forms of psychological test data, principally the California Psychological Inventory and Problem Situation Tests. The Taiwanese and San Francisco Chinese materials were for the most part identical, differing consistently from that obtained from either Japanese or Americans. For purposes of simplification, we are including only a brief analysis of the material on San Francisco Chinese. There are direct similarities between this material and that obtained in Taiwan which argue strongly for cultural continuity in interpersonal attitudes and in style of coping with interview and test situations; despite three hundred years of separation, Chinese in San Francisco and those in Taiwan have remarkably similar psychological profiles (Abbott, 1970, 1975). The Japanese material can be contrasted with either sample with very similar results.

The most directly helpful writings used as background ethnography on Chinese family behavior are those of Richard Solomon (1971), Francis Hsu (1967), and the more recent writing by Margery Wolf, based on her extensive field work in Taiwan. Her book, *Women and Family in Rural Taiwan*, is particularly helpful. The generalizations about the Japanese sample are derived largely from George DeVos's collaborative efforts with Japanese social scientists since 1953 on a number of different projects (DeVos, 1973). Although we have also collected other samples from a number of settings in Japan, in this present discussion we will compare only those materials drawn from Taipei and Tokyo.

The central purpose of this presentation is to explore, by means of stimulated stories obtained from samples in each culture, the differences between the Taiwanese and Japanese perception of relationships within the primary family. Most broadly, Chinese and Japanese have been portrayed as having an essential similarity in delineation of familial and social obligations. Responsibility to the family is great in both cultures, but when we compare responses to the Thematic Apperception Test, we find modal differences between these two cultures. There are notable differences in readiness to express concern about achievement, future time orientation, suffering, responsibility and control within the family, and perception of family harmony and discord. Using this material, we will draw inferences regarding family attitudes related to patterns of socialization within the present-day changing societies of Taiwan and Japan.

The Japanese subjects are all residents of Arakawa Ward, Tokyo, with elementary or high-school education. They are basically of the upper-lower class, with semi-skilled or unskilled jobs primarily in the small cottage industries that characterize the ward. The Japanese data were collected between 1961 and 1968. The present sample is small, but differs only in a few respects from previously analyzed materials (DeVos, 1973). We have drawn it from twenty families on which extensive life history material and projective tests were gathered over a period of several years. Our ethnographic findings are to be published in two volumes (DeVos and Wagatsuma, forthcoming).

The Taiwanese and Japanese included in the samples were control cases of families with non-delinquent adolescent male children who were matched with families containing a delinquent adolescent. The Taiwanese data were collected from the "Kuting" section of Taipei, and the families were more diverse economically than those of the Japanese sample from Arakawa Ward. The subjects chosen were mothers and fathers (with high-school education) of elementary-age children. The sample has some equivalence economically to the middle and lower strata found in the Taipei population. This sample was collected in 1968. To better match socioeconomic backgrounds, we eliminated families with either illiterate or college backgrounds. This left a total Taiwanese sample of fifty families. These families, like three-fourths of Taiwan's Chinese population, originally immigrated some three hundred years ago from China's South Fukien Province. No recent immigrants to Taiwan are included.

We were able to compare the populations on only those TAT pictures shown to both Taiwanese and Japanese. The original Murray cards with "Western" features were used in the Taiwan project. The Japanese data was gathered with a slightly modified version of the Murray cards. In this modified set, the Western faces were altered to look more Oriental, clothes were depicted to look more Japanese, and minor background changes were made to more accurately depict the Japanese scene. Seven cards are the major focus of our analysis (cards 1, 2, 3BM, 6BM, 7BM, 13, and 18F, and their Japanese equivalents).

There may be some question about the comparability of the stimulus value of the original Murray cards and the modified Japanese set. Extensive pretesting in Japan as well as subsequent research comparing both the original Murray set with a modified Japanese set has convinced the senior author that the use of the modified set was unnecessary. This became apparent when considering the consistency of results among the pictures used and the consistency between stories obtained directly with each original Murray card and its Japanese counterpart. Similarly, in the Chinese instance, the internal consistency of results between the San Francisco and Taiwanese samples, and the internal consistency of results between the pictures themselves, make it possible to conclude again that the Murray set has been validly used with Chinese to evoke interpersonal family attitudes.

Notable differences in response styles are readily apparent between the Japanese and Taiwanese. In the main, the Taiwanese tend to give brief stories, often about forty words in length. In contrast, the Japanese tend to give many more elaborated and verbose stories, often three times as long as those of the Taiwanese. Furthermore, the complexity and variety of stories given by the Japanese is generally much greater than that found among the Taiwanese. Because these differences in response styles did not vary significantly with the specific content of the different TAT cards, but instead tended to characterize the response patterns to all cards, we concluded that these differences were largely reflective of differential psychocultural attitudes toward the TAT task itself, and not the specific content of individual stories. One gains the general impression that the Taiwanese feel less free than the Japanese in the use of imaginative faculties in the composition of stories. The Chinese are more guarded in the expression of aggressive or sexual themes. This may be interpreted as conscious censorship vis-à-vis an outside interviewer, or it may reflect difficulty in allowing oneself to express ready fantasy. We return to this question in the final section. Although differences in response styles represent only a part of the data findings, such differences create some difficulty in the comparison of projective material between the two cultures.

The framework of thematic analysis that we have used in this study is one that the senior author has developed over the years through extensive research work with the TAT. The core of the system consists of ten basic dimensions of interpersonal behavior which can be usefully divided into two general categories: instrumental and expressive behavior. Briefly defined, instrumental behavior refers to behavior motivated by the desire to obtain some subsequent goal. As such, instrumental behavior is concerned with action as a means to an end, rather than action that provides pleasure as an end in itself. Note that instrumental behavior can also refer to the means whereby individuals meet societal standards by which behavior is judged. In contrast to instrumental behavior, expressive behavior can be primarily defined in terms of feelings involved rather than the consequences to be derived from the behavior. Expressive behavior refers to interpersonal behavior that is positively or negatively motivated or experienced because of qualities inherent in the act itself. Of course, instrumental and expressive qualities are both involved in much of human interpersonal behavior. However, interpersonal concerns often tend to reflect more of one than the other, and it is valuable heuristically initially to place interpersonal themes in one or the other category. The first five of the categories that follow are considered primarily instrumental, the second five primarily expressive. Furthermore, each of the interpersonal dimensions considered has what might be considered active or positive dimensions and, conversely, dimensions that are perceived as "negative" or socially unsanctioned, either of an active or passive nature (see Table 1).

1. *Achievement*. The first major category, achievement behavior, is defined as behavior or perception of social role behavior in which the actor is seen as motivated by the desire to attain a given goal positively within a given set of standards, or negatively through what is culturally defined as unsanctioned or criminal behavior.

2. *Competence*. Whereas the achievement category is primarily concerned with the internalized sense of "will or will not do," the competence category is concerned with the internalized sense of "can or cannot do." This category is designed primarily to tap feelings of adequacy or inadequacy. Along the positive dimension, we have "avowal of capacity." Within the negative category are included concerns about failing due to inadequate physical or mental prowess.

3. *Responsibility*. Social behavior can be consciously perceived as motivated by a sense of responsibility or obligation to internalized social directives. These may be in personal, familial, or community terms. The negative dimension includes guilt, avoidance or flight from responsibility, neglect due to profligacy, or irresponsible self-indulgence.

4. *Control*. This category includes behavior oriented toward the actualization of power, the exercise of authority, or the control of others, bending their purposes to one's own ends in social relationships. Control themes can depict the actor in either the dominant or subordinate role. In the subordinate role, the actor may be perceived as seeking autonomy or reacting against an unjust authority. Along the negative dimension, such behavior is sometimes perceived as rebellious reactivity. Dominant behavior may also be seen as positive or negative,

proper or irrational. It may be depicted positively as properly forceful or negatively as inept or feckless.

5. *Mutuality.* Conjoint instrumental behavior can be perceived either in cooperative or competitive terms. Positively, such behavior can be exercised within the limits of socially prescribed norms. Negatively, cooperative or competitive behavior can be seen as operating for nefarious purposes or through improper, unethical consideration of others.

6. *Harmony-Discord.* The first of the expressive concerns is harmony. A positive aspect of this dimension would be themes describing peaceful interpersonal relationships or positive behavior oriented toward the maintenance of peacefulness within a group. From the negative vantage point, this category includes discord, disharmony, aggression, violence, and possible destructiveness in interpersonal relationships.

7. *Affiliation-Separation.* This category picks up the major human concern with affiliation and contact in human relationships and the related negative concerns with isolation, rejection, or separation.

8. *Nurturance-Deprivation.* Nurturance, care, help, and comfort are all considered under the positive dimension of nurturance. Under the negative dimension is considered a sense of personal, social, or economic deprivation. Note here that although affiliation and nurturance are somewhat similar, the affiliation category is reserved for horizontal relationships wherein individuals are of equal status and the nurturance category for vertical relationships in which one person is, in some sense, above the other in an unequal status relationship.

9. *Appreciation-Disdain.* There is in human behavior very often the manifest need for recognition or appreciation from others, a need to have self-esteem bolstered by the approbation of the group. The opposite negative dimension concerns feelings of being ignored or being considered unimportant or even debased, disdained, or deprecated by others. Feelings of shame are included as a negative concern in this category.

10. *Pleasure-Suffering.* Behavior generally governed by the direct experience of pleasure or satisfaction or a sense of positive curiosity or inner creativity is included in this category. Along the negative dimension, one finds feelings of boredom and lack of interest as well as experiences of suffering and pain.

We have presented the foregoing elemental interpersonal themes as discrete units. However, in practice, one almost always finds these basic themes interwoven into complex molecular structures. Therefore, in our analysis these themes are considered repeatedly in different contexts. Our purpose in the following sections will be to present the thematic similarities and differences between the Japanese and Taiwanese as they are revealed in complex response patterns. We will confine the discussion to four overall topics. First, we will consider achievement motivation, suffering, future time orientation, and competence. Second, we will consider the themes of responsibility and control. Third, we will do a short section on the themes of nurturance and affiliation. Last, we will consider conflict and harmony.

The TAT evidence is not as complete as we would wish. The seven pictures used do not elicit a complete spectrum of the possible themes that characterize interpersonal behavior. We shall, therefore, periodically reach beyond the immediate evidence to make inferences about the two cultures.[1]

ACHIEVEMENT MOTIVATION, SUFFERING, FUTURE TIME ORIENTATION, AND CONCERN WITH COMPETENCE

Achievement Motivation

In previous work, one of us (DeVos, 1973) has stressed that, in both rural and city samples of Japanese, achievement is seen as something that requires the overcoming of personal inadequacy. One applies oneself with persistence and tenacity to tasks. As a result, over long periods of time, one succeeds by overcoming all difficulties. Sometimes suffering and sacrifice are necessary for the accomplishment of long-range objectives. Such themes are well represented in the Arakawa Ward material. Furthermore, when we compare the Arakawa and Taiwan materials, we find notable differences on cards 1 and 2 of the TAT set.

Card 1, a scene depicting a boy with a violin, evokes achievement themes in both the Taiwanese and Japanese samples. If we interpret achievement in its broadest terms, including future successful achievement of adult status, the Taiwanese manifest such concerns in 68 percent of their stories and the Japanese in 78 percent of their stories (see Table 2).[2] If we compare the internal structure of the stories, however, with respect to the means or instrumental behavior necessary to goal-

---

[1] The senior author has written at some length about Japanese status and role behavior in his recent volume, *Socialization for Achievement* (DeVos 1973).

[2] Tables 2-8 depict statistics for selected themes on each card. In this series of tables, individual stories were usually scored more than once for different thematic variables (for example, one story might be scored for achievement, autonomy, discord, long-term future concerns). Statistical findings cited in this paper were drawn largely from this series of tables. Other tables not included in this chapter for reasons of space depict the distribution of major themes for each card. For these tables, each TAT story was generally scored for one or occasionally two characterizing qualities. This series of tables, reported in Hauswald (1974), was used to guide the data analysis that led to the construction of tables 2-8.

oriented accomplishment, we see that the Japanese, significantly more often than the Taiwanese, stress the need for practice, hard work, and perseverance. This comes out in 75 percent of the Japanese stories as compared with 54 percent of the Taiwanese (P⟨.05). Interestingly, there is a discrepancy between the stories told by the Japanese mothers and fathers in Arakawa Ward, in that the mothers give such themes in 89 percent of their stories compared with only 59 percent offered by the fathers (N. Sig., P⟨.10). When comparing the Taiwanese and Japanese fathers, we find no significant difference. When comparing the mothers, however, we find that the Taiwanese mothers give only 60 percent such stories in contrast to the Japanese mothers' 89 percent (P⟨.05). In each instance, the mothers score higher than the fathers, but the Japanese mothers indicate a greater concern with self-motivated achievement than do the Taiwanese mothers.

Qualitatively the stories differ. The Japanese achievement themes are usually more complex, often involving other interpersonal concerns. Most marked is the fact that the Japanese stories include far more instances where an individual overcomes difficulties, such as his own personal incapacity, some exterior misfortune, or economic deprivation. In the Japanese stories 44 percent involve such difficulties compared with 13 percent for the Taiwanese (P⟨.001). The Japanese are especially concerned with personal inadequacy. Of the Japanese stories, 53 percent are concerned with doubts about or worry over one's capacity to accomplish. The Taiwanese, in contrast, give only 17 percent such stories (P⟨.001). For example:

> *A Taiwanese father*: This child is looking at the violin. He is thinking, thinking . . . the song was composed very well . . . don't know if I can play this song or not. . . . If I can, it will be so nice . . . he's thinking.

In the Japanese responses to card 2 (a country scene with a young woman with books in her hand in the foreground, a man in the background working in the field, an older woman looking on), one notices a distinct difference from the Taiwanese responses. The family is the primary unit in the Taiwanese stories, whereas the parent-child relationship is generally the focal point of the Japanese stories (see Table 3). From the standpoint of achievement, the Japanese stories put the emphasis on the individual and not on the family unit. However, personal achievement is closely linked with familial relationships. The figure carrying books is intent on academic success, and she must make decisions of her own to achieve or not to achieve. Decision frequently is difficult and in conflict with the desires of parents. The occupational independence of the child can be either a source of joy or discord in

SAMPLE TAT PICTURES

J1

J2

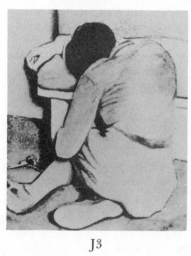

J3

J4

J6M

J7M

J8M

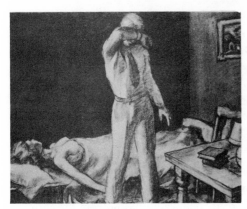

J13

J18

the Japanese family. Individual achievement is appreciated by the family if it is actualized, but such goal orientation is threatening to the family if the child neglects the parents in the pursuit of the individual goal. In the Taiwanese stories, the child is usually portrayed as achieving as part of the family unit. In the Japanese stories, the child must often leave the family to pursue his personal achievement goals.

Suffering

Card 3, a picture depicting a figure of indeterminate sex slumped against a bench, taps suffering themes with almost equal (approximately 50 percent) frequency in both the Japanese and Taiwanese samples (see Table 4). There are differences between the two groups, however, in the casual and future contexts of the suffering. The Taiwanese give 22 percent stories of suffering without cause and with no future response. The Japanese tell only 3 percent such stories (P⟨.025⟩).

A Taiwanese mother: What is this person crying for? She must be suffering, so she is crying.

A Taiwanese father: This person is a female—or male. . . . This is the blouse. This is the belt; this female is crying because she is unhappy.

In contrast, the Japanese suffering themes on card 3 more often include both some suggestion of cause and long-term future concerns. Japanese suffering themes (38 percent) include both a cause and a long-term future concern. Only 2 percent of the Taiwanese suffering themes include both a cause and a long-term future concern (P⟨.001⟩). In terms of the total sample, Japanese tell 19 percent such stories, in contrast to Taiwanese, who give only one such story (P⟨.001⟩).

A Japanese mother: She's crying—this is something, something sad happened. She can't tell her father or mother about it. So she came to her room and is crying. Then, am I supposed to say why she's crying? Well, what would be a good reason? From the impression she gives, she seems to be heartbroken. A man she fell in love with left her without understanding her. She couldn't express herself—and came home. She's in a state of sorrow and is crying, I guess. . . . Then she will recover from it and spend her youth with ardent hope. That's about all, I guess.

A Japanese father: It's the picture of suicide, but she is saved. Either because of a hard life or love affair. Judging from the shoes, it could be a co-ed. No . . . because there's a pistol. It's rather hard.

A young girl became weary of life because of a love affair. She cannot marry the man she loves because his income is not sufficient. So she decides to kill herself by shooting at her chest. But it looks as if she is going to live. Because somebody is bound to find her since it is on the street. Besides if she were dead already, she couldn't support herself with her right arm. She is living now anyway. But her future is unhappy because she is weak-minded and lacks patience despite her youth.

In place of the sexual self-indulgence and negative responsibility stories usually told by the Japanese on card 13 (a picture depicting a reclining semi-nude woman and a man with his arm raised to his forehead), the Taiwanese usually respond to this card with themes of sadness or suffering over someone being sick or dead. The Taiwanese give 40 percent such stories on this card in comparison to the Japanese, who tell only 11 percent stories of suffering over sickness or death (P⟨.005). The Japanese themes vary in other directions.

A Taiwanese father: It looks like this person is crying sadly. This female is sick.

Taiwanese father [leaning his head upon his hand and thinking]: This is probably a couple. Maybe the female is sick, and the male is worrying; very sad. So he turns his back to his wife and is crying. He fears that he might be seen by his wife.

A Taiwanese mother: This person is crying. Looks like that person is his wife who is sick and has not recovered, so her husband is crying.

The Taiwanese stories do not tie present happiness or suffering to future goals. As DeVos (1973) has reported elsewhere, suffering themes among the Japanese are often tied to future role expectations. Japanese parents are wont to practice forms of self-sacrifice that induce guilt in their children, who are impelled toward gratitude and repayment and a sensitivity to a potential hurt of parents if they do not accept the burdens of social responsibility attached to their family membership. The Japanese parents succeed in instilling within their children an unusually strong need to accomplish future goal expectations. Such a linkage between suffering, sacrifice, guilt, and achievement is far less apparent in the Taiwanese records. The form of suffering depicted in these stories exemplifies cultural variation between the Chinese and Japanese. In Taiwanese stories, fate impinges on people. It is by maintaining a stable order in human affairs that one perseveres and overcomes external disruptions. Circumstance is more often the cause of suffering than is personal action. In Japanese stories, suffering is caused by oneself or is a result of interpersonal action. If one fails to act as expected, one violates the sense of obligation and self-worth, and suffering ensues. The emphasis on expectations for individual achievement ties present unhappiness or suffering to future goals.

Future Time Orientation

Long-term future concerns are apparent on cards 13 and 3. In both instances, the Japanese far exceed the Taiwanese in the number of stories exhibiting future concerns.

The Japanese responses on card 13 (see Table 7), for example, include long-term future concerns in 50 percent of their stories. The Taiwanese give only 4 percent such stories ($P\langle.001$). This differential is probably partially a function of the two different types of themes that the Japanese and Taiwanese use. The Japanese usually give active interpersonal themes, often with an elaborated history, usually involving a personal story about two persons and society's values that somehow demands a resolution or conclusion. The Japanese stories are actual "stories," with an interpersonal plot, beginning, middle, and end.

A Japanese father: They are a couple. The husband has come back home late at night from his overtime work. His wife is lying untidily in a bed. This is not the first time but one of many times he has seen her in that manner. He was disappointed to see her lackadaisical attitude. He felt lonely and couldn't help shedding bitter tears. She can't be a good wife. They might have married for love, judging from the picture. What should the young man do? As they don't have a child, it's better for him to be divorced from her after a talk with her. If he starts over, he will be happy in the future. On the other hand, so long as she is a woman of such character, she will not be able to be happy even if she marries someone else.

A Japanese mother: This wife [lying person] is doing some business, no? She has come back drunk and is sleeping. Her husband has come back and is disappointed to see it. As the wife is also working, she is haughty and does what she wishes, I guess. She works for a teahouse, or the like. The husband works at a steady place, perhaps. His tie is neat, and there are books on the desk. He may be a sober man. . . . Though they married, made a love-marriage. . . . This sober man went to that sort of place and came to like her from the beginning and married. But now such a state! He is disappointed. As this man had no previous dissipation, he could not judge her, I guess. Therefore, their relationship will not last long. The woman will form a connection with another man and leave her husband. The husband will get a wife from a steady family and will then make a more harmonious household.

Most commonly, the Taiwanese stories on this card possessed little in the way of elaborated interpersonal causes and seldom included a long-term future concern. The most common Taiwanese story depicted someone's sickness or death and a second person's suffering over this event. With this typically Taiwanese theme, unlike the Japanese interpersonal themes, the locus of cause in the story is placed outside the influencible personal world (that is, sickness and death). The individual is not involved, as in the Japanese stories, in a complex network of interpersonal causes, many of which hinge on the protagonist's right or wrong moral behavior, but instead he is a victim of impersonal causes on which he can exert little influence. As such, his own attempts to resolve a situation are far less significant from the vantage point of fate, in contrast to the Japanese stories, where an individual's motivated behavior does matter, whether for better or worse.

A Taiwanese mother: Are these two persons husband and wife? It looks like the wife is sick. He is very uncomfortable in his heart.

A Taiwanese father: Probably his mother is sick. Very severely. Her son is crying.

A Taiwanese father: These two probably are husband and wife. This . . . probably is dead. He finds that she is dead, so he is crying. If she were not dead, he would squat by the bed to look at her. It won't be like this. If she were not dead, he would not stand to cry. . . . No more.

On card 3, with its slumping figure, we also find a differential between the Japanese and Taiwanese on time orientation (see Table 4). On this card, the Japanese give 53 percent stories suggesting long-term future concerns. The Taiwanese give only three such stories (P⟨.001).

A Japanese mother: Although it looks like a young person, something has happened outside, hasn't it? Getting a shock, I think, the person is struggling by the bed after spending a lot of energy. There is something on the floor, although I do not understand what that is beside the foot. . . . I think that person had a pretty big shock . . . then, thinking it over and over, noticing that it is not good, the person will soon be stronger and will lead a wonderful life, I think. I think this kind of thing happens to anybody.

A Japanese father: Well, this kind of picture is a bit . . . [Please say whatever you think of] Yes . . . Well, this looks like she was forsaken by her lover; judging from the bouquet [pointing at what looks like scissors or a pistol] which is dropped here. She is crying with a feeling of desperation. She looks like an office girl, and therefore she must be somewhere around twenty years old. From now on, if she is not beaten by this and if she recovers herself and finds a good man, she will be happy. However, it all depends on her effort.

A Taiwanese father: This girl probably is doing handicraft; maybe she is too tired, so she falls asleep.

A Taiwanese father: . . . This is a girl. Probably she can't pass the school exam, so she is huddling there to cry.

THEMES OF RESPONSIBILITY AND CONTROL

Every culture produces internalized standards, a sense of responsibility, and a potential for anxiety when expected obligations are not met. Every culture also functions by the maintenance of an authority system and external forms of control, directing behavior. There are important differences, however, from one culture to the next, in how and what forms of responsibility are inculcated, and how authority and dominance are exercised, or how autonomy or independence is actualized. In this section, we shall compare the Japanese and Taiwanese reflections of these concerns in TAT stories. In this analysis, we shall draw heavily on card 3 (a figure slumped against a bench) and cards 2 and 6, as they have elicited stories depicting parent-child situations.

Parental Control of Children

Findings on card 3 clearly suggest that parental control of children is a more conscious concern or point of contention among the Japanese than among the Taiwanese (see Table 4). Taiwanese tell only 2 percent such stories where parental control of children is an issue in contrast to the Japanese, who tell 25 percent such stories (P⟨.001).

A Japanese mother: He has done something mischievous and has been scolded. He sulked, cried, and fell asleep. He realized he was wrong and apologized to his mother. When he apologizes, his mother forgives him.

A Japanese father: I wonder if this is a boy or girl—I can't tell whether it's male or female—I wonder which it is. It looks like a girl, doesn't it? Or a boy? I can't tell—it looks like a girl. It doesn't look like a very wealthy family. She seems worried because she was scolded by her parents. Anyway, she was made to separate from her very close friend, her boyfriend. Her parents used their authority to make her do it. I can guess that she's suffering because of that. She looks like she doesn't know what to do from now on. In the future she is wondering whether she shouldn't go to her parents or go along with her boyfriend. Though she might suffer at the time when she goes along with her parents, she may gain happiness later if she can suppress her feelings.

Examples of Taiwanese stories without parental control themes on card 3:

A Taiwanese mother: What is this? This doesn't look like a table, chair. Looks like she is tired—She is huddling there on the table to sleep.

A Taiwanese father: What does this mean? What is this appearance? This person is sad for something. She is so sad she is huddling on the chair or the bed. This person looks like a female.

Findings on card 2 are in agreement with findings on card 3. Japanese (two men and seven women or 25 percent of the total) tell stories where parental control of children is an issue, whereas Taiwanese (one man and one woman) tell 2 percent such stories (P⟨.001).

A Japanese mother: A farming family. A father and a mother are working on the farm. They are opposed to their daughter's going to an upper school, but the daughter is firmly determined to continue her studies. She has made up her mind to leave her home to continue her studies. She goes to a higher school and completes her education. They thought that a daughter of a farming family did not need too much education, but as she has completed doing what she wanted, even though they were opposed to it, now the parents think their daughter was quite a girl.

An example of a Taiwanese story on card 2 lacking control theme:

A Taiwanese mother: This is the rice-field. The girl holds some books in her hand and is probably going to go to school. Her mother accompanies her out. Her father is plowing the field.

Findings on card 3 further suggest that the Japanese are more aware or concerned with the effects of the social or interpersonal world on the future moral behavior or character of the child, that is, the child's capacity to control and direct his behavior in culturally correct ways.

Japanese give 22 percent stories containing this theme as compared with Taiwanese, who tell only 1 percent such stories (P⟨.001).

A Japanese mother: If he goes home, worn out from playing, he will be scolded. So he stays in such a place and has fallen asleep dreaming of his ideals innocently. Therefore I wish we could let such a child sleep relaxed when he comes home after playing along so much. In such a place if a bad friend comes, he may get involved in a delinquent group.

A Japanese father: It's a girl. Her home life doesn't seem to be happy. She is an unusual girl, judging from her way of sitting. That's a bed. She must be taking a nap. She is putting on her shoes, as she is in a Western-style room. Or she may be in the sulks, having been scolded by either mother or father. Or she may have fallen into a sleep in her room after she was scolded by her parents. She is not an honest girl. She is bad and resistant, in other words. Her parents, brothers, and sisters may have trouble with her. She might have become this way because her parents were not earnest for their children. Girls like her wouldn't be able to be happy as good wives. There will be some room for her to be a good housewife if she will have been so well-guided that she will be aware of herself.

Independent Ambition as a Source of Discord

Findings on card 2, the farm scene (see Table 3), suggest that parent-child discord is an active concern for Japanese mothers. Such concern is either not present or simply not revealed in the stories given by Taiwanese mothers. Japanese mothers tell 32 percent stories involving parent-child discord, whereas Taiwanese mothers tell only 2 percent such stories (P⟨.005). Japanese and Taiwanese fathers do not vary significantly on this variable. Taken as a whole, Japanese tell 22 percent such stories in contrast to Taiwanese, who tell only 4 percent (P⟨.005). That the card depicts a girl does not impede this theme: Japanese parents today are as aware of the potentials of autonomy for women as for men.

A Japanese mother: This daughter is their child. This daughter is talking to Mother. They are talking about the work; judging from the way she looks, she cannot be a farmer; this daughter must be working in an office. It looks like a farmer's family, though. The relationship between this couple and the child is, well, it does not seem to be going well. The daughter seems to be cold. This daughter somehow looks like a person who acts very selfishly and freely. It is only from this picture, you know.

A Japanese mother: A peasant's daughter [the front left] is going
... she seems to be angry, as if she does not like a farmhouse ...
she has a book. Her mother [on the right] is turning away her face.
She may be opposed to her daughter. The central person with the
back turned will be the father. I suppose that the daughter intends
to go up to Tokyo or somewhere to attend school and to come
home after she has become successful.... Of course, she knows she
cannot pitilessly leave her parents but, at the same time, she wishes
to go to school. So the picture shows the conflicted girl at a loss.
This daughter will leave home, after all, and will come back unsuccessful.... This daughter does look so willful. This mother is
his second wife, and for that reason the father was hesitant in disciplining the daughter.... That's why she has become so willful, I
imagine. This is also a family of cold atmosphere. The future will
not be good, I guess.

All six of the discord stories told by the Japanese mothers are inextricably bound up with the possible autonomous or rebellious behavior of a daughter.

When one puts together stories about differences of opinion, occupational dislike, or desire to pursue a career different from that of the
parents, as well as the parent-child discord already considered, it is
found that on card 2 Japanese mothers give 74 percent such stories
whereas Taiwanese mothers give only 4 percent (P⟨.001). Whereas 13
of 14 of the stories given by Japanese mothers involve themes of autonomy, autonomy is *not* an issue raised in any of the stories given by the
Taiwanese mothers to this card. Also of note is that 9 of 13 of these
Japanese mothers' stories that suggest points of contention over autonomy have them resolved on a positive note. These stories are less
prominent among both Japanese and Taiwanese fathers. Japanese
give a total of 53 percent parent-child stories describing differences of
opinion, desire to pursue a career different from that of the parents,
dislike of parents' occupation, or discord, whereas Taiwanese tell 8
percent such stories (P⟨.001). Whereas autonomy was involved in 18
out of 19 of these Japanese stories, it appears as a theme in only 4
Taiwanese stories. In the 36 stories given to card 2, the Japanese told
18 autonomy-disharmony stories, 13 with eventual positive endings,
whereas the Taiwanese, out of 102 stories, used this theme only four
times, once with a positive ending—a most striking difference between
the two samples.

A Japanese mother: This girl is going somewhere. Her mother is
asking her where she is going. It does not seem that she is going to
school. She comes from a farmer's family. She is puzzled which she

should select. I think that a modern girl will study secretly if she wants to study, even if her parents object. She is very serious, so she will achieve her desire.

A Japanese father: This is a farm field. This woman has strong motivation to study. But her family is poor. She works hard in the field since her family are farmers. Though she's eager to learn she is not able to go to school. Her mother understands her feeling and wants to send her to school to study somehow. But considering how her husband feels about it, the mother is fretting very much. But the woman wants to study no matter what happens or who objects. I can tell how strong her feelings are. The mother is worrying since she loves her daughter, yet she can't disagree with her husband either. In the future I think that the woman will even leave home in order to study.

Confirming the results on this card, the Japanese see autonomy as an issue in 28 percent of the stories given on card 6 (a card depicting an older mother and an adult son; see Table 5) in contrast to the Taiwanese, who tell only 2 percent such stories ($P\langle.001$). In eight of ten autonomy stories given by the Japanese, seeking autonomy contributes to discord or disagreement.

A Japanese father: I feel that this is mother and her son. With somewhat sorrowful expression . . . the scene of the conflict of opinions. . . . The son was in the city, came back after a long while, met his mother and talked. . . . Mother is of the opinion that her son should stay home, but her son wishes to live in the city. Since they cannot come to an agreement, there arose some conflict of opinions, I imagine. I feel like this. The son has a sorrowful expression. Mother has been waiting for him in the country and has him come, but after all there is a difference in their opinions, and mother also looks sorry. This is all I feel. I don't know what will become of them in the future.

A Japanese father: Supposing they are parent and son. . . . There is expressed something which shows a disobedience to his parent's opinion. This son, though he has chosen a way opposed to his parents, seems to be himself in trouble.

Although seeking autonomy contributes to disharmony in many of the stories given by Japanese on this card, the disharmony is seen to spring from specific issues of disagreement, not the mere presence of autonomy itself in the child. The Japanese do not appear to reject a child's right to autonomy per se. Instead, they appear to accept autonomy as a fact of life, although one that sometimes causes interpersonal pain or conflict.

A Japanese mother: From now, this son wants to proceed the way he chooses, doesn't he? On the part of his mother, she misses his being away from her. She may be giving him some advice, but in her mind she is trying to overcome the feeling of loneliness and to encourage him toward future success. And she seems to be praying to God. The son is worried about leaving his old mother alone, but asks her to be excused and wants to go his own way.

Maternal Control

Japanese mothers more than fathers are apt to see the mother in card 6 as attempting some form of influence over her son. The Japanese fathers give only 6 percent active mother-domination stories on this card in comparison with Japanese mothers, who tell 39 percent such stories (N. Sig., P⟨.100 because of small sample size). In contrast, Taiwanese mothers tell 15 percent such stories, and Taiwanese fathers tell 21 percent. The Japanese fathers stand out as unusually low on the variable. One possible explanation for this differential is that Japanese fathers in this merchant-artisan sample repress or suppress direct themes of maternal dominance in such stories and emphasize instead the active autonomy of the son. Possibly this stems from a basic ambivalence felt by the Japanese male toward the mother as both a nurturing and controlling figure DeVos, 1973).

Examples of Japanese mother-dominance stories told by Japanese mothers:

A Japanese mother: This is . . . a mother is mad at her son. He is explaining what happened and apologizing to her. Well, what will be a good story. The mother found a bride-to-be for her son because he reached marriageable age. But this man doesn't want the girl no matter what. He has somebody else in mind. He is telling his mother he doesn't like the girl. So his mother is mad at him and is asking how he can refuse her offer. His face doesn't look like she is mad, though. Her son looks like he doesn't know what to do. Since he's living in Tokyo he has to go back. He's saying to his mother that he has to leave now and is telling her good-bye. Then his mother is saying "Do whatever you want," and is turning away from him. Then he goes back to Tokyo and marries the girl he had in mind. That's all.

A Japanese mother: This is the picture of grown-up's world. This man looks rather dull . . . and pessimistic. The one next to him is his mother. It looks as if they are doing something regarding his wife. The wife and the mother-in-law couldn't get along, and they came to the wife's parents' home to discuss divorce. This is not the picture of them trying to get in the house? . . . Yes, they are trying to enter because the man is holding a hat in his hands. At his wife's house, the man is looking down and is involved in thinking. The mother looks rather mean. He is pushed around by his mother and doesn't pay any attention to what his wife says. . . . It looks that way to me. Shall I tell more in detail? [If you have more, please do.] That's about it.

Despite the fact that Japanese mothers and Taiwanese mothers and fathers do not vary significantly in the quantitative number of active mother-domination stories on card 6, there is an important qualitative difference between these two groups. The Japanese mothers' stories describe the mother dominating her son in far more active terms than either the Taiwanese mothers or fathers.

A Japanese mother: [Laugh] I don't like. . . . This mother is giving advice to her son. He might return to his home late, or he might drink in a bar. I think that this boy was not an excellent student, but he got a job as an office worker by family connections. He might be advised by his mother, as he has had a lover. The mother objects to his lover. He looks worried about his situation. His father died, and he was raised by the mother. He was advised not to disgrace his father's name . . . and the family name which has continued for years. Judging from his face, he does not seem a person who meets his mother's expectations.

In contrast, the Taiwanese mother-dominance stories are described much less in terms of the mother's active behavior. The mother's dominance of her son is depicted more in terms of the son's fear of his mother.

A Taiwanese mother: This looks like his mother. Looks like he is afraid of his mother, and he dares not to speak to her. His mother is angry and doesn't speak to him.

A Taiwanese mother: The man has something to tell the old woman. Looks like he wants to tell, but dares not tell. He wants to speak but stops. The woman is very angry and is unwilling to listen to him, so she makes this man have something on his heart which he wants to tell but is afraid of being scolded, so he dares not tell.

A Taiwanese mother: What are they doing? [Thinking] He wants to go out; he tells his mother; his mother is unhappy and is thinking of something. He dares not go out. He is hesitating.

An interesting differential presents itself on card 6 between the Taiwanese fathers and mother. Taiwanese mothers, more often than Taiwanese fathers, describe the son as suffering due to his mother's refusal or rejection. Taiwanese mothers tell 25 percent such stories in contrast to Taiwanese fathers, who tell only 4 percent (P⟨.025).

A Taiwanese mother: Mother and son. I don't know what her son tells his mother. It looks like the mother doesn't allow it. The son is depressed, depressed.

A Taiwanese mother: These two persons look like mother and son. The mother looks angry. The old mother is telling something to the son, but the son doesn't listen to it. Looks like he is thinking of something and looks very sad.

A Taiwanese mother: These are mother and son. Looks like the child is telling the mother something. He wants her to understand him, but the son doesn't listen to it. Looks like he is thinking of something and looks very sad.

A Taiwanese mother: These are mother and son. Looks like the child is telling the mother something. He wants her to understand him, but the mother ignores him. The child is very upset. Maybe for a girl friend, maybe for money, but the mother doesn't permit it, so the child looks very sad.

In contrast, the Taiwanese fathers tell more stories where a son is seen as regretful or apologetic to the mother than the Taiwanese mothers, although the difference does not reach statistical significance. Taiwanese fathers tell 17 percent whereas Taiwanese mothers tell 4 percent such stories (N. Sig., P⟨.100).

A Taiwanese father: This is his mother. The son wants to go out. The mother is not very happy. Or the son is apologizing to the mother because he did something incorrectly.

A Taiwanese father: This is mother and son relationship. Their ages are so different. It must not be a love affair. The son is asking the mother for something. The mother doesn't talk to him. The son is also angry. Perhaps he's a juvenile delinquent. The mother is giving a lecture. The son seems to be sorry. That's my conclusion.

A Taiwanese father: They're an old woman and a man aged about 30. Looks like they're mother and son. His mother is very angry. Her son feels very regretful—look at his eyes [pointing at the picture]. Two hands take his hat; looks like he is anxious—the mother is looking out the window. That's all.

The foregoing differential suggests that Taiwanese women are very much aware of not only their capacity to dominate their sons but also of their capacity to make them suffer as a result of this domination. The Taiwanese fathers' high score on regret and apology (although not statistically significant) and low score on son's suffering (statistically significant) suggest that although Taiwanese sons are also aware of their mother's capacity to dominate them and of their own need to respond submissively, they often experience this dominance-submission relationship subjectively as submissive feelings of placation or self-reproach.

Another important difference is also apparent on card 6, although it is of borderline statistical significance because of the small Japanese sample size. The Taiwanese fathers and mothers tell more stories where the son is asking the mother for something physically tangible (for example, money). If we compare the previous instances where the son is refused his request for either tangible physical things or advice or permission, we find that the Taiwanese stories all suggest refusal or rejection (24 percent) in contrast to the Japanese, who tell only 3 percent such stories (P⟨.010). Taking the small Japanese sample size into account, one gets the impression that not only are Taiwanese sons more likely to be perceived as dependent-submissive on their mothers for specific things, whether physically tangible (for example, money) or psychologically tangible (for example, permission), but also that the Taiwanese mother is not regarded as amenable to discussion or persuasion. In contrast, the Japanese perceive the son as far less materially dependent on the mother and the Japanese mother as far more amenable to discussion and persuasion in the event of argument or disagreement.

A Taiwanese father: Mother and son have different opinions. The son asks the mother for something; the mother ignores him. However, the son dares not make a decision himself, so he can only stand by his mother. He's in a dilemma.

A Taiwanese father: This looks like the relationship between mother and son. . . . Looks like her son wants to discuss something with the mother, but . . . looks like his mother ignores him.

A Taiwanese mother: Are they mother and son? Looks like mother and son. The son is asking his mother for something. The mother doesn't agree.

A Taiwanese mother: That man probably is . . . that old woman's son. . . . Probably he wants to do something so he asks his mother. But his mother is not happy and ignores him.

Findings on cards 2, 3, 6, and 7 clearly suggest that child autonomy and conflicts engendered by this autonomy are more prominent concerns among the Japanese than the Taiwanese. Seen in conjunction with the prominence of parental control themes, one gets the impression that although the Japanese parents encourage achievement and attendant autonomy among their children, they nevertheless experience anxieties about the possible behavioral and social directions the autonomy might take. Although not statistically significant because of the small simple size, autonomy-related control and discord themes are more prominent among Japanese mothers than fathers, which suggests that the mother is more involved and feels more is at stake for herself in her children's correct or incorrect use of autonomy. This, of course, is probably related to the fact that a woman's success or failure in Japanese society is often judged in terms of the success or failure of her children. Moreover, it is interesting to note that conflicts over autonomy between child and parent are most often resolved in the Japanese stories. This points to the fact that not only is conflict not felt to be alien to the Japanese parent-child circumstance, but means are felt to exist whereby conflict can be resolved. The Japanese parent not only accepts conflict as part of the parent-child relationship, but also affirms that the maintenance of this relationship demands that conflicts be resolvable once they occur. Related to this is that the Japanese perceive autonomy, and conflicts over autonomy on the part of the child, as legitimate insofar as they are directed toward some socially acceptable or admirable achievement end. As was already indicated, achievement not only pervades the Japanese stories, it is also the most prominent justification for autonomy and conflict over autonomy. We might speculate further that not only does the Japanese child realize that autonomous achievement is expected of him, but also that independence of a sort can be sought or justified in the name of or under the guise of the requirement of achievement (for example, a move away from home).

Responsibility Themes

An interesting differential between Japanese and Taiwanese presents itself on card 13, the bedroom scene (see Table 7). On this card, Japanese tell 50 percent stories describing a woman as negatively responsible, whereas the Taiwanese tell only 6 percent such stories (P⟨.001). Broken down according to sex, Japanese fathers tell more such stories than Japanese mothers, but the small sample size prevents statistical significance. About half of these negative responsibility stories told by the Japanese focus on the negative effects of a woman's aggressive sexuality on the moral behavior of the man.

A Japanese father: This man was an honest youth. But since he became acquainted by chance with a girl who worked in a bar, he began to behave disgracefully. I imagine that he is regretful. . . . If he can leave the woman, he will change, but if he cannot leave her, he will continue the condition. If he has a strong will, he might be able to leave her, but if he does not . . . he will not leave her. It is hard to say which he will choose. He should leave her and study hard. The woman looks twenty-seven or thirty years old. The man looks about twenty years old.

The other half of these negative-responsibility stories tend to focus not so much on the sexual quality of the half-naked woman in the picture but instead on the impropriety of her sleeping position, or the fact that she went to bed before her husband when she should have waited for him.

A Japanese father: When one came home, the other was sleeping in a slovenly manner. One is shocked to see that. Well, I wonder if her going to bed ahead of him made him angry. . . . He looks like he is angry for her being slovenly. [What will happen now?] I wonder if he will get disgusted with her. He is disappointed with her [laugh].

A Japanese mother: . . . This man is a college student and he is married, and again thinking that he is not studying enough, he is working very hard. However, his wife has gone to bed ahead of him . . . and therefore he regrets getting married so soon; if he knew what kind of a wife she would make, he should have been a little more patient; and he wishes that he had stayed single . . . and I think he is wiping his sweat and thinking about it. [Oh, I see. Then, what will happen now?] From now on, she being such a wife, he will not pay any attention to her . . . while he is studying hard, little by little, his wife will come to realize it as she sees and listens and I think she will try to help her husband. That's right.

NURTURANCE AND AFFILIATION

With few exceptions, the Taiwanese and Japanese stories do not vary greatly along the dimensions of affiliation and nurturance. Furthermore, these are not prominent themes in the stories given by either group. Except for card 18, the cards used in this study did not tap these variables to any great degree.

Nurturance is not a prominent theme on card 1, the boy with the violin (see Table 2). However, the Japanese tell a significantly greater number of stories than the Taiwanese where parental nurturance encourages a child's achievement. Although still small in number, the Japanese give 11 percent such stories in contrast to the Taiwanese, who tell only 1 percent (P$\langle$.050).

A Japanese mother: This boy's violin concert day is coming very soon. However, er, his parents . . . er, his father is sick. . . . Well, that, er . . . he is more concerned with his father's sickness . . . and he cannot concentrate on playing. . . . And so, the boy is wondering what to do about it, but his mother knows the boy's talent . . . , er, his talent in violin . . . and so. . . . Because she knows his talent . . . she is encouraging the boy as much as she can . . . , er, . . . one day the father's condition changes, . . . er, . . . changes to worse. Then, the boy gets worse and fails a lot. And this violin, er, is something like his father's memento. Therefore, his mother tells him to think of his violin as his father and, although his illness is very bad now, to think that his father is beside him and play the violin at his best. Then, . . . one day his father suddenly dies. Then, er . . . his concert is within a few days and the boy, remembering what his mother told him, . . . to think of this violin as his father . . . reminding himself that, although he is sad, . . . er, . . . he overcomes the sadness . . . and by keeping only the violin in his mind . . . he completes his concert. This is what I have in mind.

A Japanese father: The boy has finished playing the violin. He is reflecting. He is thinking of whether he has been making enough effort and of how to be good at it. He has great hope for his future and questions, at the same time, how much talent he has. He hopes to go to a music academy. As his family seems to be in the middle class, his wish will probably be realized. His parents seem to be thinking of developing his talent as a violinist. We may suppose that he will succeed as a musician in the future by his own effort and his parent's warm understanding.

Although Japanese respondents offer more advice-giving stories in relationship to the son's socially troublesome behavior on card 7, a picture of an older and a younger man (see Table 6; Japanese 25 percent versus Taiwanese 7 percent, P$\langle$.025), these two groups do not differ significantly on the variable of advice-giving and persuasion by itself. All that we may conclude, therefore, is that although both groups do not differ significantly on card 7 (a father-son situation) on the nurturance variable by itself, the Japanese are more likely to perceive paternal nurturance in relation to and as a proper response to socially troublesome behavior on the part of the son. We see here a greater preference on the part of the Japanese for nurturance both as a means of control and a means of toning down confrontations between father and son.

A Japanese father: A young man seems to be admonished by his father. He was a nice young man, but he troubles his family because of his friends. One of his friends caused some trouble, and he was taken care of by the police. As he was asked to help the friend, he made an effort to help him. But it has resulted that he himself was involved in the trouble, and made his family worry about him. Now the father is admonishing his son for his fault, telling him his experiences. He tells the son that there are several ways to do something for other persons, and that it is now quite all right this time since it has been already done, but he should study harder from now on, making use of his experience. Keeping his father's words, the young man makes every possible effort. He becomes a good man and finally a nice old man.

A Japanese father: A difficult picture is shown. If they are not parent and child, one is older than the other. Anyway, a person of high status. The younger person seems to have a feeling of excited anger. . . . I wonder what this old man is. . . . An expression of helplessness. I will be lost if asked the reason why. So far, he is a nice man. Oh, some reason? . . . For example, he is angry because he cannot have his own way; the old man is saying it's normal. I also feel like that. [Own way about what matter, for example?] Although he thinks he is correct—the people offend him because of differences in opinion. [And what about the result?] Well, if the thing is correct and his intention is right, they can come to terms by talking with each other. The old man is also being pulled into the situation and seems lost.

Mutuality or affiliation themes are not common on card 7 and do not differ in number between the two groups to any appreciable degree. Instead, most individuals in both groups tend to describe a vertical instead of a horizontal theme or a relationship on the same status level. On the TAT, affiliation themes usually take place in horizontal relationships. Unfortunately, the large number of unspecified horizontal themes given by the Taiwanese (20 percent) on this card do not meet the requirements of true affiliative themes. Instead, these stories are little more than card descriptions, often consisting of one sentence describing two persons, often strangers, talking or thinking about something.

As mentioned earlier, the Japanese see more sexual affiliation themes on card 13, the bedroom scene, than the Taiwanese (Japanese 36 percent versus 6 percent Taiwanese, P⟨.001). However, these are usually seen as being irresponsible, self-indulgent, or pejorative in nature.

A Japanese father: The woman is not an ordinary person—from a cabaret or the softer side. . . . Suppose the man married her out of love, got together after all, but when he comes home as the woman is working in a drinking place—in a place of that kind—she is drunk and lies there lazily. This man regrets, but it's too late— nothing is to be done about it.

In contrast, in spite of the sexual press of card 13, the Taiwanese give a large number (39 percent) of sadness or suffering over sickness or death stories, whereas the Japanese tell only 11 percent such stories (P⟨.005). Many of these Taiwanese stories possess slight nurturant overtones, although formally do not qualify to be scored as nurturant.

A Taiwanese father: Probably his mother is sick. Very severely. Her son is crying.

A Taiwanese mother: This person is crying. Looks like that person is his wife who is sick and has not recovered, so her husband is crying.

A Taiwanese mother: The woman is sick and is lying in bed. The man is probably her husband. He is very anxious and seems to be crying.

Although card 18, a woman with her hands at another's throat (see Table 8), is most commonly seen as a conflict card by the Japanese, the Taiwanese most commonly give a nurturance as response to misfortune, accident, or illness story on this card. The Taiwanese give 57 percent such stories in contrast to the Japanese, who give only 8 percent (P⟨.001). If we might grant for a minute a universal press toward perception of violence on card 18, such a higher preponderance of nurturance stories and low rate of occurrence of conflict stories suggest that the Taiwanese prefer to avoid focusing on, or elaborating on, themes of violence. If we further assume that the press of the card suggests vertical mother-child relationships, we might speculate that many of the Taiwanese mother-child nurturance stories on this card exist as a psychocultural defense against a perception of violence in the mother-child relationship. The unanswered questions are still: at what psychological level does this defense occur (for example, conscious, unconscious, selective perception) and for what interpersonal or psychocultural reasons does it occur (that is, why does it occur in the Taiwanese and not the Japanese records)?

A Taiwanese father: This mother is trying to comfort her daughter. Maybe her daughter has had some hard times outside, and the mother is trying to comfort her.

A Taiwanese mother: In a poor and small house, a girl is sick and can't be cured. . . . Her mother sits before the bed every day to take care of her in order to make her daughter escape from illness and prays to God to bless her, to become well as early as possible.

A Taiwanese mother: . . . This girl seems to be the daughter of some person. It seems that she has encountered something that makes her become very sad. Her mother is trying to comfort her.

Examples of the most commonly given Japanese stories to this card are contained in the following section on conflict. As a side note, as one would expect from the vertical press of the card, affiliation themes are rarely given on this card.

HARMONY AND DISCORD

Positive Harmony Concerns

Positive harmony stories are not common responses, by either the Japanese or the Taiwanese, to the cards used in this study. Nevertheless, as the preceding materials suggest, there are some important differences between the two groups on this variable.

The strong familial emphasis of the Taiwanese responses to card 2, the farm scene, is a case in point. As indicated earlier, the mother-child relationship is the focal point of the Japanese stories on this card, whereas the Taiwanese stories emphasize the activities of the family. Of the Taiwanese stories, 34 percent simply involve a harmonious family unit doing ordinary activities. The Japanese give only 11 percent such stories (P⟨.025).

A Taiwanese mother: This looks like she is going to school. Probably the father and the mother are farming. Probably she wants to go to school. She sees her father and mother farming so hard. She's thinking that she doesn't want her parents to farm later on.

A Taiwanese father: Parents are working hard in the farm to support this girl—their daughter—to go to school. This female continues studying. After finishing her education, she will repay her parents.

A Taiwanese father: The male is farming. The female is pregnant, so she can't farm. The girl is going to school. This picture shows that the father labors so hard, the mother can't work, so the child should be filial.

One gets the impression from the Taiwanese stories that the Taiwanese prefer to depict the family as naturally harmonious, without any reference to familial conflict. Disharmony, for example, is mentioned in only one of thirty-six of the Taiwanese stories focusing on the family. As ethnographic data do not indicate that conflict is lacking in the Taiwanese households (Wolf, 1972), the near total absence of conflict themes in the Taiwanese family stories suggest that the Taiwanese find family conflict themes particularly anxiety provoking. This conclusion is consistent with the findings on card 18, a woman with her hands on another's throat, which suggest a strong avoidance of parent-child conflict themes among the Taiwanese.

Whereas the Taiwanese prefer to focus on simple family harmony, to the exclusion of conflict, one gets an almost obverse picture from the Japanese. Harmony, for the Japanese, is not something that naturally accrues to the family circumstance, but is instead something that has to be worked toward as the outcome of conflict resolution. The Taiwanese describe harmony in almost thematic isolation. In contrast, the Japanese usually depict harmony in elaborate thematic contexts. As such, Japanese harmony themes usually exist in relationship to themes of achievement, autonomy, responsibility, and conflict resolution. Examples of this Japanese pattern will be presented in the following section on conflict.

Conflict, Discord, and Violence

Conflict, discord, and, in some instances, violence place a prominent part in the stories given by the Japanese respondents on four out of seven of the cards used in this study (cards 2, 6, 7, and 18). Although such themes were present in a small number of Taiwanese stories, in general, conflict, discord, and violence were markedly absent from the Taiwanese stories.

The Taiwanese evidence a far greater preference for nurturance over violence stories on card 18. In contrast to the Japanese, who give only 8 percent nurturance stories, the Taiwanese give 57 percent such stories ($P\langle.001$). These nurturance stories are usually given in relation to and as a response to misfortune, accident, and illness.

A Taiwanese mother: Holding the daughter to cry, and looks very sad. Probably his daughter is sick.

A Taiwanese mother: . . . Is this a man? Looks like he is sick. He has a soft-hearted wife, so she holds him up to look.

A Taiwanese father: It looks like he or she is sick. Is dizzy and going to faint. The female rushes to hold. She looks like she is very sad and very much concerned. The tears are going to come out. Probably the head is congested and can't move.

Before discussing some of the psychological reasons for the absence of conflict in the Taiwanese stories, we must first note the testing context my be related to cultural differences. As with the paucity of sexuality stories, the absence of conflict themes in the Taiwanese stories might be partially a result of the fact that many of the Taiwanese tests were given to individuals while other members of the immediate family and neighbors watched on. Such a testing circumstance could understandably influence individuals to avoid such potentially touchy topics and respond with more socially acceptable, albeit, stereotypic themes, avoiding sex and aggression. The traditional antipathy that Taiwanese feel toward strangers (the interviewers were strangers) and the age-graded structure of Taiwanese society (the interviewers were far younger than the interviewees) could also compound this effect. Hence, any psychocultural interpretations of Taiwanese attitudes on these topics must recognize possible cultural differences. It must be noted that the same conditions prevailed for the Japanese, but their reactions to being interviewed may be different.

On card 2, the farm scene, as reported previously, Japanese mothers give 32 percent stories describing parent-child discord. In contrast, Taiwanese mothers give only 2 percent such stories ($P\langle.005$). Japanese fathers (with 12 percent such stories) and Taiwanese fathers (with 6 percent) do not differ significantly from each other. Taken as a whole, the Japanese give 22 percent such stories as opposed to only 4 percent given by the Taiwanese ($P\langle.005$).

Conflictual parent-child themes as a concern of Japanese mothers rather than of Japanese fathers are suggestive of the Japanese mother's greater investment in the parent-child relationship. Seen in conjunction with the fact that Japanese mothers also tell a greater number of child autonomy stories leading to interpersonal disruption, one gains the impression that the Japanese mother's concern over parent-child conflict stems from ambivalent concerns over parental control versus child autonomy. Such concerns do not seem to characterize the

Taiwanese stories, where in other contexts as well there is an absence of concern with autonomy as a desired trait.

Conflict and discord are common in both the Japanese and Taiwanese stories on card 6 (see Table 5). As this is usually seen as a mother-son card by both groups, the conflict themes on this card are usually concerned with mother-son interaction. Although both groups score high on the conflict variable, the Japanese (64 percent) nevertheless still tell a greater number of such stories than the Taiwanese (45 percent, P$\langle$.050). However, in contrast to card 2, this difference rests with the father and not the mother. Japanese fathers tell 71 percent conflict stories, whereas Taiwanese fathers tell only 38 percent such stories (P$\langle$.050). Japanese mothers (58 percent) do not differ significantly from Taiwanese mothers (51 percent) on this variable. However, it must be pointed out that the difference between Taiwanese fathers and mothers does not reach statistical significance.

A Japanese father: He looks like a man who was brought up very strictly by his mother. But something happened to make him disagree with his mother. So his mother got mad at him, saying that she didn't mean to raise her son this way. I have a feeling that he is between his wife and his mother. He is trying to make his mother feel better somehow. He's thinking desperately that he has to try hard to make a nice home. If he treats his mother nicely it seems that he can maintain peace in his family. I get the impression that he didn't go along with his mother's expectations.

A Japanese mother: This is mother, and this seems to be son. . . . The son seems to be having his own way with his parents. [Having his own way?] Yes, the child's opinion and the parent's opinion are different . . . [long silence].

A Taiwanese mother: The mother is angry with the son. Because the son did something wrong.

A Taiwanese father: The son and the mother are talking, but they have different opinions and can't get along well. The mother is about fifty years old. The son is probably twenty years old; they're foreigners.

A further difference on this card is found in the area of conflict resolution. The Japanese resolve 12 of 23 of their conflict stories in contrast to the Taiwanese, who resolve only 3 of 45 of their conflict stories (P$\langle$.001). Not only do the Japanese tell more conflict stories than the Taiwanese; they also perceive conflict interactions as resolvable in far more instances than the Taiwanese. A major conflict to be resolved is the mother-wife antipathy. Japanese seem to be more optimistic than before that such a traditionally antagonistic relationship can be resolved today.

A Japanese father: Mother at the left side and her son at the right. He seems to be very shy. He has just come back home. He is still a bachelor. He talked about his beloved girl to his mother as soon as he came back. His mother pouts, saying, "Are you going to repeat again? I have heard such a story many times. I don't like that girl." Therefore he may be thinking to ask someone to be a go-between and to get information about her family and to persuade his mother. He has been presuming upon the mother's love. His mother was born in the Meiji era, so her way of thinking is very old. It's very difficult for him to persuade his mother to accept the modern way of thinking. It is more effective way for him to ask someone else to persuade his mother. Then, they will be happy in the future since they have been a good mother and a good son. There will be some misunderstanding between his mother and his wife for the first several days or months, however. They will gradually understand each other, and the mother will come to love her as her son. [Why didn't the mother like the sweetheart?] Because her way of thinking is old and so feudalistic that she would not accept the girl as the son's wife from a different class.

A Japanese mother: These are a parent and a child. The mother wants the relationship between her son and the son's wife to . . . the mother, concerning her son and her daughter-in-law . . . the mother cannot get along well with her daughter-in-law and their life is not carried on smoothly. The son, standing between his mother and his wife . . . he is at a loss. He is always troubled this way. After all, this mother is a widow and she has been alone and she is getting old, while her son, with his wife . . . she thinks that she is out of place, she is not needed but rather a nuisance . . . but the son never thinks that way. The son and his wife always want to take good care of the mother. The mother eventually understands and thinks she was wrong and then, I always seem to make the ending positive [laugh], they will get along well, I think.

Examples of Taiwanese conflict stories that lack resolutions:

A Taiwanese father: The young person asks his mother for something. The mother doesn't agree. It is an embarrassing situation.

A Taiwanese mother: Father and son; two persons—father and son—Not father and son. Is mother and son. The child wants to speak to the mother. The mother is angry and ignores what the child said.

As with card 2, the conflict themes on card 6 are often related to child autonomy themes. Again, the Japanese tell more autonomy stories, with a score of 28 percent, as compared with the Taiwanese, who tell only 2 percent such stories (P⟨.001). Broken down further, Japanese mothers (3 of 19) do not differ significantly from Taiwanese mothers (1 of 35), whereas Japanese fathers (7 of 17) do tell a significantly higher number of autonomy stories than Taiwanese fathers (1 of 47; P⟨.001). The differences between the Japanese and Taiwanese are largely due to the high score by Japanese fathers.

Card 7 is basically not a conflict card for either the Japanese or Taiwanese respondents (see Table 6). Instead, cooperation themes are prominent in both groups. However, the Japanese respondents give 22 percent stories where parental advice is being given to a son or son-surrogate for socially troublesome behavior (for example, the son is angry, pushing a point too strongly, irresponsible, immature). The Taiwanese tell only 7 percent such stories (P⟨.025). These stories possess only a slightly discordant quality. The positive parental advice-giving element seems to be the more prominent theme. Discord in these stories does not come across as seriously or permanently disruptive.

A Japanese mother: . . . If this person is a college student [Is the person below a college student?] Yes, the person below is a college student, and this person is an educated man. . . . The student is not usually doing well at school . . . and his attitude for such is not good either and so . . . this educated man is . . . well, he could not just stand there and watch him any more . . . and so he gave the student some advice and told him, "If you continue like this, you will be finished soon . . . and your future will be poor; so you must make a fresh start with new determination." I think he is talking to this student something like that. [And, what will this student do now?] The student, bearing deep in his mind what the educated man told him . . . I think he will recover himself day by day, and he will become a fine student. By the time of his graduation, I think he will surely be a good student.

Card 18 is the only card used in this study which elicited the theme of violence with great frequency. The Japanese (69 percent) give far more stories involving violence than the Taiwanese (14 percent; P⟨.001). As in previously cited examples (DeVos, 1973), the Japanese often see the second figure as a son needing admonition.

A Japanese father: . . . It looks like a mother is strangling a child . . . well, a child. . . . Mother looks serious, so this child must be a *yakuza* [gangster or rascal] or an idiot. And so this is the scene where she is trying to kill him. If the child is a *yakuza*, then he could turn over a new leaf and start all over again to be happy, but. . . . Well, that is all.

A Japanese mother: She seems to be strangling her daughter to death. It may be a double suicide of mother and daughter. They are poor-looking.

Certain sub-themes characterize the violence and discord on this card. To begin with, 25 percent of the Japanese conflict stories (violence and/or discord) relate to husband-wife conflict. The Taiwanese give only 3 percent such stories (P⟨.001). Breaking these themes down further, we find that the Japanese give 17 percent themes where the husband's self-indulgence is perceived to be the source of the husband-wife conflict in contrast to the Taiwanese, who give only one such story (P⟨.005).

A Japanese father: . . . This picture, I think this is a picture of husband and wife quarrelling. I see. . . . Well, this is a picture of fighting. . . . This is. . . . Why are they fighting? . . . Getting drunk with *sake* . . . they had a quarrel . . . I see . . . and so . . . his wife got angry and she . . . strangled her husband, . . . she is about to strangle . . . and when things are going like this . . . well, home will be gloomy and . . . it is not very good. . . . In the future if this happens often, she will kill her husband or something of the sort . . . you know.

A Japanese mother: This is a married couple. . . . Husband drinks out every day. Wife has suffered so much by that and is wondering if she should strangle him. If nothing happens, she may strangle him.

The most prominent conflict theme on card 18, however, focuses on parent-child interaction and not husband-wife interaction, and concerns itself with violence and/or discord induced by a child's self-indulgence. The Japanese tell 33 percent stories where a child's self-indulgence induces violence from the parent to the child or discord in the relationship, in contrast to the Taiwanese who tell only 2 percent such stories (P⟨.001). As a side note, it should be mentioned that discord without violence on this card is rare. The picture stimulus, which portrays one individual with hands around the neck of a second individual, militates against a discord-without-violence response.

A Japanese father: Mother and child. The child is a delinquent girl. The mother is chastising the girl saying, "You don't even know how I feel." "Why do you do such a thing?" or "I almost feel like killing you." It must be an unhappy family. Lost the father early, and these must be the mother and the daughter. The mother has some chronic illness, could be the stomach. She has hysterical temperament, too. The reason the girl became delinquent is that she had to work in a coffee shop because of their poverty. Then she joined a delinquent gang and even found a lover. The mother won't live long, and the girl will be unhappy too.

A Japanese mother: I wonder if they are a mother and daughter. I wonder if the daughter is being scolded. Or because the daughter was fickle, mother is angry. Because of the daughter's bad conduct, mother is angry. If this is this mother's way of showing anger, I wonder if mother will eventually lose. Because this is not discussion, but violence.

Summary and Interpretation

In the preceding discussion, we have focused on the manifest content of the TAT responses. In this section, we will summarize and propose interpretations for the foregoing findings. In the concluding discussion, the senior author will further expand these conclusions in the light of other published materials.

The role of mothers as depicted in the TAT responses is portrayed quite differently by the Japanese and Taiwanese. The Japanese mother evaluates success in her own life through the success of her children. Their success is her success; their failure is her failure. Children are especially sensitive to her sacrifice and suffering. Through internalizing the mother's concerns, the child is allowed to become independent. The mother relates vicariously to his life even if he is away from the family. The child's responsibility is to correctly use his autonomy by making this vicarious satisfaction as great as possible. Thus, themes of control and concern over correct (idealized) action by the individual are dominant in the Japanese stories.

Chinese mothers are not so concerned with the independence of their children. Rather, simple nurturance and maternal control are the focus of mother-child interaction. The mother seeks loyalty and support by fostering affection and dependence in her children. Guilt is not as important an element in the Chinese family; instead, obligation and commitments are emphasized.

In Taiwanese stories, themes are presented in brief, uncomplicated summaries. Often stories simply depict daily activity and normal interaction. Achievement, activity toward a goal, is found in ordinary work and in the fulfillment of obligation to the parents. In contrast, the Japanese achievement themes are generally far more complex and often inextricably bound up with accompanying themes of autonomy, guilt, sacrifice, and future role expectations. Furthermore, the Japanese often describe achievement as demanding the overcoming of difficulties or of barriers to success (incapacity concerns, misfortune, deprivation, suffering). This finding is congruent with the fact that the Japanese, more often than the Taiwanese, emphasize the means taken for the fulfillment of achievement aspirations (for example, practice, hard work). The Taiwanese, on the other hand, seldom emphasize either the struggle or means to attain achievement.

For the Japanese, one's eventual success or achievement is largely founded on one's capacity to overcome in spite of the privations of the moment. Future accomplishment is connected to suffering, because both reflect concern with individual motivation and action. Japanese often explore the causes of suffering as well as its possible instrumental relationship to future success, whereas the Taiwanese do not connect present-day suffering with future accomplishment. Instead, they describe the expressive here-and-now of the sufferer.

Long-term future concerns are absent in many of the Taiwanese responses to all the cards. The paucity of interpersonal cause explanations and long-term future concerns, as well as the heavy emphasis on illness and death themes among the Taiwanese stories, suggest a stronger fatalistic orientation among the Taiwanese than the Japanese. On the other hand, long-term future concerns were present in numerous Japanese stories. One gains the impression that the Japanese are consciously concerned with how an individual responsibly relates to interpersonal causes and future accomplishment.

Autonomy is clearly a central theme in the Japanese configuration in this sample, taken in the early 1960's. It is through autonomous behavior that the Japanese perceive destiny to be manipulated, interpersonal causes influenced, and achievement accomplished. Autonomy is positively perceived when it relates to a desire for achievement. Success in Japanese society, from the admission examinations for kindergarten to those of the most prestigious universities or success in a business hierarchy, demands self-motivated activity. The Japanese parent assumes, even expects, a certain amount of self-motivated achievement in their children from school age on.

We have not found autonomy to be an important theme in the Taiwanese stories. Instead, as stories on card 2 suggest, there is an overriding cultural emphasis on the family as a whole rather than the individual. On card 6 (where conflict is portrayed between son and mother or grandmother—one of the few cards that elicits conflict themes from the Taiwanese), the son is usually depicted as subservient and not autonomous.

That the Japanese parent sometimes expects desires of autonomy in their children does not necessarily imply that conflict will not ensue. In fact, the seeking of autonomy on the part of a child is the single most important source of conflict depicted in the Japanese stories. Japanese parents encourage autonomous achievement, but they are consciously aware and concerned about the possibility that they will be forgotten as their children climb the achievement ladder, or that their children might choose to achieve in some endeavor of which they do not approve, or that their children might choose to become profligate.

Therefore, child autonomy, for the Japanese, is perceived as legitimate only insofar as it is justified by achievement goals. In other publications (DeVos, 1973), the senior author has demonstrated how guilt in children, aroused over parental sacrifice and suffering, is consciously and unconsciously used by Japanese parents as a means of control and influence over children. With reference to autonomy, therefore, it seems reasonable to assume that guilt felt toward parents plays an important role in the prevention of simple self-seeking use of autonomy by Japanese children and adults.

Control themes and concern over child autonomy are much less apparent in the Taiwanese mothers' stories. Autonomy does not seem to be a viable option in the fantasy of Taiwanese. We may speculate that the family is of such central importance in Taiwanese society that Taiwanese seldom consider the possibility of independence from the family. Results on card 6, depicting the Taiwanese son as dependent on the mother for physically and psychologically tangible things (money, permission, and so forth) and the mother as not amenable to discussion or persuasion in the event of conflict, further suggest that in some respects at least the Taiwanese mother is regarded by the Taiwanese son as a relatively powerful extension of the all-powerful family. We might here further speculate that Taiwanese sons are probably more likely than Japanese sons to perceive their dependence on the family in physical, concrete terms.

The Japanese mother does not have the relative assurance that her sons will not leave the family. It is part of her responsibility as a mother to instill within her children the correct motivation for autonomous achievement that will better enable them to compete, successfully, independent of the family, in the larger world. Hence, if the Japanese mother is to maintain her all-important ties with her children, she must be able to influence her children at a distance, without physical proximity. Herein we see the functional significance of the greater reliance on internalized guilt and sacrifice in the Japanese setting.

The foregoing conclusion is consistent with the fact that although the Japanese give many more conflict themes than the Taiwanese, the Japanese more readily perceive family conflict as having a satisfactory solution. This finding is integral to the rest of the Japanese configuration. If Japanese chilldren are not controlled by an immediate dependence on the family for tangibles, as in the Taiwanese situation, but instead are encouraged to be autonomous and independently make their own way in the world, means must exist whereby conflict can be resolved if ties are to be maintained in the face of disagreements that naturally follow when autonomy is encouraged.

The Japanese stories in this study are much richer than the Taiwanese stories. Hence, they may contain more information about Japanese culture than the Taiwanese stories do about Taiwanese culture. The greater number of our comparisons have indicated the presence of various themes among the Japanese stories and the absence of these same themes among the Taiwanese stories. Therefore, much of our understanding of the Taiwanese has been based on attempts to assess the psychocultural significance of the absence of selected themes. With such a methodology, our conclusions about the Taiwanese must be regarded as more tentative than our conclusions about the Japanese. This being the case, it is especially important that we compare our hypotheses about the Taiwanese with the findings of other researchers on Taiwan or China.

A Brief Examination of San Francisco Chinese Results

In interpreting the Taiwanese results, we have been concerned with how to apply them to Chinese generally. We report here results obtained from 23 male and 33 female Cantonese, living in San Francisco, also used as a control sample in our cross-cultural study of delinquency formation. After compiling the Taiwan-Japan analysis, we scored and analyzed the San Francisco stories along all of the variables differentiating the Taiwanese and Japanese.

The results show the Taiwanese and San Francisco samples to be remarkably similar in the composition of TAT stories. Except for the few trends that we shall note, the San Francisco stories were indistinguishable from the Taiwanese. For example, no trends, significant or otherwise, were found between the two groups on cards 1, 2, 3, or 7. On these four cards, the Chinese samples were alike on all variables previously contrasted with the Japanese, including the relative appearance of themes of achievement, autonomy, suffering, and conflict.

The results were basically similar for cards 6, 13, and 18, although a few differences do emerge. On card 6, one detects a larger number of conflict stories among San Francisco Chinese men, although this difference does not quite reach statistical significance (N. Sig., $P\langle.10\rangle$).

On card 13, there were two non-significant trends apparent. The San Francisco men tell fewer stories involving sadness or suffering over death or illness (N. Sig., $P\langle.10\rangle$). Conversely, the San Francisco men tell many more stories depicting rape or violence to a woman than either the Taiwanese ($P\langle.01\rangle$) or Japanese men ($P\langle.01\rangle$). These results in San Francisco contrast strikingly with the emphasis in the Japanese stories on female sexual waywardness or seductiveness on this card.

On card 18, the only difference that emerges is a slight tendency for the San Francisco sample to give more violence stories than the Taiwanese. Again, this difference does not reach statistical significance.

The differences described for cards 6, 13, 18 are not marked, and are largely outnumbered by the similarities between the Taiwanese and San Francisco Cantonese on these three cards. Both groups obtain similar scores on these cards in such areas as childhood and female self-indulgence, future time concerns, maternal dominance, and family discord.

A Discussion of Cultural Contrasts

To generalize and repeat some of what has been said here, even in this small sample, some striking differences are apparent in representations of interpersonal relationships between Japanese and Taiwanese Chinese. It is our contention that these differences in perception are due not only to differences in adult relationships but also to socialization experiences.

Further, we would like to assert that our results from Taiwan can be interpreted as more generally applicable to other Chinese. Not denying the possibility of regional differences in Chinese culture, we find that psychological tests administered to Taiwanese Chinese and Chinese originating from the vicinity of Canton, living in San Francisco, produce highly similar results. The TAT evidence reported here is buttressed by the results obtained on translated versions of the California Psychological Inventory reported elsewhere by Kenneth Abbott (1975). It is remarkable how distinctively "Chinese" profiles have been obtained from the sample of Chinese who have in the one instance migrated to Taiwan three hundred years ago and, in the other instance, Chinese from the vicinity of Canton who have come to the American continent at various times over the past hundred years. Our results affirm, first, the cultural stability of the Chinese family and basic interpersonal relationships and, second, the tenacity and persistence of this pattern despite movement overseas into highly different host settings—in one case becoming the dominant group in Taiwan and in the other case an encapsulated minority within American culture. We would describe the similarities in results and their difference from Japanese materials as highly suggestive of a basic similarity in culture throughout Southeast China. There are no Northern Chinese in our samples nor members of any group such as the Hakka. Whether one would find significant differences in such groups cannot be resolved by our data.

It must be noted that the TATs taken in San Francisco show no significant differences among the women. They do show a trend for American Chinese men to reveal a greater concern with violence expressed outside family relations, with or without heterosexual content. Such stories appear more frequently in American records, suggesting some American acculturative influence on the San Francisco Chinese men. We have no sample from Canton to test whether or not this is indeed the case, however. We have no way of predicting from our results how the new generation of mainland Chinese has been influenced toward change. We would assume profound changes have occurred. But such speculation would take us far from our present purposes. Suffice it to say, we believe our empirical results compare Chinese and Japanese.

We would like to review briefly here, therefore, some general statements that have been made concerning childhood socialization among Chinese as they may inferentially contrast with what has been described by social scientists looking at childhood socialization in Japan. Richard Solomon (1971), summarizing previous works on early socialization, states that in traditional, pre-revolutionary China (in similar terms as described for Japan) in early infancy the child was given a great deal of affection and was indulged not only by his mother but also by other members of the family. However, the Chinese continually seem to emphasize food in nurturant behavior. Solomon points out how the basic sense of social well-being and security for the Chinese remains throughout life linked to the ritual of eating. This, perhaps, finds less emphasis in Japanese culture.

In other patterns related to child-rearing, one finds striking similarities. Both Chinese and Japanese, according to the available anthropological studies, are fairly permissive about toilet training. In both cultures, the mothers seem to anticipate the child's urination or bowel movements and create little issue about sanctioning expected behavior by any harsh measures.

However, there is a basic difference between what Solomon summarizes about child-rearing (which also appears in Margery Wolf's analysis of the Chinese family in Taiwan) and what has been reported by observers in Japan. Solomon states that there is recall about having been beaten with boards, whips, or rulers or having received other forms of physical punishment in the personal histories of those informants, principally from around Canton, which he interviewed. Wolf similarly reports for Taiwanese a readiness for mother and father to resort to some form of physical chastisement should the child be unruly or out of hand. In Japan, one finds that physical punishment is the exception rather than the rule with children. According to recent theories of moral development forwarded by American psychologists, moral internalization is more apt to occur when abandonment or a sense of causing suffering are used as sanctions. Internalization is less likely to result from attempts to exercise authority by the use of force. Respect for authority even in adults needs more external reinforcement.

The senior author has extensively written elsewhere (DeVos, 1973) about the influence of a mother's suffering and self-sacrifice in arousing a strong potential for guilt and a deep internalization of social directives among Japanese. Equally, Japanese paternalism depends on invoking a strong sense of dedication and responsibility among those in authority as well as in subordinates (DeVos, 1975). Solomon does not discuss how those assuming authority internalize a sense of responsibility in Chinese culture. One senses a basic difference between the two cultures in this respect. The Japanese manifest a much greater diffusion of social responsibility throughout the society. In contrast, one witnesses in the traditional culture, at least, a much greater limitation of responsibility to expression within the family among the Chinese. Although both cultures traditionally espouse an ideology of Confucian responsibility, its behavioral manifestation in China and Japan has been quite different. The Chinese have had considerable difficulty in inducing a sense of responsibility that extends beyond the family, whereas in Japan one notes the widespread establishment of familial-like secondary "voluntary" social groups through which Japanese are organized to collective social purpose. The Maoist revolution in China has been an attempt to rectify this limited sense of social responsibility by enforcing a radically different ideology which deemphasizes the family.

In contrast to Japanese results, one does not find in the Taiwanese materials any suggestion of the mother as a self-sacrificing individual.

We infer that, along with a greater tendency for the father at all ages to apply physical punishment to a potentially wayward child in Taiwan, one finds comparatively less emphasis on controlling a child through what is termed "moral masochism." There is less espousal of a virtue of suffering in Chinese families as compared with Japanese. Certainly, the TAT materials cited here are in line with a supposition that for Chinese endurance is a necessity, not a virtue.

Solomon describes evidence of resentment toward authority in China. However, the TAT materials produce no evidence that resentment is readily expressed within the family in Taiwan. There is no permitted expression of this theme even in fantasy. The Japanese, in contrast, are freer to describe how a push toward autonomy can result in conflict within the family. There is an admitted self-conscious concern about a need to resolve differences between the generations. This theme acknowledges that change is occurring in Japan. The unquestioned authority of parents has given way. We speculate that the Japanese today are freer to consider consciously the legitimacy of the personal initiative of youth. This topic seems to be as yet taboo among the Taiwanese. The Taiwanese do not permit themselves to consider personal autonomy as a legitimate concern in the context of primary family interaction. One gains, therefore, an impression of a conscious insistence on harmony and a tendency to give more stereotyped stories with less imaginative content even in considering forms of discord to be resolved in the interests of ultimate harmony. The Taiwanese seem to be more constricted about the free expression of either sexual concerns, on one hand, or problems of aggression or discord, on the other. The Japanese, in contrast, are more willing to imagine such problems as part of an individual's social life. He must come to grips and somehow resolve consciously his personal feelings to maintain proper social relations.

In general, the data suggest that there may be considerable difference between Japanese and Taiwanese mothers in the exercise of parental roles. The use of a high sense of dedication and internalization which involves, at times, a masochistic readiness to suffer virtuously is not a theme to be elicited from Chinese subjects; the concept of hard work is not put in terms of noble suffering and self-sacrifice. In effect, many Japanese women seem to have internalized such an ideal of dedication. The Chinese woman is also not seen as the sole or primary disciplinarian concerned with the ultimate achievement of her children. Nor is the Chinese woman as responsible for the success or failure of her offspring as is the Japanese woman. In some respects, therefore, the Chinese concept of the maternal role is, in psychological terms at least, more similar to Western patterns than is the Japanese.

The striking difference in consciousness of future time orientation in the two groups emphasizes Japanese preoccupation with internal motivation, whether it is in the explanation of behavior or the sense that behavior has to be monitored to see that it remains in line with future purpose. Whereas both groups emphasize hard work, the Japanese are continually alert to its social consequences. They seem to need to maintain a vigilance concerning self-control which is not apparent in the Taiwanese records.

Another striking difference is that the Taiwanese are matter-of-fact in their statements of individual behavior, whereas the Japanese are highly sensitive to matters of morality and responsibility. In many respects, the Japanese show a much greater concern about the need to internalize social directives and about guiding their own behavior as parents to be influential in the moral training of children. One could generalize this to say that the Japanese are more idealistic in orientation as compared with the rather concrete pragmatism evidenced by the Taiwanese in their stories. Certainly the TAT material allows for some speculation in this direction.

Physical fighting among children is frequently the cause of parental punishment among the Taiwanese. From what seems stated, however, there is less a question of who is right or wrong, but more a concern with the possibilities of disruptive social conflict (Wolf, 1972). The use of physical punishment is emphasized as a deterrent to the antagonistic behavior of children. Solomon, in analyzing his interview material, indicates that individuals learn to repress hostlity or aggressive feelings before father or elder brother, but can, without compunction, release such emotions when their siblings are weaker peers. Such a pattern is noticeable in Japan as well. However, the use of any physical aggression within the family is much less in evidence among Japanese.

In describing how a Chinese mother discourages dangerous social expression of aggression in extrafamilial social relationships, Solomon and Wolf show how the mother of the "naughty" aggressive child either beats her own child in the presence of the victim or promises to do so when she finds him in conflict with other children of the community. This is rather far removed from methods used by Japanese mothers. Instead of beating her own child, very often the Japanese mother will take the responsibility for the child's bad behavior and make a public apology. Therefore, in effect, the Japanese mother arouses considerably more guilt in the offending child than if he were simply subjected to physical punishment.

Socialization through emulation of behavior is a potent means of teaching the child. Solomon states that the Chinese child observes the way in which adults handle their own feelings in external community life by preserving an emotional impassiveness. Thus, they learn to discipline their inner impulses by emulating the impassivity of their elders. Solomon does not, perhaps, sufficiently stress the inconsistency of using physical punishment within the family coupled with the necessity to express impassivity in external hierarchical relationships. One cannot easily accept the idea that the threat of physical punishment leads simply to impassivity. It is more likely that it leads to some tendency to rebellion, given the opporunity presented by weak or ineffectual leadership, a fear that the Chinese continually express in political attitudes. Conversely, the Japanese are not afraid of having a rather passive leader, as it is less likely that subordinates will be rebellious should the leader seem passive or ineffectual. The sense of dedication to group activities so apparent among the Japanese allows subordinates initiative when leadership is passive. The initiative is not in terms of potential rebellion but through a sense of loyalty to the cause which one has joined, and to which one has committed oneself with permanent adherence to a given group.

In sum, there is a major difference apparent in childhood socialization between Chinese and Japanese in relation to authority. In the Japanese family, the mother is the mediator between the father and the son, and direct conflicts are less apt to appear, for it is the mother's responsibility to see that the discipline of the child results in proper behavior in the name of the father and his line.

The direct assertion of discipline on the part of the father is far more in evidence among the Taiwanese. Curiously, in the Taiwanese projective materials, we find little capacity to express openly any sense of resentment. We infer a severely exercised taboo against any anti-Confucian sentiment. The Japanese are more ready to represent discord and opinions and desires within the primary family, which means that they are more ready to cope with them and to see them as less threatening to satisfactory harmony. The Japanese, in this sense, are optimistic that conflict can be resolved, rather than finding it necessary to bury it and pretend that it does not exist.

A further question one may ask, in terms of individuals exercising authority, is whether the Japanese have a relatively greater proneness to live up to the expectations of their subordinates, not only in the immediate family but also in the external occupational or governmental world. There are, from the psychological perspective, limitations on authority. The Japanese think, as part of dedication to role, that they must act responsibly, and therefore they are more apt to feel constrained to meet the expectations of dependency on the part of subordinates. One gains the impression from the literature, at least, that the Chinese tend to be harsher in the exercise of traditional authority relationships. The beating of subordinates did appear in the brutal Japanese army. However, this sort of behavior was most unusual. Generally, Japanese seem to have maintained considerable respect for political and administrative authority. This respect is gained, in good part, by the relative honesty of administrators, which goes back to the sense of dedication found in many administrative officials, both traditional and modern (Craig and Shively, 1970).

In closing, we must note that the TAT material did not tap many important areas of interpersonal life in Japanese and Taiwanese cultures. For example, information about self-esteem, sensitivity to "face," or deference behavior is poorly represented in our findings. However, we do believe that we have succeeded in outlining several tentative points of psychocultural difference between the two cultures. Finally, we believe that the TAT method has demonstrated its value as one useful basis for comparison of Japanese culture with other societies.

TABLE 1

BASIC THEMATIC CONCERNS IN HUMAN RELATIONS

Thematic Concerns	Positive (Socially Sanctioned)		Negative (Socially Unsanctioned)	
	Active initiated and/or resolved	Passive or unresolved	Active, initiated and/or resolved	Passive, withdrawal and/or resolution
INSTRUMENTAL BEHAVIOR				
Achievement (will do) internalized goals (S)	Goal-oriented activity	Internal conflict, over-commitment, role diffusion, daydreaming	Goal-oriented criminal activity	Anomic withdrawal, alienation from social goals
Competence (can do) internalized standards of excellence (S)	Avowal of capacity	Doubt about capacity, worry, diffuse anxiety, chagrin	Failure due to personal inadequacy	Sense of incapacity and inadequacy
Responsibility (ought to do) internalized moral standards and controls (S)	Sense of duty, assumption of obligation *Some forms of "altruistic" suicide**	Remorse, guilt, regrets over acts of commission or omission	Profligacy, irresponsibility	Avoidance, escape *Some forms of "anomic" suicide**
Control-Power (must do) external power *superordinate:* (V)	Legitimate authority, power—mastery, persuasion	Defensive insecurity	Authoritarian dominance, security, control through destruction of feared object	Failure to assert proper authority (spineless, gutless)
subordinate: (V)	Liberation, autonomy or compliance	Ambivalence about authority or power	Rebellion, trickery	Submission
Mutuality (with or against) interpersonal ethics *competitive:* (H)	Regulated competition, games, contests	Envy	Unethical competitive behavior	Capitulation, withdrawal from competitive situation
cooperative: (H)	Concerted behavior (mutual trust)	Distrust, disagreement	Plotting, deception of a cohort	Sense of betrayal

TABLE 1 *(Continued)*

Thematic Concerns	Positive (Socially Sanctioned)		Negative (Socially Sanctioned)	
	Active, initiated and/or resolved	Passive or unresolved	Active, initiated and/or resolved	Passive withdrawal and/or resolution
		Passive or Indeterminate		

	EXPRESSIVE BEHAVIOR			
Harmony (with, emotionally) (H-V)	Harmony, peaceful relationships	Jealousy, fear of threat, emotional discord	Violence, injury, revenge *Some "egocentric" suicides**	Withdrawal into hostility and resentment
Affiliation (toward someone) (H)	Affiliation, intimacy, union, re- sponsiveness, contact	Isolation, loneliness, alienation	Rejection of another	Sense of loss due to rejection or separation *Some "egoistic" suicides**
Nurturance (for someone) (V)	Nurturance, care, help, comfort, succor	Dependency	Withholding	Sense of per- sonal, social, or economic deprivation *Some "egocen- tric" suicides**
Appreciation (from someone) *others:* (H-V)	Recognition of achieved or ascribed status	Feeling ignored, neglected, un- appreciated	Disdain, dis- paragement	Sense of degradation *Some "egotistic" suicides**
self: (S)	Self-respect	Doubt about worth, sense of shame	Self-abasement, self- depreciation	Sense of worth- lessness *Some "egotistic" suicides**
Pleasure (within oneself) self-expression (S)	Satisfaction, sense of curiosity or creativity, enjoyment	Indifference, boredom	Masochistic behavior, asceticism	Suffering

	FATE			
Fortune Health, social, economic conditions	Good luck; fortunate circumstances	Anxiety over environ- mental or health conditions	Bad fortune, accident, injury, bad economic cir- cumstances	Handicap, illness, death

NOTE: In each category the relationship between actor and others changes relative to the ob-. server's perspective in the thematic concerns. Some categories are actor initiated, and some are actor responsive. There are internalized concerns (self-oriented) coded (S) and other-oriented themes concerned either with horizontal interactions coded (H) or vertical interactions coded (V).

* For explanation of types of suicide, see chapter 17 of DeVos 1973.

TABLE 2

SELECTED THEMES ON CARD 1

	Japanese			*Taiwanese*			*Significance* Chi-Square (Yates)		
	Mo	Fa	Tot	Mo	Fa	Tot			
Total N =	(19)	(17)	(36)	(52)	(48)	(100)			
Total achievement themes (including future role acquisition independent of means-ends considerations: e.g., practice, study)	17 89%	11 65%	28 78%	36 69%	32 67%	68 68%	JMo — TMo	(n.s.)	P .250
Total achievement (not including future role acquisition independent of means-ends considerations)	17 89%	10 59%	27 75%	31 60%	23 48%	54 54%	JMo — TMo JFa — TFa Ja — Tai Mo — Fa	(n.s.) (n.s.)	P .050 P .500 P .050 P .100
Stories where individual is described in goal-oriented behavior, overcoming difficulties (incapacity concerns, misfortune, deprivation, suffering) that stand in his way, and reaching some positive long-term goal	9 47%	7 41%	16 44%	8 15%	5 5%	13 13%	JMo — TMo JFa — TFa Ja — Tai		P .001 P .025 P .001
Negative capacity themes (incapacity, doubt about capacity, worry over capacity)	10 53%	9 53%	19 53%	10 19%	9 19%	19 19%	JMo — TMo JFa — TFa Ja — Tai		P .025 P .025 P .001
Role acquisition themes without means-ends themes	0 0%	1 6%	1 3%	6 12%	9 19%	15 15%	JMo — TMo JFa — TFa Ja — Tai	(n.s.) (n.s.) (n.s.)	P .500 P .500 P .100

NOTE: n.s. = not statistically significant.

TABLE 3

SELECTED THEMES ON CARD 2

	Japanese			Taiwanese			Significance	
	Mo	Fa	Tot	Mo	Fa	Tot	Chi-Square (Yates)	
Total N =	(19)	(17)	(36)	(51)	(51)	(102)		
Stories involving discord between child and parent (or parent substitute, e.g. grandmother)	6 32%	2 12%	8 22%	1 2%	3 6%	4 4%	JMo — TMo Ja — Tai	P .005 P .005
Stories involving not only parent-child discord, but also parent-child difference of opinion, occupational dislike, desire to pursue a task different from parents	14 74%	5 29%	19 53%	2 4%	6 12%	8 8%	JMo — TMo JFa — TFa (n.s.) Ja — Tai JMo — JFa	P .001 P .250 P .001 P .025
Stories where autonomy on the part of the child is an issue or causes some interpersonal disruption, as described in the two foregoing categories	13 68%	5 29%	18 50%	0 0%	4 8%	4 4%	JMo — TMo JFa — TFa (n.s.) Ja — Tai JMo — JFa	P .001 P .100 P .001 P .050
Stories where parental control of children is an issue	7 37%	2 12%	9 25%	1 2%	1 2%	2 2%	JMo — TMo Ja — Tai	P .001 P .001
Stories simply describing ordinary work or general activity (affectively flat)	0 0%	0 0%	0 0%	11 22%	6 12%	17 17%	JMo — TMo (n.s.) JFa — TFa (n.s.) Ja — Tai	P .100 P .500 P .025

TABLE 4

SELECTED THEMES ON CARD 3

	Japanese			Taiwanese			Significance Chi-Square (Yates)		
	Mo	Fa	Tot	Mo	Fa	Tot			
Total N =	(19)	(17)	(36)	(53)	(48)	(101)			
Stories suggesting parent-child relationship	7 37%	5 29%	12 33%	5 9%	4 8%	9 9%	JMo — TMo JFa — TFa (n.s.) Ja — Tai		P .025 P .100 P .005
Parent-child stories where parental control of child is an issue	6 32%	3 18%	9 25%	1 2%	1 2%	2 2%	JMo — TMo JFa — TFa (n.s.) Ja — Tai		P .001 P .001
Stories where child's moral behavior is influenced by the social or interpersonal world	5 26%	3 18%	8 22%	1 2%	0 0%	1 1%	JMo — TMo JFa — TFa (n.s.) Ja — Tai		P .005 P .001
Stories containing some sleep theme	10 53%	4 24%	14 39%	22 42%	12 25%	34 34%	JMo — JFa (n.s.) TMo — TFa (n.s.) Mo — Fa (n.s.)		
Stories containing some suffering theme	7 37%	11 65%	18 50%	20 39%	33 69%	53 53%	JMo — JFa (n.s.) TMo — TFa (n.s.) Mo — Fa (n.s.)		
Suffering with no long-term future or cause	1 5%	0 0%	1 3%	10 19%	12 25%	22 22%	JMo — TMo (n.s.) JFa — TFa (n.s.) Ja — Tai		P .100 P .025
Suffering with cause and long-term future concerns	2 11%	5 29%	7 19%	1 2%	0 0%	1 1%	JFa — TFa Ja — Tai		P .001 P .001
Stories suggesting long-term future concerns	9 47%	10 59%	19 53%	3 6%	0 0%	3 3%	JMo — TMo JFa — TFa Ja — Tai		P .001 P .001 P .001
Stories with no long-term future or antecedent cause	3 16%	1 6%	4 11%	19 36%	18 38%	37 37%	JMo — TMo (n.s.) JFa — TFa Ja — Tai		P .250 P .050 P .010
Stories without interpersonal content (Note: Child playing, someone being stabbed, and someone doing something wrong and regretting it, are all considered interpersonal and are excluded from this category)	3 16%	2 12%	5 14%	34 64%	21 44%	55 55%	JMo — TMo JFa — TFa Ja — Tai		P .001 P .050 P .001

TABLE 5

SELECTED THEMES ON CARD 6

	Japanese			Taiwanese			Significance Chi-Square (Yates)	
	Mo	Fa	Tot	Mo	Fa	Tot		
Total N =	(19)	(17)	(36)	(53)	(47)	(100)		
Stories describing mother-son interaction	17 89%	14 82%	31 86%	43 81%	41 87%	84 84%		
Stories describing conflict or discord	11 58%	12 71%	23 64%	27 51%	18 38%	45 45%	JFa — TFa Ja — Tai	P .050 P .050
Stories where conflict is resolved or ended on positive note	6 32%	6 35%	12 33%	1 2%	2 4%	3 3%	JMo — TMo JFa — TFa Ja — Tai	P .001 P .005 P .001
Stories where autonomy of child is an issue	3 16%	7 41%	10 28%	1 2%	1 2%	2 2%	JFa — TFa Ja — Tai	P .001 P .001
Stories where mother is seen as actively dominating son	7 37%	1 6%	8 22%	8 15%	10 21%	18 18%	JMo — TMo (n.s.) P .100 JFa — TFa (n.s.) P .500 Ja — Tai (n.s.) P .500	
Stories where son is suffering due to his mother's refusal or rejection				13 25%	2 4%	15 100%	TMo — TFa	P .025
Stories where son is seen as regretful or apologetic to mother				2 4%	8 17%	10 10%	TMo — TFa (n.s.) P .100	
Stories where son is seen as asking mother for something physically tangible (e.g., money)	1 5%	1 6%	2 6%	7 13%	8 17%	15 15%	JMo — TMo (n.s.) P .500 JFa — TFa (n.s.) P .500 Ja — Tai (n.s.) P .250	
Stories where son is seen as asking mother for something psychologically tangible (e.g., permission, advice)	1 5%	1 6%	2 6%	5 9%	4 9%	9 9%		
Total stories where son asks mother for something physically or psychologically tangible	2 11%	2 12%	4 11%	12 23%	12 26%	24 24%	JMo — TMo (n.s.) P .500 JFa — TFa (n.s.) P .500 Ja — Tai (n.s.) P .250	

TABLE 6

SELECTED THEMES ON CARD 7

	Japanese			Taiwanese			Significance		
	Mo	Fa	Tot	Mo	Fa	Tot	Chi-Square (Yates)		
Total N =	(19)	(17)	(36)	(53)	(50)	(103)			
Fa-son hierarchy themes	6	6	12	13	13	26			
	32%	35%	33%	25%	26%	25%			
Fa-son horizontal themes	1	2	3	17	5	22	JMo — TMo		P .050
	5%	12%	8%	32%	10%	21%	Ja — Tai	(n.s.)	P .250
Total fa-son themes	7	8	15	30	18	48	JMo — TMo	(n.s.)	P .100
	37%	47%	42%	57%	36%	47%			
Nonfamilial hierarchy roles (scholar-pupil, boss-employee, etc.)	6	2	8	0	8	8	JMo — TMo		P .001
	32%	12%	22%	0%	16%	8%	Ja — Tai		P .010
Elder-younger (older-younger)	3	1	4	5	9	14			
	16%	6%	11%	9%	18%	14%			
Unspecified hierarchical relationship	1	0	1	0	2	2			
	5%	0%	3%	0%	4%	2%			
Friends (horizontal)	1	1	2	2	1	3			
	5%	6%	6%	4%	2%	3%			
Other role (horizontal)	0	4	4	3	1	4	JFa — TFa		P .025
	0%	21%	11%	6%	2%	4%			
Unspecified (horizontal)	0	0	0	11	10	21	JMo — TMo	(n.s.)	P .100
	0%	0%	0%	21%	20%	20%	JFa — TFa	(n.s.)	P .250
							Ja — Tai		P .025
Total (including fa-son total through unspecified horizontal)	18	16	34	51	49	100			
Total hierarchy responses	16	19	25	18	32	50	JMo — TMo		P .001
	84%	53%	69%	34%	64%	49%	Ja — Tai		P .050
Total horizontal responses	2	7	9	33	17	50	JMo — TMo		P .001
	11%	37%	25%	62%	34%	49%	Ja — Tai		P .010
Stories where the individuals are simply described as thinking or talking about something (vague)	2	1	3	27	18	45	JMo — TMo		P .001
	11%	6%	8%	51%	36%	45%	JFa — TFa		P .001
							Ja — Tai		P .001
							TMo — TFa	(n.s.)	P .010
Stories describing parental advice, or parental-like advice, persuasion, or teaching in relationship to son's or sons' or son-surrogates' "socially troublesome behavior"	4	4	8	2	5	7	Ja — Tai		P .025
	21%	24%	22%	4%	10%	7%			

TABLE 6 *(Continued)*

	Japanese			Taiwanese			Significance
	Mo	Fa	Tot	Mo	Fa	Tot	Chi-Square (Yates)
Total N =	(19)	(17)	(36)	(53)	(50)	(103)	
Stories with positive tone or ending	8 42%	11 65%	19 53%	12 23%	14 28%	26 25%	JMo — TMo (n.s.) P .250 / JFa — TFa P .025 / Ja — Tai P .005
Stories describing the younger male as self-motivated (usually son or son-surrogate)	8 42%	10 59%	18 50%	9 17%	5 10%	14 14%	JMo — TMo P .100 / JFa — TMo P .001 / Ja — Tai P .001
Stories describing son or son-surrogate as passive vis-à-vis parental or parental-like nurturance, dominance, etc.	2 11%	2 12%	4 11%	11 21%	23 46%	34 33%	JMo — TMo (n.s.) P .500 / JFa — TFa P .050 / Ja — Tai P .010

TABLE 7

SELECTED THEMES ON CARD 13

	Japanese			Taiwanese			Significance
	Mo	Fa	Tot	Mo	Fa	Tot	Chi-Square (Yates)
Total N =	(19)	(17)	(36)	(53)	(49)	(102)	
Stories of a woman as the cause of or initiator of sexual self-indulgence	4 21%	9 53%	13 36%	4 8%	2 4%	6 6%	JMo — TMo (n.s.) / JFa — TFa P .001 / Ja — Tai P .001 / JMo — JFa (n.s.) P .250
Stories describing woman's negative responsibility, emphasized independently from the males (many of these cards are also double-scored as sexual self-indulgence)	7 37%	11 65%	18 50%	4 8%	2 4%	6 6%	JMo — TMo P .010 / JFa — TFa P .001 / Ja — Tai P .001 / JMO — JFa (n.s.)
Stories of sadness or suffering over someone sick or dead	3 16%	1 6%	4 11%	23 43%	17 35%	40 39%	JMo — TMo (n.s.) P .100 / JFa — TFa P .050 / Ja — Tai P .005
Stories containing long-term future concerns	7 37%	11 65%	18 50%	3 6%	1 2%	4 4%	JMo — TMo P .005 / JFa — TFa P .001 / Ja — Tai P .001
Stories describing a wife's negative responsibility, emphasized independently from husband (many of these stories are doublescored both as sexual self-indulgence and woman's negative responsibility)	3 16%	5 29%	8 22%	0 0%	0 0%	0 0%	JMo — TMo (n.s.) / JFa — TFa P .001 / Ja — Tai P .001

TABLE 8

SELECTED THEMES ON CARD 18

	Japanese			Chinese Taiwanese			Significance Chi-Square (Yates)		
	Mo	Fa	Tot	Mo	Fa	Tot			
Total N =	(19)	(17)	(36)	(52)	(48)	(100)			
Stories containing violence of some sort	15 79%	10 59%	25 69%	7 13%	7 15%	14 14%	JMo — TMo JFa — TFa Ja — Tai		P .001 P .005 P .001
Breakdown of the stories containing violence									
Mo to fa	9 47%	5 29%	14 39%	1 2%	2 4%	3 3%	JMo — TMo JFa — TFa Ja — Tai		P .001 P .025 P .001
Mo to son	2	1	3	0	1	1			
Wife to husb	1	1	2	2	0	2			
Unspecified female to male	0	1	1	2	0	2			
other	3	2	5	2	4	6			
Total	15	10	25	7	7	14			
Total stories with mother to child violence	11 58%	6 35%	17 48%	1 2%	3 6%	4 4%	JMo — TMo JFa — TFa Ja — Tai JMo — JFa	(n.s.)	P .001 P .025 P .001 P .500
Total stories with discord without violence	1 5%	4 23%	5 14%	2 4%	2 4%	4 4%			
Total of stories containing either violence or discord or both	16 84%	14 82%	30 83%	9 17%	9 19%	18 18%	JMo — TMo JFa — TFa Ja — Tai		P .001 P .001 P .001
Husband and wife conflict (discord and/or violence)	3 16%	6 35%	9 25%	2 4%	1 2%	3 3%	JFa — TFa Ja — Tai		P .001 P .001
Husband indulgence related to conflict	2 11%	4 24%	6 17%	1 2%	0 0%	1 1%	JFa — TFa Ja — Tai		P .005 P .005
Stories where daughter's self-indulgence results in violence on the part of the mother	5 26%	3 18%	8 22%	0 0%	0 0%	0 0%	JMo — TMo Ja — Tai		P .001 P .001
Stories where son's self-indulgence results in violence on the part of the mother	2 11%	1 6%	3 8%	0 0%	1 2%	1 1%			

268

TABLE 8 (Continued)

	Japanese			Chinese Taiwanese			Significance Chi-Square (Yates)		
	Mo	Fa	Tot	Mo	Fa	Tot			
Total N =	(19)	(17)	(36)	(52)	(48)	(100)			
Total parental violence induced by child's self-indulgence	7 37%	4 26%	11 31%	0 0%	1 2%	1 1%	JMo — TMo Ja — Tai		P .001 P .001
Stories where parent-child discord, without violence, is induced by a child's self-indulgence	0 0%	1 6%	1 3%	1 2%	0 0%	1 1%			
Total parent-child conflict induced by child's self-indulgence (total of all above)	7 37%	5 29%	12 33%	1 2%	1 2%	2 2%	JMo — TMo JFa — TFa Ja — Tai		P .001 P .005 P .001
Nurturance as a response to misfortune or accident	0 0%	0 0%	0 0%	10 20%	10 20%	20 20%	JMo — TMo JFa — TFa Ja — Tai	(n.s.) (n.s.)	P .250 P .250 P .025
Nurturance as a response to illness	0 0%	0 0%	0 0%	13 25%	17 35%	30 30%	JMo — TMo JFa — TFa Ja — Tai	(n.s.)	P .100 P .050 P .005
Other nurturance	3 16%	0 0%	3 8%	2 4%	5 10%	7 7%			
Total nurturance	3 16%	0 0%	3 8%	25 48%	32 67%	57 57%	JMo — TMo JFa — TFa Ja — Tai		P .050 P .001 P .001

IV

ECONOMY AND SOCIETY

The three essays in Part Four are by an economist, a sociologist, and an anthropologist. They illustrate the methodological variety within the social sciences. They also cover the sweep of Japan's modern economy: from the establishment of the pre-conditions for industrialization during the Tokugawa period to the pattern of the industrialization during the modern era to an analysis of human relations within small industries during the early postwar years.

Kozo Yamamura's essay explains the changes in the landholding systems of England and Japan that prepared the way for their respective industrializations. Looking at England between 1500 and 1760 and Japan between 1600 and 1867, he finds parallel developments: concentration of landholding, increases in productivity, the development of landless wage laborers, and the emergence of a class of rural well-to-do with an eye for profitable investments. The question he poses, in effect, is how such similar pre-conditions could emerge within such different socio-political systems.

While answering this question, Yamamura is also testing a "rational man" theory of institutional change. As "men's actions are motivated by a desire for increased gain," he argues, the institutions that evolve under given historical conditions will be those that best satisfy this desire. In reading Yamamura's essay one should keep in mind what he is trying to do and what he is not. Orthodox economics has generated powerful theories by assuming that man knows best his own advantage and acts according to it. These theories tend to ignore institutions. The theory that Yamamura tests extends the rational man hypothesis to institutions. Yamamura does not argue that man is totally rational; he claims only that we can extend our understanding of the formation of economic institutions by assuming that he is. Moreover, Yamamura is concerned to demonstrate that the same assumption works equally well in Japan and England.

Ronald Dore picks up chronologically where Yamamura leaves off. He treats the employment system of modern Japanese industry. In several ways Dore's essay would appear to differ from the other essays in this volume. Most are making initial comparisons. They take two cases, examine them in as detailed a fashion as space and method per-

mit, and then draw conclusions. Whether the conclusions are formalized as propositions or are merely put forth as descriptive comparisons, they at least implicitly contain propositions. Close to the
richness of the sources, they may be called proposition-generating
studies. Dore, in contrast, generated his propositions in his earlier
book, *British Factory, Japanese Factory* (1973), in which he contended
that the basic pattern of industrial relations in the Japanese factory
was different from the English not because of the peculiarities of
Japanese culture, character, or traditional society, but because Japan
was a late-developer. (Note here that just as Yamamura does not say
that men are totally rational, so Dore does not claim that the Japanese
employment system can be completely explained by the "late-development effect," just that it covers some of the causal factors involved.)

Dore's essay begins as a proposition-testing study. He applies the
hypothesis of a late-development effect to three other late-developers:
Sri Lanka, Mexico, and Senegal. He asks whether the employment
systems of their modern sectors, as his theory would suggest, are like
that of Japan. He finds some evidence to confirm his earlier hypotheses.
But he also finds differences. Perhaps the most interesting part is his
discussion of the provenance of these differences: the role of the state,
of culture, of incoming waves of ideas, and of the position of Japan in
history as an "early case of late-development." In sum, with rich data
on the three cases being studied in the light of his Japanese findings,
what began as proposition-testing becomes, inescapably, proposition-
generating as well.

The conference from which this book developed brought together
scholars from different disciplines and with a diversity of comparative
approaches. Unlike single-discipline conferences, where common assumptions often make for somewhat dull and routine discussions, this
diversity gave rise to lively debates. Yet no essay elicited a more enthusiastic discussion than that of John Pelzel. Pelzel began his research
in industrial anthropology by looking at small and medium sized
metal-working factories in Japan during the early fifties. Studying the
human relations of the shop, he was struck by the ubiquity of a certain
personality type and of the re-creation of this type through the system
of apprenticeship—which he found continuing even in one or another
modern guises. Listening to Pelzel describe apprenticeship, Doi ex-
claimed, "that is how doctors are formed in Japan," and others responded that it was also how graduate students really were trained in
both Japan and the United States. Having generated his propositions
from the Japanese case, Pelzel tests them against data from contemporary China. He also presents data showing the continuing impor-

tance of the small and medium-sized factory within the most modern economies. One conclusion he reaches is that in the shift from artisanal production to modern industry there are countervailing trends to the dehumanization of man by the machine. His evidence for these trends reads at times almost like passages from a novel.

Pre-Industrial Landholding
Patterns in
Japan and England*

→》《←

KOZO YAMAMURA

This chapter is a comparative analysis of landholding patterns (distribution of ownership) and systems (contractual arrangements) in pre-industrial Japan and England. As the promise of such an analysis is great, so are the difficulties. Such an examination can indeed be a rewarding comparison of the two historical paths traced by the two island nations that were the first to industrialize in their hemispheres. Because landholding patterns and systems are products of history, however, a comparative analysis runs a high risk of being caught in the web of history: a supposed comparative analysis could readily be reduced to no more than a parallel examination of two landholding systems, one affected by the Tudor monarchs and the other by the Tokugawa shogun, by the decisions of Ireton and by Ii, or by the prosperous gentry and the *gōnō* (wealthy landholding farmers).

The only means by which to reduce this risk is to employ an analytical framework capable of accounting for as many as possible of the factors affecting the landholding pattern and system. My tools of analysis shall be those applied by recent researchers to a wide range of institutions and developments in European and American economic history, that is, economic theory and the theory of institutional change based on economic theory.[1]

Although the strengths and limitations of modern (as against Marx-

* The author would like to express his gratitude for the criticism and extended discussion which this paper received from professors Albert M. Craig, Marius Jansen, Ōuchi Tsutomu, and the other participants at the Cuernavaca conference. The views expressed and the errors contained in this paper, however, are chargeable only to the author.

[1] The most influential of the literature that inspired or assisted in my analysis are L. E. Davis and D. C. North, *Institutional Change and American Economic Growth* (London and New York: Cambridge University Press, 1971); D. C. North and R. P. Thomas, *The Growth of the Western World* (London and New York: Cambridge University Press, 1973); A. A. Alchian and H. Demsetz, "Production, Information Costs, and Economic Organization," *American Economic Review* 62 (Dec. 1972); and S. N. S. Cheung, *The Theory of Share Tenancy* (Chicago: University of Chicago Press, 1969).

ian) economic theory are well known, the theory of institutional change is of recent vintage and requires a brief introduction. The meaning of *institution* is wide and includes constitutions, arrangements concerning property rights and contracts, numerous economic institutions and social conventions, and unwritten customs which evolved or were adopted to assure the working of an economy. Or, in the words of Davis and North, an institutional arrangement is:

"An arrangement between economic units that governs the ways in which these units can cooperate and/or compete. The institutional arrangement is probably the closest counterpart of the most popular use of the term 'institution.' The arrangement may be temporary or long-lived. It must, however, be designed to accomplish *at least* one of the following goals: to provide a structure within which its members can cooperate to obtain some added income that is not available outside the structure; or provide a mechanism that can effect a change in laws or property rights designed to alter the permissible ways that individuals (or groups) can legally compete."[2]

To put it concisely, the theory of institutional change states that institutional changes take place when someone or some group decides that the expected costs of changing an institutional arrangement are less than the expected benefits to be derived by changing the institution, so it pays the person or group to create a new institutional arrangement. In most instances, such innovations are designed to capture income which failed to be internalized (captured) within the existing institutional arrangements, and they typically include potential gains arising out of externalities, economies of scale, reductions in transactions costs, and new methods of dealing with risks.

Furthermore, the theory states that the speed with which an institu-

[2] Davis and North, *Institutional Change*, p. 7. In the following paragraphs, externalities refer to the gains (or losses) one realizes outside of the usual market and price mechanisms, such as an increased property value enjoyed thanks to a neighbor's investment of time and money in his garden or an ally's military protection extended at no cost for the reasons of a shared ideology. Economies of scale simply refer to the reduction in the unit costs because a good or service is provided at a larger scale. A typical example is a national defense system in contrast to individual efforts to cope against aggressors. Transactions costs are the costs of conducting business (including making contractual agreements), and they usually include the cost of obtaining necessary information about prices and potential markets, the cost of enforcing contracts or other business obligations, and the cost of negotiation (time and money) which can be high when relevant information is scarce and/or enforcement procedures are not well established. Dealing with risks can mean reducing risks by some joint arrangement, making risks insurable, or redistributing risks in such a way to benefit some or all parties without making anyone worse off. An insurance company is an example of such an institutional arrangement. For a much fuller discussion of these factors as relating to the changes in institutional arrangements, see Davis and North, *Institutional Change*, pp. 10-38.

tional arrangement is changed depends on the size and heterogeneity of the individual interests involved, the possible magnitude of gains from creating a new institution or of losses for not doing so, and the number of new alternative institutional arrangements which could accomplish the desired end. That is, when the individuals concerned are large in number and heterogeneous (in interests as well as in other relevant characteristics such as location or linguistic barriers), and when the possible gains to be realized by an institutional arrangement are relatively small and can be accomplished by one of the several methods, an institutional change is expected to occur extremely slowly or perhaps not at all. In the opposite case, an institutional change will be accomplished rapidly. The rate at which an institution changes is thus determined by various configurations of these characteristics.

The strength of the theory of institutional change is fourfold. First, the theory provides a general framework which is useful in analyzing historical changes in economic and political institutions with which economic historians are usually concerned, but about which economic theory is of not direct use. As the theory of institutional change enables analysis akin to a general equilibrium analysis, most of the relevant data can be examined under a unified theoretical umbrella and their interrelationships theoretically specified.

Second, as is expected of any theory, this theory too is useful in suggesting questions whose answers have universalistic rather than particularistic significance. A theory such as this, which is capable of suggesting hypotheses testable across temporal and spatial confines, is essential for comparative analysis.

Third, the theory is useful in predicting whether an established institution, when faced with a new disequilibrating force, will be transformed by a single decision-maker either depending on some form of voluntary cooperation or requiring the coercive power of government. Failure to obtain the predicted results will suggest either that some external consideration outside the theoretical framework is at work and dominating, or even that the theory is deficient in analyzing some set of institutional changes.

And, fourth, the theory is especially useful in dealing with a historical period for which quantitative data are either virtually nonexistent or obtainable only in limited quantity and insufficient to carry out hypothesis-testing. Given the nature of the theory, most hypotheses suggested by it can be tested by qualitative and/or limited quantitative evidence normally obtainable in existing historical descriptions.

What are the weaknesses of the theory? Many historians may consider, as a few already have done in print, that the basic assumption of the theory—men's actions are motivated by their desire for increased gain—is not acceptable in analyzing historical changes in institutions.[3] One response to the criticism follows:

"Clearly there were many institutions founded for non-economic reasons, and equally human behavior was frequently motivated by other human drives. Yet it is difficult to counter the argument that those institutions, whatever their goals, that were economically most efficient survived. Few persons and no institutions ever escape the 'scarcity' problem—all are continually faced with financial constraints. The ultimate test is whether the model we have developed is better fit to the historical evidence than other alternatives; not whether it totally explains each event. No scientific models—not even those in the physical sciences—do that."[4]

Another way of responding to the criticism is to present a case study, that is, to demonstrate the usefulness of the theory in a particular instance. If done well, this could minimize the disagreement that is bound to arise between its proponents and opponents in trying to determine whether or not a specific change in an institutional arrangement was due mostly to economic or to non-economic causes. Thus, a case study which could be useful in responding to the criticism of the basic assumption involved must present as much historical evidence as necessary to support the analysis.[5]

[3] A criticism of the theory of institutional change is found in D. R. Ringrose, "European Economic Growth: Comments on the North-Thomas Theory," *Economic History Review*, vol. 26, no. 2 (May 1973), pp. 285-292. For a sound and constructive evaluation of the theory, see A. S. Eichner's review of Davis and North's *Institutional Change* in *Business History Review*, vol. 46, no. 2 (summer 1972), pp. 326-329.

[4] D. C. North and R. P. Thomas, "Reply to Professor D. Ringrose," *Economic History Review*, 2nd ser., vol. 26, no. 2 (May 1973), pp. 293-294.

[5] I am under no illusion that such disagreements can be completely eliminated. The theory adopted here contributes significantly to explaining changes in economic institutional arrangements. However, the theory is most useful when applied against a generally determinate mix of the sociopolitical and cultural framework. That is, because these frameworks change over time and differ by region in complex ways, and because there are as yet no promising theories explaining the feedback relationships between economic motivations and the multi-faceted realities of these frameworks, one must not overstate the usefulness of the theory in discussing the reasons for economic institutional changes over centuries and across geographical boundaries. Another way of stating this caveat is that if one is to be faithful to what one learns from history, one must realize that men make many decisions which fall between the economically most rational and those which doom them to failure. This latitude could be much wider than the theory implies. However, to adopt a specific theory is to choose the rigor of analysis on a narrower range of questions over a more comprehensive analysis of wide-ranging questions, which is more satisfying in a different way. No one escapes this cost-benefit regimen; the four claims made for the theory earlier need to be and should be accepted only as relative statements stressing the benefits of the theoretical framework which I have chosen.

This essay, assisted by these theories, can help to answer several important questions in the comparative economic history of the two successful industrializers. What relationships existed, if any, in pre-industrial Japan and England between their respective landholding patterns and systems and their successful industrialization? Were the relationships similar and, if so, did they provide essential ingredients for industrialization (capital, increasing agricultural productivity, entrepreneurial talents) in a similar fashion? Were there similarities in the combination and relative importance of the factors defining and changing the landholding patterns and systems in each nation? Or, how much of the landholding patterns and systems of each nation, at a given time and their change over time, can be explained in economic terms, and how much must be explained by non-economic factors, and thus are not comparable within the analytical framework used in this essay?

These are only a few examples of major questions, and there is a host of others. Pre-industrial England, with its parliament, international trade, low interest rate, relative interclass mobility, and other seemingly unique characteristics compared with Tokugawa Japan—closed to the outside world, with its *Bakuhan* system, a rigid class structure, and rice paddies—raises for the economic historian more questions than he can hope to answer. The task of this essay is to begin to answer some of the questions.

This essay compares Tokugawa Japan (1600-1867) and England between 1500 and 1760. Each period generally covers the "pre-industrial" stage of that nation. Although the well-defined Tokugawa period is convenient, I shall begin the discussion with the conditions prevailing during the mid-sixteenth century, as they are crucial in understanding the significance and consequences of the cadastral surveys which were begun by Hideyoshi in the 1580's. That is, Tokugawa Japan is my central concern, but this shall not limit my examination to that period.

The choice of the period for England is arbitrary; approximately the same number of years as used for Japan was counted backward from 1760, the date frequently chosen to mark the beginning of the Industrial Revolution. The beginning date, 1500, is, however, a fortunate selection because it is useful in depicting the changeover from the medieval landholding pattern and system to those associated with pre-industrial England. Since the landholding pattern and system changed only slowly during the eighteenth century, 1760 could be easily changed to 1780 or even 1800 without affecting the content of the comparative analysis.

Finally, a few paragraphs should be added at this point on the precise meaning of "comparative" analysis as used in this essay and the organization and limitations of this essay. As is evident in the nature of the theoretical framework adopted, the intent of this paper is neither to ask why England and not other European nations or why Japan and not other Asian nations industrialized first in their respective parts of the world, nor to examine, à la any one of the family of stage theories, whether Japan by the end of the Tokugawa period had reached the "stage" which England had attained by the mid-seventeenth century. Rather, the central question is, taking the industrial leadership of these two nations in their respective hemispheres as a historical given, whether or not an examination of the landholding patterns and system in these two nations during their respective pre-industrial periods will yield analytically and historically significant similarities (and differences) to explain their successful industrialization. It is hoped that the analytical framework adopted will be helpful in elucidating a heretofore neglected aspect in comparing preconditions for industrialization in England and Japan, but the analysis is a narrow one compared to the wide-ranging examinations often conducted by scholars who adopt one of the various stage theories.

Much of the empirical evidence required to support the analysis could not be presented in the text due to limitations of space. Many and lengthy footnotes for the Tokugawa section and numerous citations for pre-modern England are substitutes for this missing empirical evidence. This may be useful because it allows non-specialists of Tokugawa Japan and/or pre-modern England to follow the analysis of the economic change without being slowed by the results of case studies and the scattering of available data.

It should be pointed out to those familiar with Tokugawa Japan, and especially those acquainted with the Japanese literature on the Tokugawa economy, that the analysis contained here departs significantly from the long-held view of the Tokugawa economy and the traditional explanations offered as to why the landholding patterns and system changed. The substantial differences in interpretation are due to a difference in analytical framework, that is, the basically Marxist analysis which is still prevalent in the Japanese literature in contrast to the theoretical framework here adopted.

My purpose is to compare landholding systems of pre-modern England and Tokugawa Japan within the chosen framework of analysis, so the text includes neither the Marxist interpretation of the Tokugawa economy nor the analysis of the landholding system by Japanese scholars. However, numerous and often long footnotes, summarizing and criticizing the Marxist interpretation, are added for interested readers.[6]

---

[6] There are several camps or factions of Marxist scholars, and interpretations

Tokugawa Japan

During the mid-sixteenth century, while civil wars were being waged among the *sengoku daimyō* (lords of the period of warring states), the landholding system retained vestiges of the medieval era. Lordship (or "proprietary ownership")[7] with the right to share in tax revenues was claimed over a parcel of land by a *sengoku daimyō*, by his vassal who often was a local military power, by the warriors under the command of the vassal who, in some instances, still engaged in agriculture, and in rare instances even by a surviving owner of a *shōen*, the counterpart of the European manor.[8] Although these tax claimants exerted political control over the land, the ownership of the land, with rights to work it in perpetuity and to alienate it at will, belonged in most cases to successful peasants and to some of the local warriors. The land was worked by the landless, who usually lived on the premises of the landholders (and whom Japanese scholars call "dependent agricultural laborers"), by small tenant families, and by families and relatives of the landowners.[9]

Beginning in the 1580's, however, the landholding system underwent a significant change. To use the accepted Japanese expressions, the change came in the forms of the *kokudaka* system and the *honbyakushō* system. The *kokudaka* system, which was to be firmly established by the mid-seventeenth century, refers to the new system of landholding instituted in the 1580's by Hideyoshi, who subsequently succeeded in gaining political and military hegemony over the warring *sengoku* daimyō. The promulgation of the system put an end to the remaining vestiges of the medieval landholding system because it established the principle of "one land, one ruler," that is, each major vassal (daimyō) of Hideyoshi's (and of Tokugawa Ieyasu after the Tokugawa bakufu was established) was given a fief from which to receive tax

---

offered tend to differ in nuance, in the interpretation of data, and even in conclusions, depending on the camp to which each author belongs. Except in a few instances, no effort is made to delineate these differences, as such an effort will not be productive within the context of this paper.

To note in passing, the Marxist analysis of the Tokugawa economy is analogous to the early "pessimistic" interpretation of English economic history represented in the works of Hammonds.

[7] "Proprietary ownership" refers to the *shiki*, and a lord in this context is a *ryōshu*.

[8] For a further discussion on variations in proprietary ownership and for case studies in *English*, see Nagahara Keiji, "The *Shōen-Kokugaryō* System," *Journal of Japanese Studies*, vol. 1, no. 2 (spring 1975).

[9] The specific nature of the "dependent agricultural laborers" is still fiercely debated among Japanese scholars. Some hold them to have been "slaves," whereas others believe that they were "serflike" or "agricultural servants." The most frequently used expression in Japanese is *nōdo*, a compound noun created from *nō* (agriculture) and *do* (slaves). For further discussion on this point, see footnote 11.

revenues and which he was to administer at the pleasure of Hideyoshi or the bakufu. The *kokudaka* system was so called because *kokudaka* (an assessment of the rice yield) was used, beginning with the famous cadastral surveys made by Hideyoshi, in measuring the size of the fiefs and in determining the tax burden.[10]

In a legal and political sense, the *honbyakushō* system (literally, the system of principal or basic peasants) made newly "listed" taxpayers of many of the "dependent agricultural laborers," marginal tenant-cultivators who also worked as "dependent agricultural laborers," and some of the sons and relatives of the landholders. That is, they became taxpayers to the ruling class who were newly listed, independently of the landholders, in Hideyoshi's cadastral surveys (and related tax rolls) and in similar tax registers kept by the officials of Tokugawa villages. In an economic sense, these newly "listed" peasants, in many instances, received from the landholders a small amount of land *de novo* or in addition to what they had been working at the time of listing. This meant that one important consequence of the *honbyakushō* system, which was adopted with varying rapidity depending on the region, was a reduction in the size of the average agricultural unit. (As shall be demonstrated, these newly "listed" peasants did not become bona fide owner-cultivators merely by virtue of being "listed.")

Why was the *kokudaka* system adopted by Hideyoshi and retained by the Tokugawa bakufu? Why the *honbyakushō* system? Or, to pursue the latter question: Why did the *honbyakushō* system take the specific form it did? And, was the ruling class the only beneficiary of the system?

In answering the first question, I will rephrase and adopt the view of Wakita and others *sans* the Marxist terminology which they use in presenting their view opposing the interpretations of Araki, Miyagawa, and others who form the core of the Marxist scholars writing on this question.[11] My view is that the *kokudaka* system was adopted by the

---

[10] A good discussion on the *kokudaka* system in English is found in Wakita Osamu, "Notes on Economic and Political Changes during the Period of Transition between the Medieval and Tokugawa Periods," *Journal of Japanese Studies*, vol. 1, no. 2 (spring 1975).

[11] Most of the Japanese literature on the Taikō *kenchi* and the *honbyakushō* system are concerned with their political, rather than economic, significance. Within Marxist analysis, the central question asked by Japanese scholars is whether the cadastral surveys and the *honbyakushō* system marked the beginning of a new historical stage. Some, like Araki Moriaki, argue that they did not because the Tokugawa period perpetuated the "exploitation of *slaves* by the heads of extended families" [*kafuchō-teki doreisei*], whereas a majority holds that the Taikō *kenchi* and the *honbyakushō* system signaled the beginning of a bona fide feudalism or a "transformed" feudalism. Readers interested in examining the Japanese literature are referred to Shakai Keizaishi Gakkai, ed., *Hōken ryōshu-sei no seiritsu*, (Tokyo: Yūhikaku, 1957). Wakita's article, cited in footnote 10, contains an able criticism

newly constituted military and political central authority in an effort to perpetuate itself. When supplemented with the policy of separating the samurai class from the peasants (which was adopted at the time of Hideyoshi's cadastral surveys), the system deprived possible competing powers of their regional political and economic bases. Under the new system, the *sengoku* daimyō, his vassals, and, later in the seventeenth century, the daimyō of Tokugawa bakufu were reduced to being recipients of fiefs which could be taken away from them at the pleasure of the hegemon who presided over the central government.

The questions relating to the *honbyakushō* system (the more important questions in this essay) cannot be answered equally simply. To answer why the system came into being, and why it took the specific form it did, I must first describe the basic economic forces at work during most of the 1580-1700 period.

Few specialists of the period would question that crucial changes were taking place in an economy now benefiting from the peace regained under a newly unified central government. Though demographic data do not exist for the last few decades of the sixteenth century, it appears certain that the population had begun to increase rapidly by pre-modern standards.[12] Agricultural productivity was rising through the use of improved seeds, irrigation, and agricultural techniques in general. As the more powerful of the *sengoku* daimyō had begun to do during the mid-sixteenth century, Hideyoshi and later the Tokugawa bakufu and daimyō encouraged and supported major irrigation projects and reclamation. Political powers which were confident of capturing the gains resulting from large investments understandably were willing investors in such capital-intensive ventures.

---

of the view of Araki Moriaki and Miyagawa Mitsuru, and a good bibliography on these topics is found in Nagahara Keiji, ed., *Nihon keizaishi*, (Tokyo: Yūhikaku, 1970), p. 128.

[12] Hayami Akira, "The Population at the Beginning of the Tokugawa Period," *Keio Economic Studies* 4 (1966-1967), pp. 1-28. In discussing the rate of change in population, an important variable in the analysis, I do not specify whether it is determined within my analytical model or given exogenously. The reason for this is that not enough is yet known about the relationship or the feedback mechanism between the economic, social, and other factors and demographic change in Tokugawa Japan. As discussed at length in the articles cited in footnotes 24 and 25, evidence exists supporting a hypothesis that both the samurai and the peasants in Tokugawa Japan succeeded in controlling the population, due both to the desire to maintain or elevate their living standard and to various social pressures. In this sense, the demographic changes in Tokugawa Japan were not wholly determined exogenously. That is, if the hypothesis stated here is tenable, the Tokugawa population had an effective social and institutional feedback mechanism. In analyzing demographic change during the thirteenth century in Europe, North and Thomas depict a tendency for population to grow more rapidly than the rate of economic progress. See North and Thomas, *Growth of the Western World*, pp. 69-70.

It was against this background that the *honbyakushō* system was adopted. As noted earlier, the cultivators of the newly listed small units consisted in the main of landless agricultural labor which had worked the paddies of large landholders who usually employed them for life and who provided them with the essentials of life. Some of the newly listed units were cultivated by grown and often married sons, brothers, and relatives of the head of the household which owned the land. It is important to note that when the land was divided, the cultivators of these new units usually received only a small fraction, certainly much less than half, of the land held by the landholders and that these cultivators continued to owe labor services at planting and harvesting to the original landholders.[13] Thus, although Hideyoshi's cadastral survey and the Tokugawa land law made them legally independent peasants, they were not *bona fide* independent owner-cultivators.

Given these facts, it is now possible to advance an exploratory hypothesis to explain the emergence of the *honbyakushō* system: the unequal subdivision of land resulting from the new "listing," which was vigorously pursued by Hideyoshi and the Tokugawa bakufu because it helped to increase the tax base (the total output) and also because, in most instances, it aided landholders and "dependent agricultural laborers" in making the economic institutional adjustment necessary to increase their income.

For the convenience of exposition, let us begin the analysis with the motivations of the peasants.

The basic factor motivating such an adjustment was the changing relative value of labor and land, that is, the value of labor was falling because of the relatively rapid increase in population and that of land was rising due both to the relatively slow rate of increase in paddies which were capital-consuming to create and to the increased productivity resulting from the variety of factors mentioned earlier. The new arrangement made the original landholders better off without neces-

---

[13] In addition to a few examples presented by T. C. Smith in *The Agrarian Origins of Modern Japan* (Stanford: Stanford University Press, 1959), pp. 45-46, readers are referred to the following recent case studies documenting the observations contained in this paragraph: Takeyasu Shigeji, "Kinsei zenki Kawachi ni okeru nōson shakai no kōzō," in Kimura Takeo, ed., *Kinsei Ōsaka heiya no sonraku* (Kyoto: Minerva Shobō, 1970), pp. 101-161; Hayama Teisaku, *Kinsei nōgyō hatten no seisanryoku bunseki* (Tokyo: Ochanomizu Shobō, 1966), pp. 121-144; Naitō Jirō, *Honbyakushō taisei no kenkyū* (Tokyo: Ochanomizu Shobō, 1968), pp. 152-183; Shimbō Hiroshi, *Hōken-teki shōnōmin no bunkai katei* (Tokyo: Shiseisha, 1967), pp. 21-85; Fujino Tamotsu, *Bakuhan taisei-shi no kenkyū* (Tokyo: Yoshikawa Kōbunkan, 1961), pp. 225-233; Mori Kahē, *Nihon hekichi no shiteki kenkyū*, 2 vols. (Tokyo: Hosei University Press, 1969), pp. 768-783. There have been at least forty articles in land subdivision published in various journals during the past fifteen years.

sarily making the newly listed cultivators of small units worse off than they had been, and in most circumstances the new cultivators of small units became better off as well.

First, I shall examine the case of the former dependent agricultural laborers who received land to make them cultivators of small units because, unlike subdivisions which involved family members, the basic analytics can be presented on strictly economic grounds. As real rent rose relative to the value of labor, employers found that the value received from the agricultural labor was less than that of real rent.[14] The actions which could be taken by landholders to redress this condition were severely circumscribed. The consumption bundle given to the agricultural laborers could not be reduced below the socially acceptable level which was, at any rate, not much above subsistence. Because of this, and because of the nature of agricultural employment, it was extremely difficult to reduce the imputed wage rate of agricultural laborers. On the other hand, the landholders could ill afford to sever outright their ties with the agricultural laborers because they needed a dependable supply of labor, especially during the peak periods of planting and harvesting. If the landholders chose to depend on labor supplied on a short-term basis, even if this were possible, they not only risked the possibility of being unable to obtain labor at peak periods, but they would also have incurred the cost of determining the wage-equivalent bundle of payments in kind and/or in cash, as most regions of Tokugawa Japan were yet little monetized and lacked labor markets as such.[15]

Under these circumstances, the landholders could obtain real rent only by finding a new arrangement which would satisfy their need for a dependable supply of labor and which could be adopted in a little-monetized economy. The solution adopted, the subdivision of the land with de facto labor dues, was perhaps the only possible arrangement by which the landholders were guaranteed a dependable supply of labor and were also able to increase their gains by transferring such risks as fluctuations in harvests and possible increases in taxes, and by

[14] "Real rent" refers to that amount of rent which landholders could have obtained, had it been possible for them to make a new contractual agreement with tenants accounting for the changes in the relative value of land.

[15] Even in the most advanced region, the Kinai, labor mobility and monetization of the economy were still limited in villages during the seventeenth century. Establishing wages for labor was quite cumbersome, as it involved payment in rice and in cash of various kinds, the relative values for all of which were fluctuating. See the six essays and numerous original documents cited in these essays in the Osaka Rekishi Gakkai, ed., *Bakuhan-taisei kakuritsu-ki no shomondai* (Tokyo: Yoshikawa Kōbunkan, 1963). On the process of monetization in Tokugawa Japan, see E. S. Crawcour and K. Yamamura, "The Tokugawa Monetary System: 1787-1868," *Economic Development and Cultural Change*, vol. 18, no. 4, part 1 (July 1970).

reducing or eliminating the costs of management and supervision of labor. The subdivision of land naturally reduced the total output for the original landholders, but they made certain, to the extent possible, that the loss in output resulting from subdivision would not exceed the amount formerly provided to "dependent labor."[16]

For the agricultural laborers, the new arrangement was not necessarily disadvantageous. They now had to bear the risks involved in being independent cultivators and to provide labor to the original landholders as dictated by the socially sanctioned "contracts," but they could use their labor more efficiently than before. An incentive to increase total output replaced the likely incentive to shirk under the old arrangement. These peasants were now free to plan the use of their own time, except during peak periods, and to engage in by-employments, to the extent opportunities were available. The virtual absence of peasant discontent during the seventeenth century is perhaps the best evidence that the new system did not counter peasant interests.

The cases involving blood relatives are obviously more difficult to analyze, especially if the subdivided households were headed by the sons of the original household. However, the analysis made in the cases involving former dependent laborers applies in its essential aspects.[17] The terms under which these subdivided households were established could be made more lenient by giving them more capital goods, demanding less labor, or providing more land than was given to dependent laborers. The very fact that numerous such subdivisions involving blood-relatives took place shows that land could be subdivided to make both parties better off, or at least make one party better off without making the other party worse off.[18] It is entirely

[16] As many authors have noted, the amount of land given to a new small peasant was closely correlated with the number of adult males in the newly listed household. A detailed study of this is found in Takeyasu Shigeji, *Kinsei Kinai no nōgyō no kōzō* (Tokyo: Ochanomizu Shobō, 1969), pp. 83-91.

[17] The following observation made by Smith is quite compatible with the observation made in the text: "It is obvious, therefore, that main and branch families tended to be economically complementary. Partitioning divided the resources of a highly integrated farming unit between heirs in such a way that more of some resources (capital and land) went to the main family and more of another (labor) went to the branch. Thus, critical resources that were in short supply in one family were almost necessarily surplus in the other. Since the families were kin living in the closest proximity, sometimes even in the same house, and in an economy with no market to mediate exchange, the inevitable result was continuous cooperative exchange." Smith, *Agrarian Origins*, p. 46.

[18] Even Sasaki, who argued that the *honbyakushō* system "was established with its main object to exploit taxes in kind, rice, from the *honbyakushō* who produced rice and who were in fact agricultural slaves engaged in agriculture in nuclear family units," acknowledges later in the same book that their newly gained independence became the basis from which these *honbyakushō* could begin to accumulate a

possible that in some instances subdivisions may have made the original landholders worse off, but, if this happened, such cases are yet to be found in the numerous case studies.

In short, this explanation of the *honbyakushō* system acknowledges the economic incentives on the part of the peasants involved and does not argue, as do the Marxist scholars, that political pressures exerted by the ruling class were the sole motivating force in creating the system. The *honbyakushō* system came into being in the seventeenth century because, in most instances, it was able to benefit both the landholders and the cultivators of the new small units.[19]

Those who are familiar with Japanese works know that the ruling class made a determined effort to institute the *honbyakushō* system. If my analysis is correct, the reason is that the ruling class was pursuing a policy which would provide them with larger tax revenues—a share which rose proportionately with total output. An important implication of the foregoing analysis is that it is neither necessary to argue that the peasants were unwilling and "coerced" partners in bringing about the *honbyakushō* system, nor to maintain that the system was adopted exclusively in the interest of the "exploitative" ruling class.

To maintain that the ruling class forced the new system on the peasants, one must first show that Hideyoshi possessed during the 1580's and 1590's sufficient political power to adopt a policy against the interests of the landowning peasants. Such an argument must also demonstrate that the Tokugawa bakufu also had, even during the first half of the seventeenth century, sufficient power to carry out a policy which was not in the interests of the landowning peasant class. Because of the recent works of Nagahara, Wakita, and others for the period before 1600, and because of our increased knowledge of the first fifty years of the Tokugawa bakufu made available by Fujino and others, it would be difficult indeed to support such an argument.[20]

"surplus." Sasaki Junnosuke, *Bakuhan kenryoku no kiso kōzō* (Tokyo: Ochanomizu Shobō, 1964), pp. 27, 119.

[19] As is well known, most *han* prohibited the subdividing of land if it reduced the individual holding below a specified amount and also, in many instances, while the head of the household was still alive. However, as Otake noted, "while there is the example of Kaga *han* in which the legal prohibition of land subdivision was obeyed in reality, subdivisions of land before the death of the head of the family were undoubtedly widely practiced, if not across the nation, in many regions." Otake, *Hōken shakai no nōmin kazoku* (Tokyo: Sōbunsha, 1962), p. 167.

[20] The most convenient source for Nagahara's view is Nagahara Keiji, "Village Communities in the Late Medieval Period," in John W. Hall, ed., *Japan in the Muromachi Age* (Berkeley and Los Angeles: University of California Press, 1975). For Wakita's view, see his article cited in footnote 10. Fujino Tamotsu, a historian, has criticized economic historians, especially Araki Moriaki and Miyagawa Mitsuru (the leaders among the scholars who attribute strong political power to the bakufu and the daimyō), for "deducing the existence of an abstract monolithic power"

If my economic hypothesis is accepted, no such argument needs to be made. Let me restate the hypothesis: The *honbyakushō* system emerged because it was in the interests of both the ruling class and the peasants; the rulers gained increased tax revenues, and the peasants enjoyed a larger income. The system was encouraged by the ruling class primarily because it was profitable to do so. In addition, if one accepts the hypothesis that gains resulted for both the ruling class and the peasants, it is not necessary to argue that the ruling class had sufficient political power to ignore the interests of the peasants or to ignore the fact that, even before Hideyoshi's cadastral surveys, an equivalent of newly listed cultivators was increasing in number in some provinces controlled by *sengoku* daimyō.[21] It is well to recall that, as a rule, landholding and cultivating arrangements could be changed against the peasants' interests only after subduing the utmost protest the peasants were able to mount.[22]

It should be pointed out that the preceding analysis is speculative and requires further elaboration and refinement if it is to be fully useful in analyzing the complex and multifaceted politico-economic questions which are often associated with the *Taikō kenchi*. My immediate goals in presenting the above hypothesis are to apply the theoretical framework of this essay to the economic circumstances relating to the appearance of the *honbyakushō* system, and to suggest the potential usefulness of this theoretical framework in providing a new perspective to the continuing intense debate concerning the significance of the *honbyakushō* system. I should also note that my analysis neglects the substantial regional differences which existed in the

---

without examining the process of the formation of political power at the *han* level or the changing relationships between the peasants and the ruling class. Fujino, *Bakuhan*, p. 4. For an example of economic historians who have seriously questioned the strength of the political power of the ruling class, see Gotō Yōichi, "Hōken kenryoku to sonraku kōsei," in Shakai Keizai-shi Gakkai, ed., *Hōken ryōshu-sei*, pp. 51-110. Like John W. Hall in *Government and Local Power in Japan* (Princeton: Princeton University Press, 1966), p. 346, many historians agree that the political structure and power of the Bakuhan system was in the process of consolidation until the mid-sixteenth century. Also see Yamamura, "The Increasing Poverty of the Samurai in Tokugawa Japan, 1600-1868," *Journal of Economic History*, vol. 31 (June 1971), which argues that the political strength of the samurai class was limited as judged by its inability to share in the increasing total output.

21 The system similar to the *honbyakushō* system was adopted by Oda Nobunaga a few decades before Hideyoshi instituted it. But, more significantly, the dependent labor [*genin*] was being "liberated" in Kinai and other regions well before the first cadastral survey undertaken by Hideyoshi. See Hayashiya Tatsusaburō, *Tenka ittō*, vol. 12 of *Nihon Rekishi* (Tokyo: Chūō Kōron-sha, 1971), p. 202.

22 Uprisings by peasants, called *do-ikki* (literally, the uprisings of the earth), began to increase in number during the fifteenth century because many local military powers failed to appreciate this fact. See, for example, Takeuchi Rizō, ed., *Tochi seido-shi* (Tokyo: Yamakawa Shuppansha, 1973), p. 421.

extent and timing of the *Taikō kenchi*, in resource endowments, in the degree of commercialization achieved, in the proportion of *hon-byakushō* in the peasant population, and in several other economically significant aspects. Two reasons explain this neglect. One is that, despite the clearly visible regional differences which can readily be seen in contrasting the Kinai and the Tohoku regions, the process of change and its consequences generally followed a similar course in all regions. Even the Tohoku region followed the same path as the advanced areas of western Japan, though with a considerable time lag.[23] The other reason is that the principal purpose of this essay is to analyze the general trends of change in the landholding patterns and system over time and their effects on the national economy as a whole. For this reason, I need demonstrate only that my hypothesis is tenable when applied to the national trends of change and not necessarily to every region. Though the desirability of accounting for regional differences is obvious, I must first establish whether or not my hypothesis possesses any merit as a starting point for a further examination which would take into account regional differences. More attention is paid to the regional differences in the analysis which follows, but it should be kept in mind that the goal of this essay is to analyze the subject within a national perspective.

Coming to the analysis of the landholding patterns and tenurial arrangements during the last century and a half of the Tokugawa period, I shall first summarize my view of economic change in Tokugawa Japan beginning with the early decades of the eighteenth century.[24] I shall then analyze the changes in the landholding patterns and systems which took place within the context of this economic change. Though there is no analytical necessity for it, the following analysis is conducted in the three sub-periods often chosen by Japanese scholars in order to facilitate a comparison with the Japanese view as summarized in the footnotes.

The Tokugawa economy continued to grow, if slowly by modern standards, during the last 150 years, or from the first decades of the

[23] Further discussions of the Tohoku region which are intended to support the point being made here are presented later in the text and in footnotes 30, 38, and 47. Also see Yamamura, "Toward a Reexamination of the Economic History of Tokugawa Japan, 1600-1867," *Journal of Economic History*, vol. 33, no. 3 (Sept. 1973), which analyzes the leader-follower relationship between the advanced and the less advanced regions.

[24] Though the parts relevant for the analysis of the landholding system are summarized in the text and the following footnotes, the readers interested in fuller discussions of the Tokugawa economic and demographic changes are referred to Yamamura, "Toward a Reexamination," pp. 509-546, and S. B. Hanley and K. Yamamura, "Population Trends and Economic Growth in Pre-Industrial Japan," in D. V. Glass and R. Revelle, eds., *Population and Social Change* (London: Edward Arnold, 1972), pp. 451-99.

eighteenth century to the end of the Tokugawa period. Agricultural productivity rose due to new seeds, improved tools, the increased use of fertilizers, and more efficient uses and better management of land and water. Both commerce and pre-modern manufacturing activities grew, stimulating each other and agricultural growth. The living standard of Tokugawa peasants rose steadily except for a few major setbacks caused by famine. Aiding the increase in per capita income was the slow growth rate of population due mainly to the socially enforced effort of peasants to limit their number, and due partly to the famines.[25]

Because of the declining political strength of the ruling class and because of the increasing political, as well as economic, strength of the ruled, the ruling class had little success in obtaining a share in the increasing output of the economy. The bakufu and the *han*, which had never been able effectively to tax merchants and entrepreneurs in premodern manufacturing activities, found themselves even less able to share in the profits being made by these commoners. Even in the agricultural sector, the real tax burden on peasants tended to decline. Larger surpluses remaining in the hands of commoners helped to further increase investment, productivity, and the demand for agricultural and other products. As more and more of the wealthier peasants became village entrepreneurs and investors in village commerce in response to the increasing demand for goods and services by the peasants, the Tokugawa villages—"the rice-based foundation of the Tokugawa bakufu"—were transformed into a highly commercialized agricultural economy with entrepreneurs in commerce and manufacturing who were increasingly able to challenge their counterparts in the urban centers.[26]

[25] Along with the articles cited in the preceding footnote, see S. B. Hanley, "Fertility, Mortality, and Life Expectancy in Premodern Japan," *Population Studies*, vol. 28, no. 1 (spring 1974), pp. 127-142; and the same author's "Toward an Analysis of Demographic and Economic Change in Tokugawa Japan: A Village Study," *Journal of Asian Studies*, vol. 31, no. 3 (May 1972), pp. 515-537.

[26] It is important to stress at this point that Japanese historians (with a few exceptions in recent years) have rarely concerned themselves with the rationality of peasants' economic actions. The Tokugawa peasants, as seen by many Japanese scholars, were passive victims of changing economic conditions created for the benefit of the ruling class and the merchants. The only frequently examined peasant action has been their revolts, but these are mostly seen as desperate politicoeconomic reactions. A score of existing studies examining peasants' reactions to changes in relative prices, the relative profitability of various crops, the required mix of tax payments (in cash and in kind), and so forth, have been published only during the past decade. Even today, most Japanese economic historians would perhaps subscribe to Nakamura Kichiji's view of the Tokugawa peasants: "The economic base of the Tokugawa bakufu and their daimyō was land and peasants. It [the Tokugawa society] was a samurai's feudal society in which they owned the land

Against such a background of economic change, the landholding patterns and system also changed significantly. The landholding pattern during the last 150 years of the Tokugawa period showed an unmistakable trend toward concentration. In contrast to the seventeenth century, large landholders continued to acquire even more land, whereas small and marginal peasants either left the land to become merchants or wage earners on a full- or part-time basis (in effect, reducing land worked), or became tenant farmers who worked the land of the large landholders. Tenants usually paid rent in kind, but there was a discernible tendency for fixed cash payments to increase within this period. In short, the period was characterized by what Japanese scholars call the polarization of the landholding pattern or the "disintegration" of the peasant class.

How did these changes come about? I shall analyze the process of transformation more closely, beginning with the period between the first decades of the eighteenth century and the 1760's.[27] The most significant development of this period was an increased demand for labor from the rapidly increasing commercial and pre-modern manufacturing sectors of the economy and from within the villages for the cultivating and processing of commercial crops. At the same time, the rate of growth of population seems to have undergone a perceptible decline. The demographic changes resulted because further subdivisions of the land were no longer profitable either for the peasants or the ruling class, reclamation projects to create new paddies declined

---

and the peasants." *Kinsei shoki nōsei-shi kenkyū* (Tokyo: Iwanami, 1970), p. 2. This was a reissue of the original 1938 edition.

[27] Although they examine the same phenomenon (the polarization of landholdings), Japanese scholars interpret the reasons why the landholding pattern changed during the period between the beginning of the Kyōhō period (1716-1735) and the Hōreki period (1751-1763) in a completely different way from what is about to be presented in the text. As Japanese scholars see it, small landholders were unable to prevent the loss of their land to large landholders and became agricultural laborers, marginal merchants, or underemployed tenant farmers. Whereas the large landholders gained from commercialization, the small landholders were losing because of it. This loss took place because "involvement in a cash economy" and in a market economy necessarily made them poorer due to exploitation by monopolistic and monopsonistic merchants and by large landholders who doubled as money-lenders to the hapless peasants. The statement that commercialization made the small landholders poorer is almost an article of faith among many Japanese economic historians.

Thus, according to most Japanese scholars, increasing commercialization was the main force changing the landholding patterns. The smallest landholders, owning land which yielded five *koku* (about 25 bushels) or less of rice, were the first forced off their land, and slightly larger farmers fell victim shortly thereafter. The polarization in landholding continued, creating intra-class conflicts. A new group of "wealthy farmers" (*gōnō*) emerged and continued to enlarge their landholdings on the profits made from commercial crops and money-lending. See Yamamura's work cited in footnote 24.

due to increasing costs, and commercial gains could now be realized only through a steady growth of commerce and no longer through reaping the advantages of unification and peace. However, since agricultural productivity was continuing to rise and commercial and premodern manufacturing development was accelerating, a real reason for controlling family size perhaps was that the Tokugawa villagers through their own and their grandfathers' experience had begun to see the horizon of their own and their sons' lives more clearly within the settled present and a future in which they expected no radical changes.[28]

An important consequence of what has just been described was an increase in the relative value of labor vis-à-vis that of land. This became apparent in the declining number of days which the small cultivators were required to provide to the original landholders, in the increasing difficulties in obtaining household servants, and in rising wage levels.[29] Under the circumstances, more and more small cultivators found that they could increase their income by leaving the land either completely or partly to become full- or part-time merchants for a higher imputed income per day or wage earners at the rising wage level. Significant declines in the price of rice, their main crop, during

[28] Good descriptions of the commercialization of agriculture and changes in agricultural methods and technology are found in Furushima Toshio, *Kinsei Nihon nōgyō no tenkai* (Tokyo: Tokyo University Press, 1963), pp. 167-170. For further discussion of and empirical evidence for the hypothesis concerning the apparent control of the family size, see the articles cited in footnotes 24 and 25 and Yamamura, *A Study on Samurai Income and Entrepreneurship* (Cambridge, Mass.: Harvard University Press, 1974), pp. 102-118. Though this chapter is concerned with the demographic changes of the *hatamoto* class of samurai, it contains strong supporting evidence for the hypothesis presented in the text.

[29] The gradual decline in *de facto* labor dues paid by many of the newly listed peasants *(bunke)* has long been recognized among Japanese economic historians. The reasons offered, however, for this decline are uniformly unsatisfactory: "a reflection of changes in social customs," "a decline in cohort-community identity," or "the strengthening in the degree of independence of landownership" (see, for example, Naitō, *Honbyakushō*, pp. 181-182). Even in Furushima's well-known study of *hikan* and the decline of labor dues which they paid over time, no economic analysis of the development is attempted (Furushima Toshio, *Kinsei Nihon nōgyō no kōzō* [Tokyo: University of Tokyo Press, 1957], pp. 415-504). In contrast, Smith's analysis of the declining labor dues paid by *nago* and their eventual attainment of economic independence is based on the labor shortage resulting from commercial development and increased by-employments (Smith, *Agrarian Origins*, p. 133). In reading Smith's discussion on the continuing subdivisions of land for the later periods (ibid., pp. 145-156), it becomes clear that he sees the increasing value of labor as the main factor for the continuing decline of labor dues and the eventual attainment of economic independence by *bunke*. Smith's explicit statements on the increasing difficulties of obtaining labor and on rising wages help to support the observations made in the text (ibid., pp. 108-123). And much more evidence for the increasing labor shortage and rising wages has become available since Smith wrote his book during the mid-1950's. Local histories, usually relatively free of ideological overtones, are especially good sources.

the 1720's and 1730's only hastened the process. Also, the growth of commerce and consequent monetization of the economy made it easier for small cultivators to see the opportunity costs of remaining marginal peasants. Some peasants were forced to leave the land as the result of poor harvests or personal misfortune, but it is even more important to note that more were willing to leave the land when opportunities to obtain a better income could be found.[30]

Coinciding in time with the desire of the small and marginal peasants to leave the land completely or partly in order to increase their income was the desire of large landholders to expand their landholdings and to obtain more labor because of the rising profitability of commercial farming. The motivation of the large landholders can be explained simply. Unlike the small peasants, who needed most of their land to cultivate rice for tax and rent, and who had little capital, these landholders had the capital to buy fertilizers necessary for cultivating commercial crops (cotton, tobacco, rapeseed) and holdings large enough to enable crop rotation to obtain the best yields. The decline of the price of rice only furthered the large landholders' desire to acquire more land for commercial farming. Some small peasants found an opportunity to increase their income through working for the large landholders at the rising wage level. Also, as the cost of information necessary for seeking economic opportunities in towns and in distant

[30] Although the older literature attributes poor harvests, personal misfortunes, and debts accumulated as the result of "exploitation" by merchants and the *gōnō* class as the main reasons why the peasants "lost" their land (that is, sold or left it involuntarily), recent evidence clearly shows that many peasants did indeed leave the land for better opportunities, that is, voluntarily. I shall cite only several among many examples. Nakabe Yoshiko's article "Hōken-toshi shuzōgyō no tenkai," in Osaka Rekishi Gakkai, ed., *Hōken shakai no mura to machi* (Tokyo: Yoshikawa Kōbunkan, 1960), pp. 149-219, presents convincing evidence that the sake-brewers actively competed for labor from villages with the consequence that wages were raised by 40 percent in the twenty years between 1720 and 1740. Taniguchi, writing on Okayama *han*, noted that "during the mid-Tokugawa period, because of the increases in the output of many commercial products, a rapidly increasing number of peasants became *hōkōnin* (servants) and villages suffered severe labor shortages. Several other problems connected with the rapidly rising wages of *hōkōnin* arose in Okayama. The *han* authority was at a loss in dealing with the problem [of labor outflow to towns]." Taniguchi Sumio, *Okayama han-seishi no kenkyū* (Tokyo: Hanawa Shobō, 1964), p. 473. In Kyushu, a contemporary record noted that "the peasants, who are expected to live a simple life and work assiduously on the land, are leaving the land to become merchants whose life is easier" and that "repeated pleading by the authorities had no effect because the peasants had learned the more elegant ways" of the townspeople. Saga Prefecture, *Saga kenshi*, vol. 2 (Saga Prefecture, 1968), p. 304. Even for northeastern Sendai and Tsugaru *han*, a contemporary source stated that "because agriculture yielded only meager returns . . . many chose to be merchants for the high wages. Agricultural workers became much harder to find and land remaining unattended increased." Mori also noted that the orders prohibiting peasants from leaving the land had little effect. Mori, *Nihon hekichi*, pp. 953-954.

villages was still high, working for the large landholders was at the margin a viable alternative.[31]

The next seventy years or so, roughly the period between 1760 and 1830, saw in many respects a continuation of the trends of the preceding sixty years. Further concentration of landholdings occurred as the large holders, who by this time were referred to as *gōnō* (wealthy farmers), continued to acquire land. The only significant change was a visible increase in tenant farming by households which sold a part or all of their land.[32] For the economy as a whole, this was a period of rapid increase in commercial and pre-modern manufacturing activities. Inflation, which was to characterize the 1830-1867 period, began in the 1820's.[33]

The basic reason the smaller peasants sold their land was the increase in the value of labor, which meant rising wage levels, a trend that became even more pronounced during this period.[34] This gave more marginal peasants an incentive to leave the land. As the opportunities for by-employments within the village were increasing, thanks to continued commercialization, more peasants sold a part of their land and became part-time merchants or wage earners in commerce and pre-modern manufacturing.[35] Some even left their villages alto-

[31] For peasants who left their villages illegally, there always was the risk of being forcibly brought back, though attempts to do so by the ruling class were infrequent and nearly always ineffectual.

[32] The following analysis of the reasons for the "disintegration of the peasant class" and an increase in tenant cultivators during this period summarizes the consensus among Japanese scholars, though one would find differences in nuance among them. The quotations are from Ōishi Shinzaburō, *et al.*, *Nihon keizaishi-ron* (Tokyo: Ochanomizu Shobō, 1967), pp. 93-98. "By the 1760's it became evident that the rate of increase in exploitation had its limits, however one might strengthen the methods of exploitation. Increases in exploitation, reflecting the demands made by the ruling class, could not take the portion which was necessary for peasants' subsistence. . . . Taxes demanded of the peasants necessarily caused peasants to become impoverished and to disintegrate. . . . As this impoverishment and disintegration continued, the phenomena of bankrupted peasants and unattended land resulted. These were contradictory phenomena representing a labor shortage and labor surplus. . . . As a consequence, peasants' revolts became increasingly frequent," pp. 94-95.

[33] See Crawcour and Yamamura, "The Tokugawa Monetary System."

[34] Smith, *Agrarian Origins*, p. 122. The evidence from recent studies for a rising wage level during this stage in both the advanced as well as in remoter regions is too numerous to list here. Takeyasu, one of many recent authors who found quantitative evidence of rising wages, made a valiant effort to remain within the orthodox camp by summarizing his findings in the following words: "The lowness of the degree of impoverishment of the day laborers should be noted anew." Takeyasu, *Kinsei Kinai no nōgyō no kōzō*, p. 220.

[35] Sources describing the development of the *zaikata* commerce (in towns and villages as opposed to large cities) and the consequent increase in by-employments are numerous. These developments were occurring even in the remote regions by this stage. For example, see Smith, "Farm Family By-Employments in Preindustrial Japan," *Journal of Economic History*, vol. 29, no. 4 (1969), pp. 687-715; Mori,

gether to join the ranks of the merchants and skilled and unskilled wage earners.[36] The ruling class and large landholders continued to lament the existence of uncultivated arable land; many landowners bitterly complained of rising wages and "increasingly unruly and disobedient" servants; and the ruling class in a few well-known instances ordered peasants to return to the land under the pain of punishment. The tide, however, could not be turned. Land was being sold by the peasants because it was unable to supply the peasants with the income they could earn in other pursuits. Some peasants were forced to sell their land at the time of the Temmei famine of the 1780's, but to overemphasize the significance of the famine on changes in the landholding pattern is to ignore the basic economic forces at work.

Even if the preceding can explain why the land was available for acquisition by the large landholders, it still leaves two important questions unanswered: Why did the landholders continue to acquire more land and why did some peasants choose to become tenant farmers? I shall attempt to answer these questions.

The large landholders continued to acquire more land during the 1760-1830 period because a portion of their slowly but steadily accumulating capital could be more profitably invested in land than in other alternatives. Though investments in commerce and manufacturing were continued by these landholders-*cum*-entrepreneurs in response to increasing demand in villages and nearby towns, not all of their capital could be absorbed by these opportunities. With no sudden technological changes or rapid increase in population, investment was required only to meet a slowly rising demand. In some regions, an increasing competitiveness in commerce and manufacturing deprived these landholders of a strong incentive to commit more capital to these activities.[37]

Investment in large urban centers, that is, in large-scale commerce and manufacturing, would have been a profitable alternative. This alternative, however, was closed to the village entrepreneurs for two major reasons. One was that the city guilds, though their power was weakening, were still able to rebuff the incursions of outsiders. The other was the absence of institutional arrangements to enable the transfer of capital from the villages to the cities. The banking system, which was highly developed by pre-modern standards, was suitable

Nihon hekichi, pp. 893-970; and Yagi Akihiro, *Kinsei no shōhin ryūtsū* (Tokyo: Hanawa Shobō, 1962), pp. 64-294.

[36] See the special issue of *Keio Economic Studies*, vol. 10, no. 2 (1973), entitled "Migration before and during Industrialization."

[37] Though there are numerous studies containing evidence for these observations, the handiest is Yagi, *Kinsei no shōhin ryūtsū*, pp. 63-164.

only to meet the needs of city merchants and to facilitate trade among major cities. Money-lending also became less rewarding because of the downward pressure on interest rates caused by a decline in the demand for loans by the peasants and by an increasing supply of loanable funds.[38] The inflation which began in the 1820's made lending even less promising. Under such circumstances, landholders found land the best investment even at a rent which was reduced to attract and hold scarce labor.

Rents were reduced to a level sufficiently low to attract tenants by means of a fixed rate of sharecropping, which left the increased output due to productivity increases in the hands of tenants, by increasing the proportion of rent to be paid in cash rather than rice, or by the absorption of risks due to crop failures through escape clauses favorable to tenants.[39] This, however, did not mean that the large land-

[38] For example, after a careful analysis of the existing evidence, Nakabe noted that "interest rates began to fall because of the increasing availability of cash capital" beginning in the first decades of the eighteenth century and that "this was a generally observed condition," Nakabe Yoshiko, "Genroku-Kyōhō-ki ni okeru nōgyō keiei to shōhin ryūtsū," in Osaka Rekishi Gakkai, ed., Hōken shakai, pp. 55 and 63. Describing the condition of Hachinoe han in Tohoku, Mori wrote: "The general trend was for the interest rate to decline from the beginning of the Tokugawa period and through the Genroku period. Pawnshops stayed open longer, began to value collateral at higher levels, and made loans for longer terms." During the last century of the Tokugawa period, "the han encouraged low interest policies" despite "the fierce objection of the pawnbrokers." Mori, Nihon hekichi, vol. 2, pp. 1016-17. However, on the next page, he goes on to state rather inconsistently that "as has been pointed out by many economic historians, loan sharking became rampant during the late Tokugawa period to further encourage the polarization of the peasant class," p. 1018. This type of inconsistency is common in other sources dealing with the decline in the interest rate.

[39] Important evidence accumulated during the past fifteen years shows that rent (amounts of output demanded on a sharecropping basis and/or cash) which tenant farmers had to pay tended to decline during this stage and the next, despite assertions to the contrary frequently seen in the older literature. For examples, see Yagi Akihiro, Hōken shakai no nōson kōzō (Tokyo: Yūhikaku, 1955), pp. 184-187; and Takeyasu Shigeji, Kinsei Kinai kosakuryō no kōzō (Tokyo: Ochanomizu Shobō, 1968). Takeyasu not only expresses doubts about the views of several leading scholars (pp. 254-273), but goes as far as to say that "the tenant farmers put strong pressure to reduce the portion [of the output] which had been the landlords' " (p. 228).

Takeyasu's conclusion is based on extensive empirical study. On examining the records of nearly two dozen villages in two districts in Kawachi during the second half of the Tokugawa period, he found that, "In reality, rent was determined on the basis of assessments made annually. This means that the amount of rent recorded [in the official village records] and the amount formally agreed upon when signing the tenant contract was not what was paid in fact. . . . The fact that in more than half of the villages examined in these two districts such an assessment was made after contracts were signed suggests that, at least after the mid-Tokugawa period, the contracted amount of rent was not paid in most of the villages examined. Rather, the amount in fact paid was based on an assessed amount which was less than that stipulated in the contract" (p. 8).

And even the assessed rent was not always what the tenants had to pay: "The

holders' incomes were reduced below what they had earned earlier from a given amount of land. On the contrary, their incomes tended to rise, because the total value of output was larger when tenant farmers worked the land than when hired labor cultivated commercial crops for the landholders. There were reasons for this.

 ˙ The tenants tended to plant more rice (whose price was then rising due to increases in per capita consumption, sake-making, and a run of poor harvests in some regions) than did the landholders, who had their land worked by hired labor. Tenant cultivators preferred rice to commercial crops because it required less capital and less specialized knowledge than did commercial crops and because the risks of yield and price fluctuations of rice were appreciably smaller than those of commercial crops.[40] That rice cultivation required, over the year, more labor—well-motivated to plow deeply, weed conscientiously, and har-

---

annual assessed rent was the projected rent and it was not necessarily paid in full. There were some arrears of course. But, even for those who paid, the amount in fact paid could be less than the assessed amount either because of a reduction in the rent base or because of a flat reduction. At times, the rent reduced by these means was even further reduced and these additional reductions were given benevolently [by landowners] and were called yōsha or make [both meaning "concessions"]. . . . These additional reductions were mostly given individually, but there were cases in which these reductions were given for all tenants in a village as a reward for not falling in arrears" (p. 45).

Many sources, while not explicitly stating that the land rent declined, note favorable changes in the cash-rice mix of rent which in effect reduced the rent. This is a subject on which investigation was begun only during the past decade, and many more studies are needed in order to show fully that the effective land rent declined in most regions. Because anyone reexamining the effective rate of land rent is questioning one of the fundamental building blocks of the orthodox view, not many younger economic historians are willing to undertake such a reexamination. Some economic historians have failed to go beyond examining changes in nominal rates, thus failing to estimate changes in effective rates due to changes in the mix of rent (cash and in kind), inflation, benefits accruing from the redistribution of the risks of crop failures, etc. Also, a reduction in land rent was possible partly because the taxes on land by this stage were not rising due to the increasing inability of the ruling class to raise taxes in order to capture the surplus accruing to peasants as the result of rising productivity.

40 Though not pursued here, there are other theoretically interesting questions concerning the changing methods of payment for labor and the changing patterns of the distribution of risks. For example, why did tenants not demand a fixed wage instead of a sharecropping arrangement in order to avoid risks of fluctuations in yield? One answer could be that an increase in total output under the incentive provided by the sharecropping arrangement enabled labor to obtain a larger income than could be earned in the form of fixed wages which shifted all the risks to the landholders. Rice, which is easier to measure and evaluate than a mix of commercial crops, was also more conducive to sharecropping arrangements. However, had the landholders who planted various commercial crops attempted to adopt sharecropping arrangements in order to minimize the risks involved in fixed wage payments, they would have found the transaction costs so high as to make this arrangement nearly prohibitive. On these and related theoretical issues, interested readers are referred to Cheung, *Theory of Share Tenancy*.

vest and winnow with care to maximize the yield—also was a crucial factor explaining why the large landholders who depended on hired labor (which was less motivated than the tenant cultivators) tended to rely more on other crops than rice.

Of course, in some regions such as Kinai, which had significant comparative advantages in planting commercial crops because of climate, soil, easy access to supply of fertilizers, and proximity to markets, commercial crops continued to be planted by hired labor and by tenant farmers. In these places, however, the land worked by tenant farmers tended to increase very slowly and, as a Japanese scholar put it, "Landlords cultivated their own land [by hired labor] and the rise of parasitic landlords" was less visible than elsewhere.[41]

Though the answer to the question why some peasants became tenant-cultivators is contained in the preceding discussion, I shall restate it explicitly: some peasants chose to become tenant-cultivators because the rent demanded by the large landholders was sufficiently low to make tenant-farming more attractive than or equal to other pursuits. Although some peasants found better opportunities in commerce and manufacturing and left the land completely or partly—and this was more pronounced in some regions than in others—many peasants in many regions found it more profitable to become tenant farmers. As tenants, they could fully use all of their household labor, enabling them to work an additional parcel of paddy in lieu of engaging in by-employments (which were not always available or dependable) or to remain in the village of their birth, provided the income earned by doing so was not significantly lower than that which could be earned elsewhere.[42] That is, the cost of finding new and suitable opportunities outside the village and the difficulty of obtaining sufficient capital to relocate were still significant factors in the decision-making of peasants.

Perhaps an accurate assessment would be to view this period as one in which alternatives for peasants were increasing, and in large numbers. They were leaving the land, engaging in part-time by-employments, becoming tenant farmers, or even increasing their landholdings in response to the changing relative levels of returns which could be earned in these pursuits. This assessment seems especially warranted

[41] Kimura, ed., *Kinsei Osaka*, p. 265.

[42] Smith wrote: "But if the large holder could not support the burden of rising production costs, one wonders how the small holder—especially the tenant—managed. The answer to this question has several parts. For one thing the small holder was far more willing, if need be, to absorb higher costs at the expense of his standard of life. Poverty was his usual condition" (*Agrarian Origins*, p. 127). For Smith to say this and then in the following pages to observe that wages were rising to increase the income of the *hōkōnin* and that by-employments supplemented small holders' earnings leaves theoretical ambiguities.

because during this period there were significant variations by region in the pace of the concentration of landholdings and in the increase in the number of tenant farmers. Within the broad trends, regional differences were marked, depending on the availability of opportunities for commercial and manufacturing activities either on a full- or part-time basis, and individual responses were varied.[43] However, all the calculations involved in adjusting their economic activities were done within economic circumstances which were generally characterized by an undeniable trend toward a rising wage level and by a general trend toward lower rents offered by large landholders as a measure for obtaining and keeping tenant farmers. The changes in the landholding patterns took place because both the landholders and peasants were actively seeking ways to maximize their gains.

During the last years of the Tokugawa period, from about 1830 to 1867, the economy continued to grow, albeit slowly. The living standard rose for most, despite the Tempō famine of the mid-1830's, because of increasing commercial and manufacturing activities and the increasing productivity of agriculture. Population, partly due to the famine, continued to increase only slowly, which resulted in a continuing labor shortage and a rising real wage level.[44] New factors at work during this period were rampant inflation and an increased competitiveness in commercial and manufacturing activities due to the decline of the guilds and the rise of the village entrepreneurs who began ef-

[43] This is the reason why one invariably finds, in the recent empirical studies, that some small holders increased their landholding whereas others reduced it or left the land entirely. Contrary to frequent observations made in the older literature that small holders were systematically subjected to economic pressures to give up their land, the changes in the landholding pattern of the small holders were quite varied, reflecting the many factors which came into the decision-making process of each peasant. A frequently added qualification on changes in the landholding pattern of small holders is one made by Shimbō after examining the changes observed in one village: "Changes in the landholding of those who originally held [an amount of land yielding] 3 to 5 koku [of rice] and 1 to 3 koku were most frequent during the 1760-80 period, and the number of those who increased their holdings was nearly equal to those whose holdings were reduced. In both classes of holders, upward and downward changes were manifest," Shimbō, Hōken-teki shōnōmin, p. 146. Contrast this to the following categorical statement made by several leading Marxist scholars: "The characteristic of the disintegration of the peasant class which became pronounced during the 1760-80 period was the polarization that was continuing to create the wage earners versus capital owners relationship. This was a process of disintegration caused by the continued impoverishment of peasants." Ōishi, Nihon keizaishi-ron, p. 98.

[44] For evidence of an unmistakable rising trend in the real wages of construction workers, see Sano Yōko, "The Changes in Real Wages of Construction Workers in Tokyo, 1830-1894," Management and Labor Studies, English series no. 4 (Jan. 1963), Institute of Management and Labor Studies, Keio University. Despite the fact that this is an extremely valuable source of important empirical evidence for analyzing the economy of the period, I have not seen any reference made to it by Japanese economic historians.

fectively to challenge the dominance of city merchants.[45] The Tokugawa bakufu, whose political power continued to wane at an accelerating pace, was responsible for both the inflation and the death of the guilds.

The effects of these economic forces on landholding patterns and contracts were predictable.[46] As increased competitiveness, inflation, and the generally uncertain climate of the economy seemed to have discouraged the wealthier landholders from investing in commerce and pre-modern manufacturing in nearby cities, and as money-lending had become riskier and less rewarding, the large landholders chose to continue to invest in village-based commerce, the processing of agriculture products, and land, despite the stronger demands made by wage-earners for higher wages and by cultivators for lower effective rents. More land was available for sale, because more peasants were beckoned to non-agricultural pursuits on a part- or full-time basis in and around the villages and because the Tempō famine reduced the numbers of cultivators and forced some to sell their land in those regions which were hardest hit.

The labor remaining in agriculture stood to gain. If the rent was paid in fixed amounts of cash, even only in part, the real burden of the rent declined in this period of rapid inflation. Even in the northeast, the poorest region of Japan, the terms improved for tenants because commercial and pre-modern manufacturing activities finally be-

[45] This refers to the growth of the *zaikata* merchants. See B. Hauser, *Economic Institutional Changes in Tokugawa Japan* (London and New York: Cambridge University Press, 1974), pp. 143-173.

[46] Japanese scholars' analyses of changes in the landholding pattern during this period are much less economic than those advanced for earlier periods. This is because much academic energy has been expended in debates on the nature of the *gōnō* (were they pre-industrial landowner-money lenders or incipient bourgeois capitalists?), and the nature and degree of industrialization achieved by the end of the Tokugawa period (did manufacturing, in the strict sense of the term, exist?). These questions, first debated during the early 1930's, were considered important to Japanese economic historians who were attempting to determine the politico-economic nature of the Meiji Restoration (was it a bourgeois revolution à la Western models or a uniquely Japanese "absolutist" revolution?) and to assign the Restoration to a specific stage in the Marxist framework of historical change.

As many Japanese economic historians have continued to be preoccupied with such debates, if at a much subtler and sophisticated level than in the pre-war years, the economic explanation offered for the polarization of landholding and the continuing increase of tenant farming during this stage is still a direct extension of the explanation offered for the third stage. The best analyses of the debate, i.e., the well-known debate between the Rōnō-ha (Labor-peasant faction) and the Kōza-ha (Lecture faction) are found in Ishii Takashi, *Gakusetsu hihan Meiji ishinron* (Tokyo: Yoshikawa Kōbunkan, 1961). What can be labeled the orthodox interpretation of the changes in the landholding pattern and the economy of this period is presented in a readable fashion by Kitajima Masamoto in *Bakuhan-sei no kumon* (Tokyo: Chūō Kōron, 1966), pp. 442-509. Nagahara, ed., *Nihon keizaishi*, pp. 147-153, also presents the dominant view with clarity.

gan to increase perceptibly, drawing labor out of agriculture, and because the population was reduced by the famine of the 1830's.[47] The price of rice was rising steadily, and the larger landholders were anxious to have their land worked by tenant-cultivators even if the rent in real value was declining.[48]

PRE-INDUSTRIAL ENGLAND

The major economic and political factors contributing to the changes in the landholding pattern and system of England during the sixteenth century were (1) an increasing population, in sharp contrast to the preceding centuries which had suffered from the Black Death (1348-1349), the Hundred Years' War (1337-1453), and the War of the Roses (1455-1485); (2) diminishing returns in agriculture, which was limited by the three-field rotation; (3) a secular rise in the price level (the Price Revolution); (4) increasing international trade, though only very slowly and yet limited in absolute quantity; and (5) political stability which rested on the delicate balance of power between the Tudor monarchs and the House of Commons dominated by the landed gentry and the merchant class. It was a combination of these factors which brought about the slow but steadily accelerating changes in the landholding pattern throughout the course of the century.[49]

[47] The terms of contract for both *nago* and tenant farmers improved during this period. Even in Nambu *han*, which has often been cited as a strong case in support of the traditional view, the remaining *nago*, who ranked below tenant farmers economically and socially, found their economic lot improving during this period to the point of being able to achieve *nago-nuke* (getting out of the *nago* status). By the 1830's, *nago* even in the mountainous regions were succeeding in becoming tenant farmers who paid a land rent in cash and who were increasingly able to add to their income through by-employments. Also, tenant farmers found it easier to renegotiate contracts after a poor harvest in order to effectively reduce the land rent.

The following statement from Takeyasu, who made one of the recent studies on land rent in the advanced Kinai region during this period, is revealing of the contrast between the orthodox view and the recent empirical reexaminations: "Mr. Araki has noted that the distribution of tenant farmers' agricultural output in the regions around Osaka during the last decades of the Tokugawa period was one-third for taxes, one-third for land rent, and one-third for the necessities of the tenant farmers. However, [my own case studies of several villages in this region] showed that the ratio was 1 for taxes, 1.4 for landholders and 2.6 for the tenant farmers. These of course are not absolutely reliable numbers and further large-scale examination of historical evidence must yet be continued." Takeyasu, *Kinsei kinai kosakuryō no kōzō*, pp. 245-246.

[48] The price of rice rose at an accelerating rate from 70-80 silver *momme* per *koku* in the early 1830's to 467 *momme* per *koku* in 1866. The prices of commercial crops were also rising, but the costs (labor and fertilizers) of cultivating these crops were rising equally rapidly and profits were under a strong pressure downward because of the competitive market. Yamamura, *A Study of Samurai*, pp. 52-55.

[49] The most useful sources consulted in writing this section on pre-modern Eng-

Before tracing the changes, however, I shall first establish a few relevant facts pertaining to the beginning of the sixteenth century. The War of the Roses had changed the landholding pattern significantly; some of the old noble families lost, the gentry gained, and Church holdings were diminished. But the Church was yet to suffer the wholesale confiscation of its vast holdings as it later did at the hands of Henry VIII in the name of the English Reformation.[50] For 1500, no English historian appears to be willing to make even an educated estimate of landholding by class of landholders. The first quantitative speculation is offered for the mid-sixteenth century, but even this is expressed in comparative terms vis-à-vis the beginning of the seventeenth century.

The basic tenurial system consisted of freehold, leasehold, and copyhold. The freeholders, who are estimated to have been a little over 20 percent of the total number of cultivators, enjoyed permanently secure tenure to their land. The leaseholders, consisting of less than 20 percent, had temporarily secure tenure but no claim to remain on the land which they cultivated. The remainder were copyholders or customary tenants whose claim to tenure was based more on custom than on law. Their tenure, however, was more secure than the leaseholders', and they were, by 1500, no longer serfs. They paid rent in cash and not in labor dues.

The changes in the landholding patterns and system during this century took three basic forms. The first was the gradual increase in landholding by the gentry; the second was the enclosure and/or reorganization of tenurial arrangements of demesne by the nobles and some gentry; and the last was the enclosure of commons and arable land. I shall examine each in turn.

The increase in landholding by the gentry was by far the most significant development. In terms of the total acreage affected, the en-

---

land were G. E. Mingay, *English Landed Society in the Eighteenth Century* (London and Toronto: University of Toronto Press, 1963); Phyllis Dean and W. A. Cole, *British Economic Growth, 1688-1959* (London: Cambridge University Press, 1964); E. L. Jones and G. E. Mingay, eds., *Land, Labor, and Population in the Industrial Revolution* (London: Edward Arnold, 1967); L. S. Pressnell, ed., *Studies in the Industrial Revolution* (London: Athlone Press, 1960); J. D. Chambers and G. E. Mingay, *The Agricultural Revolution, 1750-1880* (London: B. T. Botsford, 1966); E.C.K. Gonner, *Common Land and Enclosure* (London: MacMillan, 1962); and scores of articles published in the *Journal of Economic History* and the *Economic History Review* since the end of the Second World War.

[50] F.M.L. Thompson, "The Social Distribution of Landed Property in England since the Sixteenth Century," *Economic History Review*, 2nd ser., vol. 19, no. 3 (Dec. 1966), p. 512. This article (pp. 505-517) is one of the most useful for obtaining a general outline of changes in the landholding patterns from the sixteenth to the nineteenth centuries. Also see J. P. Cooper, "The Social Distribution of Land and Men in England, 1436-1700," *Economic History Review*, 2nd ser., vol. 20, no. 3 (Dec. 1967), pp. 419-440.

closure of commons, which aroused the passion of the time and of later historians, was a relatively minor factor in transforming the landholding pattern during this century. Far more important was the acquisition of land by the gentry. The consensus is that the landed gentry's income from land became three times as large as that of the peers by 1600, and that the peers' landholding declined from about one-third of the total land to one-twelfth between 1500 and 1640, on the eve of the civil wars.[51] Although this was the trend, there were, of course, exceptions. Some peers, benefitting from office income and other favors from the Court and from their own managerial interests and talents, increased their landholdings. And not all of the gentry increased their landholdings. But even with this proviso, I must answer a crucial question before I can examine the reasons for the changes in the landholding pattern. This is: Who were the gentry?

Tawney's answer was that the gentry "varied widely in wealth" and "though ragged at its edges, it had a solid core." The core consisted of,

"The landed proprietors, above the yeomanry, and below the peerage, together with a growing body of well-to-do farmers, sometimes tenants of their relatives, who had succeeded the humble peasants of the past as lessees of demesne farms; professional men, also rapidly increasing in number, such as the more eminent lawyers, divines, and an occasional medical practitioner; and the wealthier merchants, who, if not, as many were, themselves sons of landed families, had received a similar education, moved in the same circles, in England, unlike France, were commonly recognized to be socially indistinguishable from them."[52]

Tawney's definition is sufficient for the purpose of my analysis, provided one remains aware, as critics have pointed out convincingly, that there were some lesser gentry whose landholdings declined and that some gentry became peers, facts which some believe invalidate Tawney's oversimplified analysis, which in effect argued that most gentry increased their landholdings and that the peers as a group clearly stood apart from the gentry.[53]

Why did the gentry, or some of the gentry, increase their landholdings while many nobles tended to lose their land? The answer is that they had the means, the opportunities, and the motivation to do so. The capital used by the gentry to acquire land came from their ac-

---

[51] Thompson, "Social Distribution," pp. 509-511.

[52] R. H. Tawney, "The Rise of the Gentry, 1558-1640," in E. M. Carus-Wilson, ed., *Essays in Economic History*, vol. 1 (London: Edward Arnold, 1954), p. 176.

[53] The critics are represented in Lawrence Stone, ed., *Social Change and Revolution in England, 1540-1640* (London: Longmans, 1965). See especially section 1, which contains essays by H. R. Trevor-Roper, R. Zagorin, and L. Stone, pp. 19-32, 45-59, and 63-80.

cumulated earnings in the steadily expanding domestic and international trade, professional earnings, and income earned through skillful management of the land. Their opportunities came in the form of the Crown land which was put on sale; financial embarrassment suffered by the nobles (the causes of which I shall describe shortly) who were forced to sell their holdings; confiscated Church lands sold to the highest bidder; and the land which could be acquired from lesser gentry and freeholders who either chose to, or were forced to, sell their land. The gentry's motivation was their confidence that their talents could make the land pay, as well as their desire for country life and the social standing which came to large landholders. In Tawney's eloquent words:

"The Government of the first two Stuarts continued, on a more majestic scale, the Elizabethan policy of turning Crown estates into cash. So far from deprecating the acquisition of land by the business world, it threw land at its head. It was not surprising that a successful merchant, who had made his pile in trade, should prefer the risks of commerce to the decorous stability of what was regarded as a gilt-edged investment. By the middle years of James, if not, indeed, earlier, it is difficult to find a prominent London capitalist who is not also a substantial landowner."[54]

It is important to stress that the gentry's "commercial turn of mind" tended to justify their confidence and enabled them to make profits, and thus keep and enlarge the holdings once acquired. The increase in population also worked in favor of these shrewd men. Tenants were no longer scarce, and the increasing supply of labor in this century enabled these new landholders to negotiate more profitable terms with their tenants. Although many nobles had to contend with the copyholders, who were still protected by custom which was far from cost-free to change, the gentry's land could be worked by leaseholders who were more exposed to competitive pressure.[55]

The story for most nobles was quite different. "The value of all customary and non-commercial payments tumbled down"[56] because of the falling value of money which their copyholders paid. Raising quit rents and waiting out the lives of copyholders to recontract with their sons benefitted the peers only too slowly. Many peers had little inclination or aptitude for slaving over account books, reorganizing landholding by buying out freeholds, or engaging in mining or in timber-cutting as a minority of nobles did with great success. The ma-

[54] Tawney, "Rise of the Gentry," p. 188.
[55] For an excellent analysis of these developments, see D. C. North and R. P. Thomas, "The Rise and Fall of the Manorial System: A Theoretical Model," *Journal of Economic History*, vol. 31, no. 4 (Dec. 1971), pp. 777-803.
[56] Tawney, "Rise of the Gentry," p. 179.

jority let their holdings dwindle to pay for steady or even rising expenditures due to extravagant tastes, ostentatious waste, and mounting debts.[57] "Some groups can adapt themselves to the new tensions and opportunities; others cannot. The former rise; the latter sink."[58]

The process of this rising and sinking was facilitated by the development of the market and the necessary institutional development to facilitate the transfer of property. As the volume of land sales rose, lawyers emerged who specialized in dealings involving land, and laws protecting the involved parties against malpractice were enacted, both of which reduced the transactions costs significantly. The Act of 1585, for example, voided fraudulent conveyances, imposed penalties on the guilty, and required all mortgages to be entered with the clerks of recognizance.

Many peers, under strong pressure to increase their income, began to change the tenurial arrangements on land which had once been demesne. The former demesne often had been divided up among a large number of serfs who had, by the beginning of the sixteenth century, became copyholders. It had been profitable for the manorial lords of the fifteenth century to exchange labor dues for a fixed cash rent, because cultivators were hard to come by and the value of money was relatively steady. The peers in the sixteenth century, however, found this arrangement unsatisfactory, because tenants were easier to find and inflation was eroding the value of the fixed rent. The peers, therefore, proceeded to reduce the number of small copyholds and to have the land cultivated by a smaller number of more efficient leaseholders working larger plots of land who were able to invest their capital to improve the land and to pay higher rents. These leaseholders were obliged to recontract periodically to account for the changing value of money, land, and labor. Of course, these changes in tenurial arrangements desired by the peers did not come about overnight. In some instances, the peers chose to proceed slowly, respecting all the customary rights of the copyholders, but in more and more cases they chose to invoke their legal rights to circumvent custom.

With regard to the enclosure of commons and arables, I need to point out only the few aspects of this well-known development which are significant within the framework of this analysis. Put simply, enclosure took place because the price of wool rose sufficiently during most of the sixteenth century to justify the costs involved in altering the existing pattern of land use and the institutional arrangement

[57] A useful source that enables one to see the increasing economic difficulties of the nobles in the early sixteenth century is Ian Blanchard, "Population Change, Enclosure, and the Early Tudor Economy," *Economic History Review*, 2nd ser., vol. 23, no. 3 (Dec. 1970), pp. 427-443.

[58] Tawney, "Rise of the Gentry," p. 179.

called commons. When the price of wool began to rise, the first step was to accommodate this new economic factor within the existing institutional framework. The device, known as "stinting," came into being in order to limit the number of grazing animals. The voluntary arrangement, however, was difficult to enforce, and so long as the pasture was being used communally, a natural tendency was to set a limit higher than what was desirable in maximizing the collective return from grazing.[59]

As the price of wool continued to rise and the weakness of stinting became obvious, landholders took their second step, the enclosing of commons, in order to maximize their returns from the land. The economic logic behind this action was this: if a common is used exclusively by a single decision-making unit, the rent—in the economic theoretical sense of the term—is maximized, in contrast to a case in which multiple decision-making units dissipate all the rent. That is, when the right to graze on the commons is non-exclusive, "rent becomes a residual with every decision-making unit maximizing the portion left behind by others."[60] Therefore, from a society's point of view, an exclusive common used by a landowner is more desirable—more efficient—than a common used to graze sheep belonging to many. What took place was a profound change in institutional arrangements, i.e., the common became exclusive private property.

An important reason enabling this fundamental change in institutional arrangements was the precedent existing in the common law, from as far back as the Statute of Merton of 1235, permitting the enclosure of pastoral commons. Previous rulings required that the copyholders be given "sufficient" alternative land, but what was "sufficient" was often a matter of interpretation. And the interpretation could be quite flexible when legal claims of many copyholders were far from ironclad and when the copyholders were in no position to engage in costly legal battles. Records exist to tell us that when what landholders hoped was "sufficient" alternative land failed to satisfy the copyholders, "persuasion, intimidation, destruction of copy rolls, and other devices within and outside of the law" were resorted to by the enclosing landholders.[61] However, lest the preceding give the impression that this essay subscribes to the view that enclosure was the prime cause of the social ills of the century, it should be added that the areas suitable for sheep-grazing were in many instances sparsely populated

---

[59] For a theoretical analysis of the tendency described here, see the source cited in footnote 60.

[60] S.N.S. Cheung, "The Structure of a Contract and the Theory of a Non-Exclusive Resource," *Journal of Law and Economics*, vol. 13, no. 1 (April 1970), p. 59.

[61] Dudley Dillard, *Economic Development in the North Atlantic Community* (Englewood Cliffs, N.J.: Prentice-Hall, 1967), pp. 135-136.

and for this reason obtaining the necessary consent from a small number of persons affected did not constitute "class robbery."[62] Amicable agreements were easier to obtain when only a small number of persons was affected, and the low population density promised a good chance of providing the required sufficient alternative.

To recapitulate, the sixteenth century witnessed a gradual increase in landholding by the gentry; copyholds, either in former demesne or otherwise, declined; leaseholds rose slowly; and, though affecting only a small portion of the total land, the enclosure of commons and arable took place. These changes reflected the changed economic and political circumstances of the sixteenth century. The transformation of commons into exclusive private property was a significant step forward, as was the increase in the number of leaseholds. Both were indications of the English society's ability to respond to a new set of economic stimuli.

What I have described in the preceding pages also applies to the years between 1600 and the Civil War. The political and economic factors characterizing the sixteenth century prevailed in the main for the 1600-1640 period, as did the trend of change described in the preceding paragraph. The Civil War was a momentous upheaval in political history, but its consequences were yet to be seen in the landholding patterns of the years that followed.

Between the beheading of Charles I (1649) and the Glorious Revolution, the power of Parliament became supreme in the realm. The interests of the landed were well represented, and the merchant class too had its members in that body. The merchants also had the means to influence Parliament. Together, they imposed policy in their interests, and laws against their interests often failed to pass. If some laws not to the liking of the landed and/or the merchant class did chance to pass, there was little likelihood of their being enforced. Naturally, taxes on the landed and the merchants tended to remain low.

It is not warranted to say that the civil wars drastically changed the landholding patterns, because most of the royalists managed to buy back the lands which were confiscated, but the heavy fines imposed on the royalists and the fragmentation of Church and Crown lands tended to favor the new peers and the gentry. In Mingay's words:

"The effects of the civil wars and the subsequent political developments thus exercised an influence on landownership until well into the eighteenth century. The changes, however, came about slowly and gradually, and resulted in a revolution in landholding. The principal

[62] "Enclosure . . . was a plain enough case of class robbery" (E. P. Thompson, *The Making of the English Working Class*, New York: Random House, 1963, p. 218).

consequence was that the properties of the impoverished owners who were forced to sell were either bought up by newcomers from outside the landed classes, or were absorbed into the large estates."[63]

Another product of the civil wars and the new complexion of Parliament was the Act of 1695, which destroyed the customary rights of tenants of confiscated lands and virtually made them tenants-at-will. The act did not materially affect many cultivators; some copyholders were already in fact tenants-at-will and others could count on custom to help them, if less effectively than it once did. The crucial fact, however, was that such an act was passed.

If Thompson is correct in characterizing the latter half of the seventeenth century as "a period of stability" in landholding patterns and systems,[64] most significant was the visible increase in agricultural productivity which began sometime around the middle of the seventeenth century. In the words of E. L. Jones:

"The middle of the seventeenth century seems the most appropriate starting-point for the infinitely expansible improvement of farming practice. . . . Documentary evidence bears this out. The crucial innovations pertained to the supply of fodder, partly the diffusion of turnip as a field crop but much more important at that early date the first widespread cultivation of clover, sainfoin, and ryegrass, with the vigorous 'floating' of water meadows (i.e., the irrigation of streamside pasture). These crops and practices, with later additions like the swede (a much hardier root), went on spreading into new counties, new estates, new farms, and new fields."[65]

The rising price of livestock was an important factor in this change. The relatively slow population increase, the gains from international and domestic trade, and the stable or declining prices of the steadily increasing cereal output contributed to a stronger demand for meat and grain per head.[66] The well-known agitations and parliamentary acts relating to the Corn Laws of this period do not contradict these observations, for these were the laws, in the final analysis, which protected and increased the income of the landed class, then dominating Parliament.

Increasing agricultural productivity—the tempo of which seems to have accelerated as one piece of new knowledge was built upon another—and the consequent rise in the income from landownership were the prime movers in changing the landholding pattern during

[63] Mingay, *English Landed Society*, p. 43.

[64] Thompson, "Social Distribution," pp. 509-510.

[65] E. L. Jones, "Introduction," in E. L. Jones, ed., *Agriculture and Economic Growth in England 1650-1815* (London: Methuen, 1967), p. 7.

[66] See A. H. John, "Agricultural Productivity and Economic Growth in England 1700-1750," in Jones, ed., ibid., pp. 172-193.

the first sixty years of the seventeenth century. Before I analyze the changes in the landholding pattern, I shall first establish the characteristics of the change, generally and quantitatively, and provide a brief sketch of the economic conditions of the 1700-1760 period against which the causes of the changing landholding pattern must be analyzed.

According to Mingay, a leading student of the economic history of eighteenth century England:

"The late seventeenth and early eighteenth centuries have been characterized as a period of marked change in the structure of land-ownership. The great landlords' domination of government and political life was matched by their growing stake in the countryside, and the decline of small estates was the corollary of the amassing of land in fewer hands. In this process, the substantial gentry generally held their own, although the gap between them and the great lords tended to widen. It was the small gentry and occupying owners who fell in number, and whose land to a considerable extent was absorbed into the estates of the large landlords. The general drift of the land market was in favour of large accumulations of property in the hands of existing large owners and wealthy newcomers."[67]

If one is to give credence to the quantitative "guesses" made by Mingay, the change in landholding pattern was substantial. Though he was willing to speculate only for 1690 and 1790, one learns from his figures that the landed class's income from land nearly doubled during the century. This means that, even given the steady but slow rate of increase in rent, the collective landholding of the landed class as of 1790 must have just about doubled over that of the preceding century.

The pattern of landholding and income range of the various land-holding classes as of 1790 were as follows:[68]

1. Four hundred great landlords had annual incomes ranging from 5,000 to 50,000 pounds, and they jointly owned 20 to 25 percent of the total cultivated land in England and Wales. A great landlord is a landowner whose annual income exceeded 5,000 pounds and whose style of life distinguished him from others in the landed society.

2. The gentry class could be separated into three sub-groups consisting of 700 to 800 wealthy gentry families, each having an annual income of 3,000 to 5,000 pounds; 3,000 to 4,000 squires, each having an annual income of 1,000 to 3,000 pounds; and 10,000 to 20,000 gentlemen, each having an annual income of 300 to 1,000 pounds. The

[67] Mingay, *English Landed Society*, p. 50. Also see H. J. Habakkuk, "English Landownership, 1680-1740," *Economic History Review*, 2nd ser., vol. 10, no. 1 (Jan. 1940), pp. 2-6 and 15-17.

[68] These data are from Mingay, *English Landed Society*, pp. 25-27.

whole gentry class together owned 50 to 60 percent of the total cultivated land.

3. There were two types of freeholders. Mingay called one group
the "better sort," which had annual incomes of 150 to 700 pounds;
about 25,000 families were in this group. The other group, the "lesser
sort," had annual incomes of 30 to 300 pounds; about 75,000 families
belonged to this group. Both types of freeholders together owned
about 15 to 20 percent of the total cultivated land.

The general economic condition of England during the first half of
the eighteenth century, which is essential in understanding the motivation of the large estate owners, can be summarized as follows. During
the period, agricultural output rose relative to domestic and foreign
demand, despite the fact that foreign demand more than doubled between 1700 and 1760. Also, because population was growing relatively
slowly—an annual increase of 5,000 to 8,000 in contrast to 60,000 per
year after 1760—the agricultural output was running "slightly ahead
of demand," that is, the prices of agricultural products tended to remain stable or even fall.[69] As population did not rise relative to the
total number of people lost to urban centers plus those who continued
to be demanded by agriculture, the real wage rose. (Nominal wages
remained stable or declined less than prices of agricultural products.)
A. H. John would add here that the increase in real wages was extremely important because it increased the demand for manufactured
goods, providing a crucial stimulus for the beginning of the Industrial
Revolution which followed.[70]

The preceding suggests that English agriculture of this period was
in a situation analogous to a competitive industry with an excess capacity and facing a declining price for its product. Short of a sudden
increase in demand, such an industry is bound for a prolonged period
of struggle toward efficiency which hopefully will help some to survive
the rough waters until the successful, possessing sufficient initial scale
and the necessary capital for improving productive efficiency, can absorb the market share of their weaker competitors. A sufficiently large
initial scale—those landholders whose holdings grew most had at least
300 acres—was crucial because it meant that the holder could use his
capital efficiently or could borrow the capital required to increase
production efficiency, could realize economies of scale in marketing,
and could offer better-equipped farms which were important in attracting the best tenants.[71]

---

[69] E. L. Jones, "Agriculture and Economic Growth in England, 1660-1750: Agricultural Change," in Jones, ed., *Agriculture and Economic Growth*, p. 158.

[70] John, "Agricultural Productivity," pp. 174-175.

[71] Mingay, "Size of Farms," pp. 470-471, and the same author's "The 'Agricultural Revolution' in English History: A Reconsideration," *Agricultural History*,

It is beyond dispute that the increasing agricultural efficiency of the period required substantial capital. Capital was needed to buy new seeds, "to rear and maintain more animals, and to carry a greater stock of implements. Landowners were involved in the planting of hedges, in the building of roads and farms, and in a more extensive policy of maintenance."[72] Economies of scale were also important. To cite only one example:

"Contemporary writers argued that in the marketing of his produce, the large farmer had greater bargaining power in dealing with middle-men, and he could grade his produce and take advantage of market fluctuations by waiting for the highest price. He was also more efficient in his use of labor and capital. He could hire the best laborers in the neighbourhood, take advantage of their natural aptitudes by employing them in specialized work, and so to a degree practice division of labour. Moreover, with a large acreage, he found it possible to utilize more economically his teams, wagons, carts, ploughs and other implements."[73]

And in borrowing capital—this important factor must be stressed because of the falling interest rates and the rapidly developing capital market—the largest landholders had a decided advantage:

"The attractions of mortgages were further enhanced by the development of the capital market and the fall in the rate of interest. Consequently, with mortgages more secure, easier to arrange, and cheaper to service, they came to play a major role in enabling landowners to shoulder a heavy burden of debt without resort to large sales of land. . . . In the last years of the seventeenth century about six per cent was the usual rate of interest on mortgages and personal bonds. In the eighteenth century, however, the rate on mortgages fell in line with the fall in yields on the Funds to five per cent, and never moved far from this moderate level, although at some periods favoured borrowers could obtain a mortgage for as little as four per cent. There were usually many investors, landholders, professional men and businessmen, retired officers, and widows, seeking good mortgages in which to place their surplus money. The transactions were generally on an impersonal basis, and were arranged through a London banker or lawyer, or a country attorney. Mortgages were not necessarily kept in being for long terms of years but were often rearranged with surpris-

---

vol. 37, no. 3 (July 1963), pp. 123-133. The latter cites numerous articles that deal with changes in agricultural methods, technology, and efficiency.

[72] A. H. John, "Aspects of English Economic Growth in the First Half of the Eighteenth Century," in E. M. Carus-Wilson, ed., *Essays in Economic History*, vol. 2 (New York: St. Martin's, 1966), p. 362.

[73] Mingay, "Size of Farms," p. 471.

ing rapidity, usually in order to pay off a pressing mortgage or to secure a more favourable rate of interest."[74]

In addition, the larger landholders were better able to distribute
the risks imposed by nature than were the smaller owners. Sharp declines in the prices of agricultural commodities, as happened several
times during the 1700-1760 period, were much less likely to cause financial insolvency among the larger landholders. For economic and
social reasons, marriages often helped to join land with land or land
with fresh capital. In a society in which interclass boundaries were
easy to cross and "virtually all peers were related through marriage
and younger sons with the wealthier gentry,"[75] class did not stand in
the way of enlarging the landholdings through well-chosen spouses.
The process of increasing the holdings among the landed class was
also aided, as Clay pointed out (admonishing Mingay who stressed
economic reasons, marriages, and inheritance), by the demographic
trend found by Hollingsworth:

"In the middle decades of the seventeenth [century] their [English
peers'] natural rate of increase rapidly fell off; and . . . the generations
born between 1650 and 1724, who were fathering children from the
early 1670's onwards, were failing to maintain their numbers by an increasing margin. By the second quarter of the eighteenth century, indeed, only four sons were born to every five males of the previous
generation. This tendency towards extinction was reversed around the
middle of the century."[76]

If the relative efficiency of large farms over smaller holdings can
be accepted, my analysis of an increasingly important development
for change in the landholding pattern of eighteenth-century England
—the Enclosure Movement—can be reduced to asking: Why did enclosure proceed at a relatively slow pace during the 1700-1769 period?[77] The answer, stated simply, is that the costs of enclosing—the·
costs of meeting legal requirements—were relatively high compared to
the gains which could be realized from enclosure, i.e., from the increased efficiency in using resources. Unlike the enclosure of the sixteenth century, which primarily enclosed common pastures, the eighteenth-century enclosure involved arable land. Under such circumstances, the common law required that an agreement consenting to enclosure be obtained from the persons affected. Thus, depending on the

---

[74] Mingay, *English Landed Society*, p. 37.

[75] Ibid., p. 9.

[76] Christopher Clay, "Marriage, Inheritance, and the Rise of Large Estates in
England, 1660-1815," *Economic History Review*, 2nd ser., vol. 21, no. 3 (Dec. 1968),
p. 514.

[77] For the data on enclosure bills during this period, see Dean and Cole, *British
Economic Growth*, p. 94.

difficulty or ease with which such an agreement was obtained, enclosure was exemplified by one of two methods: piecemeal exchange or one simultaneous exchange of land. The first method was painfully slow, and the second required an agreement involving a large number of persons.

The simultaneous exchange was much more desirable than piecemeal exchanges, because the former enabled the landholders to realize various economies of scale immediately and otherwise to increase the productivity of their resources more in speed and magnitude than the latter. The difference in the gains realized by these two methods apparently was crucial, because enclosure could and did increase when legal changes were made to reduce the costs of simultaneous exchange. Such changes came in time. The law required four-fifths of the affected persons to agree to enclosure until the mid-century, but it was changed to require only three-fifths in 1773. The General Enclosure Act, which substantially eliminated the legal costs of having each enclosure bill enacted by Parliament, was finally passed in 1801. The rapid rise in enclosure after the mid-century, therefore, was due to these legal changes, along with the declining cost per enclosed acre of surveying and fencing, as the size of each enclosure increased.[78]

Returns from enclosure were high. McCloskey made an assessment of the magnitude of the returns:

"If rents doubled on the 14 million or so acres enclosed after 1700, assuming as a low estimate that they earned typically a rent of 10 shillings an acre before enclosure (this before the inflation of the Napoleonic Wars), the increase in rent yields a lower bound on the increase in the value of agricultural output of around £7 million each year. Only opportunity costs need to be subtracted from this total (transfers of income, although they affect the rate of enclosure, do not detract from its social benefit), which may be put at around £2 an acre for each enclosure. If they were put higher it would matter little for the results, because to convert this capital sum into a stream of income comparable to the yearly increase in output it must be multiplied by the interest rate. Conceding that the rate of interest on consols, typically well under five per cent, is a riskless rate and therefore too low, one might still doubt that the relevant rate was much above 10 per cent. The 14 million acres enclosed, then resulted in a stream of income foregone of (£2) (14 million) (.10) or £2.8 million each year. Therefore, the net gain to national income, if one had the temerity to ignore the many qualifications necessary in view of the

[78] Donald N. McCloskey, "The Enclosure of Open Fields: Preface to a Study of Its Impact on the Efficiency of English Agriculture in the Eighteenth Century," *Journal of Economic History*, vol. 32, no. 1 (March 1972), pp. 27-29.

argument of this essay, could be put around £4.2 million a year. . . .
To put the matter another way, the return to enclosure was high; an
expenditure of £2 an acre (ignoring here transfer costs) yielded an
increased rent accruing to the landlord of 10 shillings in each year
following, for a rate of return of 25 per cent per year."[79]

McCloskey's findings help one pursue the relationships between the
changes in landholding patterns and such developments as rises in
productivity, the accumulation of capital, and increased output and
rises in real wages, all of which are crucial in understanding the
reasons for the successful Industrial Revolution which soon came. But
as it is not the intent of this essay to review the massive literature on
the relationships between agricultural change, in the widest sense of
the phrase, and the Industrial Revolution, I shall conclude this section
on pre-modern England by quoting two English scholars whose reflections are most valuable in comparing the experiences of pre-modern
England and Tokugawa Japan. Mingay, speaking on the role of landowners in industrialization, wrote:

"There is ample ground for saying that landowners played a very
significant part in the industrial developments of the later seventeenth
and early eighteenth centuries. As the industrial revolution gathered
momentum there appeared more men from outside the landed classes
with sufficient capital to undertake the risks of enterprise, and the
landlords, for the most part, fell into the background as lessors and
investors. In many respects their role in industrial development was
similar to that in agriculture: to encourage enterprise and efficiency,
and to be the providers of the basic capital facilities necessary for
progress. As innovators they were not prominent—technical problems
generally were outside their field; essentially they were promoters and
investors; but even so some landlords were still among the leading
entrepreneurs of the later eighteenth century, particularly in the newer
industrial areas. Over the whole period it might well be argued that in
some vital spheres of the economy, in mining, iron and transport, as
well as in agriculture, the landlords' contribution was itself crucial to
the process of expansion."[80]

And in a well-known essay written in 1965, A. H. John wrote at a
more general level:

"Given the technnical and financial resources of early eighteenth
century England, increases in real income as a consequence of a rise
in agricultural productivity, far from slowing down growth, had their
own special contribution to make to it. The buoyancy of the domestic
market, compared with conditions abroad, provided a favourable en-

[79] Ibid., pp. 34-35.
[80] Mingay, *English Landed Society*, p. 201.

vironment for introduction of new kinds of goods and improvement of techniques which encouraged import substitution."[81]

As many economic theorists of economic growth have emphasized, industrialization can begin and succeed only if it is aided by robust agriculture.

A COMPARATIVE ANALYSIS

Through an examination of nearly three centuries of changes in the landholding systems in Tokugawa Japan and pre-modern England, one particularly salient common denominator emerges. That is, despite economic, political, social, and institutional differences which existed between these two nations, both succeeded in transforming the landholding patterns and the institutional arrangements between landholders and cultivators in such a way as to increase the total output of the agricultural sector, which, in turn, raised the living standard of the population and provided the essential foundations, in the form of capital, labor, institutions, and potential demand, for the industrialization which followed.

In both nations, the most significant change observed in the landholding pattern was a trend toward concentration in landownership. Concentration in landholding was achieved in England through the enclosures in the sixteenth and eighteenth centuries and through a gradual acquisition of estates by the landholding nobles and successful gentry. In Tokugawa Japan, a steady acquisition by the wealthy landowners was the principal method by which the landholding pattern in the villages came to be highly skewed.

The increasing size of landholdings in most cases raised the productivity of each of the factors in agricultural production. Specialists of English economic history agree that the enclosures increased the productivity of land, capital, and labor, and that the larger farm units which came into being after the mid-seventeenth century were able to realize various economies of scale. In Tokugawa Japan, the large landholders managed to use their resources more efficiently because their large holdings enabled them to rotate crops, to use all-important fertilizers more economically, to acquire new seeds and improved tools, to undertake irrigation and reclamation, and to take advantage of economies of scale in processing and marketing their output.

That it was the wealthy farmers of Tokugawa Japan and the nobles and the gentry of pre-modern England who became the large landholders is no less important than the fact that large holdings increased the efficiency of resources. These large landholders were men "with a

---

[81] John, "Agriculture and Economic Growth," p. 178.

commercial turn of mind"; they sought to increase their holdings for economic gain; and they never ceased, even after they accumulated land and capital, to seek even more profitable opportunities for their capital and talents. These opportunities came, for example, in the budding industries in Yorkshire and the thriving commerce in the Kinai. In whose hands the surpluses of an economy are accumulated is often more important than how much surplus exists, if one is to seek reasons for economic growth. In this regard, both Japan and England were fortunate.

An integral part of the changes in the landholding patterns in both England and Japan were the changes in the contractual agreements between landowners and cultivators in these nations. These changes were made in response to changing economic circumstances, with the result of improving the allocation of resources and providing the incentives necessary to make better use of resources. When the changes in contractual arrangements are seen within the perspective of three centuries, these changes appear to have come almost methodically in response to changing economic forces.

Just as the decline of the manorial arrangement was in response to the rising value of labor and the growth of markets, as North and Thomas have ably shown,[82] the increased use of leaseholds in preference to copyholds was in response to the declining bargaining power of labor and the rising price level. The rights of copyholders were lost over time because they stood in the way of more productive uses of the land. And just as "customs" eroded in the face of changing economic circumstances, the economy demonstrated the ability to equate the marginal returns of labor and capital from agriculture and other pursuits. Recent studies—Chambers's well-known work included[83]— show that changes in contractual arrangements, as well as enclosure, helped to make the allocation of labor more responsive to the relative income which could be earned in agriculture and in cities. The Poor Laws and the parish registers did their best to obstruct the market forces by impeding the mobility of labor, but, in retrospect, their ability to impede was limited and short-lived.

The changes in contractual agreements in Tokugawa Japan also followed the path suggested by the analytical framework adopted in this essay. The emergence of the *honbyakushō* system, the gradual decline of labor dues required of the newly "listed" peasants by the landowners, the growth of tenant-cultivators, and a tendency for rents to be paid more in cash than in kind—all are developments explain-

---

[82] North and Thomas, "The Rise and Fall of Manorial Systems," pp. 777-803.

[83] J. D. Chambers, "Enclosures and Labour Supply in the Industrial Revolution," *Economic History Review,* 2nd ser., vol. 5, no. 3 (Aug. 1953), pp. 319-43.

able within the analytical framework. The factors affecting and determining these developments were the relative values of labor and land, the rate of increase in population, the relative advantages in planting labor-intensive rice or capital- and land-intensive commercial crops, inflation, and not the inevitable "contradictions" involved in "feudal agriculture" or the tendency of landholders to "exploit" the landless.

There is another similarity between Japan and England which was important in facilitating the changes in landholding patterns and contractual agreements to make more efficient uses of resources. That is, for two very different reasons, the dominant political authority in both nations did not prevent, or was unable to prevent, these changes, and thus contributed to the growth of the economy, either actively or passively.

In England, the Parliament—the supreme political power in the realm—reflected the interests of the landed throughout the period. It was an active participant, as clearly shown in the enclosure movements, in redefining the rights of copyholders and otherwise altering the contractual arrangements between landowners and cultivators. The Tokugawa bakufu, in contrast, was a passive partner. It could not prevent the landholding patterns and contractual arrangements from changing. Because its political power was weak, the laws forbidding the transfer of land were little observed and rarely enforced. The bakufu's and daimyo's restrictions on peasant mobility were relatively ineffective from the beginning of the Tokugawa period and became progressively less effective over time; the more peasants moved, the more land changed hands. Also, the ruling class of Tokugawa Japan was not composed of landowners but of the collectors of land taxes. For them, changes in landownership and contractual arrangements mattered little as long as they received their dues. In short, either actively or passively, economic forces were free or little constrained in molding the landholding patterns and contractual arrangements.

These similarities which existed between Tokugawa Japan and premodern England provide students of Japanese economic history with an important insight. When one realizes that Tokugawa landholding patterns and contractual arrangements continued to be transformed, as in pre-modern England, it would be expected that Japan would be ready to take its first significant steps toward industrialization as soon as the opportunity was presented through the opening of the nation to the West, knowledge of Western technology, and a chance to reap the large gains to be captured from international trade. It is possible to argue that Japan was following the English path of economic growth about a century behind. Roughly, both the effective end of the medieval landholding system and the gradual attainment of a highly rational use of resources followed an analytically similar course in these countries, except that these developments in Japan came between the late sixteenth century to the mid-nineteenth century in contrast to England, where they occurred between the early sixteenth century and the later decades of the eighteenth. Thus, Japan was introduced to the industrializing world economy when most of its preparations for taking its first steps in this direction had been completed.

Because of the changes in the landholding pattern and contractual arrangements which had been accomplished, and because of what these changes implied in terms of increasing demand, the accumulation of capital, and resource mobility, Japan after the Meiji Restoration was able to depend on agriculture as the prime supplier of capital and labor needed for her industrialization.[84] It is not surprising that during the last decades of the nineteenth century the large landholders became the important organizers of and providers of capital for the rapidly increasing number of banks, as well as active participants in the budding international trade and the silk and cotton textile industries.[85]

My analysis is equally instructive in highlighting the significance of a few crucial differences which existed between these two nations. The most important is that Japan was closed to the outside world prior to its industrialization, whereas England was one of the most active participants in the international market. The difference is important not because of the international trade per se—Dean and Cole deemphasized its importance in the economic growth of England during the period with which I am concerned[86]—but because it kept modern

[84] For Japanese historians, it should be stated explicitly that although the wage level and the living standard of the Tokugawa peasants rose, I do not argue that the Tokugawa peasant became happier or more satisfied with life. As amply shown by numerous peasant revolts and other indications of dissatisfaction, which have often been used mistakenly to suggest "increasing immiserization," a higher real income is only a partial indicator of human well-being. I am also the first to admit that there are numerous exceptions to the inferences and observations made in this essay and that the analyses presented here are applicable only to the most dominant patterns identified and the major factors at work. Economic change, however important, was only one among many factors determining the totality of the lives of people in Tokugawa Japan. Ironically, the point made here is the same as that made in E. P. Thompson's critique of the "optimists'" literature of the English industrial revolution: "It is quite possible for statistical averages and human experiences to run in opposite directions. A *per capita* increase in quantitative factors may take place at the same time as a great qualitative disturbance in people's way of life, traditional relationships, and sanctions. People may consume more goods and become less happy or less free at the same time." E. P. Thompson, *The Making of the English Working Class* (Middlesex: Penguin, 1963), p. 231.

[85] See part 2 of Yamamura, *A Study of Samurai*, pp. 137-194.

[86] Dean and Cole, *British Economic Growth*, p. 310.

technology from Japan while it stimulated the growth of technology-promoting import substitutions in England, which already was a leader among the effective innovators. Had Japan had access to Western technology and had returns from capital been higher in manufacturing, the increasing amounts of capital being accumulated by the wealthy landholders would undoubtedly have flowed to the cities rather than to land. Thus, the comparative study I have made here helps one to see more clearly the significance of technology in affecting the landholding patterns and in shaping the course of subsequent economic change.

Another difference, which had a substantial effect on the landholding patterns and contractual agreements in the two nations, was the relative ease with which the English crossed class barriers, in contrast to the rigid class differentiations which persisted in Tokugawa Japan. In England, many a son of a noble married a daughter of a wealthy merchant, uniting land with capital, but this was virtually impossible in Tokugawa Japan. Such social constraints arising from the rigid class structure forced the Tokugawa economy to maximize its output with severe handicaps. The political weakness of the Tokugawa ruling class mitigated its handicaps, but the samurai did their best to slow the mobility of labor and capital in search of higher returns. The costs of circumventing the laws prohibiting the sale of land and restricting the mobility of peasants were low, but they were always there.

Another significant difference was that the samurai class was not a landowning class as was the English ruling class. In the period preceding industrialization, this difference did not matter since in neither nation did the ruling class impede efforts toward more efficient use of resources in agriculture. The difference, however, is important in explaining the ease with which the Meiji Restoration was accomplished and the rapidity with which industrialization took roots in Meiji Japan.

Because the samurai class lived on the income obtained from the right to tax and not from landownership, it had little economic reason to object to a change in political institutions as long as there was an assurance or a good chance that it could obtain an income even after the political change. Thus, unlike the landed interest of England, which bitterly objected to various political and economic measures introduced by the increasingly potent manufacturing interests, the samurai took an active part in bringing about the Restoration and in the post-Restoration industrialization. In discussing the landholding system and industrialization of Japan, singly or comparatively, no one can neglect the importance of the fact that the ruling class in Japan was landless. In too many nations, the landed ruling class delayed or even effectively stopped the political changes necessary for industrialization and the process of industrialization itself.

Yet another difference worthy of specific discussion in this essay is the significantly more advanced financial institutions in England compared to those found in Tokugawa Japan. This is not to say that the *ryōgaeya* (money-exchangers) of Tokugawa Japan were unsophisticated. They had their own functioning quasi-reserve system by the early eighteenth century and were indeed highly sophisticated by premodern standards. Their bills, issued against the reserve in amounts equal to several times their reserve, facilitated trade among major cities. The money-exchangers of Edo (Tokyo) and Osaka were able to establish a smoothly operating mechanism for adjusting the relative values of their bills, one backed by gold and the other by silver, which tended to reflect the trade balance between eastern and western Japan.[87]

However, even with its sophistication, the Tokugawa financial institutions were no match for those found in pre-modern England. Before the end of the seventeenth century, England had its central bank, and the London and country banks were functioning as deposit banks and were already rendering many of the services which modern banks were to perform.[88] Mortgage loans, unknown to Tokugawa money-exchangers, were made by English bankers in the eighteenth century. There is little doubt that the cost of using the services of financial institutions was appreciably lower in pre-modern England than in Tokugawa Japan. A landed gentleman in search of a borrower or a lender enjoyed the services of a bank at a lower cost than did a *gōnō* seeking a borrower. It is reasonable to conjecture that not many *gōnō* ever thought of using a third party in putting their capital to use.

In pre-modern England, money flowed freely from one sector of the economy to another in search of the highest returns. Landholding became concentrated because larger landholdings were more efficient, and not because surplus capital tended not to move out of agriculture but to be invested in land as in Japan. In Tokugawa Japan, capital did not move freely from agriculture to the cities because it could not, due, to an important degree, to the limited institutional capabilities of the financial institutions. That agricultural capital was over-invested in land (or that it could have earned higher returns elsewhere) is clearly demonstrated by the fact that the *gōnō* capital rapidly moved

[87] See Crawcour and Yamamura, "The Tokugawa Monetary System."
[88] Dillard, *Economic Development*, pp. 152-159.

into the nascent industries and international commerce after the Meiji Restoration, which brought a modern banking system to Japan.

Any discussion of differences is much more difficult than a comparison of similarities, because any specific differences which can be singled out are usually deeply rooted in the unique historical background of each nation. Even if Western technology had come to Japan a century earlier, it is conceivable that the rampant inflation and other political and economic factors of the late Tokugawa period would have occurred anyway and would have motivated landowners to choose to acquire more land rather than to make investments in manufacturing industries. In an examination comparing two distant nations, separated by seas, culture, and factor endowment, a list of differences could indeed be a long one.

Such a list is not presented here, primarily because what is significant are not the differences but the similarities. In both nations, each of which became the leader in industrialization in its respective hemisphere, landholding patterns and contractual arrangements were changed to make agriculture increasingly efficient. That is, the political institutions in both nations were such that it was possible, with little or no resistance, for economic forces to be allowed to raise the productivity of their precious resources. One way to express this is to state along with Crouzet, "In English society [and one should add Tokugawa Japan] there was a more 'capitalist,' a more commercial, a more acquisitive spirit; and according to contemporary accounts there was in England a harshness, a ruthlessness, a concentration on the pursuit of gain, which was absent in the more easy-going France of Ancien Regime."[89]

A part of the outcome owes to the good fortune of both nations. In both nations, once the process of the increase in output had begun to help accumulate capital and to raise the living standard, the population did not increase at a rate which drew on savings or reduced the living standard. The peace in Tokugawa Japan was rarely disturbed and the government was stable, allowing the Japanese to pursue their economic goals. By European standards, the English too fared much better than her neighbors. Both countries were also fortunate in hav-

[89] F. Crouzet, "England and France in the Eighteenth Century: A Comparative Analysis of Two Economic Growths," in R. M. Hartwell, ed., *The Causes of the Industrial Revolution in England* (London: Methuen, 1967), p. 159. Also see Yamamura, "Economic Responsiveness in Japanese Industrialization" in L. P. Cain and P. Uselding, eds., *Business Enterprises and Economic Change* (Kent: Kent State University Press, 1973), pp. 173-197. This article argues, using examples from the medieval and the Tokugawa periods, that Japanese peasants have shown their capacity to respond rationally (i.e., to maximize their incomes) to changing economic circumstances.

ing homogeneous populations, each with a single language, because this, though rarely stressed, substantively reduced the costs of conducting commerce, of the development of the necessary economic institutions, and of factor mobility. Success is often made much easier when accompanied by good fortune.

Industrial Relations in
Japan and Elsewhere*

-»» «««-

R. P. DORE

Some people are interested in the particular, some in the general. But even if they neatly sort themselves out—the particularists in history departments and the generalizers in departments of sociology—they still need each other, at least as long as the particularizers want to explain as well as to describe.

This essay, perhaps, will appeal more to those interested in the general determinant of patterns of industrial relations than to those interested in the particulars of Japan's own history, but it is rooted in those particulars and returns to them and, I hope, illuminates them, while illuminating one or two other things on the way.

My starting point, some years back, was the question: How did the Japanese employment system come to be the way it is? Of course, the starting point is really farther back than that. The nature of the Japanese employment system became problematic only because of what I knew about employment systems in Western countries and because I knew them to be different: one did not ask, after all, why the Japanese produce their electrical generators in places called factories, or why the female proportion of the labor force is greater in textiles than in mining, because in those respects Japan is *not* different from other countries.

Hence a comparison is implicit even in the initial posing of a question seemingly purely about Japan. It was explicit in my attempts to answer it by means of a detailed comparison between the British and the Japanese situation. I was looking for "concomitant variation"—other factors, plausibly related to employment systems which also differentiated Japan from Britain. From this emerged certain generaliza-

* The introductory section summarizes some of the argument in my book *British Factory—Japanese Factory: The Origins of National Diversity in Industrial Relations,* 1973.

Most of the data used in this paper were collected by Susantha Goonatilake, Maureen Mackintosh, and Miguel Sanchez-Padron. They are not responsible for the conclusions, however, though they would probably agree with them more than with those of the first draft, as their criticisms helped greatly in the process of revision.

tions about the differences between early and late developers—generalizations the plausibility of which one could reasonably assess only by looking at other late developers: hence the present essay, concerned chiefly with Sri Lanka, Senegal, and Mexico; with what the study of their employment systems tells us about the effects of late development *in general*; and with the significance which that in turn has on our understanding of how the Japanese system got to be the particular way it is.

Let me begin by summarizing what emerged from the earlier British-Japanese comparison on the major characteristics of the two types of employment systems. For reasons which will be obvious, I call them respectively market-oriented and organization-oriented.

The Sources of Institutional Difference

So much for characterization of the differences. What causes them? Three explanations are on general offer.

The first is that espoused by ethnocentric stage-theorists of the West and xenocentric stage-theorists of Japan (those who speak of Japan's as a "distorted" form of capitalist development, deviating from the normative forms described in the textbooks and supposedly exhibited in the history of Western countries). According to this view, paternalism is characteristic of the early stages of capitalism in all societies. Most societies grow out of it quickly. Japan is suffering from a case of arrested development, but it is unlikely to last. Eventually the Japanese too will become "modern" and succeed in changing their system to conform to the sensible principles on which Westerners (so productively and harmoniously) base their industrial activity. Behind such reasoning lies a whole range of theoretical assumptions about the continuing unilineal trends which define increasing "modernity"—increasing emphasis on achievement rather than ascription; affective neutrality and specificity rather than affective diffuseness of roles; universalism rather than particularism of norms; a growth in individualism at the expense of group identifications; the *gleichschaltung* of all individuals before the law and the norms of the market, etc.

Luckily, few people believe that reasoning anymore—neither optimists nor pessimists. In any case, even in its own terms, the argument will not work. It is sociological sloppiness to describe by the same term, "paternalism," both the discretionary benevolence of the small employer of nineteenth-century Britain or twentieth-century Japan or India, and the rule-bound, bureaucratized enterprise welfare received by the employees of Mitsubishi. The paternalistic employer proper seeks to evoke a personal loyalty by benefits which he can give or withhold depending on how much he likes the color of a man's eyes or

British market-oriented type	*Japanese organization-oriented type*
Unitary; a single national system in which all firms operate in the same labor markets.	Dualistic, with a market-oriented system in the small firms and an organization-oriented system in the large.

IN LARGE ENTERPRISES

High labor turnover, with the average employee changing jobs (returning to the market) every three or four years.	Low turnover: lifetime employment of permanent workers institutionally differentiated from temporary workers and the employees of on-site subcontractors.
Wages and salaries representing a "going market rate" for particular skills; differentials reflect market differential; "equal pay for equal work" the only intra-enterprise principle of consistency.	No concept of a "going rate" for skills; consistency in principles of wage determination sought within the organization; those principles emphasize seniority, age, and "merit" as much as, or more than, function, which means that a wage rate is an attribute of a person, not of a job.
Training, which enhances a man's market value, is at his own, or the public, expense.	Training provided by the firm, which expects to benefit from the trainee's superior performance.
Entry into firm at all levels.	Entry only at fixed lower entry ports; higher positions filled by promotion. Firm provides prospects of a "career" for manual as well as for white-collar workers.
Social security primarily the responsibility of the worker or of the state.	Firm assumes responsibility for workers' security and welfare.
Unions seek to unite all those who have similar skills to sell in the market.	Unions based on individual enterprise.
And seek national or regional agreements covering firms in the same industry.	And bargain at the enterprise level, albeit with some coordination between similar firms.
Among secondary identifications a man's professional identity, craft consciousness, class consciousness, or regional loyalty likely to be stronger than his enterprise consciousness.	Vice-versa, and management policies deliberately seek to foster a sense of "involvement" in the firm.
Individual material self-interest seen as the most reliable work-motivator, involving: (a) frequent use of payment-by-result systems; (b) clear delimitation of individual responsibilities, especially those of managers; (c) use of sanctions, in extreme cases of demotion and dismissal, for failure to fulfill these individual responsibilities; (d) and also of individualistic interpersonal competition for, e.g., promotion.	Workers also expected to be motivated by a shared group interest in the firm's prosperity and prestige, and to this end: (a) payment-by-result systems are group-based, rarely based on individual performance; (b) and responsibilities are assigned (e.g., in organization charts) to sections and groups rather than to individuals; (c) the rarity of demotion and dismissal engenders a sense of security; (d) and opportunities for interpersonal competition are institutionally restricted (by emphasis on the seniority criterion for promotion) and group cooperation emphasized.

values his skill or the loyalty in his heart. The "welfare corporatist" Japanese firm has institutions which seek to evoke a loyalty to the *firm* as a whole, by benefits which are received as of right, as part of the contract, through no particular person's personal benevolence. And, of course, rights thus institutionalized are not prone to "fade away" as the discretionary benevolence of small employers might be when they cease to be small or become more all-embracing in their rationality.

The second favorite explanation for the difference in employment systems is just that the Japanese are peculiar people. Differences in employment patterns, it is argued, simply reflect differences in those enduring elements of national character which differentiate modern Japan from modern Britain, as they differentiated the Japan of 1800 from the Britain of 1800.

This is not an argument to be dismissed lightly, but it needs some refinement. Clearly is it not a matter of instinctual behavior, or the simple inertia of earlier institutional patterns or habits of mind; Japan's employment system in 1900 was pretty much as market-oriented as Britain's. It was conscious institutional innovation which began to shape the Japanese system in the first two decades of this century, perfected the system of enterprise familism (or what one might call corporate paternalism) in the 1930's, and revamped the system to accommodate the new strength of unions in the late 1940's to produce what is called here the "welfare corporatism" of today. So the "reflection of national character" argument has to be disaggregated. It can mean either that the managers (and in the postwar period union leaders) whose decisions produced the institutions in question in response to new situations, were concerned to create institutions which embodied their own (widely shared, Japanese) values, or, alternatively, that the institutions created were such as to be effective (in maximizing the firm's profits or whatever else it was seeking) given, and only given, the values and behavioral dispositions which were widely shared by Japanese workers—or both of these things. To put it another way, one argument is that they were created *by* the Japanese character, the other that they were created *for* the Japanese character.

There is a good deal of truth in both of these arguments, particularly the second. The question is *how much* truth, for there is a competing explanation for the emergence of the "Japanese system," an explanation in terms of a "late-development effect."

There are, runs this argument, good reasons for expecting that in any late-developing country a Japanese type of employment system will emerge. In part it is the "last gets the best" phenomenon. Later industrializers not only take over the very latest machine technology but also the very latest social technology from the most industrialized countries. Their institutions, created anew, can embody the latest "transnational received wisdom" in a way impossible for older industrialized countries whose institutions, molded to the norms and assumptions of an earlier age, have already acquired some rigidity. But that is only one part of the late-development effect: other parts of it are the consequences of importing advanced capital-intensive technology, population growth rates and the labor supply-and-demand balance, the implication of creating modern school systems ahead of modern factory systems. Instead of trying to document, as I have done elsewhere,[1] the particular historical circumstances of Japan to which the management innovators might be seen to be responding, let me instead try to spell out in more detail those general characteristics of late developers just hinted at—those characteristics which distinguish Japan (and a fortiori even later developers) from Britain and the other earliest developers, and which might be thought to make it "rational" for late-developer managers—and union leaders—to opt for a Japanese-type system of employment.

1. First, late-developer industrialization starts dualistic in organizational form. On the one hand, there are the small firms started by indigenous entrepreneurs, developing, as has been argued here, an open type of labor market. But whereas in the early industrialization of Europe there was little else besides the small entrepreneurial firms so that it was they which set the pattern of labor market operations and industrial relations, in the mid-twentieth-century starter the little firms are typically dwarfed by big enterprises—sometimes the successful large enterprises of indigenous industrial pioneers, more often expatriate firms, state corporations, or state-sponsored consortia.

2. Some of the characteristics of firms in the large-scale sector derive from their bigness:

(a) they are too large for personal paternalistic relations to exist between "employer" and "employee";

(b) they are big enough to be able to develop career structures and promotion ladders within their organization;

(c) they represent such a substantial chunk of invested capital that (1) they command considerable political influence, and (2) even if they did not, no government could afford to allow them to collapse, for both of which reasons they can be fairly sure of having their domestic markets protected—and this stability allows them to give fairly firm guarantees of employment to their workers.

[1] *Ibid.*, the last two chapters.

3. Some of the characteristics of these big firms derive from their contemporaneity—from the fact that they are big organizations of 1960 vintage, not of 1860 or 1910 vintage:

(a) they are likely to be organizationally complex and bureaucratized in the sense of relying, in personnel matters, on formal written rules, not on verbal understandings;

(b) they are likely to have specialized personnel managers, which were unheard of in early industrializers (toward the end of Britain's second century of industrialization, specialized personnel management was still such a new development that membership of the Institute of Personnel Management doubled between 1963 and 1970);

(c) the doctrines of personnel management to which these specialized personnel managers adhere are likely to be influenced by (1) ILO doctrines concerning the rights of workers and of unions, the importance of consultation and participation, much of which is likely to be embodied in legislation which large firms (unlike the small) cannot ignore, and by (2) the new "tender-minded" personnel management doctrines gaining increased currency in the richer countries (in which, of course, LDC personnel managers might well have received some training), doctrines which see the art of management as depending not just on the harnessing of the single-minded desire for gain by Taylorian "science," but on harnessing a wider range of other motives —the desire for security, for self-realization.[2]

4. Some of their characteristics derive from the circumstances of their birth—they are frequently the offspring either of governments or of large multinational corporations (whose management structures often resemble the civil services of governments), and certain characteristics of these parent organizations are likely to transmit themselves to their offspring, such as:

(a) planned career structures and incremental salary scales, based on the assumption of life-long service;

(b) a preponderance of power in the hands of salaried managers who are not profit-takers and whose salary increases may, indeed, be proportionate to increases in manual wages;

(c) the greater likelihood of a "planning ethos." The salaried managers, recruited from among university graduates, are likely to be calculating organization men, not the fittest survivors of thrusting entrepreneurial competition, and the stable prospects of protected firms give added incentives to careful foresighted prudence—hence, a

---

[2] On the shape and importance of these influences, see the papers by Kassalow and Dore in Japan Institute of Labour, *Social and Cultural Background of Labour and Management Relations in Asian Countries* (Proceedings of the 1971 Asian Regional Conference), 1971.

greater propensity toward the sort of long-run calculations of advantage which might justify expenditure on training schemes and welfare schemes. Hence also, perhaps, a further push toward tender-minded industrial relations policies of worker involvement and judicious concessions. The thrusting entrepreneur throve on competition and conflict; the manager on cartels and compromise.

5. With big organization goes high technology. The late developer is required to make a technological leap quite different in its consequences from the slow shuffling technological advance of the early industrializers. In Britain, for example, the smooth progression from the artisan skills of eighteenth-century Britain to the factory engineering skills of the next century is reflected in the continuity of apprenticeship system and modes of skill certification throughout the transition from guilds to unions. New inventions came gradually and in penny packages; the workmen acquired the new skills, as they evolved, as a topping up of their existing skills, and passed them on to their successors. But in the late-development situation, no such gradualist solution is possible, and in the typical import-substituting industrialization pattern, with only one or two plants in each industrial branch, probably widely separated geographically, there may be little chance of poaching skilled workers from a rival. The enterprise is likely, therefore, to *have* to do its own training (quite apart from the snow-balling mystique of training, analyzed by Berg in his *Education and Jobs*,[3] which—the diffusion effect again—is likely to communicate itself to LDC managers, too). And having invested money in training its young workers, the firm acquires an interest in keeping them—and hence in the devices of seniority increments, career promotion prospects, and welfare benefits which would help to keep them.

6. Universal primary schooling was late to emerge in the history of Western industrialization; in the late developer it may become an aspiration and a policy even before the nation acquires its first half-dozen factories. Industrialization with an already developed school system is likely to lead employers (as they are likely to have to do their own training anyway) to prefer to do their recruitment among young, newly graduating school leavers:

(a) because their literacy and numeracy is an advantage;

(b) because their schooling has disciplined them to habits of timekeeping and steady application which make of them better factory workers than peasants straight off the fields;

(c) because they see a modern sector job as the only outcome and purpose of their schooling. They are "committed" in anticipation. And

[3] Ivar Berg, *Education and Jobs: The Great Training Robbery* (1970; Penguin edition 1973).

as their numbers increase with an increase in enrollments far exceeding the increase in modern-sector job opportunities, (1) the wage needed to hire these young bachelors (from families which could afford, at any rate, to keep them at school for 6 or 8 years) may well fall, and (2) the employer can select to make sure that the training he is going to give is invested in the most promising trainees. And to help in this process whereby the larger enterprises "cream off" each age group, school records and teachers' reports can be used to supplement the personnel manager's battery of selection tests.

The fact that the employer has skimmed the cream off the age group is a further reason, additional to his investment in training, for wanting not to lose his workers. To keep them he must raise their wages from the low level at which he can hire a teenage single man to a level, at marrying age, at which it is possible to rear a family. Incremental scales are an obvious way of doing that. They offer, too, an advantage in flexibility of great importance when union organization becomes powerful. When an increasing number of school-leavers are clamoring around the bottom-rung entry-ports, it is possible to respond to this buyers' market by lowering (usually, failing to raise in inflationary conditions) starting wages—the wages of those not yet union members —without risking the desertion or disaffection of the established workers: in effect steepening the gradient of the incremental scale, as happened in Japan quite markedly in the young-labor-surplus conditions of the mid-1960's.

The personnel management philosophy of employer responsibility, the "workers are just as much human beings as staff members" approach, provides, of course, additional reasons for the adoption of incremental scales.

7. When trade unions develop, as they are likely to be allowed to do, given the pressures for international respectability, they are likely to be:

(a) confined to, or at least strongest in, the large firm half of the labor economy;

(b) because of the prevailing recruitment patterns, low turnover, and the small number of (often geographically isolated) firms in each industry, organized on an enterprise basis with, whatever the national federation structure, effective bargaining taking place at the enterprise or plant level;

(c) quite happy, because of low mobility and the absence of any active market for established skills, each with its proper price, to accept wage structures which are entirely enterprise-specific, including incremental scales, promotion systems, etc.;

(d) and in a situation where the large-sector wage-earners are an *elite*, envied by the mass of unemployed, by small-sector employees, and by underemployed rural workers, the union is likely to be as much, or even more, concerned with getting guarantees of job security as with higher wages.

8. At the risk of overdetermining the outcome, I shall add two more factors tending to produce the large-sector employment patterns postulated here. Late developers' early factories use expensive imported machinery. Labor costs are therefore likely to represent a smaller proportion of total costs than they did for the early manufacturers of the new developed countries; hence, perhaps, a greater willingness to increase labor costs by expenditure on welfare facilities, for example, or seniority increments, or family allowances, the return for which (in loyalty, motivation, etc.) is inherently incalculable.

9. A further aspect of cost structures: having a machine left idle from absenteeism is more serious the higher the ratio of the loss incurred by leaving capital unutilized to the saving from not paying the wages of the worker who would otherwise have worked it, and the more closely the operations of various machines are integrated with those of others in work-flow processes. From both points of view absenteeism and the disruption of high turnover are likely to be more costly to the modern LDC employer than to employers in the early days of Western industrialism. He buys his machines from high-wage foreign countries and employs cheaper local labor. He is more likely to have a planned integrated production flow process—hence an additional incentive for him to find ways of "stabilizing" even semi-skilled machine-minding workers.

Late Development in General, Japan in Particular

Let me stress again that these are generalized statements of features, common to most late developers, thought likely to conduce to a Japanese type of employment system. Clearly not all late developers share all of these characteristics, and it may be as well (to forestall the objections of those who would in spite of what was said earlier take this as a comprehensive list of the features explaining Japan's particular pattern of development),[4] to list just some of the ways in which Japan, being an earlier rather than a later late developer, deviates from the general statement of the conditions of late development given here.

1. Big-firm dominance was a good deal less marked in 1900 Japan than in, say, 1960 Kenya.

2. Similarly, the dominance of the salaried manager, though great as the *zaibatsu* bureaucratized at the turn of the century, was a good

[4] For my historical account, see *British Factory—Japanese Factory*, chaps. 13, 16.

deal less complete than in many contemporary developing countries today because there *was* a good deal of small entrepreneurial enterprise—more proportionately than in modern Mexico probably, though far less than earlier in England.

3. Another aspect of lesser big-firm dominance: there was a more fluid labor situation; there were few industry branches in which a small number of firms in isolated parts of the country were the sole employers of certain skills. Some shipyard skills might be usable only in Nagasaki, Kure, or Yokosuka, but in textiles, for example, there were hosts of small employers competing for labor (when they were not temporarily patching up no-poaching agreements).

4. The "planning ethos" is less well-developed. Even big Mitsui enterprises did not have quite the gilt-edged security of, say, a Sri Lanka state corporation.

5. The ILO convention influence, on workers' rights and trade union organization, though not negligible in the 1920's, was less important in the early stages in Japan, though it had a decisive effect on the definitive revamping of the system in the late 1940's. So too for the modern doctrines of management by involvement, etc.

6. Likewise the technological gap was less than in most contemporary developing countries—both because of the high level of Japanese traditional skills (compared with Africa, say) and because of the less developed nature of imported Western skills.

7. Similarly, in the world at large school systems were much less commonly and universally defined as job-certification mechanisms or manpower-training institutions in the 1910's than in the 1960's. Japan was a hesitant pioneer of practices which were later taken for granted.

Comparisons and Conclusions

In all these ways, then, the "logic of the situation" for late developers differs from that of Japan just as Japan's differed from that of Britain—but by and large in the same direction—that is to say that one can modify many of these static propositions about late development as a static condition, to dynamic propositions about changes in that condition: the later . . . the more. The later development starts, the greater the degree of big-firm dominance in the framing of employment institutions, the more certain it is that trade unions will be given some legitimate role in the system, etc.

The interesting question is, though, how *much* causal influence to attribute to factors like this in explaining the emergence of particular national systems. I spoke here of the "late development" explanation as one which "competes with" the "national culture" explanation. In fact, of course, there is no necessary contradiction. Both sets of factors could be mutually reinforcing; alternatively, each could be primarily responsible for some aspects of the system and not of others. Moreover, one cannot ignore the importance of another set of factors which are unlike the national culture and late development sets in being neither easily categorized nor of such universal application. I refer to the "random" effects of historical accident—the incidence of wars, of business depressions, or of union-repressing governments at particularly crucial times in the development of a country's institutions. (It has been argued, for instance, that employment practices in that other late developer, the United States, were moving rapidly in a Japanese direction in the late 1920's and would have continued to do so but for the depression.)

Can one ever sort out these varying strands of causation? To some extent one can. At the very least, one can test the likely strength of the "late-development" explanation by looking at other late developers. What follows is a summary of preliminary impressions (a better word than findings from research, in three countries chosen to be as different as possible in degree of industrialization, types of pre-industrial social structure, and source of metropolitan influence: Mexico, Sri Lanka, and Senegal.) If one finds emerging in all three the same syndrome of features as makes up the Japanese employment system, one will have a strong *prima facie* case for seeing some merit in the late-development explanation in general; minor variations in the features found should give clues to the importance of the various different causal mechanisms subsumed under the late-development label; major deviations from the model will point to the importance of the "national culture" or "historical accident" factors. It is an exercise which looks two ways. It looks to Japan's past insofar as it should tell one something about how the Japanese system got to be the way it is. It looks to the present and the future of the developing countries, for if it helps to understand the forces at work in shaping their institutions, it should also help those who are trying to control their own fate to handle, modify, combat, or even adapt to those forces.[5]

There are indeed—to begin with the broadest conclusions—a good many of the characteristics of the "organization-oriented system" in these three countries. In all three, for instance,

1. there is a fairly clear dualism within the manufacturing sector. Within the large-firm sector;

[5] Or even just monitor them! Many developing countries collect wage statistics in ways taught them by metropolitan countries, which start from the assumption that they have a market-oriented wage system in which it is meaningful to calculate average wages by skill and industry, when the significant parameters are more likely to be age, educational certification level, and scale or type of enterprise.

2. the distinction between permanent and temporary workers is firmly institutionalized;

3. turnover of permanent workers is low;

4. bottom-level recruitment and internal promotion, providing institutionalized career possibilities for both manual and white-collar workers, are fairly common features;

5. so is an emphasis on seniority;

6. a number of firms provide a good deal of general as well as specific training;

7. and welfare facilities;

8. and plant or enterprise-based union organization is a good deal stronger and more effective than industrywide organization.

It is clear, however, that the broad similarities of form conceal differences of "meaningful" content. This will become apparent if we look at some of these features more closely.

Dualism

Let us begin with dualism and an attempt to define terms. What one expects to find are systematic differences between firms which can be summarized in the following list of contrasts.

LARGER FIRMS	SMALLER FIRMS (TYPICALLY LESS THAN TWENTY WORKERS)
Bureaucratically organized and rule-bound	Run by individual (perhaps paternalistic) employers little bound by established rules
Unionized	Un-unionized
Higher wages and fringe benefits	Lower wages and fringe benefits
Workers get full benefit of state social security, employment protection, etc.	Workers unprotected

To some extent these contrasts hold in all three societies. Alongside the large bureaucratically organized and unionized firms which, as subsequent discussion will show, share many features of the Japanese system with their Japanese counterparts, there are also a good number (probably more in Mexico than in Senegal or Sri Lanka) of small workshops much more informally run by individual owner-entrepreneurs. But the extent to which this contrast is accompanied by a sharp difference in wages and fringe benefits depends on a variety of factors.

The first is the level of law enforcement. In Mexico or at least in some parts of Mexico, even small employers are likely to pay minimum wages, to inscribe their employees on the social security rolls and to pay up their social security contribution, if only because it can be risky not to. In Sri Lanka enforcement is perhaps slightly looser; in Senegal most nominal of all.

A second major variable is the extent to which trade unions have succeeded in raising wages in the large-scale sector. This very much depends on the role of the state. In Sri Lanka, where the trade union federations have had considerable freedom to bargain and have exercised very strong political influence as a basis of support for left-wing governments, the wage gap is considerable. In Senegal, where the unions were "tamed" and subordinated to a one-party government in 1968, the gap still reflects the success of union pressures before that date, and although the gap has not been *much* widened in subsequent years, the government has recently had to grant wage increases which have maintained and perhaps even widened differentials. (This illustrates one important element of the late-development effect: the irreversibility of changes of consciousness. The expectations of workers in the large firm sector for a certain level of income, even for an increasing level of income—initially raised, perhaps, by union leaders in direct contact with the union organizations of advanced countries—are not immediately altered by a statutory limitation of union power. Disappointment of those expectations causes resentment. Resentment has the potential of political unrest which even a would-be authoritarian government may have to take into account.) In Mexico the picture is mixed; the union movement, though coopted, still manages to press for substantial increases which are forced on the large-firm sector by presidential pressure, but the legal minimum wages paid by the small firms increase also. Strong plant unions can, however, especially in the state-managed sector, quite effectively raise wages above the general level.

A third factor is the extent to which employers in the large sector—with capital-intensive production techniques and high labor productivity, which allows them to pay high wages without it hurting too much—choose in fact to do so in order to recruit, keep, and claim the loyalty of, a high-quality labor force or to enhance the firm's prestige. The Monterrey Group, whose declared policy is to pay thirty percent above local rates, is an example, as are some of the multi-nationals in Sri Lanka and Senegal. An additional factor in Sri Lanka may be the threat of nationalization; at least one firm saw a union whose members might stand to lose if they were put on state corporation wage scales as useful insurance against government takeover.

This third factor, of course, brings us close to the heart of the matter, to questions of the goals and values of managers and workers. Of this, more later.

Lifetime Employment

To give the conclusions first. Labor turnover in the large-firm sector is very low in all three countries, especially for manual workers. But lifetime employment is not, or at least not always, to be assumed to be synonymous with lifetime commitment in spirit.

First, on the workers' side, the rarity of voluntary leaving is largely a function of the scarcity of job opportunities, of the fact that anyone who is lucky enough to have a job does not easily abandon it. But those who *do* have an opportunity to move—skilled maintenance fitters and electricians, engineers, and experienced managers—change jobs fairly easily.

Equally, the employer's virtual abandonment of the traditional managerial prerogative to fire as well as to hire, the fact that permanent employees have a fairly well guaranteed security of tenure, is a reflection of the same labor surplus situation; of the fact that trade unions are preeminently concerned with job security; and of the fact that they have been able to mobilize government power on their behalf. In all three countries, dismissal on the grounds of redundancy is possible (if unions dispute it) only after arbitration by government officials, and the terms of compensation are likely to be a considerable deterrent. Similarly, dismissal on disciplinary grounds is liable to challenge in labor courts. "Catch a man redhanded going out of the gate with a pair of stolen shoes under his arm and you can try sacking him, but don't be surprised if you find the court ordering you to take him back in twelve months' time, entitled to full back pay," said one Ceylonese manager, and although he was exaggerating wildly, it is true that the courts in Sri Lanka do tend to put the onus of proof on the employer and to give the benefit of the doubt to the worker. In Mexico the leanings of the courts vary from state to state or, for those industries with federal tribunals, from industry to industry. In Senegal cases have tended in recent years to pile up, with frequent postponements—a fact which may not be unconnected with the weakened power of the unions since 1968. But still, in Mexico and Senegal too, the law stands as a sizable deterrent to hasty dismissal, particularly for such less easily provable causes as not working hard enough.

Hence, in fact, great security of employment and low labor mobility. And, indeed, the two forces identified here as producing that result—job scarcity and the emerging transnational normative view that job security is a worker's right and an employer's duty—were both probably of some importance in the Japanese case too. (Japan, as an earlier late developer, by institutionalizing job security at an early stage, probably contributed to the establishment of that international consensus—certainly more than did Britain's institutional example, as suit for unfair dismissal became possible only in 1971 in Britain, long after Mexico, Senegal, or Sri Lanka.) But the Japanese system, whatever it may *originally* have been a response to, has developed two further important elements: (a) managerial policies deliberately de-

337

signed to keep turnover to a minimum. (b) an ethic which places a positive value on loyalty and discerns something suspicious and reprehensible in an employee's *wish* to change jobs—which perception, of course, when once diffused through a society, acts as a powerful deterrent to job-changing.

The first element is not hard to discern. For the most part such policies are not necessary, as few workers are disposed to leave their jobs anyway, but at the more mobile higher skilled levels, managers are generally concerned to reduce turnover. This is in line with the Japanese precedent: it was concern at the loss of skilled men which prompted the Nagasaki shipyards to develop their labor-stabilizing devices—and for the same reason that their training represented a heavy investment of the firm's resources. One firm in the Monterrey Group calculated that they had, on average, to keep a worker for four years to recoup the costs of training and, with a claimed loss of only 0.5 percent of its labor force to other firms every year (and another 2 percent to emigration to the U.S. or to self-employment), they seemed with their high-wage, high-fringe-benefit policy to be successful in protecting their investment. And where that policy prevails, of course, entrance to the firm in the first place is likely to be highly selective; educational qualifications are likely to be insisted on, and/or there is rigorous selection by tests. (One leading Sri Lanka firm which received 1800 applications for two clerk's posts tested 100 and interviewed 25.)

In all these countries there is a correlation between: (a) paying relatively high (even for the large firm sector) wages; (b) having a well-developed training policy; (c) using careful selection procedures; (d) consciously trying to keep turnover low. But only a few firms in each country clearly exhibit these characteristics. There are others—the Mexican subsidiary of an American automobile parts manufacturer, for example—which are cost-conscious in a traditional sense: they see no point in any calculated stance of demonstrative generosity in the matter of wages and pay as little as they have to; they are somewhat grudging in their investment in training and look to the market and the technical schools to fill their needs as far as possible, and by the same token philosophically accept that some of their most valuable workers are likely to leave, that all being part of the game.

And even in the firms closest to the Japanese model one sees only the faintest glimmer of the second additive in the Japanese system—the loyalty ethic. That glimmer comes, once again, from the Monterrey Group, which has been cited several times already. Consider this manager's statement of the firm's ideology:

"I've never found a better definition of industrial relations than this: maintain a work force that is satisfied and satisfactory and the rest is just a matter of auxiliary techniques. This is why we put so many obstacles in the way of those entering the company, because once in it's difficult to get out. We don't like giving anyone the sack, and its something we try to avoid. You see, we think of our work force as a family, united not just for work reasons but also by emotional relations. Here we never talk about 'obreros' because of the pejorative connotation the word has; here we are all equal as employees or as members of the 'Sociedad' [the firm's welfare and recreational society]."

One can see the emotional logic leading from profit-maximizing interest to sentiments and ethics. Keeping people means making them privileged; emphasizing how privileged they are means invoking pride; and a sense of pride enhances the sense of belonging to the group which shares the source of pride, which also reinforces the propensity to stay with the firm, and invests the act of leaving it with emotional significance; the assurance of not being thrown out is a pre-condition for family feeling; the expectation that no one would voluntarily leave is a validation of the existence of that pride and family feeling—so that when anyone *does* leave it can be seen as a betrayal, a flaunting challenge to the pretensions to superiority which underpin the pride and the family feeling.

But even the Monterrey Group has not managed to take many Mexicans far along the road to the Japanese ethic. Perhaps the emotional logic hypothesized here is not sufficiently compelling to make them try hard enough. Or perhaps the individualistic assumptions of Mexican society—the assumption that every man has a natural right to "better himself," to lead his own life—are too strongly entrenched.[6] Clearly one has to evoke that much-documented strain of "groupishness" in the Japanese national character to explain this ethical element of the Japanese system, but—remember the state of employment relations in 1900—not that alone. Without the constellation of circumstances which presented a similar "logic of the situation" to both Japanese employers and the Monterrey Group,[7] neither would have started on such similar roads. Without Japan's particular cultural traditions, however, she is unlikely to have got so far along it in the direction of translating managerial policy into ethics.

[6] It might even be, I suppose, that the Mexican psychologist was right when he argued that North American personnel doctrines stressing the need for involvement in the firm are inapplicable in Mexico because Mexicans, unlike North Americans, are blessed with a warm family life which satisfies all their needs for belongingness. Rogelio Díaz-Guerro, *Estudios de psicología del mexicano*, 1972, p. 69.

[7] And, indeed, to employers in the advanced industrial countries. See the literature on labor market dualism in the United States.

Wages

"Equal pay for equal work" is a compelling slogan, a principle to be achieved as an object of policy in a socialist society, a principle which supposedly the invisible hand of market forces achieves automatically in a capitalist society. The essence of a Japanese-type organization-oriented wage system is that it breaches this universalistic principle explicitly. Men are paid for being older, even though there is no clear evidence that the experience they accumulate in any way improves their work performance; they are paid for being loyal and cooperative, even though there is no obvious difference in the quality of a loyally produced gasket and a disloyally produced gasket; they are paid for having children because their needs are greater, not because father-hood improves work capacity. Above all, the system of payment ensures that future-oriented men can always have some *improvement* in their lot to look forward to, to console them for their present frustrations, to enhance their commitment to a judiciously responsive organization, and to reduce the likelihood that they will seek greener pastures elsewhere.

If one is looking for signs of organization-oriented wage systems in our three countries, one can certainly find them. In fact, one way of describing the wage systems of big firms in all the three countries studied is to say that many of them *look* like more or less halfhearted attempts to achieve the objective of providing for even manual workers a steadily increasing wage packet as they get older without breaking— or at least without too obviously flouting—the principle of "equal pay for equal work," though whether that is the result of conscious managerial efforts to achieve that end is an open question.

The first feature which fits this description is the incremental scale. For each job there is a minimum and a maximum wage; one starts at the minimum and receives annual increments until one reaches the maximum. This is the common practice in Sri Lanka's state corporations. It can still be accommodated, if a little uncomfortably, in an "equal pay for equal work" framework. As a man acquires experience in a job, the better he gets at doing it. Consequently the length of scales differ, being longer for workers of higher skill. At a ceramics factory, for example, the lowest grade of manual worker had a six-step scale; a foreman, on the other hand, is presumed to go on "maturing" for sixteen years. In fact, of course, most of the Grade I workers master their job and achieve peak productivity well within their first month in the factory, hardly over the course of six years. It is hard to see the payment for experience as anything other than a fiction designed rather to serve the "sustain expectations" purpose of the organization-oriented system.

The incremental scale for manual workers is a device fully institutionalized only in the state corporations of Sri Lanka among our three countries, and appears to derive historically from British colonial practice spread from the colonial bureaucracy itself to the railways and docks and their attendant workshops. In Senegal there are the beginnings of such a system in the payment of *sursalaire* over and above the basic rate-for-the-job, but these are generally discretionary payments to senior workers, in only one of the more bureaucratized firms routinized into a regular pattern of seniority increments and in any case adding only marginally to the wage.

The chief device which in all three countries serves the "sustain expectations" principle while not breaking the "equal pay for equal work" principle is to divide all jobs into grades, to recruit only into the bottom grades, and to make it possible for most workers in the course of their lives to be promoted from job to job and thus enjoy a steadily rising income. A multinational shoe manufacturer operating in both Sri Lanka and Senegal had a system of ten job grades in the one country, eight in the other. In the state corporations in Sri Lanka, where there are incremental scales for each grade, the number of grades is fewer, but the combined effect in one corporation is that a manual worker can, by dint of moving through the four grades, receive annual increments for twenty-eight years in succession, ending up with double his starting wage, and for another six years, taking him up to 230 percent of his starting wage if he is appointed as a foreman.

The job category system *in itself* implies neither deviation from a straightforward rate-for-the-job "equal pay for equal work" principle, nor adherence to a "motivate by sustaining expectations" policy on the part of management. In Senegal, for instance, French-type wage systems are crystallized into industrial collective agreements which are worked out under the aegis of the state and given the force of law, and which establish the job categories and the rates of pay for each category, industry by industry (market by market). Some managers, indeed, see the system as *no more than* a means of orderly regulation of the market designed to establish the going rate for particular skills and consider it quite natural that they should bring in outsiders for a vacancy if they are more suitable than any internal candidate for the post. In other firms the job-category system is used deliberately to create promotion chains which provide predictable career structures, recruitment from outside being limited to cases where higher levels of educational certification than those normally held by shop-floor workers are thought to be necessary. (It is a frequent cause of dispute whether or not foremen's positions come in that category.)

So much for methods of accommodating a "sustain-expectations" policy within a *strict* rate-for-the-job, "equal pay for equal work" framework. One can see the organization-oriented system struggling to get out of the body of a market-oriented system even more clearly in some firms where the rate-for-the-job framework is bent.

The first device is best explained by illustration. In a railway truck factory in Mexico a man starts in the tool room in category four as, in effect, an apprentice learning to use all the complex tools in the shop. Fifteen or twenty years later he may end up as a category-one toolroom fitter, a highly skilled man with three quite testing promotion exams behind him, at double the starting wage. Another man in the same factory might start at the same category-four wage in the paint shop, spraying undercoat on the trucks. After the same lapse of time he too may reach category one and double his wage—at which point, after passing three nominal tests concerning painting hygiene and the chemical constituents of paint, he will have the privilege of using the same sort of paint spray *plus a stencil* to write *Ferrocarriles de Mexico* on the side of the truck—still "equal pay for equal work" in the narrowest sense that everyone who uses a stencil will have the same pay, but certainly not in the sense of equal pay for work of equal difficulty. The difference in skill level between a category-one painter and a category-one toolroom fitter is great—whether one measures skill level in terms of the proportion of the population who have the minimum capacity to learn to do the job adequately or the average length of time required to be trained to an adequate level of competence, or whether one adds in other standard job evaluation criteria such as responsibility and danger. Clearly this system of categories is designed not, as is the "stricter" Senegalese system, to embody what would, in a free market, be the "going rates" for particular skills, but rather to provide equal chances of promotion to all—within a framework of semi-insulated departmental promotion chains (in any vacancy those in the next category down within the same department have priority; only if none qualify can those of the same category in other departments apply; only if none of those qualify might outsiders be brought in).[8]

A second device is to create category distinctions in what is, in effect, a spectrum of skills and functions. This applies preeminently in maintenance jobs, where there is a genuine difference between the

[8] From the manager's point of view the rationale for this is that those *in* the department can learn the job in anticipation of promotion more easily than outsiders. From the worker's point of view it responds to group feeling (which the management also may deliberately seek to encourage) that "jobs in our department belong to us."

beginner who can mend a limited range of faults which he only painfully and uncertainly diagnoses and the highly skilled man who diagnoses swiftly and accurately and can deal with anything. And these
skills do accumulate with experience. All the same, the precise number
of categories into which one divides that continuum of skills is essentially an arbitrary matter, for there is rarely any precise division of
functions between maintenance men. The choice of how finely grada-
tions of competence are separated is very much influenced by "sustain
expectations" purposes. The collective agreement at the railway truck
factory in Mexico, in fact, makes no attempt to define the degrees of
skill for maintenance categories; it simply specifies *how many* men
should be in each skill category, the distribution being designed to
allow adequate promotion opportunities.

The third device is ad hoc recategorization. Many factories, on strict
"equal pay for work of equal skill/responsibility/danger, etc." principles, would have very large numbers of people in the lower categories, very few in the higher, and hence limited chances of promotion.
In a world in which more and more manual workers *do* have career
prospects so that even more workers come to see themselves *entitled*
to them (an idea which would have been foreign to British workers
in 1850—or even 1950), a man who stays in the same job at the same
wage for seven, ten, fifteen years is likely to become restive, whether in
Mexico, Sri Lanka, or Senegal. The union can often be persuaded to
take up his case (it is, indeed, one of the commonest of union activities in all three countries) and personnel managers can often be persuaded to see the justice of it. (Rigid managers partly concerned to
stop wage drift, but even more, one suspects, with the justice of the
equal pay for equal work principle, will not.)[9] The most pragmati-
cally flexible will simply recategorize a job temporarily as a straight
"merit award" to the incumbent without seeking any more subtle
justification than that the *man* deserves it. Those with a stronger sense
of propriety will discover some way in which the nature of the job has
changed or was improperly evaluated in the first place. The subterfuge
is usually transparent to all. When a Sri Lanka state corporation listed
its "cadre" in the budget document it sends to the ministry for approval, one section ran as follows. No one really supposes that changes
in the security situation required beefing up of the cadre, but nevertheless the fiction that a worker's pay depends on the job he does was
decently preserved.

[9] And may well find themselves with difficult disputes on their hands. This applies equally to France, the source of the Senegalese system, vide the protracted
dispute in 1973 at the aluminum smelting firm.

Title of Post	Number of Posts	
	1973 actual	*1974 proposed*
Chief security officer	01	01
Security officer	01	02
Assistant security officer	02	01

Finally, there are four instances (the only four out of over twenty firms studied in the three countries) of the organization-oriented principle of the wage rate as a *personal* attribute being asserted in defiance of the "equal pay for equal work" principle. The first, and clearest, is—who would have guessed? the only Japanese subsidiary in our sample of firms—in Mexico. The girl operators are paid on a three-step wage scale, the top wage being some fifteen percent above the bottom rate. Promotion depends on a merit and skill assessment, not on the job performed at any one time.

The second instance is an American subsidiary in Mexico in which the strength of managerial authority was so great and the union officials so effectively "fixed" that what was intended to be a strict equal-difficulty-equal-category system was used by the manager to give category increments based entirely on his and supervisors' assessment of how cooperative and loyal a worker was. And, unlike the Japanese subsidiary, the decisions so reached did not appear to accord with the workers' sense of legitimacy—or to be designed so to accord. The personnel manager thumbed his nose at his workers' sense of legitimacy.

A third instance is the garment manufacturer in Senegal where the supervisor's discretionary grant of category promotions seemed to be—though entirely subjective—much more widely accepted as fair by the workers. In this firm, the fluctuating nature of the jobs to be done partly explained the looseness of the connection between job function and wage category.

The last instance is—again no surprise, given what has been said about these firms earlier—from the Monterrey Group. Firms in this group run a cut-price grocery shop for their employees. The larger the family, the bigger one's grocery bill, the more one benefits from it. This is of less significance for its actual effect in altering the distribution of real wages than for the explanation of the system given by a manager. He claimed that it was deliberately intended as "a device to break the legal obligation to give equal pay for equal work and to move on to the idea of a family wage based on need." Whether or not this is a historically accurate account of the origin of the grocery stores is less important than the declaration of managerial policy. In this case the source of this particular piece of management ideology is clear. The Papal Encyclicals on social questions have developed the notion of the employer's duty to provide a "family wage"—though not, as here, directly counterposing it to the "equal pay for equal work" principle.

We are left with two questions:

1. If the implication of the "struggling to get out" metaphor of the previous discussion is accurate and there *are* strong forces pushing in the direction of an "organization-oriented" wage-as-personal-attribute system, what explains the continuing strength of the rate-for-the-job principle?

2. What *are* the underlying forces pushing in an organization-oriented direction?

The answer to the first question is partly given in the last quotation from the Monterrey manager. In all three countries the "equal pay for equal work" principle has the backing of the law. In Mexico it is clearly inscribed in the labor code; in Senegal and Sri Lanka it is embodied in the legally enforced industrywide collective agreements and wage-board awards. Thus, the argument might run, the norms implicit in earlier, market-oriented-because-genuinely-market-based wage systems[10] become codified in law and hence continue to have a constraining influence even though patterns of organization change with the emergence of the large corporation in a way which makes those norms inappropriate.

The only trouble with that explanation is that the Japanese labor code also enshrines the principle of "equal pay for equal work." It was, indeed, briefly insisted on by some mining unions in the 1950's but later abandoned. Clearly one has to invoke other explanatory factors. One perhaps is that the Japanese law distilled the norms, not of Japanese experience, but of the liberal New Dealers who drafted it in the headquarters of the American occupation army, and hence as an alien law it is more easily selectively interpreted.

But there is clearly something more to it than that. Mexico (a country where streets are named Avenue Article 123!) is a country where the law has had tremendous importance in regulating conditions of work and the management-union bargaining process. In Mexico, a lawyer is the most obvious choice as a personnel manager, and inquisitive sociologists can be driven mad by trade-union leaders who will answer any question concerning what actual practice is by endless citation of the legal code which says what it *ought* to be. Sri

---

10 In the case of Senegal and Sri Lanka, the wage systems of which the legal norms are the distilled experience are predominantly those of France and Britain, respectively.

Lanka and Senegal are not very different, but Japan is considerably different.

Again, one might invoke a "national culture" factor. There *are* different degrees of "litigiousness" between societies. But there is here, too, a late-development effect. In Britain, what one might broadly call the process of adjusting feudal notions of a master-servant relationship to the changing political relationships of the nineteenth century, of transforming them into employer-employee relationships which could be considered to conform to bourgeois democratic notions of "equality of condition," was carried out by tough grass-roots power struggles between workers and their employers *before* the device of using state power to regulate a reasonable division of power was thought of or accepted.[11]

Once the device had been invented, however, it spread. Once it was accepted into the international consensus (given institutional expression in the conventions and resolutions of the ILO from 1920 onward) that it was a proper function, indeed the duty, of the state to regulate employment relations, in "new" states like post-revolutionary Mexico or post-independence Sri Lanka or Senegal, unions did not have to push very hard to get a complete kit of labor laws, and (to conform to the conventions of the international consensus) these laws generally embodied principles which were well "ahead" of (more protective of workers than) existing practice. Hence many disputes which in, say, Britain could be settled only by strikes were matters for appeal to the law; hence the much greater importance of the law in Mexico than in Britain, with Japan, an earlier late developer where a good deal of the present body of worker rights owe their recognition to strikes rather than to lawsuits, somewhere in between in terms of the law's importance.

For all the general importance of the law in the three countries, however, it needs more than that to explain the continuing strength of the "equal pay for equal work" principle, its much greater strength than in Japan. Again one might appeal to national cultures. One might expect that as a universalistic principle of justice the equal pay for equal work criterion has a *more* compelling attraction the more universalistic the value system of the society is. This is very tricky ground, but if one speaks *as if* one could measure the unmeasurable and operationalize the inoperable, I would be prepared to grant that the dominant values in the modern sector enclaves of Sri Lanka and

[11] And the unions and employers' organizations that achieved this task of stabilizing custom and practice through the process of free collective bargaining acquire a strong vested interest in resisting forever the introduction of that device—witness the fate of Britain's 1971 Industrial Relations Act now being ingloriously repealed as this is written.

Senegal were more universalistic than those of Japan, but hardly that Japan was a more particularistic society than Mexico.

An alternative explanation, of course, is that it is not so much the "equal pay for equal work" principle that is *stronger* in these countries than in Japan, but that the managerial urge to seek an alternative expectation-sustaining system is *weaker*.

Which brings us to the second question: what *are* the forces pushing wage systems in an organization-oriented direction? Here the most interesting question is the relative importance of managerial innovation, on the one hand, and of union pressure, on the other. The two questions are really inseparable because of the "expectations factor"; some policies become advantageous to managers only *because* workers, as a result of union activity, have acquired certain expectations; and this change in workers' expectations alters the cost to managers of different managerial policies.

Why should managers be concerned to provide career prospects, even at the expense of "breaking the equal pay for equal work" principle, as the Monterrey manager put it?

1. Because the security of tenure which workers by and large enjoy, given the legal restraints on dismissal and the bother of dealing with union complaints against any attempt to discipline by fines or suspensions, in effect rules out the use of punishment and dismissal as a means of motivating work. One is forced to rely on positive sanctions —on giving people some attachment to the organization by making them feel they have prospects in it.

2. The particular form of "prospects" which consists of moving from job to job up a promotion chain has great advantages because it offers a cheap solution to the training problem. Men can be induced to train themselves for the job next up the ladder—very conveniently, too, if they are working in the same department.

3. Perhaps more importantly, workers have come to expect, and unions to demand, career prospects, so that not offering them brings costs.

A rather rare instance of an explicit statement of the motivating rationale may be found in a Nigerian government report, that of the so-called Morgan Commission in 1964. (The italics are mine.)

"Persons in the wage-earning class, in the same way as persons in the salary-earning class, are entitled to certain prospects in respect of their employment . . . a remuneration sufficient to *maintain an ever-increasing family*. . . . A person who is engaged as a labourer should be given . . . a long scale with efficiency bars . . . to act as an *inducement to greater effort, greater productivity and the inculcation of a sense of duty*; more so as the Nigerian labour force is increasingly going to be made up of school-leavers rather than illiterates as at present."[12]

The last remark points up one of the reasons why (point 3 here) *workers'* expectations have changed. Presumably, school-leavers are likely to be more prudent, future-oriented men who *have* expectations, whether employers like it or not, expectations which an employer will disappoint at his peril. Note also the phrase, "in the same way as persons in the salary-earning class." The egalitarian impulse which in the newly democratized Japan of the late 1940's led to the amalgamation of white-collar and manual unions and the creation of unified wage systems for all grades is *also* part of the international consensus, affecting the consciousness of modern-sector workers in the developing countries and shaping the expectations that employers have to reckon with.

In this explanation, all the initiative is assumed to lie with the managers; the workers appear as people whose expectations have to be reckoned with. It is clear, however, that some of the features described here derive from *direct* union pressure. For example, Sri Lanka unions always press for a lengthening of incremental scales; it is *one* way of getting more pay piecemeal and by the back door when overall rates are frozen. Similarly, several managers in Senegal who believed firmly in the justice of rate-for-the-job wages and deplored pressures to re-categorize the jobs of long-service workers, claimed that there would be no such pressure if there were the possibility of a general rise in wages to keep up with inflation.

Similarly, in Mexico, the category system in the paint shop clearly derived from union pressures. The causal sequence seems to go like this. Labor surplus, low turnover, de facto lifetime employment rule out the possibility for the ambitious of making careers the "traditional" way—by moving from job to job. Internal promotion is the only hope. Unions press hard to stop employers from appointing to higher-level vacancies from outside. Employers bow to this demand—and are happy to do so, given the training advantage. The unions then press for promotion by seniority because that reduces the managers' discretionary power and is, among equals, a generally acceptable (because objective and egalitarian) means of allocating scarce goods over time.

This much is nothing very new in the world. Unions have been trying to achieve these ends for a long time in many countries. In some industries, such as the railways in Britain and America, and the

[12] Government of Nigeria, Commission on the Review of Wages, Salaries, and Conditions of Service of the Senior Employees of the Government of the Federation and in Private Establishments, *Report*, 1964, p. 8.

steel industry in Britain, they succeeded in the mid-nineteenth century. What is new is that (largely owing to the victories of unions in early industrializers) these principles should be embodied in the law—both the preference to internal candidates in filling vacancies principle and seniority-selection in the Mexican law, and the first but not the second in the legally binding collective agreements reached by the tripartite commissions in Senegal. The second new thing is that the unions' demands and workers' expectations move forward one step from asking simply that *insofar as job structures permit* career possibilities should be provided to asking that *job structures should be designed* so that career possibilities are provided.

This enlarged demand is still not very strong in most firms of the three countries—least strong in Senegal as are workers' consciousness of and willingness to assert rights in general—but as there are more instances of institutions which *do* meet that demand so one might expect workers' *expectations* for the enlarged principle to grow, and hence the pressure on managers to make such institutional arrangements no longer as (in terms of Herzberg's distinction) a positive motivating device but as what he calls a hygienic device—something necessary to avoid positive resentment.

So far there are not many managers in the three countries who show anything like the concern for these motivational factors that Japanese managers have done. For most it is an intermittent concern revealed only in their acknowledgment that it is a genuine problem if a man gets stuck for twelve years in the same category at the same wage. Again, the Monterrey Group is the Japanese exception in explicitly attaching positive importance to the sustaining expectations principle.

Equally the concern of unions with pressing what was called here the "enlarged demand" varies from union to union, though as a general rule the stronger the union the stronger its demand for these just as much as for other benefits.

One might think that the end result is the same, whether the career possibilities are developed by union pressure or managers' foresight. In fact this is not so. There is one crucial respect in which the institutional arrangements preferred by the two sides diverge. Managers would generally prefer a career system in which they retain complete discretion to give or withhold advancement. Unions would prefer an automatic system regulated exclusively by that most legitimate of all egalitarian principles, seniority. In fact, we find a whole spectrum with at least six distinguishable bands.

1. Advancement depends on seniority alone (as with an automatic incremental scale).

2. Ditto, except that for serious misconduct an increment or promotion can be withheld as an explicit sanction.

3. Advancement depends on job promotion, which depends on seniority *plus* the demonstration of competence in a formal test, training for that test being provided at the employer's expense and the test being jointly agreed and administered by management and union.

4. Ditto, except that training is at the employee's expense and/or the test is unilaterally determined by the employer.

5. Advancement is regulated by two principles, a minimum guaranteed rate of advance determined entirely by seniority, plus faster rates of advance for those judged—unilaterally by superiors—to be worthy of faster advance.

6. Advancement depends unilaterally on the discretion of managers.

Unions seek to be as far up the spectrum as possible and managers as far down as possible (except that corrupt union leaders will settle for arbitrary managerial power provided that they are allowed to share it). Most Japanese firms come in band 5; most Senegalese firms in band 6; most Mexican firms either in bands 3 or 4 or band 6. Position on this spectrum is, in fact, a good litmus indicator of the strength of unions in a particular firm. It is to that question that we now turn.

Unions

The three salient characteristics of industrial relations in a Japanese-type, organization-oriented system are:

(a) the autonomy of the plant or enterprise union (or union branch) run by employees of the company (as opposed to its subordination to a national organization), the union being concerned, fairly narrowly, with increasing the workers' share in the company cake, without unfairly increasing the effort they have to put into making it;

(b) managers' acceptance of the legitimacy of the union and its right to bargain in the interests of workers;

(c) the unions' willingness to cooperate with managers in promoting the firm's prosperity and maintaining and enforcing agreed on rules.

The degree of autonomy is perhaps the least ambiguous characteristic to try to measure. In all three countries it is much more limited than in Japan, and the major reason seems to be that which was already hinted at in the last section—namely, the greater role of the law, and of the executive power of the state, in regulating industrial conflict. The circumstances in the three countries are different, however.

In Mexico a constraining factor in some industries is the action of the state in institutionalizing patterns of an earlier period, and an important fact about Mexico is that it *does* have an earlier period, a history of industrialization and of trade-union activity nearly as old as Japan's and certainly a good deal older than the other two countries. In textiles, for instance, unions became organized and acquired enough solidarity to conclude effective bargains with employers' federations before the state was much involved in the labor field. Since the industry was very much a small-enterprise industry with a good deal of labor mobility at the time, it was naturally an industrial agreement between unions and a federation of employers. Any subsequent tendency which there might have been for big enterprises, as they emerged, to break away from the industrial bargaining system in order to strike more favorable bargains at the plant level has been checked by the official institutionalization of the bargaining process in the *contrato-ley* system. The government now takes part in the biennial textile negotiations, and the collective agreement which results is given the force of law and made obligatory even for firms not in the federation. There may still be large firms where the plant union branch does autonomously bargain for rates above the basic minimum set by the agreement, but there was none such in my sample. In the textile firm which was in my sample the plant branch did bargain autonomously over recruitment and job allocation (indeed, actually controlled both), but the wages were determined by the official collective agreement.

Outside the textile and half-a-dozen other industries, however, the collective agreement regulating hours and pay and conditions is an enterprise or plant agreement; to that extent the situation conforms to the organization-oriented model. Equally, membership is in a union organization at the place of work: there is normally only one union for the manual workers of any enterprise; the union shop is part of the agreement, and workers do not normally retain their union membership while out of a job and "in the market," as one might in an industrial union (except in, for example, the construction trades where there is great mobility and where unions have closed-shop agreements so that the purchase of union membership is a purchase of job-seeking rights).

Generally, however, the Mexican union organization at the plant is not a formally independent union, but, on the North American pattern, a local of an industrial federation and, perhaps more importantly, affiliated to the regional center of a general federation of labor. There are two major reasons *why* unions need to maintain such an affiliation, neither of which has much to do with the traditional "market-oriented" union purpose of regulating the price for skills required in certain industries throughout the market.

The first is the importance of the law for regulating disputes over dismissals, holidays, compensation, etc.; the second is the involvement of the major trade-union federations (notably one of them, the CTM) in maintaining political support for the regime. The CTM is an integral part of the ruling party. Politicians depend on it for support; its nominees fill the union's seat on the tripartite labor courts; its officials can, in return, claim political patronage, if necessary in the form of executive pressure on employers or on judges. The courts are more important for the unions of smaller firms which cannot possibly hire their own legal services; the possibility of mobilizing political support is more important to unions of bigger firms, whose disputes are likely to attract the attention of the president and his entourage. On the other hand, if a firm is *that* important—a Volkswagen, say— its union may not need a privileged political pipe to the centers of power and can afford to be (as the Volkswagen union is) completely independent.

There is, perhaps, yet another factor determining the external affiliations of Mexican unions: a sense, on the part of at least some union leaders, of the need for class solidarity vis-à-vis the government. One does not *need* to belong to any national federation to benefit from the wage increases which follow every official raising of the minimum wage, but there is, perhaps, some sense of obligation to play a part in putting pressure on the government.

If one is talking, however, not of formal links but of actual functional independence, it appears from my sample that there is a correlation between the degree of autonomy a factory union branch exercises and the extent to which its leaders are democratically representative of its members. The firms (usually either small or with a predominantly female work force) in which the outside union organizer played the predominant role in collective bargaining were also the firms in which that organizer colluded with the employers to keep "trouble-makers" away from the factory, and received sizable sums of money accounted for as "contributions to union sports activities" in the company budget and not accounted for at all in the union budget. (The belief that *all* professional union organizers are such Hoffa-like *charros* is widespread in Mexico and, though untrue, is not implausible.) By contrast, the unions where the collective agreement was renegotiated almost exclusively by a committee elected from employee union members without outside help were unions where the bargaining was tough and genuine and internal discussion quite open.

This contrasts, of course, with the general assumption that an autonomous enterprise union is more likely to be corrupted by the employer than one which is linked to a national organization and dominated by full-time officials. One case, however, conforms to those general assumptions—the case of the "white unions" of the Monterrey

Group, which have their own federation of plant unions entirely un-related to any other union body. These are unions which have fully accepted the role of "loyal opposition," with the emphasis on the loyalty rather than on the opposition. Union dues are lower and the company subsidizes its funds; the company also pays half the salary of a "union advisor" who is supposed to help it fight for its rights. The union does not, unlike most unions, claim control over recruitment, and it enters negotiations for a renewal of the collective contract not with a specific wage demand but with a statement of the increase in the cost of living and a request to the company to make an offer. Nevertheless, the grievance procedures seem to be fairly and vigorously operated; union officials do not seem to gain personally from their office, and they have a general reputation for being public-spirited and uncorrupt—which is noteworthy given the rarity of such reputations in the Mexican trade union world.

Once again the Monterrey Group emerges as the most Japanese in pattern, though in the extent to which they have domesticated the union, they stand well toward the right-of-center, management-dom-inated end of the Japanese spectrum.

The pattern in Sri Lanka is quite different—though equally shaped by the fact that the political power of the government is the most potent force in regulating industrial conflict. The contrast between the dominance of a single federation in Mexico, with a single union in each factory, and Sri Lanka's fragmented system, with as many as four or even five unions competing for the same members in a single fac-tory, simply reflects the difference between a hegemonic dominant party system of national politics and a competitive party system where power really does change hands at elections, or shift marginally from party to party within coalitions in between elections. Each Sri Lanka union federation quite simply is linked (frequently via one or two outstanding lawyer-politicians) to a particular political party or ex-traparliamentary political faction.

In the state corporations managers simply have to accept this frag-mentation of the unions as a fact of life—particularly if three of the competing unions belong to the three parties in the ruling coalition. To appear to show favor to any one of them might be to jeopardize a career, political influence being notoriously important in determining state corporation appointments at the higher levels. Some managers, on a divide-and-rule principle, may even welcome the fragmentation.

It is noticeable, however, that the three major private-sector firms in the Sri Lanka sample have eliminated, or avoided, union competi-tion. They have a single union for manual workers and another for clerical workers. (How far this was deliberately engineered by the management we did not find out). They each have their own separate collective plant agreement. In each case, however, the union is affiliated to a national union, and the outside union officials, as well as taking up legal cases, also play a larger role in negotiating the plant collective agreement than in comparable types of firms in Mexico. The fact that Sri Lanka is a small country and that all three of the firms mentioned were only a short bus ride away from the national general secretary's office partly explains this. The ideological factor mentioned apropos of Mexico is important too. Sri Lanka is a more politicized society: the working-class consciousness nurtured by the Marxist ideologies of the (middle-class lawyer or LSE economist) leaders of the unions can derive real emotional energy from the status group division of Sri Lanka society—the resentment of the Sinhalese Buddhist worker for the anglicized and English-speaking products of the elite schools who shape the ethos of the managerial class. Ceylonese unions, for example, do not give rise to the professional money-making union boss of the Mexican charro type.

One final point about Ceylonese unions. There are some industrial unions which (like the textile unions or miners' unions in Mexico) reflect a market-oriented stage of union organization—the plantation workers, the bank employees, the clerical workers. In the match company in the sample, the union was formerly a branch of a match-workers' union which also organized two other firms in the industry. Since there is a match industry wage board, there is, indeed, still a genuine basis for such an organization. This union, however, has disintegrated. The union of the company in the sample, a multinational which is a good deal more capital-intensive than its competitors and can pay higher than wage board minimum wages without much difficulty, now goes it alone—and secures much more advantageous plant agreements than in other match firms. Its only links—important ones —are, as explained here, with a political confederation. One additional factor in this may be that the wage-board structure has been largely superseded as a locus of genuine bargaining by across-the-board cost-of-living allowances granted in the government sector and automatically extended by wage board agreement to the private sector.

In this last respect Senegal is similar to Sri Lanka. There is a nominal structure of industrial union federations with an obvious raison d'être in the existence of legally binding collective conventions which set wage rates and define job categories *industry by industry*. The conventions have not been revised for years, however. Wage increases come from general percentage all-round increases decreed by the government. The bodies which exist to put pressure on the government to make such decrees are political confederations. As in Mexico there is only one such which really counts, and as in Mexico it is firmly integrated into the structure of power. In Senegal the president is the minister of national education. The political confederation, in other words, has effectively superseded industrial unions or federations of unions—if, indeed, superseded is the right word. Historical research will show that. It seems probable that even when the collective conventions were being negotiated, the industrial federations never played a very big role; the national political role of unions has always been of the highest importance because of the large part they played in the national independence movement. Unions in Senegal—as in Sri Lanka, and for the same reason—were born political. Nevertheless, the industrial federations continue to exist, although there has been no bargaining at the industry level for a decade. Full-time union officials usually wear at least two hats: one by virtue of a position in an industrial federation, one by virtue of a position in the political confederation. It is their activity wearing the second hat—pressing the government for wage rises—which most affects the welfare of their members. Their other hat chiefly determines which particular factories they keep liaison with, though some industrial federations hold regular meetings of their factory representatives in the Dakar area, and this contact is useful to the plant representatives. Concessions in one firm can be cited to support claims in another; and it *is* a more compelling argument for the union in a peanut-oil firm to argue that another peanut-oil firm does such and such than to cite a firm in a quite different industry.

The autonomy of these factory-level branches in Senegal is strengthened by the law. Employers have a statutory obligation to arrange for the selection of a committee of worker delegates and to discuss matters concerning the work and pay and welfare of the workers with them. Naturally the unions tend to preempt these posts, and the delegates' committee is usually the effective union committee for the plant.

With only one exception, the Senegalese factory committees of the firms in the sample did not, on the Mexican or Sri Lanka model, make formal collective agreements of a comprehensive kind with employers —partly, no doubt, because basic wage rates are effectively state-regulated and taken out of the collective-bargaining process. But they do reach formal ad hoc agreements on a wide range of matters— grievance procedures, disciplinary procedures, production bonuses, job categorization, shift working, holiday loan advances, and so on. And all of this, of course, is bargained over at the plant level, and generally without much formal intervention by outside officials; the latter are brought in chiefly for the resolution of grievance disputes, particularly those which are likely to be carried to the labor tribunal.

A summary answer can now be given to the first question about the patterns of union organization and the locus of bargaining. That part of the "late-development effect" thesis which argues that market-oriented patterns of industrial unions and industry-wide wage setting will not get established or if established will lose their importance would seem to be true (though the law can *sometimes* "fossilize" such patterns established in the early stages and prevent their disappearance). The other part of the hypothesis—that these will give place to an enterprise union/enterprise bargaining structure—is, however, wrong, or only half-true. It overlooks another "late-development" principle: the later deliberate industrialization/modernization starts, the greater the role of the state.

That principle was invoked in my original hypotheses about industrial relations only insofar as it partly explains the security of prospects of large firms and the rapid establishment of the institutional *framework* of industrial bargaining. What has been overlooked is the large role of the state in determining the *outcomes* of bargaining—much greater in the three countries with weaker trade unions than in Britain, where the institutionalized strength of trade unions has destroyed the incomes policies of both major political parties in turn, or in Japan, where the union movement is, according to one's point of view, strong enough for the government not to have had the courage to try an incomes policy or weak enough for no such policy to have been necessary.

But state action and national-level negotiation and agitation are not everything. The bargaining process also shifts in part from the industrial to the plant or enterprise level, and in Sri Lanka and Mexico, where big firm unions can negotiate substantially higher-than-average wages, that part is the bigger part.

And insofar as plant bargaining does assume greater importance, the reasons seem to be those one would expect. In a dualistic structure, the unions of the big firms, which have everything to gain by going it alone, are likely to do so. The expansion of the subject matter of bargaining (to embrace not just wages and hours but a wide range of other matters too: welfare provisions, working conditions, grievance procedures, discipline) means that agreements can be made only at the plant or enterprise level. Labor immobility makes recruitment into the firm a major concern replacing the traditional concern with regulating the numbers entering a craft to prevent any "flooding of the market." And insofar as there is leeway in wage bargaining by state regulation, it comes from manipulating a structure of wages and job categories specific to the organization, which can only be bargained over within the organization.

The answer to the second question about unions—whether or not they are accepted by employers as an inevitable and legitimate part of their factory's organizational structure—should be fairly obvious from the preceding discussion. No large firm manager in any of the countries sees a no-union option as open to him. Small firm owners in Mexico and Sri Lanka do see themselves as having such an option (not so easily in Senegal, where the law prescribes the election of delegates, though some may simply ignore the law). But a Mexican small-firm owner is likely to prefer to take out insurance against a genuinely militant union by inviting the local CTM official to organize his factory, and even a Ceylonese works manager who was determined not to have a union in his factory of 120 engineering workers (a determination which he said came from his bitter personal experiences as an engineer in one of the state corporations best known for being riven by the struggles of competing unions) nevertheless claimed that his workers' welfare society and its committee effectively did all the representational jobs that needed doing. Few people any more, in other words, are prepared to say flatly, "I am running this firm, it's my job to manage, they can just take it or leave it."

But, of course, the *degree* to which unions are accepted, the extent to which they share in decision-making, the extent to which there is genuinely "constitutional management," varies considerably. One cannot separate this question from the last one listed at the beginning of this section: the union's willingness to cooperate with managers in making the firm prosper.[13] Perhaps the best way to handle this particular discussion is to give a number of type cases.

Perhaps the most fully accepted, most fully cooperative, example in all three countries was a Senegalese garment manufacturer who had delegated disciplinary powers to a committee on which the union delegates were well represented. The initiators of disciplinary proceedings were the foremen and the Senegalese chief supervisor, who had also

[13] As an example of the feedback relationship between managers' acceptance of unions and union willingness to cooperate, this comment by a union official in the Monterrey Group: "At the beginning, in the thirties, the employers were full of ideas of economic liberalism and Taylorism. In the working-class movement there was a lot of confusion with anarchists, Marxist-Leninists, and so on. . . . Employers were frightened of us too, despite the fact that our ideas were based on a Christian humanism. Little by little the ideology of the employers changed, thanks to the diffusion of the papal encyclicals and the influence of the unions. Now . . . the workers are no longer considered the 'work force' but as heads of families. The company and union have gradually formed themselves into a team, and little by little the company has acquired a disposition toward change which the union has accelerated."

become a major shareholder in the firm. It was perhaps the effective, not overly authoritarian, authority of the latter which ensured that there was enough of a genuine consensus between workers and managers over the norms to be sanctioned for the system to operate effectively. It had been set up by the French part-owner general manager. Perhaps his acceptance of the principle that a constitutionally shared authority can claim a more genuine legitimacy than an arbitrary one owes something to the racial situation. When the social distance between French manager and African supervisior is so much greater than between the latter and his workers, the sharing of disciplinary authority between the latter two levels may seem, to the general manager, a small step to take. Colonial rulers of the most authoritarian kind, when they opted for the conveniences of indirect rule, were not much concerned with the question whether the local chiefs ruled democratically or arbitrarily, provided the system worked.

Perhaps the same sort of explanation applies to another firm, a small textile firm in Mexico, which was almost at the same end of the spectrum. It was operated by its owner, a man of strong and highly articulate opinions, a part-time economics professor who saw himself as a nineteenth-century entrepreneur, who deplored all the creeping manifestations of socialism apparent in Mexican society, who openly expressed his contempt for his workers and in return was personally quite widely disliked by them. He, nevertheless, had delegated to the union not only control over recruitment (which is fairly common) but also over job and shift allocation and the calculation of piece-rate wage entitlements. Rather than face disputes arising from union challenges to supervisors' decisions, he found it more convenient, and cheaper, to let the union sort things out within its *own* authority structure. A similar system exists in the match company in Sri Lanka, where there is a whole-factory *daily* production bonus depending on total output, and the managers happily delegate to the union the responsibility of disciplining all those who are not "pulling their weight." One could see these examples, of course, as a revival of widespread early industrial practices of indirect hiring through labor contractors. It makes a big difference, though, that the union leaders were responsible elected officials.

At the opposite end of the spectrum to these three examples are unions which avoid any kind of commitment in the matter of discipline and work organization, defend all workers against management sanctions of any kind—and are by the same token treated by management as bodies whose sphere of competence is to be kept as limited as possible. The assumption is, on the union side, that the duty of worker solidarity vis-à-vis managers far overrides any *shared* interests workers and managers might have in, for instance, preventing theft or violence or shoddy workmanship in the factory; on the manager's side that the workers are naturally concerned to get as much money for as little work as possible and will "get away with" anything they are allowed to get away with. This, roughly, is the situation in some of the state corporations in Sri Lanka; unions exhibit a general syndrome of militancy, which expresses itself also in the suspicion that any managerial plan to alter work allocations is almost certain to be to the disadvantage of the worker and as such should be resisted—or at least consented to only after the exaction of the highest possible price. (Thus, in the steel corporation, for instance, when one department lacked essential raw materials the union delegates insisted on their right to be idle and it took over a month before they were persuaded to agree to transfer to work in other departments.)

In part this reflects the genuineness of class feeling in Sri Lanka between the anglicized managerial class and the Sinhala-speaking underclass. Britain transmitted the most extreme form of its class divisions to Sri Lanaka—the military form with its division between a hereditary officer caste and the "other ranks" living in quite separate social worlds—and the institutional traces of that legacy are still apparent in the state corporations today. Although practices are gradually changing, managers are still referred to as "officers" and have their own "officers' clubs" in some corporations; disciplinary sanctions involve "charge-sheeting" in court-martial style, and so on. Add to this the ideological input, the fact that egalitarian ideals (originating, perhaps, in another part of British traditions) are stronger in Sri Lanka than in the other countries. The demand from some unions for *flat-rate* production bonuses to replace bonuses proportional to salary may be seen as an example of this, as is the widespread resentment of the gap between workers' and managers' salaries—much more marked than in, say, Mexico, where the actual pay differentials are a good deal greater.

There are two other factors in Sri Lanka. First, competition for members between rival unions can easily lead to demonstrative "we *really defend* our members, right or wrong" activity. Second, no union leader or worker can easily be convinced that his prosperity depends on the corporation's prosperity, because he knows that the corporation's "prosperity" depends not on how hard he works but on how readily the state allows price increases or subsidizes the corporation's losses—particularly when he deals with managers who are equally happy to keep things ticking at a ritualistic level of activity, as if they thought that somehow or other their status as university graduates gives them a prebendary *right* to a state pension in the form of a corporation salary.

That situation can be changed, however, even within the context just described. Dynamic top management in one corporation altered the work habits and sense of pride of junior managers and altered the attitudes of the union—initially because of top managers' skill in dealing with them (conceding for instance, the egalitarian flat rate bonus scheme), increasingly as the corporation began to gain a national reputation for its successes because they came to feel "involved." They were willing to accept that some dismissals were justified (and dismissals were, in fact, far more frequent than in other corporations) and willing to accept changes in work arrangements to enhance productivity—even though this corporation too, had several unions competing for members.

There are many intermediate positions between the garment-maker in Senegal and the Sri Lanka steel corporation. In the majority of firms in all countries the union either formally agrees to, or is at least consulted about, the disciplinary code of the factory, while leaving its application exclusively to managers so that it reserves complete freedom to challenge any particular decision—even though it will in practice calibrate its challenge according to what it concedes to be the "justice" of the managers' case.

But generally in the middle range, there is no apparent correlation between (a) the actual power a union has, (b) the managers' wish to involve the union in decision-making, and (c) the cooperativeness of the union. This is largely because *most* of the powers that unions possess have either been given to them by the law or won in their *own* interests, not voluntarily given by managers in the interest of efficiency through involvement. The control which most Mexican plant unions exercise over recruitment (and which some Sri Lanka's unions are increasingly pressing for, and getting) is a right won by workers concerned with jobs for their sons, not a planned devolution of powers; so also is the control which many Mexican unions exercise, to a greater or lesser degree, over promotion.

The Monterrey firms are most interesting in this regard. Here the ideology of union involvement is strongest. Managers point out that even the security guards are in the union, and that they do not choose lawyers to be personnel managers—both pieces of evidence that they do not have a "confrontational" view of union-management relations. But in practice the union shares less in decision-making than in other companies where "confrontation" is expected. Union officials take part in productivity committees, and there is an effective system of department grievance committees—which in effect sanction disciplinary action and can in theory act as a brake on work intensification—in which the unions play a major role. But they do not have control over recruitment and promotions as unions do in many other firms. Managers explain that the grant of such powers would corrupt union leaders. The fact remains that the union accepts a wide range of managerial authority as unchallengeable and as such in the Mexican context would justifiably be considered weak.

So it would in a Japanese context. One can find many Japanese unions which were just as deferential to management authority and had carved out just as small a share of power as the Monterrey "white" unions, but many of the large Japanese firms do have unions which, while holding the same ideology of partnership and absence of confrontation as the Monterrey unions, and leaving a wide range of production decisions to the unchallenged authority of managers, nevertheless combine with this the bargaining toughness over wages of the stronger Mexican or Sri Lanka unions.

Some of the circumstances which have made this possible, and conversely the circumstances which determine in the three societies studied the emergence of something different from the pure type "organization-oriented" model which one might have generalized out of the Japanese example, will have become clear in the foregoing discussion.

The relative unimportance in Japan (as compared with later developers) of the state and the courts in the regulation of industrial relations has enhanced the completeness of enterprise-union separatism in organization and made less likely strong external links which would have helped to keep alive a genuinely class-conscious conception of workers' interests and a confrontational view of industrial relations.

To this should be added the relative unimportance of state enterprise—as compared with Sri Lanka, where state corporations are dominant pace-setters. In both Sri Lanka and Mexico state firms are more likely than private firms to have slack managers who are (a) willing to give in to union demands "for a quiet life," thus encouraging confrontational militancy, and (b) quite unable, thanks to their own example of self-interested ambition and lack of concern with the corporation's prosperity or reputation, to offer any plausible arguments about cooperation for the good of the company.

The absence in Japan (as compared particularly with Sri Lanka, and even with Mexico) of inherited class divisions—with clear cultural, status-group divisions between classes—meant that there was a lesser likelihood that divisions of interest would be much exacerbated by resentments deriving from the pretensions or arrogance of managers and the sense of status inferiority of workers. Compare, for instance, the remark of a Japanese manager in Mexico:

"University graduates are a problem. They expect 4,000 pesos a month immediately after they graduate—and they can get it. They expect a room of their own and a personal secretary. They put *licenciado* or *ingeniero* on their calling cards. Can you imagine a Japanese graduate doing that? And Japanese graduates, anyway, only start at 3,000 pesos—in a country where the average wage level is much much higher. It seems that in Mexico, when you graduate from a university you move into a different social class—and nobody questions the justice of these wage differentials."

Perhaps, also, Japan's long pre-industrial tradition of bureaucratic legalism (compare the arbitrary *caudillismo* of Mexican local government traditions) has predisposed Japanese workers more effectively to accepting the legitimacy of institutional rules (rather than seeing *all* social outcomes as the result of power inequalities) and hence toward cooperating to make them work. Again, the same Japanese manager, after he had given me a long explanation of their hiring rules—a ban on rehiring, not more than one person from the same family, and so on:

"No, I'm afraid I can't give you a copy of these rules. They aren't properly set out anywhere. I agree with you that it's very important that they should be. As a matter of fact I've drafted a set of rules once or twice. But my Mexican colleagues have been all against it, and I've had to drop the idea. They say: you're right that if you set out the rules clearly you constrain the workers. But you also constrain management too. You limit our powers of discretion. So the rules are all unwritten. It does have advantages. You can be more humane, for instance. You can show *ninjō* 'human sympathy' to a worker off sick. Social security guarantees him 60 percent of his wage, but he might have several children and be sick for a couple of months. If he's a good worker, there's nothing to stop us making up his wage.

"Resentments if you do it for some and not others? Well to start with, people keep these things secret. Then there's a basic difference between countries like England or Japan, where there's a basic spirit of equality and here where there isn't. People here don't think they have a *right* to equal treatment."

Also one might invoke a general syndrome of deference to authority which may well be more strongly institutionalized in Japan and more salient a part of the "modal personality" than in the other three countries, and which may explain, therefore, a greater willingness to accept unquestioningly the authority of managers in some spheres. Once again our Japanese manager, this time on the difference between Japan's Confucianism and the "deformed kind of Catholicism" of modern Mexico.

"How does it show itself concretely? Well. I'll give you examples. A man comes late; you ask him why. In Japan he would say: 'I'm sorry, I'll try to do better tomorrow.' He may not in fact do better and you know he may not, but at least he admits he's in the wrong. But here they'll say, well, yes, as a fact I'll admit my lateness—but I left home at the same time as usual. It was the bus. It's not my fault.

"Or, say, production over the month is down to 80 percent. You call the factory manager and ask him why. A Japanese factory manager would say: 'yes, I'm sorry, my powers of command have not been adequate to cope. The actual circumstances were such and such.' But here it's, 'Well, it's not my fault. I did my job properly. The materials we got this month were defective. Four percent of the work force left; the personnel manager didn't get us the replacements soon enough. . . .' "

Also, it is worth recalling that the present fairly stable (in private industry) modus vivendi between Japanese management and workers represents a point of compromise, a swing back of the pendulum *after* the period of the late 1940's, when managers were demoralized and the new unions swept all before them. This may have confirmed the basic rights of unions to a place in the system, and reconciled managers to it, more effectively than the more gradual, often legally directed and grudging, advance of union rights in the other countries.

Finally, one must, again, come back to the strong strain of "group-ishness" in Japanese culture—the greater propensity which Japanese seem to show, as compared certainly with the three nationalities considered here, to merge themselves in a group and to work together for collective rather than individual goals. This cannot fail to have predisposed Japanese unions more easily to integration, or cooptation, within the structure of the enterprise:

"Yes, I've thought a lot about that. The first reason, I think, is that the Mexicans are 'dry' [*dorai*, emotionally uninvolved and calculating, as opposed to *uetto*, susceptible to sentimental considerations]. Then, I think, Mexicans don't think 10 or 20 years ahead; they're more likely to be seduced by the prospect of 500 pesos extra now than by their prospects of advancement in 10 years' time. Third, in Japan the whole social system—and I mean the organization of the firm as well as of the society—protects a man and gives him security and a place. Here there is no security: people feel they have only themselves to rely on. Fourth, there is no orderly progression by promotion. That's all because of personal loyalties. For example, if someone is hired on the recommendation of the chief accountant and he goes to work in the personnel office, then in Japan his chief loyalty would be to the personnel manager and the accountant would expect that to be the case. But here no. His first loyalty is to the accountant. That sort of thing destroys the system. It means that you can only trust people of your own group. If a Mexican were to take over from me, you would see all the top jobs change—to bring in his own people. So—to get back to the mobility thing—if you're a factory manager, you've no *calculable* prospects of becoming a director or chairman; you're a factory manager, and if somebody offers you an extra 1,000 pesos to be a factory manager somewhere else, you'll take it.

"Finally, another thing is that there's no sense of the firm being a public organization which belongs to everybody. In our firm, as you know, the original founder is still alive, but it's not really *his* firm in the way that Mexican firms *belong* to their owners. So there isn't any sense of loyalty to the firm. Well, that's an overstatement; there is some, but the sense of loyalty to individuals—to oneself or one's family—is stronger. Take what happens to profits. In Japan a large proportion of profits are retained—they go to the *firm*. In Mexico, by contrast, all the profits are taken out as dividends by the owners. I suppose you could say that the Japanese system is semisocialistic."

Involvement: Work Motivation

The loyalty aspect, indeed, deserves separate treatment.

Negative sanctions—dismissal, fines, and demotions—are hard to apply in the big firm sector in all three countries—as in Japan. If the stick is ruled out, what alternatives do managers resort to as a means of enhancing workers' willingness to work? The brief answer is,

(a) Carrots: cash production incentive schemes.

(b) Some firms do try other motives such as a sense of commitment to the enterprise as an ongoing successful *gemeinde*, whose successes and failures, joys and sorrows, are shared equally by all its members.

(c) But these latter attempts frequently have indifferent success:

(i) partly because the extent to which the joys are *not* shared equally —salary differentials between workers and managers—is too great to accord with current conceptions of fairness; (ii) partly because managers still hanker after punitive sanctions, use them as far as possible within the constraints to which they are subject, and hence perpetuate a legalism in management/work relations which seems inimical to the sort of commitment they seek to evoke; (iii) and equally they perpetuate individualistic competitiveness and the idea that responsibilities should be individually divided, the records for success and the responsibilities for failure being clearly pinnable on individuals— rather than seeking to enhance cooperation.

The Mexican textile firm and the Sri Lanka match factory are good examples of managers setting up relatively efficient Taylorite systems of piece rates to encourage a high level of production, are happy enough to rely on the unions to police it, and show no interest whatever in giving workers any feeling of belongingness.

But doctrines of the need for identification, participation, self-actualization, etc., are sufficiently widely diffused for many of the big firms in all three countries to do something to evoke enterprise-consciousness. This was more obviously the case in Mexico than in Sri Lanka, and in Sri Lanka than in Senegal. (In the latter two countries there was the possibility of comparing the way different branches of the same multinational interpreted the policies of their company, which was generally very strong on identification.) These differences perhaps reflect the cultural gulf between managers and workers: the French in Senegal are more likely than Ceylonese managers to have a contemptuous view of their workers as unreachable except by the crassest of financial incentives, and the latter (possibly, though the difference is probably small) than Mexican managers.

The one group of firms which came closest to succeeding was, once again, the Monterrey Group. First of all, they invested a good deal of money. Not only did they provide high wages, but their workers also enjoyed up to four weeks of paid holiday, retirement benefits, subsidized meals, clinics, insurance, free transport, home loans, grocery stores, and a vast range of sports and leisure facilities. Moreover, these benefits are administered by a separate society whose main officers (and in theory controllers) are elected from among the employees. There are also, in their mixed committees of unions and managers at departmental level, attempts to keep workers informed of the company's plans and to "consult" with them about changes in work schedules.

These measures have some success if low levels of turnover, absence of work stoppages, and high productivity are any guide. It is noticeable, however, that both workers and managers—the former as a matter of course, the latter as evidence of a partial failure—see the Welfare Society as a piece of company paternalism; few show much disposition to take their democratic rights to participate in its management very seriously.

The more interesting failure to develop an effective sense of "involvement" may be seen in the Sri Lanka state corporations. It ought, perhaps, to have been easy; managers are not profit-takers; the corporations could be represented as the pride of a developing Sri Lanka. In fact, however, the effort has been half-hearted. Workers' councils were started after instructions to create them were received from the Ministry of Industries. Some younger managers have tried to make them work, but the whole traditional style of authoritarian management is too deeply ingrained for an effective spirit of cooperation to be generated. Suspicions run too deep. Works councils feel that one of their main aims is to get involved in the tendering process in order, as a vigilante committee, to ferret out managerial corruption. Factory council meetings can all too easily become a display of mutual recrimination, to pin down the blame for a maintenance failure, with the electrical repair men showing a solidary front in blaming the mechanical repair men, and vice versa.

Only one corporation has managed to create a different atmosphere, largely by generating some enthusiasm among managers and by company achievements (judiciously publicized) which have given some sense of satisfied pride. This has been achieved also by being ahead of some other firms in sharing the benefits (with a flat-rate production bonus—the same number of rupees for the general manager and the gatekeeper) and by such devices as a corporation "family news sheet." It is notable, however, that this was achieved despite the tough use of dismissal as a sanction—though not so much for non-performance as for clear sins of commission—corrupt abuse of responsibilities, chiefly.

The Uses of Comparison

From comparisons several points emerge about the general model of the late-development pattern. The first is that the original formulation very much underestimated the role of the state in shaping employment systems. Here, clearly, is an important difference between late and later development. The later that development takes place, for a wide variety of reasons, the more likely the state is to play a predominant role in the development process and the wider the conception of the state's "proper sphere of competence" in the "international concensus" is likely to be. Its impact on the employment field is likely to be much wider than the basic establishment of workers' and trade-union rights and the setting of the basic framework for industrial relations envisaged in the thesis. The state does a lot of the training which the late-development model assumes the employer has to do (not only in schools: in Sri Lanka and in Senegal also in the government arsenal and railway workshops). The state guarantees job security; it lays down detailed framework legislation, controlling such matters as hiring and promotion procedures, the election of union representatives, the handling of redundancy. And it is likely to go further and control what happens *within* the frame work—setting, effectively, levels of wages from outside the firm.

But, of course, the freedom the state has to maneuver is often distinctly restricted; wages cannot be screwed down for too long during inflation; dualistic differentials cannot be reduced too fast or too far without risk of political trouble—even in countries where the state does not obviously base itself on popular consent. Which point suggests a second reflection—on the diversity of the *modes of diffusion* of institutional forms. The original model assumed several forms of international diffusion of norms and organizational forms, but only at the upper levels. Governments enact legislation under the inspiration of the ILO; management brings organization directly from the rich countries in multinationals through technical experts, through management training courses. To add to the diversity of channels—though still upper-level channels—we found in Mexico some influence from papal encyclicals.

The interesting diffusion mechanism which I had overlooked, however, is the molding of *workers' expectations* by influences from richer countries. These expectations, once established, may *force* certain policies on managers because the cost of disappointing these expectations (in low morale, non-cooperation, etc.) becomes too great. For example, in all three countries, we found the assumption that a man was hard done by if he stayed at the same wage rate in the same job for seven or eight years; we found the assumption that people had a *right* to job security; we found the assumption that every renewal of a collective agreement should bring an *additional* benefit to the workers as part of the general progress of society.

How did expectations such as these—expectations hardly common among British workers, say, twenty years ago—get implanted? Is it because of the "advanced" labor legislation which implicitly or explicitly gives some of these expectations the status of "rights?" But, if so, how did these laws get transplanted? Was it because trade unionists, with knowledge of the laws of other countries, were thereby given targets to aim at? Was it the odd employer, transferring practices from other countries, who conferred on workers certain "rights" which, conceded in one firm, raised expectations in others? Or was there more direct "people-to-people" diffusion, along trade-union channels, through *Readers Digest*, and other demonstration-effect-producing international media?

And, anyway, how *much* has the diffusion of organizational forms and norms to answer for? The infrastructure/superstructure question is usually an insoluable and generally an unprofitable one. In the original formulation the hypothesis about a late-development organization-oriented pattern laid more stress on the "logic of the situation" in late developers: the technological gap, the pattern of industrial ownership, the prerequisites of training. In fact, the more one thinks about the three countries, the more the direct diffusion of ideas —values, attitudes, knowledge about organizational forms seen as good in themselves—seems to be the more important factor. This is true especially when one includes the last-mentioned mechanism, the diffusion of expectations, which is an example, too, of the indivisibility of the two aspects, (a) diffusion and (b) independent arrival at the same solutions in a given "logic of the situation". The diffusion of expectations to workers *creates* the "logic of the situation" for the manager. At any rate, if international convergence of social forms *is* taking place, it is more likely to be, not, as most convergence theories have suggested, because of the imperatives of technology but because of the diffusion of ideas.

The last point to be made about the general model is that there is a great deal which *neither* diffusion *nor* the "logic of the situation" explains—a great deal which has to be ascribed to local cultural traditions, particular intellectual influences, "national character." The individualism/groupishness dimension is one which crops up incessantly in comparisons of Japan and anywhere else. The different nature of racial and class divisions in the five societies considered here clearly reflects itself in managers' choices of organizational forms, in the quality of the relationship between superiors and inferiors, the sentiments those relations invoke. The presence or absence of a strong religious-moralistic middle-class left-wing tradition clearly affects the different character of the trade-union movements in Mexico and Sri Lanka. And so on.

A second set of reflections springs from the question: What light does all this reflect on the history of Japan and the origins of the Japanese system?

The most obvious point is the last one made about the model in general stood on its head. There *is* a lot in the Japanese system which has to be ascribed to cultural traditions, national character, modal personality, or whichever of those nowadays suspect terms one chooses to use. One suspects that it was the character of the workers rather than of the managers that was important; that is to say that the predisposition of workers formed part of the "logic of the situation" for managers and helped to set limits to what would and would not "work" in a Japanese industrial situation and that national character was important in that way, rather than because it determined managers' perception of what was just and fitting. But that, again, needs historical examination of particular instances of institutional innovation.

Then, again, a number of other suggestive hints arise from the comparison. Having seen, for example, the large part played by unions in introducing seniority principles in Mexico, one is prompted to look again at the early development of the *nenkō joretsu* system in Japan and to see what the unions have to do with it.

But perhaps the most important general conclusion is that if one can ascribe some features of the Japanese system to late development, one must ascribe others to the fact that Japan's was an *early* case of late development. Some of those features listed at the beginning of this essay were crucial. The state did not play such a vital role in forming Japanese institutions as it does in late late developers. As a consequence, there was no minimum wage legislation, for instance, and no enshrinement in Japanese law (until after the system was established) of the "equal pay for equal work" principle, embodying a notion of fairness established by workers' struggles in the early developing European countries and spread through the world by the ILO and associated influences. That made the establishment of steep seniority wage scales in Japan much easier. Seniority wage scales were established by permitting straightforward personal rather than job-related wages; the absence of a minimum wage, by allowing employers to hire young school-leaving bachelors at the very low going market rate for such labor (a wage far lower than that necessary to sustain a family) *provided that* they offered prospects of increments up to a family wage by the time marriage was likely. Had there been a legal minimum wage, calculated to provide at least a bare *family* subsistence, that option would have been foreclosed.

And so, from general features and general preconditions explaining them, one inevitably moves back to more particular features and conditions—from late development *tout court* to development at a particular historical juncture which never repeats itself.

But, all the same, there is enough which repeats itself in rough outline for the exercise of making and breaking hypotheses to be worthwhile. Whether those hypotheses about "trends" and "forces" are confirmed or falsified, one can learn something. If comparison with Japan prompts managers or trade unionists in Mexico or Senegal to see in their wage systems a career-providing personal wage system "struggling to get out" of an "equal pay for equal work" framework, then they might start questioning all those principles in a new way. Irrespective of whether they choose to go along with the trend, or to dig in their heels and stick to equal pay for equal work principles, they might at least be doing consciously what formerly they were doing only by inertia. By my lights, at least, any increase in rationality is a good thing.

Factory Life in Japan
and China Today

※ ※

JOHN C. PELZEL

Introduction

This essay presents three case studies of factory work life in Japan and China today. It has seemed useful to do so perhaps discursively, because all are situations little known in the Western literature and two—the smallest Japanese shop and the Chinese works—in any literature.

Those parts of the work life in which I have been particularly interested here are the careers of workers, and the ways in which people relate to one another in the plant. My material, deriving as it does from factories of different sizes, is obviously not the stuff out of which controlled comparisons are made. In point of fact, hypothesizing that both type of industry and size of plant are independent variables of some strength, the broader study[1] from which these cases are sampled has focused upon small and medium-sized[2] modern metals and machinery operations. Events have, however, not been kind enough to bring forward suitable cases of small shops in the People's Republic of China, and until they do I therefore proceed through the more ancient method of natural history studies, i.e., clinical interpretation.

In the course of asking questions about work lives, I have come to

[1] The study has to date comprised two distinct types of research: In Japan, a field study in the city of Kawaguchi, at various periods between the late 1940's and late 1950's; in China, a study of factories in the People's Republic, carried on via interviews with refugees who had recently worked in these plants, during the early 1960's, in Hong Kong. I received valuable local assistance on other parts of both studies, for which my gratitude will be expressed at the proper time and place, but the Okuda and Ch'ang-sha works were done by me. The material given here on the Nagai plant is, on the other hand, excerpted from Nakano Takeshi, 1956. Professor Nakano and I did our work in Kawaguchi at the same time, as part of the same loosely structured study team under the direction of Professor Odaka Kunio of the University of Tokyo. Nakano Takeshi, "Rōdō kumiai ni okeru ningen kankei" (Human Relations in a Labor Union), pp. 201-69, Odaka Kunio, ed., *Imono no machi* (A Casting Town), Tokyo, 1956.

[2] Standards by which factories are classified as "small," etc. refer to numbers of personnel, but vary appreciably by country and period. I tend to take any plant under 50 to be "small," and any over 500 to be "large," but the diagnostic power of such size categories seems to me extremely limited.

feel that the material presented here is relevant to a major historical hypothesis, which I shall therefore briefly outline and discuss.

An evolutionary stereotype that has been much in favor in the industrial West in recent generations posits a historical change from manufacturing by men to production centering on machines. The worker was once a "craftsman" or "artisan," the argument goes, relying primarily on his own skills and energy, and imparting to the work process and the product a recognizably individual style. His role in work society was one of relative independence, based upon the ability of each artisan to identify and to solve production problems unaided. Respect and self-esteem flowed from these conditions, and the artisan was perhaps best defined in terms of his image of himself and his fellows as men who could accomplish production of high quality alone.

By way of contrast, the proposition continues, it is today the machine which, fed by inanimate energy, supplies the skills and force for production. The opportunity to meet new mass market demands with this technology has caused manufacturing to be carried out in large factories, and engineers and managers have built uniform skills and products into the machine, and programmed the production process to an ahuman routine. The production worker—the "worker" par excellence—has been demoted from creator to be the servant of the new creators: the machine, and the gods of the machine upstairs. Lewis Mumford chills us with his characterization of this new society as "authoritarian,"[3] as Charlie Chaplin wryly amused us two generations ago with his portrayal of one of the new breed of workers, so dehumanized by his work role as no longer to be able to differentiate a woman's nipple from the steel nut it is his job to tighten.

As it is designed to be, the stereotype is terrifying to the humanist. One hears also, with a sinking heart, the hypothesis that a similar evolution will occur wherever modern industry develops throughout the world.

I react with the assumption—which colors this work—that to the extent such predictions come true, men will find compensation and in the process promote a counter movement. Certainly the growth of manufacturing occupations has been exceeded in all modern societies by the concurrent growth of tertiary occupations, many of which offer people at work new opportunities for independent and skilled task performance. As my colleagues have reminded me,[4] some of the

[3] Lewis Mumford, "Authoritarian and Democratic Technics," reprinted, pp. 50-59, in Melvin Kranzberger and William H. Davenport, eds., *Technology and Culture*, New York, 1972.

[4] I am grateful for these and other comments to the participants in the Social Science Research Council conference on the Comparative Uses of the Japanese Ex-

workers I will describe who still bear much of the supposedly obso-
lescent stamp of the artisan are in critical ways not greatly unlike persons in many contemporary liberal professions—scientists and scholars,
lawyers and doctors, entertainers and artists, to say nothing of the
engineers, designers, etc., who today supply much of the skill to large-
scale manufacturing the production worker himself is alleged to have
lost.

I have, moreover, felt able to present evidence even from the factory floor that does not conform to the stereotype. These examples are
not, be it noted, in dying handicraft industries, but in modern metals
and machinery lines, turning out products as contemporary as gun
mounts, refrigerator motor housings, marine valves and machine
tools. They are in Japan and China, one of which has been modernizing for a century and both of which have been more successful at
creating modern industry than any other non-Western area of the
world, in economies that moreover, during this same period, have
showed great competitive strength vis-à-vis those of the Western home-
lands of modernity.

It is not my intention, in underlining these factors, to try to refute
the hypothesis of a unilinear industrial evolution. The material is
totally inadequate for such a purpose. There is also nothing, to my
mind, wrong with the thesis. It requires only the antithesis, derived
from an awareness of the dialectical instinct through which men continually re-engineer the conditions under which they live.

The Role of the Small Factory
in Japan and China

One point of entry to the study of this engineering is the small factory. There are technological, economic, social, and even physical factors peculiarly at home in it that create the very conditions that tend
to keep production an affair of men rather than of machines. Small
plants do not compete well for the capital that would permit them to
substitute the machine for the skilled workman. They do not because
the small shop cannot normally participate independently and directly
in the standardized mass markets to which the large factory is suited.
Instead, small operations must usually confine themselves to local,
specialized, or otherwise restricted markets; or act as marginal producers to satisfy overflow demands for which it would be uneconomi-
cal for large firms to build the same marginal capacity; or sub-contract

perience, at Cuernavaca, Mexico, in September 1974, and especially to Professors
Nakane Chie, Doi Takeo, George DeVos, Ronald Dore and Albert Craig.

for large producers, supplying them with often technically simpler parts or materials, more cheaply or more conveniently than they could themselves manage.

In all such demand situations, the small manufacturer faces alternative periods of intensive activity and idleness, a rhythm that not only reduces the economic advantage of machinery but also requires for success at busy times the human motivation of pride in hard work, and encourages in bad times the equally human resentment of the worker against "society's" breach of its implicit contract with him. In all such situations, moreover, the small plant must be able to mobilize the skills to shift from one product to another, as marginal demand for one slumps and that for another increases, and as the custom orders of specialized markets present continually changing production problems.

To the same effect, the small shop must, and can, operate with a tiny decision-making leadership, perhaps typically centering on one person, the entrepreneur or manager himself, with final authority and responsibility. He is unlikely to have the talents or the time to make all production decisions himself, and must therefore employ workers with independent abilities, and give them a measure of autonomy. He will, moreover, spend much of his time as a regular participant in the work group on the floor of the plant, in face-to-face relations with at least a few senior workmen, who in their turn are likely to have similar relations with most of the rest of the work force. Such dyadic human relations impel everyone involved to take into consideration, when developing work habits and rules, not only the work problem but also varying individual abilities, situations, and personalities, to build the work process and organization as much around the actors as around the acts they perform.

In other words, and to whatever extent the thesis that size of production unit comprises variables of great independent strength is correct, one datum to be built into hypotheses about industrial evolution concerns those factors that tend to destroy, or to perpetuate and re-create, the small plant form.

If the small shop provides an environment in which the skilled artisan, related to his work and his companions with great independence, can flourish, such lives cannot constitute an insignificant proportion of those in the manufacturing work force even in the West today. Of the more than 14,000 factories active in New York City in 1974, only 25 employed more than 500 workers each, and all but a tiny minority in fact gave work to fewer than 50.[5] Of greater relevance here, the data of the last generation or two from Japanese and Chinese

5 *New York Times*, August 3, 1974, p. 29.

374

areas demonstrate that the small plant has continued to play a very large role there, and even in industries near the core of modern product lines and markets.

In Japan by 1940, the economy was already dominated by industry, and the emphasis was on heavy manufacturing. Yet in all lines of manufacture, 80 percent of plants employed fewer than 5 persons each, and 99 percent fewer than 100. It is true that the smallest category of plants, by size, turned out only 7 percent of Japanese manufacturing output by value, and were thus of only incremental utility to the gross national product. Yet they gave employment to 22 percent of all Japanese manufacturing workers,[6] and livelihood and status to the overwhelming majority of the Japanese entrepreneur-manager class, that mainstay of the conservative-capitalistic cultural and political systems of the day.

Moreover, this situation was not brought about by any dominance over manufacturing by "backward" sectors; it was in fact very nearly as characteristic of the most "advanced" fields. In evidence: the metals-machinery component of manufacturing is of course the leading edge during a period emphasizing heavy industry, and even quantitatively dominant during a period of war and preparations for war such as Japan was then experiencing. In 1940, for example, metals-machinery work occupied 30 percent of all manufacturing plants, employed 53 percent of all Japanese at work in manufacturing, and turned out over 60 percent of the total value added by that part of the economy.[7]

By 1955, Japanese industry was fully recovered from defeat and just beginning, in the Jimmu Boom of that year, the direction of the development it still follows today. In the new peacetime orientation of 1955, the metals-machinery component was the business of only 16.4 percent of all Japanese factories, employing only 30.2 percent of all manufacturing workers, and turning out only 34 percent of the value added by Japanese manufacturing.[8] Yet, if it was no longer technologically the leading edge of an economy it utterly dominated, it was still, obviously, very central to that economy.

In 1951, midway both of my own study and of the alteration of Japanese manufacturing, metals-machinery plants employing fewer than 5 persons each comprised 44 percent of all such factories, and 97.4 percent of such establishments employed fewer than 100.[9] The

6 Sōrichō Tōkeikyoku (Statistical Bureau, Prime Minister's Office), *Nihon Tōkei Nenkan* (Japan Statistical Yearbook), Tokyo, 1949, pp. 294-297.

7 Tsūsanshō jūkōgyōkyoku (Office of Heavy Industry, Ministry of International Trade and Industry), *Nihon no kikai kōgyō*, Tokyo, 1960, I, 5-7.

8 *Ibid.*

9 Tsūshō-sangyō daijin kambō chōsa tōkeibu (Research and Statistics Division,

average metals-machinery plant midway of its devolution, therefore, was somewhat larger than had been the average of all factories, in all industries, eleven years before. Yet, even after three generations of the most rapid development, what had to that time been the dominant part of the economy and was thereafter to be near its core was a realm overwhelmingly of small, and even of tiny, plants. Clearly to this advanced stage of industrialism, in one of its most advanced sectors, the small factory had by no means been made a "relic."

The data from mainland areas of China are only impressionistic. Indeed, and as is so extensively and drearily true, they are not even comparable with those from Japan, for the material from that portion of China is classified in terms of "modern" and "handicraft" industry, categories into which the often subjective evaluation of product and process enters, rather than the objective criterion of plant size alone. Yet such data allow at least an indicative sort of comparison, for "handicraft" plants are generally small, and "modern" ones large.

During the early 1930's—the last reasonably "normal" period of the pre-socialist economy—it is estimated that 21 percent of the Chinese labor force, producing 35 percent of the net domestic product by value, was engaged in non-agricultural pursuits.[10] China was obviously only at the start of industrial development at that time.

It is impossible, from estimates now available, to differentiate the roles of manufacturing, transport, and trade. Nonetheless, the "modern" sector of all three combined is believed to have produced about 60 percent of all non-agricultural output and "handicraft" operations 40 percent, while the proportions of the non-agricultural labor force they employed were, respectively, 38 and 62 percent.[11] "Handicraft" establishments, therefore, gave employment to almost two-thirds of the non-agricultural working population, though they produced somewhat less than half of what at least an economist would recognize as quantifiable non-agricultural output.

"Handicraft" manufacturing was a most diverse category. It included not only (mainly small) factories, usually located in cities, but also the work of many full-time artisans operating alone rather than in plants, found in both city and country, as well as the industrial work carried on by farmers in their spare time, whether for their own use or for the market. I cannot even guess at the relative roles of these

---

Minister's Secretariat, Ministry of International Trade and Industry), eds., *Kōgyō tōkeihyō* (Census of Manufactures) Tōkyō, 1951, I, Tables 4-5, and *Japan Statistical Yearbook 1953*, Table 74.

[10] Order of magnitude estimates only, made from Chen Nai-ruenn and Walter Galenson, *The Chinese Economy under Communism*, Chicago, 1969, pp. 28-29, and citing the Liu-Yeh estimates for 1933.

[11] *Ibid.*, 10, fn. 9.

several types of operations for the early 1930's, but in the admittedly atypical year 1949 it is estimated that factories and full-time artisans together turned out 85 percent of the value of all Chinese "handicraft" manufacturing, with factories alone accounting for almost 50 percent of the total.[12] In other words, manufacturing by the part-time farmer was no longer of significance in the economy, or, alternatively, the role of part-time rural manufacturing was beyond the capacity of the economist to calculate.

Chen and Galenson have argued, somewhat as I have done here in the introduction, that there are good reasons why handicraft or small-scale manufacturing is not destroyed by the development of a modern large-factory system.[13] They suggest that the small factory was probably not, as has often been claimed, in decline during the pre-socialist period in China. They go further, to suggest that it has maintained, and probably even increased, its relative position in the Chinese economy under socialism. They note that, in spite of the phenomenal growth of modern large-scale industry under the first five-year plan, in 1957 "handicraft" manufacturing contributed 29 percent of the total value of all PRC industrial output, and, together with a growing small-scale manufacturing in the rural sector, may have contributed as much as 48 percent of that output, a larger proportion of a vastly larger total industrial production than in the early 1930's. They go on to suggest that this trend continued during the 1960's,[14] as it became customary for rural brigade and commune organizations to operate small-scale "sideline" industries, employing both part-time and full-time workers; as local administrative organs set up small- and medium-sized factories, especially in support of agriculture, in provincial cities; and as huge factories on the Russian model, to support heavy industrial development, fell somewhat out of official favor.

In one formal sense, their suggestion leads to an incorrect conclusion about the size of work units. From the mid-1950's, as privately owned shops in cities were taken over by units of local government, such as the so-called "Resident Committees," they were on the whole amalgamated into much larger administrative units. Four or five garment shops, for example, each employing perhaps a few persons full-time and 40-50 part-time workers, would be joined together into administrative organizations employing perhaps 200-300. In both city and country, moreover, the hitherto numerous independent artisans were on the whole absorbed into such units, and on the farm into brigade and commune sideline organizations. Gross statistics on size of industrial units, therefore, would undoubtedly reveal few "small" plants at all in the PRC anymore.

12 *Ibid.*, 10, fn. 10. 13 *Ibid.*, pp. 14-15.
14 *Ibid.*, p. 68.

Yet for the most part new construction has not been provided, and these organizations therefore continue to operate physically in dispersed and separate work units, in small groups. It is in such terms that Chen and Galenson's suggestion is not inconsistent with the admittedly limited and haphazard impressions of visitors to the People's Republic during the early 1970's. I was myself moved—as small factories slid by my car windows, as I peeked into some of them on my evening walks, and as my official itinerary took me to several medium-sized plants—to the deep impression that I was back again in the industrial world of Japan that I had known in the 1950's. No doubt many irrelevant factors entered into this impression. Nonetheless, there were clearly vast numbers of small factories in both city and countryside, and they were busy. By contrast with American—and increasingly today with large-scale Japanese—practice, it was clear they invested little or nothing in such immediately unproductive capital equipment, or its upkeep, as elbow space for workers, amenities, storage, white-collar tools, and in this they resemble closely the small Japanese plant of twenty-five years ago.

Rest rooms are often open privies. The enclosed space per worker is only a fraction of that deemed minimal in the contemporary West. Heat (or cold), noise, and dirt, unabated by pollution-control investment, overwhelm the inexperienced visitor. Boxes serve as file cabinets in offices naked even of adding machines, let alone typewriters and the more recent marvels of IBM and Xerox. Rows of clerks laboriously write by hand everything that needs to be recorded and communicated. Raw materials and finished products are stored in the open, thus avoiding expensive enclosures. These conditions are moreover as pervasive in even quite large factories as they are in tiny household operations. The product may be modern, and where it needs be the production machinery, but everything else derives from a parsimony of capital and a plethora of labor for which one would have to go far back in American industrial history to find analogues.

If there is only impressionistic evidence that small production units have retained, or even improved, their role in the greatly expanded socialist industrial economy of the People's Republic, there is clear proof of their significance in the contemporary capitalist economies of Taiwan and Hong Kong.

Between 1952 and 1969 Taiwan moved into the column of "developed" nations. Employment in agriculture declined from 61 to 45 percent of the total work force and the value of agricultural products fell from 36 to 20 percent of net domestic product. During the same 17 years, while those employed in manufacturing rose only from 9 to 12 percent of the work force, their production increased from 18 to

32 percent of the national output.[15] In 1966, the last year for which figures on size of plant are available, 96 percent of all manufacturing enterprises employed fewer than 100 workers each, in the aggregate gave employment to 42.7 percent of the manufacturing work force, and turned out about 25 percent of manufacturing output by value. Indeed, 94 percent of all manufacturing firms employed fewer than 50 apiece, and in aggregate 34 percent of the manufacturing force was at work in such small plants.[16] It is true that in the late 1960's the government of the Republic of China mounted a campaign to "rationalize" industry by encouraging amalgamation of very small plants, but it is to date unclear how much effect the movement has had.

In the utterly and deliberately laissez-faire economy of Hong Kong, in 1968 91.6 percent of all factories, employing 36.4 percent of all industrial workers, were under 100 each in size, while those under 50 alone comprised 84 percent of the total, and employed 24 percent of all manufacturing workers.[17] Even in the new industrial suburb of Kwun Tong, developed only during the 1960's to give space specifically to more "modern," i.e. larger, plants, in 1971 almost 72 percent of plants employed fewer than 50 workers each and only about 7 percent were larger than 200 apiece.[18]

This rather close correspondence among the situations of at least Taiwan and Hong Kong today and Japan in the early 1950's is the more impressive in that it also extended to Hong Kong metals-machinery plants. In 1971, almost one quarter (22 percent) of all the new plants in Kwun Tong were in metals-machinery trades, and their distribution by size was very close to that of all Kwun Tong factories.[19] One may indeed argue that metals-machinery work was not, in the Hong Kong of 1971, quite the "leading edge" of industry that it had been in Japan in the 1940-1950 period, yet it is also clearly not a "backward" sector of the contemporary economy.

In summation, and *pace* data that is not always fully comparable, it does seem a defensible thesis that the small factory is the dominant form of enterprise management and/or ownership, and the locus of employment for a substantial minority of all industrial workers, in both China and Japan. This has remained true from early into ad-

15 Robert H. Silin, *Leadership and Values*, Cambridge, Mass., 1976, Table 1, citing *Taiwan Statistical Data Book 1971*.

16 *Ibid.*, Table 4, citing *General Report on the Third Industrial and Commercial Census of Taiwan, Republic of China*, 1968, xxii.

17 England, Joe, "Industrial Relations in Hong Kong," pp. 207-259 of K. Hopkins, ed., *Hong Kong: The Industrial Colony*, Hong Kong, 1971, Table 5.5, citing *Annual Report 1967-68* of the Commissioner of Labour.

18 Victor Mok, *The Nature of Kwun Tong as an Industrial Community*, Hong Kong, Social Research Centre, The Chinese University of Hong Kong, 1972, Table 1.

19 *Ibid.*

vanced stages of industrialization in both countries, and under varied ideological, political, and property systems. This proves true not only in industry as a whole, but also in so relatively advanced a sector of manufacturing as metals-machinery work. The small factory, in other words, is an important organizational form of the modernizing society of the Far East, up to some stage that has not yet been reached in Japan (in 1970, 73 percent of all factories employed fewer than 10, and 16 percent of all manufacturing workers were in such shops).[20] The situation in the People's Republic of China is in many ways even more favorable than that of Japan for the continued development of industrial production in relatively small units, a fact which its current governmental policies, with their emphasis upon local production initiatives and a "Chinese way" to industry, recognize; one therefore might expect the small plant to be one of the key forms through which industrial growth continues there for the foreseeable future.

JAPAN: KAWAGUCHI, A SMALL METAL TOWN

The two Japanese cases to be described here are both small metals-machinery plants in the city of Kawaguchi, Saitama prefecture. As a part of the work lives to be depicted, the community itself deserves some comment.

Kawaguchi was at the time a microcosm of that sector of Japanese industry occupied by small plants. Indisputably a manufacturing town, on December 31, 1951, 46 percent of its work force were employed in its 1,623 active factories. Equally, it was specialized to the metals and machinery trades, 72 percent of its plants, and 79 percent of its manufacturing workers being so engaged. Most of its few commercial and service establishments in areas other than household consumption were likewise ancillary—as raw material suppliers, marketing wholesalers, etc.—to its main industry.

Kawaguchi's plants were also small. Only 3 of the 1,161 factories active in metals-machinery work employed over 500 each, and 99.3 percent (compared with the national average for this branch of manufacturing of 97.4 percent) gave work to fewer than 100 apiece. Sixty-one percent of Kawaguchi's plants, in fact, employed fewer than 10 workers each, and 31 percent 3 or fewer.[21]

The prevalence of small plants, moreover, was not an artifact of the youth of an enterprise, or even of an early state in the development of the metals-machinery industry. Iron-casting and hand-forging were

[20] *Japan Statistical Yearbook 1973-74*, Table 121.

[21] Data on employment from *Population Census of 1950*, Tokyo, 1952-1953, VII, Pt. 11, Table 11; data on factories at the end of 1951 from records of the Department of Industries, City of Kawaguchi.

the dominant technologies of pre- and early industrial periods, and retain significance today, so that Kawaguchi is still known as an *imono* (iron-casting) town, but over time these techniques have been joined by a variety of other procedures for turning out basic metal forms in new kinds of iron and in non-ferrous metals, with a wide range of performance characteristics. Somewhat more than half (55 percent) of the local plants were indeed specialized in iron-casting, but the rest were in non-ferrous metal and machinery lines, and there was no strong correlation between plant size and variety of technology. In iron-casting, for example, several plants, each employing many hundreds, did nothing but produce basic pig for sale to other processors, but 40 percent of the plants so specialized employed under 10 persons each. One plant concentrating on the production and machining of parts for, and the assembly of major components of, internal combustion engines employed over 500 workers, but 24 plants with fewer than 10 workers each performed parts or all of the same task.

Similarly, though iron-casting is the oldest part of the industry, it has exhibited vitality at all periods of the development of metals work. Of such plants still active in 1951, 4.5 percent had been founded before 1904; 15.3 percent between that date and the end of World War I; 38.7 percent in the inter-war years before the start of the full-scale "China Incident" in 1936; 28 percent during the war years; and 13.6 percent after 1945.[22] By way of comparison, of *imono* factories employing fewer than 30 persons each in 1951, 4 percent had been founded before 1904; and 15 percent between then and 1920. Larger casting plants showed greater variability, having been established in about equal numbers at every stage of the industry, but their absolute numbers were too small for meaningful comparison by age of foundation with casting plants as a whole. Certainly the distribution of casting plants by size had remained almost constant over the 20 years preceding this study, as the following table shows:

Imono Distribution, by Size, 1932 and 1951[23]

Persons Engaged	1932	1951
Over 100	1.0	0.7
99-30	14.0	11.4
29-10	33.0	44.1
— 9	52.0	43.8
	100.0	100.0

22 From records of the Kawaguchi Imono Trade Association, as of December 31, 1951.

23 For 1932 see Kyōchōkai (Conciliation Society), *Kawaguchi imonogyō jitchi chōsa* (A Field Study of the Iron-Casting Industry of Kawaguchi), Tokyo, 1933, p. 70. For 1951 see Department of Industry records in Kawaguchi City Hall.

It was impossible, on the basis of the records available, to go further and demonstrate changes in the size of given plants over the years since their establishment, for any considerable proportion of Kawaguchi's factories. Some enterprises had indeed started small and grown, and they were the cynosures of ambition. Others had started large and fallen on evil days. The majority, by the report of local enterprisers and my own impression of individual histories, seem to have started, or quickly attained, the size that would thereafter be characteristic of them, often in 1951 under the second or even later generations of management. The small factory in Kawaguchi is by no means an artifact, then, of either now-fossil stages of the technology, or of youthful immaturity.

A special case is presented by that 30 percent of the total of metals plants which employed three or fewer persons each. In many instances they turned out on inspection to be no more than an independent artisan, working alone or in most cases with only one or two family helpers or learners. More than half of such enterprises were specialized in the newer light metals and alloys, and in advanced machine work. Some were master mold makers, who often had to design the machine part for which they were preparing the mastermold, and one could find the better ones any day poring over Japanese and foreign catalogues and journals, searching for examples and inspiration. Others were smeltmasters, hired by the job by small plants, but they were among the highest-paid persons in the industry, and their competences extended to all varieties of metal. Many of these independent artisans were indeed casters, who took custom orders from a number of factories, and rented space and bought smelt from one or more of them. Some, of course, were not master artisans at all, but only *chūnen no mono* (men who had come to the industry only in their later years, without a "proper" apprentice training), who took home a batch of castings to clean and polish on contract. Yet many of even these smallest of all "enterprises" operated in advanced technological sectors of the industry, and many others would prove to be the seed of new larger factories, in time, the very model, we shall see, of the way that many Kawaguchi people felt a true factory should, and often did, start.

One hardly needed the arithmetic given here about Kawaguchi's industry to reach many of the basic conclusions to which they lead, for the city was physically almost as easy to comprehend by inspection as a village. A third of its census population of 120,000 was that of small rural villages annexed only administratively. Its capital-poor parsimony of space, controlled by landlords who owned both urban and farm lands, had always jammed the rest of its population into a tightly built urban core of one- and two-storey wooden buildings that covered scarcely more than 1½ square miles. On three sides, this core ended almost as abruptly as if a wall had intervened in typical Musashino farmsteads hardly changed from those of Tokugawa period prints. On the fourth, the Arakawa River marked the boundary with Tokyo prefecture. Even men in their 30s could recall that the land across the river had in their youth been farmland, and that the built-up section of Tokyo city had been hardly visible off to the south. By 1940, the city had of course grown up to its river border, but only briefly, for during the last years of the war the fire-bombings had destroyed almost all structures south of the river, and in 1950 one could again see nothing but farmed-over rubble in that direction.

Kawaguchi itself had been almost totally undamaged by the war, protected not only by the river from the spread of the Tokyo fires, but also by the ease with which its own people, thoroughly used to their furnaces, had put out such fire bombs as fell here. The physical plant of urban Kawaguchi was thus much as it had grown over the generations, from its foundation as a post town in the 11th century, through the establishment of an iron-casting industry there during the Tokugawa period, into the adventurous years of growth as a modern metal workplace after Meiji. A few of the oldest iron-masters still treasured guild patents issued by Tokugawa governments, and every period of growth since the 1870's could show factories built at that time and still in operation. Kawaguchi was not only physically comprehensible, then, but comprehensible historically and socially as a factory town reasonably independent of the adjacent Tokyo metropolitan sprawl. Men could remember that before 1940 local people hardly ever went as far away from home as Tokyo, and then usually only for a night, every year or two, to the Yoshiwara. Enterprisers had had as little reason as their workmen to go into Tokyo, and then usually little farther than to the northern shopping center of Akabane, and only for such rare purchases as new furniture when at last they had reached prosperity. Only the larger wholesalers had regular business with their Tokyo counterparts. Kawaguchi had not even had to play host to the refugees who fled Tokyo during the last years of the war, for this town was still too close to the danger for their comfort, and in any event, booming with war business but prohibited by shortages from any except essential construction, Kawaguchi in those years had been too crowded with its own people to take in outsiders.

The early 1950's was a period of national recovery and business was booming for an undamaged workshop like Kawaguchi. Though its buildings and machines had run down somewhat, they were still operable for workmen used to making their own repairs. The city was still piled high with raw material consigned to it for war production too late to be so used—a fact it was assumed the destruction of records in Tokyo (and curiously also, of relevant records in Kawaguchi's undamaged city hall, controlled by factory owners) would prevent government accountants from discovering. The market for everything from *shōji* runners and tea pots to industrial machinery was insatiable. Its wartime workers remained, and those who had gone away to war had by now come home again.

In this environment, furnaces roared and belched columns of soot and, by night, fire in almost every block. Polishing machines and lathes filled every neighborhood with their high-pitched screams, coating everything and everyone with rust and grey dust and converting the very ground of the city to a mat of iron filings. Hills of ore, pig, and haphazardly-piled metal products, stored in the cost-free space of the narrow and unpaved city streets, made an obstacle course for a steady river of carts, bicycles and trucks loaded to the collapsing point (a frequent diversion) with the paraphernalia of metal work. No specialization seemed to characterize the flow of human activity. Clouds of women, in summer unconcernedly bare from the waist up, and naked scabby-headed children gossiped and played in the only space they had, the street and factory grounds. Housewives tossed slops, including often the morning pot, into the passing parade with hardly a prior glance to ensure that the space aimed at was not already occupied. Male workers, in summer naked save for a gee-string, came out from work or from sleep to urinate in the public gutter and roar greetings while doing so to passing friends in voices trained to carry above the factory's noise. At night, on the long way from work to home across the street, if possible through the local *sangyō chitai* (Yoshiwara) with its cheap yellow entrance pillars, men happily laid open the scalps of foe and friend (and not infrequently policemen and their own bosses) alike. Kawaguchi's can-of-worms life style was indeed "low," as middle-class Tokyoites and a few of its own more precious children said in disgust, but most local people at the time perhaps agreed with the more satisfied judgment, "it's lively; always something doing." There was work, lots of money to be made, and life now beat that of wartime, as life here beat that of the villages and workless slums of which many had memories. In any event, every sense told one Kawaguchi was a factory town, specialized to the metal trades, its plants mostly small, its life an undifferentiated amalgam of work, family, and excitement.

The times were good in 1951, but this could not be seen as a historical anomaly. Times had been either boom or bust for as far back as anyone could recall. Recovery and the start of a peacetime orientation to industry were giving the town a new direction, but this represented no more than another of those shifts—a result of policy, technology, or market changes—which had come every few years for almost a century, and to which adjustments were made within the tradition. Though at times embarrassed by their smallness, Kawaguchi's enterprisers also maintained that in smallness there is an adaptability that can "weather any storm."

The Owner of a Very Small Shop

The first Japanese case,[24] the Okuda Junzō Imono, is a very small shop, with a total work complement of only 12 persons. As seems often true in such cases, the plant, its work and its society, are intensely personal, essentially an outgrowth of the enterpriser himself and of his own life experience. The description of such a case must, therefore, focus on the owner. As background, it has seemed useful to try and outline an ideal-typical pattern for a life career in this sector of the industry.

Career Patterns from Apprentice to Enterpriser: The career mystique of this trade, probably like that of any other, envisages a range of goals to fit a range of individual life chances, and prescribes ideal methods for their attainment. Though it is recognized that few careers conform precisely to the ideal, deviations are treated as to some extent the result of weakness, whether of life chance or of character. The lack of prestige and, in the actor himself, of self-esteem occasioned by such failures are, however, mitigated in several ways. For one thing, there is a strong strain of pragmatic nihilism in this poor, rough, and dangerous society, which gives virtue also to resignation to what cannot be changed, or which alternatively debunks all ideals one has not oneself chosen, or been able, to attain. For another, some members only gain a living in the trade, but gain their more intimate satisfactions from non-work goals. And in a time of more-or-less rapid and radical social change, there arise such a plethora of competitive or alternative ideal career mystiques that one can hardly speak of *the* ideal career pattern at all. The following paragraphs present no more than the public ideal—to which even their own career seldom conforms precisely—of successful small and medium-sized enterprisers in the metals trade of the present generation.

The minimal *role* in this society is that of *zatsueki*, the "handyman" who breaks up iron, hauls coke, stacks loads of finished products, etc. A slightly higher level of this role is that of the "finisher," who cleans burrs off of castings in a rattle box, polishes surfaces, etc. This is not

---

[24] The time referred to in both the Okuda and Nagai studies is about 1950. In both case studies, all names of persons have been changed.

really the minimal *goal* of anyone entering this society, however; rather, it is the fate of the true failure, from this or some other occupational course, in recognition of which the handyman is referred to generically as *chūnen no mono*, someone who entered the occupation in his (or her) later years, after having accepted failure to attain anything better.

The minimal career goal is to be a *shokunin*, "artisan," the ideal attributes of which are that he is not afraid of very hard work, and that he has, in youth, acquired one of the "good techniques"—as a molder-caster, as a smelter, or as a master-mold maker. Most of the artisans in a casting plant are molder-casters, who form the (usually) one-time negative mold around the master-mold or *tane*, pour the molten metal into the negative, and break it out when cooled. Only moderate-sized plants can afford their own smelter, who is thus often an independent artisan, loading, firing, and tapping a number of customers' furnaces by the job. Only the larger plants can keep their own master-mold makers, who are thus usually independent artisans.

The process of acquiring the technique must be carried out as an apprentice, *totei*. In recruiting a boy (no one has ever heard of a girl *totei*) into this training, one looks for evidences of physical hardiness, of a sound head and steady hand, and such qualities of character as patience and perseverance. Two other criteria, however, define the social and human limits within which a search for the recruit is made. A candidate must be recommended by someone with personal ties— of kinship, neighborhood, or friendship—with an already-established member of factory society—whether the owner, a principal workman, or a labor recruiter who himself has such ties. And to be finally accepted after a brief probationary period, the candidate must prove to be personally compatible with that already-established member; artisans are not teachers, after all, paid to cram some minimal level of skill into a boy, and the two must find that it is at least not unpleasant to work together to make the whole process worthwhile.

Once in apprenticeship, a boy must show another attribute—a strong motivation to acquire the technique, strong enough to overcome obstacles deliberately put in his path to test for this quality. Attached to a particular artisan, the boy is at first used only as a menial hauler and personal servant, and the artisan in fact tries to hide what he at least pretends to be key steps of the process from the boy's knowledge. To succeed, the boy must show enough determination to "steal the technique," "spying" on his master and sneaking back to work after hours to experiment on his own, until he has succeeded well enough to exhibit his work to his mentor. If he does not show this degree of ambition, he will be sent home if he does not leave of his own accord. Only if he shows and persists in this interest will the artisan begin to give him on-the-job training.

For Okuda's generation, the ideal apprentice came from a poor family with no other prospects for advancement. Though the 1920's and 1930's were periods of unprecedented migration for work from the farm to the factory in Japan,[25] in this industry at any event there was no prescription or expectation that the learner should necessarily come from the farm; rather, it was expected that he might come from a city worker's family quite as often. In the factories known to me, both mature artisans and learners seemed to derive about equally from rural and urban backgrounds. Likewise, the census of 1950 shows that, of the population of the urban core of Kawaguchi, approximately half had been born within the present-day city limits (which include large areas still rural), and 40 percent in other prefectures—with 15 percent of the total born in Tokyo prefecture (which at that time also had large rural areas), and 10 percent each born in other Kantō and Tōhoku prefectures.[26] This industry, at any rate, was therefore already recruiting heavily from established city worker backgrounds.

The ideal apprenticeship for this generation of mature artisans, moreover, was of 6-8 years' duration, extending from the age of 12 or 14, when a boy completed the then-compulsory 6 years of elementary schooling, to age 20, when he went away for his compulsory military service. The perception of those who held this view was that apprenticeship with all these characteristics had in fact been general during their own youth, in the 1920's.

It does seem likely that the proportion of on-the-job learners to mature artisans had always been high in this industry, as it remains high today. As late as 1932, a city-wide survey listed 23 percent of all persons employed in casting plants as *totei*,[27] and although there are no comparable figures today, in factories I knew the proportion of learners ranged from a high of around 50 percent, in small shops, to 10 percent in even very large plants. Though numbers may always have been high, career biographies do show that men who were apprentices between the wars very often did not live up to one or more of the ideal criteria, even the formal ones. Many entered apprenticeship late; many remained an apprentice only a few years; many were apprenticed to independent artisans, wandering from factory to factory and

25 Nojiri Shigeo, *Nōmin rison jisshō-teki kenkyū* (A Study of Farmer Emigration from the Village), Tokyo, 1942, gives a comprehensive study of internal migration during this period. Also cf. Irene Taeuber, *The Population of Japan*, Princeton, 1958, Chaps. 7 and 8.

26 *Population Census of 1950*, VII, Pt. 11, Table 15, modified by exclusion of 16 percent of the population estimated to be living in rural areas of Kawaguchi.

27 Kyōchōkai, *op. cit.*, p. 172.

often without work at all for considerable periods during their formal apprenticeship, rather than to factory owners themselves. In other words, even in the 1920's, when many older men today claim the system was in its ideal prime, there may have been few whose actual experience exactly fitted that ideal.

The ideology of apprenticeship was of course already under attack during the 1920's by the Marxists, who then as now considered it a form of "exploitation" (the apprentice was paid nothing above his food, clothing, and housing, all at minimal levels, and a tiny bit of pocket money, the profits of whatever technique he acquired going to swell his artisan's income). The system was even more basically attacked by facts in the 1930's, as more and more children stayed in school beyond the compulsory years, as the war demand for production led to the truncation of the more unproductive elements in apprenticeship, and as the military itself proved that boys can be taught (rather than motivated to learn) complex skills in a fraction of the time the ideal apprenticeship required.

Responding to these pressures, the key elements of the ideal *totei* system were abolished by law in 1939, a disposition confirmed by the post-war Labor Standards Law. Among other things, this requires that entering learners be at least 18, that they sign their own learning contracts with the master, that they be paid a fair wage for the work they produce while learning, and that they may not be required to live in the plant under the personal supervision of their master after work hours. Formally, these conditions are observed in the case of all learners known to me, and they are officially called *minaraiko*, "trainee workers," and in the scornful vernacular of the old-timers *kayoi totei*, "commuter apprentices."

These provisions—and even more, changing conditions—are having their effect. Nonetheless, it is still possible to follow the criteria for recruitment and training outlined here, even for the new trainees in the small factory. Where there are dormitory facilities, many learners seem willing to live in them, at least as long as alternative housing is in short supply and expensive, and given the fact that personal moral supervision of boys as old as those now in the factory was probably never very strict. Learners are everywhere called *totei*, and in their relations with others generally still continue the old naming rules (*ani* or *aniki* to senior age-grade companions, even *oyakata* to the master when no one likely to accuse them of a "feudal" mentality is around), and perhaps as much of the deference conforming to these rules as career biographies suggest was common even a generation ago. It proves still to be possible for the master to get rid of a learner who does not measure up to expectations.

Once a man has achieved the goal of full-fledged artisan status, his career is perceived as opening up along any of several different lines. Everyone recognizes that artisans in fact present a wide range of competence, from the barely-skilled to the highly-talented. Many of the former will have to be content with whatever benefits seniority, loyalty to the boss, etc. can bring them, and such individuals are theoretically protected in their unequal competition with their fellows by the ideal that an artisan can always remain in, or return to, the factory in which he did his apprenticeship, so long as the master is on his feet financially. What is much less often stated is that the choice of an adult career is also a projection of elements of the individual personality, or of the salience in it of non-work goals. There may be a presumption that artisans who settle into their old master's plant are less self-confident at the prospect of being independent, less tolerant of the insecurities of aloneness, more committed to family than to occupational goals. It is also clear from career biographies that whether an artisan remains in his master's factory or not depends powerfully upon personal compatibilities, personality rivalries, etc. Many artisans say frankly they left the old master's plant because they could not stand him, and many masters that they are glad the artisan did not stay because he got above himself too often.

Yet if a man without too much ambition or skill does choose this course, he can expect that growing seniority alone will bring increasing benefits. He should be given the better work, offering more income. He should have apprentices assigned to his supervision, or even young artisans of whom the master is not yet sure, and a proportion of their earnings will come to him. True, he cannot expect seniority alone to bring him the position of foreman—though few plants of under 20 workers need foremen—since a foreman must also have at least the reputation of being as skilled, or better skilled, than the men he directs. The trade-off among skills, seniority, and loyalty is always a difficult one for management, but it also can be handled in a variety of ways. It is not infrequent, of course, for a master or senior artisans simply to get rid of a too highly skilled junior, or for the master to put the less skilled senior in a corner by himself, at a very good rate of pay.

Unquestionably, however, the higher public ideal for men of the current enterpriser generation was for a mature artisan to gain some sort of independence. The basic requirement was a superior skill and an unusual ability to produce. And given these prerequisites, a man might move in any of several directions.

Some seem to have been satisfied merely with independence, quite apart from wealth or power, and for many of these a respectable and satisfactory career could be made as a smelter or master-mold maker, working alone or with an apprentice or young artisan or two, for a number of outside customers. As already noted, a high proportion of Kawaguchi's "establishments" were in fact of this nature.

A career of this sort is more difficult for a caster, however, for he must have access to a furnace, and space for his molds beyond that he can find in his own home. An alternative, therefore, is for him to work in other men's factories, but in the form of the *henreki*, "pilgrimage," that is, to move restlessly from factory to factory, and even from casting town to casting town, assured everywhere by his reputation as a highly skilled and productive worker of a job for as long as he wants it. Unquestionably there are personality factors at work in this choice as well, for an uncommonly high proportion of men who take this course stress in their autobiographies their rebelliousness against authority, their intolerance of routine, their cupidity (the "right due their skill" as they would put it) for earnings as high as possible, as well as the fringe benefits such a career offers through the joys of *yoi-goshi no kane* ("here today, gone tomorrow"). They tend, in other words, to be high-living and often deliberately egocentric, loners or rebels by nature. Curiously perhaps, an enormous fondness for such men creeps through the reminiscences of many of the very masters whom they insulted, tricked and robbed, as if there, but for the grace of my shackles, go I.

The highest ideal goal is however that of independent entrepreneurial status, with one's own factory, no matter how small, one's own furnace, one's own men working alongside and under one, one's own apprentices coming up the ladder, and of course one's own family as to a closer or more distant degree the cell from which the factory grows. This obviously requires a great deal more than a superior casting technique, though owners usually maintain, in the small plant at any rate, that such superiority is a prerequisite, without which they could not control their men.

It certainly requires ability in selecting and/or handling men. For one thing, if the master must ensure that his technique is superior to that of any of his workmen, he must be careful to hire no artisan better than he or—as we shall see Okuda did—institute a recruiting program that would result in all his workmen being his own apprentices, those who surpass him being "encouraged to seek better opportunities elsewhere." But even where every design has been used to try to ensure an orderly hierarchical community, few places are more destructive than the small factory of the simple foreign stereotype of the "solidary and cooperative Japanese group." Abrasions and suspicions hang unspoken in the air. Violence flares, undeterred by middle-class manners. Human affection can consume the work group as quickly as hatred. At any rate, life in the small plant is not dispassionate, and the preservation of even a minimal level of work efficiency requires constant inter-personal engineering.

The small factory also, of course, requires ready-made markets, for its enterpriser has not the time or ability, or the staff, to make contact with the ultimate consumer of his product. He may from time to time receive government orders parcelled out through his enterprisers' association, but for the most part he must depend upon sub-contract orders from large plants, which do have contacts with government or still larger firms, and upon orders from large wholesalers. Above all, of course, the small enterpriser requires money—for start-up costs and thereafter, as steady infusions of operating capital, to pay for raw materials, labor, taxes, etc. between receipt of an order and payment thereof, in a business that is notoriously seasonal or cyclical, or both.

Once one has started, operating capital can be gotten via prepayments from the prime contractor or the wholesaler. These cost the small enterpriser a great deal, of course. He must in effect pay a high interest upon the money advanced him, and enough additional to make it profitable for the large manufacturer or wholesaler to utilize his service rather than to build and operate a similar capacity himself —by producing and selling the product more cheaply. Small enterprise thus depends upon the entrepreneur and his workmen being willing— or constrained by their total situation—to accept lower incomes, and substitute their own labor for many processes that in the large factory would be performed by capital or outside service facilities. But for many these "sacrifices" are either inevitable or worthwhile in terms of such benefits as a degree of independence and self-determination.

In any event, for the artisan, the big hurdle to enterpriser status is the initial one. Few small enterprisers of this generation had access to loans from banks, savings societies, or "small-business" activities of government. They were dependent upon personal savings, personal or familial loans or guarantees, or upon their willingness and ability to enter into what could be expected to become long-term relations of dependency with large manufacturers or wholesalers who thereby acquired some control over their future output via sub-contracting or wholesale orders.

The latter types of dependency are unquestionably unwelcome to many artisans who would otherwise like to become enterprisers, and deter many from the step. It is fashionable for enterprisers to inveigh violently against such dependency upon wholesalers—reflecting status attitudes held over from the farm, and even from the Tokugawa period. Yet all admit that "when the small enterpriser is in trouble (as he usually is), he runs crying to the *tonya* (wholesaler) like a small child to its mother." It is equally fashionable for this generation to extoll such dependencies on larger manufacturers, for it keeps the "bridge between worker and capitalist" in repair. But whether fashionable or not, such dependencies, from start to end of the small enterpriser's career, are a fact of life. Figures upon the extent of such dependencies are impossible to obtain, for only at this time are many small entrepreneurs incorporating. Nevertheless, it is generally accepted around town that one very large manufacturer has investments, sub-contract ties, etc. with well over a hundred small factories, and that one very large wholesaler-manufacturer has perhaps twice that many links.

At the start of his entrepreneurial career, however, it is the rare artisan who is well enough known or likely enough to develop reliably for a well-to-do owner or wholesaler to want to go very far out on a limb in advancing initial capital to him. What was most common in the years at least between the two world wars was for an ambitious artisan who had saved up a little money and who could borrow a bit more from family or friends to "go out to *kaiyu* (the molten metal tapped from the furnace)." This involved buying the necessary initial stock of master-molds, renting a corner in someone's else factory in which to make one's molds, and buying melt whenever the factory owner's furnace was tapped. Most good artisans could get together the personal savings for master molds, but needed a deposit to ensure payment for rent and melt that might be procured from family loans, guarantees by personal friends, loans by wholesalers, or credit with the factory owner. The artisan at *kaiyu* sold his product wherever he could—perhaps to the lender wholesaler or creditor manufacturer—and kept the proceeds for himself, after payment of wages to whatever apprentices, or perhaps a young artisan or two, he had brought with him to *kaiyu*. Hopefully, in time, he would have saved enough, or earned enough credit, to rent or buy a factory building, with its furnace, of his own.

Once well established as a factory owner, the small enterpriser may of course have further ambitions primarily of an economic character. He may wish to grow large, though as suggested earlier it was uncommon for a plant to change greatly from the scale which its initial capital permitted to it. More likely, his economic goals thereafter would be for the kind of solidity that Okuda seems to have obtained, leaving it to the next generation to modernize and hopefully to grow. But for an ambitious man who has reached his goals before he has exhausted his energy it is hard to be satisfied with a "no-growth" stance thereafter. One can, of course, find suitable diversion in keeping a mistress, but for the many who, like Okuda, found their satisfaction in work rather than diversion it would have been an unfulfilled life in late and successful maturity were it not for one thing: one can, at this point, switch one's ambition from economic goals that have already been assured at a satisfactory level to political goals.

Since Meiji, the political leadership of the town—which also played an important role in the prefecture and at least a minor role nationally —has been shared among a coterie of "old families" comprised of landlords, major shopkeepers and wholesalers, and large manufacturers. Though in recent years some of the landlords and shopkeepers have been eliminated by economic changes, a few of both have for long been heavy investors in local industry, and could therefore see their farm lands confiscated and their shops sink into insignificance with indifference. In any event, the core of political leadership revolves around manufacturing and wholesaling wealth.

There are of course some of the largest factory owners and merchants who profess no interest in politics, and a few of these seem to be sincere, though it is debatable whether this is even economically a wise policy, given the salience of government in the economy of Japan. On the other hand, there are a number of manufacturers and merchants participating carefully in politics who profess to see this as merely one of the prices they have to pay for maintenance of a reasonably sound and secure business and this, for the same reason, seems at least a more practical stance, though possibly no more sincere.

Perhaps the great majority of small enterprisers who are already soundly established, however, participate today in a local Liberal (conservative) Party organization of formidable size and, to date, success. It is not even locally accepted as a coincidence that the leaders of this organization are the same largest manufacturers and wholesalers who have investments, sub-contracting and wholesaling ties with large numbers of small enterprisers, or that the channel from top party leadership to ward and neighborhood political leaders follows the channel of economic links from prime contractors and wholesalers to the small plant owners who are their clients.

The Okuda Junzō Imono

The *Okuda Junzō Imono* was founded in the early 1930's by its present owner, who is almost 50. It has usually employed somewhat more than 10 workmen, and reached as many as 18 at one point during the war. In 1951 its workers numbered 12, including a smeltmaster who also tends the furnaces of several other small plants, on a piecework basis. Half of the complement has usually been, as it is today, composed of boys in a learner status.

During the war, the shop worked mainly on machine castings, done on sub-contract for larger factories with government-derived orders.

However, Okuda is quite aware that his own technical qualifications are rather limited; he barely finished elementary school in his home village in the Chichibu Mountains of western Saitama Prefecture, where his father was a rather poor part-owner, part-tenant farmer, and his own apprenticeship, as we shall see, was scrappy. He seems quite relieved, therefore, to have been able to take advantage of the booming reconstruction demand for simple castings of household items, with which he feels technically more at ease, and most of which he markets through one of the city's larger wholesalers. Okuda still does some machine castings on sub-contract, however, principally he says in order to keep his ties with certain large factory owners in repair.

By all accounts and evidence, Okuda has done extremely well during the last twelve to fifteen years, in both wartime and reconstruction. He himself says that work was slow for only two to three years just before and after the end of the war, but some of the workmen he would otherwise have felt obligated to keep on the payroll were in service or did not return. He owns the land on which his factory sits, something that is still uncommon for the small owner, and a good stand of forest land, managed by his elder brother near the home farm. His factory compound, surrounded by a board fence, is larger than he needs at present—large enough for a small baseball diamond almost constantly in use by factory personnel or their children, for the great piles of stores that he has accumulated, and for a factory building, a dormitory for the young learners, a large family house, two small houses for the families of senior workmen, and a good-sized bath house used by everyone connected with the plant, all structures built in 1937 and in good repair. On top of these evidences of financial solidity, he has been able to send those of his own six children old enough and suited to higher education to good schools in Tokyo; similarly he has sent his favorite apprentice and expected successor—Mitchan, now twenty-one—to higher technical schooling; he seems to look forward with confidence to funding the capital improvement plan that it is hoped Mitchan will be able to devise; and he has become a minor but apparently respected figure in the local organization of the Liberal Party.

Okuda, as a younger son of a poor farmer, says he never seriously considered farming as a career; his elder brother, after all, was healthy and liked farm work, and could therefore be expected to succeed to the family farm. He remembers no especial preference for a career as he was growing up, but admits that he was only an indifferent student, and was therefore probably in his own mind headed for some sort of manual career. That was in any event practical, for he was a strong, healthy boy who liked to work with his hands, and his family were too poor to conceive of being able to send him on to higher schooling. When, at the age of sixteen, he was told by his father to go to Kawaguchi and become an apprentice to his uncle—who in his own youth had been similarly apprenticed so that Okuda's father could inherit the family farm—he seems to have gone without demur.

Okuda is decidedly not fond of his uncle, and tends to picture him as the wrong way to go about a career in the small metals trade. Allowance must certainly be made for personal animus, due to their experiences with the uncle by both Okuda and his wife, who was the uncle's step-daughter. Nevertheless, the accounts of others—of factory owners who have known all concerned, and of Okuda's elder brother's family—tend to confirm the allegory of two artisans, uncle and nephew, as the wrong and right ways to search for success in this kind of life.

Okuda's uncle, with whom he began his apprenticeship at the age of sixteen, near the end of the First World War, seems to have been something of a tough customer (*nigate*) even as a youngster, rebellious of discipline and routine at home and in school, and not averse, rumors in his village still have it, to anything that promised to be exciting. He was, however, a physically powerful lad who, when he worked at all, worked hard and well. Apprenticed to a well-known casting master in Tokyo, where it is said discipline was often enforced with fists, he became a mature artisan with a good reputation for skill and productivity, a reputation that seems to have preceded him wherever he went for the rest of his life. As so often with such artisans, he embarked upon his "pilgrimage," moving restlessly from one casting town and factory to another, always ensured by his reputation of a good job.

When Okuda joined him as an apprentice, he was working in what was then—and still is—one of the largest factories in Kawaguchi, that of the Takagi family. The family is still a famous one in town, not only for its wealth but because, during the 1930's and before the end of the war, the son became an important figure in local and prefectural politics. Okuda feels they were well treated there, but the uncle soon found some excuse for picking a fight with the owner, and moved on to another plant. He was drinking and womanizing heavily at the time, and there was often not enough money for the apprentices' food; in consequence, Okuda's companion apprentice, an unrelated boy from the same village, finally gave up and went home. Perhaps somewhat shaken by this defection, the uncle settled down to work, moved to still another factory, and for a year or so uncle and nephew were busy and prosperous.

This factory was a famous one in local legend. It had been founded by the inventor of a cast-iron stove that burned rice husks, who was inordinately proud of his invention. During World War I, he had turned over management of the factory to his two sons, who decided to modernize and turn to machine casting, which at the time was coming into heavy demand. This "madness" and "treason" against their father so enraged the old man that, after a long and fruitless attempt to dissuade them, he threatened to destroy the furnace, the heart of the factory. A compromise was thereupon reached, whereby the factory was divided down the middle, one half, under one son, continuing to manufacture the father's invention, the other modernizing. The old owner hung about the factory constantly, and in order to encourage the workmen making his invention—who included Okuda and his uncle—repeatedly slipped them large sums of extra money out of his own pocket. The son managing that part of the factory also "took a liking" to Okuda's uncle, and put four or five young artisans under his supervision, a device which allowed him to pocket a part of their earnings.

Within a couple of years, the uncle had saved enough money to try for independent enterpriser status himself. Having bought his *tane* and put away enough for his rent and melt, he went out to *kaiyu* with the one apprentice—Okuda himself—and one young artisan, a scale of operations said to have been about average for the time.

At just this point, however, the uncle began to drink and to womanize again. More important, these diversions kept him short of money and of product to sell, and he began to welsh on the rent and payments for molten iron, and so precipitated fights with the owner of the factory in which they were working. In consequence, they moved to another factory, where the same process was repeated, then to another factory, and so on until at last all doors were closed to them. No one would rent them space or sell them iron, or even give them a job as ordinary workmen. In disgust, Okuda himself went back home, after only about three years of apprenticeship, and worked on the family farm for six months.

He had to find his own job, however, and the iron was in his blood. He flatly refused the pleas of his uncle to come back, but instead went to the Takagi factory, where he had first worked. Through the introduction of a boy he had known there, he got to meet the sister of the old owner. She took an interest in him, got him a job in the factory, and remained until her death one of his most trusted advisors. He was taken on at the factory as a regular artisan, no longer an apprentice, but at first he was assigned to an older workman, who therefore took a part of his earnings, but after a while the owner allowed him to operate alone.

Okuda says he had already made up his mind to become a factory owner himself. He therefore worked hard for five years, and scrimped on everything he could—even living in the dormitory with the apprentices because the Takagis charged him ¥16 a month less for room and board there than he would have had to pay outside. He also during this time paid his father back ¥250 his uncle had "borrowed" when accepting Okuda as an apprentice, a sum his father had been able to raise only by mortgaging part of the farm. Eventually, Okuda bought his own *tane* and saved enough to dare to venture out to *kaiyu* on his own.

In the meantime, however, Okuda's uncle had again straightened out, and had even come to own his own factory. He had persuaded the old owner of the Kuroda plant to let him work there on *kaiyu*, and had done well enough that he was able to go for some time charging, rather than paying for, his rent and melt, using the money owed Kuroda to buy his own small plant. He of course left owing Kuroda money, which he never paid, but he had his own plant out of this thievery. Moreover, at about this time Okuda's grandmother died, and as a mourning penance the uncle vowed not to touch liquor or women for three years, a vow he in fact did keep. In consequence, he began to make a good deal of money. Okuda decided he would do better if he invested his savings in the uncle's factory and became a junior partner than if he went out to *kaiyu* on his own, and did so.

There followed three years, during the late 1920's, of real prosperity. In 1929, however, precisely as the depression struck, the uncle simultaneously decided to buy a small branch factory and, his vow of abstinence at an end, to start drinking again. Okuda went to manage the branch factory, but within six months they were in dire straits and knew they would have to close the branch, keeping only the main factory open. This presented a ticklish problem, however. Times were hard; factories everywhere were closing; and most closings precipitated a strike. They were afraid that a strike by the branch workers would lead to one at the main installation.

They tried to handle the problem in a way that Okuda now says, laughing, he realizes was incredibly stupid. They decided to trick the branch workers: They pretended that there were no raw materials to be had for either plant; when supplies ran out, they "regretfully" closed both plants "temporarily," until supplies should be available again, meanwhile privately telling the main factory workers they would keep them on the payroll. As expected, the branch workers struck and the main plant workers did not. Negotiating sessions with the branch workers ended in a brawl, during which much of the office furniture was broken over people's heads, so to pacify the workers the Okudas gave them written promises to hire them back, *in preference to the main plant workers.*

Predictably, the latter heard of this trickery, and themselves went on strike. At the negotiating session, Okuda and his uncle told them the written promises were only a ruse that would not be honored, and this satisfied all but four of the strikers. Disgusted with them, Okuda and his uncle threw them bodily out of the plant. These men then told the branch plant workers, who at that point raised the red flag, marched to the factory, and occupied it. Okuda called the police, thus effectively ending the matter.

They re-opened the main factory, but times were so hard that they were desperately poor, with hardly enough money even for the simplest food. Okuda's son fell ill and they could not afford to take him to a doctor; in consequence he is today almost stone deaf. When their eldest child, a daughter, fell ill, the mother insisted that she be taken to a fortuneteller (*yogensha*), and under his ministrations the girl recovered.

The *yogensha* was even then, and remains today, well thought of by a number of Kawaguchi people, including the owners of several of the largest factories and the wartime mayor, all of whom say quite without embarrassment that when they have a problem they consult him. A quiet, rather self-effacing little man, whose house and life style seem no different from those of a barely comfortable farmer or shop-keeper, he is seated invariably at the place of honor when he is invited to the large homes of the rich.

Okuda says that for some time he was skeptical of the *yogensha's* powers, but since the man merely gave advice, which often tended merely to reinforce and make reasonable what Okuda himself had wanted to do, he did continue to go to him. At last, the overhead of his uncle's factory and family was so heavy that, with the fortuneteller's and old "Aunt" Takagi's concurrence, he decided to leave and go out on *kaiyu* on his own. The decision was taken in August, and he planned to start in October, but the fortuneteller gave one of his rare flat orders (*iitsuke*), to start in September. It meant working day and night to get ready but he did make the September date. A couple of weeks later, when Okuda would on his own schedule still have been with his uncle, the uncle's wife had a serious stroke. If he had persevered in his own timetable, rather than accepting that of the *yogensha*, he would never have been able to leave.

Since then, Okuda says he has never had the slightest doubt that the fortuneteller, in addition to being a fine advisor, has certain real powers. Okuda ascribes both the nature and timing of every key decision of his subsequent career to the *yogensha*—the foundation of his own factory, buying the forest land, buying the land (then vacant) on which his present factory compound sits, building his present factory, etc. More specifically, perhaps, he seems to feel that his success is the result of a combination of his own hard work and successful execution of the key decisions to which the *yogensha*, by some unerring power, has led him.

Turning to the situation today: factory and household are of course intimately intertwined, and the management of both is a joint enterprise of Okuda and his wife. The workmen and apprentices—by now all from Okuda's home district, though none is a kinsman (incompatible employees, even from the home district, have been gotten rid of)—live in or close to the factory compound. All draw water from its well, share its communal bath, play on its field, and during the years of shortages divided up communally procured supplies of rice and vegetables. Mrs. Okuda is thus constantly in touch with worker wives and children, who play with the Okuda children, as Okuda is with the men. Though the apprentices sleep, cook and eat separately, Mrs. Okuda constantly checks their food, housing, and health, and though the boys are old enough to be allowed to go out as they wish at night, the grapevine soon brings her news of any goings-on considered untoward—and standards are much more tolerant than in the middle classes—and ensures at least a lecture.

Okuda is a powerful, bull-like man not yet at all gone to fat, and his perpetually grime-impregnated hands, body covered with the scars of old metal burns, and hours spent working on the floor of the plant almost every day lend credence to his claim that he is still "only a workman." He and his wife, a comfortable, calm woman, talk over matters concerning home or factory more as incidents to the other business of daily living than formally, and what is done seems to follow any preference she may have expressed about as often as one he holds. Perhaps they are aided to what, to an American, seems a very equal relationship, by Okuda's own character as a man. He has never drunk or smoked, and questioning about town elicited no suggestion that he has ever played around with other women. Moreover, he is obviously extremely shy in any social gathering—whether a business meeting of the enterpriser's association or small parties at the houses of even those few important people who have been his trusted patrons for many years. He can become so passionately absorbed in any conversation about work, communal business, etc., that he salivates and must constantly wipe his mouth, but he appears to have utterly no light conversation at all, being unable to enter even into jests and banter with the family of his elder brother, with whom he is otherwise quite at ease. Clearly he is not a man for whom there is much life other than that of family and whatever he considers work.

On only one point could I detect that Okuda and his wife may be in basic disagreement, and on this, at least, she seems to have accepted a decision by him. Their elder son, who became almost deaf in infancy, is now nineteen. The mother treats him with normal maternal concern, but Okuda seems incapable of looking at or speaking to the boy without signs of near-rage. He says the boy is a "fool," and has for several years forced him to live in the dormitory with the apprentices. Yet Okuda says he is incapable of becoming a regular apprentice, and has him working as an assistant to Hei-san, the husky and rather simple-minded *zatsueki* who breaks up iron and hauls heavy loads. The family doctor and his schoolteachers say that the boy, Hatchan, is in fact perfectly normal, even as to intelligence, though his deafness made it so difficult for him to get anything out of school that he was finally allowed to leave on a medical discharge. Though Okuda could afford to do so, and has been so advised, he has refused to send the boy to a hearing specialist, or even to have him taught hand signs, etc., saying "he's too much of a fool." In fact, Hatchan is an unusually healthy-appearing, and even handsome, boy, who reacts warmly and naturally to anyone who treats him with the least consideration.

In any event, having decided that Hatchan cannot succeed him, and being unwilling to wait until the younger son, now only six, is old enough, Okuda has informally designated Mitchan, his favorite apprentice of several years, his successor, and as noted is putting him through a good technical school so that the boy can modernize the plant. Okuda has not yet decided how to accomplish the succession, and the usual way—marrying him to the eldest daughter—may be stalemated by that girl's character. As headstrong as her father, she twists him easily about her finger, and maintains she hates Kawaguchi, and wants to marry a Tokyo salaryman, and in fact spends as much of her time as she can get away with, at school and after, in Tokyo. When not in school, Mitchan works in the factory, and is clearly a good and hard worker. Also as clearly, he is very intelligent and ambitious, and carefully attentive to his master's moods.

Okuda manages the floor of the plant, but in the normal course of things this involves little supervision of the regular workers. His main labor-management task has been completed when he has selected and trained apprentices; thereafter he must assign particular batches of work—any one of which may take days to complete—to different workmen in terms of their relative rewards and pleasantness, and tend to any squabbles that arise. The furnace is tapped every few days, when work is extremely hectic for hours, as the artisans and apprentices carry molten metal from the furnace to the molds they have spent days preparing. Okuda is invariably present when the furnace is prepared and tapped—as one of the prime symbolic duties of the owner—but smeltmasters will brook no supervision of their work, perhaps particularly by an owner, so there is little for Okuda to do, if he is not himself working as a caster that day, but watch and iron out any small kinks that develop.

His main tasks are thus to ensure that the buildings are kept in good repair, and to deal with the all-important outside contacts that keep the floor of the plant at work. Supplies must be ordered and stored for use. Orders must be procured and when they involve new master-molds, supplies, etc., these requisites must be bought. Payments must be made to suppliers and workers, and received from customers. Visits must be made to government offices or to the Imono Enterprisers' Association office to learn the latest facts of importance, fill out forms, etc. Petitions must be made in person to major patrons when there is any hitch in orders or finance, or, if there is no necessary contact for too long, one must drop by deliberately in order to remind them of one's continued existence.

In very many of these tasks Mrs. Okuda, rather than the master himself, is the person responsible. She keeps records and accounts, or meets minor suppliers and customers, in the tiny room off the vestibule of the home which is their only office. She makes trips to government offices or outside contacts on routine matters, or in those frequent cases which Okuda himself finds unpleasant, if in fact protocol will permit of her substitution for him. Perhaps in her performance of these apparently routine tasks, and informal talks during the household occasions of the day, she exerts a far greater influence over the management of the business even than it seems, for the large manufacturer Takagi, their patron of many years, says "Okuda is an artisan, but his wife is the businessman of the family."

This career biography thus ends at the point when Okuda, still young and vigorous and already economically solid, is preparing to turn a plant that is in many ways little more than an expansion of his own family, natal and, through his apprentice-workers, "adopted-in," to one of the latter as a successor. He now spends a good deal of time as a minor functionary of the local organization of the ruling Liberal Party. What ambitions he has in the latter line, he plays very close to his chest. Whether he will in fact be able to free himself from the factory, or if he does, be able to get very far in politics, remains to be seen.

It is not so much that Okuda's plant is anachronistic. There are still many small factories with a technical level and social organization not unlike those he maintains. Nor is his plant merely a fossil, a hold-over into the present of something that was average when it started; his uncle's factory, and the earliest form of his own, were far less "traditionalistic" socially than the one he operates today. Rather, his plant seems deliberately atavistic. Caught in a world of rapid change, with a still rather primitive technique and no desire or opportunity to improve it—and, one must suspect, a deep distaste for the human world he saw emerging around him—Okuda self-consciously and suc-cessfully used a blueprint from the past, to create a home in which he could live more or less on his own terms. It also does not seem a co-incidence that, at the point where it will be increasingly difficult to preserve this sanctuary, he is preparing for technical modernization—and probably for social modernization as well—by turning his plant over to an outsider, and eyeing a new career. Seen in the light of this hypothesis, Okuda seems in fact as modern an individual as those Westerners who fled to "communes" in the 1960's.

The Society of a Barely Medium-Sized Plant

The Nagai plant[28] is also a family-owned firm, and with only 123 employees it is not enormously larger than Okuda's, but in many ways it presents sharp contrasts. For one thing, its size may well have passed a low threshold beyond which an organization must have a more complex managerial organization. For another, it is technologically far more sophisticated; founded in 1889, in Tokyo, to manufacture an advanced silk-weaving machine invented by its first owner, it is said to remain even today, though small, near the forefront of precision machine plants. In consequence, its personnel are highly skilled and extremely well paid. Moreover, it is unionized. While technically it may be somewhat above average for Kawaguchi's plants, it is much more nearly representative of the local factory society of the last twenty years than is Okuda's shop. It will be useful, before describing Nagai in more detail, to outline some of the features of that society which are not observable at Okuda's.

The First World War boom gave Kawaguchi its first taste of rapid growth. Between 1915 and 1920, the population of the town's urban core grew from 9,000 to 16,000, the number of metal plants likewise increased by about 70 percent, and for the first time machine plants came to join the town's traditional casting factories in some numbers. This growth proved not to be merely flash-in-the-pan, to tap the war's quick profits, moreover, and after a brief pause just after the end of the war, growth continued. Between 1920 and 1931, the population

[28] Excerpted from Nakano, *op. cit.*

grew to 28,000, and the number of metal and machinery plants—with the latter now quite important elements of the whole—again increased by about 70 percent. The town was now three times as large, with three times as many factories, as only sixteen years before. It was in fact at the very end of this period, in 1931, that the Nagai factory, finding its Tokyo quarters cramped and noting that most of its castings came from Kawaguchi, moved to the town.

Old Kawaguchi enterprisers date the beginnings of a "deterioration of the worker" from the period of explosive growth during the First World War, and say that during the succeeding inter-war years this decline reached proportions essentially unmanageable by means at their disposal. To their minds, it was therefore essential, if the Japanese community as a whole were to develop in an orderly manner, for the state to align itself with them through its Peace Preservation Laws. The town's labor leaders are quite as willing to date a sharp change in the character of the worker from this period, but they couple it with a "deterioration of the employer," and a changed definition of the goals of the two classes relative to one another. "Fortunately," from their standpoint, Marxism came along at this point to instruct the worker in the nature of his situation, and in what to do about it.

During the slow growth before 1915, most owners and workers alike had been *Kawaguchiko* (Kawaguchi natives), or at least born and raised in neighboring villages. There had been time to train apprentices slowly from youth, and enough stability to ensure a lifetime career in the industry—if not in a given plant—for worker and owner alike. Even if this picture is—and it probably is—over-idealized, there had been no viable Marxist message to give workers a different vision of the future. On the other hand, it is certain that during the next sixteen years a high proportion of both the new workmen and the new employers were outsiders with minimal personal contacts with one another previously, whether they were like Okuda from the farm or like Nagai and his cohorts from the city. In a great many cases they were inevitably even newcomers to the industry who, like the "Rosie the Riveters" of another time and place, could not even expect that their involvement with the industry would outlast a boom that would certainly end soon. It was at this time that the distinction between "permanent" and "temporary" employees began to grow up—though less in terms of the level of job done in a given plant than in terms of whether they were career metal workers or not.

Above all, it is significant that the labor movement began here in 1917, with the foundation of a local chapter of the *Yūaikai*. This was essentially only a "workers' uplift" society, departing from the same perception as the enterpriser that the worker's quality had "deteriorated," though with more understanding of the total environment in which this had happened. It was joined by a number of other attempts by local influential people, including employers, to "raise the worker's level." Employment in the iron industry did not, of course, end with the war for most of the new people who had come into it, but by that time a number of individuals had begun to arrive at new perceptions of the situation, and of the advantage that they personally might expect from it, and new patterns were beginning to be set. Among the latter was a pattern of organized violence. Individual violence had never been scarce in this rough society, but during the brief post-war slump a number of plants had to close or let their non-career employees go, and numerous disorganized and ineffective strikes resulted, as has already been described in Okuda's case.

It was not until around 1925, however, that there were enough individuals in Kawaguchi imbued with at least faint perceptions of a permanent change to begin to organize avowedly Marxist unions. The catalyst seems to have been the unionization of the Noda Brewing Company of Chiba and a strike against it, which spread to a company brewery in Kawaguchi's neighboring village of Yokosone. A number of the town's present leaders of metal unions recall vividly going out to watch the strike. Most claim that they had previously had only an abstract interest in the labor movement, derived from reading and some desultory talk with a few other workers, but the Noda strike made it all suddenly concrete and realistic, and began a new train of personal development in them. Within a few months cells began to form in factories here and there, each consisting of only three to five men who now found it exciting to talk about these matters with one another. In 1926, a branch of the *Tōkyō Tekkō Kumiai* (Tokyo Iron-Workers' Union) was set up in town, and these hitherto-isolated cells began to join it.

In 1927, these cells felt strong enough to begin organizing strikes. There were the usual schisms in the movement itself; the *Kantō Kinzoku Sangyō Rōdō Kumiai* (Kanto Metal-Workers' Union) was formed in rivalry to the Tokyo Iron-Workers, and the internal competition engendered was itself one major cause of the strike activity. Nonetheless, during 1927 and 1928 business was still good, and strikes were held to gain new and positive benefits from the employers rather than to prevent losses to the worker, and certain gains were made. After 1929, as the depression settled in, strikes reversed their character and became shriller and more violent, with the usual panoply of lockouts, sit-ins, imported "goon gangs," the martyr's bloody *hachimaki* (head-band) as a standard, etc. Labor leaders frankly admit that during both

404

periods the unionization of any considerable proportion of a plant's workers and a strike were coterminous. Either a union was formed to direct a strike already agreed upon, or a strike was fomented to justify the formation of a union, and there was still only very minor interest on the part of most workers in unionism as an on-going element of the life of the work place rather than as an organization for combat. Yet, apart from large accretions to membership that were only temporary, there persisted a hard core of union men, scattered as small cells among a number of plants, who were rather closely tied to one another across plant boundaries by the city-wide union organization. The "enterprise union" of the post-1945 period was not, in Kawaguchi at any rate, yet in existence, and the union was an industry-wide organization.

Given these qualifications, both unionization and strike activity developed about as strongly in Kawaguchi as anywhere else in Japan during the five years from 1927 to 1932. There are no official figures for Kawaguchi to compare with the national figures showing 8 percent of the industrial labor force unionized in 1931, but in 1933, when the union movement was already moribund under government repression, 6 percent of Kawaguchi's factory force was reported as unionized.[29] Local labor leaders likewise boast that for a time Kawaguchi was "the most struck town in Japan." That this view does not contain too much poetic license is suggested by the fact that in 1930 Kawaguchi was the scene of 10 percent of all strikes recorded in Japan.[30] Clearly, the small, "solidary and cooperative" factories of Kawaguchi were not unresponsive to the joys of civil war.

From its very beginning, unionism in Kawaguchi had been inseparable from Marxist politics. In 1927, the two branches of iron-worker's unions had founded local chapters of the *Shakai-minshū tō* (Social Democratic Party) and the *Nihon rōnō tō* (Japan Labor-Farmer Party), and in 1931 a small element of the Japan Communist Party had even succeeded in setting up locally as a clique within the Kanto Metal-Workers' Union. In fact, union activity and the strike were used as much to advance the political ambitions and interests of labor leaders as they were to advance the workers' union movement. When, in 1932, the two Socialist parties joined together nationally, the local parties and unions dutifully followed suit, but this marked the end of both. The unions maintained formal existence until 1940, when they were proscribed, but the union-Marxist movement was at an end by 1932. The general climate was mainly responsible, but the forced amalgamation of the local labor movement contributed its bit. During the preceding five years of rivalry between the two union-party groups,

29 Kyōchōkai, *op.cit.*, p. 159.   30 *Ibid.*

the most bitter personal animosities had been engendered, and many drifted out of the movement entirely rather than have to work together.

In fact, many of the labor and socialist party leaders of those days became, during the business boom of the next ten to twelve years, factory owners. These men today tend to give defensive explanations. After all, they had been superior technicians, or the workers would not have followed them into the union at all, the technical bias of this society being what it is. What more natural, therefore, than that they should, like other superior technicians, take advantage of the boom and of the followers they had attracted, and admit the impossibility of further union-Socialist activity, to found their own factories?

Against this enormously abbreviated background of a society much more complex than that revealed in Okuda's plant, we may now look briefly at the Nagai Company.

The firm today is owned and, in spite of its legally incorporated form, controlled by two brothers in their fifties, the sons of the old inventor and founder. Both sons trained as apprentices in the machine shop, and can thus claim the background of skilled workers, but both also received a good higher technical education, and grew up with money in Tokyo. The younger brother has little to do with the firm, spending most of his work time in other business ventures with a high technical and modern-taste component, e.g., sound-recording equipment. The elder brother is president of the firm, but leaves most of the routine business of management to a managing director, who came up under their father and has been with the company for more than thirty years. The president seldom appears at the plant, living in Urawa—a much more pleasant residence than Kawaguchi or, at this time, much of Tokyo—commuting to other businesses in Tokyo or living the life of a "sportsman." He draws much of his remuneration from the company in the form of goods and services paid for by the firm—his house and automobile, his *machiai* (geisha house) and club bills, and six personal servants, including two *tobi* (a colorful roughneck) who are bodyguards and factota; though carried on the company rolls, these retainers never appear at the plant and by union regulation do not belong to that organization.

The owners are thus quite unlike the often equally or even more wealthy local factory owners and wholesalers. They are not tied to Kawaguchi's can-of-worms life style, or involved in its ruling economic and political networks. But though atypical of the town's past and present leaders, the owners represent a trend that is today growing so rapidly that it may in time destroy the old social community of Kawaguchi, as the town becomes at last merely a specialized cell of the metropolitan region.

The firm operates out of three locations—a *general office* in Tokyo; the main *machine shop* in Kawaguchi, which will be the primary object of this description; and a small *imono* near the latter but organized as a separate company division. The machine shop takes all the output of the *imono*, and also contracts for most of the production of four other, but entirely independent, casting (not all in iron) and machine shops.

The general office is small. It houses only the managing director, who visits the Kawaguchi installations every few days and is otherwise in frequent communication with them, and the firm's Finance and Sales Departments, a total of two executives and six clerks. Finance and sales personnel are seldom in direct contact with the plant, but require a certain amount of clerical, etc., work out of plant personnel.

The machine shop at the moment employs eighty-six persons. One is struck by the fact that fewer than half of these, forty persons, are production workers per se, organized into lathing and finishing-assembly sections, though another five—the foreman and four section chiefs—are also workers in intimate contact with the floor. These are, from the workers' point of view, the backbone of the factory.

The machine shop must also, however, maintain a wide range of functions in support of their work. Another twenty-four workers are engaged in making packing crates, painting and packing the product, and transporting it and raw materials from suppliers; their skills are however obviously less specialized or valuable, and their social standing in the plant is therefore appreciably lower. In addition, the plant must carry on its own record-keeping and accounting for in-plant purposes, as well as whatever the general office may require of it, and support plant executives in their work, and nine persons of clerical status, all directly attached to one executive or another, are employed. They, together with the ancillary workers, are members of the plant union, but there are great differences between clerks and workers in life style, in the closeness of their relations with executives, and consequently in their community of interest with one another.

The multiplicity of functions—which also include research and development, quality control, logistics, cost accounting, etc.—combined with size, require a considerable managerial component of eight executives, each formally in charge of a specialized activity, and including the chief of production and the plant head himself. Whether this proportion—almost 10 percent—is high for the executive roster or not I am not in a position to say. The administrators themselves, of course, argue that it is not. The number of distinct functions that must be performed, combined with the high technical component of most of them and the need to maintain the company's reputation for excellence in all of them, inevitably lead to the segregation of the work process into compartments, each under a specialist, and the need for their coordination. The multiplication of liaison occasions brought about by the physical spread of the firm among several locations adds greatly to the total executive load. The information explosion has the same effect. Government requirements—and increasingly employer association "suggestions"—as to record-keeping, in the form of ever-changing regulations, etc., still further swell the burden.

Every observer will admit that these things are true. Nevertheless, the burden of most such tasks can neither be measured nor proved, and varies greatly with the subjective state of the administrator, itself subject to a variety of influences related and unrelated to the work-place. In this connection, one must point out that the executives in this company have all been with it between fifteen and thirty years. Such long-term employment cannot fail, in and of itself, to encourage the proliferation of supervisory positions and levels—as individual abilities harden and specialize in certain directions, as mid-career crises arise and must be solved, as inter-personal relations achieve a particular pattern of inclusions and exclusions, and as individuals must be promoted merely in order to maintain motivation. One even wonders if these incentives to the growth of bureaucracy have not been allowed to develop further than they might otherwise have by the divorce from the management of the plant of the one person whose profit interest may be adversely affected by such growth, the owner.

The executives here are set apart from the workers not only by their managerial status, which is also true in a plant like Okuda's, but by their class and sub-culture, and by their curious failure to per-form some of the most important functions of the manager, things that seldom separate the worker from small owner-managers like Okuda.

In part, both of these executive characteristics stem from the fact that the technical level of the plant is high. Even the core workers are much more highly skilled than those of the *imono*, while the execu-tives for the most part have university or higher technical school de-grees. Yet even the difference in knowledge between them is not mere-ly the matter of a continuum, but the true discontinuity between work with the hands and work with the mind. The workers, for ex-ample, seem convinced that no executive could handle a lathe without ruining the billet or choking the machine. By way of contrast, the foreman Taguchi, or Morita, the precision lathe section chief, though supervisory personnel, could brush aside a young workman puzzled by a problem and quickly show him how to run the machine so as to solve it.

Coupled with this, biographies of the workers show that they are not, in family backgrounds or gross experience, appreciably different from the workers in technologically simpler plants. Most came from farmer or worker backgrounds and trained as on-the-job apprentices. The difference between them and Okuda's workers is that they emerged from apprentice training with a somewhat better-than-average technique, which by individual application and the luck of their being in this environment, they have been able still further to improve. They are more skilled, but they are culturally, and identify themselves socially, as workers. The executives, by contrast, are mainly from families of middle-class status, or ambitious for that status, and have gone through the education necessary to maintain or attain it.

Perhaps most important, the executive-worker discontinuity has been institutionalized in the management process itself. The company, receiving an order for, say, 2,500 machined marine valves, passes the work to the foreman, with suitable technical, scheduling, etc., instructions. It concurrently negotiates with him a lump sum payment for the labor involved. The assignment of this work to sections and individual employees is thereafter his job, as is the allocation of piece-work rates to each worker. It seems correct to say, therefore, that executives and workers are linked in the central work process only as customer and supplier, almost as if they were two separate firms. As an impersonal machine for carrying out production, the plant is indeed a hierarchically organized unit. But as a managerial process, it consists to a high degree of two distinct though related groupings.

It is because of this situation that it is arguable that the president plays *the* vital role in the plant, even though he is seldom there and takes little part in its routine operations. As noted, he trained as a skilled workman in the plant, and moreover at a time when some of the most senior of the workmen were also there. The workers therefore say that he could handle a lathe himself, and so could certainly manage the plant if he wanted to. The older workers are perhaps a bit tongue-in-cheek about his ability still to handle a lathe, but essentially he does have a fraternal identification with them as well. Moreover, his behavior, and apparent personality, are such as to reinforce this identification. He frequently turns up to play sand-lot baseball with them, and takes them all on outings at the appropriate seasons. When he is with them, he mixes very easily, even being able to drift into local class dialect without seeming affected, to talk about sports and the other kinds of things that interest them, and to play the matey patron. The fact that he is known to be, on his own time, an avid sportsman, to frequent *machiai*, and even to retain two *tobi* as personal servants, suggests that this behavior is not merely a pose but reflects a set of tastes that come close to those ideal for a rich *oyakata* of artisans in the traditional style.

Yet he is also a well-educated and sophisticated urbanite who can with equal ease preside over a discussion with his executives. An observer often wonders—not, of course, "Which is the real president?"—but to what extent the roles he plays are sincere expressions of the different facets of a rich personality, and to what extent instruments consciously employed. In any event, he is the president for both social elements in his plant, identifiable and in communication with both. I do not know enough about the history of this arrangement to know if he has deliberately engineered it, so as to allow each section of the plant to go about its largely independent work, governed by its own internal structure, and permit him to stay out of the routine business of management, or if it arises from some other source. Since the development of the union, however, it is clear that a new *modus vivendi* is emerging in the plant, and he has stepped in to help manage its development, as we shall see.

The internal organization of the core workers is ordered, in the first instance, by their formal and functional structuring into four sections, two each of lathers and finishers, for precision and industrial machinery, each with its own section chief, under the general direction of the foreman. This organization does seem to be the principal one for the ordering of the work process itself, individual work and pay assignments being made by the foreman and section chiefs acting as a committee. These are skilled workers, and each man, unless he asks for help from the chief, is usually left alone to do his work as he wishes. This, and the fact that most could certainly sell their skills elsewhere easily, may go far to explain the relatively open, frank, and even individualistic atmosphere of this plant, in marked contrast with the reticence and guardedness—and, when pressed, the *"shikaku ga nai"* (I don't know) evasions—of Okuda's workers. So too does the fact that almost half of Nagai's core workers were trained elsewhere, and so have no elder-younger brother ties through apprenticeship, with their chiefs, or with one another. One must add that only a few—the trainees and one or two young bachelors—live in the factory dormitory where they might develop close personal attachments; most of the workers commute to widely-scattered homes, at distances of as much as an hour's ride up the Tohoku Line.

Seniority in terms of years of service in the plant is an important criterion of status and influence within the group, but it is only one of several such factors. It is certainly not the sole criterion for appointment to a supervisory position. Taguchi, the foreman, has been here nineteen years, but two other men have been here even longer and are not even section chiefs. Morita and Satō, two of the section chiefs, have been here sixteen years apiece, but they are outranked in years of service by four others with no supervisory jobs. The two other section chiefs, with twelve years each, are outranked or equalled by eleven other non-supervisory personnel. Certainly, reputed skill, within broad limits of seniority, is a determining criterion, and Taguchi and Morita have that special reputation that came from long years spent on the "pilgrimage" before they settled down in this plant. In the workers' eyes, it is a mark in their favor that Taguchi worked in more than fifty different plants, and Morita in more than twenty.

Apart from these factors, Taguchi and Morita appear aided in being the most influential men in the worker group by the fact that each has clear relational talents. The foreman gets along very well with the president. Recently, for example, the latter, noting that Taguchi is getting along in years and has to spend much of his work time on supervisory tasks, offered to put him on salary. Likewise, when approached about the formation of a union in the plant, the president, unlike many another company president in this situation, is reported to have said "I don't mind, if Taguchi will be union president." Yet the foreman seems able to retain the workers' trust, perhaps because—as an example—when offered a salary, he refused, saying that since he must negotiate the piece-work wages for the workers, he could not do so in the workers' best interest if his own income was not also affected by the deal he was able to make with the company.

On the other hand, Taguchi does not seem personally close to any of the workers. Business-like, straightforward, and fair, he does not encourage discussion of personal problems, and is in fact frequently curmudgeonish in such situations. Only five workers, whom he trained himself before he became acting foreman many years ago, can be said to show him even the formal deference due their teacher, an obeisance he moreover does not seem to want. He is, unquestionably, an individualist, a type that one must recognize had very high prestige in the old society of artisans.

Morita, by way of contrast, seems a very different type of ideal personality in that society, that of the personally involved *oyaji* (the old man) of a permanent work group, and his close relations include almost half the workers at Nagai. Many, almost a quarter of the total, were in fact trained under him, but he has gathered many more adherents by the fact that he shows concern for the human problems of others, whether they are his apprentices or not. Recently, for example, he noted that one of the young workers seemed peckish, and persuaded him to go to a doctor, and then to have the operation he proved to need, and paid for the treatment out of his own pocket until such time as the worker could afford to pay him back. More recently, he has acquired a powerful new tool for the expression of this side of his character; it was decided to use the money accumulated from union dues as a welfare fund, and Morita was easily elected to administer it.

It has been fortunate for Taguchi, and probably for the workers as a whole, that the foreman and Morita seem to have got along very well with one another, each leaving the other to play his own role, and cooperating amicably in managing the plant floor between them. There are two other networks of section chiefs and the men they have trained, but neither is large, and both seem content to work under the leadership of the two "bosses."

At the time of this study, this order was being subjected to new strains occasioned by the union. Curiously they were not—or not yet—those so usual at this time elsewhere, between management and the workers. As noted, the president had not objected to the formation of the union, or to its affiliation with the conservative Sōdōmei national organization. There have been no strikes or threat of strikes, and the monthly meeting of the Management Coordinating Committee with the president, representatives of management, and union representatives, including the foreman and section chiefs—seems to have been able to iron out all labor-management problems to date. It is aided to this result, as are all group-decision situations in this plant, through the device of the preliminary informal meeting among the leaders, so that the formal session can pass proposals almost without discussion, spending the rest of the meeting time listening to a rambling monologue on this and that by the president.

The strain has developed, rather, among the workers themselves. Professor Nakano is probably correct in saying that hitherto order had prevailed among the workers because they had confidence that their leaders would handle properly the kind of problems that had hitherto arisen. This confidence, born of the old work group, was ratified when the union was born, and the structure of the work group merely extended to that new organization. The workers elected the same men to union leadership—Taguchi as president and Morita as treasurer—to whom they had extended work leadership.

Within a short period, however, it became apparent that many workers were dissatisfied with this arrangement. The first casualty was Taguchi. Some workers began to grumble that he was too cozy with the president of the company to represent their interests—a complaint which seems never to have arisen before, when he represented them as their foreman—and he, in dudgeon, resigned the presidency of the union. A former apprentice of Morita's, now a section chief, was elected in his place, clearly under Morita's aegis, and Taguchi was elected *komon* (advisor) to the union. In his dual roles as union counsellor and plant foreman, Taguchi continued to play a central part in company-union relations, and the Taguchi-Morita cooperation continued to guide the work of both the work group and the union. Shortly, however, the same voices began to be raised against the new union president, as a "tool of the bosses," and therefore, for the first time, against those "bosses" themselves. Things went so far that an "out" clique began to form, and put forward an opposition candidate for the union presidency. Morita thereupon tightened his network and again ensured election of his follower, but the workers' group was now split, and moving in a new direction.

One need not be surprised, of course. Prior to the entry of the union, the workers had been organized only as a work group. Its objectives were to employ the men's skills to produce goods and earn individually disposable income for them. Its internal hierarchy was chosen to effect those ends—in terms of skill, seniority of experience, and the relational abilities, external and internal, which helped to achieve those purposes. The union, however, has very different objectives. Its basic purpose is to increase the worker's share of the pie of status—income and prestige—in an open-ended competition with management; it is intrinsically an organization of competition, and potentially of combat, and this central function can be denied only by euphemism or superior force. In addition, by its very existence, it creates new goods that did not exist before—union funds and hierarchical positions within the union—that must be allocated differently among the union members, by competition.

The abilities that can order the production and work processes are almost certainly not those that can successfully lead an open-ended competition with management for a different allocation between them of general social goods. In any event, agreement must be reached through experimentation upon what those new abilities are, and each man with an interest in the outcome is free to put forward his own proposals. Faced at the same time with a new set of union-controlled goods, that were not assigned by general agreement to any particular type of leadership control, ambitious men who do not—or not yet—qualify for leadership of the work group inevitably turn to this new prize in hope; it multiplies the sum total of prizes open to the worker.

PEOPLE'S REPUBLIC OF CHINA:
A METAL WORKS IN "CH'ANG-SHA"[31]

Newly constructed under the First Five Year Plan, in 1958, and designed to produce machine tools, the Ch'ang-sha works is an example of the emphasis of the years when Soviet models were still considered persuasive, on the development of a Western style of heavy industry. Located in an interior province not previously identifiable with modern manufacturing, it also illustrates a determination, which has persisted, to disperse industry and to bring all parts of the country into the mainstream of modern life.

This factory had about 650 employees in the early 1960's, and so is well beyond the size range dealt with elsewhere in this essay, but is discussed here in the absence of adequate data on smaller metals plants. It was also at the time, for reasons that will become apparent, in process of sharply reducing its personnel complement.

There were also causes why any Chinese factory engaged in modern manufacturing at that time, and especially where, as in the case of the Ch'ang-sha works, it was isolated from other centers of such production, was obliged to be larger than would have been necessary for a Japanese enterprise turning out the same volume of a similar product. An integrated metals operation, the Ch'ang-sha works was built around a series of shops (ch'e-chien) for turning out basic metal parts by casting, forging and in steel, and for finishing and assembling them. To this point, it was quite like many of the medium-sized works in Kawaguchi. It also, however, included other shops performing ancillary technical functions—making tools for use in the plant, repairing buildings, maintaining machinery and motors—that might more easily and cheaply have been bought on the open market or sub-contracted

---

[31] I put the name Ch'ang-sha in quotation marks because that is not the city in which this works is located. I have made this change, and avoided certain other comments which might conceivably allow identification of my refugee informants, in accord with my promise that their anonymity would be protected. In doing so, I follow practice honored in many other societies, and do not thereby imply that such anonymity is peculiarly necessary in the People's Republic of China. As in any other such case, the student must himself be responsible for guaranteeing that informant anonymity has not been coupled with informant irresponsibility. On the basis of both internal evidence and comparative material (on other plants, from other informants unconnected with one another) I believe that such irresponsibility has here been reduced to a minimum. The reliability of any informant, in any situation, is another and not necessarily related problem. I have come to believe that this kind of "study of culture at a distance," or in the present instance "China-watching," produces a roughly accurate picture of many things. It can never substitute for participant-observation by a trained student who observes with prior knowledge of the questions he wants answered, a fact I am fully aware this study demonstrates.

out to separate firms in the technically richer environment of a Japanese manufacturing city, but that probably in Ch'ang-sha at this time could have been procured only if incorporated into a self-sufficient factory.

There remained, however, a large number of separate offices in the Ch'ang-sha works engaged in administrative service functions. Most—planning, product design, quality control, technical control, the chief engineer, personnel, finance and supply, general administration, security, the emergency clinic, the plant manager—represented functions performed in any factory, but they by no means had to be performed, as here, in separate administrative offices, with specialized personnel of executive (*kampu*) rank in each. Others—wage regulation, enforcement of the national industrial charter (the so-called "70 Regulations"), to say nothing of a distinct party apparatus—represented accommodations to a specifically Chinese Communist matrix, as indeed did the extreme size of some of the other offices (e.g., planning). In all, there were more than 100 persons of executive rank in the Ch'ang-sha works, a much higher proportion than in Nagai's smaller plant, but not than in factories of comparable size in Hong Kong.[32] Perhaps there was something to be said for the comment of cynics, that there were so many separate offices because so many executives were covetous of the additional prestige title of *k'e-chang* (section chief). Certainly those who engineered the Cultural Revolution, in the late 1960's, with its marked down-grading of bureaucracies, must have agreed that the situation in this regard had gotten out of hand and required rectification.

The Changing Matrix: The works here was built, and is owned and controlled, by the provincial government, and is thus answerable to the Industrial Office of that headquarters. Indeed, this is a system in which all industrial establishments, great and small, are owned and controlled by some unit of government—from state enterprises, directly under a central ministry no matter where located physically in the country, through provincial units like the present one, to plants under city governments, resident committees in cities, rural communes and brigades, etc.

This is of course a "planned economy." Ch'ang-sha began opera-

---

[32] Mok, Victor, *The Organization and Management of Factories in Kwun Tong*, Hong Kong, Social Research Centre, The Chinese University of Hong Kong, 1973, in a useful study of the structure of factories in the Kwun Tong section of Hong Kong, finds that over 19 percent of the personnel of operations employing 200-499, and almost 25 percent of those in factories employing over 500, are "administrative" and "technical" personnel, perhaps roughly equivalent to the *kampu* posts of the time in the People's Republic. Cf. especially Mok, Table 22.

tions almost concurrently with the enthusiastic birth of that economy in 1956, and in the early 1960's was still, at least in part, operating according to its terms.

This meant, for one thing, that its operations were governed by written plans, which had annually to be worked out with, and approved by, the Industrial Office of the provincial government as coordinate and appropriate parts of its own master plan for all industrial establishments (other than those owned by the state) in its territory, whether owned by itself, as in this case, or by subordinate units of government. In its turn, the province's plan had to be worked out with and approved by various ministries of the central government, as likewise fitting in with the national plan. On this basis, the Ch'ang-sha works was expected annually to produce a certain number of units of output of stipulated types and quality. It would market them to other organizations, in amounts and at prices which had been negotiated between them under government supervision, and for which written contracts were for the most part in hand before the production year was far along.

In order to accomplish this plan, the factory was authorized by it to employ a given number of personnel of specified ranks and pay grades, within a complex national system covering all occupations. There was, at this time, a basic distinction between executives (kam-pu) and workers. Worker ranks began with apprentices, of which there were three grades (with No. 1 as the highest), and went on to mature workmen in eight grades (of which No. 8 was the highest), each grade being further subdivided into a senior (cheng) and junior (fu) class. Executives were seriated among twenty-six grades, with No. 1 again as the senior (a rank believed to be held by only one person in China). Executive grades were further subdivided into administrative and technical categories, the latter beginning with four grades of technician, and leading into three grades of engineer, in both cases with No. 1 as the most junior. These grades, to each of which was assigned a given monthly income (though it varied somewhat by industry and region), remained with an individual until he was promoted, regardless of his specific job assignment. The highest personal executive rank of anyone in the Ch'ang-sha works in the early 1960's was No. 13, half-way up the national list, held by the plant party secretary.

The Ch'ang-sha works received the personnel to fill these slots, and let them go, at the direction of a nation-wide personnel allocation machinery. In the case of the graduate of a technical college controlled by the state, for example, several months before graduation he would have been asked to fill out a form, with spaces for three choices each for geographical location of assignment and for the type of work preferred (e.g., teaching, administration, technical), and to write an essay explaining why he had made these choices. At least some of the more sophisticated urban college students of bourgeois background at the time considered that the reason that would be judged most appropriate would be an elaboration of the theme "my wish accords with the Fatherland's need." During the summer after graduation his class would meet regularly for sessions to continue discussion of the same topic until, toward the end of the summer, his school would receive notification of the assignment of its graduates that year. It appears that people did in fact very frequently receive at least one of their choices. Others did not. The immediate assignment in this case would be to the Industrial Office of the provincial government, which would then make—or notify the applicant of—his further assignment to the Ch'ang-sha works. Observation was unable to establish how applicants with other backgrounds entered the personnel allocation system, whether directly into the national roster or as parts of some provincial, etc. quota. Certainly the national roster itself did however service even isolated and lower-level plants, for graduates of state-run technical colleges often in those years found themselves sent directly by the machinery described to rural commune and brigade, and other technically-primitive, shops.

It would appear, in other words, that this mechanism eliminated every vestige of older Chinese systems for hiring and firing, and for local and *ad hoc* differential treatment and pay of workers. Little evidence was adduced, in this or other organizations, of the employment of key workers through personal ties, through labor contractors, or by simply tacking "Help Wanted" signs on the factory gate. It is possible, of course, that better observation would alter this conclusion. For example, there was also no evidence of the old distinction between "permanent" workers, with monthly rates of pay, extensive fringe benefits, and the expectation of lengthy employment, and "temporary" workers, with only daily wages and a precarious tenure. Yet, as will be described later, some workers at the Ch'ang-sha works did indeed prove to have only temporary jobs there.

A factory's purchase of raw materials, supplies, and equipment was likewise regulated by its plan, and as with the sale of its products to its own customers, its purchases were for the most part also made from designated enterprises, in amounts and at prices stipulated in contracts drawn up under government supervision, prior to or early in the production year. Similarly, the plan authorized the factory to negotiate approved capital and operating budgets with local branches of the state banks, on schedules tied to its own schedule of production and of payment from its customers.

In carrying out all these plans, moreover, the plant was obliged to operate according to a plethora of procedural regulations conforming to standard national models. Such rule-books, for example, stipulated the intervals between personnel promotions and the methods to be followed in making them, measures to be taken to ensure quality control of goods, etc., etc.

The economy in which the Ch'ang-sha works sat was thus the very model of a nationally and "rationally" integrated mechanism. Not a sparrow should rise or fall save by plan or without record, and a factory was merely another office of a nation-wide bureaucracy with totalitarian purview.

As has already been suggested, the internal organization of the works seemed suited to link it to that matrix. More basically, as in every echelon of government and all major organizations, the internal structure was a dual one. That is, there was a functional management organization as we too would understand that term, headed by a plant chief (ch'ang-chang), or in this case a board of four plant chiefs. There was also, however, a distinct party organization, which in the first instance handled, without reference to the functional table of organization, internal party and league matters—e.g., recruitment, training, discipline, etc. Only a minority of the personnel of the plant were believed (though this was a matter not widely discussed) to be members, and thus this aspect of the activities of the Party organization was of little moment to most workers.

The party, however, defined a number of other things to be also of primary concern to it, and exerted frank initiatives and controls over them. One was the continuing assessment of the political status of all personnel of the enterprise, and measures to ensure that this status be considered a matter of substance in all personnel decisions. Thus, each worker was covered by a dossier, which recorded not only the usual items of a curriculum vitae but also the class status of his immediate ancestors and family, and his own political activities and attitudes at each stage of his career to date. Few observers, in this or other organizations, did not accept it as axiomatic that assignment to "sensitive" positions was available only to individuals with a "good" political background and record, and that all other personnel dispositions, including especially promotion to the better jobs, were matters in which, other things being equal, good political status would tip the balance.

This is not the same as saying that "only those with a good political attitude can get the good jobs." The observations of too many people, in very different situations, substantiate the great emphasis placed upon ability to do the (non-political) job, and every organization, including the Ch'ang-sha works, had men in even high positions who were not party members, who had "bad" (e.g., landlord or bourgeois) backgrounds, and who in cases were even forgiven distinct political errors. Assignment was rather, as summarized, a matter of the situation and of the balance between political and other abilities. In any event, the importance from the point of view of the party of political attitude and activity was constantly and frankly held up to people's attention. At a time of re-assignment, or when he was due for promotion, for example, a worker was often called before a committee, including but not limited to party officials, and asked to justify the disposition of his case on both technical and political grounds, and he would be openly praised and criticized by the board on both counts.

In addition to these aspects of plant life in which the party took leadership, it was also accepted as axiomatic by all observers, in this and other organizations, that the party side of its structure exerted effective control over even usual operational activities. The formal mechanism through which this control was exerted was an interlocking directorate between top management and party executive positions. By no means were all management posts, even senior ones, manned by party members, but key party executives did fill some of the key management posts, from which they could observe and participate in all matters of importance in the plant. It was also widely reported, though with less evidence, that party members up and down the line kept the party secretariat informed through their own channels on all matters of significance throughout the works.

In any event, it was reported from most organizations, including the Ch'ang-sha works, that the party secretary, who normally did not hold any formal management position, was frankly treated as the undisputed executive focus of everything, and was the "busiest and hardest-working man in the outfit." Certainly these dual hierarchies within a single organization seem to have been reasonably well coordinated and to have worked together without undue friction. Moreover, even observers unfriendly enough to the regime to have left the country often felt that the dual executive apparatus reached its decisions in a manner that was not only "centralist" but also "democratic," that is, through persuasion rather than by party fiat. It is difficult to define simply the wellsprings of conformity to regnant trends in any society. As a special factor in this case, there is little doubt that in the PRC negative sanctions for infractions of political substance could be condign and were feared by many, or that a wide variety of acts, not normally considered "political," were from time to time and especially during campaigns so re-defined. Yet there is also evident a fund of respect for the wisdom of the party, and for the primacy of its definitions of the situation.

Though the Ch'ang-sha works still, in the early 1960's, operated within this pervasive matrix of governmental, party and national initiatives and controls, it must be recognized that the Chinese economy and society have remained plastic throughout the generation since Liberation. Subject to the pulling and hauling of a variety of macro-societal factors which have by no means as yet found an easy accommodation with one another, and to conscious experimentation, they have changed repeatedly. "Planned economy," even "bureaucracy," seems somehow inappropriate to describe the whole range of what the plant has experienced in the fewer than twenty years of its existence.

The initial attempt to apply the nationally centralized system of bureaucratic planning and control had hardly begun before the frenzy of "politics in command" of the Great Leap Forward, 1958-1960, effectively shelved it. Plans were disregarded. Bent on producing as much as possible, with little attention given to product quality, or often even to a market or use for it, local officials whipped themselves and their workers to an exhausting pitch, wore out machinery, and used up scarce materiel, on projects that were *ad hoc*. This was no longer planning or centralization. It was often not even bureaucracy, but the mob in the hands of fanatics.

The early 1960's was a period of very slow recuperation from that excess. All goods, including food and basic raw materials, were in catastrophically short supply. Managerial and technical skills had been revealed inadequate to ensure "rational" production, and a failure of nerve seemed pervasive. Factories, in consequence, found it difficult or impossible to get the materiel, supplies, etc., they needed, or to organize production of adequate volume and quality. Plants were thus considerably under-employed, and workers even had to spend much of their time growing their own food.

Concurrently, the economy was being given a rather fundamental re-orientation. With its ties to the Soviet cut and aid from that source at an end, with the Soviet pattern of development discredited, and with its food and raw material base shown to be inadequate, the regime was mid-stream of a thorough-going shift. Priority was to be given to the primary sector, and manufacturing re-directed to its support, e.g., for agricultural tools, fertilizers, etc. A parallel way to production, "our own road," dependent more upon the labor, skills, and motivation of workers and less upon machinery and administrative tinkering, was to be developed. Much more authority was delegated to lower-level units, which were also encouraged to take advantage of their own, often local, most advantageous factors of production by being permitted to keep the income of production over quotas. Piece-work rates of pay for workers, rather than the flat monthly wages described earlier, were allowed. Convinced that a responsible cost accounting was essential, the government required organizations to live within whatever incomes they were able to make, and banks were given authority to police money flows in terms of realities rather than of plans. It is true that much of the planning, allocation, and procedures outlined earlier remained on paper and were even adhered to wherever possible. But the system was made far more diverse than had been the standard. For most decisions, it became more many-headed. "Economically rational" factors, including the incentive for gain at least at the level of the organization, were built in to it. Certain traditional human values, never really denigrated but left only to wither, were now once more praised, as in the campaign to "learn from old workers."

Caught by the depression, the Ch'ang-sha works had found it impossible to turn out machine tools of acceptable quality in sufficient numbers, nor did such work any longer have the priority it once had. The provincial government, perhaps at the time only groping toward accommodation to the emerging national priorities, turned the plant to the manufacture of simple consumer and agricultural goods—skillets, plows, etc.—work in which it was engaged much of the time it was under observation. The plant's experience during the subsequent Cultural Revolution of the late 1960's is unknown, but it would be surprising if it escaped the general trends of that period, during which bureaucracy itself was down-graded, and the party lost much of its organizational control of affairs. Information suggests that in recent years, as the Chinese economy has not only made a substantial recovery but in fact reached new levels of productivity, the Ch'ang-sha works has again been re-directed to the production of more complex agricultural machinery, and so fulfills something of the role as an integrated metals plant for which it was designed.

During its fewer than twenty years of life, then, the Ch'ang-sha works has suffered vicissitudes as great as any of those experienced by the capitalist plants of Kawaguchi. Some of the sources of these changes in the two cases of course differ, but others are strikingly similar—e.g., the wasteful frenzies of "politics in command" of the Second World War and the Great Leap Forward.

The results have also differed to a degree, but not totally. During a depression as severe as that of the early 1960's in China, Japanese workers might have been let go in large numbers, while those retained would certainly have had their wages drastically reduced. In fact, a considerable proportion of the Ch'ang-sha workers were also let out, usually by being sent down (*hsia fang*) to lower-level and technically more primitive units, and even to the farm, where their skills were in cases used as little as if they had in fact been un-employed. Moreover, those so sent down were for the most part apprentices and probationary workers, and a much higher proportion of the females than of the males in these categories; for whatever reasons, therefore, the greatest hardship was visited upon the same persons who would have been "temporary" workers and received similar treatment in capitalist Chinese and Japanese factories. The wages of workers retained at the Ch'ang-sha works were not cut, it must be emphasized. They were, however, also not raised, as by national regulations they should have been, and consumer goods were now either unavailable or available only at much higher black market prices.

The conclusion seems inescapable that the Ch'ang-sha workers have also experienced "boom or bust" cycles, and radical realignments of their use and work lives. It is thus a reasonable hypothesis that they have faced many of the same problems that over the years the workers in Kawaguchi's capitalist plants have also faced—motivations cycling from enthusiasm to disillusion and resentment, the necessity to develop and use now one and now another of a broad range of skills and competencies, etc.

The Work Life: Prior to Liberation, China like Japan had ideally trained skilled workmen through apprenticeship, even in modern industries, and a worker without that background was by definition to be considered, in some way, unskilled. In the stereotype of observers too young to have experienced that system, an apprentice, who was usually if not invariably male, was recruited at around the age of twelve or thirteen, through some sort of personal tie—kinship, a co-villager, etc.—between the recruiter and the boy's family. The recruiter might be the owner of the shop in which apprenticeship was to be served, or a mature artisan working there, or a labor contractor for one of the large modern factories.

During apprenticeship, which ideally extended to the boy's late teens, he lived with other apprentices in a dormitory, under the watchful eyes of the owner and his wife, whom he called respectfully and intimately *lao pan* and *shih mu* (craft mother). He addressed apprentices senior to himself as *shih hsiung* (craft elder brother) and mature artisans as, for example, Yang *shih fu* (artisan Yang). Assigned to an artisan, he was typically used only as a menial helper, key elements of the technique being even "hidden" from him, until and unless he showed enough ambition to "steal the technique," practice it surreptitiously on his own time, and succeed well enough to show his work for his master's scrutiny. When he had passed this motivational and skill test successfully, and was therefore worth taking some trouble with, the artisan might get the boy to sign a contract, guaranteeing to pay his teacher something after attainment of mature artisan status, in return for a somewhat less adversary learning relationship between them. After graduation, a workman might ideally remain in his old master's shop. The resemblances between this stereotype and that held by Japanese workers about their own former apprenticeship system are obvious.

Since establishment of the PRC, the former apprenticeship arrangements are considered to have been exploitative. Especially under the First Five Year Plan, a large number of new technical schools were founded, at both the middle school (roughly, the American high school) and college level. Graduates of such schools, however, would still be few enough to man only the technician (executive) ranks, and persons destined for worker status continued to be trained on the job. Normally to remain in the trainee status for a minimum of three years, and ideally progressing each year along the three trainee ranks, they were here paid from JMP 18 a month in the first rank to 22 for the third. It was also recognized that even graduates with technical degrees would need further on-the-job training in the requirements of a particular factory, and they too spent the first year after assignment in a probationary status, at rates of pay that ranged from JMP 28 to 41, depending on the level (middle school or college) of the degree held and the quality of the school that had awarded it. Given the facts that the lowest worker rank was paid almost twice as much as a worker trainee in his highest level, and that the highest-ranking worker received three to four times as much as the lowest, levelling tendencies were not at this time and in this industrial context obtrusive. By the same token, trainee workers were either being "exploited," or were being paid in terms of the saleable value of work they were expected to produce rather than in terms of need. That income was of considerable and frank importance to the workers was evidenced by the constant complaints, here and elsewhere, that a trainee worker really could not live on his wage without outside help of some kind, and by the fact that, when the monthly wage was replaced by piece-work pay in 1962, production is reported to have increased greatly in both quantity and quality.

A very large proportion of the personnel of the Ch'ang-sha works at this time were new recruits—trainee workers brought in on their three-year terms during the Great Leap Forward, and probationary technicians now being turned out by the new schools, in numbers apparently greater than were for the moment needed. These trainees had come from a great variety of sources—the farm, nearby provincial cities, and many even from distant large cities like Shanghai. Almost half of all trainee personnel were girls, a stunning departure from tradition. The Ch'ang-sha works was considered to be a rather good assignment, even by people from the arrogant coastal metropolis, at any rate by comparison with the rural sideline industries to which many urban middle-school and college graduates were at the time being sent. It is indeed clear that China's leaders had not yet been able to eradicate the disdain many urban people, even those born and raised under the new regime, felt for the provinces and life on the farm, or to counter the magnetic attraction of the city.

This was a society in which bureaucratic and party position gave appreciable power. A caricature of the arrogance this power sometimes brought to its holders was that of the person of executive rank, "inspecting" the work of the floor with measured tread, arms folded high behind his back and nose slightly in the air. A less amusing caricature was that of the high executive who sneaked around to the back door of the dining hall, to use his rank to get a cut of the best meat for his private family table.

To counter-balance this, however, one must also report the caricatures of the worker: The old workman who, when peremptorily asked by an executive "Why don't you do it this way?" would reply "Fine, section chief, please show me how you would have it done," knowing full well that the executive was incapable of operating the machine. Or the workman who steadfastly refused all requests to work one minute beyond official quitting time, and who, because he was always prompt, and worked steadily and well on shift, could not be reprimanded. There was even the experienced worker who, in this time of acute food shortages, refused the bonus he had won, by over-fulfilling his quota, of a month of free meals of superior quality in the Labor Union dining hall, saying that he was quite able to make enough money out of his own work alone to be able to afford an egg every day if he wished, and had no need for "charity." In fact also, one of the four men with the official title of plant chief, an old worker, still chose to retain his personal rank as a worker rather than an executive, and exerted his authority on the floor of the plant in the comradely manner of a man who could, and often did, show his workers how to do a job that was troubling them.

Certainly respect for skill and hard work with one's hands, and for the autonomy of the mature workman, was said to be everywhere evident in the workplace itself. Foremen were all old and experienced

personnel. Workmen were left alone at their jobs by foremen and
their fellows until they asked for help. Most workers are said to have
been quite prompt for their shifts and to have worked steadily
throughout, but even if one were repeatedly late, or frequently
botched a job, it was unlikely that the foreman would do more than
seem a bit sad, and leave any overt reprimands for political activists
in small group sessions.

There was much else that reminded one even more forcefully of the
pre-Liberation system. Trainee workers were called colloquially "apprentices" (hsueh-t'u, or orally t'u-ti), and were trained by attachment
to an older workman. Even probationary technicians spent at least
half their trial year assisting a technician in one of the basic metal
shops, only going on for the rest of their tutelage to one of the service
offices if they were destined for assignment to it. Mature workers were
regularly addressed, at least by apprentices and other workers, as for
example "Yang shih fu" (artisan Yang) rather than as "comrade"
(t'ung-chih).

If I can be forgiven for projecting into the Ch'ang-sha works of the
early 1960's something of the atmosphere of a very similar type of
factory I visited in Shanghai in the early 1970's, I can only characterize the attitudes of these Chinese workers as remarkably like those
I had come to know among Japanese iron workers almost a quarter of
a century earlier. In both, master artisans are immediately identifiable
by the unquestioning assurance with which they work their benches
and direct their helpers, as if certain that their skill deserves the
friendly respect it evidently receives. Lesser workers such as casters
appear to accept with equanimity a work role that brings very low
material rewards. Young learners show an awkwardness that admits
their status as only half-finished human beings, and rush and strain at
a senior's hardly perceptible gesture in substitution for our conveyor
belts and fork-lift trucks. Above all, I sensed in both a satisfaction
with and respect for themselves and for one another that I tend to
ascribe in the PRC less to the ideology of the regime than to the ancient self-confidence and comradeliness of the artisan, rooted in a real
world with which he knows he or any of his fellows could cope alone.
I fantasized at the time that a Kawaguchi smelter or caster of 1950
could have been set down at a stand in the Shanghai Tractor Works
in 1973 (or the Ch'ang-sha works in the early 1960's) and could have
begun work at once, feeling quite at home with his tools, his physical
surroundings, and his role among his fellows.

Throughout the PRC, an effort has been made to create a near total
community for the life of the individual around the work place—to
train, to participate politically, to have his friends and most of his

recreation, to live and to work together with the same people, in the same location, a concept not radically different from that of the ideal pre-Liberation artisan workshop. This has been impossible of complete realization in many urban plants, white-collar establishments, etc. Like most newly constructed factories, however, the Ch'ang-sha works was able to lay the groundwork for such a community. The entire complement of the plant lives in company housing within the compound, surrounded by a wall, the gates of which are closed at about midnight (though security guards are usually lenient about letting personnel in later). The plant also maintains a large dining hall capable of serving all meals to plant personnel. There is plenty of space within the compound for sports, including the omnipresent basketball courts, and for garden plots assigned to families or to bachelor room units.

Dormitories consist of a series of flimsy wooden buildings of two stories each, divided into small rooms, with one toilet and two simple kitchens—with cold running water and a couple of coal braziers—to a floor. Some buildings are for married personnel, invariably one family to a room, while others are for workers who are unmarried or living away from their families, with usually four persons, in double-decker bunks, to a room. Residents had to procure or build their own furniture, bedding, etc., and were responsible for tidying up their own areas; livelihood discipline, at least at this time, was somewhat headless, however, so that some were able to perform this task perfunctorily or not at all without reprimand, and it was difficult to get anyone at all to clean halls, toilets, etc.

In this period of acute food shortages, the factory dining hall fed only workers on shift at meal time, and such customers had to turn in individual ration meal coupons and make a small payment for side dishes. The Labor Union also operated a separate dining room which provided better meals to a small number of persons who had won this privilege as a prize, for overfulfillment of quotas, etc., and usually for only one, or at most three, months running. All other meals had to be provided by personnel for themselves. Apart from an occasional purchase of cooked snacks from the portable stalls some private entrepreneurs had set up just outside the gate, or a very rare meal in a restaurant in town, workers cooked for themselves, often as individuals rather even than by dorm units. They bought rationed uncooked rice, but most of the rest of their food consisted of vegetables each person or family grew itself, and consumed itself, and a few chickens most people also kept.

Living conditions were thus primitive, at the level more of the rural village than the city. Though the plant complement lived physically together, a pervasive independence could be seen in their relations with one another. Except for an occasional fist fight between workers and lower-ranking service personnel such as cooks or clerks, aggression seems not to have hung in the air between dormitory mates any more than it did between workers on the floor of the plant, but, equally, there seemed to be none of that compulsive attempt to create routines that would require active cooperation between individuals in close contact so often apparent in similar Japanese situations.

In spite of the power, income, etc., differentials between executives and workers, party and non-party personnel, there was also a pervasive equality in other than certain work and political situations. Except that a high-ranking executive might have a slightly larger room for his family, there was no discrimination whatsoever in living, dining hall, etc., arrangements. Dormitories were segregated only with regard to married or unmarried status, not as between executives, party members, workers or even trainees.

Critical institutions of this plant community, and those at which power and even aggression were most likely to be exerted on a systematic basis at this time, when the party was still in firm control, were the small group (hsiao tsu) mechanism for political education and assessment, and at special occasions, the campaign for peak political mobilization. The organizational base of the small group was the functional organization of the plant itself, a shop or a combination of several offices forming a "large group," which would itself be broken down into a number of small groups, again insofar as possible along the lines of the functional organization, and so as to number somewhere between 5 and 15 persons. Rank distinctions were strictly observed here, a given small group always being formed only of persons of executive grade, or only of workers. Each small group had both a senior and a junior leader, elected by the membership from a slate of candidates presented in the name of the branch secretary of the party organization and equal in numbers to the numbers of posts to be filled. A small group did not need to include a party member, though it was assumed that if it did he would be thus "elected" its leader; the leader of an executive group was normally the head of a shop or of an important office of the factory administrative organization, who was thus often a party member. The party branch secretary in principle attended executive group sessions, but did not those of workers.

Conferences, meetings, etc., were in any event a constant fact of life, even on the work side of the plant's activities. But for everyone there was also the special kind of meeting of the small group for political education and assessment. Though the "70 Regulations" limit the amount of time to be spent in meetings unrelated to the work of the factory to four hours a week, in this plant workers spent at least one hour a day, five or six days a week, in their small group meetings, always after regular work hours, and officers spent a great deal more time in such sessions, though usually during work hours, no doubt in good part timed to accommodate the need of the branch secretary to attend them.

Most small group meetings were concerned with "study" (*hsueh-hsi*), and pursued a fairly routine round of subjects. A couple of meetings a week usually dealt with political matters or the study of current events. Other sessions had to do with labor union activity, production matters, or problems concerning livelihood. Whenever a problem of discipline arose, however, the small group meeting was likely to turn from study to a "boring-in" (*chien-t'ao*) session, which was also common during a campaign of any sort. As an example of a disciplinary "boring-in" session: a worker of high rank, who was normally assisted by several apprentices, had given a piece of work to them to do while he remained idle. He had done this before, and the apprentices had ruined the jobs, so on this occasion he had been given a rare order by his foreman to do the work himself. The apprentices again ruined the job. The worker was therefore fined a percentage of what the failure cost, and in addition was subjected to a series of boring-in meetings in his small group, then by the workers of his large group as a whole, and finally in a meeting of all the workers in the factory. In such cases, the one being disciplined would be accused of insubordination, and made to speak out himself in each session, admitting that he had been greedy and selfish, wrong in his political thinking and in his assessment of the important role of work leadership. No similar treatment of an executive was reported from this factory, and when one young female executive was caught stealing clothing from another the matter was quietly hushed up.

Small group meetings were reported, here and elsewhere, to follow a set pattern. The leader would open the session by stating, usually rather simply and without expressing an opinion with regard to the substance of the discussion, what the subject would be that day. He would then ask for someone to speak on the matter, though he seldom called on a specific individual. Everyone was expected to say something during the session, but it was often some time before anyone would volunteer to speak, respondents believed because everyone wanted to be quite sure that he said exactly the right thing, no more and no less. Remarks by one member would also not necessarily be immediately followed by those of another, and in fact much of the time of many meetings passed in dead silence. Unlike Americans in such situations, members did not seem to feel embarrassment at such silences, or an obligation to fill up every minute with talk. In the end, the branch secretary (in an executive meeting) would give his opinion on the matter, one that was normally, respondents felt, already well known to everyone, and the leader often ended the meetings by saying that he heartily agreed with everything the branch secretary said.

Small group meetings at the Ch'ang-sha works, and indeed in many other adult work organizations at this time, were far more relaxed than they seem often to have been in the early years of the regime or than, for example, in schools. They were frequently late getting started, people drifting in at the last possible moment and (in the case of executive sessions) the branch party secretary not being called until everyone else was present. The secretary often, in fact, did not attend executive meetings, and in such a case even group leaders might stay away.

Unlike the impression sometimes given of relations in the People's Republic, I did not conclude that observers at Ch'ang-sha, or in many other organizations at this period, lived in marked fear of their surroundings. Most denied, convincingly, that they felt anyone was deliberately "spying" on them. In informal situations, or even in small group sessions not attended by formal leaders or by individuals who wore the party on their sleeves, ties of equality and solidarity—old school mates, co-workers, personal friends—seemed able to ensure one protection from being harmed, and even of a relative freedom to discuss otherwise sensitive political matters.

As in many another type of society with a distinct power elite controlling access to better life chances, however, when one was not sure of the stance of a vis-à-vis, it seemed wise to consider him a *hsiao jen* (petty man), who may report one's laxity as one of the measures he takes to advance. And when the elite took its formal stance, the atmosphere might come to be characterized by great tenseness, and especially in those great party rituals known as "campaigns," which seem to have occurred in an organization like the Ch'ang-sha works two or three times a year. Then, one had to make oral and written reports adumbrating the correct ideology, even if not a direct target of attack. For such occasions, it was said by many to have been well to keep a written record of all the reports one had made in the past, and to refresh one's memory of them before each new encounter since, in one observer's words, "what you say is often not true, and it is hard to remember what you have said earlier that is not true."

CONCLUSION

I have emphasized in these three factories a type of workman who resembles rather closely the traditional artisan, even though he now works with modern tools to create modern goods. Okuda and his uncle were such men, as were the core of the workers in Nagai's incompletely bureaucratized plant. Though I am unable to provide the detail about their work lives that would demonstrate this assertion for the Ch'ang-sha works, such men seem also to have held the floor there, even though they were at the time embedded in an enormous bolus of politicians, bureaucrats and technicians.

The artisan is usually defined in terms of his ability, aided by tools that only extend but do not replace his own hand and brain, to cause inanimate matter to be or to do something that did not exist before. This skill is of course essential, but it is not all that is needed to describe the artisans of legend or, I believe, those shown here. Theirs is a kind and degree of skill which allows each to do his work alone, even though it may often be part of a coordinated team effort. And the artisan is proud of that skill, which seems to him a satisfactory and sufficient definition of what he is in the world of work. The ideal artisan, in his own and his fellows' eyes, is the worker whose skill needs no aid, and who needs no other assurance of his value.

It was this independence that made the artisan something of a sport in traditional Far Eastern life, with its pervasive matrix of kin and neighborhood ties, the necessity for group work in the major tasks of rice agriculture that was the principal occupation of most of its people, and with its many hierarchies. Though I would argue that in general independence is far more deeply institutionalized in traditional Chinese than Japanese society, in the ideal artisan I see little difference in this essential. The work itself made its own personality and social role.

To man the class in the next generation, recruits were selected through personal ties. Though this may also have fostered nepotism, it increased the chance that the boy selected would be one perceived to have at least the germ of a personality suited to this kind of work. Apprenticeship was clearly, and it would appear consciously, conducted so as to select for it, and to reward those who proved that they were determined to learn the skill on their own, rather than persisting only as the menial dependents of others, and rather than needing to be passively force-taught. One is reminded of the similarity of approach in the university-level training of scholars and other professionals today, and one wonders if there is any other way to ensure self-reliance in the adult worker.

The traditional industrial class as a whole, of course, could not be composed entirely of ideal representatives of the type. Varying aptitudes and proclivities for independence would result among those who were able to proceed through the training, and there would be changes in even the ideal artisan over his lifetime. Those who failed the apprenticeship course might be used, though as the lowest sub-class, as "handymen." Those who achieved a minimal skill, though without the concomitant of the independent spirit, might remain as workmen in their old master's shadow. Those who, at least with age, developed a need to serve as a nurturant figure, and so to exercise influence, could do so in later life in the roles of the paternal foreman or owner. Those who also wanted economic power might become enterprisers in their own right, and those for whom even this power was insufficient could, in pre-modern times, aspire to a position as guild-master or, as in China, as entrepreneurs licensed under State monopoly. It is only a step from the latter, in contemporary society, to becoming directly involved in politics, whether that of Japan or, in the People's Republic, that of the party.

In the case of Japan, these patterns have been able to retain considerable strength. Basically, of course, they have done so because of the happy circumstances that Japan was untroubled by over-population, colonial exploitation, internal political instability, etc., and did also create a burgeoning industrial sector with room for many small, as well as large, enterprises. In China, environing conditions were not so kind for the growth of industry, and much of the modern industry that did grow up, under colonial and comprador aegis, was not of a type to appeal to a self-respecting workman, or to create in its work force this kind of independent spirit. Nonetheless, it is a reasonable hypothesis that much of an older and more traditional industry survived, and that in it Chinese maintained recognizable ties with the ideals of the past. Where conditions have permitted, as in contemporary Hong Kong[33] and (I hypothesize) Taiwan, they have come close to re-creating some of the old artisan society to make new goods. Even on the mainland they were able to do so down into the mid-1950's, and one would be surprised if they have not continued to do so in the very many rural sideline and small-city industrial establishments of the present day.

Even where, as in the Ch'ang-sha plant, industry was for at least a time forced into a bureaucratic, large-factory mold, it seems clear that this strait-jacket merely contained, and had not yet destroyed, much of the old artisan spirit. Except in certain restricted types of situations, which seem to have reached only modestly into the routine of daily work, relations were determinedly egalitarian and such as to permit wide sectors of individual independence. Moreover, in the apparently

---

33 Cf. Barbara Ward, "A Small Factory in Hong Kong: Some Aspects of Its Internal Organization," pp. 353-385, in W. E. Wilmott, ed., *Economic Organization in Chinese Society*, Stanford, 1972, for a study of one small Hong Kong shop; Mok, 1973, *op.cit.*, and D. J. Dwyer and Lai Chuen-yan, *The Small Industrial Unit in Hong Kong, Patterns and Policies*, Hull, 1967.

basic re-orientation of the Cultural Revolution, and of the industrial design of "walking on two legs," there seem renewed opportunities for the work context to stress the ancient qualities of the artisan. "Iron Man" Wang of Taching[34] is patently a lineal descendant of theirs, and like them he too operates under the banner "self-reliance."

The work may, as I suggested earlier, create the public personality and the social role. If men were infinitely plastic, perhaps nothing would be lost then in a world of "authoritarian" factories. To revert at the end to personal value judgments, I assume an obdurate individuality in men. Some will work best through their hands, and alone with inanimate matter which they compel to creative new forms. And among these, some will be happiest if they can make their own big decisions, whatever the consequence, while some will also prefer relational simplicity, directness and equality in their dealings with others. I feel confident such men will in each generation devise conditions that permit them these choices.

[34] A famous labor hero of the post-Cultural Revolution period.

List of Contributors

ORIN BORDERS is writing his doctoral dissertation in clinical psychology at the University of California at Davis.

ALBERT M. CRAIG is Professor of History at Harvard University and Director of the Harvard-Yenching Institute. He is the author of *Chōshū in the Meiji Restoration* (1961), co-author of *East Asia: The Modern Transformation* (1965) and *Japan, Tradition and Transformation* (1977), and co-editor of *Personality in Japanese History* (1970).

GEORGE A. DE VOS is Professor of Anthropology at the University of California at Berkeley, and is the co-author of *Japan's Invisible Race* (1966), *Socialization for Achievement* (1973), *Japan's Minorities* (1974), and *Heritage of Endurance* (forthcoming).

TAKEO DOI is Professor in the Faculty of Medicine of Tokyo University; his publications include: *Seishin bunseki to seishin byōri* (1965), *Seishin ryōhō no rinshō to shidō* (1967), *The Anatomy of Dependence* (1973), and *The Psychological World of Natsume Sōseki* (1976).

R. P. DORE is a Fellow of the Institute of Development of the University of Sussex, and is the author of *City Life in Japan* (1958), *Land Reform in Japan* (1959), *Education in Tokugawa Japan* (1964), *British Factory—Japanese Factory* (1973), and editor of *Aspects of Social Change in Modern Japan* (1967).

LIZABETH HAUSWALD is writing her doctoral dissertation in the Department of Anthropology at the University of California at Davis. Her topic is "A Comparative Study of Family Systems in Single- and Two-Parent Households."

MARIUS B. JANSEN is Professor of History at Princeton University. He is the author of *The Japanese and Sun-Yat-Sen* (1954), *Sakamoto Ryōma and the Meiji Restoration* (1961), *Japan and China: From War to Peace 1894-1972* (1975), editor of *Changing Japanese Attitudes Towards Modernization* (1965), and co-editor of *Studies in the Institutional History of Early Modern Japan* (1968).

TAKEHIKO NOGUCHI is a Professor of Modern Japanese Literature at Kobe University, and is the author of *Mishima Yukio no sekai* (1968), *Kyōsui no ato* (1969), *Ishikawa Jun ron* (1969), *Hoegoe sakebigoe chinmoku* (1971), *Edo bungaku no shi to shinjitsu* (1971), *Shūkaku no toshi* (1973), *Rai San'yō* (1974), *Tokugawa Mitsukuni* (1976), and *Hata wa kurenai ni moete* (1977).

JOHN C. PELZEL is Professor of Anthropology at Harvard University, and has written widely on economic anthropology, kinship, and myth in Japan and China.

SEISABURO SATO is Professor of Political Science at Tokyo University, and is a frequent contributor to Japanese journals in the areas of intellectual history, foreign policy and educational policy, and the co-author of *Kindai Nihon no kaigai taido* (1974).

HENRY D. SMITH II is Professor of History at the University of California at Santa Barbara. His publications include *Japan's First Student Radicals* (1972).

EZRA F. VOGEL is Professor of Sociology and Chairman of the Council on East Asian Studies at Harvard University. His publications include *Japan's New Middle Class* (1963), *Canton Under Communism* (1969), *Japan as Number One: Lessons for America* (1979), and (ed.) *Modern Japanese Organization and Decision-Making* (1975).

KOZO YAMAMURA, Professor of Economics at the University of Washington at Seattle, is the author of *Economic Policy in Postwar Japan* (1967), and *A Study of Samurai Income and Entrepreneurship* (1974), and co-author of *Economic and Demographic Change in Preindustrial Japan, 1600-1868* (1978).

Index

Abbott, Kenneth, 215, 253
Academia Sinica (China), 146
achievement motivation, 218, 220-224
Act of 1695 (England), 309
agriculture, comparisons: Communist
  China, 140-141; England, 284, 309
amae, 158, 187
ambition and parental discord, 230-233
Amherst College, 201
architecture, 68, 70, 89-90
Arishima Takeo, 160, 178, 179, 180-181
Augustine, Saint, 208

bakufu, 110-111, 114, 125-126
banks, 321-322
Basil II, 36
Baynes, Norman H., 42, 45
Billington, James, 36
Bonhoeffer, Dietrich, 210-211
Booth, Charles, 86
Buddhism, 38-39, 43-44, 73-74, 120
buke-chi, 89, 90-91
bureaucracy, comparisons: Communist
  China, 137-140; Korea, 118-124
Byron, Lord, 171-172
Byzantine culture, 18-47 passim

Catholicism, 162, 167, 345, 363
censorship, 120, 148-149
census data, 143
Ceylon. See Sri Lanka
Chen and Galenson study, 377
China, People's Republic of, 130-153;
  factory life, 371-380, 414-432
Chinese Civil War, 133-135
Chinese cultural models, 9-10, 18-47
  passim, 61-62
Ch'ing dynasty, 115, 116
Choe Ik-hyŏn, 116
Chŏng Yag-yong, 121-122
Chōshū, 113, 125-126, 133-135
Christianity, 158-159, 161-164, 182-213
citizen participation, 76, 83, 149
city planning, 82-83
civil service examinations, 118-119,
  126, 138
Clark, William S., 193, 201
Clay, Christopher, 313, 315-316
Cockney, 84-85, 87
Communist Party of China, 130-153

conflict, family, 230-233, 243-249
Confucianism, 44, 106, 108, 114, 116-117,
  126-127; and family socialization,
  214-215; and romantic novel, 164-169
Corn Laws (England), 309
"Country," 55-56, 92, 97-98
cultural development, 147-149
cultural diffusion, 3, 157-158
cultural models, 9-12, 18-47
Cunliffe, Marcus, 162, 163

daimyō, 69, 89-90, 123
Davis and North study, 277
Diary of a Japanese Convert. See How
  I Became a Christian
discord, family, 219, 230-233, 243-249
dissidence, political, 150-151
Don Juanism, 162, 164, 165, 171-172, 173
"Dutch studies," 40, 47, 114

Eberhard, Wolfram, 215
economic development, comparisons:
  Communist China, 140-143; England,
  290-291, 296-297, 311, 318-323;
  Korea, 122, 125
Edo. See Tokyo
Edokko, 84-85, 87
education, 145-147, 330-331
Emerson, Ralph Waldo, 170, 173, 174
emperor-system, 158
employment systems, 324-370
enclosure (England), 306-308, 313-314
England, comparisons: 108, 113, 128;
  industrial relations, 325-333, 346,
  348-349, 356, 359; landholding pat-
  terns, 280-281, 302-316. See also
  London
English Civil Wars, 308-309
Enlightenment, 114-115, 120, 128
Erikson, Erik, 188-189, 199
Eros and Thanatos, 166, 171, 175, 176
exclusionism, 108-109, 111-112, 114, 118

factory life, 371-432; Communist China,
  414-429; Japan, 380-413
family socialization, 214-269
faubourg, 89
Fiedler, Leslie A., 161-163, 165, 171, 178
financial institutions, 321-322
France, 108, 111-112, 128, 358, 365

Fukuzawa Yukichi, 7, 47
future time orientation, 226-228

"Garden cities," 82, 93
General Enclosure Act (England), 314
gōnō, 276, 295, 321

han, 123-125
harmony, family, 219, 242-243
Hawthorne, Nathaniel, 177-178
Hideyoshi, 282-283
Hikaru Genji, 166
honbyakushō system, 283, 284-290
Hong Kong, 379
How I Became a Christian (Uchimura
    Kanzō), 182-204
Howard, Ebenezer, 82, 93

ILO, 329, 333, 346, 367, 369
imperialism and anti-imperialism,
    135-137
industrial development, 141-142
industrial relations, 324-370
Industrial Revolution, 315
institutional change, theory of, 276-279
institutional development, comparisons:
    Communist China, 137-147; Russia,
    44-46
Iwano Hōmei, 173
Izumi Kyōka, 175-177

Japanese Constitution, 150
John, A. H., 311, 312
Jones, E. L., 309

Kapsin Reform, 128
Kawaguchi, Japan, 380-413
Kerlin, I. N., 200
Kierkegaard, 210
Kim Yun-sik, 114-115
Kitamura Tōkoku, 169-172, 173
Kojiki, 30
kokudaka system, 282-284
kokugaku, 10, 41, 42, 106, 117
Korea, 31-32, 105-129, 135
Korean War, 134, 144
Kumazawa Banzan, 9-10
Kunikida Doppo, 178-179
Kuomintang (KMT), 133, 134, 144
Kyoto, 61, 63, 72, 73

labor-management relations, 324-370
Labor Standards Law, 388
labor unions, 333, 336, 348-349, 350-364,
    404-405, 412-413
landholding patterns, comparisons,
    276-281, 316-323; England, 302-316;
    Japan, 282-302

language, 44
"Late-development" model, 327-328,
    333-334, 366-367
Lawrence, D. H., 178
Le Corbusier, 82
legitimation, 147-148
Levin, Harry, 174, 175, 176, 178
Lin Piao, 132, 144, 150
Liudprand, 25
London, 49-99
Low, Frederick, 113
Luther, Martin, 188, 192, 198-199,
    203-204, 206-207, 209

machi, 53, 84, 97, 98
Magazine for Women Students, 168
Marañon, Gregorio, 164
Marxism, 281, 288, 354, 388, 403, 404,
    405
maternal control, 233-237
Mayhew, Henry, 86
McCloskey, Donald N., 314-315
Meiji Restoration, 128, 130-153, 320
Mexico, 334-366 passim
militarism, 131, 143-144
Ming dynasty, 115-116
Mingay, G. E., 308-309, 310, 312-313,
    315
misogyny, 177
missionaries, 111-112, 167, 168, 169
modernization, 3-5, 151-153
money-exchangers, 321
monogamy, 167-173
Monterrey Group (Mexico), 336,
    338-339, 344, 345, 347, 349, 352-353,
    360-361, 365
Mukyōkai, 194, 205, 208, 210, 212

Nagai Company, 402-413
Nagai Kafū, 177
Nara, 61, 73
National Academy of Sciences
    (China), 146
"National character," 327, 333-334
nationalism, 117-118
Nigeria: Morgan Commission report,
    347-348
novel, romantic, 160-181
nurturance and affiliation, 219, 239-242

Obolensky, Dimitry, 23, 33-34, 42-43, 45
Oda Nobunaga, 72, 74
Ogyū Sorai, 38, 117
Okuda Junzō Imono, 393-402
Oliphant, Laurence, 91
omote and ura, 191-192
Opium War, 107, 110-111
Osaka, 71, 72

Pak Chi-wŏn, 115
parent-child discord, 230-233
parental control, 218-219, 228-237
parks, 75
Pascal, Blaise, 209
paternalism, 325-326
Paul, Saint, 208
Peking, 61-62, 108, 111
Perry, Commodore, 111
Peter the Great, 39-40, 45
Poe, Edgar Allan, 163, 174, 175-176
political opposition, 150-151
polygamy, 165
Poor Laws (England), 317
Primary Chronicle (Vladimir), 23, 24, 29, 30
Protestantism, 162, 166-173
public security, 143
Puritanism, 162-163, 167, 173-174, 178

religion, comparisons: Communist China, 145; England, 72-76; Russia, 43-44
responsibility, concept of, 218, 228, 237-238
Ricci, Matteo, 113-114
Richardson, Samuel, 162-163
Rougemont, Denis de, 163-164, 165
Roze, Pierre, 112
rurality, 53-61
Russia: and Japan, 18-47, 107; and Korea, 111, 128. *See also* Soviet Union
Russo-Japanese War, 184, 205

Saigō Takamori, 150, 151
Saitō Ryokuu, 177
samurai class: and bureaucracy, 123-125, 137, 150; and cities, 89-90, 91; and Communist Party, 131-133; and Confucianism, 126; and landowning patterns, 320-321
San Francisco Chinese, 215, 252-253
Sapporo Agricultural College, 186, 193
Sapporo Independent Church, 194-195
Sasaki Nobuko, 178-179
Satsuma, 113, 133-135, 150
Scarlet Letter (Hawthorne), 177-178
Seeley, J. H., 201
Senegal, 334-366 *passim*
Sengoku daimyō, 282
Shanghai, 425
Shimazaki Tōson, 168
Shintō, 41, 44, 74
shogun, 69
Sino-Japanese War, 128, 135, 204
Sirhak, 113, 114
slums, 85-86

Solomon, Richard, 254-255, 256, 257
sonnō jōi, 113, 118
sovereign power, limited, 68-69
Soviet Union, 135-136. *See also* Russia
Sri Lanka, 334-336 *passim*
suburbs, 88-96
suffering, concept of, 219, 224-226
Sugita Gempaku, 40, 47
suicide, 166, 171, 172, 173, 176, 180
symbolism, 176

Taewŏn'gun, 110, 112
Taikō-kenchi, 289, 290
Taipei: "Kuting" section, 216
Taiwan, 133, 135; factory life, 378-379; family socialization, 214-269
Tawney, R. H., 304-305
technology, 113-114, 330
Thematic Apperception Test (TAT), 215, 216-217, 220-249, 252-253
Tokugawa Ieyasu, 40, 63-64, 74
Tokyo, 49-99; Arakawa Ward, 216
Tokyo Imperial University, 137-138, 145
Transcendentalism, 174
Treadgold, Donald, 43, 46
Tristanism, 164, 165
Tsukamoto Toraji, 206

Uchimura Kanzō, 158, 172, 180, 182-213
Unitarianism, 167, 168
United States: and China, 135-136; employment practices, 334; and Japan, 111; and Korea, 108, 113; and romantic novel, 160-181
urban populations, 71-72

wages, 340-350, 369, 423
War of Roses (England), 302, 303
Warring States period, 107, 282
Weber, Max, 76-77
Western cultural models, 11-12, 62-63
Westernization: of Japan, 5-7; of Russia, 39-40
white-collar workers, 92
Wolf, Margery, 215, 255
Woman, A (Arishima Takeo), 160, 178, 179, 180
woman, cult of, 173-177

Yamagata Aritomo, 144
"*yamanote*," 91-92
yangban, 110, 118-119, 121
Yi Ik, 113
Yi Toe-gye, 108
yogensha, 398-399
Yokoyama Gennosuke, 86

437

LIBRARY OF CONGRESS CATALOGING IN PUBLICATION DATA

Main entry under title:
Japan, a comparative view.

   "Based on a conference sponsored by the Joint Committee on Japanese
Studies of the American Council of Learned Societies and the Social Science
Research Council."
   Includes index.
   1. Japan—Civilization—1868-   —Addresses, essays, lectures.
2. Comparative civilization—Addresses, essays, lectures.
I. Craig, Albert M.   II. SSRC-ACLS Joint Committee on
Japanese Studies.
DS822.25.J36   952.03   78-70285
ISBN 0-691-05271-9